The Biology of Psychological Disorders

The Biology of Psychological Disorders

David Linden

*Professor of Translational Neuroscience,
Department of Psychological Medicine &
Neurology and School of Psychology,
Cardiff University, UK*

This book should not be used as a primary source for prescribing, dispensing or administering drugs. While all reasonable care has been undertaken to ensure accuracy, the Publisher and Author cannot accept any legal responsibility or liability for any errors or omissions that may be made.

First published 2012 by
PALGRAVE MACMILLAN

Palgrave Macmillan in the UK is an imprint of Macmillan Publishers Limited, registered in England, company number 785998, of Houndmills, Basingstoke, Hampshire RG21 6XS.

Palgrave Macmillan in the US is a division of St Martin's Press LLC, 175 Fifth Avenue, New York, NY 10010.

Palgrave Macmillan is the global academic imprint of the above companies and has companies and representatives throughout the world.

Palgrave® and Macmillan® are registered trademarks in the United States, the United Kingdom, Europe and other countries.

ISBN: 978–0–230–24640–9

This book is printed on paper suitable for recycling and made from fully managed and sustained forest sources. Logging, pulping and manufacturing processes are expected to conform to the environmental regulations of the country of origin.

A catalogue record for this book is available from the British Library.

A catalog record for this book is available from the Library of Congress.

10 9 8 7 6 5 4 3 2 1
21 20 19 18 17 16 15 14 13 12

Printed in China

Brief Contents

Figures

Tables

Plates

About the Author

David Linden is a psychiatrist and neuroscientist. He is Professor of Translational Neuroscience at Cardiff University where he specialises in neuroimaging and neurophysiology and their combination with other techniques of biological psychiatry.

Acknowledgements

I am grateful to several colleagues who contributed pictures from their laboratories and invested time and expertise in their preparation: Professor Ralf Galuske (histology), Professor C. Harker Rhodes (neuropathology), Professor Derek Jones, Luke Dustan and Tim Vivian-Griffiths (diffusion tensor Imaging), Professor Thomas Dierks (positron emission tomography), Professor Robert Rafal (clinical neuroimaging). For the clinical vignettes I received advice from several colleagues: Julie Evans suggested examples of EEG traces from our EEG service at Ysbyty Gwynedd, Bangor. Dr Craig Roberts and Dr Rudi Coetzer of the North Wales Brain Injury Service were involved in the care of the patients whose histories feature in Chapter 21, and Becca Henderson administered the research patient panel at Bangor University. I am particularly grateful to the featured patients for consenting to the use of their EEG traces or MRI scans in this book.

Publisher's Acknowledgements

The publishers are grateful to the organisations listed below for permission to reproduce material from their publications:

American Medical Association for Figure 2.9. Original source is Haenschel, C., Bittner, R. A., Haertling. F. et al. (2007). Contribution of impaired early-stage visual processing to working memory disfunction in adolescents with schizophrenia: A study with event-related potentials and functional magnetic resonance imaging. Archives of General Psychiatry, 64, 1229–40. Copyright 2007 American Medical Association, all rights reserved.

Elsevier for Figure 1.12. Original source is Hornby, P. (2001). Central neurocircuitry associated with emesis. American Journal of Medicine, 111 Suppl 8A, 106S–223S.

Elsevier for Figure 2.10. Original source is Sack, A.T. and Linden, D. (2003). Combining transcranial magnetic stimulation and functional imaging in cognitive brain research: possibilities and limitations. Brain Research Reviews 43, 41–56.

Elsevier for Figure 2.11. Original source is Dierks, T., Linden, D. E., Jandi, M. et al (1999). Activation of Heschel's gyrus during auditory hallucinations. Neurom, 22, 179–94.

Elsevier for Figure 10.2. Original source is Haenschel, C. and Linden, D. (2011). Exploring intermediate phenotypes with EEG: Working memory dysfunction in schizophrenia. Behavioural Brain Research, 216, 481–95.

Elsevier for Figure 16.1. Original source is Rask-Andersen, M., Olszewski, P., Levine, A. and Schiöth, H. (2010). Molecular mechanisms underlying anorexia nervosa: Focus on human gene association studies and systems controlling food intake. Brain Research Reviews, 62, 147–64.

Elsevier for Figure 17.1. Original source is Itier, R. and Batty, M. (2009). Neural bases of eye and gaze processing: The core of social cognition. Neuroscience and Biobehavioral Reviews, 33, 843–63.

National Academy of Sciences for Figure 15.3. Original source is Nestler, E., Barrot, M. and Self, D. (2001). DeltaFosB: A sustained molecular switch for addiction. Proceedings of the National Academy of Sciences USA, 98, 11042–46. Copyright 2001 National Academy of Sciences USA.

Every effort has been made to obtain necessary permission with reference to copyright material. The publisher and author apologise if, inadvertently, any sources remain unacknowledged and will be glad to make the necessary arrangements at the earliest opportunity.

Preface

The biology of psychological disorders is likely to become one of the core scientific disciplines of the twenty-first century. Although great progress has been made in the second half of the twentieth century in the understanding of the basic principles of life and disease, including the sequencing of the entire human genome, we are only just beginning to understand how disruptions in biological mechanisms influence our thoughts, feelings and actions and in certain cases, can lead to mental disorder. At the same time mental health is assuming an ever more central position in public health debates in the developed – and increasing also in the developing – countries. We can say with some justification that mental disorders account for about half of the most pressing health concerns of the industrialised world: depression, dementia, schizophrenia and alcohol and drug abuse are constantly in the top ten public health issues, and all have devastating socio-economic effects. The market for antidepressants is one of the biggest drug markets with worldwide sales amounting to tens of billions of dollars. The identification of new disorders such as attention deficit/hyperactivity disorder (ADHD) or social phobia over the last decades has brought further expansion of mental health services and new markets for psychotropic drugs. Another completely new market, partly legal and partly illegal, for psychotropic substances is being created by the increasing demand in the United States and elsewhere for performance enhancing drugs. If we want to understand and critically discuss these developments, basic knowledge of the techniques, principles and recent finding of biological psychiatry is indispensable.

Part I therefore provides an introduction to basic neuroscience from the molecular to the systems level, and Part II specifically deals with chemical signalling in the brain and the ways of influencing it with psychotropic drugs. Part III explains what we know and what we do not know about the biological underpinnings of the most frequent psychological disorders, including schizophrenia, depression, anxiety, substance abuse, autism and ADHD, about the degenerative mechanisms leading to dementia and about the basic biological principles of personality and its disorders. It describes the structural and functional brain changes, genetic and environmental risk factors, neurochemical changes and treatment approaches, and explores how biological mechanisms may relate to the specific symptoms and deficits observed in clinical practice. The chapter that makes the closest links between specific brain structures and psychological and behavioural changes is perhaps that on neuropsychiatry (Chapter 21), which discusses the consequences of focal brain lesions from trauma and other causes. Chapters 18 and 19 concern two groups of disorders that are of great clinical relevance but too often overlooked in psychological and medical training: disorders of sexual function and orientation and disorders of sleep. A central aim throughout the book is to link the basic science with clinical applications, and to explain the methods behind the evidence for biological alterations in mental disorders. This book looks very different from how a textbook on the same topic would have looked only five years ago, and it is highly likely that future editions will present different models in many of the chapters of Part III. However, the main principles and problems of the neuroscientific investigation of human psychology and behaviour are likely to remain unchanged, and it is hoped that readers of this book will be well equipped to deal with them when faced with new results from preclinical and clinical studies.

This book is intended to accompany undergraduate and postgraduate modules in biological psychiatry/biological bases of psychological disorders or psychopharmacology, and will be useful for students of psychology, biology or neuroscience. It also covers the background in neuroscience, pharmacology and psychiatry required in most undergraduate psychology courses. Students from other related disciplines with an interest in neuroscience or psychiatry can use it to gain graduate-level knowledge in these fields. Medical students and doctors can use this book to prepare for their final exams in psychiatry, as a guide through their specialist training in psychiatry and for the preparation of their membership exams. The book covers sections 3 (Basic neuroscience), 4 (Clinical psychopharmacology), and parts of sections 5 (Mental health problems and mental illness) (a–d), 7 (Child and adolescent psychiatry) (c–d), 8 (Old age psychiatry) (a), and 9i (Addictions) (a–b) of the areas of core medical knowledge required by the Royal College of Psychiatrists of the United Kingdom for specialist training in psychiatry. The biology of psychological disorders draws on many different scientific disciplines, including biochemistry, physiology, pharmacology and neuroanatomy. The basic concepts of these disciplines are explained as clearly and accessibly as possible, making this book suitable for readers from a wide range of scientific backgrounds as well as for lay readers interested in the biological mechanisms and treatments of psychological disorders.

Introduction

BIOLOGICAL PSYCHIATRY INVESTIGATES THE BIOLOGICAL CAUSES AND MECHANISMS OF PSYCHOLOGICAL DISORDERS

At a certain level of explanation all of psychiatry is biological. All our thoughts, feelings and actions have a biological substrate in the electrical and chemical signals of the nervous system. Mental disorder, tentatively defined as disturbance of perception, thought, affect or behaviour, would therefore always be accompanied by changes in these biological processes. In this sense, all mental disorders are indeed brain disorders, as the German neurologist and psychiatrist Wilhelm Griesinger (1817–68) famously observed as early as the mid-nineteenth century. However, it is less clear whether such biological changes are always the main causative factor in the development of mental disorder. Some disorders may have a strong genetic component, which determines a faulty development of the brain resulting in mental abnormalities. However, for other types of disorders environmental changes or psychological stress may play a major role as well. This apparent conflict has led to often heated debates between proponents of 'biological' models of mental disorders and those preferring psychological accounts. In reality any environmental or psychological factors would have to affect the biological processes in the nervous system in order to alter the mind, and thus any biological/psychological dichotomy has to be regarded as entirely artificial. A more enlightened view would be that all mental disorders probably arise through a combination of underlying vulnerability and the additive effects of biological or psychological stressors – the vulnerability-stress model (Zubin and Spring, 1977). The vulnerability could stem from an individual's genotype, early subclinical brain damage or hormonal imbalance, for example, and any of these biological risk factors except the genotype would have been influenced by the environment. In simple terms, the causation of any mental disorder can be broken down into a genetic (G) and an environmental (E) contribution. However, we also know that an individual's genotype can influence how they react to environmental stressors, and thus a third term, gene × environment interaction (G×E), needs to be taken into account.

THE DEFINITION OF MENTAL DISORDERS IS BASED ON PATIENT'S SELF-REPORT AND OBSERVED BEHAVIOUR

The investigation of the biology of psychological disorders faces two main difficulties that are not (or rarely) encountered in other fields of medicine. These are how to define psychological disorders and how to find biological markers for them. For most of medicine, a disease is defined by a number of more or less specific complaints (symptoms) and/or signs, and normally also by specific physiological or chemical changes. For example, the symptoms of diabetes mellitus might be lethargy or nausea, its observable signs polydipsia and polyuria (increasing drinking and passing urine), and the chemical change an increase in blood glucose levels. For most mental disorders, psychiatrists and psychologists have to make do without the chemical or physiological changes, and thus definitions are solely based on reported symptoms and observed signs. These can relate to any aspect of a person's experience and behaviour. For example, a patient with depression might complain of a low mood and inability to enjoy things that used to be pleasurable and observable signs may include slowing of speech and movements (called 'psychomotor retardation') and altered sleep patterns. This approach entails several problems. First, the signs of mental disorders are often less easily quantifiable than those of classic medical diseases. For example, how do we determine whether a person is slowed down when we meet them for the first time? We can certainly ask them or their relatives, but it is still easier to measure someone's weight or water intake than quantify their psychomotor retardation. Second (and partly resulting from this first issue), psychiatric diagnoses were found to be less reliable than those made in other fields of medicine. This has resulted in the formulation of diagnostic manuals such as the *Diagnostic and Statistical Manual* of the American Psychiatric Association, currently in its 4th edition (DSM-IV) (2000) and soon to be in its 5th, or the *International Classification of Disease* of the World Health Organization (1993), currently in its 10th edition (ICD-10) (1992). These manuals, which are widely used in mental health practice, provide catalogues of symptoms and signs, and a patient would fall into a diagnostic category if he or she ticks a sufficient number of boxes (for more detail see the tables in Part III). Although this approach has resulted in improved reliability of the diagnostic process and aided standardised treatment programmes, it does not take account the individual nature of psychopathology. One classical criticism is that two patients who do not share a single symptom could both be labelled as suffering from schizophrenia according to the defining criteria of the DSM-IV or the ICD-10. It may still be justified to include them in the same diagnostic category – because of shared genetic risk factors or because they respond to the same treatment, for example – but it presumably will make it harder to find biological correlates for any of these heterogeneous categories. Third, the present diagnostic approach assumes a qualitative difference between normal and abnormal experience, when many of the phenomena in question, for example the propensity to develop hallucinations or to endorse magic beliefs, may be quantitative traits that are continuously distributed in the population. Proponents of this more quantitative approach to alterations in personality and mental illness seek to replace the traditional categorical diagnostic system, which goes back to the German psychiatrist Emil Kraepelin (1856–1926) and survives in the modern manuals, with multi-factorial dimensional systems. Finally, a main challenge to all diagnostic systems in mental health remains how to deal with people who do not regard themselves as being ill but still come to the attention of the services and fulfil diagnostic criteria for a mental disorder. For such cases, diagnostic systems implicitly or explicitly assume a range of socially acceptable or functional behaviours and convictions, and classify those who fall outside as suffering from a mental disorder. This problem is particularly apparent in the case of delusional disorders where people may hold a conviction that is not shared by the majority of their contemporaries, but what is classified as a delusion today may be socially acceptable in other times or cultures. To a certain extent, thus, mental disorder will always be defined by social norms.

It might make sense in this context to introduce a distinction between mental disorder (or disease) and mental illness. Although these terms are often used interchangeably, illness has been used sometimes to denote a person's subjective experience of their disease. Such a distinction is meaningful in some fields of general medicine but particularly in mental health. There are certainly examples of people suffering from medical diseases – chemically defined – without being aware of it and thus without feeling 'ill'. Similarly, the patient mentioned above who would be classified by mental health professionals as suffering from a delusional disorder may not feel impaired or distressed at all, and thus not be appropriately called mentally ill. Such lack of insight is an important problem in mental health and can lead to difficult conflicts between duty of care to the patient and to those around him who may be endangered by the patient's beliefs or actions. The converse scenario is also conceivable, with a person complaining of a mental illness that does not map onto any of the diagnostic groups. Such cases sometimes lead the way to the definition of new disorders, when behaviours that were previously socially acceptable (or whose potential to cause distress had been under-recognised – the interpretation depends on one's position in this debate) become pathologised. The debate whether excessive shyness was rightly classified as a mental disorder – social anxiety disorder – in the DSM-IV is a case in point (see Chapter 13).

THE DIFFERENCE BETWEEN PSYCHIATRY AND NEUROLOGY IS FLUID

If all mental disorders are – at least in some sense – brain disorders, what is the difference between psychiatry and neurology? The two fields arose from common roots in the nineteenth century, and most of the founding fathers of psychiatry were also neurologists. In continental Europe, there were joint departments of psychiatry and neurology right into the 1960s, and it is still relatively common for junior doctors to undergo training in both disciplines. Classical neuropsychology started in the nineteenth century as the science of associations between deficits in perception (e.g., agnosia, inability to recognise objects), attention (e.g., hemineglect, failure to attend to one half of peripersonal space), or cognition (e.g., amnesia, loss of memory, or dyscalculia, difficulty with calculations) and brain lesions. The study and rehabilitation of patients with such deficits is today known as 'Behavioural Neurology'. Yet, what about patients who develop changes in personality and social behaviour after a brain lesion, like Phineas Gage, the American railway worker who suffered damage to his frontal lobes in 1848 after an explosion had driven a tamping iron through his skull and subsequently was reported to show a complete change of character? Such patients have 'neurological' lesions but primarily 'psychiatric' or 'psychological' symptoms. Indeed, the same psychiatric syndrome (e.g., depression with paranoia) could potentially be caused by a brain tumour and thus by a detectable lesion ('neurological') and/or by the transmitter abnormalities leading to a mood disorder ('psychiatric').

The present distinction between neurology and psychiatry is largely pragmatic. In addition to disorders of the peripheral nervous system (such as neuropathies or myopathies, damage to nerves or muscle) and the spinal cord, neurologists treat those brain disorders that have a clear correlate in brain pathology. Psychiatrists conventionally treat disorders whose brain correlates cannot be ascertained by standard diagnostic tests. In addition, the symptoms of psychiatric disorders tend to be 'in the mind', as denoted by the term 'mental' disorder, for example delusions, hallucinations or complaints of low mood. However, this is not a clear-cut criterion because motor (e.g., catatonia in the case of schizophrenia), sensory (e.g., pain) or vegetative (e.g., loss of appetite, loss of libido) symptoms may feature prominently in psychiatric disorders. Conversion disorders, where patients present with classical neurological symptoms such as numbness or paralysis but no conventional neurological cause is found, can even mimic the clinical presentation of neurological disorders completely. The rationale for assigning them to the realm of psychiatry is not so much based on their symptoms but on the absence of diagnostic tests to bring out their brain correlates. What, then, if ultimately advanced imaging techniques will show us brain correlates even of symptoms traditionally labelled as 'functional' or 'psychological', as in the case of hysteric paralysis? At one level, we might say that psychiatry will then disappear into neurology, and the unity between these two disciplines be restored. At another level, one might redefine the scope of psychiatry in the age of ever more refined biological models and tests as the science and care of those brain disorders whose development and course is strongly influenced by psychological factors such as the individual's personality and life history.

What do these considerations mean for the future of the mental health professions? Psychiatrists will need to become 'neuropsychiatrists' again. This term is used here in a broader sense than the current clinical definition of neuropsychiatry, which covers the psychiatric consequences of classical neurological disorders such as brain tumours or injury, epilepsy, Parkinson's disease, or stroke. The same pattern of thought, which always aims to elucidate the biological substrate of psychiatric symptoms and their interplay with a person's biography and life events, needs to apply to mental disorders generally. Along similar lines, clinical psychologists would have to be at the same time neuropsychologists and move on from purely behavioural and cognitive accounts of mental illness to models that incorporate the brain substrates for the different behavioural and cognitive abnormalities. Ultimately, the aim for all researchers and clinicians in the field will be to provide a biological framework for the natural history of psychiatric diseases and environmental influences in order to improve understanding of the disorders and the mental states of the patients and their care.

Part
I

BASIC NEUROSCIENCE AND RESEARCH METHODS

1 NEUROANATOMY

PREVIEW

A solid knowledge of the structure of the brain at several levels of description is a key to understanding its functions and dysfunctions. This chapter will therefore deal with the anatomy of the brain from the level of single cells, the neurons or the non-neuronal cells of the brain (the glia), through that of groups of cells, for example small networks or cortical layers, to that of anatomically or functionally defined brain areas or pathways. For each level of anatomical description, we will also discuss the relevant tools of investigation, for example the different microscopic techniques (see Box 1.1), staining methods or neuroimaging techniques, and the relevance to the biology of specific mental disorders.

1.1 THE NEURON IS THE BASIC BUILDING BLOCK OF THE NERVOUS SYSTEM

The basic building block of the nervous system is the nerve cell, or neuron. It is estimated that the human brain, which weighs on average 1.5 kg or 2% of body mass in an adult, contains about 80 billion (1 [American] billion = 1,000,000,000) neurons and about the same number of glia cells. The cerebral cortex (with the underlying white matter) accounts for about 80% of brain mass but only about 20% of the number of neurons, whereas about 80% of neurons are in the cerebellum, which makes up only 10% of brain mass. The rest of the brain, including the basal ganglia and the brainstem, accounts for less than 10% of brain mass and less than 1% of brain neurons. This large difference between the proportions of brain mass and neurons found in different regions of the brain indicates that factors other than the sheer number of neurons influence brain size and weight. These include the ratio of glia cells to neurons (over 3:1 in cortex and about 1:4 in cerebellum) and the size of the neurons, particularly their dendritic trees and axons. For example, the white matter contains mainly axons originating from cortical neurons and glia cells, but few neurons for its vast size (Azevedo et al., 2009). The human brain is the largest primate brain and, although several mammals (e.g. elephants and whales) have larger brains, recent estimates indicate that they may actually have lower overall numbers of neurons (Herculano-Houzel, 2009). Thus, number of neurons, rather than brain size, may correlate most closely with intellectual abilities.

1.1.1 Neurons share many features with other cells

Like all other eukaryotic cells, the neuron has a nucleus that contains the chromosomes and thus the genetic information coded in its DNA (see Chapter 4). The cell body (soma) also contains the mitochondria, which are the main site of the generation of adenosine triphosphate (ATP), the main energy storage molecule, through the metabolism of pyruvate, a product of the breakdown of glucose (glycolysis) in the Krebs cycle. Through glycolysis and the various steps of the Krebs cycle and cellular respiration 1 glucose molecule can yield up to 38 ATP molecules. This is the main source of energy for the signalling processes within and between neurons (see Chapter 2). Cellular respiration (also called oxidative metabolism) is the main process where oxygen is consumed. Essentially in the process glucose is oxidised to carbon dioxide and water. This oxidative (or aerobic) metabolism of glucose is far more efficient than the anaerobic pathway to lactate, which needs to be taken when oxygen supply is scarce but results in only 2 ATP molecules per glucose molecule. The brain, which normally receives about 20% of the body's blood supply, is particularly vulnerable to even short drops of blood (and oxygen) supply, which can result in hypoxic brain damage. Because of their specific function and separate structure with their own membrane mitochondria are counted amongst the 'organelles' of the cell. Other organelles include:

- the rough endoplasmic reticulum (ER), which is covered with ribosomes, the sites of protein synthesis, but also hosts a variety of enzymatic processes, including the production of precursors of peptide neurotransmitters;
- the smooth ER, site of the synthesis of phospholipids, steroids and fatty acids and carbohydrate metabolism, and involved in membrane receptor trafficking;
- the Golgi apparatus, which plays an important part in the modification, transport and excretion of macromolecules such as proteins or lipids (Figure 1.1).

Figure 1.1

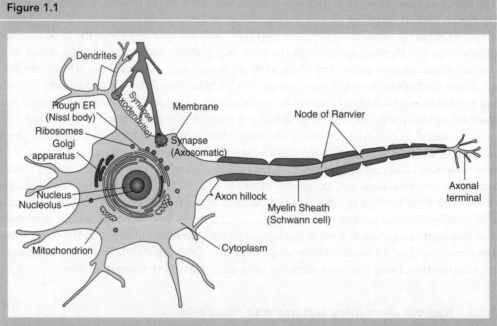

Structural elements of neurons

This schematic drawing shows the basic structure of a neuron (light grey) and its main elements, whose functions are explained in Section 1.1.1. Neurons have many dendrites, which relay input from other neurons (e.g. from the dark grey axon in the upper half of the figure), but normally only one output path (the axon), which branches out into multiple terminals.

Figure 1.2

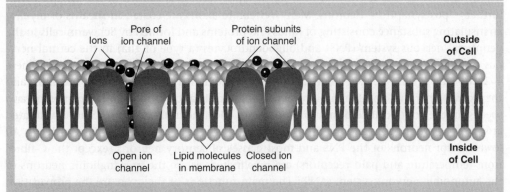

The cell membrane

The membranes of neurons and other cells (and of intracellular structures such as the nucleus and vesicles) consist of a lipid bilayer. The lipid molecules are drawn schematically with a head and tails. The head is hydrophilic (water-loving) and points outwards (to the extracellular fluid space, above, or the intracellular fluid, below), whereas the hydrophobic (water-avoiding) tails point inwards. Interspersed are transmembrane proteins, for example ion channels (shown in open conformation, left, and in closed conformation, right), for the transport of polar molecules (ions shown as black balls).

Like all animal cells, the neuron has as its outer boundary a lipid bilayer membrane, which separates the cytoplasm from the extracellular environment. The bilayer structure results from the composition of the membrane out of phospholipid molecules that are hydrophilic at one end and hydrophobic at the other. The hydrophobic tails pair with each other, while the hydrophilic heads point to the watery extra- and intracellular environments (which are essentially solutions of electrolytes and proteins). Interspersed in this phospholipid bilayer are intra- and transmembrane proteins, which can serve as receptors for neurotransmitters or ion channels (or both, in the case of ionotropic receptors). The cell membrane is largely impermeable to electrically charged and otherwise soluble molecules, meaning that electrolytes, amino acids and polar macromolecules such as proteins will pass only through the dedicated channels or other passive or active transport mechanisms (Figure 1.2).

1.1.2 Dendrites and axons are the specific projections of neurons

The two prominent specific structural elements of the neuron are its processes, the dendrites and the axon (there is normally only one). These projections are supported by the cytoskeleton, which is formed by three main protein-based structures: the microtubules, neurofilaments and microfilaments. The dendrites (derived from *déndron*, the Greek word for tree) form tree-like patterns, branching out from the cell soma in all directions, with tapering diameter and ever finer ramifications whose number per cell can go into the thousands. They receive input from other neurons through synapses formed with the synaptic terminals of the axons of those 'presynaptic neurons'. The dendritic membrane is then called 'postsynaptic'. The main function of dendrites is to generate and integrate postsynaptic potentials and intracellular signalling cascades, which are discussed in more detail in Chapter 2. The axon (Greek for axle) is a single projection which can vary between micrometres (μm) (for local intracortical projections) and over 1 metre (for motor or sensory neurons in large animals) in length. It grows out of the axon hillock and then maintains an equal diameter across its length, branching out at the end into the synaptic terminals that form the synapses with further – 'postsynaptic' – neurons. Many vertebrate axons are coated in sheaths of myelin, an insulating substance consisting of lipids and proteins and formed by Schwann cells in the peripheral nervous system (PNS) and oligodendrocytes (a type of glia) in the central nervous system (CNS). The myelin sheath is interrupted by gaps called 'Ranvier nodes'. These 1–2 µm-long myelin-free segments allow for the exchange of ions between the axon and the extracellular milieu. Myelination increases the resistance of the axonal membrane and speeds up the conductance of neuronal currents. Most neurons of the CNS are myelinated at some point during development, although CNS myelination is fairly sparse at birth. All lower motor neurons of the PNS and most classes of sensory neurons (except the C-fibres from temperature and pain receptors) are myelinated, as are the preganglionic neurons of the autonomic nervous system (ANS). The main functions of the axon are the propagation of action potentials and the transport of neurotransmitters or their precursors along the cytoskeleton.

1.1.3   Neurons are classified according to their projections, shape and functions

Neurons can be classified structurally according to the number and position of projections. Unipolar neurons have only one process, from which both the axon and the dendrite emerge. They are found in the dorsal root ganglion of the PNS and convey signals from sensory receptors to the dorsal horn of the spinal cord. The dendrite is structurally and functionally akin to an axon, and thus these cells can be conceived as having a single axon projecting from the periphery into the spinal cord. Bipolar neurons have two processes. One example is the retinal bipolar cell, which conveys inputs from rods or cones to the ganglion cells. Most brain cells are multipolar, integrating information from a great number of dendrites, with a single axonal output path. Although the dendritic tree is normally confined to the local area, the length of the axon can vary widely, with the pyramidal cells of the cerebral cortex, the Purkinje cells of the cerebellum and the lower motor neurons in the anterior horn of the spinal cord all having long-ranging projections. Conversely, interneurons are multipolar neurons that project locally in the spinal cord, cerebellum (e.g. granule, stellate or basket cells) or the cerebral cortex.

1.2   GLIA CELLS ARE THE NON-NEURONAL CELLS OF THE NERVOUS SYSTEM

The non-neuronal cells of the nervous system are summarily called 'glia' (from Greek *glía* = glue). They have mainly structural, immunological and metabolic functions, although recent evidence suggests that they may be involved in signal transmission as well. A basic distinction according to size divides the glia cells into micro- and macroglia.

1.2.1   Microglia mediates the brain's immune response

The microglia cells are part of the immune system and have the capability to ingest solid material, for example bacteria, dead cells or protein plaques, through a process called phagocytosis. Because the brain is separated from the rest of the body by the 'blood–brain barrier' (the endothelial cells of the cerebral vessels) relatively few infectious agents can reach the brain, which gives it a natural protection from systemic infections. However, the blood–brain barrier is also an obstacle to large proteins like antibodies, which gives the microglia a particular importance as first line of the immune defence of the brain. Microglia is are also activated when large amounts of debris are produced by the brain as a consequence of a neurodegenerative disorder, for example Alzheimer's disease (AD), where it disposes of the amyloid plaques. Activated microglia can be detected in vivo with positron-emission-tomography (PET), and hotspots of microglia activation are correlated with progressive loss of brain volume (Cagnin et al., 2001). Whether brain inflammation in AD is one of the processes that trigger loss of neurons and not just a reaction to the consequences of brain degeneration, is currently intensely debated.

Another type of microglia are the ependymal cells, epithelial cells that line the ventricles and the spinal canal. The ependyma does not constitute a barrier to fluid exchange between the brain and the ventricles and spinal canal, which is why investigations of cerebrospinal fluid (CSF), for example through a spinal tap, can provide good estimates of neurochemical processes (e.g. inflammation, neurotransmitter metabolism) in the brain. The CSF is produced in the choroid plexus of the ventricles, a convolution of capillaries and ependymal cells shielded against the ventricles by tight junctions, a kind of seal produced by neighbouring stretches of cell membrane, thus restricting the exchange of molecules and acting as the 'blood–CSF barrier'.

1.2.2 Astrocytes have structural and metabolic roles and regulate blood supply

We have already encountered two types of macroglia: the oligodendrocytes, which make up about 75% of CNS glia, and Schwann cells, the most important glia cell in the PNS. In the CNS, astrocytes are the second most common type of glia. They surround the neurons and link them to supplying vessels. Beyond this structural role, the astrocytes are also involved in the regulation of blood supply through the release of vasoactive substances, in the removal and metabolism of excess neurotransmitters and in the supply of nutrients to the neurons. The main source of energy for the body is the glucose that is taken up with food (or obtained from food carbohydrates through enzymatic breakdown). A traditional model assumes that glucose is extracted from blood by astrocytes, which maintain a glucose pool and supply the neurons as needed. The neuron then metabolises it through mainly aerobic processes; however, depending on the availability of oxygen, there would always be some anaerobic processing as well, resulting in the production of lactate, which is transported back into the astrocyte. According to an alternative model, the astrocytes produce lactate and supply it to the neurons, which then derive their ATP from oxidative metabolism of lactate (astrocyte-to-neuron-lactate-shuttle hypothesis by Pellerin and Magistretti). In either scenario, it is interesting to note that the glucose pool would last for only 150 seconds of brain activity in the event of a stop of the glucose supply, with the lactate pool providing another 75s and the glycogen stored in astrocytes another 500s (Barros and Deitmer, 2010). Because the brain, unlike the liver, lacks the enzymes required for glucose synthesis, the glycogen would enter the ATP production pathway in the form of lactate. Areas with high resting state activity are, of course, especially vulnerable to this limited energy supply, which is the reason why the hippocampus is particularly affected by prolonged hypoglycaemia, as after accidental or suicidal overdoses of insulin.

Astrocytes have their own electrochemical communication system through gap junctions (direct communication points between cells without intervening synaptic cleft), and the main molecules involved are the second messengers inositol triphosphate and calcium (Chapter 7). Glial calcium levels also change in response to neural activity and this can lead to the release of classical neurotransmitters such as glutamate and gamma-aminobutyric acid (GABA) or co-agonists such as D-serine, which can in consequence be called 'gliotransmitters'. Through such gliotransmitter release, astrocytes can in turn modulate neural activity, although little is known about the conditions under which this takes place (Deitmer and Rose, 2010).

1.3   UNCONTROLLED PROLIFERATION OF BRAIN CELLS RESULTS IN TUMOURS

All types of brain cells can enter uncontrolled proliferation resulting in tumours, although tumours derived from nerve cells seem to be confined to medulloblastomas, which are

---

Box 1.1   Techniques for the investigation of cell structure: light and electron microscopy

The resolution of our visual system is limited by the density of photo receptors – luminance sensitive rods and colour sensitive cones – on the retina. It is highest – about 200,000/mm^2 – in the foveal area in the centre of the retina, which is why we see things best when we look directly at them. Because the retina of one eye does not 'know' how distant the image is, resolution or 'visual acuity' is quantified in fractions of visual angle rather than physical size. A single foveal cone covers about 0.4 arc minutes, but psychophysical measures yield even lower visual acuities, due to integration processes in the visual cortex. Another limitation is the distance at which we can focus objects, which is given by the optical apparatus of the eye (lens and cornea) and has a lower limit at around 7 cm. Even large neurons with a diameter of 100 μm would thus be at the lower limit of our visual resolution, and we would certainly not be able to recognise any detail without optical aids. These optical devices range from a simple convex lens (magnifying glass) to complex combinations of objective and eyepiece lenses in light microscopes, but they all have the common purpose of bundling the light from the observed objects and directing it onto a higher number of photoreceptors than would be on its natural path. Another way of describing the effects of a microscope is that it produces a virtual image (the one inspected by the eye) that is larger than the real image (Figure 1.3).

Figure 1.3

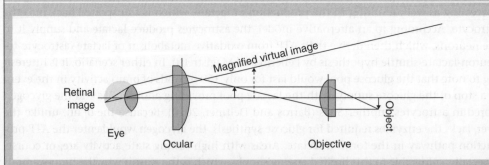

The light path through a light microscope

The light microscope magnifies the real image (indicated by the downward pointing arrow on the right) to a much larger virtual image (the one inspected by the eye). This is achieved through a combination of objective and ocular (eyepiece) lenses.

However, the art of visualising neurons does not stop with the design of microscopes of good magnification and illumination. In order to visualise single neurons against the background of neuropil (dendrites and axons of other neurons) and glia cells, we need to stain them. The classical method for this was developed by the Italian physician Camillo Golgi (1843–1926). Golgi's method, impregnating fixed nervous tissue with potassium dichromate and silver nitrate, selectively stains neurons, allowing for a detailed inspection of their processes (Figure 1.4, Plate I). This method allowed the Spanish physician Santiago Ramon-y-Cajal (1852–1934) to produce the first drawings of neural networks in the hippocampus. Both men shared the Nobel Prize in Physiology and Medicine in 1906. Other staining methods, which are used for other bodily tissues as well, do not distinguish between cell types but between their molecular content. For example, the Nissl stain, developed by the German neuropathologist Franz Nissl (1860–1919), colours ribosomal RNA dark blue and thus highlights cell bodies, but does not differentiate between neurons and glia (Figure 1.5, Plate II).

If we want to stain cells more selectively, we can link fluorescent dyes to antibodies and thus image the distribution of specific molecules. It is also possible to link antibodies to 'reporter' enzymes such as horseradish peroxidase that catalyse colouring reactions. All proteins and polypeptides and most smaller molecules that are of interest for neuroscience can thus be targeted by antibodies and stained. For example, interneurons can be classified according to their calcium-binding proteins, and selectively visualised by immunostaining (Figure 1.6, Plate II). Such chemically selective staining techniques enabled Dahlström and Fuxe in the 1960s to label different cell groups in the brainstem and diencephalon that contained dopamine, norepinephrine, or serotonin, respectively. For example, cell groups B1-9 are all serotonergic and mostly located in the raphe nuclei. This terminology is still often used in neurochemistry (Fuxe et al., 2010). Sometimes chemical reactions of interest can even be visualised by standard staining techniques. For example, melanin appears brown or black (giving the substantia nigra its name 'black substance'), allowing inferences about cells with active dopamine synthesis (Figure 1.7, Plate III). Impregnation with silver selectively stains myelin sheaths and thus visualises myelinated axons and large fibre tracts both in cortex and in subcortical white matter (Figure 1.8, Plate III).

One crucial limitation of light microscopy is its dependence on visible light, whose wavelength determines a minimum resolution of about 0.2 μm and maximum magnification of about 1000. Electron microscopy, which is based on the focusing of an electron beam on the imaged object by a system of electromagnetic lenses and subsequent magnification through another lens system, can resolve structures down to 0.2 nanometres (nm), yielding subcellular structures in high detail and even images of large molecules. Images are black and white, and the darkness reflects the deflection of electrons by the tissue, which is determined by its atomic mass.

composed of primitive nerve cells from foetal development (neuroectodermal cells) and mainly seen in children. Tumours derived from glia cells, mainly from astrocytes, oligodendrocytes and ependymal cells, make up about 80% of malignant primary brain tumours. The meninges, the membranes that surround the brain, can also produce tumours. These meningiomas are the commonest type of primary brain tumour in adults, and the majority are benign, although even benign brain tumours can have devastating consequences, depending on their impact on functionally important tissue. Primary brain tumours can also arise from tissue that is not brain-specific such as lymph cells, and there are many cancers from other parts of the body that can spread metastases to the brain through the blood system. Such secondary brain tumours are actually the commonest type of brain cancer in adults. Brain tumours can result in many psychiatric symptoms in addition to a wide range of neurological deficits, and we will return to them in Chapter 21 on neuropsychiatry.

1.4   THE NERVOUS SYSTEM

The main division of the nervous system, which is both functional and anatomical, is into the PNS CNS and ANS. The PNS, composed of peripheral nerves (including the cranial nerves) and ganglia, mainly carries inputs and outputs to and from the CNS. Even the simplest input–output loops, for example the patellar reflex or 'knee jerk', require at least one connection through the CNS, in this case the synaptic connection between the sensory nerve and the motor neuron of the femoral nerve. The CNS is composed of the spinal cord and brain. The spinal cord bundles the pathways to and from the periphery into specialised tracts to the brain, but also controls simple independent actions, such as the spinal reflexes alluded to above, whereas the brain performs more complex computations and controls voluntary and multi-step actions. The ANS is composed of nerves and ganglia supplying the internal organs.

1.4.1   The PNS transmits signals between the CNS and muscles and peripheral sensory organs

Neurons do not function in isolation. In the PNS they form bundles of axons, called nerves, and clusters of cell bodies, called ganglia. Motor neurons that have their cell bodies in the anterior horn of the spinal cord project axons that leave the spinal cord (and thus the CNS) through the ventral root, whereas the axons of sensory neurons enter the spinal cord through the dorsal root, whose ganglia are formed by their cell bodies. Further towards the periphery, the motor and sensory axons travel together in spinal nerves. They leave the vertebra at their 31 (in humans) segments and are thus called C1-8 (for the eight cervical segments, starting with C1, which arises between the skull and the first cervical vertebra), T1-12 (thoracic), L1-5 (lumbar), S1-5 (sacral) and Cog (coccygeal). The spinal nerves join together in the cervical (C1-4), brachial (C5-T1), lumbar (T12-L4) and sacral (S1-4) plexus, which then taper into branches and nerves, which connect to the end organs (muscles for motor neurons, receptor cells for sensory neurons). Schwann cells provide the myelin sheath for the myelinated axons, and groups of axons (called fascicles) are surrounded by a layer of connective tissue, called perineurium. The outer layer of connective tissue that surrounds the entire nerve is called epineurium and it often merges with the connective tissue of accompanying arteries and veins. Although knowledge of the PNS is mainly of relevance to neurologists, neurosurgeons and orthopaedic surgeons, mental health clinicians need to be aware of its basic anatomy and functional principles in order to understand phenomena such as pain and neurological symptoms, which come to their attention in the context of conversion or somatoform disorders. This is a group of disorders where patients present with symptoms that are commonly associated with physical illness, but no medical cause can be established.

1.4.2   The ANS regulates the function of the internal organs

The main divisions of the ANS, according to function and neurochemistry, are into the sympathetic and parasympathetic system. Acetylcholine is the preganglionic neurotransmitter in both systems and the postganglionic (from nerve to effector organ) transmitter for the parasympathetic system, which is therefore 'cholinergic'. The postganglionic transmitter for the 'adrenergic' sympathetic system is noradrenaline (also called norepinephrine). Generally, the sympathetic system increases cardiac output, constricts blood vessels, relaxes the bronchi, reduces motility of the gastrointestinal tract and stops the voiding of the bladder, whereas the parasympathetic system has the opposite effect, although there are exceptions. The two systems are also anatomically distinct. The parasympathetic ganglia are located close to or in the effector organs and fed by nerves from the sacral spinal cord or by cranial nerves, most prominently the vagal nerve, which carries parasympathetic fibres for the organs of the thorax and abdomen. The sympathetic ganglia, which receive axons from the entire spinal cord, are located in two strands on either side. In addition, the celiac, superior mesenteric and inferior mesenteric ganglia, which are located in the abdomen, contribute to the control of abdominal and pelvic organs. A third system of the ANS is the enteric nervous system (ENS), which is located in the walls of the gastrointestinal tract, and uses a variety of neurotransmitters, including acetylcholine, vasoactive intestinal peptide (VIP), nitric oxide and ATP. It can control a wide range of functions, including motility of stomach and bowels, local blood flow, fluid uptake from the gut lumen, secretion of gastric acid and hormone secretion. It is the only part of the ANS or PNS that is capable of functioning without the CNS and has therefore been dubbed the 'second brain'. Knowledge of the ANS is important for understanding the biology of psychological disorders, not least because autonomic symptoms are prominent in many mental disorders and several psychotropic drugs have important side effects on this system.

1.4.3   The spinal cord connects the brain with the remainder of the body

The CNS consists of the spinal cord and the brain. The spinal cord connects the brain with the PNS and the ANS, and thus enables it to receive sensory input, effect actions and regulate internal organs. The only input and output of the brain that is independent of the spinal cord is that through the 12 cranial nerves, which exit the brain directly and connect with the sensory organs of the head and the muscles of the head and neck. The tenth cranial nerve, the vagus nerve, is an exception in that it travels all the way to the stomach, giving off parasympathetic fibres to the internal organs of the thorax and abdomen along the way. The spinal cord is nested in the vertebral column, which gives it mechanical protection. Its main features are the white matter tracts, axons travelling from the cell bodies in the dorsal horn up to the brain, or from the brain down to the lower motor neurons in the ventral horn, and the butterfly-shaped central grey matter, which is subdivided into the anterior ventral and the posterior dorsal horns (Figure 1.9).

The motor fibres travel along the lateral tract or funiculus. Their cell bodies are in the primary motor cortex in the precentral gyrus of the contralateral hemisphere, and the fibres cross sides in the pyramids, a structure of the brain stem, giving this tract its name 'pyramidal tract'. The main somatosensory pathways are the anterolateral and posterior tracts. The axons that carry information about pain and temperature enter the spinal cord through the dorsal root and then cross over one or two segments above, where they synapse onto dorsal horn neurons. From there the axons travel up along the anterolateral or spinothalamic tract to the ventral posterolateral nucleus of the thalamus (VPL), where they synapse onto tertiary somatosensory neurons. Conversely, the axons that carry information about

Figure 1.9

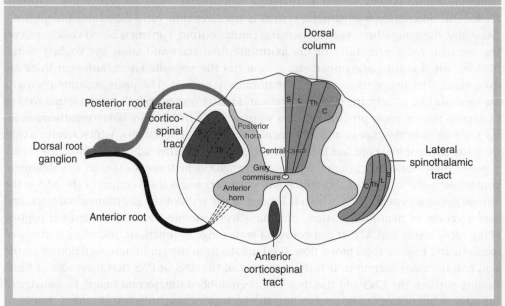

Transverse section through the spinal cord in the neck
This schematic drawing shows the major ascending fibre tracts in the dorsal column and lateral spinothalamic tract and the major descending (anterior and lateral corticospinal) tracts. The tracts are topographically organised according to the segments where they receive/ give off their fibres (C: cervical; Th: thoracic; L: lumbar; S: sacral). The central and peripheral (anterior root) motor pathways are shown in dark grey, the central and peripheral (posterior root) sensory pathways in middle grey, and the central grey matter in light grey.

touch, vibration or proprioception travel up to the medulla oblongata in the ipsilateral dorsal column (fasciculi cuneatus and gracilis) and then synapse onto secondary somatosensory neurons in the nucleus cuneatus or gracilis. Their axons cross to the other side and travel up to the thalamus through the medial lemniscus. In the VPL they synapse onto tertiary somatosensory neurons that project to the primary somatosensory cortex in the postcentral gyrus. Knowledge of these ascending and descending pathways is important in order to appreciate the distribution of motor and sensory symptoms after traumatic brain or spinal injuries, stroke, multiple sclerosis, brain tumours, or other focal pathologies of the brain or spine.

1.4.4   The vertebrate brain has six parts

The vertebrate brain has six parts, the medulla (or medulla oblongata), pons, cerebellum, midbrain, diencephalon and cerebrum (Figure 1.10). The medulla, pons and midbrain are often collectively termed the 'brainstem'. In developmental terms, medulla (myelencephalon) and pons (metencephalon) constitute the 'hindbrain' (rhombencephalon), the midbrain the mesencephalon, and diencephalon and cerebrum (or telencephalon) together the 'forebrain' (prosencephalon).

Figure 1.10

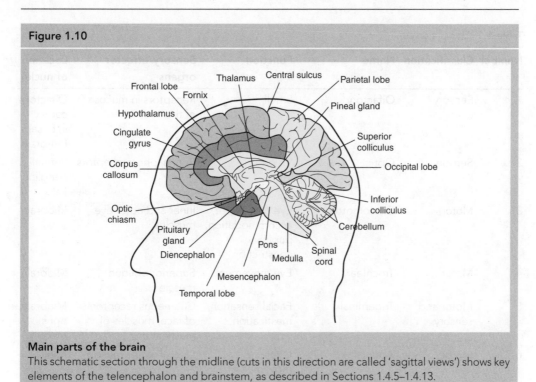

Main parts of the brain

This schematic section through the midline (cuts in this direction are called 'sagittal views') shows key elements of the telencephalon and brainstem, as described in Sections 1.4.5–1.4.13.

1.4.5   The medulla is a relay centre for sensory information, site of cranial nerve nuclei and important regulator of autonomic functions

The medulla oblongata is essentially a continuation of the spinal cord, or medulla spinalis (hence its Latin name *oblongatus* meaning extended). In its lower portions it contains the tracts we have encountered in the spinal cord, for example the lateral (motor) tract, the spinothalamic tract and the fasciculi gracilis and cuneatus, which end at the nuclei gracilis and cuneatus of the medulla. Both the crossing of the motor fibres in the decussatio pyramidum and the crossing of sensory fibres from the nuclei gracilis and cuneatus in the lemniscus medialis are located in the lower medulla. The upper part of the medulla contains nuclei of the lower cranial nerves (see Table 1.1), the lower part of the olive, which is connected with the cerebellum, and the reticular formation, a central arousal system that extends into the pons.

The medulla controls crucial autonomic functions, including respiration, blood pressure, heart rate, vomiting, defecation and urination. One main structure for the control of autonomic function is the solitary tract, which receives inputs from mechano- and chemoreceptors in the walls of the cardiovascular, respiratory and gastrointestinal systems. Its dorsal respiratory group mainly controls inspiration through the phrenic and intercostal nerves. In addition, a group of nuclei in the ventrolateral region of the medulla, termed the ventral respiratory group (VRG), control both inspiration and expiration. Blood pressure is determined by the resistance of blood vessels and the cardiac output volume. It is controlled both by peripheral and central mechanisms. Peripheral mechanisms include the regulation of fluid secretion and retention in the kidneys, which influences blood volume, and secretion of vasoactive substances such as angiotensin II. One of the main central regulatory circuits for

Table 1.1 Cranial nerves

Number	Classification	Name	Function	Sensory/effector organs	Location of nuclei
1	Sensory	Olfactory	Smell	Receptors in mucosa of the nose	Olfactory cortex in basal forebrain
2	Sensory	Optic	Vision	Retinal photoreceptors	Retinal ganglion cells
3	Motor	Oculomotor	Eye movement, accommodation, pupillary constriction	Inner and outer eye muscles	Midbrain
4	Motor	Trochlear	Eye movement	Superior oblique muscle	Midbrain
5	Motor and sensory	Trigeminal	Facial sensation, mastication	Cutaneous receptors of face, muscles of mastication	Midbrain, pons, medulla
6	Motor	Abducens	Lateral eye movements	Lateral rectus muscle	Pons
7	Motor and sensory	Facial	Face movements, taste, secretion of tears and saliva	Facial muscles, taste buds on anterior 2/3 of tongue, salivary (except parotid) and lacrimal glands	Pons
8	Sensory	Vestibulocochlear	Hearing and balance	Hair cells of the inner ear	Pons
9	Motor and sensory	Glossopharyngeal	Swallowing, sensation of pharynx and adjacent areas, taste, secretion of saliva	Stylopharyngeus muscle, mucosal receptors of pharynx, taste buds on posterior 1/3 of tongue, parotid gland	Medulla
10	Motor and sensory	Vagus	Swallowing, vocalisation, parasympathetic innervation of internal organs, taste	Most muscles of pharynx and larynx, thoracic and abdominal internal organs, taste buds on epiglottis	Medulla
11	Motor	Accessory	Neck and shoulder movements	Sternocleidomastoideus and Trapezius muscles	Medulla
12	Motor	Hypoglossal	Tongue movements: swallowing and articulation	Tongue muscles	Medulla

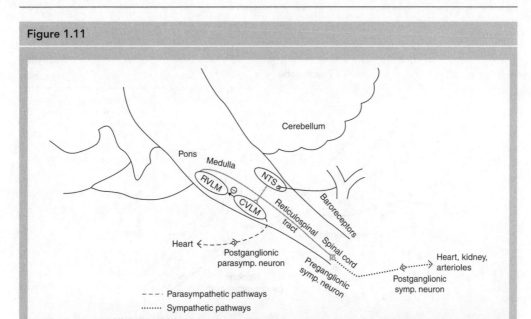

Figure 1.11

The circuit of the baroreflex is an example of the regulation of physiological functions in the brainstem

Baroreceptors in the aortic arch and carotid sinuses are sensitive to pressure of the blood flowing past them. They project to the nucleus of the solitary tract (NTS), which in turn activates neurons in the caudal ventrolateral medulla (CVLM). The CVLM neurons regulate blood pressure in two ways. They inhibit neurons of the rostral ventrolateral medulla (RVLM), which control the sympathetic input to the blood vessels and peripheral organs. This inhibition thus reduces peripheral vasoconstriction. The CVLM and NTS (projections not shown) neurons also excite parasympathetic neurons that oppose the effects of the sympathetic system, for example by reducing heart rate.

blood pressure (the 'baroreflex', see Figure 1.11) starts with baroreceptors in the aortic arch and carotid sinuses, whose activity triggers a negative feedback loop that is mediated through the nucleus of the solitary tract (NTS) and results in decreased activity of the sympathetic neurons of the rostral ventrolateral medulla (RVLM) and thus reduced peripheral vasoconstriction. The baroreflex is crucial for the short-term regulation of blood pressure, for example to avoid dangerous peaks that might otherwise arise from the increased sympathetic tone that is part of intense emotions (Guyenet, 2006). NTS neurons also excite parasympathetic cells in the dorsal motor nucleus of the vagus and nucleus ambiguus, triggering heightened parasympathetic tone (e.g. reduction of heart rate).

The circuits for vomiting (synonym: emesis) also run through the NTS, which receives afferents from the vagus nerve that respond to gastric tone and intestinal content and from the area postrema at the floor of the fourth ventricle, which is outside the blood–brain barrier and whose chemoreceptors can thus pick up circulating emetic agents such as dopamine agonists, opiates or anti-cancer drugs. In addition to these mechanic or chemical effects, vomiting can also be triggered by movement (motion sickness), hormonal or psychological changes (Figure 1.12). The complex sequence of muscle contractions of the digestive system is not controlled by a single 'vomiting centre', but by groups of neurons in the medulla that form a 'central pattern generator' (Hornby, 2001).

Figure 1.12

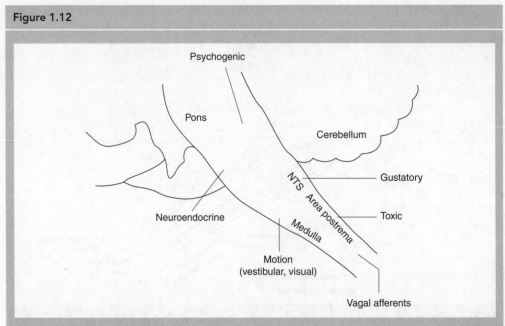

Vomiting can be triggered by a multitude of environmental and homoeostatic factors
Several groups of neurons in the medulla control the motor processes involved in vomiting. Mechanic or chemical effects can trigger vomiting in the NTS or Area postrema. Vomiting can also be triggered by movement, mediated through vestibular centres in the brainstem, or hormonal or psychological changes, conveyed from higher brain centres in the di- and telencephalon Adapted from Hornby (2001) with kind permission from Elsevier.

Neurons in the VRG, in addition to their role in the control of respiration, also control the anal and urethral sphincter muscles and are involved in central reflex loops that maintain continence during coughing and vomiting (Iscoe, 1998). In sum, the medulla is not only a central transfer area for motor and sensory pathways of the spinal cord, but also crucial for the control of many autonomic functions.

1.4.6   The ascending and descending tracts run through the pons

The pons (Latin for 'bridge') connects the medulla with the midbrain. The corticospinal (pyramidal) tract runs through it as do the corticopontine fibres that end at the several cranial nerve nuclei located in the pons. Both major ascending sensory tracts, the spinothalamic tract and the medial lemniscus, also run through the pons. The auditory pathway (cochlear nerve) enters the pons at the cerebellopontine angle and then continues from the cochlear nuclei through the lateral lemniscus to the inferior colliculus of the midbrain.

The seamlike central part of the medulla and pons is called raphe (Greek for 'suture'). A group of centrally located 'serotonergic' nuclei in the medulla, pons and midbrain are called raphe nuclei and are characterised by the neurotransmitter that they release, serotonin. The lower raphe nuclei (in the medulla) project to brainstem and spinal cord, whereas the pontine and midbrain raphe nuclei project to the di- and telencephalon. The raphe nuclei play a central role in pathophysiological models of depression because many antidepressant agents increase serotonin concentrations in the synaptic cleft.

Another neurochemically important structure is the locus coeruleus (Latin for 'blue', because of its appearance in unstained brain slices), located in the dorsal wall of the upper part of the pons, and the main producer of the neurotransmitter noradrenaline. Because many antidepressants are also enhancers of noradrenergic activity, the locus coeruleus features prominently in models of depression as well, in addition to being implicated in anxiety, stress and trauma.

In sum, the pons is the origin of important neuromodulatory (serotonergic, noradrenergic) pathways and the bridge between the midbrain and lower parts of the brain as well as the lower cranial nerves.

1.4.7   The cerebellum is crucial for motor coordination and learning

The cerebellum contains about 80% of the neurons of the human brain and plays a central role in motor control and learning, as well as balance and posture and probably a number of cognitive functions. The cerebellum can be divided into three main portions, based on function, connections and evolutionary age. The oldest part is the archi- or vestibulocerebellum, which is mainly made up of the flocculonodular lobe. Its main input is from the vestibular nuclei of the eighth cranial nerve, and its function is the regulation of balance and spatial orientation. The next oldest part is the medially located palaeo- or spinocerebellum, which receives proprioceptive input from the spinal cord and trigeminal nerve and contributes to the fine-tuning of movements. The youngest and (in humans) by far largest part is the neo- or cerebrocerebellum, which occupies the lateral parts of the cerebellar hemispheres. It receives input from the cerebral cortex and projects back to primary and higher motor areas through the thalamus. It also projects to the red nucleus of the midbrain, which sends off fibres to the spinal cord (rubrospinal tract). The output from the cerebellum is relayed through the deep cerebellar nuclei of their respective side, the nuclei dentatus (neocerebellum), emboliformis and globosus (palaeocerebellum) and fastigii (archicerebellum).

The cerebellum is connected with the rest of the brain through three paired white matter tracts – the superior (upper), middle and inferior (lower) cerebellar peduncles. The superior cerebellar peduncle carries fibres to the contralateral pons, midbrain and diencephalon. The middle cerebellar peduncle carries fibres from the contralateral pontine nuclei to the cerebellar cortex. Because the neocerebellum thus interacts with the contralateral motor cortex, its actions affect the ipsilateral part of the body. The only afferent tract in the superior cerebellar peduncles is the anterior spinocerebellar tract. The posterior spinocerebellar tract enters the cerebellum through the inferior cerebellar peduncle. Both spinocerebellar tracts mainly convey proprioceptive information. The inferior cerebellar peduncle also carries fibres from the inferior olive, vestibular nucleus and reticular formation and an efferent tract to the vestibular nucleus. Because the fibres of the anterior spinocerebellar tract run partly ipsilateral and, partly contralateral to their dorsal horn neurons (and thus their peripheral input) each side of the palaeocerebellum receives information from both sides of the body.

Patients with cerebellar lesions mainly have problems with balance, posture, motor learning and coordination. However, cognitive functions, especially those involving timing or actions or assessments of temporal intervals, can also be affected. Although the cerebellum has not been a classical component of neuropsychological models of mental illness, an influential model of schizophrenia implicates it in the genesis of cognitive dys-coordination (Andreasen and Pierson, 2008).

1.4.8 The midbrain is a source of dopaminergic projections and a relay station for sensory and motor signals

The midbrain connects the telencephalon and diencephalon with the lower parts of the brainstem. It has four parts, from anterior to posterior the cerebral peduncles (or crura cerebri), substantia nigra, tegmentum and tectum (Figure 1.13). The cerebral peduncles carry the fibres from the cerebral cortex to the spinal cord (corticospinal tract), pons (corticopontine tracts), and to cranial nerve nuclei (corticonuclear tracts). The substantia nigra is a nucleus of dopaminergic neurons, which project to the caudate nucleus and putamen in the basal ganglia (nigrostriatal dopamine system), and forms part of the extrapyramidal motor system. Loss of dopaminergic neurons in the substantia nigra constitutes the primary pathology of Parkinson's disease (PD). Adjacent to the substantia nigra in the tegmentum is the ventral tegmental area (VTA), which also contains dopaminergic neurons and projects to the nucleus accumbens. This 'mesolimbic' dopaminergic pathway has been widely implicated in mental disorders, ranging from schizophrenia to addiction. The tegmentum also contains the main afferent pathways to the thalamus, the medial (somatosensory) and lateral (auditory) lemnisci and the spinothalamic tract (pain and temperature). It also houses important oculomotor pathways and the medial longitudinal fascicle, which carries vestibular fibres and coordinates the different eye movement control centres. The periaqueductal grey (PAG) contains opioid-sensitive neurons that are involved in the central modulation of pain afferents. The red nucleus (or Nucleus ruber), which was mentioned above for its connections with the cerebellum, is involved in the control of posture and

Figure 1.13

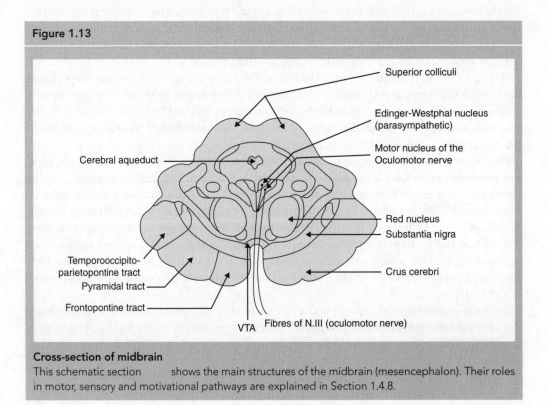

Superior colliculi

Edinger-Westphal nucleus (parasympathetic)

Motor nucleus of the Oculomotor nerve

Cerebral aqueduct

Red nucleus
Substantia nigra

Temporooccipito-parietopontine tract
Pyramidal tract
Frontopontine tract

Crus cerebri

VTA   Fibres of N.III (oculomotor nerve)

Cross-section of midbrain
This schematic section   shows the main structures of the midbrain (mesencephalon). Their roles in motor, sensory and motivational pathways are explained in Section 1.4.8.

movement and gives off the rubrospinal tract, which crosses to the contralateral side in the tegmentum. The tectum is composed of the inferior and superior colliculi. The inferior colliculi are relay stations for the auditory pathway (lateral lemniscus). The superior colliculi are involved in the control of eye movements, especially in reflexive reactions to auditory or visual stimuli.

In sum, the midbrain houses relay stations for sensory pathways, eye movement and general motor control and connects the prosencephalon with the rhombencephalon. In addition, it is the main origin of dopaminergic projections.

1.4.9   The diencephalon contains the thalamus, hypothalamus and epithalamus

The largest structure of the diencephalon (Figure 1.14) is the thalamus, which is the brain's main sensory relay station. The right and left thalami sit on either side of the third ventricle and border on the internal capsule of their respective hemisphere. Several structures on the dorsal aspect of the thalamus and towards the corpus callosum form the epithalamus, whereas the subthalamus (mainly containing the subthalamic nucleus) is located below it, adjacent to the mammillary body. The subthalamic nucleus, a main target for deep brain stimulation (DBS) in PD, is functionally a part of the basal ganglia and will be

Figure 1.14

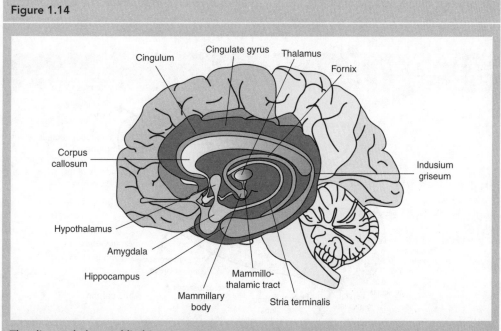

Cingulum
Cingulate gyrus
Thalamus
Fornix
Corpus callosum
Indusium griseum
Hypothalamus
Amygdala
Hippocampus
Mammillo-thalamic tract
Mammillary body
Stria terminalis

The diencephalon and limbic system
The diencephalic and telencephalic structures around the lateral and third ventricles are summarily described as the 'limbic system', which regulates emotion and memory. The anterior nucleus of the thalamus, anterior cingulate gyrus, cingulum, hippocampus, fornix, mammillary body, and mammillothalamic tract (projecting back to the thalamus) form Papez's circuit. For a discussion of the function and clinical relevance of these structures see Sections 1.4.9 and 1.4.12.

discussed in that section. Another important structure is the hypothalamus, which forms the most ventral part of the diencephalon anterior to the mammillary body and is the centre of the ANS.

The nuclei of the thalamus are divided into an anterior, lateral and medial group, in addition to the centrally located centromedian nucleus (Figure 1.15). The lateral group has mainly sensory and motor functions, whereas the anterior and medial group are connected with prefrontal, autonomic and limbic areas. The caudal part is composed of the pulvinar and the medial (MGN) and lateral geniculate nuclei (LGN), relay stations for the auditory and visual pathways. The LGN receives fibres from the temporal retina of the ipsilateral and from the nasal retina of the contralateral eye through the optic tract, and projects retinotopically to the primary visual cortex (PVC) along the calcarine sulcus of the occipital lobe (Figure 1.16). The MGN receives frequency-specific (tonotopic) fibres from the ipsi- and contralateral ears and projects to the primary auditory cortex in Heschl's gyrus of the temporal lobe. Another main relay station between peripheral afferents and primary sensory areas is the VPL nucleus, where the axons from all somatosensory tracts (medial lemniscus, spinothalamic and trigeminothalamic) synapse onto neurons that project to the primary somatosensory cortex in the postcentral gyrus. The VPL and ventroposterior medial (VPM) nuclei also project to higher somatosensory areas in the parietal lobe. Projections from the pulvinar reach extrastriate visual areas in the occipital lobe (Brodmann areas [BA] 18 and 19) and multisensory areas in the parietal lobe (BA 39 and 40) and thus also subserve higher sensory functions and multisensory integration. The motor nuclei (ventrolateral and ventral anterior nuclei and parts of VPL) of the thalamus receive input from the basal ganglia,

Figure 1.15

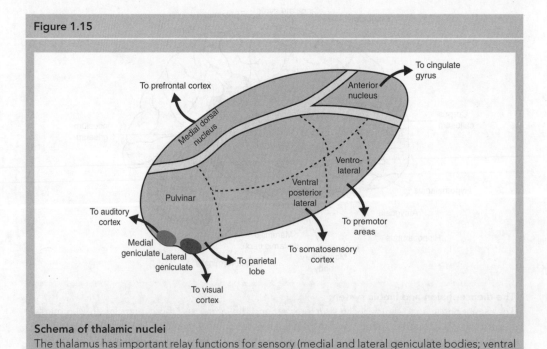

Schema of thalamic nuclei
The thalamus has important relay functions for sensory (medial and lateral geniculate bodies; ventral posterior lateral nucleus), attentional (pulvinar), motor (ventral lateral) and cognitive/motivational (medial dorsal and anterior nuclei) functions.

Figure 1.16

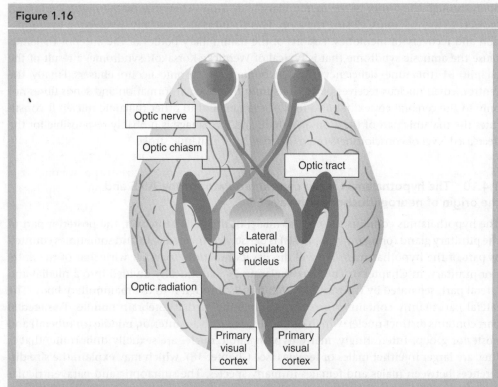

Optic nerve

Optic chiasm

Optic tract

Lateral
geniculate
nucleus

Optic radiation

Primary
visual
cortex

Primary
visual
cortex

The visual pathway

Signals from the eye travel along the optic nerve to the optic chiasm, where the fibres from the nasal (medial) parts of the retina cross over to the other hemisphere. They continue in the optic tracts with the temporal (lateral) fibres of the same side to the thalamic relay station, the LGN. Fibres from the LGN travel through the optic radiation and terminate in the primary visual cortex (PVC) along the calcarine sulcus of the occipital lobe (Brodmann area 17). A lesion to the PVC of one hemisphere results in blindness for the opposite hemifield (homonymous hemianopia) because it affects the temporal fibres from the same and the nasal fibres from the opposite side. A compression of the medial part of the optic chiasm by a pituitary tumour, affecting the nasal fibres from both eyes, which carry information from the lateral parts of the visual fields, results in blindness for the lateral parts of the visual fields and sparing of the centre (bitemporal hemianopia).

midbrain (substantia nigra) and cerebellum (dentate nucleus) and project to primary and premotor areas in the frontal lobe for motor planning and learning.

Of particular relevance to the study of cognition and mental disorders, the medial dorsal nucleus is reciprocally connected with the prefrontal cortex (the part of frontal cortex anterior to the premotor cortex). Lesions in this area can produce neuropsychiatric symptoms similar to those observed after lesions of the frontal lobe ('frontal lobe syndrome' with disinhibition, executive dysfunction and personality changes). The medial dorsal nucleus also receives projections from the hypothalamus. The anterior nucleus is a relay station of the circuit of Papez, one of the central emotion-controlling circuits of the limbic system. It projects to the anterior cingulate gyrus, from where fibres run through the cingulum to the parahippocampal gyrus, which in turn projects to the entorhinal cortex and hippocampus. The hippocampus sends fibres through the fornix to the mammillary body, from where the mammillothalamic tract projects to the thalamus, closing the loop. This circuit is also crucially involved in the formation and recovery of memories. Lesions of the mammillary bodies or the anterior thalamus cause the amnesic syndrome that is typical of Wernicke-Korsakoff syndrome, a result of the vitamin B1 (thiamine) deficiency often encountered in chronic alcohol abusers. Finally, the centromedian nucleus receives projections from the reticular formation and sends fibres not only to the cerebral cortex but also to the striatum, and to other thalamic nuclei. It constitutes the thalamic part of the arousal system, and its damage is probably responsible for the decreased level of consciousness often observed after thalamic stroke.

1.4.10   The hypothalamus is the central regulator of the ANS and the origin of neuroendocrine pathways

The hypothalamus contains the central nuclei of the ANS. Moreover, the posterior part of the pituitary gland (or neurohypophysis) is densely connected with and sometimes counted as part of the hypothalamus. We will discuss its function, together with that of the anterior pituitary, in Chapter 3. The hypothalamus is anatomically divided into a medial and lateral part, separated by the fornix, which travels through it to the mammillary body. The lateral part mainly contains fibres, for example the medial forebrain bundle. The medial part contains distinct nuclei, which can be divided into an anterior, middle (or tuberal) and posterior group. Interestingly, many hypothalamic nuclei are sexually dimorphic, that is they are larger in either males or females (see Chapter 18), which may explain the size differences between males and females in many species. The supraoptic and paraventricular nuclei of the anterior group produce the hormones vasopressin (also called antidiuretic hormone, ADH) and oxytocin and secrete them into the neurohypophysis. Oxytocin is important for the regulation of pregnancy and lactation, but has also been implicated in social behaviour. The suprachiasmatic nucleus controls circadian rhythms (see Box 1.2) and sends projections to the pineal gland in the epithalamus, which secretes the hormone melatonin that is also implicated in this process. This diencephalic system for sleep–wake cycles is a main target for research into sleep disorders as well as the disturbance of the circadian rhythm in depression. Melatonin is used to help reset circadian rhythms after long-distance travel ('jet lag').

The nuclei of the middle group (dorsomedial, ventromedial, arcuate and lateral nuclei) are involved in the control of eating and drinking behaviours, although not all their functions are well understood. They also contain neuroendocrine cells that secrete dopamine (in this case to inhibit the release of prolactin), growth hormone-releasing hormone (GHRH, to stimulate the release of growth hormone, GH) or the release factors for the sex hormones luteinizing hormone (LH) and follicle-stimulating hormone (FSH) to the anterior pituitary. The nuclei of the posterior group (mammillary nuclei and posterior nucleus) contribute to thermoregulation and blood pressure control. Hypothalamic neurons also seem to be instrumental in controlling the 'fight or flight response'. This response, assumed to be a general response to stress and threat in all higher animals, consists in a general activation of the sympathetic nervous system, resulting in a general state of hyperarousal with acceleration of heart beat, flushes, dilatation of the pupils, suppression of digestion, and constriction of blood vessels. Such a response would require the coordinated sympathetic input to the heart and adrenal glands, and neurons capable of activating both systems have indeed been found in the hypothalamus (Jansen et al., 1995).

Box 1.2   Circadian rhythm, sleep and mental health

The regulation of sleep–wake cycles in humans relies on two main components, the arousal system and the circadian clock. Inhibition of the arousal system leads to sleep, which can be classified into phases with rapid eye movements (REM) and generally higher arousal levels (and dreams) and into non-REM (NREM) sleep. NREM sleep in turn has been classified into three stages according to its EEG features, with stage 3 being classed as deep or 'slow wave sleep' (SWS). The latter is commonly thought to be crucial for the (poorly understood) role of sleep in the restoration of physiological processes. REM phases increase towards the later part of the night. Sleep and its disorders will be discussed in more detail in Chapter 19.

The ascending reticular arousal system (ARAS) is a system of projections from the brain stem to cortex through the following main pathways:

1. Cholinergic projections to thalamus from brainstem (laterodorsal tegmental and pedunculo-pontine nuclei) – these are most active during wakefulness and REM sleep, and less so during SWS.
2. Cholinergic projections to neocortex from the Nucleus basalis of Meynert (NBM) in the basal forebrain, which receives ARAS afferents – the activation pattern is similar to the brainstem projections to the thalamus (1).
3. Monoaminergic projections to hypothalamus, basal forebrain and neocortex – these are most active during wakefulness, less active in REM sleep and almost silent during SWS.
4. Peptidergic hypothalamic neurons with the same pattern of activity as the monoaminergic projections (3) – the main neuropeptide is orexin (hypocretin)
5. Melatonin-containing hypothalamic neurons, which are active during REM sleep.

It is inhibited at various levels by the GABA-ergic sleep system in the ventrolateral preoptic (VLPO) nucleus. The preoptic nuclei are located anterior to the most anterior group of hypothalamic nuclei and sometimes counted amongst them, although they developmentally belong to the telencephalon rather than the diencephalon. The mutual inhibition between these two systems works as a switch between ON or OFF states, with relatively little time spent in bistable states – we are normally either asleep or awake.

Although healthy adults are asleep about 30% of the time (and newborn babies over 80%), the function of sleep is still poorly understood. From animal studies it is known that sleep is crucial for survival because sleep-deprived rats die after 2–5 weeks. They develop a complex syndrome that includes weight loss, changes in body temperature and hormones, and reduction of white blood cells. Thus, restoration of energy (particularly glycogen) stores, thermoregulation and immune functions have all been attributed to sleep. Energy demanding activities with the resulting breakdown of glycogen may lead to sleep signals through the nucleic acid and neurotransmitter adenosine, which inhibits the basal forebrain and activates the VLPO. Caffeine and theophylline have a purine structure like adenosine and thus block some of its receptors, which may explain their arousing effects.

The SCN is the pacemaker of the mammalian circadian clock. Several clock genes code for proteins that regulate their own secretion with a circadian rhythm and thus lead to rhythmic neuronal activity even in the absence of environmental stimuli. Under normal conditions, light functions as 'zeitgeber' (literal translation from German – 'time giver') for the SCN. Visual input during daytime is transmitted through the retino-hypothalamic tract from photosensitive ganglion cells. The SCN sends signals to the pineal gland, which secretes melatonin during the night and thus provides the signal for darkness. A main role of the circadian clock seems to be the regulation of activity levels in the ARAS and of feeding signals through the projections from the SCN to the dorsomedial hypothalamus. In the absence of a zeitgeber, for example in prolonged blindfolding experiments, some circadian rhythmicity is preserved, but its cycle will depart from the 24-hour cycle of the earth's rotation.

Sleep disturbance affects approximately 20% of the population of industrialised countries and is a major factor in the morbidity of mental disorders. Patients with depression are most affected, with up to 90% reporting difficulty falling or staying asleep and/or early morning wakening. They also have shortened REM latencies, and thus the sleep that they do get may be less refreshing because of the lower proportion of SWS. Primary sleep disorders also commonly lead to fatigue and low mood and can even result in a full-blown picture of clinical depression. Psychological and pharmacological approaches to the treatment of sleep disturbance are therefore a major area of ongoing research, with pharmacological research focusing on drugs that have a lower addictive potential than the commonly used benzodiazepines. Some antidepressant drugs may have a place here because they suppress REM sleep. Conversely, stimulants such as modafinil, which suppresses the sleep neurons in the VLPO nucleus, are effective for disorders of excessive daytime sleepiness such as narcolepsy. Because clinical symptoms of depression often fluctuate over the day and are particularly bad in the morning, and because of the phenomenon of winter blues (seasonal affective disorder), disruptions of circadian pacemakers have been postulated as mechanisms of depression. The non-pharmacological treatment methods of sleep deprivation and light therapy, which were developed on this basis, are often effective for short-term alleviation of symptoms. EEG changes during sleep are amongst the most promising candidate biomarkers for depression.

1.4.11   The basal ganglia form the extrapyramidal motor system

'Basal ganglia' is the collective term for the grey matter nuclei that are embedded in the deep white matter of the telencephalon, located between the insula and the lateral ventricles. The caudate nucleus and putamen are connected by fibres traversing the internal capsule that give it a stripy appearance on coronal cuts, which has resulted in the term 'striate body' or 'striatum' for these two structures. The putamen and globus pallidus (GP, or 'pallidum') are sometimes collectively termed the 'lentiform nucleus', again because of their (lentil-shaped) appearance. Because of their function and connectivity, the subthalamic nucleus (STN) (part of the diencephalon) and the substantia nigra (part of the midbrain) are also often counted amongst the basal ganglia. The basal ganglia form the 'extrapyramidal motor system', a system of motor control loops that complements the corticospinal motor system of the pyramidal tract. In addition to these motor loops, the basal ganglia also contain circuits for cognitive control and motivation. The latter, mainly in the ventral pallidum and ventral striatum, are densely connected with the limbic system and their function will be discussed in Section 1.4.12, below.

The striatum is the main input node of the basal ganglia. It receives projections from the cerebral cortex (mainly primary and premotor areas), thalamus (centromedian nucleus), substantia nigra, pars compacta (SNc), VTA brainstem and amygdala (to the ventral striatum). The striatum projects to the GP and substantia nigra. The internal GP (GPi) projects to the ventral and centromedian thalamus, and the external GP (GPe) to the STN, which activates the substantia nigra, pars reticularis (SNr). The SNr also projects to the thalamus, but also to structures in the midbrain (superior colliculus) and brainstem (pedunculopontine nucleus). Because the pathway from the striatum to the thalamus through the GPi, the 'direct pathway', involves a double inhibition it activates the excitatory thalamic projections to the cerebral cortex. Conversely, the 'indirect pathway' through GPe and STN involves three inhibitory steps and thus inhibits the thalamic output (Figure 1.17). The interplay between these two main extrapyramidal circuits, which is not understood in all its details, is crucial for motor control. Its disturbances can lead to severe movement disorders, for example

Figure 1.17

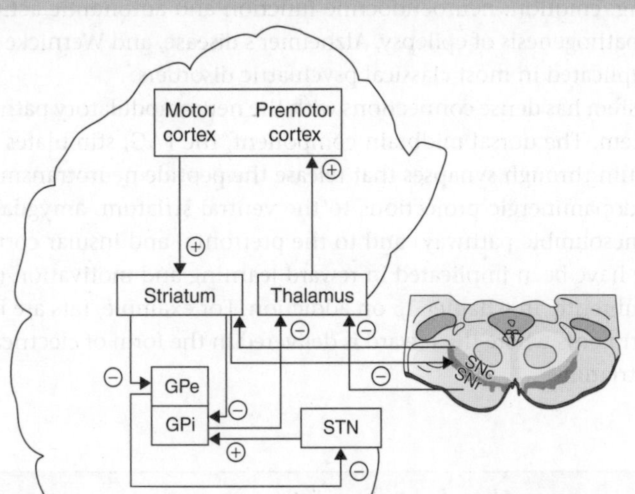

The direct and indirect pathways of the basal ganglia are important for the understanding of Parkinson's disease

The basal ganglia (striatum: putamen and caudate nucleus; globus pallidus, external and internal parts [GPe, GPi], subthalamic nucleus [STN] and thalamus) form an important loop for motor control (in addition to other sensory and homoeostatic functions not shown here). The striatum is the main input station of the basal ganglia and receives excitatory (glutamatergic) input from motor cortex. The main output station is the (ventrolateral/ventral anterior) thalamus, which sends excitatory projections to (pre-)motor cortex. The striatum regulates the thalamic motor nuclei through a direct (through the GPi) and an indirect (through GPe, STN and GPi) loop and further loops through the substantia nigra, pars reticulatea (SNr). The striatal function is modulated by dopaminergic input from the substantia nigra, pars compacta (SNc), which is disrupted in Parkinson's disease.

Huntington's disease, caused by degeneration of the caudate nucleus, and PD caused by loss of dopaminergic neurons in the SNc.

1.4.12 The limbic system is central to pathophysiological models of mental disorders

The limbic system is a network of forebrain areas that border on the lateral ventricles (the Latin word *limbus* means border). Its core includes the hippocampus, amygdala, cingulate gyrus, indusium griseum and the pathways of the Papez circuit. Adjacent areas and regions that are densely connected with the limbic system, such as the parahippocampal gyrus, the ventral striatum and pallidum, the septal nuclei, the hypothalamus, and the VTA and PAG in the midbrain, are also commonly counted among its components.

With the discussion of the functions of the limbic system we move into the key territory of biological psychiatry and neuropsychiatry. The limbic system not only has a central role in memory, learning, emotion, neuroendocrine function and autonomic activities, but is also involved in the pathogenesis of epilepsy, Alzheimer's disease, and Wernicke encephalopathy, and has been implicated in most classical psychiatric disorders.

The limbic system has dense connections with the neuromodulatory pathways that ascend from the brainstem. The dorsal midbrain component, the PAG, stimulates the raphe nuclei to secrete serotonin through synapses that release the peptide neurotransmitter enkephalin. The VTA sends dopaminergic projections to the ventral striatum, amygdala, hippocampus and cingulate (mesolimbic pathway) and to the prefrontal and insular cortex (mesocortical pathway). These have been implicated in reward learning and motivation (see Box 1.3) and will feature prominently in Chapter 15 on addiction. For example, rats are highly motivated to perform experiments where the reward is delivered in the form of electrical currents to the VTA or ventral striatum.

Box 1.3   Dopamine, reward learning and prediction errors

Much of elementary learning is mediated through pairings of stimuli that have no intrinsic value ('conditioned stimulus', CS) and natural rewards (e.g. food, 'unconditioned stimulus', US). These associations are learnt without overt behaviour in schedules of Pavlovian conditioning (Ivan Pavlov, Russian physician and physiologist, 1849–1936, Nobel Prize in Physiology or Medicine in 1904). The dog in Pavlov's famous experiments, which started salivating to the ring of a bell that predicted the delivery of food, is a classical example. Here, salivation in response to the smell of food is the natural or 'unconditioned' response (UR), and its transfer to the CS constitutes the 'conditioned' response (CR). In instrumental or operant conditioning, delivery of the reward depends on the response of the animal to the CS, and the CR is reinforced by its association with the reward. Although CRs have traditionally been investigated at the level of behaviour (pushing a button) or peripheral physiology (salivation), they can also be probed at the level of neuronal responses. The most impressive results come from striatal dopaminergic neurons. Their firing mirrors the timeline of the acquisition and extinction of associations between CS and rewards. In particular, they are assumed to mediate learning because they aid the computation of a 'prediction error', which reflects the mismatch between an expected and delivered reward and figures prominently in learning rules of current learning theories (Figure 1.18).

When the reward is unconditioned and thus unexpected, the neuron responds with phasic discharges at a high rate. After approximately ten trials, the neuron starts responding in a similar manner to the conditioned stimulus (e.g. a particular visual object or sound), but firing in response to the reward returns to baseline. When the expected reward is missing, firing is suppressed. If the reward is discontinued, the conditioned response becomes extinguished and the response to the reward, which is now not expected any more, returns to baseline as well. The reward response thus reflects the amount and direction of deviance from an expected reward, the prediction error. This explains the baseline firing after an expected reward. This pattern is also observed in some OFC neurons. However, most reward-responsive neurons in the amygdala or cortex do not make this distinction and fire indiscriminately after predicted and unpredicted rewards. Other neurons, mainly in prefrontal and cingulate cortex, fire whenever a reward is missed because the animal makes an error in instrumental tasks. Correlates of this negative prediction error can be measured non-invasively in humans using event-related potentials (see Chapter 2), especially the 'feedback-related negativity'(Holroyd and Coles, 2002). The prediction errors of dopaminergic and cortical neurons are not only important for the understanding of the neurobiological mechanisms of reward learning but also for its putative deficits in disorders such as substance abuse (Chapter 15), eating disorders (Chapter 16) and ADHD (Chapter 17).

Figure 1.18

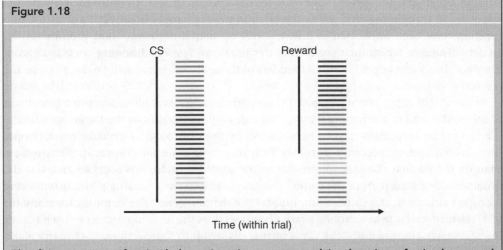

CS

Reward

Time (within trial)

The firing pattern of striatal dopaminergic neurons explains learning of stimulus-reward associations

This schema shows idealised responses of a dopaminergic neuron to a conditioned stimulus (CS) and a subsequent reward over 30 trials of a conditioning paradigm, as described by Schultz et al. (2006). Each line denotes one trial. Darker grey denotes higher firing frequency. In the initial trials, when the reward is unexpected, the neuron responds with phasic discharges at a high rate. After approximately ten trials, the neuron starts responding in a similar manner to the CS, but firing in response to the reward returns to baseline. On trials when the expected reward is missing, firing is suppressed, and if this happens several times, the conditioned response becomes extinguished and the response to the reward returns to baseline as well.

The amygdala is located below the ventral striatum and pallidum, separated just by the narrow band of white and grey matter that is known as the substantia innominata ('unnamed substance'), and forms part of the anterior border of the inferior horn of the lateral ventricle. Its constituent nuclei form a corticomedial (cortical, central and medial nuclei) and a basolateral (lateral, basal and accessory basal nuclei) group. The amygdala receives input from the olfactory cingulate and perirhinal cortex, the basal forebrain and insula, the hypothalamus, the thalamus, and the brainstem. In addition, many neocortical areas, including medial prefrontal cortex, orbitofrontal cortex, and visual and auditory association fields, project to the lateral and basal nuclei. The amygdala projects to the hypothalamus and dorsal thalamus, the striatum, prefrontal and orbitofrontal cortex, visual and auditory cortex, and most paralimbic areas (e.g. cingulate, entorhinal and perirhinal cortex). The amygdala is furthermore reciprocally connected with the subiculum, the most important projection area of the hippocampus. The central nucleus, which is rich in dopamine, projects to brainstem areas, including the VTA locus coeruleus, PAG, NTS and vagus nuclei. Most cortical projections arise from the basal and lateral nuclei, whereas most hypothalamic projections start in the corticomedial group. The classic function of the amygdala is in the acquisition and maintenance of affective dispositions, for example fear conditioning. Its connections with the hippocampus are presumed to be instrumental in the formation of memories for emotionally salient events. The projections to the hypothalamus and brainstem have been implicated in the generation of fight or flight responses and in the suppression of pain in stressful situations. The direct input from higher sensory areas is supposed to facilitate fast responses to threatening changes in the environment. Changes in amygdala structure and function have been implicated in a wide range of mental disorders, most prominently in anxiety disorders, which may result from dysfunctional fear conditioning, and depression. They are thus a key target for animal models of these disorders and will be discussed in the respective chapters.

Although the hippocampi (Figure 1.19) are part of the cerebral hemispheres and form part of the medial wall of the temporal lobes, they are distinguished from the largely neocortical (i.e. having six identifiable layers) hemispheres by their histological structure (mainly only three layers) and connectivity. Together with the other main allocortical (i.e. having less than six layers) area, the olfactory cortex in the basal forebrain, it is counted amongst the evolutionarily oldest parts of the cortex. The hippocampus itself consists of two interlocking C-shaped structures: the cornu ammonis and the dentate gyrus. The name cornu ammonis (CA) refers to its shape (resembling a ram's horn), as does the term hippocampus itself (Greek for 'seahorse'). Histologically, the CA is further divided into four sections: CA1 (particularly well developed in humans and other primates) to CA4.

The hippocampus is connected with the hypothalamus through the fornix and with the cingulate gyrus through the cingulum. Together with the adjacent entorhinal cortex, which receives rich input from neocortical association areas, the hippocampus is a key region for the formation of long-term memories. This fact became clear in a dramatic way through the fate of the patient HM who had the hippocampi of both sides (along with other parts of the medial temporal lobes) removed in 1953 because of intractable epilepsy. Removal of part of the medial temporal lobe, a frequent site of epileptic foci, is still a relatively common

Figure 1.19

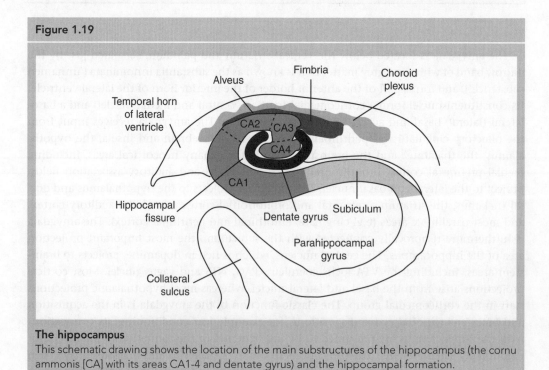

The hippocampus
This schematic drawing shows the location of the main substructures of the hippocampus (the cornu ammonis [CA] with its areas CA1-4 and dentate gyrus) and the hippocampal formation.

procedure to control epileptic attacks that are supposed to arise from there and do not respond well to anticonvulsant medication, but is today confined to one side because of the devastating effects of memory observed in HM. He was tested after his surgery by Scoville and Milner who documented a complete anterograde (i.e. for the time after the surgery) loss of memory for new events and a partial retrograde amnesia, which was worse for events closer to the surgery. This suggested that the hippocampus and adjacent areas are crucial for episodic memory. Conversely, anterograde semantic memory was partially spared, and his motor learning and language comprehension were not affected at all. This suggested that other aspects of memory, in particular procedural memory and the lexicon, are stored in other, presumably neocortical areas.

The hippocampus is of great relevance to neuropsychology and biological psychiatry because of its involvement in focal pathologies, for example related to temporal lobe epilepsy, limbic encephalitis or herpes-simplex encephalitis, neurodegenerative disorders, particularly Alzheimer's disease, and its increasing implication in classical mental disorders like depression and schizophrenia.

1.4.13 The cerebral cortex contains primary sensory and association fields

The cerebrum consists of the basal ganglia, which develop from the ventral part of the telencephalon (subpallium), and the cerebral cortex with its underlying white matter, which develop from its dorsal part (the Latin word *pallium* means 'coat'). Most of the cerebral cortex is composed of six-layered neocortex and 2–5 mm thick. Its main types of neurons are excitatory pyramidal neurons (approx. 80%) and the smaller inhibitory interneurons (approx. 20%, different types: smooth stellate, basket cells, chandelier cells, double bouquet cells). The layers are counted from the outside (pial surface) to the inside (boundary with the white matter) and are called molecular (I), outer granular (II), outer pyramidal (III), inner granular (IV), inner pyramidal (V) and multiform (VI) layers. Most afferents from subcortical areas, mainly the thalamus, end in layer IV, which is particularly thick in primary sensory areas and almost absent in primary motor areas. It is characterised by another type of (excitatory) interneuron, the spiny stellate cell. Layer V is the main source of long efferent projections, for example the corticospinal (or pyramidal) tract that arises from the particularly large pyramidal cells (called Betz cells) of the primary motor cortex, and layer VI is the main source of cortico-thalamic projections. The upper layers (III, II and the almost cell body-free layer I) receive input from other cortical layers and areas and project back to them. With some simplification, the lower layers (IV–VI) thus serve the communication with the rest of the nervous system, the upper layers (I–III) the communication within and between cortical areas. The 'cortical column', a section of approximately 0.5 mm diameter perpendicular to the cortical surface, has been proposed as a basic functional unit of the cerebral cortex. According to this model, first advanced by Vernon Mountcastle in the 1950s and explored in detail for the visual cortex by David Hubel and Torsten Wiesel (Nobel Prize for Medicine or Physiology 1981), neurons with a larger distance do not normally share a representation in the periphery, at least not for the same feature. For example, the PVC is organised into columns that are specific for input from one eye, or for stimuli with a specific orientation. This implies that retino-thalamic projections enter the cortex in a columnar organisation.

The next higher level of functional organisation, which again is exemplified by the visual cortex, is the division of the cerebral cortex into areas. For example, the left visual area V1 has a full retinotopic representation of the right visual field. Its dorsal part, above the calcarine sulcus, represents the right lower quadrant from the horizontal down to the vertical axis (or from three to six o'clock). The adjacent dorsal part of area V2 starts with a representation at the vertical axis, which then travels back to the horizontal axis. The border between V1 and V2 is thus formed by the vertical axis of retinotopic representation, whereas that between V2 and the next higher visual area V3 is formed by the horizontal axis. Each of these lower and intermediary visual areas has a full retinotopic representation, but has different functional specialisation. V2, for example, may extract information about contour from visual stimuli, whereas V3 is more involved in the extraction of motion information. Areas further downstream, such as the 'extrastriate body area' at the occipitotemporal junction, and the 'fusiform face area' and the 'parahippocampal place area' in the respective gyri of the temporal lobe respond selectively to particular types of visual information, and their lesion may result in inability to perceive a particular visual category, for example prosopagnosia, inability to perceive or discriminate faces. Other sensory systems, particularly the somatosensory cortex in the parietal lobe and the auditory cortex in the temporal lobe, have similar principles of functional organisation, moving from 'primary' or 'lower' areas with a full representation of basic stimulus features to 'higher' or 'association' areas that integrate information across space (and in the case of auditory stimuli sound frequency) and basic features and extract more complex properties, for example the 'human voice area' in the superior temporal sulcus.

The attempts at understanding the functional organisation of the cerebral cortex go back at least 150 years. They started with observations in patients with brain lesions, for example Paul Broca's work on a patient with severe disruption of speech production who was later – at post-mortem – shown to have suffered a stroke to his left ventrolateral prefrontal cortex (although some researchers argue that his lesion was more medial, affecting the insula). This case formed the basis for the association between motor aphasia and 'Broca's area' in the inferior frontal gyrus of the dominant hemisphere. This classical neuropsychological approach of identifying associations between functional deficits and lesion sites was later complemented by direct cortical stimulation during neurosurgical procedures (justified mostly by the need to map out functional territories when planning the resection of pathological tissue), which resulted in the famous motor and sensory homunculi of primary motor and sensory cortex and detailed maps of the putative functions of association areas. For example, in the 1940s and 1950s the Canadian neurosurgeon Wilder Penfield elicited various types of auditory and visceral hallucinations by stimulation areas in the temporal lobe. Such work was of great use for the understanding of the clinical presentation of temporal lobe epilepsy and potentially also for the role of altered brain structure in psychiatric disorders. The study of structure–function relationships in the brain has recently been taken to a new level by the development of non-invasive functional neuroimaging techniques, most notably functional magnetic resonance imaging (fMRI), that allow for the measurement of regional brain activity during perceptual and cognitive tasks and a wide range of mental states (Chapter 2). These techniques, jointly with the higher temporal resolution methods of non-invasive electrophysiology (electroencephalography, EEG and magnetoencephalography, MEG), have greatly enhanced our understanding of the information processing deficits of mental disorders and the neural correlates of altered mental states, and their results will be discussed in more detail in the clinical chapters.

The broadest anatomical (and to some extent functional) classification of the cerebral cortex is into its four lobes (occipital, parietal, temporal and frontal). The frontal lobe is separated from the temporal lobe by the Sylvian fissure, a large sulcus, and from the parietal lobe by the central sulcus (sulci are fissures between the cortical gyri and filled with CSF). The parietal lobe is separated from the occipital by the parietooccipital sulcus, whereas the occipital and temporal lobes have no clear landmark as their boundary. A more refined anatomical classification of cortical areas was proposed on purely histological grounds by the German neuroanatomist Korbinian Brodmann in 1909. Using the Nissl stain, Brodmann had observed that the absolute and relative thickness of layers varied across the neocortex and that certain types of neurons were particularly prominent in specific regions. On the basis of these observations he classified the neocortex of humans (and other primates) into over 40 areas, which are still in use today. For many of these areas, functional correlates have been identified as well. For example, BA 17 along the calcarine sulcus in the occipital cortex is the primary visual field and characterised by a particularly thick layer IV, or BA 4 in the precentral gyrus is the primary motor cortex. In the current functional imaging literature, four terminologies can be found:

1. The functional terminology based on functional specialisation
2. The cytoarchitectonic terminology of Brodmann areas
3. The lobar terminology, based on lobes and their topographic parts
4. The anatomical terminology, based on gyri and sulci

Thus the activation in the face-selective higher visual area might be located in the 'fusiform face area' (1.), 'BA 37' (2.), 'inferior temporal lobe' (3.) or the 'fusiform gyrus' (4.). Another example would be activation related to eye movements, which might be described as being in the 'frontal eye field' (FEF) (1.), 'BA 6' (2.), 'dorsal premotor cortex' (3.) or 'precentral sulcus' (4.).

1.4.14 The visual system is functionally and spatially specialised

1.4.14.1 The visual pathway leads from the retina to the occipital lobe

Specialisation for different aspects of visual information begins in the retina, with the photoreceptors that are specialised for luminance differences or specific wavelengths (rods and cones). The retinal ganglion cells constitute the second level of processing after the photoreceptors. The ganglion cells extract information about local contrasts in the intensity of incoming light. Their axons form the optic nerve. Ganglion cells receive input from several photoreceptors (principle of 'convergence'). The part of the visual field where changes in the intensity of light elicit activity changes in these photoreceptors, is called the 'receptive field' of a particular ganglion cell. This term is used analogously for the neurons in visual cortex. The receptive field of most ganglion cells has a 'centre–surround' structure, which means that changes in the intensity of light in the centre of the receptive field, or its periphery, produce the opposite effects on the activity of the cell. Consequently, homogeneous illumination of the entire receptive field will have a smaller effect on a cell's activity than a differential illumination of centre and periphery (thus, a high contrast). The ganglion cells can therefore be considered to be contrast detectors, with 'on centre' cells being activated by illuminating the centre, 'off centre' cells by illuminating the periphery or switching of the illumination of the centre. Both types of ganglion cells are about equally common in the retina, and each photoreceptor has connections to both 'on' and 'off centre' cells (principle of 'divergence'). The ganglion cells are thus the first level of processing where both specialisation and integration occur.

Integration of information from several photoreceptors results in a new function, contrast detection, but at the same time in a new level of specialisation, for decreasing and increasing intensity, which is the basis for further higher order processing steps.

The ganglion cells are the source of a further specialisation that is also of importance for the functional architecture of the visual cortex, the distinction of M (magno) and P (parvo) cells. M cells have large receptive fields and respond mainly to differences in illumination. P cells have smaller receptive fields and respond specifically to particular wavelengths, which makes them suited to transmitting information about details of visual scenes such as shape and colour.

The optic nerve, formed by the axons of the retinal ganglion cells, partly crosses sides in the optic chiasm and then reaches the LGN the visual part of the thalamus. In the optic chiasm, axons from the nasal part of the retina cross to the other side whereas axons from the temporal side stay on the ipsilateral side. This has the effect that visual information only from the contralateral visual field reaches the thalamus (Figure 1.16). This separation is carried through to the PVC and beyond, although higher visual areas do integrate information from both visual hemifields through interhemispheric connections.

This lateralisation of the visual system underlies the clinical phenomenon of homonymous hemianopia, blindness for the contralateral visual hemifield after unilateral damage to the visual pathway after it passes through the optic chiasm, for example a stroke affecting the occipital lobe of one hemisphere. This spatial division of visual processing points to a further level of specialisation in the brain, the hemispheric specialisation for contralateral space. This lateralisation is fairly strict for the visual and somatosensory modalities, less pronounced for the auditory pathways and probably absent in the olfactory and gustatory modalities. Information is integrated across hemispheres through cortico-cortical fibres, most of which pass through the corpus callosum.

The axons from the retinal M and P cells reach different layers of the lateral geniculate body, the magnocellular layers 1 and 2 and the parvocellular layers 3 through 6. There they synapse onto neurons whose axons end in PVC. The properties of the thalamic M and P cells nicely illustrate the degree of specialisation. P cells respond to differences in colour (largely regardless of luminance), whereas M cells respond even to subtle changes in luminance. P cells moreover have a higher spatial resolution (they differentiate stimuli with higher spatial frequency), whereas M cells have a higher temporal resolution (they differentiate luminance changes occurring in close temporal succession).

The visual pathway reaches the telencephalon in PVC. The PVC has the six-layer structure characteristic of neocortical areas. The thalamic neurons mainly project to layer 4, with axons of M and P cells ending in separate sublayers. The parallel nature of the magno- and parvocellular systems is thus preserved at the level of the PVC. Whereas these neurons with direct thalamic input show similar excitation patterns to those encountered in retina and visual thalamus, most neurons in the PVC are specialised for asymmetric stimuli with a preferred direction. These neurons can be distinguished into 'simple' and 'complex' cells. Simple cells respond best to rays of light of a particular orientation at a particular location. Complex cells, however, respond best to rays of light of a particular orientation that move in a particular direction. This property of complex cells may be a result of the convergence of the projections of a number of simple cells. In any event, the integration achieved by the simple and complex cells of the PVC already seems to provide a basis for solving some of the elementary problems of vision. It allows for the differentiation of contours and the preservation of their constancy during motion through the visual field. However, the level of specialisation achieved in PVC is not sufficient to support some of the global perceptual functions that are needed in an ecological context, such as recognition of structure from motion (of which biological motion perception seems to be a special case) or viewpoint invariance. In order to understand these, we will need to follow the magno- and parvocellular paths beyond the the PVC.

1.4.14.2　The dorsal and ventral visual pathways process different features

After leaving PVC, these paths split into anatomically distinct brain regions. The neurons of the magnocellular sublayer project onto area MT ('middle temporal', named for the location of its analogue in monkeys) and thence to the posterior parietal cortex, whereas those of the parvocellular sublayer project onto area V4 (and thence to inferior temporal cortex). Because of this anatomical separation the magno- and parvocellular pathways are also called 'dorsal' and 'ventral' path, respectively. The brain area MT is specialised for the analysis of moving visual stimuli. Most neurons in MT respond to a particular direction of motion by detection luminance contrasts and have receptive fields that are about ten times as large as those of PVC neurons. Loss of function of MT (e.g. in patient with bilateral strokes affecting posterior cortex) results in a severe restriction of the perception of moving objects (measured as correct detection of the direction of motion). A functioning area MT thus seems to be required for the perception of visual motion. Yet, is it also sufficient? This question can be answered by introducing the clinical phenomenon of 'blindsight'. Patients with this phenomenon are affected by a homonymous hemianopia (see Section 1.4.14.1 above) due to a postchiasmatic lesion to the visual pathway, normally at the level of the optic radiation (the tract from the LGN to the PVC) or the PVC itself, but sparing MT. Unlike most patients with homonymous hemianopia, however, they can detect direction of motion in the blind hemifield. This can be measured by asking them to 'guess' the direction of a moving display, which they can do with above chance accuracy. This is particularly striking because they will deny consciously perceiving any stimulus in that hemifield. These patients have a preserved ability to discriminate motion direction but no conscious awareness thereof. A functioning MT alone thus does not suffice for motion perception to occur. Coactivation of MT and PVC and perhaps additional visual areas seems to be required for conscious perception of visual motion.

The ventral path runs from the PVC through areas V2 and V4 to the inferior temporal lobe (IT). Neurons in area V2 respond particularly to contours. Area V4 also processes contours and more complex visual shapes. Moreover, it plays an important role in the discrimination of colour. IT neurons also respond to shapes and colours. One of the characteristic features of IT neurons reported in neurophysiological recordings from monkey visual areas is its high specificity for a particular shape or colour. Neurons that respond specifically to a particular object category, such as faces, or particular exemplars have also been reported. We have to remember, though, that these results do not necessarily reflect the properties of the brains of animals in their natural habitats. Under laboratory conditions, monkeys are often confronted with the same visual stimuli over and over again. Some of the findings of specificity might thus be artefacts of repeated exposure and training. Interestingly, receptive fields of IT neurons are much larger that those of early visual areas, sometimes comprising the entire visual field. This property is supposed to support the constancy of object perception independent of the position and orientation of the object in the visual field. It has been mentioned above that the segregation of the dorsal and ventral paths largely parallels that into magno- and parvocellular systems. According to our current neuroanatomical knowledge the dorsal path receives only magnocellular input and would thus be 'colour blind'. The dichotomy is not complete, though, because the ventral path is not exclusively parvocellular but also receives magnocellular input, which explains why IT neurons can discriminate objects whose contrasts are based on subtle changes in grey values.

1.4.15   The parietal lobe subserves sensorimotor integration

The parietal lobe is divided by the intraparietal sulcus into a mediodorsal (superior parietal lobule, SPL) and a ventrolateral part (inferior parietal lobule, IPL). Its most anterior part between the postcentral and central sulci is the postcentral gyrus, site of primary somatosensory (BA 1, 2 and 3) and in its ventral part (parietal operculum) of secondary somatosensory cortex. The SPL (BA 5 and 7) can be considered to be a part of the dorsal stream of visual processing, which has also been interpreted as a 'vision for action' pathway. Its functions include spatial attention and transformation and the spatial analysis of visual scenes, as well as the coordination of visually guided motor acts such as saccades and reaching. Because of the complexity of these functions and their overlap (e.g. almost all of them require spatial attention) it has been difficult to pinpoint them to specific parts of the parietal lobe, and considerable functional overlap between SPL and IPL is likely. The IPL (BA 39 and 40), which comprises the angular and supramarginal gyri, has traditionally been associated with multimodal integration (between vision, hearing and touch) and higher symbolic functions such as writing and counting. For example, lesions to the IPL of the dominant hemisphere lead to Gerstmann's syndrome, which is characterised by agraphia (inability to write), acalculia (inability to perform mathematical operations), finger agnosia (inability to distinguish the fingers of the hand) and right–left confusion. However, lesions of the IPL, like those of the SPL, mainly of the right hemisphere can also lead to attention deficits for the opposite side of the body or space (hemineglect), which suggests that the IPL, too, has visuospatial functions. The parietal eye fields of humans probably span the SPL and IPL as well. Some authors have suggested a division of attention into a more dorsal (SPL and FEF) pathway that subserves both overt (involving saccades) and covert spatial shifts of the attentional focus and a more ventral (IPL and ventrolateral prefrontal cortex, VLPFC) pathway that subserves target detection and orienting to novel stimuli. The same anatomical division also seems to subserve the allocation of attention to far and near space.

1.4.16   Temporal lobe functions include hearing, comprehension, higher vision and memory

Parts of the temporal lobe have already been discussed in previous sections. IT forms part of the ventral pathway of visual processing and contains category-selective areas; the mesial temporal cortex, including hippocampus and entorhinal cortex, forms part of the limbic system. The remainder of the temporal lobe is mostly concerned with auditory processing and language. The auditory fibres from the MGN reach the primary auditory cortex (PAC) in Heschl's gyrus (BA41) and the anterior superior temporal gyrus (BA42) in tonotopic (frequency-specific) organisation, matching the tonotopic organisation of the sensory organ in the inner ear (cochlea). The auditory cortex in each hemisphere receives projections from both ears, but these can be excitatory or inhibitory. Some neurons are excited by input from both ears, whereas another group is excited by input from one and inhibited by input from the other. These groups of neurons are organised in stripes, whose functional significance is not well understood (most computation of binaural differences to determine the spatial origin of sounds seems to happen in the superior colliculus of the midbrain rather than the PAC). The PAC is surrounded by a 'belt' area with less strict tonotopic organisation, which receives input both from PAC and MGN and probably subserves the analysis of complex sounds. Higher auditory areas without direct thalamic afferents are located along the superior temporal sulcus (STS), for example the 'human voice area' that specifically responds to human voices and may be the auditory analogue of the fusiform face area. The STS is also a key region for audio-visual integration, for example to enable lip reading to aid auditory perception of language. Further dorsal, the posterior part of the superior temporal gyrus, also called planum temporale (PT, BA 22), is specifically involved in the extraction of semantic meaning from sounds and thus in the comprehension of words. Lesions to the PT and adjacent areas can lead to Wernicke's aphasia, where patients can still produce sentences with a correct structure, which are, however, devoid of meaning (therefore also termed fluent aphasia). The comprehension of speech is very poor in these cases (receptive aphasia). The PT of most healthy people is larger in the dominant than the non-dominant hemisphere. This PT asymmetry may be reduced or even absent in patients with schizophrenia (Oertel et al., 2010). Findings like this, together with the theoretical attraction of linking the many language-based symptoms to changes in temporal lobe structure and function, have made the temporal neocortex a central target for the neurobiological study of schizophrenia.

1.4.17   The frontal lobes support motor functions and decision-making

The frontal lobe can be functionally divided into primary motor cortex (PMC), premotor cortex, prefrontal cortex (PFC) and orbitofrontal cortex (OFC). These regions matches an anatomical division from posterior/caudal to anterior/rostral. The PMC in the precentral gyrus is the starting point of the corticospinal tracts for motor signals. Anterior to it, the dorsal premotor cortex along the precentral gyrus and in the superior frontal and medial frontal gyrus controls movement planning and the execution of complex sequences. It includes the frontal eye field (FEF), which is actually the primary motor field for eye movements (the brainstem oculomotor neurons are the only lower motor neurons that do not receive input from the PMC), the supplementary eye fields (SEF) and the supplementary motor area (SMA). These areas have also been implicated in a range of cognitive functions, most notably spatial attention. The ventral premotor cortex in the inferior frontal gyrus has classically been associated with language production (Broca's area in the dominant hemisphere). More recently, it has been postulated that it also contains 'mirror neurons', which had originally been described in monkeys as being active not only during execution but also during observation of the same actions. Their role in social cognition and empathy is currently intensely debated (see Box 1.4).

Box 1.4   Mirror neurons, empathy and autism

'Mirror neurons' were first observed almost accidentally during experiments with macaque monkeys who were trained to execute specific movements. Neurons that fired selectively during these movements also fired when the monkey saw the experimenter executing a similar movement. The analogy of the mirror is actually double-faceted. Such cells that fire both when the monkey executes and observes an action may allow him to understand how it feels for the other person to be executing this action – or to reflect on his own actions. Mirror neurons have been observed in premotor areas such as the inferior frontal gyrus and in parietal cortex. They have mainly been documented for object-related hand movements (e.g. grasping) and mouth movements of ingestion and communication and fire slightly less strongly during observation of those actions in human experimenters or conspecifis. Most of them also respond to related actions and even when only the preparation of the motor act is observed and the actual action is hidden. Because some mirror neurons fire differently when the same action is associated with different intentions it has been suggested that this system extracts the intention from the context of motor acts. This system may also support imitation learning because, although monkey mirror neurons do not respond naturally when actors use tools, they do after lengthy training periods in the laboratory, where it is almost unavoidable that monkeys would see human experimenters using tools to achieve goals. The mirror neuron system is of obvious fascination to students of motor behaviour and social interaction. Thus, one key question was whether it also exists in other species, notably humans. Direct evidence from invasive recordings (which are possible only in very specific settings of pre-surgical functional mapping) is still scarce, but functional imaging studies of action observation and imitation suggested the presence of a mirror system in the ventral premotor cortex and anterior parietal cortex as well. Experiments with transcranial magnetic stimulation (TMS), a non-invasive technique for the short-term excitation or inhibition of groups of neurons, also suggest a functional significance of this system in imitation learning. However, critics have questioned the specificity of the mirror neuron concept and suggested that the experimental data can be explained by a general facilitation of motor and premotor areas during movement observation. Furthermore, single cell recordings in monkeys are not quantitative and do not easily allow for estimates of the proportion of neurons that have mirror properties in a particular brain area. Functional magnetic resonance imaging (fMRI) studies in humans do not easily resolve this issue because of the spatial resolution of this technique (see Chapter 2). Similar activation on a spatial scale of millimetres could still be produced by different, albeit neighbouring, groups of neurons engaged in action observation and execution, respectively.

It will be important to obtain more clarity on this issue, for example by more quantitative approaches. The theory of the mirror neuron system is very powerful in explaining the acquisition of social skills and has therefore dominated the emerging discipline of social cognitive neuroscience. The mirror neuron system would be the ideal neural implementation of classical psychological models for the understanding of the mental states of others ('theory of mind') that are based on simulation. For example, contagious emotions could be produced by the necessity to imitate the facial expressions of others in order to understand their emotions. Deficits in theory of mind, extraction of social meaning from day-to-day communication, interpretation and expression of emotions and other core social cognitive skills have been observed in autism, schizophrenia and other developmental and mental disorders. Some forms of autism are also characterised by deficits in language acquisition and motor skills, and the premotor mirror system is therefore a key candidate region for research into its biological underpinnings. One study indeed reported reduced activity in the inferior frontal gyrus in children with autism during imitation of emotional facial expressions, although they performed as well as controls, which calls the functional significance of these findings into question (for an overview of functional neuroimaging studies in autism see Verhoeven et al. (2010)).

The PFC can be divided into a lateral and a medial part, and these further into dorsal and ventral divisions, yielding dorsolateral (DLFPC), ventrolateral (VLPFC), dorsomedial (DMPFC) and ventromedial (VMPFC) PFC. The lateral PFC subserves a range of cognitive functions often collectively termed 'executive', such as working memory, rule learning, and decision-making. Its function can be tested with neuropsychological tests of rule shifting (such as the Wisconsin Card Sort Test, WCST) or interference suppression (such as the Stroop test, where participants have to name the colour in which a colour word is printed, e.g. 'red' printed in green). These tests of executive function are often used to evaluate the degree of cognitive impairment after brain lesions or chronic toxic damage (e.g. from alcohol abuse), but also in classical mental disorders such as schizophrenia. The specialisation of the DLPFC and VLPFC, which are separated by the inferior frontal sulcus, is less clear because lesions often span both parts of the lateral PFC and functional imaging experiments of frontal lobe function often produce rather global and overlapping activations. However, based on their different connectivities (the DLFPC more to the parietal lobe, the VLPFC more to the temporal lobe) it has been proposed that they are continuations of the 'dorsal' (spatial) and 'ventral' (object) stream of visual processing. The medial PFC plays a key role in motivation. This is known from the amotivational syndrome observed in strokes of the anterior cerebral artery, which supplies this territory. Other functions include introspection and generally self-referential cognitive processes. The functions of the medial PFC overlap with those of the OFC, which has been implicated in learning, reward processing and the control of social behaviours. Lesions to these areas can thus result in inappropriate or disinhibited behaviour and loss of social skills, and according to some authors, even acquired sociopathy. They also often lead to labile mood and irritability.

1.4.18 Fibre tracts connect brain areas within and across lobes

Brain areas are connected by intracortical fibres between adjacent areas, short association tracts within a lobe and several long association tracts linking the frontal lobe with the parietal lobe, the limbic cortex (uncinate fascicle and superior occipitofrontal fascicle), the temporal and occipital lobes (superior longitudinal and superior and inferior occipitofrontal fascicles) and the anterior temporal and occipital lobes (inferior longitudinal fascile) of the same hemisphere. The anterior branch of the superior longitudinal fascicle, also called arcuate fascicle because of its shape (Latin *arcus* = arch), connects the ventral premotor cortex and PT and thus in the dominant hemisphere Broca's and Wernicke's areas (Figure 1.20, Plate IV). Its damage leads to disruption of communication between speech production and comprehension centres and thus to a phenomenon termed 'conduction aphasia', where patients are unable to repeat words and may have difficulty reading aloud. The arcuate fascicle has also attracted the interest of biological psychiatrists because several studies have reported that it may be one of few, or the only, area, where connectivity is actually increased in schizophrenia. Studies with diffusion tensor imaging, an MRI technique that is sensitive to water diffusion and can thus track the integrity of myelinated fibre tracts, have otherwise shown widespread changes in schizophreniathat support earlier neuropsychological models of a 'dysconnectivity' syndrome.

The two hemisphere are linked by homotopic (between homologous areas, for example those representing the vertical meridian of the visual field) and heterotopic connections, which run through the commissural tracts. The corpus callosum, the largest commissure by far, is topographically organised. Its posterior parts (splenium and isthmus) carry fibres from the occipital and temporal lobes, its middle part (truncus or midbody) carries fibres from the parietal lobe and motor cortex, and its anterior parts (genu and rostrum) connect prefrontal and limbic areas. Limbic interhemispheric connections also run through the anterior commissure. Alterations in size and connectivity of the corpus callosum have been implicated in mental disorders, most notably in schizophrenia (Rotarska-Jagiela et al., 2008).

Experiments on patients who underwent a resection of the corpus callosum (callosectomy, sometimes used in intractable epilepsy to prevent spread of the seizure to the other hemisphere), the so-called 'split-brain research', have provided impressive confirmation of the lateralisation of certain cognitive functions. When such a patient sees an object only in the left visual hemifield, which is represented in the right cerebral hemisphere, she is unable to name it because the information does not travel to the (commonly) language-dominant left hemisphere. However, she can still grasp it because each hemisphere alone is capable of visuomotor coordination. These deficits occur only in specific testing situations with strictly unilateral visual input and do not translate into major difficulties with everyday functioning. Although the split-brain research has supported theories of hemispheric specialisation (left: language and arithmetic operations; right: visuospatial skills), some researchers have drawn too far-reaching conclusions from it, for example claiming that the right hemisphere is more 'holistic' or 'emotional' than the left. Another outcome of the split-brain research was the discovery of the ability of each hemisphere to function independently on many tasks.

1.5   THE BRAIN RECEIVES ABOUT 20% OF THE BODY'S BLOOD FLOW

Although the brain represents only about 2% of body mass, it receives about 20% of the body's blood flow. Because of the high demand on aerobic glycolysis for neuronal signalling, even brief disruptions in cerebral blood flow can have devastating effects. Aerobic glycolysis is the metabolism of glucose to carbon dioxide and water, which requires oxygen and yields far more energy than the anaerobic metabolism of glucose to lactate.

The blood supply to the brain is divided into an anterior (through the internal carotid arteries) and a posterior (through the vertebral arteries, which fuse to form the basilar artery at the level of the medulla) circulation. The posterior circulation supplies the brainstem, cerebellum, thalamus, occipital lobe and anterior and inferior temporal lobes, including the hippocampus, and the anterior circulation supplies the medial (anterior cerebral artery) and lateral (middle cerebral artery) aspects of the frontal and parietal lobes, the superior and lateral parts of the temporal lobe, and the anterior basal ganglia. The two circulations are linked with each other and across hemispheres through the circle of Willis, providing some redundancy of blood supply in cases of stenosis (narrowing) or thrombosis of one of the major supplying arteries. However, occlusions of arteries distal to the circle of Willis will normally result in ischaemic (from lack of blood supply) strokes. The ensuing loss of cognitive functions and disability will depend on the functional specialisation and relevance of the affected areas and on the ability of other parts of the brain to take over some of the function (neuroplasticity). For example, a stroke in the territory of the left middle cerebral artery in a left language-dominant patient can lead to global (production and comprehension) or partial aphasia, or a stroke in the territory of the posterior cerebral artery, which supplies the PVC, may lead to hemianopia for the contralateral hemifield. Cerebrovascular disease is one of the main causes of mortality and disability in old age (e.g. through vascular dementia) and the reduction of its risk factors, which include high blood pressure, high cholesterol levels, smoking, diabetes and gout, therefore a major public health concern.

Learning points

In this chapter we have covered some of the basic principles of the structure of the nervous system. Its basic building block is the neuron, which is a cell specialised for the conversion and transmission of electrical signals. Its characteristic structural features are its processes for input (the dendrites) and output (the axon). Through these processes and the synapses formed between them, neurons are linked into neural networks. In the cerebral cortex, these often follow the principle of functional columns. Long axons from many neurons are assembled into fibre tracts, which form links between different brain areas and between the brain and the periphery. Areas rich in cell bodies form 'grey matter' and areas that mainly contain fibre tracts form 'white matter'. In addition to the neurons, the nervous system contains many other cells that subserve its structure, nutrition, blood supply and immune response, collectively termed 'glia'.

The nervous system is divided into three parts, the central (brain and spinal cord), autonomic (sympathetic, parasympathetic and enteric) and the peripheral nervous systems. The brain is connected with the PNS through tracts to the nuclei of cranial nerves (the cranial nerves that supply the sensory and motor organs of the head and neck are part of the PNS) and through the spinal cord. The central control areas of the ANS are mainly located in the hypothalamus and the medulla oblongata of the brain.

The brain consists of the telencephalon (cerebral cortex and underlying white matter and basal ganglia), diencephalon (thalamus, hypothalamus and epithalamus), brainstem (midbrain, pons and medulla oblongata) and cerebellum. All its part are densely connected and do not function in isolation. However, lesion studies can tell us about parts of the brain that are crucially required for certain functions. For example, the cerebellum is involved in motor learning and coordination and the midbrain in the control of eye movements. The different lobes of the cerebral cortex have functional specialisations that are related to their input and output pathways, for example the occipital lobe for vision, the temporal lobe for hearing, the parietal lobe for visuomotor integration and the frontal lobe for decision-making and motor functions. The limbic system, which contains medial parts of the telencephalon and parts of the diencephalon, is important for learning and emotions. Such relations between brain, function and behaviour are at the core of research into the biological mechanisms of mental disorders.

Revision and discussion questions

- How can we study the structure of the human brain? What are the different techniques available for in vivo and post-mortem studies and what can they tell us?
- What are the main components of the human brain and what are their key functions?
- Why are the brain's energy metabolism and blood supply relevant for neuropsychology and neuropsychiatry?
- Some functions of the brain are conscious but others (and probably many more) are unconscious. What do we know about their different implementation in specific brain areas and pathways?

FURTHER READING

Germain, A. and Kupfer, D. (2008). Circadian rhythm disturbances in depression. *Human Psychopharmacology*, 23, 571–85.

Holroyd, C. B. and Coles, M. G. (2002). The neural basis of human error processing: reinforcement learning, dopamine, and the error-related negativity. *Psychological Review*, 109, 679–709.

Iacoboni, M. and Mazziotta, J. (2007). Mirror neuron system: basic findings and clinical applications. *Annals of Neurology*, 62, 213–18.

Nieuwenhuys, R. (1986). *Chemoarchitecture of the Brain* (Berlin: Springer).

Nieuwenhuys, R., Voogd, J. and Huijzen, C. V. (2007). *The Human Central Nervous System* (Berlin, London: Springer).

Schultz, W. (2006). Behavioral theories and the neurophysiology of reward. *Annual Review of Psychology*, 57, 87–115.

Schwartz, J. and Roth, T. (2008). Neurophysiology of sleep and wakefulness: basic science and clinical implications. *Current Neuropharmacology*, 6, 367–78.

2 NEUROPHYSIOLOGY AND BASIC NEUROCHEMISTRY

PREVIEW

Neurophysiology is the science of neurons in action and deals with the way in which they generate and transmit electrical and chemical signals. This chapter will review the basic properties of neuronal membranes and the ion currents that contribute to the excitation and inhibition of neurons. We will move from excitatory and inhibitory synaptic potentials to the generation of action potentials and the signal transmission from neuron to neuron and neuron to muscle. We will review the principles of electrochemical transmission and the classes of neurotransmitters involved, including their basic chemistry. The boxes will focus on non-invasive ways of assessing brain function that can be applied in human studies and are therefore of particular relevance to psychiatric research (Boxes 2.1–2.3).

2.1 NEURONS TRANSMIT INFORMATION

Although the ways in which the brain processes information are still clouded in mystery, and the translation of these neuronal processes into phenomenal awareness is largely a matter for philosophical debate, the basic principle of neural functioning seems clear enough. Any single neuron can be conceived as an input–output machine, which receives chemical and/or electrical signals and converts them into an output (normally NT release) in an all-or-nothing fashion. The mechanism behind this all-or-nothing mode is the action potential, which is a unitary electrical event that occurs only if the incoming signals exceed a certain threshold.

2.1.1 The reflex arc is a simple model of information processing

The monosynaptic input–output loop that leads to sensorimotor reflexes such as the knee jerk can serve as a simple model of information processing by neurons. This particular reflex arc (Figure 2.1) starts in the muscle spindle of the quadriceps muscle, which is stretched by the tap on the tendon that connects it with the tibia bone. The muscle spindle is part of a bipolar neuron with its cell body in the dorsal root ganglion. It is connected with an axon that carries an action potential into the grey matter of the spinal medulla and forms a synapse with a motor neuron in the anterior horn. The action potential (AP) leads to release of the neurotransmitter (NT) glutamate from the presynaptic (sensory) neuron, which in turn effects an excitatory postsynaptic potential (EPSP) in the postsynaptic (motor) neuron. This EPSP (in fact, the sum of a large number of EPSPs) triggers an AP at the axon hillock of the motor neuron, which travels back to the muscle and leads to release of acetylcholine, another NT, at the neuromuscular endplate, which effects the contraction of the muscle and the extension of the lower leg. Another synapse of the afferent axon activates an inhibitory interneuron,

Figure 2.1

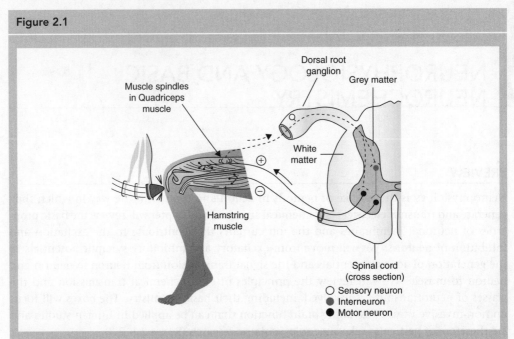

The reflex arc of the knee jerk illustrates basic principles of excitatory and inhibitory neuronal activity

A tap on the tendon of the quadriceps muscle below the patella stretches the muscle, which activates muscle spindles. These are connected to sensory nerves (broken lines) that project through the dorsal root (see Figure 1.9) onto motor neurons in the anterior horn (black) and inhibitory interneurons (grey). They activate the innervation of their own muscle which then contracts to counteract the stretch, resulting in the 'knee jerk'. At the same time, the motor neurons for the antagonist (hamstring muscle) are inhibited by the activated interneurons.

which releases glycine and leads to an inhibitory postsynaptic potential (IPSP) in the motor neuron innervating the leg flexor muscle.

2.1.2   Changes in membrane potentials underlie signal transmission

In order to unravel the component processes of information transmission in and across neurons we need to distinguish three basic events that are largely separate in space and time, the EPSP or IPSP, the AP and the electrochemical transmission, and the release of NT molecules into the synaptic cleft and their reaction with post- and presynaptic receptors. These events are all enabled by the specific properties of the lipid bilayer membrane, especially its selective barrier function for molecules. Water, soluble gases like oxygen and carbon dioxide, small polar molecules like ethanol and lipophilic substances can all freely diffuse across the plasma membrane. Conversely, the membrane is almost impermeable for charged particles, even atomic ions like Na$^+$ (sodium), K$^+$ (potassium), Ca^{2+} (calcium) or Cl$^-$ (chloride), and larger polar molecules like sugars. These substances can pass the membrane only by way of selective transport through so-called channels (e.g. sodium, potassium, chloride or calcium channels), transmembrane proteins with microscopic (< 1 nm diameter) pores. Finally, large molecules, such as NTs, can enter and exit the neuron through the formation of vesicles that are coated

Figure 2.2

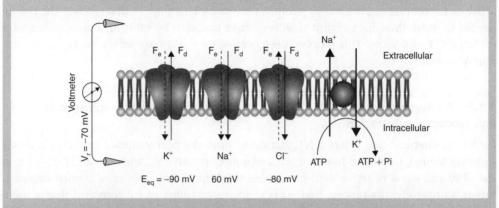

The resting membrane potential

The resting membrane potential V_r is around −70 millivolts (mV). The membrane potential is governed by the distribution of charged particles (ions) on the outside (extracellular) and inside (intracellular) of the membrane. V_r occurs when there is no additional input from synaptic or action potentials or opening of ion channels caused by neurotransmitter binding. Particles travel along concentration gradients (F_d) to areas of lower concentration and along electrostatic gradients (F_e) to areas of opposite charge. The negative V_r thus results in electrostatic attraction of positively charged ions (Na^+, K^+) and repulsion of negative ions (Cl^-). Because extracellular concentrations are high, Na^+ and Cl^- are driven into the cell by a concentration gradient, whereas the opposite is the case for K^+. The equilibrium potentials E_{eq} are explained in Section 2.1.2. The concentration gradients are maintained through the Na^+/K^+ pump, which moves Na^+ out of the cell and K^+ into it.

with a lipid bilayer that fuses with or separates from the membrane, a process termed exo- or endocytosis.

The kinetic of the diffusion of molecules through the membrane is governed by the concentration gradient of the substance (i.e. the concentration difference between the intra- and extracellular space) and, if it is charged, by its electrostatic gradient (i.e. whether the charges inside and outside the membrane are positive or negative). For example, if the concentration of a positively charged ion is higher inside the cell, but the cell is overall negatively charged, the ion will be driven out of the cell by its concentration gradient (F_d) but pushed into it by the electrostatic gradient (F_e; see the example of K^+ in Figure 2.2). Because there are no channels for the negatively charged large organic ions (proteins) the membrane potential is mainly governed by the distribution of Na^+, K^+ and Cl^-. Each of these ions has an equilibrium potential (E_{eq}), at which the electrostatic and concentration gradient add to zero. The potential at which these gradients add to zero across all ions involved is called the membrane potential, V_m. The resting membrane potential V_r, which occurs when there is no additional input from synaptic or action potentials or opening of ion channels caused by NT binding, is approximately −70 millivolts (mV). By convention, the outside of the cell is the zero point, and the negative V_r thus denotes a preponderance of negative ions inside the cell.

Because the E_{eq} for K^+ is more negative than V_r (approx. −75 mV), and the E_{eq} for Na^+ far more positive (approx. 60 mV), K^+ ions diffuse out of the cell, whereas Na^+ ions diffuse into the cell. Diffusion processes would thus ultimately lead to equal concentrations for these positive ions on both sides of the membrane, which would make the triggering of fast responses (AP) impossible. The concentration gradients are therefore maintained through an active transport process, the Na^+/K^+ pump, a transmembrane protein that receives the energy needed to move these ions against their respective gradients by splitting a phosphate group off from ATP molecules. This process is responsible for a large part of the energy consumption of neurons.

2.1.3   Postsynaptic potentials can lead to action potentials through spatial and temporal summation

Let us consider the case where a NT that docks onto the postsynaptic membrane opens a sodium channel, leading to influx of Na^+ and a more positive V_m, and thus an EPSP. Because the EPSP still has a negative sign, just less so than the V_r, this process is termed depolarisation. Conversely, the process that leads to increased influx of Cl^- ions and thus a more negative V_m is called hyperpolarisation. It makes firing of an action potential less likely and is thus inhibitory (IPSP). Because IPSPs are normally produced by a combination of Cl^- entering and K^+ leaving the neuron, the largest hyperpolarisation through this process is equivalent to the E_{eq} for K^+. Both EPSPs and IPSPs summate over time and space. Summation over time occurs if a further postsynaptic potential is generated before the previous one has been completely discharged. Whereas the postsynaptic currents (EPSC and IPSC) normally last for only 1–2 ms, the PSPs take longer to discharge. Their time constant (time until decrease to 1/e or approx. 37% of the peak) is in the range of 5 ms, which is also the approximate time window for temporal summation. Spatial summation occurs if PSCs from several dendrites meet downstream (e.g. at the axon hillock between soma and axon) to create a PSP that is larger than any of the original ones alone. Depolarisation of the axon hillock that exceeds a threshold of approximately −40 mV triggers an AP (Figure 2.3). The ion movements across the membrane that sustain the AP do not occur through chemically gated channels, as in the case of the PSPs, but through electrically gated channels. Such voltage-dependent sodium channels that open when the threshold depolarisation is reached allow for the massive influx of Na^+ into the neuron, leading to further depolarisation up to approximately 40 mV, which is slightly below the E_{eq} of Na^+ at 60 mV. This leads to compensatory K^+ efflux with repolarisation and even a slight after-hyperpolarisation. Restitution of the resulting concentration imbalance to resting levels is one of the functions of the Na^+/K^+-ATPase. The hyperpolarisation constitutes a relative refractory period, during which it takes a higher EPSC to reach the voltage threshold to open the sodium channels and trigger a new AP. During the repolarisation phase of the AP the sodium channels are shut and no new AP can be triggered (absolute refractory period). The whole AP/refractory period cycle takes only a couple of milliseconds, and thus the maximum firing frequency of a neuron is in the range of 500 Hz (Hz [Hertz] is the unit for frequency; 1 Hz = 1 cycle/s).

From the axon hillock the AP has to travel, often over many millimetres or even metres, in the case of very long motor or sensory axons, along the axon to the synapse. This propagation is achieved by bidirectional spreading of the electrotonic potential. However, the refractory sodium channels prevent a new AP at the site of its origin and the AP can thus travel only along the axon. Thus, a new AP will originate at the next non-refractory sodium channels and thus propagate all the way to the synapse at a speed of approximately 1 mm/s. However, transmission speed can be much higher (up to 100 ms/s) in myelinated axons. Here the myelin sheath works as insulation and prevents formation of APs. Thus, the AP has to

Figure 2.3

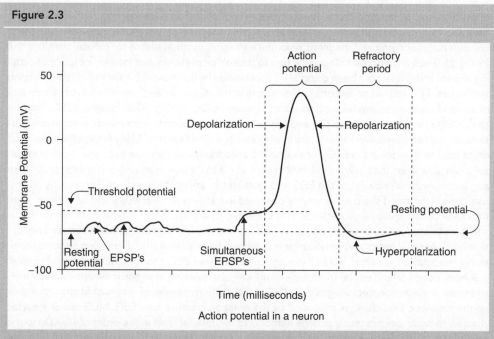

Action potential in a neuron

The action potential

This schema shows the idealised change of membrane potential over time during an action potential (AP). The initial isolated excitatory postsynaptic potentials (EPSPs) are insufficient to trigger an AP, but then the summation of a sufficient number of simultaneous EPSPs brings the membrane potential to a threshold at which voltage-gated ion channels allow the influx of Na$^+$, leading to rapid depolarization. The membrane then repolarizes, even hyperpolarizes, through K$^+$ efflux. During the refractory period no new AP can be triggered in the neuron.

spread electrotonically to the next node of Ranvier, where a new AP will be triggered. This process is, of course, limited by the inevitable loss of depolarisation over distance, but given a close enough spacing of nodes of Ranvier will reliably propagate APs, and much faster than in non-myelinated axons.

Box 2.1   Non-invasive techniques: EEG, MEG

Although even single channels can be recorded in preparations in vitro, and single cells in invasive recordings from animals, most neurophysiological research in humans has to rely on non-invasive techniques. Electroencephalography (EEG) measures the cortical potential changes on the scalp, but requires the spatial summation of large numbers of synchronous postsynaptic potentials for a sufficient signal-to-noise ratio. EEG uses electrodes (made of silver, lead, zinc, or platinum, for example) and amplifiers, which were originally connected to an oscillograph and nowadays to a computer. The result is a visual picture of brain wave. Already the inventor of the EEG, the German psychiatrist Hans Berger (1873–1941) observed that these brain waves changed dramatically if the subject engaged in mental activity, compared to rest. The resting rhythm was in the alpha frequency (8–12 Hz), also termed 'Berger rhythm', whereas cognitive activity and attention were accompanied by faster activity (beta: 12–30 Hz). Slow waves in the theta (3.5–7.5 Hz) and delta (< 3.5 Hz) ranges occur during deep relaxation and sleep, but also during certain pathological states and as a consequence of psychotropic or narcotic drugs. Frequencies even higher than beta (gamma range: 30–100 Hz) have also been associated with cognitive activities. In the time before modern neuroimaging with computed tomography and magnetic resonance imaging (both available for clinical use since the 1970s), EEG was an important diagnostic tool to determine presence and location of space occupying lesions. In this role it has been completely superseded by the more accurate and reliable imaging techniques. EEG still has an important clinical role in the diagnosis and classification of seizure disorders and some neuropsychiatric disorders, for example Creutzfeldt-Jakob disease (CJD). There is also an EEG renaissance in cognitive and clinical research because the observed neuroelectric patterns can be compared with those found in vitro and in animal research. Many prescription and illicit drugs lead to changes in the EEG; for example, benzodiazepines increase beta activity, anticonvulsants can slow down the background rhythm from alpha to theta frequencies and antipsychotics are also associated with slowing of the EEG and increases in epileptiform activity. This activity resembles the synchronised sharp wave activity observed in patients with epilepsy, and sometimes even the characteristic spike–wave patterns. This epileptiform activity, which is most common (in about a third of treated patients) under clozapine and olanzapine, is thought to reflect a reduced seizure threshold. Antipsychotics and antidepressants indeed have a small risk of inducing seizures (commonly thought to be below 1%) but in most patients these EEG changes will remain subclinical.

A more complicated (and far more expensive) way of measuring changes in synaptic activity noninvasively is magnetoencephalography (MEG). MEG systems consist of arrays of sensors that pick up the magnetic field changes produced by the synaptic currents. Like EEG, MEG needs synaptic changes to occur synchronously in large numbers of neurons (at least in the order of 10,000s), but it has the advantage that the attenuation of magnetic signals depends only on the distance from the source, and not on the type of surrounding tissue. MEG thus allows for a more reliable reconstruction of cortical sources of scalp signals than EEG.

Sensory stimuli evoke synchronous activity in the central nervous system that can be measured on the scalp by EEG electrodes. These so-called evoked potentials (EPs) have mainly been described for the visual, auditory and tactile domain, but can in principle be measured for all sensory channels. EPs are normally described as positive or negative going (denoted with the letters P or N), according to the direction of the deflection in standard referencing procedures. This convention is unrelated to the contribution from excitatory vs. inhibitory neural activity, though. The letter is followed by a number that denotes the latency in milliseconds or the position in a sequence of positive or negative deflections. For example, the P100 or P1, generated in primary and higher visual areas, is a positive deflection with latency from stimulus onset of about 100 ms (Figure 2.4). Even subtle changes in the physical stimulus can evoke large changes in neural activity, for example through violations of expectancy. The classical way of studying such 'event-related potentials' (ERPs) is through so-called oddball paradigms, where a train of regular 'standard' stimuli (e.g. tones of a particular frequency) is disrupted by a deviant 'oddball' (a tone at a different frequency). These oddballs are associated with the P300 response, which can be elicited in all sensory modalities, and the auditory 'mismatch negativity' (MMN). The P300 is probably the most widely studied neurophysiological biomarker of mental disorders (see, for example, Chapter 10 on its uses in schizophrenia research). The MMN is also of great neuropsychiatric interest, for example because of its modulation by glutamate antagonists at the NMDA receptor, and its potential use as a prognostic marker for coma patients.

EPs/ERPs have a place in the clinical diagnosis, for example of demyelinating disorders such as multiple sclerosis, where information transmission from the periphery to the CNS is delayed because, as explained above, speed of AP propagation depends on the insulation from the myelin sheath. They are also widely used in psychiatric research to pinpoint the locus of disrupted information processing. In the example below (Fig. 2.9), the P1 component of the visual ERP was used to highlight disruptions of visual processing in schizophrenia. That information processing may be disrupted in sensory (rather than only in frontal and limbic) systems in schizophrenia is a relatively recent outcome of this type of non-invasive research.

Figure 2.4

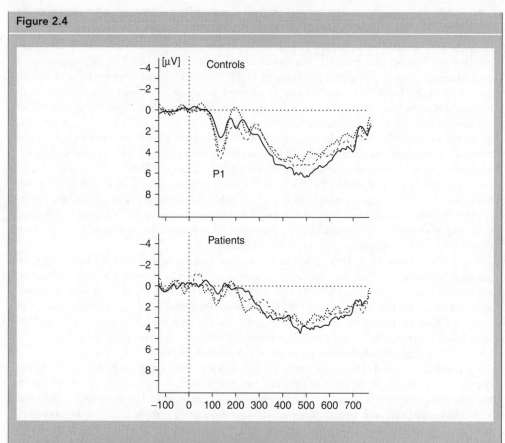

An example of event-related potentials (ERPs)

The P1 component of the visual ERP from a visual working memory task where participants had to encode one, two or three visual objects ('load 1–3'). The ERPs, recorded at the central occipital electrode Oz (over visual cortex), are shown for the encoding phases of load 1 (black line), 2 (dotted line) or 3 (broken line). Patients with schizophrenia showed overall smaller amplitude and less load modulation than control participants. Note that positive deflections go down, following a convention in ERP research.

Source: Modified from (Haenschel et al., 2007), with kind permission of the American Medical Association.

2.1.4   Electrochemical transmission occurs at the synapse

When it reaches the synapse, the AP induces opening of voltage-dependent Ca^{2+} channels. Ca^{2+} induces the release of NTs from presynaptic membrane vesicles through exocytosis into the synaptic cleft. The released quantity of transmitters depends on the concentration of Ca^{2+} in the presynaptic terminal, which increases with the duration and frequency of the APs. A delay of a few milliseconds is involved in the electrochemical synaptic transmission because the Ca^{2+} influx starts only towards the end of the AP, and although the ensuing exocytosis occurs within fractions of a millisecond, the diffusion of NT molecules to the postsynaptic membrane takes some time. NT molecules travel through the synaptic cleft (approx. 20 nm wide) and bind to postsynaptic receptors. The NT/receptor complex has an impact on post-synaptic membrane permeability and can thus trigger a new EPSP or IPSP. Then the cascade from postsynaptic to action potentials to NT release can start in a new neuron.

Box 2.2   TMS

Whereas EEG measures changes in synaptic activity, transcranial magnetic stimulation (TMS) can induce them. TMS works according to the laws of electromagnetic induction. The TMS apparatus is a bank of capacitors that discharge a strong (up to 10,000 Amperes [A]) and very brief (approx. 200 µs) current into a coil that is held over the head. This current generates a magnetic field that induces an electric field in the tissue under the coil. If this tissue is conductive (as is the case for nervous tissue) this electric field will lead to an electric current, which can affect the V_m and cause local membrane de- or hyperpolarisation. Depending on the orientation of the coil and the stimulated neurons, and of the stimulation parameters, the effects of TMS can be excitatory or inhibitory. For example, we can elicit movements of the contralateral hand by applying single pulses of TMS to the hand area of the primary motor cortex. The net effect of this stimulation was thus excitatory. Similarly, stimulation over the visual cortex may induce perceptions of flashing lights, called phosphenes. Conversely, repetitive stimulations at intermediate frequencies (e.g. 1 Hz) or the more recently developed 'theta burst' (3 cycles per second of fast bursts of 5 pulses) are thought to have inhibitory effects, for example to slow down cognitive operations that rely on the stimulated area.

In cognitive neuroscience, TMS is used as a 'functional lesion' method. Whereas neuropsychologists traditionally had to base their studies on opportunistic samples of patients with clinical lesions, experimental neuropsychology with TMS can now manipulate brain activity as the independent variable and assess the resulting cognitive deficits (or enhancements). TMS is thus a unique method to assess the brain structure–function relationship systematically. With the use of single pulse (sp) TMS researchers can disrupt or facilitate neural processing at particular points of time, whereas repetitive TMS (rTMS) disrupts or enhances neural processing during a train of stimuli and beyond.

In a psychiatric context rTMS is also used as experimental treatment method for hallucinations and depression. In both cases the aim is to target an area that is supposed to be under- or overactive. In the case of depression, the model is that the frontal cortex is underactive (hypofrontality), which leads to problems with executive function and motivation and generally inability to rein in the uncontrollable emotions presented by the limbic system. Thus, the aim is to enhance prefrontal function with high-frequency (10 Hz) rTMS. There are some promising reports of clinical improvement (and some evidence for a biochemical correlate, increased dopamine release, but only in animal experiments), but rTMS has yet to pass the standard tests for an evidence-based treatment method. Based on neuroimaging findings of a role of temporal lobe activity in hallucinations, rTMS of left temporoparietal cortex has been attempted for a reduction in severity and frequency of hallucinations. Again, the first clinical results are promising, but problems like the design of a placebo condition, quantification of clinical effects, and sample size of studies make it difficult to demonstrate improvement definitively.

2.2   NEUROTRANSMITTERS CONVEY INFORMATION BETWEEN NEURONS

Not all synaptic molecules are NTs. In order to qualify as an NT a substance needs to:

- be synthesised and stored in the neuron
- be released from the neuron upon electrical stimulation
- have postsynaptic receptors
- be deactivated after release and action
- have selective inhibitors.

There are two main classes of NT receptors. In the case of ionotropic or ligand-gated receptors, the same protein acts as receptor and channel. Binding of an agonist will directly lead to opening of the channel and higher permeability for an ion and a postsynaptic current.

Its action and termination are fast and it is thus involved in short-term information transmission and neural plasticity. Conversely, metabotropic receptors are not themselves ion channels, but indirectly control channels through G-proteins. G (GTP-binding)-proteins are central regulating molecules. When they are activated by a metabotropic receptor, they bind guanosine triphosphate (GTP) and split off a phosphate group from GTP. In this process G-proteins also release a subunit that activates other molecules, for example an ion channel. However, this subunit can also activate other proteins and thus trigger cascades of so-called second messengers (the NT molecules are the 'first' messengers), which can influence gene expression or lead to other lasting biochemical changes in the postsynaptic neuron. These second messenger systems include cyclic adenosine monophosphate (cAMP), inositol triphosphate (IP3) and diacylglycerol (DAG). Because of their effect on second messenger systems the metabotropic receptors are supposed to support long-term neural plasticity. It is still a moot case whether psychotropic drugs such as antipsychotics or antidepressants, which all influence synaptic transmission, act through alteration of postsynaptic potentials or through more long-term plastic changes (the onset latency of most clinical effects would support the latter view). These issues will be discussed in more detail in Part II.

Modulatory processes at the presynaptic membrane can inhibit or enhance NT release. Inhibition of calcium channels or hyperpolarisation of the membrane through increased K^+- or Cl^- permeability (leading to K^+ efflux or Cl^- influx, respectively, and thus more relative negative charge inside) decrease Ca^{2+} influx or sensitivity. Conversely, direct increase of Ca^{2+} permeability or closing of K^+ channels, increased duration of the AP or high-frequency stimulation of the presynaptic neuron all lead to increased Ca^{2+} influx and thus enhance NT release.

2.2.1 NTs come from different chemical classes

The classical NTs are the monoamines dopamine, noradrenaline/norepinephrine, adrenaline/epinephrine (collectively termed catecholamines) and serotonin, the amino acids glutamic acid, glycine and gamma-amino-butyric acid (GABA), and acetylcholine. The monoamines derive their name from the single amine (one nitrogen and two or three hydrogen atoms) group at their tail. The catecholamines are named for the catechol ring (carbohydrate ring with two hydroxyl-groups), whereas serotonin or 5-hydroxytryptamine (5-HT) has the structure of an indoleamine. All amino acids have an amine group at one end (the amino-terminal) and a carboxy (COOH) group at the other (the carboxy-terminal) (Figure 2.5). Acetylcholine is chemically an ester (combination of two molecules via an oxygen bridge) of choline and acetic acid (Figure 2.6). The enzyme that splits it into its components is therefore called acetylcholine-esterase, and drugs that inhibit this enzyme are called acetylcholine-esterase inhibitors (AChEI). AChEI are the main class of anti-dementia drugs, based on the assumption that cholinergic (acetylcholine-based) neurotransmission is disturbed in Alzheimer's disease.

2.2.2 Dopamine, noradrenaline (norepinephrine) and adrenaline (epinephrine) are catecholamines

Catecholamines are synthesised in the synaptic terminal from a common precursor, the amino acid tyrosine, which shares a transport system into the brain with the other hydrophobic amino acids, for example tryptophan. Tyrosine reaches the synaptic terminal through active transport in the cytoskeleton of the axon. Depending on the availability of the enzymes

Figure 2.5

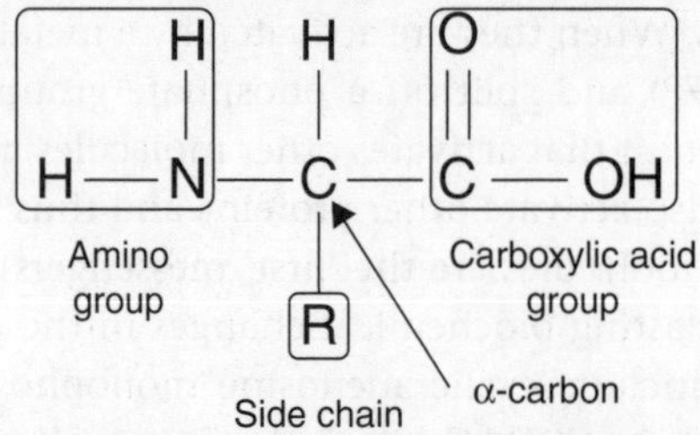

Amino acids, the building blocks of proteins
The basic structure of amino acids consists of a carbon atom with a carboxylic acid group, an amino group and a side chain. The 20 amino acids that make up human proteins are all alpha amino acids, meaning that the same (alpha) carbon atom carries the carboxy- and amino groups. The negatively charged salts of amino acids that result from the loss of the proton of the carboxy-group are often termed with the suffix 'ate', for example 'glutamate'.

Figure 2.6

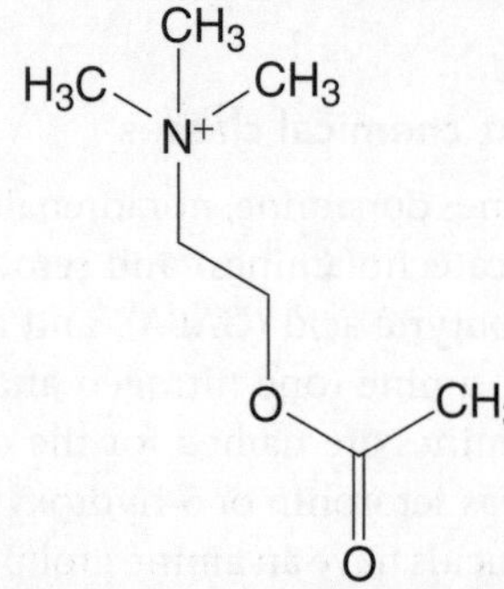

The neurotransmitter acetylcholine is an ester of a choline group (top) and acetic acid (bottom)

that catalyse the respective reactions, tyrosine will be converted to dopamine (through the intermediary step 3,4-dihydroxyphenylalanine, DOPA), and further to noradrenaline/ norepinephrine (NE) and adrenaline/epinephrine (E) (Figure 2.7). Because dopamine does not pass through the blood–brain barrier, dopamine replacement therapy in Parkinson's disease, which is characterised by loss of dopaminergic neurons in the substantia nigra and elsewhere, uses DOPA. DOPA can be easily converted to dopamine by the enzyme DOPA-decarboxylase (also called aromatic L-amino acid decarboxylase [AAAD]). In order for this to happen only in the brain (and not in the general circulation, where dopamine would cause unwanted side effects, for example on blood pressure), AAAD inhibitors, which unlike DOPA do not pass through the blood–brain barrier, are normally given at the same time (see also Section 6.4).

Figure 2.7

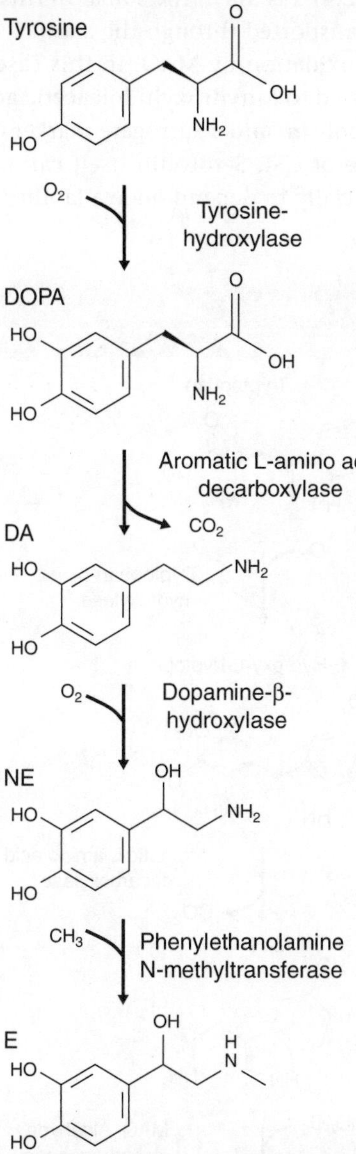

Catecholamine biosynthesis starts from the amino acid tyrosine

The respective enzymes are listed to the right of the arrows. The step to DOPA, catalysed by tyrosine hydroxylase, is rate limiting, meaning that a dysfunction of this enzyme would result in a deficit of catecholamines. DOPA decarboxylase is of clinical importance because inhibitors of this enzyme are added to DOPA in the therapy of Parkinson's disease in order to avoid conversion to dopamine in the periphery. Dopamine (DA) is further converted to noradrenaline by addition of a hydroxyl group to its beta carbon atom, and noradrenaline to adrenaline/epinephrine (E) by addition of a methyl group. Noradrenaline is a member of the group of phenylethanolamines.

2.2.3 Serotonin is an indoleamine

The conversion of tryptophan to 5-HT (serotonin), through the intermediary step 5-hydroxytryptophan (Figure 2.8), occurs in the soma. In this case therefore, the final NT rather than the precursor is transported through the axon. Its degradation starts, as with the catecholamines, through oxidation by MAO, in this case to 5-hydroxyindoleacetaldehyde, which is further oxidised to 5-hydroxyindoleacetic acid (5-HIAA), the main end-product of indoleamine metabolism, and a surrogate marker of serotonin concentrations that can be measured in urine or CSF. Serotonin itself can be measured in blood platelets. Serotonin levels seem crucially to depend on availability of tryptophan. Tryptophan

Figure 2.8

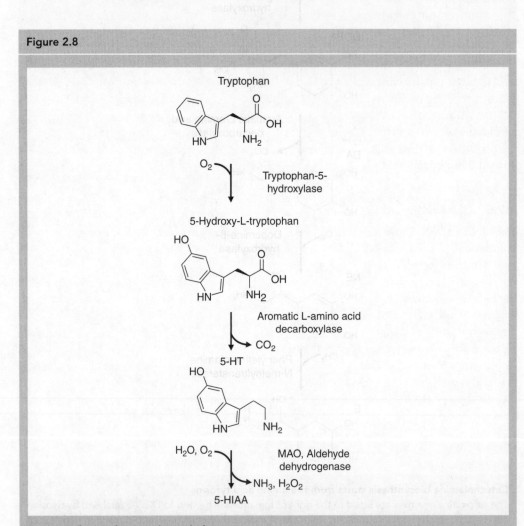

Serotonin biosynthesis and metabolism

The first two steps (hydroxylation and decarboxylation) are analogous to the conversion of tyrosine to dopamine. Serotonin (5-hydroxytryptamine, 5-HT) can then be metabolised through MAO and in a further step aldehyde dehydrogenase to 5-hydroxyindoleacetic acid (5-HIAA), which can be measured in blood or CSF as a surrogate marker of serotonergic activity. Another pathway leads from 5-HT to melatonin.

depletion has been used as an experimental model of depression, based on the theory that depression is caused by monoamine deficiency (monoamine deficit model of depression, which will be discussed in more detail in Chapter 11).

2.2.4 The action of NTs can be terminated through enzymatic degradation

Enzymatic degradation is one of the main mechanisms for the termination of NT action. Other enzymes that are targets of psychotropic drugs include monoamine-oxidase (MAO) and catechol-O-methyltransferase (COMT). MAO removes the amine group from monoamines and thus converts them into aldehydes, which can be oxidised further to the corresponding acid (e.g. 5-HIAA, see Figure 2.8) or reduced to the corresponding alcohol. COMT adds a methylene (CH_3) group to the catechol ring. Through these enzymatic processes catecholamines can be converted into methylated alcohols or methylated acid. In neurons, the main metabolic pathway for dopamine leads to the methylated acid 3-methoxy-4-hydroxyphenyl acetic acid or homovanillic acid (HVA). For NE, the main metabolic pathway in neurons yields 3-methoxy-4-hydroxyphenylglycol (MHPG). Both HVA and MHPG can be measured in urine as surrogate markers of catecholamine production. MAO inhibitors are used in depression in order to maintain high levels of monoamines in the synaptic cleft, and COMT inhibitors are used in Parkinson's disease with the same rationale.

2.2.5 Glutamate and GABA are produced by central metabolic pathways

The amino acid L-glutamate is the product of the transamination of alpha-ketoglutarate, a component of the Krebs cycle, the common pathway of glucose, protein and lipid catabolism. Humans therefore do not depend on the glutamate that is ingested with food, unlike for the 'essential' amino acids, for which they do not have a pathway of biosynthesis, for example tryptophan or phenylalanine, the precursor of tyrosine. Decarboxylation of L-glutamate, which is catalysed by the enzyme glutamate decarboxylase I in nervous tissue and needs pyridoxal phosphate as coenzyme, yields GABA (Figure 2.9). Its action is terminated by reuptake into the presynaptic neuron or further enzymatic conversion to succinyl-CoA, another ubiquitous component of the Krebs cycle. It is therefore impossible to draw any conclusions about glutamate or GABA activity in the brain from measuring its metabolic products. The same is true for glycine, which is the simplest amino acid and a basic building block for many

Figure 2.9

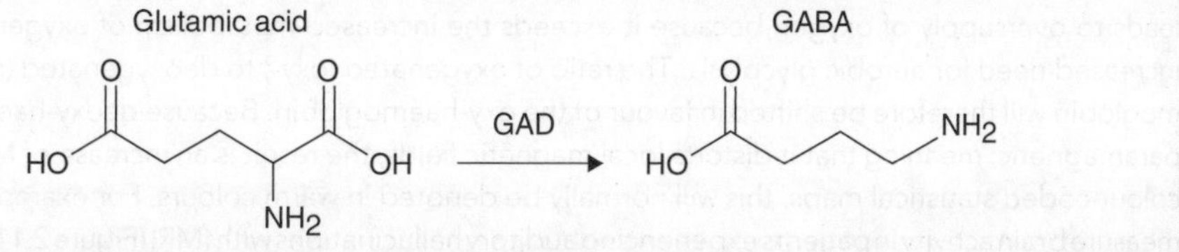

Glutamic acid   GABA

Glutamic acid and GABA (a gamma amino acid) are the most important amino acid NTs in the brain. Their reaction is catalysed by glutamic acid decarboxylase (GAD).

more complex biomolecules. One of its catabolic reactions is catalysed by D-amino acid oxidase (DAO), which is also involved in the metabolism of the amino acid D-serine, a co-factor required for the activation of the NMDA receptor by glutamate. Some post-mortem evidence suggests that the activity of DAO may be increased in schizophrenia.

Glutamate is the main excitatory NT of the CNS, GABA the main inhibitory NT of the brain, and glycine the main inhibitory NT of the spinal cord and the PNS. Acetylcholine and the monoamines are the NTs of specific (cholinergic, dopaminergic, serotonergic, noradrenergic) neurons and can have a range of inhibitory and excitatory effects. They are therefore sometimes classified as 'neuromodulatory'. Another group of NTs with a largely modulatory effect are the peptide NTs. They seem to modulate the function of the classical NTs through poorly known mechanisms, but also have their own receptors, for example the enkephalins, which bind to opioid receptors. The neuropeptides play a major role in the transmission and modulation of pain perception, especially the enkephalins and substance P. Some of the neuropeptides, for example angiotensin II, vasoactive intestinal peptide (VIP), somatostatin and cholecystokinin (CCK), also have functions outside the nervous system and straddle the boundary between NTs and hormones. We will revisit them in Chapter 3 on neuroendocrinology.

Box 2.3   Metabolic imaging

EEG and MEG have exquisite temporal resolution (in the range of the underlying synaptic events) and can thus trace neural activation in real time. However, their spatial resolution and localisation accuracy are limited. Functional magnetic resonance imaging (fMRI) can trace neural activation at a spatial resolution that is about one order of magnitude higher (in the millimetre range), but suffers from limitations in its temporal resolution because it relies on a sluggish vascular response. However, with the echo-planar imaging (EPI) technique, functional images of the whole brain can be acquired within 1–2 s, which is sufficient to capture complex cognitive processes or changes in mental states. The hallucination study described below is an example of such an application. PET has even lower spatial (and temporal) resolution (Figure 2.10), but can yield excellent molecular resolution (discussed in chapter 7). The temporal resolution of TMS ranges from tens of milliseconds in the case of single pulse (sp) TMS to several minutes in the case of virtual lesion protocols with repetitive TMS (rTMS). An invasive method that, like fMRI, relies on vascular signals and has an excellent spatial resolution is optical imaging. In animal studies it can be combined with direct intracerebral recordings to yield both global activation maps and information about fine-grained temporal activation patterns, but this is not possible in human studies. However, even in humans it may be possible to explore the blind spot in the left lower corner of Figure 2.10 and trace brain correlates of perception or thought at millisecond and millimetre resolution through the combination of fMRI and EEG.

FMRI provides an indirect measure of neural activity. Synaptic activity leads to the release of vasoactive substances such as nitric oxide that lead to local vasodilatation. The ensuing influx of fresh blood leads to oversupply of oxygen because it exceeds the increased metabolism of oxygen due to the increased need for aerobic glycolysis. The ratio of oxygenated (oxy-) to deoxygenated (deoxy-) haemoglobin will therefore be shifted in favour of the oxy-haemoglobin. Because deoxy-haemoglobin is paramagnetic, meaning that it distorts local magnetic fields, the result is an increase of MRI signal. In colour-coded statistical maps, this will normally be denoted in warm colours. For example, when we measure brain activity in patients experiencing auditory hallucinations with fMRI (Figure 2.11, Plate V), we can detect a hotspot in their auditory cortex (even without any change in external auditory stimulation).

Another technique for metabolic imaging is positron emission tomography (PET) with radioactively labelled glucose (fluorodeoxyglucose, FDG) or water. FDG-PET picks up the increased con-

Figure 2.10

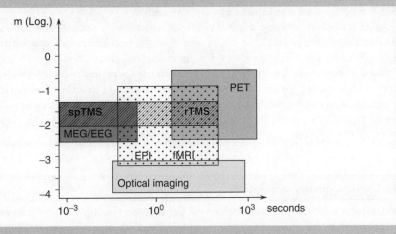

Temporal and spatial resolution of the most widely used non-invasive neuroimaging/ neurophysiology techniques

Notes: EEG: Electroencephalography; EPI: Echo-Planar Imaging; fMRI: Functional Magnetic Resonance Imaging; MEG: Magnetoencephalography; PET: Positron Emission Tomography; sp/rTMS: single pulse/ repetitive Transcranial Magnetic Stimulation.

sumption of glucose in activated brain areas. Although it was the most widely technique of metabolic imaging into the late 1990s PET has now been largely superseded by fMRI because of its ease of administration and absence of radioactivity. PET still very much has a place in psychiatric research as a tool for receptor mapping.

FMRI has already contributed significantly to our understanding of psychopathology (e.g. hallucinations). It provides information that cannot be obtained from structural imaging and/or neuropsychology alone. FMRI can also reveal the networks involved in cognitive operations that are affected by neuropsychiatric disorders. Although fMRI has no diagnostic use yet, clinical applications in the monitoring of pharmacological and psychological interventions are currently being explored.

Learning points

Mental disorders are disorders of perception, thought, action and emotions. All these functions are supported by complex interplay of information processing by neurons in the CNS. Although very little is known about the mechanisms of higher cognitive functions, the basic elements of neuronal signal processing are relatively well understood. A neuron converts chemical input (docking of a receptor to their dendritic membrane) into chemical output (NT release from synaptic boutons) through electrical signals. NT binding to a receptor can lead to excitatory or inhibitory postsynaptic potentials. The excitatory potentials can sum up (temporal and spatial summation) to yield an action potential, which travels along the axon to the synaptic terminal, where it triggers influx of calcium, which results in release of NT. This NT can in turn bind to postsynaptic receptors, starting a new cycle.

NTs come from different chemical classes, including amino acids, monoamines (molecules with one amino-group, $-NH_2$) and peptides. The amino acids glutamic acid and GABA are the main excitatory and inhibitory NTs of the human brain. The monoamines can be further subdivided into catecholamines (derived from the amino acid tyrosine) – dopamine, norepinephrine, epinephrine –

and indoleamines (derived from the amino acid tryptophan) – serotonin. Each monoamine has its specific brainstem nuclei that project onto cortical excitatory or inhibitory neurons. The monoamines and acetylcholine are also regarded as 'neuromodulators'.

Although we cannot study neuronal excitation directly in humans, several non-invasive techniques are available for the investigation of the neural correlates of information processing and its dysfunctions. These include techniques with high temporal (EEG, MEG) and high spatial resolution (fMRI). TMS is a method that allows testing brain–behaviour relationships through virtual lesions and also has potential clinical applications, for example in depression. These techniques can be complemented with neurochemical approaches, such as the measurement of NT metabolites in CSF, blood or urine, or radioligand imaging of NT receptors, in order to further the understanding of the molecular basis of information processing and its disturbance in mental disorders.

Revision and discussion questions

- Describe a full cycle of electrochemical transmission starting with the generation of an action potential in the presynaptic neuron and ending with an action potential in the postsynaptic neuron.
- What are the main biochemical classes of NTs and how does the human body get them?
- What are the advantages and disadvantages of the non-invasive techniques for the investigation of human brain function?

FURTHER READING

Floel, A. and Cohen, L. (2006). Translational studies in neurorehabilitation: From bench to bedside. *Cognitive and Behavioral Neurology*, 19, 1–10.

Ford, J., Krystal, J. and Mathalon, D. (2007). Neural synchrony in schizophrenia: From networks to new treatments. *Schizophrenia Bulletin*, 33, 848–52.

George, M. and Aston-Jones, G. (2010). Noninvasive techniques for probing neurocircuitry and treating illness: Vagus nerve stimulation (VNS), transcranial magnetic stimulation (TMS) and transcranial direct current stimulation (tDCS). *Neuropsychopharmacology*, 35, 301–16.

Kandel, E. R., Schwartz, J. H. and Jessell, T. M. (2000). *Principles of Neural Science* (New York and London: McGraw-Hill, Health Professions Division), Parts II and III.

Linden, D. E. and Fallgatter, A. J. (2009). Neuroimaging in psychiatry: From bench to bedside. *Frontiers in Human Neuroscience*, 3, 49.

Sack, A. T. and Linden, D. E. (2003). Combining transcranial magnetic stimulation and functional imaging in cognitive brain research: Possibilities and limitations. *Brain Research Reviews*, 43, 41–56.

Thaker, G. (2008). Neurophysiological endophenotypes across bipolar and schizophrenia psychosis. *Schizophrenia Bulletin*, 34, 760–73.

3 NEUROENDOCRINOLOGY

PREVIEW

Hormones are an important bridge between the CNS and various effector organs and they regulate key metabolic processes. Changes in hormone levels are important for many psychological disorders, for example those associated with the menstrual cycle, and some of the key hormonal regulation systems feature prominently in current theories of affective and stress-related disorders. Hormones and their receptors have also recently become a target for drug development in biological psychiatry. This chapter describes the central role of the hypothalamus in providing the release factors for pituitary hormones and the three main systems arising from it, the hypothalamic-pituitary-adrenal (HPA) axis, the hypothalamic-pituitary-thyroid (HPT) axis and the hypothalamic-pituitary-gonadal (HPG) axis. It then focuses on the role of the HPA axis in mediating the stress response and that of the HPG axis for the impact of sex hormones on mental health.

3.1 HORMONES AID COMMUNICATION BETWEEN CELLS

Like neurotransmitters (NTs), hormones communicate between cells, but not just between neurons. Hormones can act on the cell that neighbours the secreting cell (paracrine), on the secreting cell itself (autocrine), or they are secreted into blood and act on cells that are further afield (endocrine). Peptides (chains formed from up to 100 amino acids), amino acid derivatives and steroids are the commonest forms of hormones. They are synthesised in endocrine glands such as the pituitary, thyroid, adrenal or gonadal glands, or by endocrine cells that are interspersed in the various tissues. In their target organs the hormones bind with extracellular or intracellular (cytosolic or nuclear) receptors and regulate the metabolism of the target cell.

3.2 THE HYPOTHALAMIC-PITUITARY SYSTEM REGULATES BASIC FUNCTIONS OF THE LIFE CYCLE

The hypothalamic-pituitary system is the main neuroendocrine system. It regulates basic functions of the life cycle – growth, procreation and survival. The hypothalamus is the main link between the neural and endocrine systems. Its secretory cells are activated by NTs and release hormones, some of which, the so-called release factors, stimulate the pituitary to release other hormones into the blood. Both the hypothalamic release-promoting or -inhibiting factors and the pituitary hormones are peptides (with the exception of dopamine) (Table 3.1). The other main neuroendocrine system is the sympathetic adrenal-medullary (SAM) pathway, which controls the release of adrenaline and noradrenaline.

The pituitary and peripheral hormones control the secretion of the hypothalamic release factors, and thus their own release through feedback loops. Although all the

Table 3.1   The release factors and hormones of the hypothalamic-pituitary systems

Hypothalamic release factor	Pituitary hormone (upregulated unless stated otherwise)	Target organ and function of pituitary hormone
Corticotrophin releasing ractor (CRF), Vasopressin (AVP)	Adrenocorticotropic hormone (ACTH)	Adrenal cortex (zona fasciculata): Cortisol production
TSH releasing hormone (TRH)	Thyroid-stimulating hormone (TSH); Prolactin	Thyroid gland: Production of the thyroid hormones T_3 and T_4
Luteinising hormone-releasing hormone (LHRH)	Luteinising hormone (LH) Follicle-stimulating hormone (FSH)	*Male* LH: Leydig cells of testicles: Production of testosterone; FSH: Sertoli cells of testicles: Spermatogenesis *Female* LH/FSH: Ovary – regulation of menstrual cycle
Growth Hormone Releasing Hormone (GHRH)	Growth hormone/ Somatotropin (STH)	Liver: Production of insulin-like growth factors (IGF); Cartilage: Stimulates division of chondrocytes
Somatostatin	STH and TSH (downregulation)	See above
Dopamine	Prolactin (downregulation)	Mammary glands: Lactation; Brain: reduction of dopamine release from hypothalamus (short feedback loop), otherwise unknown

hypothalamic-pituitary-peripheral gland systems are of immense importance for physical and mental well-being, those most directly related to mental disorders and their treatment are the tuberoinfundibular dopamine-prolactin system and the HPA axis, which will therefore be described here in more detail.

3.3   THE TUBEROINFUNDIBULAR DOPAMINE PATHWAY REGULATES LACTATION

Dopamine is synthesised in the arcuate and periventricular nuclei of the mediobasal hypothalamus (the 'tuberal region' from *tuber* (Latin) = lump) and released into the system of portal veins that connect the hypothalamus with the anterior pituitary through the pituitary stalk (also called *infundibulum* (Latin) = funnel). Because the anterior pituitary is outside the blood–brain barrier dopamine can exert direct effects on the prolactin producing pituitary cells, which are called lactotrophs. Lactotrophs have a high baseline activity, which may explain why hypothalamic inhibiting factors (mainly dopamine) are generally more important than the factors that stimulate prolactin release (thyrotropin-releasing hormone, TRH and vasoactive intestinal peptide, VIP). Lactotrophs comprise up to half the cell population of the anterior pituitary, and some are more responsive to the inhibitory effects of dopamine, whereas others are more responsive to the stimulating effects of TRH. Unlike in the HPA axis, there is no hormone produced by the target gland (like cortisol) to regulate the hypothalamic release (or in this case: inhibiting) factor. Hypothalamic dopamine secretion is thus under the direct control of prolactin, a mechanism termed 'short-loop feedback' (Fitzgerald and Dinan, 2008). The dopaminergic neurons of the arcuate and periventricular nuclei possess prolactin receptors, and increasing prolactin concentrations enhance their activity, and vice versa, producing a negative feedback loop (increasing prolactin production leading to enhanced release of the inhibiting factor). The mechanism through which prolactin stimulates dopaminergic activity in the hypothalamus seems to be activation and induction (stimulation of the gene expression) of tyrosine hydroxylase, which is the rate limiting enzyme for dopamine synthesis (see chapter 2). Prolactin secreted from the pituitary travels through the blood stream to the choroid plexus where it enters the CSF and diffuses to the hypothalamus – amongst other parts of the brain, where it is almost ubiquitous. Its enhancing effects on tyrosine hydroxylase seem confined to the dopamine producing hypothalamic nuclei.

The tuberoinfundibular pathway is of great importance for clinical psychiatry because of the antidopaminergic effects of antipsychotic agents. The dopamine effects on the lactotroph are mediated through D2 receptors, which are blocked by all typical antipsychotics. The resulting disinhibition of prolactin production leads to side effects that can include growth of breasts and even milk secretion in men, impotence in men and infertility in women, and persistent milk secretion, lack of libido and vaginal soreness in women. Of the atypical antipsychotics, some (risperidone, sulpiride and aminosulpiride) frequently lead to increased prolactin levels, whereas others (e.g. olanzapine, quetiapine) show this problem much less. One explanation may be that the blood–brain barrier is less permeable for the former class, necessitating higher levels of the antipsychotic agent in the circulation (and thus in the anterior pituitary) in order to obtain a given central dopamine receptor occupancy (and antipsychotic effect). However, even those antipsychotics that do not lead to lasting increases in prolactin levels and the associated side effects produce a marked transient increase. The transient nature of this initial prolactin increase may be explained by the fast dissociation from the D2 receptor that is a pharmacokinetic property of some of the atypical antipsychotics. Furthermore, prolactin is also under the control of the serotonergic system. Stimulation of 5-HT$_2$ receptors promotes prolactin release, and this effect is utilised by the fenfluramine test that assesses the viability of the serotonin system through its ability to increase prolactin levels.

3.4 THE HPA AXIS REGULATES METABOLISM AND THE STRESS RESPONSE

The paraventricular nucleus (PVN) of the hypothalamus secretes corticotrophin-releasing factor (CRF) and vasopressin (also called arginine vasopressin, AVP or antidiuretic hormone, ADH) into the infundibular portal veins. The adrenocorticotropic hormone (ACTH)-secreting cells of the anterior pituitary, called corticotrophs, express receptors for CRF and AVP, which act synergistically to stimulate the release of ACTH. ACTH is secreted into the circulation and stimulates the adrenal cortex to release glucocorticoids, a class of steroid hormones (Table 3.2). Glucocorticoids increase blood glucose levels, counteracting the effects of insulin. They also contribute to the regulation of water and electrolyte homoeostasis, increase blood pressure and can suppress immune responses. Several effects on the CNS have been postulated, for example in the formation of new memories, but also damage to the hippocampus after longer periods of upregulation. The best documented psychiatric effect is probably the acute psychosis that can arise from high levels of glucocorticoids owing to overproduction

Table 3.2 Steroid hormones

Class	Main production organ	Target organ	Receptor	Function	Examples
Glucocorticoids	Adrenal cortex	Ubiquitous	Glucocorticoid receptor (intracellular): forms complex with glucocorticoids	Gluconeogenesis, anti-inflammatory, immune suppression	Cortisol (human), corticosterone (rodents)
Mineralocorticoids	Adrenal cortex	Kidneys	Mineralocorticoid receptor (MR) (intracellular): forms complex with gluco- or mineralocorticoids	Sodium retention, potassium secretion	Aldosterone
Sex hormones Androgens	Testicles (Leydig cells)	Ubiquitous	Androgen receptor (intracellular)	Male secondary sex characteristics; Anabolic	Testosterone
Oestrogens	Ovaries, placenta	Ubiquitous	Oestrogen receptor (intracellular); GPR30 (G Protein-coupled Receptor 30)	Female secondary sex characteristics; Regulation of menstrual cycle	Oestrone [E1], oestradiol [oestradiol-17 beta, E2], oestriol [E3]
Gestagens	Ovaries	Ubiquitous	Progesterone receptor (intracellular); MR (high affinity blockade)	Regulation of pregnancy	progesterone

(e.g. from overstimulation of the adrenal glands by an ACTH-secreting tumour of the anterior pituitary, Cushing's disease) or medical use (e.g. as immunosuppressant in autoimmune disease). The effects of glucocorticoids on the brain can be mediated through the glucocorticoid - (GR) or the mineralocorticoid receptor (MR). The affinity of glucocorticoids for the MR, which is mainly expressed in the pituitary, hippocampus and amygdala, is much higher than that for the GR. The MR is thus probably saturated most of the time, whereas the GR, which is more widely expressed in the brain and in peripheral tissue, is mainly activated during times of peak concentration in the early morning or during stress. GR binding of cortisol in the hypothalamus, anterior pituitary and adrenal cortex lead to downregulation of the HPA axis (Figure 3.1), constituting a negative feedback loop (Thomson and Craighead, 2008).

Figure 3.1

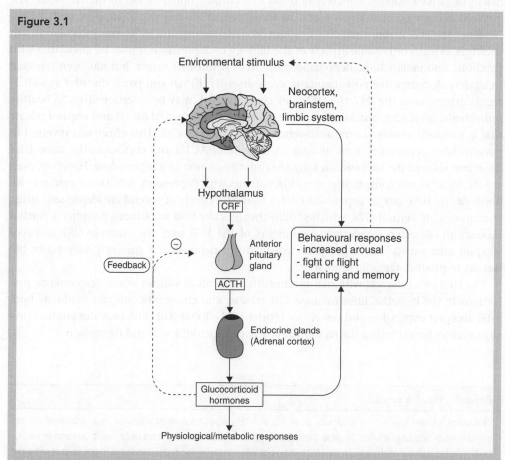

The hypothalamic-pituitary-adrenal (HPA) axis mediates the stress response

The production of glucocorticoids (cortisol) in the adrenal cortex is stimulated by the pituitary hormone ACTH, which in turn is under the control of the hypothalamic hormone CRF. The CRF-producing cells in the hypothalamus receive input from other brain regions. This cascade is regulated by a negative feedback loop because higher cortisol levels lead to reduced ACTH production. It mediates the physiological and behavioural responses to environmental stress.

The synthesis and secretion of CRF and AVP increase after exposure to stressful stimuli, for example encounter with a predator or immobilisation. The HPA axis has thus been implicated in the 'fight or flight' response, a common response pattern to threat that was first described by the American physiologist Walter Bradford Cannon (1971–1945) in 1915. Stress and in particular dysfunctional coping with and adaptation to stress play a key role in psychological models of anxiety and depression, and it was therefore natural to probe changes in the HPA axis in these disorders. Normally, blood cortisol levels show a clear diurnal pattern with a peak in the morning and a second, smaller peak in the evening. Studies in patients with depression found a less pronounced circadian cortisol rhythm and reduced suppression of CRF and ACTH secretion in response to glucocorticoids. This is typically tested with the dexamethasone suppression test (DST). Dexamethasone (DEX) is a synthetic steroid that has glucocorticoid function and suppresses CRF and AVP release from the PVN. Reduced suppression of cortisol levels after intake of dexamethasone thus indicates insufficient negative feedback, which may result in a chronic upregulation of the HPA axis. The elevated urinary cortisol levels found in some patient studies would support such a link. However, the DST is abnormal only in about 50% of patients, and HPA axis dysregulation can therefore explain only some aspects of the biology of depression. It may be associated with psychotic and melancholic depression more than with other forms, but has been reported in anxiety disorders like post-traumatic stress disorder (PTSD) and panic disorder as well. A recent extension of the DST, the DEX/CRF challenge test, may be more sensitive. In healthy individuals, prior administration of DEX suppresses the increased ACTH and cortisol release that is normally observed after intravenous application of CRF. This effect was reversed in patients with depression, who showed an increase of ACTH and cortisol at the same DEX dose, and showed the suppression only after administration of a higher dose. However, even the DEX/CRF is not consistently altered in patients with depression. Additional evidence for a role of the HPA axis in depression comes from the effects of several antidepressant drugs that upregulate central GRs, which should theoretically lead to reduced peripheral cortisol production. Research developing modulators of the HPA axis, for example CRF and AVP receptor antagonists, into a potential treatment for depression is currently very active but has yet to produce tangible results.

The HPA axis interacts with neurotransmitter systems at various levels. Serotonergic projections to the hypothalamus increase CRF release, and glucocorticoids can modulate both 5-HT receptor expression and sensitivity (Porter et al., 2004). This link provides another possible avenue for exploring the relationship between cortisol levels and depression.

Box 3.1   What is stress?

The term 'stress' is used in a variety of ways. We talk about stress at work or in a relationship, or stressful periods of our lives. In laboratory settings, stress can be induced in animals by cold or heat, bright light, painful stimuli such as electroshocks or immobilisation. Imminent danger to our lives or those of our loved ones produces stress, and even the past experience of threatening situations can result in ongoing stress, as in 'post-traumatic stress disorder'. What these scenarios have in common is that they consist in perceived or real threats to the homoeostasis, the balance of bodily functions, and ultimately to survival. Although 'stress' is sometimes used to denote maladaptive responses to environmental changes, its psychological (e.g. heightened arousal) and physiological (e.g. increased heartbeat) components can serve important purposes, for example the flight from a predator. It thus makes sense to follow the endocrinologist Hans Selye (1907–82) and distinguish adaptive 'eustress' from maladaptive 'distress', which results from insufficient coping with challenging life situations and can lead to avoidance behaviour and anxiety. It is the latter type of psychological stress that has been mostly implicated in the genesis of mental disorders.

A stressor thus cannot be defined by its intrinsic properties but only by the response it evokes in the organism concerned. One person might find a five-minute journey in an underground train extremely stressful, whereas this is a perfectly routine undertaking for the majority of the population. The biological cascade that defines the stress response and has the goal of returning the body to homoeostasis relies on three main neuroendocrinological systems. In addition to the HPA axis, these are the noradrenergic brainstem pathways and the neuropeptide system (particularly α-melanocyte-stimulating hormone and β-endorphin) (Chrousos, 2009).

The stress response involves many important changes in the CNS and peripheral organs that can subserve a fight or flight response. The psychological effects of heightened arousal, vigilance, aggression and memory probably arise from the activation of positive feedback loops involving the central nucleus of the amygdala by CRF, by stimulation of the ascending reticular activating system through heightened noradrenergic tone and by activation of the mesolimbic and mesocortical dopamine systems. At the same time the growth hormone, thyroid (HPT) and reproductive (HPG) axes arising from the hypothalamus and pituitary are inhibited at various levels. Important effects of the cortisol and catecholamine release on peripheral organs include increasing blood pressure and heart rate and increased blood glucose levels.

As with all homoeostatic processes, the stress response can be described as an inverted U-shape function (Figure 3.2). For example, both too little and too much fear can be bad for an animal's survival. An insufficient stress response may lead to lack of vigilance for dangers in the environment, whereas an exaggerated response could exhaust the resources of the body prematurely and lead to long-term damage to the CNS (as hypothesised for the hippocampus in PTSD) and peripheral organs.

Figure 3.2

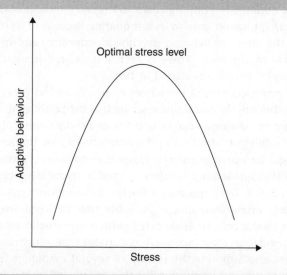

The inverted U-shape model of the stress response
In this highly simplified model, increasing stress first leads to more adaptive behaviour until an optimum is reached and then to a collapse of adaptive behaviour (and possibly mental illness).

Modulations of the stress response are a part of coping styles. More aggressive animals will show a more proactive response style to potential threats and tend to activate the stress response at lower environmental thresholds, whereas less aggressive animals with a more avoidant response style will show a fight or flight response only when absolutely necessary. The proactive coping style is commonly associated with higher sympathetic tone, whereas the avoidant or reactive coping style has been associated with higher reactivity of the HPA axis. However, these endocrine changes may also depend on the outcome of the coping behaviour. Different coping styles are adaptive for different types of environment. Proactive responses will work better in stable environments where actions and their consequences are highly predictable, whereas the more cautious and avoidant approach seems more appropriate for new or rapidly changing environments (Koolhaas, 2008). Coping styles seem to remain stable over relatively long periods, though, ranging from months in rodents to years in domestic animals, and may be fixed personality characteristics in humans from a relatively early time in development.

The stress response seems to have evolved for the important function of protecting an organism and restoring homoeostasis in the short term. However, chronic overactivity, or lack of feedback suppression, of the stress pathways can lead to physiological and psychological changes that result in obesity and type 2 diabetes mellitus, hypertension and cardiac ischemia, autoimmune disorders and allergies, anxiety and depression, insomnia and fatigue, and possibly even to addiction (through the overstimulation of the reward system) (Chrousos, 2009). Many of the disorders on the list of the top ten common diseases in Western societies thus have a potential link with stress, although the important contribution from unhealthy nutrition and lifestyle and genetic vulnerability factors must not be neglected.

3.5   THE NEUROENDOCRINE AND IMMUNE SYSTEMS INTERACT

Mutual links between psychological well-being and immune function have long been postulated. The first observations of the influence of emotions on the immune system and on the conditioning of immune responses go back to the early decades of the twentieth century, but systematic research took off only in its last quarter. Because of its considerable potential clinical relevance, the interface between psychoendocrinology and immunology has since received a great deal of attention. There is even a dedicated journal with the title *Brain, Behaviour, and Immunity*, which was started in 1987.

Several lines of evidence suggest influences of psychological processes on the immune system. Similar to other physiological processes such as the famous salivation of Pavlov's dog (see Chapter 1), immune responses can be conditioned (Adder and Cohen, 1993). For example, the immunomodulatory effect of cyclophosphamide, an immunosuppressant, could be elicited by a sugar-flavoured drink in a classical conditioning paradigm. Modulation of immune responses through sensory imagery or specific hypnotic suggestions has also been claimed (Zachariae, 2009). Emotions may influence inflammatory responses as well.

However, the best established link is probably that between stress and the immune system. The white blood cells or leukocytes, which are crucial to the cellular immune response, are upregulated after acute glucocorticoid administration. Glucocorticoids and catecholamines also suppress the release of several cytokines (messenger molecules between the different types of immune cells) that are proinflammatory (promote immune responses), tumour necrosis factor (TNF), and Interleukin (Il)1, Il6, Il8 and Il12. The relationship between hormones and cytokines is bidirectional. One example of the effects of hormones on cytokines is that increased STH release from lymphocytes can lead to higher production of interferon-gamma-alpha. One influence in the other direction is the effect of IL6 and TNF-alpha, which are both produced in the human adrenal gland, on the local regulation of glucocorticoid secretion. Furthermore, cytokines can suppress the expression of the GR.

The effect of chronic stress on the immune system is harder to evaluate than that of acute stress, in particular in humans, where a considerable number of confounding effects such as lifestyle, nutrition and general health play a role. Coping styles may lead to different patterns of immune response. Proactive coping style has been shown to facilitate the experimental induction of the autoimmune disease EAE (experimental allergic encephalomyelitis) in experimental animals, perhaps because of its association with higher noradrenaline and proinflammatory cytokine levels. However, mice with proactive coping style also showed slower growth of experimentally induced tumours, which could be a beneficial effect of the enhanced immune response. Reliable data in humans on the clinical association between personality factors and emotional reactivity and tumours or autoimmune disorders are difficult to obtain for the reasons mentioned above. Although there are thus clear biological links between the homoeostatic systems of the brain and the immune system and psychoimmunological interaction therefore entirely possible, the clinical relevance of such mutual influences is still awaiting confirmation.

3.6 SEX HORMONES HAVE AN IMPACT ON MENTAL HEALTH

Many mental disorders have uneven gender distributions. Depression, for example, is about twice as common in women, whereas the pattern is reverse for mania or alcohol addiction, and autism is even four times more common in boys than girls. Although psychosocial factors may explain some of these differences, genetic (e.g. relation to Y chromosome) and hormonal factors have been implicated as well. In females, at least three distinct syndromes point to a link with sex hormones and their fluctuations. These are postpartum depression (PPD), premenstrual syndrome (PMS) or premenstrual depressive disorder (PMDD) and menopausal depression.

About 10% of women suffer from a depressive episode after childbirth, which can have all the features of melancholic depression, including somatic symptoms like sleep disturbance or loss of appetite, inability to enjoy anything and feelings of guilt (see Chapter 11). Although again psychosocial factors may play a role, most researchers implicate the sudden drop in the concentrations of oestrogens and progesterone after the birth of the child. However, it is not entirely clear how such oestrogen or progesterone 'withdrawal' could bring about psychological changes. Perhaps downregulation of the gonadal steroid receptors during pregnancy plays a role. PPD is normally treated with psychotherapy and/or classical antidepressants, although some studies with hormone replacement, which is still in the experimental phase, are underway. Depression can also occur during pregnancy, again in about 10% of cases, which shows that high concentrations of gonadal steroids are not automatically a protection against depression. The biological mechanisms behind this antenatal depression are unknown and may involve the overactivity of the HPA axis during pregnancy (Kammerer et al., 2006). However, we must not forget the life-changing effect particularly of the first pregnancy, which can induce considerable anxiety and ensuing depression in its own right.

Oestrogen withdrawal has also been adduced to explain menopausal depression. Women in the late menopause, when the organism has to adjust to the declining levels of gonadal steroids, show a peak in the incidence of depression. Although this association between the transition to menopause and depression (as well as anxiety) has been well documented (Harsh et al., 2009), it is not clear whether this is confined to a single episode, or whether the hormonal change triggers a new, recurrent depressive illness. Hormone replacement improves not only the physical symptoms of menopause, for example the hot flushes, but also the depression and anxiety. This 'antidepressant' effect of oestradiol might be mediated through monoamine systems, but the reported effects on serotonin transporters and receptors are inconsistent. Oestradiol may also act directly on brain cells through the α- or β-oestrogen receptors, which are expressed in the limbic system, amongst other brain regions. Finally, oestradiol may enhance concentrations of brain-derived neurotrophic factor (BDNF) and contribute to dendrite formation in the hippocampus. BDNF is a crucial activator of neural growth and survival and its deficient function has been implicated in both affective and psychotic disorders. Through its effects on BDNF, oestradiol may counteract the effects of chronic overstimulation of the HPA axis, which has been implicated in hippocampal damage. However, we must not forget that the 'female' gonadal hormones are not the only ones to decrease in menopause. Their precursor 5-Dehydroepiandrosterone (5-DHEA), which is also the prohormone for testosterone and acts directly on androgen receptors, is also reduced by about 50%, and thus reduced androgen activity may play a role in female mental disorders as well.

Symptoms of dysphoria, anxiety, tension, lability, irritability, apathy, changes in appetite and sleep, which can amount to a full-blown depressive syndrome, make up PMS or PMDD. 'Premenstrual' is not a particularly precise temporal term and can essentially denote the whole second half of the menstrual cycle. The precise hormonal correlates are therefore impossible to ascertain, particularly as hormone levels do not differ between women with and without PMS. The rising or falling phases of progesterone and oestrogens as well as alterations in the progesterone metabolite allopregnanolone have all been implicated. A hormonal origin is further suggested by the frequent observation that PMS becomes worse or even arises first after the birth of the first child. Because allopregnanolone interacts with the GABA$_A$ receptor, which may have reduced sensitivity in PMS, benzodiazepines, which are GABA$_A$ agonists, have been tried with some success. PMS is also helped by selective serotonin reuptake inhibitors (SSRI) and worsened by tryptophan depletion (Cunningham et al., 2009), which again points to a role for the serotonin system in the interaction between sex hormones and mental health.

Learning points

Hormones, like NTs, convey signals between neurons, but their action is not confined to the nervous system. Some neuropeptides with effects both inside and outside the nervous system can be conceptualised both as NTs and as hormones. Most classical hormonal pathways start in the hypothalamus, where their release or inhibition factors are secreted to the pituitary. This hypothalamic control of pituitary hormone release provides an important link between the nervous and endocrine systems. The pituitary hormones and the hormones they stimulate in effector organs regulate important functions of the life cycle, such as growth (growth hormone, TSH/thyroid hormones), stress responses (ACTH/ cortisol), sexual functions (LH/FSH and gonadal steroids) and metabolism (ACTH/ cortisol, TSH/thyroid hormones), to name just a few. Hormonal function and dysfunction is the topic of a separate medical subspecialty, endocrinology, but its impact on mental health is considerable and neuroendocrinology thus of great importance to psychiatrists and clinical psychologists. The hypothalamic-pituitary-adrenal axis in particular, which regulates cortisol release, has been implicated in stress-related disorders including PTSD and depression, and the affective disorders associated with the menstrual cycle and pregnancy also point to a role for gonadal steroids in mental health and illness. Finally, interactions between the hormonal and immune systems are important in determining the multifaceted relations between mental and physical health.

Revision and discussion questions

- What are the main neuroendocrine systems that start in the hypothalamus?
- Discuss the relationship between hormones and mental health.
- What distinguishes adaptive from maladaptive stress responses?

FURTHER READING

Brown, R. E. (1994). *An Introduction to Neuroendocrinology* (Cambridge: Cambridge University Press).

4 GENETICS

PREVIEW

Amongst the common diseases, psychological disorders have some of the highest heritabilities. Heritability estimates from quantitative genetic studies constitute the most reliable findings in the biology of psychological disorders, and they are increasingly being complemented by evidence for specific genetic variants from genome-wide association studies (GWAS). This chapter reviews the basic genetic mechanisms underlying heritability, including recombination and transmission of genetic information across generations. We follow the path of gene function from the storage of genetic information in the macromolecule deoxyribonucleic acid (DNA) to its transcription into ribonucleic acid (RNA) and translation into proteins. One key aspect of this chapter will be the explanation of the techniques of molecular biology that allow for the identification and manipulation of gene sequences and of the specific techniques of psychiatric genetics, where often many genes are expected to contribute relatively small effects, necessitating the large numbers of patients required for current GWAS.

4.1 MOLECULAR GENETICS

4.1.1 Deoxyribonucleic acid (DNA) carries the genetic code

The genetic information of all cellular organisms is contained in their DNA, which is contained in the nucleus in eukaryotes. DNA is a macromolecule that consists of two chains of nucleotides. Nucleotides are composed of a 5-carbon sugar (e.g. deoxyribose), a base (adenine, thymine, guanine, cytosine or uracil) (these together are termed 'nucleoside') and one to three phosphate groups. For example, the energy storing molecule ATP (Chapter 1) is a nucleotide. In the case of DNA, the nucleotides form a chain or 'strand' through single phosphate bridges (Figure 4.1) between the fifth (5′) carbon atom of one sugar and the third (3′) carbon atom of the next. By convention, the sequence of bases is described in a 5′–3′ direction. The two strands are linked by hydrogen bonds between specific base pairs. Adenine (A) binds thymine (T) and guanine (G) binds cytosine (C). These two complementary strands form the famous double helix structure, discovered by James D. Watson (born 1928) and Francis Crick (1916–2004) in 1953 (Nobel Prize jointly with Maurice Wilkins in 1962).

The sequence of bases (about 3000 million in humans) is equivalent to the genetic information. It is distributed into about 30,000 genes, which are contiguous stretches of DNA that code for a particular protein. This genetic information will lay dormant unless it is transcribed and translated into proteins, which are the main functional units of any organism because of their importance for the structure and function (through their enzymatic activity) of the cell.

Figure 4.1

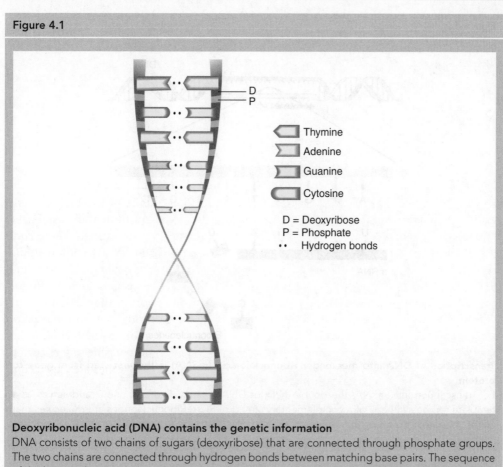

Thymine

Adenine

Guanine

Cytosine

D = Deoxyribose
P = Phosphate
•• Hydrogen bonds

Deoxyribonucleic acid (DNA) contains the genetic information
DNA consists of two chains of sugars (deoxyribose) that are connected through phosphate groups.
The two chains are connected through hydrogen bonds between matching base pairs. The sequence
of the bases adenine, cytosine, guanine, and thymidine, or A,C,G, and T forms the genetic code.

4.1.2   DNA is transcribed into messenger ribonucleic acid (mRNA)

The first step of the expression of a gene is the transcription of a stretch of DNA into mRNA,
another nucleic acid that differs from DNA by its sugar (ribose), the replacement of one base
(uracil for thymine) and its secondary structure (single strand rather than double helix).
Transcription is initiated when one or more proteins called transcription factors bind to
the promoter region at the 5′-end of the gene. This allows the enzyme RNA polymerase to
interact with the template DNA strand and initiate the synthesis of an RNA molecule, whose
base sequence is identical to that of the complementary DNA strand (the coding strand),
except for the replacement of thymine by uracil. RNA polymerase travels along the DNA template strand to add more ribonucleotides to the RNA strand until this process is terminated
(Figure 4.2) (little is known still about the mechanisms of this termination). Each mRNA has
untranslated regions (UTR) at either end.

The resulting mRNA molecule is processed in several ways, called 'post-transcriptional
modification'', to yield mature mRNA. The most important one is the removal of sequences
that are not required for the translation into a functional protein through a process called

Figure 4.2

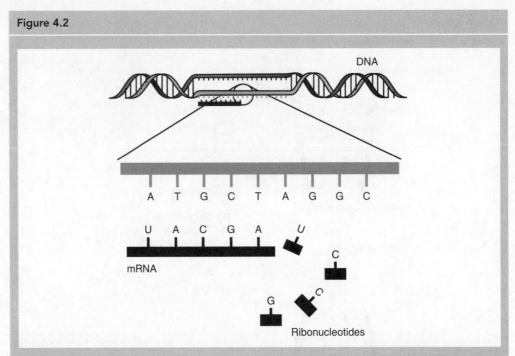

Transcription of DNA into messenger ribonucleic acid (mRNA) is the first step from gene to protein

For transcription into mRNA, the double helix of DNA is unravelled and one strand serves as a template for the synthesis of a complementary strand of RNA. RIbonucleotides are molecules that consist of one of the bases (the ones known from DNA, with the exception that uracil, U, replaces thymine), the sugar ribose and phosphate groups.

'splicing". A gene commonly has several of such sequences that are not used for the protein product, so called 'introns" (Figure 4.3). Only the remaining 'exons" determine the sequence of amino acids in the protein. Splicing errors, for example caused by mutations, can result in dysfunctional mRNA molecules. Splicing also introduces additional flexibility into the transcription process because many genes allow for different splicing patterns (alternative splicing) and can thus code for different proteins. Further modifications that enhance the stability of the RNA molecule are the addition of one nucleotide, called cap, to the 5′ UTR and a long stretch of adenosines, called 'poly-A tail', to the 3′ UTR.

4.1.3   mRNA is translated into proteins

Protein synthesis occurs in the cytoplasm and requires two other types of RNA in addition to the mRNA, ribosomal RNA (rRNA) and transfer RNA (tRNA). The ribosomes, which are the sites of protein synthesis, consist of rRNA and proteins and bind the mRNA. Many tRNA molecules bind to the mRNA strand at consecutive binding sites. These are three-bases long ('triplets') and correspond to an 'anti-codon sequence' on the tRNA. Each type of tRNA molecule carries a specific amino acid. These amino acids are polymerised into polypeptide chains and ultimately into proteins (defined as chains of over 100 amino acids) (Figure 4.3).

Figure 4.3

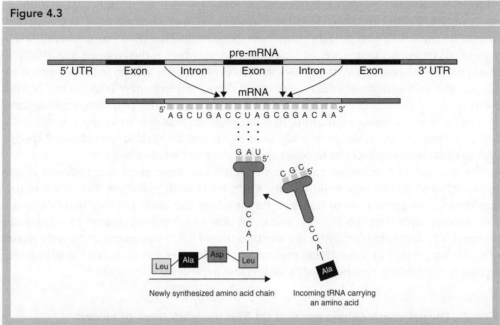

Translation results in a new protein, whose sequence of amino acids is determined by the sequence of base triplets in the mRNA
Upper panel: Splicing removes intronic RNA. Lower panel: The translation process: Transfer RNA (tRNA) molecules carry specific amino acids and bind to specific base triplets (codons) on mRNA. The sequence of amino acids is determined by the sequence of codons.

The sequence of amino acids in a protein, and thus its structure and function, are determined by the sequence of triplets on the mRNA. There are 64 (4^3) possible triplets or 'codons', which code for 20 proteinogenic amino acids. Although there are three 'stop' codons and one 'start' codon (which also codes for the amino acid methionine), this leaves eukaryotic cells with many more codons than needed for the specification of the relevant amino acid. The result is that several codons refer to the same amino acid. This type of code, where several 'symbols' confer the same 'meaning', has been called 'degenerate'. The idea of a 'code' is useful here because the base sequence can be read in different ways, depending on the starting point, resulting in completely different amino acid sequences.

4.1.4   The genetic sequence of an individual can be studied with a variety of molecular methods

4.1.4.1   Restriction enzymes allow for the analysis of specific DNA fragments

Single cell organisms have restriction enzymes, which cut DNA at specific nucleotide sequences. If the recognition sequence contained the site of a potential genetic variant (single nucleotide polymorphism or base substitution mutation, see Section 4.3.1), which would make it dysfunctional, digestion with the restriction enzyme can be used to determine whether this variant is present. Gel electrophoresis, a method to separate polar macromolecules with different molecular weight through a voltage gradient, will show whether the DNA has been cut properly or whether unrestricted fragments are present, which would indicate the dysfunctional variant. Cutting by restriction enzymes is also used in a technique called 'Southern blot' (named for the British biologist Edwin Southern, born 1938). Here the electrophoretically separated DNA fragments are transferred onto a membrane, which is then infused with relatively short (100–1000 bases) single strand DNA molecules of a specific known sequence, which are labelled with radioactivity or a fluorescent dye. If these complementary DNA 'probes' hybridise with one of the fragments on the membrane, they can be detected by autoradiography or fluorescence microscopy, indicating that the sequence was present in the original DNA. Similar techniques are available to study gene expression through identification of specific RNA strands ('northern blot') or to detect specific proteins ('western blot').

The Southern blot technique can be carried further to detect restriction fragment length polymorphisms (RFLPs) across individuals. RFLPs result from mutations affecting a restriction enzyme recognition site or from genetic variations that affect the length of DNA (variable number tandem repeats [VNTR], insertions, deletions, translocations or inversions, see Section 4.3.1). Southern blotting for the identification of RFLPs was crucial in the early phases of molecular genetics in determining the sites of disease genes and for genetic identification, but has now been largely superseded by faster gene sequencing techniques.

4.1.4.2   The polymerase chain reaction (PCR) is the work horse of modern molecular genetics

PCR is a method for the amplification of DNA. It is catalysed by one of the DNA polymerase enzymes in a reaction that requires two brief primer sequences of DNA (identical to the 5′-ends of the original DNA strands), the nucleotides that make up DNA and a small quantity of the original DNA. One round of this reaction duplicates the targeted DNA fragment, but it can be repeated many times, resulting in exponential amplification.

PCR can be used for genotyping in different ways. It can be used to measure the length of a VNTR in an individual. The relevant section of DNA is amplified using a primer that is labelled with a fluorescent dye. The resulting fragments are then separated by gel electrophoresis, where the distance they travel is inversely related to their molecular weight (or number of bases). This allows the length of the repeat to be assessed. PCR can also be used to identify the alleles of single nucleotide polymorphisms through the restriction enzyme approach, where it has largely replaced the Southern blotting technique.

4.1.4.3   DNA microarrays enable the parallel genetic analysis of multiple loci or genomes

The DNA microarray follows the same principle as the Southern blot, that is, a short DNA probe will bind more efficiently to a perfectly complementary DNA strand than to a slightly different one, even if this difference may consist in allelic variation at only one locus. The microarray is a matrix of thousands of DNA fragments that are applied to a surface (e.g. silicone or glass), normally by a robot. These can be fragments of the same locus from different individuals or fragments of different loci from the same individual's genome. In the first scenario, the same pair of fluorescent-labelled probes (each complementary to one of the possible alleles) can be used for all positions of the array, and subsequent confocal laser scanning will determine the colour of the bound probe at each position, which determines the genotype for the respective individual. In the second scenario, different pairs of probes have to be used for each position, and the analysis will yield the genotype at each of the probed loci.

4.1.4.4 Sequencing

A classical method for DNA sequencing is the chain termination method, developed by the British biochemist Frederick Sanger (born 1918) in the 1970s. The basic reaction is similar to one round of PCR, with the exceptions that there is only one strand of DNA to be copied and the nucleotides are radioactively or fluorescently labelled. The key point is the addition of a modified nucleotide that terminates the elongation of the copied DNA strand. Dideoxyribose, which cannot form phosphodiester bonds with subsequent sugars, is used for this purpose. Because only one such dideoxynucleotide is added to the reaction, the sequence can terminate only at this specific base. Assuming that this will happen at random positions and that enough reagents are available, the resulting mix will have DNA fragments terminating at all positions that have this base. Separation by electrophoresis, followed by visualisation (e.g. autoradiography) will reveal all positions with this base. If this reaction is repeated three times with the dideoxynucleotides of the other bases and the resulting mixes separated on different columns of the gel, the full sequence can be read (Figure 4.4). This technique is not fully accurate and is limited to about fragments of up to 1000 bases because of the resolution of electrophoresis, but it revolutionised DNA sequencing. Automated versions of the chain termination technique or other more recent approaches are used in modern high throughput sequencing.

Figure 4.4

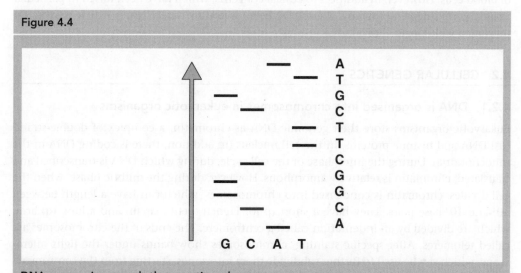

DNA sequencing reveals the genetic code

On this schematic representation of an electrophoresis gel, fragments of DNA travel along an electric field, whereby shorter fragments travel faster and thus further in the direction of the gradient (indicated by the arrow) than longer fragments. The four lanes G, C, A and T were filled with DNA fragments where the respective nucleotide was replaced with a dideoxynucleotide (with dideoxyribose replacing deoxyribose), which terminates the chain. For further explanation of this 'chain termination' or Sanger method see Section 4.1.4.4.

4.1.4.5   Recombinant DNA can be used to produce human proteins in bacteria

A fragment of human DNA, obtained by digestion with a restriction enzyme, can be inserted into the genome of other organisms to yield a sequence of recombinant or artificial DNA. Common vectors for the creation of recombinant DNA are the plasmids of bacteria, circular DNA molecules that can replicate independently of chromosomal DNA. This insertion of DNA from one organism into another for subsequent replication is achieved through techniques of molecular cloning. The key steps are the digestion of DNA with restriction enzymes to obtain fragments of the desired length, which are then ligated with the vector DNA. The target cell is then transfected with the vector that contains the recombinant DNA. In order to ensure selective replication of cells with the vector, a gene for antibiotic resistance is often added to the vector before transfection, and the cell culture then treated with this antibiotic.

If a full gene is inserted into the plasmid, the bacterium will express the respective protein, which can be used to study the function of unknown genes. Another use is the massive replication of plasmid DNA with the purpose of mass production of therapeutically relevant proteins (genetic engineering). One of the first such applications was the production of human insulin in Escherichia coli bacteria, which started in the 1980s and has since replaced the use of animal insulin in the treatment of diabetes mellitus. Another potential use of the recombinant DNA technology is gene therapy for disorders brought about by dysfunctional or missing genes. Here a functional copy would be inserted by a vector, for example a virus, into germ line cells (sperm or egg) – and thus affect the genome of the offspring and subsequent generations – or into somatic cells. One example of the latter is the attempt to treat monogenetic immune disorders with gene therapy of bone marrow cells, which are the precursors of blood cells. However, in addition to ethical concerns, which have been raised in particular against germ line gene therapy, there have been important safety issues which have so far precluded widespread clinical use.

4.2   CELLULAR GENETICS

4.2.1   DNA is organised into chromosomes in eukaryotic organisms

Eukaryotic organisms store their genomic DNA as chromatin, a complex of double-strand (ds) DNA and histone proteins, in the cell nucleus (in addition, there is coding DNA in the mitochondria). During the interphase of the cell cycle, during which DNA is transcribed and translated, chromatin is relatively amorphous. However, during the mitotic phase, when the cell divides, chromatin is condensed into chromosomes, which can have a length between 10^4 and 10^9 base pairs. They have a short (p for French 'petit': small) and a long (q) arm, which are divided by an indentation called a centromere. The ends of the chromosomes are called telomeres. After specific staining, chromosomes show bands under the light microscope, which can be used to further subdivide them into zones, starting from the centromere. Thus, 2q1 would be the band that is closest to the centromere on the long arm of chromosome 2. Maps of chromosomes (called karyograms) can be assembled according to homology and show the organism's karyotype (from Greek *karyon* = kernel, equivalent to Latin *nucleus*). The karyotype describes the number of homologous (identical save for recombination effects, see Section 4.2.3) autosomes (22 in humans) and the number of sex chromosomes, which determine the organism's gender. In humans, presence of the Y chromosome determines male gender. Most human cells are diploid (have two sets of autosomes), and thus the human karyotype is 46,XY for males and 46,X for females. Deletion or addition of a sex chromosome during meiosis leads to karyotypes that commonly result in infertility and other clinical features (e.g. Turner syndrome: 45,X; Klinefelter syndrome: 47,XXY).

4.2.2 Mitotic cell division yields genetically identical daughter cells

Dividing cells need to replicate their DNA. This happens during the interphase of the cell cycle in a reaction catalysed by the DNA replicases. After the chromatin is condensed into chromosomes, the replicated chromosomes have two identical 'chromatids' that are linked at the centromere, forming the characteristic 'H'-shaped structure (Figure 4.5a). These 'sister chromatids' align in a plane defined by the microtubular complex, which pulls them apart after the protein links between the sister chromatids have been cleaved. Each of the chromatids (now chromosomes) of a sister chromatid ends up in one of the new nuclei. The two daughter cells thus receive exact replicas of the genome of the original cell.

4.2.3 Meiosis produces genetically different haploid gametes through cross-over of chromatids

Germ line cells have a different way of dividing the DNA amongst its daughter cells, called meiosis, which is instrumental in the creation of the haploid (only one set of chromosomes) gametes (sperm [karyotype: 23,Y] and egg [karyotype: 23,X]). During the first stage of meiosis (meiosis 1), homologous sister chromatids align. During this process, they can exchange fragments (recombination or 'cross-over'), which means that the resulting four chromosomes are all different, and none has the sequence of an original chromosome. The aligned sister chromatids are distributed onto the daughter cells such that each has one set of sister chromatids, yielding a haploid cell with double DNA content. This first generation then divides without further DNA replication through a process similar to mitosis (also called meiosis 2) to yield cells with a single set of chromosomes (Figure 4.5b). To be precise, this description is accurate only for the generation of sperms because during division of female germ line cells most of the cytoplasm is divided onto one daughter cell (the future egg), whereas the smaller daughter cells ('polar bodies') do not divide further.

4.2.4 Allelic variation gives rise to genetic (and phenotypic) diversity

During fertilisation of an egg by a sperm, the two haploid genomes are fused and the resulting zygote is thus diploid again. Because our genome is thus based on the combination of single chromosome sets from genetically different individuals, we have two copies (alleles) of each gene, which may be slightly different. Although humans agree on about 99.9% of base pairs, the remaining 3 million loci can produce considerable phenotypic diversity. Individuals who have two identical alleles at a particular locus are called 'homozygous'; those who differ at this locus are called 'heterozygous'. If the two alleles result in a different function, for example a different protein sequence, two main scenarios can arise: (i) Only one gene influences the phenotype, which is then called 'dominant' (the other is called recessive because it influences the phenotype only when it occurs in two copies). (ii) Both genes influence the phenotype to some extent ('co-dominance'). These concepts are important for the study of inheritance patterns of monogenetic disorders.

Figure 4.5

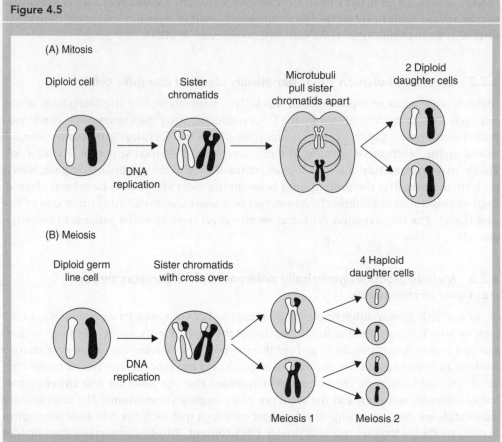

Mitosis and meiosis

(A) Mitosis results in the distribution of identical sets of DNA to the two daughter cells of a cell division. In this simplified description, only the key stages are indicated. DNA replication leads to sister chromatids, which have identical DNA sequence and are connected by a centromere (the short horizontal bar in the 'H' structure). These are separated by pull from the microtubule, and a new nucleus and cell form around the separated sets of chromatin. All the genetic information from the original cells are preserved in the daughter cells, which again have two sets of chromosomes ('diploid').

(B) Meiosis leads to haploid gametes and allows for recombination. During the alignment of the chromosomes, parts can be exchanged between homologous (and sometimes also between non-homologous) chromosomes. This recombination allows for a new 'mix' of genetic information. In the first step of Meiosis, homologous sister chromatids are separated, resulting in two nuclei with a single set of sister chromatids each ('haploid'). In the second step, analogous to Mitosis, the sister chromatids are separated to yield daughter cells with a single set of chromosomes.

4.2.5   Embryonic cells are totipotent until differentiation starts

Mitotic division of the zygote gives rise to the development of the embryo. The first 4 cell divisions occur without notable growth and thus yield a 16-cell complex of equal size to the zygote, called morula (from Latin *morulus* = blackberry, named for its spherical, cleaved appearance). The cells of the morula are still totipotent (that is, can develop into any kind of tissue including the placenta). Division of the morula yields the blastocyst, which contains the embryoblast, the precursor of the foetus, and the trophoblast, the precursor of the placenta. The cells of the trophoblast, which forms in the later part of embryonic week 1, are thus the first differentiated cells. The embryonic stem cells from the embryoblast are pluripotent, that is, they can develop into any tissue except the placenta. Differentiation of the embryoblast into the three germ layers (ectoderm, endoderm, mesoderm) that later give rise to specific organs starts at the stage of the gastrula in week 3 of human embryogenesis. The further development of the embryo (during months 1–3) and foetus (months 4–9) is highly relevant to the topic of this book because of the many theories about altered neurodevelopment in relation to mental disorders. However, developmental neurobiology is a huge field in its own right and would thus be impossible to cover in this book. Interested readers are referred to the Further Reading section at the end of the chapter. Yet it was important to cover the first stages of differentiation to familiarise the reader with the principles behind the toti- or pluripotency of embryonic stem cells, which play an increasing role in neurobiological research and as a potential vehicle for the restoration of neurodegenerative processes. There is considerable controversy around the use of stem cells in general, and those from embryos in particular. Some lines of adult stem cells are almost as pluripotent as embryonic stem cells, including those from umbilical cord blood or bone marrow, and may be developed into a viable alternative for future therapeutic use. However, therapeutic successes with embryonic (or other) stem cells in neurodegenerative disorders, such as Parkinson's disease, have so far been obtained only in animal models.

4.2.6   Meiotic non-disjunction can give rise to monosomies or trisomies

Let us return now to meiotic cell division. If homologous chromosomes fail to separate during meiosis 1 or sister chromatids fail to split during meiosis 2, gametes with extra or missing chromosomes will result. If such a gamete contributes to a zygote, the resulting embryo will have an aneuploid (imbalanced) karyotype. The most common types are monosomies (where one chromosome is missing) or trisomies (with an added chromosome). The most frequent autosomal abnormality is Down's syndrome or trisomy 21 (three chromosomes 21). Sex-chromosomal abnormalities include monosomy (Turner's syndrome) or different trisomies (Klinefelter syndrome, Triple-X syndrome, and the 47,XYY karyotype). The clinical features of these chromosomal abnormalities vary widely and range from largely normal phenotypes (Triple-X and XYY) to mild/moderate learning disabilities and health problems (Down's syndrome) and to serious medical complications in some of the rarer autosomal abnormalities. Chromosomal abnormalities are the topic of clinical genetics, but a basic understanding of mechanisms, risks and syndromes is important for clinicians in mental health because of their prevalence in learning disability services, and because of their importance for genetic counselling and pre- and postnatal maternal mental health.

4.2.7   Mitotic non-disjunction can lead to mosaics

If sister chromatids fail to separate during a mitosis in early embryogenesis, one of the daughter cells will be trisomic and the other monosomic (the latter usually does not divide any further). Thus, all cells derived from this stem cell will be trisomic, and the body thus have a 'mosaic' pattern of different genotypes. Chromosomal abnormalities in mosaic form usually have a less pronounced phenotype than those affecting the whole body. Polyploidy (one or two complete extra sets of chromosomes: triploidy/tetraploidy) occurs physiologically in liver and bone marrow cells.

4.2.8   Imprinting is the silencing of the paternal or maternal chromosome

We have one set of autosomes from our mother, and the other from our father. The X chromosome can come from either of them, whereas the Y chromosome is always paternal. Normally it does not matter whether a gene is paternal or maternal, except when it comes to tracing inheritance patterns of Mendelian disorders (see Section 4.3.2). However, for some genes, less than 1%, the paternal or maternal allele is not transcribed. This 'silencing' is achieved through epigenetic modification (see Section 4.4.5). Imprinted genes may play an important role in brain development (Wilkinson et al., 2007). Imprinted genes are vulnerable to genetic disorders because if the expressed copy is lost through a deletion or other genetic variation, no active reserve copy is available. This is the case in several developmental disabilities such as Angelman's and Prader-Willi syndromes (discussed in Chapter 17).

4.3   GENETIC VARIATION AND PATTERNS OF INHERITANCE

4.3.1   Genetic variations can be classified into base substitutions, short insertions and deletions, chromosomal breakage and whole-chromosome abnormalities

Alongside the addition or subtraction of whole chromosomes from the karyotype discussed above, several smaller chromosomal aberrations are possible. Chromosome breakage along the path to the gamete can result in losses of DNA (deletions), reattachment in the opposite direction (inversion) or duplication or exchange of fragments between non-homologous chromosomes (translocation). If the translocation is imbalanced, the offspring will miss part of one and have added material from another chromosome (partial monosomy and partial trisomy), which can lead to phenotypic consequences. These rearrangements of chromosomal structure, which commonly affect one ore multiple genes, are called 'large-scale mutations'. They can lead to 'copy number variations' (CNV), where fewer or more copies of one or several genes are present on a chromosome. The resulting lower or higher gene expression can affect the phenotype and has been implicated in risk of cancer, schizophrenia and Alzheimer's disease.

Substitutions of a single base are called 'point mutations'. These can result in a change of amino acid in the coded protein if the substitution affects a change in the genetic code ('missense mutation') or truncation of the protein if the change is to a stop codon. Sickle cell disease, for example, is caused by a missense mutation in the beta-haemoglobin gene. Single-base substitutions with a minor allele frequency of over 1% are called 'single nucleotide polymorphisms' (SNPs), and if the frequency is over 5% these are considered as 'common'. Several SNPs (or other genetic variants) together form a haplotype. The stability of haplotypes across individuals is maintained because of linkage disequilibrium, which results from the lower rate of meiotic recombination between neighbouring loci. Thus, two SNPs are in linkage disequilibrium if they occur together more often than would be expected from a random allocation of alleles.

Point mutations occur across life, both spontaneously and promoted by mutagens such as radiation or toxins. Insertions or deletions of single bases or short nucleotide sequences alter the reading frame of a gene and make its product dysfunctional. Insertions of triplets can add amino acids to the gene product. A very relevant neuropsychiatric example is the CAG repeat in the Huntingtin gene on chromosome 4p16.3. CAG codes for glutamine, and the insertion thus leads to polyglutamine expansions of the protein. Once this CAG repeat exceeds a certain length, the person affected will develop Huntington's disease (HD). Genetic testing for the number of CAG repeats can identify individuals who will develop HD before they develop symptoms. Because HD is an autosomal disorder, which means that 50% of offspring will be affected, and normally develops long after sexual maturity, this is an important issue for genetic counselling in individuals with a family history of HD.

4.3.2   Monogenetic disorders can be recessive or dominant

Based on the effect of an allele on the phenotype, different patterns of inheritance can be established for monogenetic disorders (those that are caused by variation in a single gene). If a dominant allele produces the pathological phenotype, one copy will lead to the disease, as in HD, and affected individuals will thus be heterozygous. Homozygous embryos normally do not survive. Because their gametes can contain either allele, they have a 50% chance of passing on the disease allele, and their offspring thus a 50% chance of having the disease (Figure 4.6). In the autosomal recessive case, a single copy of the disease allele does not produce the phenotype. Heterozygous individuals are thus called 'carriers'. However, the offspring of two carriers has a 25% risk of having the disease (and a 50% chance of being carriers again). These figures are based on the probability of combination of disease alleles from the parents. Some forms of early-onset Parkinson's disease (PD) are autosomal recessive,

Figure 4.6

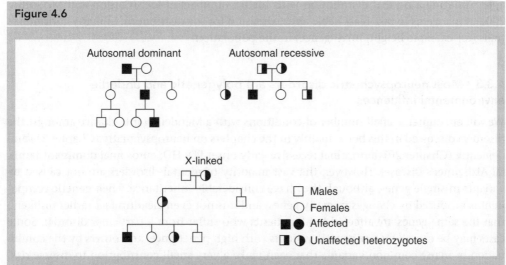

Mendelian inheritance patterns can be inferred from pedigrees
In the autosomal dominant case, any carrier of the allele is also clinically affected. The risk of having affected offspring is 50%. In the autosomal recessive case, only those with two copies are affected. If two carriers mate, the risk of affected offspring is 25%. In X chromosome-linked recessive disorders, only males are affected (because they only have the one X chromosome). Female carriers have a 50% risk of affected male offspring (and a 50% risk of passing the gene on to female offspring, making them carriers again).

for example. In recessive X-linked diseases, mainly males are affected, and only females are carriers, but very rarely affected themselves (this could only happen if a carrier had children from an affected male). Male offspring of a carrier have a 50% chance of having the disease, and female offspring a 50% chance of being carriers themselves. Red–green colour blindness and haemophilia are famous examples of X-linked recessive phenotypes. X-linked dominant or Y-linked patterns are less common. For example, fragile-X syndrome is (see Chapter 17) X-dominant. Here the FMR1 gene, which is involved in neural development, is affected by a trinucleotide repeat, making the long arm of the X-chromosome more susceptible to breaks. The clinical phenotype includes changes of facial features and learning disability. Females are almost as frequently affected as men, but less severely because they still have a functional copy of the FMR1 gene in those cells where the unaffected X-chromosome is not silenced.

These classical inheritance patterns are called Mendelian, after the Austrian priest and scientist Gregor Mendel (1822–84) who discovered dominant and recessive inheritance through simple plant breeding experiments, long before anything was known about chromosomes, let alone DNA. They apply to phenotypes that are controlled by a single genetic locus, but in reality may be distorted by variable penetrance (the degree to which a dominant allele produces the phenotype).

Many traits are neither dominant nor recessive but continuous. The simplest continuous pattern is additive, for example where one allele results in a less efficient but still active enzyme, and thus heterozygous individuals have intermediate levels of enzyme activity. In the population, the alleles are distributed according to the Hardy-Weinberg equilibrium. For example, for an equal distribution of an allele, the frequency of the three possible genotypes (AA, Aa, aa) is 1:2:1. If more than one locus determines a trait and alleles are equally distributed, genotypes (and thus levels of the continuous trait) will be binomially distributed, approximating a normal distribution with higher numbers of loci (Cardno and McGuffin, 2004). This seems to be a reasonable approximation for the distribution of many continuous traits (for example height, intelligence) in the population.

4.3.3   Most neuropsychiatric disorders are polygenetic and underlie environmental influences

We will encounter a small number of conditions with a Mendelian inheritance amongst the disorders discussed in this book, mainly in the chapters on neuropsychiatry (Chapter 21) and dementia (Chapter 20) (autosomal recessive early onset PD; HD; autosomal dominant familial Alzheimer's disease). However, the vast majority of mental disorders are not caused by variants in single genes, although they have considerable inheritance. Their genetic component is produced by changes in many genes, and it is not even clear (in fact rather unlikely) that the same genes are affected in all patients who suffer from a particular disorder. Some cases may be caused by rare genetic variants with high penetrance, and others by the combination of many common variants that each make a very small contribution to disease risk. These concepts will be discussed in more detail in the chapter on schizophrenia (Chapter 10), because schizophrenia genetics is the field where these models have developed farthest. In addition to the polygenetic influences, environmental factors play a major role. Individuals with almost identical genomes (monozygotic twins, who are genetically identical, save for epigenetic modification and mutations occurring after separation of the embryos) may differ on clinical phenotypes. For example, the risk of a monozygotic twin of a patient with schizophrenia to develop the disorder is 50%, which is considerable but far away from the 100%

that would be expected if the penetrance was complete. The remaining variance needs to be explained by environmental (including epigenetic) influences and interactions between genome and environment (G×E interactions). An example of G×E would be the observation that adverse upbringing leads to antisocial behaviour only in individuals with a particular genotype. G×E are an important factor in current causal models of mental disorders. They have to be distinguished from mere gene–environment correlations, for which three general types have been distinguished. This correlation is called 'passive' when parents transmit a congruous environment together with the gene. For example, a parent transmitting a gene for antisocial behaviour may also behave antisocially and thus shape the rearing environment. An 'evocative' correlation describes the changes in the environment evoked by the trait. For example, the family may respond in a hostile manner to traits of antisocial behaviour in the child. Finally 'active' correlation occurs when the traits leads the affected individual to shape their environment in a way that is congruous with the trait.

4.3.4 Heritability can be estimated from family, twin and adoption studies

Long before the advent of tools of molecular genetics, population genetics has been applied to study the heritability of quantitative traits such as intelligence or height and categorical phenotypes such as the presence of absence of a particular disorder. These heritabilities still count amongst the most important and replicated findings of biological psychiatry. They were essentially achieved through a combination of family, twin and adoption studies.

Family studies consist in the identification of index cases of a particular disorder and assessment of their relatives. The prevalence of the disease in family members of the patient can be compared to that in the family members of a demographically matched healthy control person (or to the prevalence in a population, although the validity of this comparison depends on the characteristics of the population). Higher prevalence in family members of the index patient can be an effect of genetics, shared environment (including the potential stress of having a mentally ill close relative) or both. This can be unravelled in twin or adoption studies. In addition, family studies suffer from several potential confounds, which derive from the selection of cases and the effects of the disease. Patient selection can introduce biases towards the more (e.g. in-patient recruitment) or less severe (e.g. higher functioning patients are more likely to volunteer for research) forms of an illness. The mortality and age of onset of a disorder influence the a priori likelihood of detecting individuals with the disorder in a sample, and thus prevalence rates in the sample have to be corrected for the lifetime morbid risk. Finally, certain diseases may affect the reproduction rate of affected individuals. In this case parents would be under-represented amongst the affected relatives of index patients. This may explain the lower rate of affected parents (6%) compared to siblings (10%) and children (13%) amongst the relatives of patients with schizophrenia (Cardno and McGuffin, 2004).

Monozygotic twins have largely identical genomes, but dizygotic twins are as genetically different as any other sibling pair. The difference in association of a trait between monozygotic and dizygotic twins is thus commonly used as an estimate of heritability, based on the assumption that both groups of twin pairs essentially share the same environment (although this may not be true in all respects, for example regarding the environment in the uterus). Another assumption is that a disease is not generally more common in twins, or monozygotic twins in particular, which is a reasonable one for mental disorders. The heritability is then calculated by comparing the concordance rates (twin pairs concordant for the phenotype/total number of twin pairs) for monozygotic and dizygotic twins.

Adoption studies provide a way of dissociating genetic and environmental effects. For example, if the biological relatives of an adoptee with a particular disorder have a higher prevalence of that disorder than the adoptive relatives, this would suggest strong genetic influences. Conversely, higher rates in the adoptive family would suggest environmental influences. Adoption studies are limited by the specific psychosocial antecedents and consequences of adoption such as a socially disadvantaged background and the biological mother's health behaviour during pregnancy.

4.4   CURRENT RESEARCH METHODS IN PSYCHIATRIC GENETICS

4.4.1   Linkage analysis reveals genetic maps and chromosomal loci associated with specific phenotypes

In a strict Mendelian model, all traits are transmitted to the next generation independently from each other. However, this is only true if their genes are not located on the same chromosome. For example, if a chromosome contains two dominant alleles, the resulting phenotypes will be coupled in the next generation, unless the alleles are separated by cross-over during meiosis. The likelihood of this happening increases with distance on the chromosome. In fact, it provides the standard measure for chromosomal distance, named for the American biologist Thomas Hunt Morgan (1866–1945), who discovered this process. The Morgan describes the frequency of cross-over events between chromosomal loci. The standard unit, centiMorgan (cM), is defined by one cross-over in 100 meiotic events. It corresponds roughly to 1 million base pairs or one Megabase (Mb). Such crossovers allow for segregation of two genes, even if they are on the same chromosome (although double crossovers will cancel this recombination). The frequency of recombination of two loci can be described by the *recombination fraction*, which ranges between 0 (at 0 Morgan) and 0.5 (chance recombination, e.g. for loci that are on different chromosomes or widely separated on the same chromosome). The distance between two loci in cM can be estimated from the recombination fraction, and this can be the basis for linkage maps of the human genome that show the relative position of genes to each other.

The most likely recombination fraction can be computed from the information about the proportion of joint and segregated transmission of a trait in a pedigree. The statistical procedure is based on the lod (logarithm of odds) score, which compares the likelihood of obtaining the data under a given recombination fraction to that occurring from chance recombination. The recombination fraction with the highest lod score will be chosen, with lod scores over 3 normally accepted as being highly significant. This classical linkage approach needs to be modified for complex modes of transmission or traits that are continuous (e.g. scores on an anxiety scale) and the underlying 'quantitative trait loci' (QTL). This is described in more detail in textbooks of behavioural and psychiatric genetics (see Further Reading section at the end of the chapter).

Linkage analysis can be used to identify chromosomal loci that are associated with a phenotype (e.g. a disease) and thus define the area in which the gene or genes are likely to be localised. This search for candidate regions for genetic associations has also been called 'positional cloning'. For this purpose, marker alleles (e.g., common SNPs) are used and the recombination fraction with the phenotype computed. A high lod score denotes a high probability that the gene is indeed close to this marker. Genome-wide linkage studies test up to 10,000 SNPs and thus have a chromosomal resolution of about 300 kb (kilobases). However, they have insufficient power to detect genes of very small effects.

4.4.2   Association studies test the co-occurrence of genotypes and traits in a population

Unlike linkage studies, association studies do not need information from pedigrees (although this can be helpful) but assess the frequency of a particular allele or alleles in two samples of the population. One sample is affected by the disease ('cases') and the other is unaffected. The classical approach is the case-control design, whereby cases and controls are demographically matched. This is important because biased samples of the population may have different allele frequencies ('population stratification'), which can inflate or hide real associations. The frequencies of the marker allele (or haplotype) and the phenotype (cases vs. controls) can be entered in a contingency table, and a chi-square test will reveal whether the allele is significantly associated with the phenotype. Such an association does not imply that this genetic variant also causes the disease. The actual locus of the gene contributing to disease risk may be many thousand base pairs away from the marker allele as long as that area is still in linkage disequilibrium with the marker. However, association studies detect genetic association only up to about 1 cM distance from the marker, whereas linkage studies can detect them over distances of over 10 cM. The advantage of association studies is their greater power to detect genes of small effects that explain less than 1% of variance (Sham and McGuffin, 2004). Up to 500,000 SNPs are nowadays tested in genome-wide association studies. This confers considerable resolution of chromosomal distance, but also the necessity to correct for a large number of statistical tests (correction for multiple testing). Based on the estimate of 1 million independent SNPs in the human genome, the conventional p-value of 0.05 has to be divided by 1 million, yielding a standard p-value for genome-wide significance of 5×10^{-8}. This requirement often makes sample sizes in the tens of thousands necessary for sufficient power to detect risk variants with small effects.

4.4.3   Candidate gene studies are based on hypotheses about disease mechanisms

For diseases where researchers have clear hypotheses about the potential biochemical and genetic mechanisms, one can look directly for associations between the phenotype and variants on a specific gene. This obviates the need for linkage markers but also limits the approach to the gene in question. Genes coding for monoamine transporters and receptors have been targeted with this approach in the study of ADHD, depression, anxiety and schizophrenia, or genes coding for GABA receptors in association with alcohol use disorder, or those coding for opioid receptors in association with opioid abuse. Many of these studies have detected associations between the disease (and in some cases a treatment response: pharmacogenomics) and variants in the candidate gene, but replication has often been problematic, pointing to the possibility of type 1 errors (false positives). For this reason, the field is gradually moving from candidate to the more conservative genome-wide association studies.

4.4.4   Endophenotypes may help overcome the heterogeneity of clinical phenotypes

Why is it so difficult to obtain strong and replicable associations with gene loci for mental disorders that have a heritability of 50% or higher, as demonstrated by population genetics? One reason might be locus heterogeneity, whereby different genetic variants cause the disease in different families. Other reasons might be that the effect of any individual gene is just very small and thus needs very large association studies to be detected, or that a strong contribution of G×E interactions means that many unaffected individuals still carry risk loci. Finally, the problem may be in the definition of the clinical phenotype. We will learn in the chapters of Part III that most mental disorders are defined by catalogues of symptoms, not all of which will be present in each individual case. It is even possible for two people who do not share any symptom to receive a diagnosis of schizophrenia. How should these people then be expected to have shared genes? The issue is not this clear cut, though, because the genetic influence may still operate through some shared upstream mechanism (e.g., dopamine regulation), that just is expressed in different symptoms, depending on environmental influences. The approach to the definition of a 'case' for a genetic study will thus depend very much on where researchers see the phenotypical elements that are influenced by the putative genes, at the level of the symptom, at that of clusters of symptoms called 'syndromes' or even at a larger, more dimensional level. The last approach, replacing diagnostic categories with dimensions, has been applied to anxiety and mood disorders, which have been grouped along dimensions of 'distress' and 'fear', which can then be used as quantitative traits in association studies.

In addition to this need to reconsider the clinical phenotypes, researchers have also turned to so-called endophenotypes (Gottesman and Gould, 2003). These are phenotypes that are not the direct targets of clinical intervention, or not even directly observable by a clinician (for example, a change in functional neuroimaging signals (Meyer-Lindenberg and Weinberger, 2006) or an eye movement test (Klein and Ettinger, 2008)), but are associated with a disease. There are several criteria for the definition of endophenotypes, for example that they are heritable, co-segregate with the disease in families but are also found in unaffected family members more frequently than in the general population. A specific type of endophenotype is the *intermediate phenotype*, which is supposed to be an element in the chain of causation from genetic variant to clinical phenotype, for example higher dopaminergic activity in schizophrenia (assuming that it fulfils the general endophenotype criteria, which has not yet been established). The attraction of the endophenotype concept is that these biological or cognitive markers may be more reliable than the clinical phenotype, mechanistically closer to the gene and less susceptible to environmental influences. An association study with an endophenotype should then give a clearer picture of potential risk genes for a disorder. Although theoretically appealing the endophenotype concept has not as yet produced stable additional genetic information. However, intermediate phenotypes may play an important role in the elucidation of the function of the newly discovered loci that are brought up by genome-wide studies. For example, a functional imaging or cognitive study with unaffected carriers and non-carriers of a risk allele may point to the brain areas where this gene is differentially expressed or to the functional domain that it controls.

4.4.5   Epigenetic mechanisms modify gene expression

Although the genome of an organism does not change over time, except for the accumulating effect of somatic mutations, gene expression patterns do vary across time and cells. Otherwise, the differentiation of the embryo into different cell types and organs would not happen. These processes are under the control of epigenetic mechanisms, which include the chemical modification of DNA through addition of methyl groups and the remodelling of chromatin through modifications of the histone proteins. Gene expression regulation through transcription factors, and post-transcriptional modulation of RNA by small stretches of anti-sense RNA (small interfering RNA) can also be counted amongst the epigenetic mechanisms. DNA methylation seems to affect the ability of transcription factors to bind to promoter regions.

The main target for methylation are dinucleotides (2 base sequences) of cytosine and guanine (CpG). Clusters of 'CpG islands' are found in the promoter regions of many genes, and most of the CpG dinucleotides are methylated. Exceptions are those in the promoter regions of so-called housekeeping genes, which are transcribed in most cells. CpG methylation may thus play an important role in the regulation of transcription. Epigenetic mechanisms are inherited, but exactly how they are regulated is not yet known. There is currently considerable interest in the role of epigenetics in mental disorders (Tsankova et al., 2007).

4.4.6 Transgenic animals permit the investigation of gene function

One of the most important techniques for the identification of gene functions is the use of transgenic animals, mainly rodents, where genes are switched off or on, altered or added, and the neurobiological and behavioural consequences observed. There are two main strategies for the design of transgenic animals: the addition of genes to the original genome of an organism, and the modification of parts of the original genome (gene targeting). The first approach is similar to genetic engineering, but the transgene is injected into a mouse embryo rather than a bacterium or yeast. In the case of gene targeting, a vector with the modified original gene is introduced into an embryonic stem (ES) cell. These ES cells with the modified genetic information are then injected into mouse embryos, yielding chimeric animals (a type of mosaic where cells in an organism are derived from different cell lines), where a fraction of the cells have the mutated gene. If the mutation is integrated into the germ line, this will give rise to transgenic offspring. This technique is often used to produce knock-out mice, lacking a particular gene. However, it can also be used to introduce mutations, for example mimicking those of single-base mutations in human homologue genes, which is called the knock-in approach (Elder et al., 2010). These animals can then be tested for behaviour, development of clinical features, changes in gene expression and protein patterns and other biological consequences of the mutation or loss of the gene. The recently developed technique of optogenetics (Box 4.1) gives researchers control over the activity of the gene products with high temporal and spatial precision.

Box 4.1   Optogenetics – switching cells on and off with light

Recombinant genetic technologies allow for the manipulation of single molecules in cells or entire organisms but once the modification has been achieved it cannot be reversed any more. Recent developments of optic control of single molecules allow this field of research to move one step further by essentially switching molecules, for example ion channels, on and off in living cells. One way of achieving this is through delivering receptor ligands in molecular 'cages' that will open in response to light of specific wavelength. The release of the ligand can thus be controlled with very fine temporal resolution. In many smaller animals, for example the fruit fly drosophila, this approach is even entirely non-invasive because it is sufficient to shine the light onto the animal from outside. Further specificity can be achieved when a particular cell type, for example dopaminergic cells, are modified to express the receptor, which is not present on other neurons. The illumination will then selectively activate these neurons, allowing for the behavioural consequences of activation of a particular cell type to be observed (Deisseroth et al., 2006).

Figure 4.7

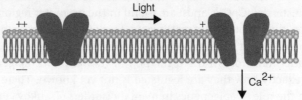

(A) Light-activation of a photosensitive cation channel

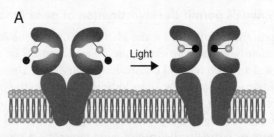

(B) Light-activation of a receptor by a photoisomer-tethered ligand

Optogenetics enables the control of cellular processes through light
(A) Schema of light-activation of a photosensitive cation channel (channelrhodopsin 2).
(B) Schema of light-activation of a receptor by a photoisomer-tethered ligand. The ligand (black ball) is bound to the receptor via the photoisomer (white ball) but only the conformation change induced by light (black arrow) will allow it to dock onto its binding site (right). Conformation change back to the original state induced by another wave length will remove the ligand from the binding site again (left).

Another approach uses naturally occurring light-sensitive proteins. For example, an ion channel of algae that is chemically related to retinal photoreceptors opens in response to blue light (Figure 4.7). If this channel, channelrhodopsin 2 (ChR2), is inserted into cells of an experimental animal by recombinant techniques, its opening can be controlled by illumination. This approach has been used to probe dopaminergic pathways in vivo. If the virus carrying the ChR2 gene is injected into a circumscribed region of the rat brain including the substantia nigra (SN) but sparing the VTA, and if added precision is derived from local photostimulation, specific nigrostriatal projections can be investigated. Stimulation then led to dopamine release in dorsal but not ventral striatum and also to whisker twitches (Bass et al., 2010). This technique thus allows researchers to probe the physiological, neurochemical and behavioural consequences of activation of specific types of neurons with high spatial and temporal precision.

Optogenetics is currently confined to naturally occurring light-sensitive proteins, but its scope has been broadened by the recent availability of channels with hyperpolarising (inhibitory properties). A more flexible use of optic control of proteins may be through the addition of switchable ligands ('photoisomer-tethered ligands'). This technique uses so-called photoisomers, short molecules that change their conformation in response to a particular wavelength. One end of the photoisomer is linked to a ligand and the other to the receptor. The light-induced conformation change will then determine whether the ligand binds to and activates (or blocks) the receptor or not. This approach would allow activation and blockade of ion channels and other signalling proteins at a temporal precision that is not available with classical pharmacology because of the slow dissociation rates of high-affinity ligands (Gorostiza and Isacoff, 2008).

It is an intriguing question whether these techniques will ever be available for clinical use. It has been speculated whether they will, for example, provide a more targeted alternative to deep brain stimulation in PD. Work with experimental animals has shown that it is possible selectively to activate dopaminergic neurons. However, all previous attempts at therapeutic genetic modification of cells in humans have encountered major difficulties. Major safety issues would arise if one was to inject non-human proteins with viral vectors into the human brain. Furthermore the photostimulation would still require the permanent placement of fibre optic devices, similar to the present use of deep brain electrodes. Thus, the main hope for benefits from optogenetics for the not so distant future would be through the elucidation of pharmacological pathways of behaviour and the mechanisms of action of new, more specific neurochemical agents.

4.5   GENETICS IN CLINICAL PRACTICE

4.5.1   Prenatal screening can detect genetic risk before implantation of the embryo

During in-vitro fertilisation procedures, the first stages of embryogenesis occur in the laboratory, and a cell from the early embryo can be harvested for genetic analysis. This method permits the identification of embryos with one or two copies of a disease variant. It is then possible to select embryos without the disease variant, for example those with less than 35 CAG repeats of parents with HD. In this way, the risk of the offspring of an affected individual to develop an autosomal dominant disorder can be reduced from 50% to zero. This procedure comes at the cost (financial, psychological, physical) of having to undergo the IVF procedure, which can compromise the mother's and infant's health. It also has important ethical implications because universally acceptable criteria for genetic selection have not yet been defined. It is likely to be considered only for the most severe and disabling of inherited disorders with known and stable genetic markers. Another, more widely practised, application of prenatal screening is to determine the genetic pattern (most frequently chromosomal aberrations) of cells from a normally conceived foetus. These can be obtained through sampling amniotic fluid or through biopsies from placenta tissue. These procedures carry a small risk of spontaneous abortions. The information obtained allows parents to decide whether they want to abort a foetus that is affected by a disease-related variant. The most common application is in the early identification of trisomy 21.

4.5.2   Genetic counselling is based on the pattern of inheritance and impact of a disease

Genetic counselling in the traditional sense concerns the decision of individuals or couples who may carry genes for an inherited disorder whether to have children. Three main scenarios are possible:

- An individual is already affected by a dominant or recessive disorder
- An individual has relatives with an inherited disorder
- A couple already has children who are affected by an inherited disorder.

The first task will be to determine the genetic risk of the offspring. In the case of an individual with an autosomal dominant disorder it will be 50%, in the case of an autosomal recessive disorder it will be negligible (equal to the frequency of the risk allele in the general population), even for further generations, as long as inbreeding is avoided. If only relatives are affected so far, it is important to analyse the pedigree in detail. For example, if a person has a parent with HD, their own risk will be 50% and that of their offspring 25%. This scenario is common for disorders that manifest after the standard reproductive age, such as HD. In this and similar cases, where the genetic variant is known, the carrier status of the parent can be determined by genetic testing, resulting in a more specific risk prediction for the offspring (50% if the parent is affected, zero if he/she is not). If a couple already has affected children, and if this is the first occurrence in the pedigree, the mechanism is most likely recessive, and the risk for each further child would then be 25%. These risks then have to be balanced against the couple's wish for offspring, psychosocial circumstances and the impact of the actual disorder on quality of life. These decisions, which ultimately have to be taken by the couple themselves and for which the geneticist can only explain the science and provide points to consider, are never easy. The recent advances in prenatal screening provide additional options, but involve IVF and pre-implantation diagnosis or the willingness to abort the foetus.

Another more recent version of genetic counselling concerns the person's individual risk of developing a disorder. With increasing numbers of risk loci identified, a full genome screen of an individual should in principle allow estimates of genetic risk for a multitude of disorders. However, the only established variant in psychiatry that predicts a clinically relevant risk is the Apolipoprotein E epsilon 4 isoform, which is associated with an increased risk and earlier onset of Alzheimer's disease (AD). As long as no specific preventative treatment for AD is available, this information can be used only for general advice on risk reduction (healthy lifestyle) and possibly financial and care planning. Incidentally the effect of this genotype on individual risk is about as high as that of having two parents affected with AD. The relative risk conferred by the other common genetic variants associated with mental disorders is much lower, even if several are considered together, and full genome scans are thus presently not informative from the point of view of neuropsychiatric genetic counselling.

4.5.3 DNA banks allow for the identification of individuals and the testing of disease associations

More and more people are being asked to provide DNA for DNA banks. DNA banks are repositories of DNA, fully sequenced or typed for the pattern of SNPs or VNTRs, and linked to information about the person and their disease state. Forensic databases for the identification of criminal offenders from material retrieved at the crime scene preserve personal information, whereas research databases, for example for association studies of a particular disease, preserve clinically relevant information (e.g. whether someone is a 'case' or not). DNA banks are important for psychiatric research because of the large numbers of cases and controls needed for GWAS and because more refined sequencing techniques are becoming available more cheaply, allowing for increasingly extensive sequencing of the genome, thus providing a higher chance of detecting new genetic associations. DNA banks that are linked to clinical cohorts can also serve other important functions, such as genetic predictions as to who is going to respond to a particular intervention.

Learning points

Genetic information is stored in DNA, which is transcribed into mRNA and translated into proteins. Proteins provide structure to cells, catalyse biochemical reactions in the body (enzymes) and regulate metabolism, gene expression and signalling. Changes in DNA (mutations) that result in changes in the amino acid sequence of proteins or in levels of expression can therefore have profound functional consequences. Although some neuropsychiatric disorders are caused by variants in a single gene (and thus in a single protein), most are polygenetic (have contributions from many genes), with additional important contributions from environmental risk factors.

Heritability estimates based on family, twin and adoption studies are still amongst the most stable and important findings in biological psychiatry. A great deal of effort has been devoted to the discovery of the underlying genes. So far the result for most mental disorders has been that many common variants explain a small fraction of the variance of each. This information is presently not clinically relevant for risk prediction in individual cases. However, it may lead to the formulation of new biological models of these disorders and eventually to the development of new treatments. Such 'translational' applications of neurogenetics are a key target of current research programmes.

Revision and discussion questions

- Describe the steps from the gene to the protein.
- What is the difference between mitosis and meiosis?
- How can the heritability of a disorder be estimated?
- Discuss possible ways of gene–environment interaction.

FURTHER READING

Deisseroth, K., Feng, G., Majewska, A., Miesenböck, G., Ting, A. and Schnitzer, M. (2006). Next-generation optical technologies for illuminating genetically targeted brain circuits. *Journal of Neuroscience*, 26, 10380–386.

Gorostiza, P. and Isacoff, E. (2008). Optical switches for remote and noninvasive control of cell signaling. *Science*, 322, 395–99.

McGuffin, P., Owen, M. J. and Gottesman, I. I. (2004 [2002]). *Psychiatric Genetics and Genomics* (Oxford: Oxford University Press).

Plomin, R. (2008). *Behavioral Genetics* (New York: Worth Publishers; Basingstoke: Palgrave Macmillan [distributor]).

5

ANIMAL MODELS OF HUMAN BEHAVIOUR AND MENTAL DISORDERS

PREVIEW

This chapter discusses the opportunities and difficulties of modelling human behaviour and its dysfunctions in animals. It explains the rationale for trying to model complex human diseases in animals, which allows for a level of invasive biological investigation that would not be possible in humans, including the creation of transgenic animals. It introduces the criteria of face, construct and predictive validity used to evaluate animal models. After explaining some of the basic setups, it goes on to describe selected animal models for behaviours associated with specific mental disorders, for example reduced feeding as a model of depression, and ways of inducing them, for example with chronic stress. An important part of this chapter is the discussion of the ethical aspects and limitations of animal experimentation.

5.1 BEHAVIOURS ASSOCIATED WITH MENTAL DISORDERS CAN BE STUDIED IN ANIMALS

An animal model permits the investigation of the biological mechanisms of a disease with a level of detail that is not available in humans. In animals researchers can assay the function of molecules, cells and systems at almost any level, ranging from in-vivo recording from single ion channels to the removal of whole organs. A wide range of manipulations that would be impossible or require extensive safety checks in humans is also possible, including the administration of new or experimental drugs or modification of the genome of the animal (transgenic animals, see Chapter 4). However, animal research poses important ethical (see Box 5.1) and, methodological problems, particularly in biological psychiatry. It might be relatively straightforward to model a somatic disease with a known biological marker and a putative pathomechanism, for example to design a diabetic mouse that has lost its ability to produce insulin and thus has chronically increased glucose blood levels. However, how does one go about this for behavioural and mental disorders where, as in almost all cases, there is no unequivocal biological marker? Moreover, lack of communication with animals means that we can rarely ascertain whether they suffer from the same symptoms as humans. Most of the face validity (plausibility) of animal models of mental disorders thus derives from the behavioural changes they display. For example, if we wanted to design an animal model of Alzheimer's disease we might aim for deficits in spatial learning. Similarly, for an animal model of anxiety we might use mice that show exaggerated conditioned fear responses, or for mania exaggerated motor activity. The two classical ways of identifying and selecting strains with the desired behaviour were through inbreeding of animals with specific phenotypes or through the analysis of many available strains for phenotypic differences. The inbreeding approach allows for more control of the desired phenotype but is also far more time consuming, requiring many generations of breeding often over several years. More recently, targeted neurobiological manipulations (pharmacological, lesions, genetic) have become more widely used, but these normally require good hypotheses about the biology underlying the disorder and/or the relevant phenotype.

This constitutes a central conundrum of animal models in psychiatry: the most relevant models are those that are based on the biology of the disorder, but often one of the main aims behind the animal research is to find out just about this biology. This circularity is difficult to overcome. Animals that exhibit behavioural features of a mental disorder may provide new leads to its biological mechanisms, assuming that the behaviour is subserved by the same biological processes in the animal, for example a rodent, and humans. This assumption is called 'homology' in evolutionary biology, whereby structures and functions in different species have evolved from a common genetic ancestry. However, the alternative assumption of convergent evolution is often equally plausible as long as the biological mechanisms are not known. Here evolutionary pressure leads to analogous functional (and possibly underlying structural) adaptations, but the molecular genetics behind them may be very different. For example, the wings of insects and birds are analogous in that they serve similar functions (locomotion through air) but their evolution started after the ancestries of the two classes separated. Studying wings of insects thus may reveal a great deal about general principles of biomechanics, but very little about the molecular mechanisms of wing development in birds. A researcher who wants to make inferences about the biology of human stress responses from those of rodents will encounter the same difference if they are merely the product of convergent evolution.

5.2   ANIMAL MODELS OF MENTAL DISORDERS REFLECT ONLY PARTS OF A CLINICAL PHENOTYPE

The above examples also make clear that, except in the cases where a mental disorder consists in one very specific symptom (e.g. simple phobias), researchers will never be able to model behaviourally the whole syndrome. Rather, they might obtain animals that display features of the loss of motivation and exploration typical of depression, for example reduced feeding and foraging, but no clear behavioural correlate of the remainder of the depressive syndrome. Alternatively, they may have animals that display some but not all features of several related disorders, for example depression, anxiety and bipolar disorder. A recent approach to animal models goes beyond the investigation of a specific phenotype to take into consideration the full range of adaptive behaviours in response to environmental challenges, termed 'ethogram' (Desbonnet et al., 2009b). In some cases researchers can also supplement cross-species behavioural observation with neurobiological markers that can be obtained in both animals and humans. In addition to levels of hormones and other circulating molecules, these comprise electrophysiological measures such as evoked potentials and the frequency profile of the electroencephalogram.

5.3   CONSTRUCT AND PREDICTIVE VALIDITY DETERMINE THE USE OF A MODEL IN PHARMACEUTICAL RESEARCH

The design of animal models of complete syndromes or disorders relies on the knowledge of the biological mechanisms and the feasibility of inducing the relevant alterations. Such animal models are only available for disorders with known biological mechanisms, for example for Parkinson's disease (through dopamine depletion) or hereditary Alzheimer's disease.

However, even these models, which should have a high 'construct' (biological) validity, do not always display the same behavioural or neurological features as expected from the human presentation. Even if an animal model has good face and good construct validity, its practical use will still need to be established. Its utility for drug discovery is largely based on the model's 'predictive validity', that is whether the animal reacts to factors that influence the disease, notably medical treatment, in the same way as affected humans. Thus, a mouse with reduced mesencephalic dopamine production, difficulty to initiate movements and a good response to dopamine would constitute a model of Parkinson's disease with good construct, face and predictive validity.

5.4 MANY ANIMAL MODELS ARE BASED ON LEARNING THEORY

Most animal models probe changes in behaviour through one of the two classical models of associative learning, Pavlovian (or classical) and operant (instrumental) conditioning, or their combination. In a typical Pavlovian paradigm, a natural or unconditioned stimulus (US, e.g. food) is paired with another environmental stimulus (e.g. a sound), which after a sufficient number of pairings becomes a conditioned stimulus (CS) and will evoke the physiological and/or behavioural response to the US (e.g. salivation) without its presence (see

Figure 5.1

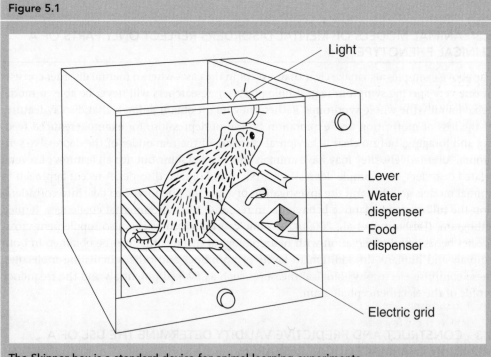

The Skinner box is a standard device for animal learning experiments
In this example, the experimental animal has to press a level in response to stimuli (e.g. light flashes) in order to obtain a food or drink reward (positive reinforcement). Learning schedules based on adding (punishment) or removing (negative reinforcement) negative consequences can also be tested, for example with electric shocks.

Box 1.3 in Chapter 1). A large body of studies by Pavlov and his followers has analysed the parameters (e.g. timing, duration, intensity, length of pairing schedule) under which conditioning occurs, and also the time course of the disappearance of the automatic responses to the CS when the contingency between the US and the CS is disrupted (extinction learning). The classical application to mental disorders is through the paradigm of fear conditioning (where normally innocuous stimuli such as air puffs are conditioned to elicit behavioural and physiological fear responses, for example through pairing with electric shocks), which has been suggested as a model for anxiety disorders.

Classical conditioning does not require the active engagement of the animal with the stimulus. Conversely, operant conditioning is based on the contingency between the animal's response and the obtained reward. In the typical testing setting in the Skinner box (Figure 5.1), the animal has to respond with a lever or other similar device (the 'operandum' or 'manipulandum') to stimuli, and will get the natural reward (e.g. food or water) only if it performs the right motor response. Manual responses are most often conditioned in this way, but any other motor act such as eye movements or vocalisations can be used in an analogous way. It is possible to condition only a particular motor response or a particular stimulus–response association, for example when a reward is given only if the lever is lifted after a red or pressed after a green stimulus. Although both classical and operant conditioning can be used to study an animal's ability to discriminate between stimuli, only operant conditioning allows to model complex behaviour and is thus the main technique to study behavioural disorders, such as substance abuse or ADHD. The most widely used animal models of drug-related reinforcement will be discussed in Chapter 15, and the biological information obtained from specific disease-related animal models will feature throughout the chapters of Part III.

5.5 ANXIETY DISORDERS CAN BE MODELLED THROUGH EXAGGERATED STRESS RESPONSES AND REDUCED EXPLORATORY BEHAVIOUR

Rodent models of anxiety have the longest tradition in the modelling of human disorders in animals. Several laboratory tests assess exploration-based and threat responses (Kalueff et al., 2007). For example, in the open field test (OFT), the animal has to explore a large new area, and parameters of locomotion and defecation are used as surrogate markers of anxiety. The OFT also assesses hyperkinetic behaviour, which is a feature of several mental disorders, or stereotyped motor behaviours, which may model Obsessive Compulsive Disorder (OCD) (Szechtman et al., 1998). The elevated plus maze (EPM) is another classic test of anxiety. The animal is put in a plus-shaped maze with two unprotected elevated arms and two enclosed arms. The ratio of time spent in the enclosed over the unprotected arms is used as a measure of anxiety. The novelty-suppressed feeding test (NSFT) assesses the latency to eat familiar food in a novel environment. The classic animal test of exaggerated threat response, which is assumed to underlie phobias and panic disorder, is fear conditioning, where the time of freezing in response to a conditioned fear stimulus is measured.

Some of these tests have a good predictive validity. For example, the latency on the NSFT is reduced by anxiolytic drugs, such as benzodiazepines, which are also effective for human anxiety disorders. An attempt to introduce a model of anxiety with good construct validity has been the development of serotonin transporter knock-out rats. These rats show higher anxiety-related behaviour on the OFT and EPM and higher extracellular serotonin levels. They may thus demonstrate a link between abnormalities in the serotonin system and anxiety, which had been postulated on theoretical grounds and because of the clinical effects of drugs that affect the monoamine systems. However, the current monoamine models of anxiety and depression postulate a deficit in serotonin and noradrenaline (which would be compensated by the effects of serotonin and noradrenaline reuptake inhibitors), which is difficult to square with higher anxiety in animals with reduced serotonin reuptake. We will discuss this issue further in Chapter 13 on Anxiety Disorders. In general the predictive validity of animal models of anxiety has been better for benzodiazepines than for other classes of anxiolytic drugs. One exception is the modelling of stereotypic motor behaviours. Repetitive movements and hoarding are features of OCD that can be observed both in rodents and primates. Even if primates are not purposefully socially isolated (which raises ethical issues), any rearing in captivity can result in repetitive behaviours such as excessive grooming. This model has a good predictive validity because, like human OCD, the stereotypies can respond to SSRI treatment.

5.6 DEPRESSION-LIKE FEATURES ARE INDUCED BY CHRONIC STRESS

Animal models of depression have been derived both from behaviour resembling that of depressed patients and from putative environmental depressogenic events. Examples of the first scenario are tests modelling despair such as learned helplessness or Porsolt's forced swim test (FST). Learned helplessness occurs after repeated exposure to unescapable stress, which can lead to failure to withdraw from *escapable* stress as well. The FST follows a similar principle and assesses the duration of immobility in a water tank after prolonged exposure to inescapable stress. Rearing in deprivation or under chronic environmental stress are examples of the putative causal animal models of depression. Other causal approaches include manipulations of the HPA axis or monoamine system. There is considerable overlap between the animal models of anxiety and depression, and even transitions from one to the other have been observed (Kalueff et al., 2007). For example, mice that experienced social defeat developed features of anxiety after ten days of exposure, but features of depression after twenty. Such transitions are relevant as models of the differential effects of acute and chronic stress, and of the comorbidity and syndromal overlap between anxiety and depression.

5.7 ANIMAL MODELS OF SCHIZOPHRENIA USE PUTATIVE ENDOPHENOTYPES

It may seem counterintuitive at first that a disorder that is as closely linked with altered speech and thought patterns as schizophrenia should be modelled in animals at all. However, animal equivalents have been proposed both for its characteristic positive (e.g. hallucinations or delusions) and negative (e.g. apathy, anhedonia) symptoms (Desbonnet et al., 2009a). Exaggerated responses to novel stimuli may mimic positive symptoms, whereas failure to approach and investigate conspecifics has been adduced as a model of deficient social functioning in schizophrenia. These behaviours have limited face validity and specificity because they could reasonably be used to model anxiety and depression as well. Increased sensitivity to drugs that can induce psychosis in humans, such as amphetamines, may mimic psychotic syndromes more directly, but only for the subgroup of schizophrenia patients who are likely to be affected by such a hypersensitivity to psychotomimetic substances.

Because of these difficulties, animal models of schizophrenia have made ample use of the endophenotypes concept (see Section 4.4.4). Endophenotypes are behavioural or biological features that are observed in patients (and often in an attenuated manner in their relatives) but they are not part of the clinical phenotype (that is, would not warrant treatment as such). Examples include the reduced pre-pulse inhibition of the startle reflex and reduced sensory gating (Geyer, 2008). The startle reflex, which can be measured by eye blinks in humans and whole body flinch in animals, is triggered by loud noises or other sudden environmental changes. It is attenuated if the triggering sound is preceded by another, warning, sound. This pre-pulse inhibition (PPI) is reduced in schizophrenia. Sensory gating is normally measured in the auditory domain, where the P50 component of the auditory event-related potential, which can be recorded with electrodes on the scalp of humans or animals, is reduced to the second of two sounds. This reduction is less pronounced in schizophrenia, which is commonly interpreted as a 'gating' deficit. What these potential deficits have in common is that they concern the processing of environmental context and thus may reflect inability to filter out irrelevant information and attribute salience to the more relevant stimuli. Thus, such cognitive deficits may contribute to the symptoms that eventually form the clinical phenotype of schizophrenia. The PPI model has been widely tested pharmacologically in animals and derived some predictive validity. PPI is disrupted by various psychotomimetic (psychosis-inducing) drugs, such as dopamine agonists, hallucinogens (serotonin agonists) and NMDA-receptor antagonists, and improves with some (atypical) antipsychotic agents.

The design of animal models with good construct validity is difficult in schizophrenia, similar to anxiety and depression, because of the patchy knowledge about the biological mechanisms of the disease. Over expression of dopamine D2 receptors and hypofunction of the NMDA-receptor or its glycine binding site have all been implicated in schizophrenia and tested in animal models (Desbonnet et al., 2009b). Hyperdopaminergic models generally lead to hypervigilant, hyperlocomotive and anxious behaviour that may resemble features of psychosis, whereas disruption of glutamate signalling additionally leads to broader impairments of social interaction and memory. Again, some of these behaviours improve after administration of antipsychotics, but results have been inconsistent.

5.8   ANIMAL MODELS HAVE ALSO BEEN DESIGNED FOR ADHD, ADDICTION AND MOST OTHER MENTAL DISORDERS

Hyperkinetic and impulsive behaviour, as observed in Attention Deficit Hyperactivity Disorder (ADHD), can be modelled with exploratory motor behaviour and responses to delayed reinforcement. For example, patients with ADHD show impaired delay discounting – they will prefer a smaller reward now over a considerably larger reward in the future, even if the delay is not that long. Some mouse strains also display hyperactivity and impulsivity on such tasks with delayed rewards, as well as exaggerated orienting to new stimuli. It will be interesting to test the predictive validity of such ADHD mouse models by assessing behavioural improvement after treatment with dopaminergic psychostimulants.

Addiction is in some ways the area of mental health that lends itself most easily to animal modelling because of its circumscribed behavioural patterns. For example, some rodent strains have higher voluntary alcohol intake when they have the choice between ethanol and water on alcohol self-administration tasks. However, addiction is not defined by the amount of intake of the relevant substance alone but also by the associated physiological and psychological responses. Psychological withdrawal symptoms in particular are much harder to model in animals.

Animal models have been designed for almost all neurological, psychiatric and developmental disorders, ranging from autism to dementia. We will discuss their validity and the extent to which they have elucidated the biological mechanisms of these disorders and the underlying genetics in the respective chapters of Part III.

Box 5.1   Ethics of animal research

Most animal experiments ultimately lead to the death of the experimental animal, and experimenters often cannot exclude that the animal will suffer as a consequence of the procedures involved. How then can such experiments be morally justified? One could argue from a utilitarian perspective: The suffering and sacrifice of animals is justified for the greater good of saving humans from suffering, illness or premature death. However, this is a perspective that we do not accept for comparisons between humans. For example, it would be illegal – and by most considered to be morally wrong – to test a new vaccine against a life-threatening infection, say the human immuno deficiency virus (HIV), on a non-consenting human, even if a successful test could save millions of lives. The situation may become different if the 'human guinea pig' were to consent to this experiment, which would involve inoculation with the vaccine and then infection with the virus, and thus potentially result in a life-threatening illness if the vaccine did not work. Actual guinea pigs, of course, are never asked for their consent, and thus this option does not apply in animal experimentation.

Animal experiments can thus be morally acceptable only if we concede to animals no rights at all or rights that are subordinate to those of humans. The radical view that animals have no rights at all, which would allow researchers to treat them like plants or other objects, is probably a minority position even in the camp of supporters of animal experiments. Most would favour a gradual increase of rights according to the animal's position in the evolutionary hierarchy (normally measured by its genetic and behavioural similarity to humans), which would allow for quantitative assessments of harm–benefit ratios and safeguards against suffering. For example, whereas it may seem acceptable to kill one thousand fruit flies in the service of a small step towards a new cancer drug, the situation may be judged differently for one thousand monkeys. Furthermore, procedures for reduction of pain and natural rearing may become more important with increasing complexity of the organism. Finally, there is general agreement that invasive research with great apes is not permissible and even strong movements to ban any research with these close genetic relatives of humans, even purely observational, barring very exceptional cases. Although most of the animal models of mental disorders are rodents, behavioural neuroscience also uses 'higher' animals like cats – because of their well-developed sensory systems – and macaque monkeys, who have a well-developed frontal lobe and can learn complex tasks. This raises issues about animal welfare. For example, is it acceptable to deprive an animal from a crucial function or constituent of its environment? Monkeys (like humans) are quintessentially social animals, and thus would be greatly affected by social isolation, which, however, may be a particularly relevant manipulation to study brain/environment interactions and their influence on behaviour.

Although the most common argument for animal experiments is based on their direct or indirect translation into new drugs or other important medical (diagnostic or therapeutic tools), some researchers argue in favour of a general right to use animals to understand more about the principles of nature. According to this position we cannot alter the fact that humankind has taken on the stewardship of this planet, for better or worse, and knowledge about the basic principles of its biology is needed for the right decisions on the future of the planet as a whole. However, the majority of the population would probably react sceptically to such claims.

The main ethical argument of the opponents of animal experiments is that we have no basis for assigning different levels of rights to different creatures, including those that are potentially capable of suffering pain and feeling other emotions just like us. According to the Australian philosopher Peter Singer, the statement that humans have rights that deserve a higher level of protection just by virtue of being humans would be akin to similar statements made about race, and thus amount to 'speciesism'. If, however, we wanted to base such a statement on our ability to communicate with these other humans, Singer would query the basis for including infants or severely mentally disabled people under this protection. Because most of us would recoil from the proposal to conduct experiments on infants or handicapped people, Singer would then argue that the same rights need to be afforded to animals that are capable of suffering (Singer, 1989). Interestingly, this argument goes back to the founder of utilitarianism, the English philosopher Jeremy Bentham (1748–1832). The argument that people kill animals all the time for supposedly less honourable reasons than scientific knowledge or medical progress – that is, for the enjoyment of their meat – does not convince the representatives of the animal liberation movement because to them it is an argument for vegetarianism rather than for vivisection. Opponents of animal experiments often also adduce other weaknesses of this approach, such as the difficulty of making inferences from animals to humans and the possibly overstated role that animal experimentation has played in the history of medical progress, but for an assessment on strictly moral grounds these points should not matter greatly.

There are two main positions in the animal rights camp, which are based on fundamentally different assumptions about the foundations of ethics, but lead to the same conclusions. One is the utilitarian position (Singer's), where judgements on actions are based on their consequences, particularly whether they maximise pleasure and minimise pain, and this includes that of animals. The other position is 'deontological', meaning that it bases morality on general rules that need to be followed for their own sake, for example to respect the rights of others. This position was originally devised, for example by the German philosopher Immanuel Kant (1724–1804), to include only humans. However, if one accepts the animal rights position set out in the preceding paragraph that there is no valid criterion for denying similar rights to animals, they would have the same moral rights as humans.

Regardless of the controversy around animal rights, there is widespread political agreement that animal experiments should be conducted in a strictly controlled environment and under supervision by independent committees, and efforts should be made to find alternative ways of biological and medical research. The '3 R's' of 'Reduction, Refinement and Replacement' summarise this approach. Efforts to replace animal experiments through alternative techniques are currently being made along three lines of development. Non-invasive techniques that can be used in humans (functional imaging, TMS) may allow for direct testing of neural models of human behaviour without the transfer into monkey models but will never attain the same spatial resolution. Likewise, computational modelling may aid the investigation of many perceptual, motor and cognitive functions, but neurochemical inferences will always be indirect. These can potentially be made through the increased use of stem cells and in-vitro models, which may ultimately lead to the creation of organs and whole organisms in the laboratory. The 'brain in the Petri dish' is already partly reality (DeMarse et al., 2004), but such developments are likely to raise their own ethical issues.

Learning points

Many techniques of biological investigation are not available for the study of living humans, which limits researchers in their ability to find biological correlates of mental disorders. Furthermore, the introduction of biological changes that may trigger symptoms of mental illness is generally banned in humans, except for reversible manipulations such as dietary restriction or single doses of a psychoactive drug given in controlled settings. These restrictions apply much less to animal research, which is the reason why animal models are in widespread use for the study of the mechanisms of mental illness and the discovery of new psychotropic drugs.

The design of animal models is particularly difficult in psychiatry compared to other fields of medicine because so little is known about the biological mechanisms of most mental disorders, and because the crucial symptoms cannot be ascertained without communication with a patient. Thus, animal models of mental disorders are largely based on the behavioural features associated with these disorders, such as reduced exploratory behaviour and enhanced responses to threat in anxiety disorders. However, these behavioural features are not necessarily specific for a particular disorder, and their 'face validity' will depend on their ability to capture a behavioural phenotype that is characteristic of the disorder. A model's 'construct' validity describes its fit with the putative biological mechanisms of a disorder, and the 'predictive' validity depends on the response of the behavioural change to standard treatments for the disorder. Eventually, animal models may turn out to be more useful for modelling dimensional traits of mental illness rather than categorical disease entities.

Revision and discussion questions

- How can animal models help elucidate the mechanisms of a mental disorder?
- Describe the concepts of face, construct and predictive validity.
- Can animals be mentally ill?

FURTHER READING

Kalueff, A., Wheaton, M. and Murphy, D. (2007). What's wrong with my mouse model? Advances and strategies in animal modeling of anxiety and depression. *Behavioural Brain Research*, 179, 1–18.

PSYCHOPHARMACOLOGY

6

GENERAL PRINCIPLES OF PSYCHOPHARMACOLOGY

PREVIEW

Psychopharmacology is the study of the chemical mechanisms of neural information processing in relation to psychological processes and their disturbance. It is therefore at the heart of the understanding of the mechanisms of mental disorders and their biological treatment. In this second part of the book we will revisit some of the topics encountered in Chapter 2, but in considerably more detail. Chapter 6 deals with the general principles of neurotransmitter action and the presynaptic regulation of NT release. In the context of this book we will be particularly concerned with theories of altered signalling in psychological disorders and its remediation through drugs. These drugs, which influence mental activities or consciousness, are called 'psychotropic'. We have already learnt in Chapter 1 that specific neuroanatomical pathways contribute to certain motor, sensory and cognitive functions and that some of these pathways are also neurochemically specific. We also discussed the basic principles of communication between neurons that apply both to the communication between the central and peripheral nervous systems and within the CNS (Chapter 2). One basic principle is that of electrochemical signal transduction, where an electrical signal is converted into a chemical signal (neurotransmitter release) at a synapse, and back into an electrical signal in the postsynaptic neuron. Chemical communication between neurons (and other cells) uses NTs and other signalling molecules, including hormones and growth factors. These signalling molecules bind to specific receptors on the membrane or in the cytoplasm of the neuron. In this chapter we will discuss how signalling molecules that are produced by the body (endogenous) and analogues administered as drugs (exogenous) bind to receptors, how this binding may be disrupted by endogenous or exogenous antagonists, how the action of signalling molecules is terminated and how psychotropic drugs are metabolised. The therapeutic use of different classes of psychotropic drugs – antipsychotics, antidepressants, sleep-inducing drugs (hypnotics), anti-anxiety drugs (anxiolytics), stimulants and anti-dementia drugs – and their molecular mechanisms will be explained in the sections on treatment in the relevant chapters of Part III.

6.1 THE FORMATION OF LIGAND–RECEPTOR COMPLEXES FOLLOWS THE 'LOCK AND KEY' PRINCIPLE

The basic principle of receptor binding is depicted in Figure 6.1A. A signalling molecule (the ligand) binds to a receptor molecule. The receptor and ligand have matching geometrical structures like a lock and key.

Receptors are always proteins, whereas their ligands can be from a wide range of molecule classes. Neurotransmitters can be amines, peptides or single amino acids, for example. Growth factors (neurotrophins) are proteins, and hormones can be steroids (e.g. cortisol or gonadal

Figure 6.1

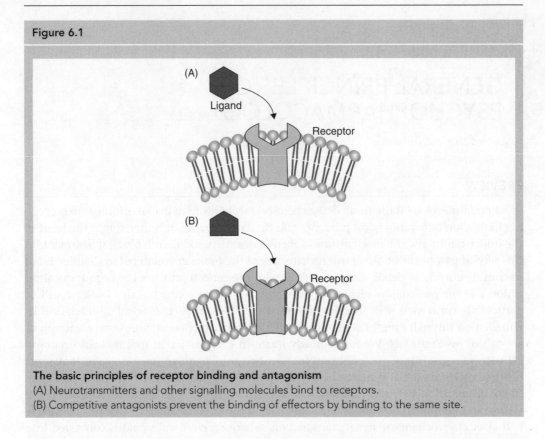

The basic principles of receptor binding and antagonism
(A) Neurotransmitters and other signalling molecules bind to receptors.
(B) Competitive antagonists prevent the binding of effectors by binding to the same site.

steroids), amino acids (the thyroid hormones) or polypeptides (growth hormone, oxytocin). Ligand binding changes the conformation of the receptor and leads to a number of chemical processes in the postsynaptic cell, for example ion currents where the receptor is an ion channel ('ionotropic receptor') or a modulator of an ion channel and/or second messenger cascades, where the receptor is coupled with a G-protein that triggers further metabolic processes ('metabotropic receptor'). These processes will be discussed in more detail in subsequent paragraphs, and the different types of receptors (e.g. ionotropic vs. metabotropic) will feature prominently in Chapter 7. Some molecules possess the key configuration but their binding does not result in the necessary conformation changes in the receptor B in Figure 6.1. To keep within our analogy we might say that this key fits in the lock but cannot be turned. Such molecules are called 'antagonists' because they prevent effective ligands – the 'agonists' – from binding to the receptor and thus maintain its function in the baseline state (e.g. prevent an ion channel from being opened). For example, the muscle relaxant curare, which is used by South American Indians for poisonous arrows and by anaesthetists during the induction of narcosis, is an antagonist of the nicotinic acetylcholine receptor and thus prevents signal transduction at the neuromuscular endplate. The result is complete paralysis of all skeletal muscles.

Whereas an antagonist has no effect on the postsynaptic neuron, an inverse agonist will bind to the receptor and have the opposite effect to the agonist, for example reducing the activity of a receptor-coupled G-protein below its baseline level. Far fewer inverse agonists than antagonists have been identified. Many psychotropic drugs are receptor antagonists, but further research may show that some of them have inverse agonist properties as well.

Another group of substances that bind to the receptor but do not exert the full agonistic effect are the so-called partial agonists. When concentrations of agonists are low, they can increase receptor activity but not to the same extent as a full agonist, but when agonist concentrations are high, they will have an antagonistic effect because they prevent the more effective full agonist from docking onto the receptor. The antipsychotic agent aripiprazole is such a partial agonist on the dopamine D_2 receptor. This mechanism of action is attractive where instability of neurotransmitter concentrations rather than generally increased levels is suspected. For example, one of the main models of dopamine function in schizophrenia posits dopaminergic hyperactivity in limbic but hypoactivity in prefrontal pathways. A partial agonist might thus regulate both.

Most receptors do not have one but multiple binding sites for ligands. Molecules that bind to sites other than the main agonist binding site are called 'allosteric' (from Greek: other space) modulators. They can have agonistic or antagonistic effects. For example, benzodiazepines increase the activity of the $GABA_A$ receptor by docking on their binding site and are therefore positive allosteric modulators (PAM) (Figure 6.2). The benzodiazepine antagonists compete with the benzodiazepines at their binding site and can therefore be considered to be negative allosteric modulators (NAM).

Whereas the $GABA_A$ receptor can be activated in the absence of its PAMs, other receptors require PAMs, which are also called co-transmitters in this scenario, in order to respond to their ligands. A notable example is the NMDA glutamate receptor, which requires the presence of the co-transmitters glycine or D-serine in addition to glutamate (and membrane depolarisation) in order to open its ion channel.

Ligands and receptors do not form a new molecule through a classical covalent bond (such as would occur if one added an amino acid to a protein by a peptide bond, see Figure 6.3). Rather, they form a complex that is held together by weaker bonds such as hydrogen bonds, electrostatic interaction and van der Waals forces. For example, the hydroxyl (OH) group of the catechol ring of NE can form a hydrogen bond with a hydroxyl group of the amino acid

Figure 6.2

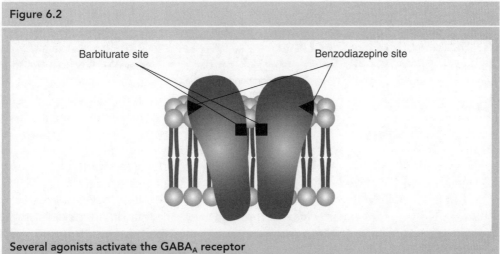

Barbiturate site   Benzodiazepine site

Several agonists activate the $GABA_A$ receptor
In addition to its binding site for $GABA_A$, the receptor also has 'allosteric' binding sites for benzodiazepines and barbiturates. These GABA agonists have various clinical uses.

Figure 6.3

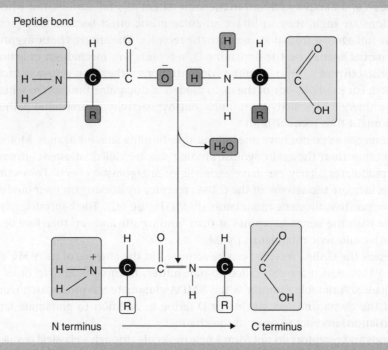

Peptide bond

N terminus ⟶ C terminus

The peptide bond is the basic structure of peptides and proteins
The upper panel shows two amino acids (alpha carbon atoms are depicted as black circles, see
Figure 2.4). The peptide bond is formed between the carboxyl group of the amino acid on the left
and the amino group of the amino acid on the right. This is an example of a covalent bond by which
two molecules form a new molecule (lower panel; in this case a dipeptide, formed by two amino
acids, the simplest form of peptide).

Figure 6.4

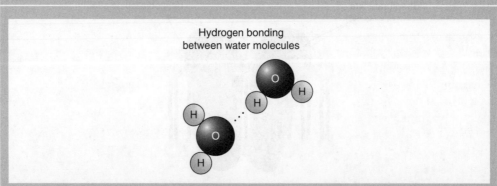

Hydrogen bonding
between water molecules

The hydrogen bond
Hydrogen bonding between water residues (hydroxyl groups), as indicated here by the dots between
a hydrogen (H) and an oxygen (O) atom, is one of the mechanisms for ligand-receptor binding.

serine of adrenergic receptors. This sounds complicated but is essentially the same mechanism by which water molecules are held together (Figure 6.4). An example of electrostatic interaction is that between the positively charged nitrogen atom in the choline part of acetylcholine and negatively charged amino acid residues in the nicotinic receptor. Van der Waals forces are caused by small and transient dipolar moments in apolar molecules, for example carbohydrates. They can be responsible for interactions between steroid hormones and apolar amino acid side chains in receptors.

6.2 DIFFERENT LIGANDS HAVE DIFFERENT AFFINITIES TO THEIR RECEPTORS

The binding of ligands to and dissociation from their receptors can be described by receptor kinetics. Because their binding energies are lower than those of covalent bonds, receptor–ligand complexes are less stable and tend to dissociate. The complex and its components (receptor and ligand) are in an equilibrium that can be described by the dissociation constant K_D, which is the quotient of the product of the concentrations of ligand ($[L]$) and receptor ($[R]$) and the concentration of the complex ($[C]$):

$$K_D = [L][R]/[C]$$

When $[L]$ equals K_D, half the receptor will be occupied by the ligand. The unit for concentrations is molar = mol/l. The mol is the base unit for the amount of a substance, and 1 mol of a molecular substance contains approximately 6.022×10^{23} molecules. The kinetics of such equilibria are the same as those governing the competitive inhibition of enzymes, and thus the term 'inhibitor constant' K_i is also commonly used as equivalent to the dissociation constant. The dissociation constants for ligands with a high affinity to a receptor, for example for the antipsychotics haloperidol or amisulpride at the dopamine D2 receptor, are normally in the nanomolar (nM) range. By comparison, the affinity of dopamine to the D2 receptor is 100 times weaker. The K_i database of the Psychoactive Drug Screening Programme (PDSP) of the National Institute of Mental Health (NIMH) of the United States, which is hosted by the University of North Carolina (http://pdsp.med.unc.edu/pdsp.php), is a useful search tool for anyone interested in the affinity of endogenous or experimental ligands and drugs to the various receptors and transporters. Students will not normally be expected to know exact or even approximate K_i values but will come across them in scientific papers and thus a basic understanding is helpful. For example, it is important to remember that lower K_i values denote higher affinity, and that a substance with a lower K_i will replace that with the higher K_i from its receptor binding site, regardless of whether it is an agonist or an antagonist. It is also interesting that affinities for the endogenous ligands are relatively low, and that for most receptors more specific ligands with higher affinity have been synthesised. For example, the affinity of raclopride to the D_2 receptor is about 1000 times higher than that of dopamine, but its affinity to the D_1 receptor is several orders of magnitude lower. This is the rationale for the use of radioactively labelled raclopride as a marker of D_2 receptors in positron emission tomography (Chapter 7).

6.3 THE ACTION OF NEUROTRANSMITTERS CAN BE TERMINATED IN SEVERAL WAYS

The equilibrium between ligand and receptor can be influenced by the removal of the ligand from the local area. In the case of complexes between transmitters and membrane receptors, this can occur through diffusion from the synaptic cleft, uptake into presynaptic neurons or neighbouring glia cells or enzymatic degradation of the NT. The reuptake of NTs into the presynaptic neuron, which is the main target of the most widely used antidepressants and many drugs of abuse, is an active (that is, energy demanding) process. It is mediated by transport proteins and many of the principles of ligand–receptor binding apply, with the exception that receptors do not normally transport their ligands. A substance can be a substrate, competitive or non-competitive antagonist at the transporter proteins, and its affinity can be described with dissociation constants.

6.3.1   The reuptake of neurotransmitters is an active transport process

The main transporters on the cell membrane are coded by genes from two families, SLC (solute carrier) 1 and 6. The members of the SLC 'superfamily' of transporters are linked by their function of transporting soluble molecules across extra- or intracellular membranes but have little else in common. However, within each SLC family, there is a certain overlap of gene sequence (20–25%) and thus transporters will share some of their protein structure. The SLC1 transporters have a high affinity for glutamate and are also called 'excitatory amino acid transporters' (EAAT). They have six transmembrane domains and are located on the presynaptic and glial membrane, and also on the postsynaptic membrane. Thus, glutamate can be transported into the postsynaptic neuron through this mechanism. The transporters of the SLC6 family are sodium- and chloride-dependent monoamine, glycine and GABA transporters. They have 12 transmembrane domains (Figure 6.5) and are found on presynaptic and glial cells. Both families transport Na^+ along a concentration gradient from the extra- to intracellular milieu together with their main substrate. This 'co-transport' provides the energy for the active transport of the substrate against a concentration gradient. In the case of SLC6 transporters this is furthermore coupled with co-transport of Cl^- ions into the cell. For example, the dopamine transporter moves two Na^+ ions and one Cl^- ion with each dopamine molecule, whereas norepinephrine and serotonin are co-transported by their respective transporters with one Na^+ ion and one Cl^- ion (Torres et al., 2003). The SLC1 transporters (and amongst the SLC6 transporters the serotonin transporter) use counter-transport

Figure 6.5

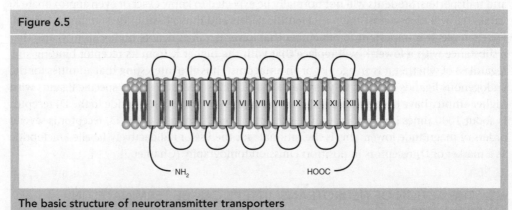

The basic structure of neurotransmitter transporters
Neuorotransmitter transporters from the SLC 6 family have twelve transmembrane domains (Extracellular is above), but it has not yet been clarified through which of them the substrate is transported into the cell.

of K$^+$ ions (Gether et al., 2006). These co- and counter-transport mechanisms rely on the restitution of the concentration gradients by the Na+/K+ ATPase (see Chapter 2). This ATP-dependent ion pump thus indirectly provides the energy for the active transport of NTs into pre- and postsynaptic neurons.

The SLC6 family includes the monoamine transporters, which are at the centre of pharmacological models of affective disorders and drug addiction and central targets of antidepressants. The serotonin transporter (SERT) has high affinity for serotonin, whereas the norepinephrine (NET) and dopamine (DAT) transporters have the catecholamines as substrates. For example, the affinity of dopamine to the NET is similar to that of norepinephrine, which explains reuptake in areas like prefrontal cortex where NET, but not DAT, is expressed. Monoamine transporters are expressed mainly by the neurons that also release the respective transmitter. For example, SERT is expressed in the raphe nuclei, NET in the locus coeruleus and DAT in the substantia nigra, VTA, striatum and habenula. In cortex, DAT expression seems to be confined to dopaminergic axons to the cingulate and medial prefrontal cortex, whereas NET and SERT expression is more widespread in hippocampus and cerebral cortex (Torres et al., 2003).

6.3.2 Many monoamine reuptake inhibitors have antidepressant or stimulant properties

Most antidepressants are negative allosteric modulators of SERT, NET or DAT, although in many cases their precise binding sites have not yet been identified. The selective serotonin reuptake inhibitors (SSRI) have a high affinity for SERT and much lower affinities for the other monoamine transporters. For example, the K_i of the SSRI citalopram for SERT is about 5 nM, whereas it is in the micromolar range for NET and DAT, denoting about 1000 times lower affinity for the catecholamine transporters (Torres et al., 2003). Conversely, the affinity of selective norepinephrine inhibitors (NRI) like reboxetine is high for the NET and lower for SERT and DAT. Bupropion is an antidepressant with a slightly different mechanism because it blocks both NET and DAT. Although its affinity is only in the micromolar range, it is still an order of magnitude higher than for SERT, giving bupropion a relatively selective catecholaminergic mode of action, which may be desirable for some depressive syndromes. The tricyclic antidepressants (TCA) block both SERT and NET (and DAT with much lower affinity), although some of them (e.g. desipramine and nortriptyline) have higher affinity for NET and some of them (e.g. imipramine, clomipramine) for SERT. Because blockade of the presynaptic and glial transporters results in higher availability of the transmitters in the synaptic cleft these reuptake inhibitors are indirect monoamine agonists. They also have multiple other pharmacological effects at pre- and postsynaptic receptors for several neurotransmitters, which may contribute to their therapeutic effects but even more so to their side effects. This is particularly the case for the TCAs, which also have important anticholinergic and antihistaminergic effects. The implications of these different pharmacological profiles for clinical use of antidepressants will be discussed in Chapter 11.

Most of the (legal and illegal) drugs with stimulant properties are also inhibitors of SLC6 transporters. Whereas cocaine has similar affinities for all three monoamine transporters, 3,4-methylenedioxymethamphetamine (MDMA, 'ecstasy') has highest affinity for SERT and amphetamine, methamphetamine ('speed') and methylphenidate (Ritalin®) have highest affinity for DAT and NET. Amphetamine blocks catecholamine reuptake by promoting phosphorylation of DAT, which inactivates the transporter, and also acts as a competitive inhibitor. Amphetamine competes with dopamine for transport into the presynaptic cell, and its transport is accompanied by release of dopamine. Thus, it effectively reverses the reuptake of dopamine rather than merely blocking it (Figure 6.6). Amphetamine also blocks the vesicular monoamine transporter (VMAT) and thus promotes the release of dopamine from its storage vesicles (see below). The mechanisms of action and clinical effects of stimulants and related illicit drugs will be discussed in detail in Chapter 15.

Other members of the SLC6 family include several GABA and glycine transporters. One of the GABA transporters (GAT1) is the target for an antiepileptic drug, tiagabine. GABAergic agonism is generally one of the therapeutic principles to control seizures. The glycine transporters, although not yet targets for any drugs that are marketed for therapeutic use, are being explored because of the role of glycine as co-transmitter at the NMDA receptor. Current pathophysiological models of schizophrenia implicate hypoactivity of glutamatergic transmission at the NMDA receptor (Chapter 10). Whereas enhancement of glutamate release entails too high a risk of promoting seizures and excitotoxicity, glycine release may be a more specific mechanism for NMDA agonism. Although malfunction of the EAAT has been implicated in various neurological disorders such as Amyotrophic Lateral Sclerosis (ALS) or epilepsy, no drug currently in therapeutic use targets the SLC1 transporter family. Again, the reason may be that direct interference with glutamate release has too many global effects.

Figure 6.6

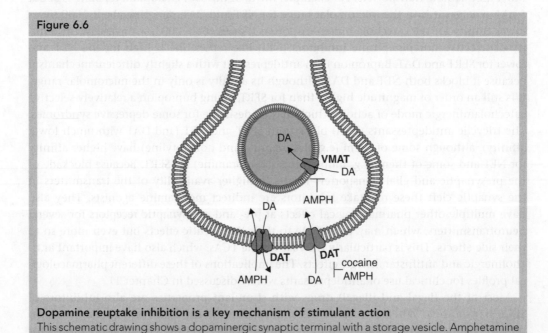

Dopamine reuptake inhibition is a key mechanism of stimulant action
This schematic drawing shows a dopaminergic synaptic terminal with a storage vesicle. Amphetamine (AMPH) reverses the dopamine (DA) transport into the presynaptic cell by acting as a substrate for the dopamine transporter (DAT) and blocks its storage blocking the vesicular monoamine transporter (VMAT). Cocaine is an allosteric inhibitor of monoamine reuptake.

6.3.3 Several synaptic enzymes break down neurotransmitters

Another important factor in the termination of neurotransmitter action is the presence of enzymes that degrade the neurotransmitter. These can be located in the synaptic cleft or in the presynaptic neuron, in which case they act in concert with the reuptake mechanisms explained above. One clinically relevant example is monoamine-oxidase (MAO), which is mainly located on the mitochondrial membrane in neurons and astroglia. MAO catalyses the oxidative deamination of monoamines to aldehydes, which do not have neurotransmitter functions, and thus inactivates them (see Chapter 2). Of the two types, MAO-A has all monoamines as substrates, whereas MAO-B is selective for dopamine. MAO inhibitors (MAOI) are used in the treatment of depression and Parkinson's disease (PD). Another enzyme that breaks down catecholamines is catechol-O-methyltransferase (COMT). It transfers a methyl group onto a hydroxyl group ('O-methylation') of the catechol ring and thus deactivates the catecholamine. The reactions catalysed by MAO and COMT are shown for dopamine in Figure 6.7. COMT inhibitors are used in the treatment of PD, although concerns about liver damage have resulted in the withdrawal of one of them, tolcapone. Furthermore, current trials explore their use in schizophrenia for patients who may have genetic variants leading to higher COMT activity and thus lower dopamine levels.

The main enzyme for the breakdown of acetylcholine is acetylcholinesterase (AChE), which is released into the synaptic cleft and can thus inactivate the neurotransmitter in the absence of reuptake mechanisms. AChE splits acetylcholine into its components choline and acetic acid and thus reverses the synthesis of acetylcholine that is catalysed by choline acetyltransferase (CHAT). AChE inhibitors, which have indirect cholinergic effects, are a main class of anti-dementia drugs (Chapter 20).

Figure 6.7

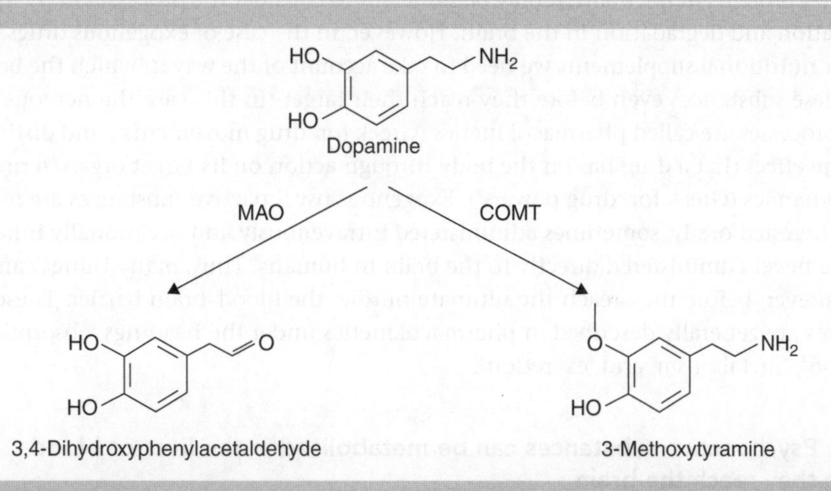

Metabolism of dopamine

MAO (monoamine oxidase) and COMT (catechol-O-methyl transferase) are the main enzymes for the degradation (inactivation) of monoamines.

6.3.4   Neurotransmitters are released from presynaptic vesicles

After synthesis and transport into the synaptic terminal, neurotransmitter molecules are stored in vesicles, and the balance between storage and release is another target for drugs that regulate neurotransmitter levels. The intracellular vesicular transporters come from three families and transport amines (SLC18), the inhibitory amino acids GABA and glycine (SLC32) and glutamate (SLC17) (Gether et al., 2006). The vesicular inhibitory amino acid transporter (VIAAT), the only member of the SLC32 family, exchanges a GABA or glycine molecule against a proton. The SLC17 family comprises a number of glutamate transporters that co- or counter-transport protons with glutamate. Because of their widespread expression in striatal, hippocampal and neocortical glutamatergic neurons they are thought to play an important role in the regulation of glutamatergic signalling, but a specific clinical significance has not yet been determined. Conversely, the clinical importance of the SLC18 family, which comprises the vesicular monoamine transporters VMAT1, expressed in the peripheral sympathetic nervous system, and VMAT2, expressed in the brain and the vesicular acetylcholine transporter (VAchT), is well established (Eiden et al., 2004). The anti-dopaminergic drugs tetrabenazine and reserpine are VMAT2 inhibitors. Tetrabenazine is used for relief for the hyperkinetic symptoms of Huntington's disease (Chapter 21). Reserpine is a formerly popular antihypertensive drug, whose depressogenic effects triggered the interest in monoamine deficit models of depression in the 1950s. Although by inhibiting the VMAT these drugs may lead to temporarily increased cytosolic dopamine concentrations, they lead to less efficient dopaminergic transmission because dopamine cannot be stored in vesicles for timely release. Conversely, the amphetamines, which are substrates of VMAT and are counter-transported with monoamines (Partilla et al., 2006), lead to enhanced dopaminergic transmission through their effect on the VMAT and on the DAT.

6.4   PHARMACOKINETICS DESCRIBES THE FATE OF DRUGS IN THE BODY

If we want to understand the actions of endogenous, locally synthesised ligands at receptors and other proteins in the brain, it may be sufficient to consider the processes of NT synthesis, dissociation and degradation in the brain. However, in the case of exogenous drugs, medications or nutritional supplements we need to take account of the way in which the body deals with these substances even before they reach their target (in this case the nervous system). These processes are called pharmacokinetics (Greek for 'drug movements') and distinguished from the effect that a drug has on the body through action on its target organ, termed pharmacodynamics (Greek for 'drug powers'). Exogenous psychoactive substances are most commonly ingested orally, sometimes administered intravenously and occasionally inhaled. Yet, they are never administered directly to the brain in humans. Thus, many things can happen to them even before they reach the ultimate hurdle, the blood–brain barrier. These various processes are generally described in pharmacokinetics under the headings 'absorption', 'distribution', 'metabolism' and 'excretion'.

6.4.1   Psychoactive substances can be metabolised in the liver or blood before they reach the brain

Unless inhaled or injected, psychoactive substances have to be absorbed from the gastrointestinal system. The fraction of a drug that is absorbed is its 'bioavailability'. The speed of this process can be influenced by the formulation of a drug. For example, a slow release version of methylphenidate was created by coating the tablet in wax, resulting in slow liberation and absorption of the active substance. The aim of this formulation was to protect against addictive effects. Conversely, rapidly disintegrating preparations of benzodiazepines that can be absorbed through the oral mucosa may be desirable to produce immediate anxiolytic effects. This aim has been realised with the fast release form of lorazepam. It is also important to consider the effect of concurrent food intake on the absorption of drugs. Once a substance has been absorbed into the blood vessels of the gut, it has to pass through the portal vein through the liver. Some of it will be metabolised during this 'first pass'. The rest gets distributed through the systemic circulation and enters the fluids and tissues of the body. Intramuscular and, even more directly, intravenous administration of drugs delivers drugs into the systemic circulation and thus results in quicker and often more potent physiological effects. However, this comes at the cost of the more invasive administration, which can be experienced as particularly aversive by psychiatric patients, and a higher risk of anaphylactic side effects.

The distribution of a substance in the body is governed by its chemical properties, for example its hydrophilic or hydrophobic nature, and by factors of the body, for example the availability of transport proteins. In the case of psychoactive substances, the aim would normally be for a high proportion of the substance to pass through the blood–brain barrier and as little as possible to enter other organs where it might cause side effects. The concentration of a substance in blood plasma may thus be only an indirect indicator of its effectiveness. Once in the brain, the substance, which might be an NT agonist, could be degraded in the same way as described above for the endogenous substances. Its metabolites would then ultimately show up in CSF and, through the resorption of CSF in the arachnoid granulations of the superior sagittal sinus, return into the blood circulation. However, the brain is not the only place where psychoactive substances are metabolised. Like any drug that is carried in the blood circulation, they can be metabolised directly in the blood, liver or kidneys. The various challenges of getting an exogenously administered neurotransmitter into the brain are exemplified in the dopamine treatment of PD. Here the aim is to replace the missing dopamine in the brain. However, dopamine does not pass through the blood–brain barrier. Therefore its precursor L-DOPA (see Chapter 2) is used as a drug. It would normally be converted to dopamine before it reaches the brain by the circulating enzyme Aromatic L-amino acid decarboxylase (AAAD). This peripheral metabolism of L-DOPA needs to be prevented because it would reduce the amount of dopamine available for the brain and cause undesirable dopaminergic side effects in peripheral organs. Therefore, an AAAD inhibitor such as carbidopa is normally added to the preparation.

6.4.2   Drug metabolism in the liver relies on the cytochrome system

Drug metabolism in the liver occurs in two stages, termed phase I, where a drug is converted into a more polar state, for example through oxidation or hydroxylation, and phase II, where a group from another molecule is added, for example conjugation with glucuronic acid. Phase I can result in active metabolites. For example risperidone is hydroxylated to paliperidone, which has almost the same affinity for D_2 (and $5HT_2$) receptors and has been developed into an antipsychotic drug in its own right. Conversely, phase II leads to inactivation of the compound. Most psychotropic drugs are oxidised by an enzyme of the cytochrome P450 (CYP) group, which is a superfamily of enzymes with a central heme group. It is important for the prescriber of psychiatric drugs to keep track of the metabolic pathways because metabolism can be delayed if several substances compete for the same CYP enzyme, or accelerated if a patient is also prescribed a drug that induces a CYP enzyme, for example the anticonvulsant carbamazepine. Furthermore, polymorphisms on the CYP genes may result in more or less active enzyme forms. For example, individuals who lack CYP2D6 or CYP2C19 or have less or more functional versions will be 'poor' or 'rapid' metabolisers, respectively. Such individuals will need higher or lower doses to reach the same plasma level of a drug. Poor metabolisers for the CYP2D6 system appear to be rare in all ethnic groups except Caucasians, where they make up 5–10% of the population. Conversely, defective alleles in the CYP2C19 seem to be more common in Han Chinese and may result in longer half life of benzodiazepines. Adjusting medication and its dosage to the genetic profile of a patient is called 'pharmacogenetics'. The deficit in aldehyde dehydrogenase 2 production, which is essential for the metabolism of alcohol, in many East Asians is another example of ethnic differences in the response to psychoactive substances.

6.4.3   Induction and blockade of cytochrome enzymes alters blood levels of drugs

Several antidepressant and antipsychotic drugs are metabolised by CYP2D6, which is inhibited by the antidepressants fluoxetine, paroxetine or bupropion. CYP2C19 metabolises several antidepressants and benzodiazepines. Other CYP enzymes important for the metabolism of psychotropic drugs are CYP1A2 and CYP3A4. For example, CYP1A2 metabolises the antidepressant duloxetine but is inhibited by the SSRI fluvoxamine and fluorochinolone antibiotics. CYP3A4 is induced by several drugs, including the anticonvulsants carbamazepine, phenytoin and barbiturates and the antidepressant St John's Wort. This induction may reduce plasma levels of drugs that are metabolised by this system, which include several antidepressants, antipsychotics, benzodiazepines and mood stabilisers (De Leon, 2009).

6.4.4   The kidney makes important contributions to drug metabolism

Unless drug metabolites accumulate in fatty tissue, which is not normally the case under physiological conditions, they are eliminated through excretion with urine or, less commonly, bile and faeces. In addition, the kidney has systems for phase I and II drug metabolism. Thus, doses need to be adjusted in patients with reduced kidney function for any drug, but particularly those with exclusively renal elimination such as the AChEI rivastigmine. Because listing all the pharmacokinetic pathways and resulting drug interactions would exceed the scope of this book, any readers who prescribe psychotropic medication should consult the relevant formularies and prescribing guidelines of their countries. However, the principles outlined here may aid in the understanding of basic ideas of pharmacogenetics and highlight the importance of therapeutic drug monitoring.

6.4.5   The half life of a drug in the body is an important parameter for prescribing decisions

The elimination of a drug from the body normally follows a logarithmic process that can be described by the half life (T½), which is the time it takes for the concentration to reach half its original value. This parameter is important to determine the duration of the effects of a drug. For example, the T½ for the Z-hypnotics zaleplon and zolpidem is 2 hours, whereas it is between 20 and 100 hours for diazepam. This explains why the Z-hypnotics work more selectively against early insomnia and are less likely to lead to sedation during the next day than diazepam. Long-term effects of a single administration of a drug can also be the consequence of long half life of active metabolites, or of slow release from tissue stores. For example, the TCAs are lipophilic. After overdose, patients need to be monitored for cardiac arrhythmia for 72 hours because of slow release of the substance from fatty tissue. The half life is also important for the decision how long to wait for the washout of a drug before a new one is started. For example, after unsuccessful treatment with an SSRI a psychiatrist may consider switching to a MAO inhibitor (MAOI). Fluoxetine has a half life of 1–3 days, which becomes longer after long-term use because fluoxetine inhibits its own metabolism through CYP2D6, and is even longer for its active metabolite. SSRIs must not be combined with MAOIs because of the risk of life-threatening serotonin syndrome, and thus patients have to wait five weeks after discontinuing fluoxetine before they can start taking an MAOI.

6.5   OVERDOSING, TOXICITY AND ANTIDOTES

Insufficient awareness of pharmacokinetics by a prescriber or overdosing by the patient can lead to toxic concentrations of a substance. Toxicity can be defined in various ways. The acute toxicity in animal experiments can be described by the median lethal dose or concentration (LD_{50}/C_{50}), at which half of the tested population dies after a specified duration. The levels of safe clinical dosage are normally established in phase I and II clinical trials, where human subjects get doses that are a fraction of the minimum harmful dose in animals. However, some drugs have a narrow therapeutic range, meaning that the minimal dose required for a clinical effect is close to the minimal toxic dose (see Figure 6.8). For example, lithium normally has a mood stabilising effect from plasma concentrations of 0.4 mmol/l onwards and the target concentration for adult patients is between 0.4 and 1 mmol/l, but toxicity can occur at levels of 1.5 mmol/l and even lower. Thus, administration of another drug that

---

Figure 6.8

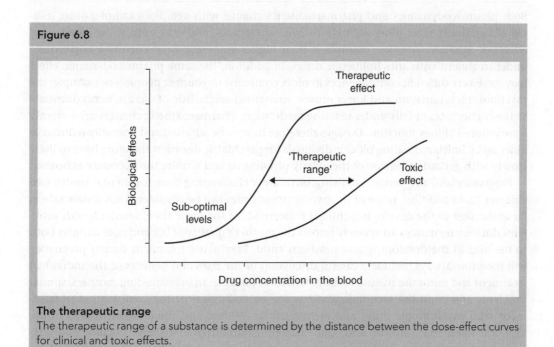

The therapeutic range
The therapeutic range of a substance is determined by the distance between the dose-effect curves for clinical and toxic effects.

affects kidney function may easily move lithium levels from the therapeutic into the toxic range, making monitoring of plasma levels and clinical signs of toxicity very important.

Many mental disorders carry with them an increased risk of self-harm and suicidality, which poses particular challenges to the safe prescribing of psychotropic drugs. One of the reasons for the higher popularity of SSRI than TCA antidepressants amongst prescribers is the lower cardiac toxicity of the former. However, ultimately any drug can be ingested in toxic quantities and thus particular care needs to be taken in patient and carer education and restricting availability for acutely suicidal patients. Some patients try to 'self-medicate' with recreational drugs, for example drinking alcohol to combat depression or smoking cannabis to calm themselves down during psychotic episodes. Although this practice may yield short-term respite, in the long term these substances exacerbate the problems they are supposed to alleviate: alcohol can lead to depression and cannabis can trigger psychotic episodes and disorders. Furthermore, the uncontrolled ingestion of legal or illegal recreational drugs poses a particular challenge to pharmacotherapy because they may interfere with the metabolism of the prescribed drugs and compound their toxicity.

Intoxication with psychotropic medication can sometimes be treated with specific antidotes, for example flumazenil, a competitive antagonist at the benzodiazepine binding site of the GABA$_A$ receptor, or the competitive opioid receptor antagonist naloxone. However, in the majority of cases general emergency procedures aiming at preventing absorption and promoting elimination, for example through activated charcoal in some cases, and providing general life support will be the only methods available. These are outside the scope of this book, and the interested reader will find more information in textbooks of clinical toxicology and emergency medicine.

6.6 OLD AGE AND PREGNANCY POSE PARTICULAR CHALLENGES FOR DRUG TREATMENT

Both pharmacodynamics and pharmacokinetics change with age. For example, older individuals generally react more strongly to benzodiazepines, and may even show paradoxical effects of agitation. Another example is their higher vulnerability to cognitive impairment under treatment with anticholinergic drugs. In addition, the same pharmacodynamic effect may have very different consequences in older compared to younger people. For example, the psychomotor retardation and lower muscle strength characteristic of old age may contribute to the higher rates of falls under sedating medication. Pharmacokinetic changes arise mainly from reduced kidney function. Dosages therefore have to be adjusted and normally reduced in older age. Clinicians treating older individuals for psychiatric disorders therefore have to liaise closely with geriatricians (care of the elderly physicians) and acquire the necessary expertise.

Pregnancy and the period following birth are a challenging time for mental health (see Chapter 3). In addition, none of the psychotropic drugs can be considered absolutely safe as far as damage to the developing child is concerned. At the same time, mental health problems during pregnancy can severely impair the mother's quality of life and pose dangers both to her and to the developing and newborn child. Psychiatric treatment during pregnancy will therefore always include a careful discussion of the risks and benefits of the individual treatment and minimise the use of drugs wherever possible. In breastfeeding mothers, similar problems arise, and the recommendations are generally against the combination of treatment with psychotropic drugs and breastfeeding. Lithium and the anticonvulsants in use as mood stabilisers (valproic acid, carbamazepine, lamotrigine) all have documented teratogenic (damaging the development of the embryo) effects when taken during the first trimester and should therefore generally be avoided during pregnancy.

6.7   PRESCRIBING CONTROLLED DRUGS

Drugs that have a high potential for abuse but also established medical applications pose particular challenges to regulators. We will discuss them using the example of the UK (Misuse of Drugs Regulations 2001), but similar schemes are in place in most countries. Opioid analgesics have traditionally been the main class of controlled drugs. They are used for a wide range of anaesthetic protocols in surgical procedures, for perinatal pain control, in intensive care and the treatment of chronic pain. Some opioids are also approved for substitution therapy for opioid dependence. Methadone is the opioid most widely used for this purpose, but some countries also have substitution programmes with buprenorphine or diamorphine (heroin). Other groups of controlled drugs include amphetamines, increasingly used for the treatment of ADHD, cocaine, used for substitution therapy, anabolic steroids, barbiturates, benzodiazepines and z-hypnotics, although the last two groups with few exceptions are subject to minimal controls. Controls are tightest ('schedule 1') for drugs which do not have an established medical use, such as hallucinogens, which can be used only for research and by practitioners holding a special licence. 'Schedule 2' drugs, which include diamorphine and several other opioids as well as amphetamine and cocaine, need to be kept in safe storage, and prescription documented in a special register. Drugs that fall under schedules 3–5 are assumed to have less potential for abuse and require less strict controls by prescribers, dispensers and manufacturers. There are dedicated forms for the prescription and dispensing of controlled drugs, and prescriptions for all schedule 2 and most schedule 3 drugs, which include most barbiturates, the opioid buprenorphine and the hypnotic midazolam, need to carry the handwritten signature of the prescriber. Further regulations apply for the dosage, transport and destruction of controlled drugs. In the context of the present book, it is of primary importance that readers are aware of the importance of minimising the potential of abuse of controlled drugs and of adhering to operating procedures and good clinical practice. In addition to the self-regulation by professional bodies, these are subject of legal regulation in most countries. Prescribing practitioners will need to update themselves in regular intervals on the legal requirements in force in their respective countries. The current guidance for the UK can be found on the website of the Department of Health (http://www.opsi.gov.uk/si/si2006/20063148.htm) and for the United States on the website of the Drug Enforcement Administration (DEA) (http://www.justice.gov/dea/pubs/abuse/index.htm). At the European level, the European Union's European Monitoring Centre for Drugs and Drug Addiction (EMCDDA) provides information about the different drug legislations in member states through the European Legal Database on Drugs (http://eldd.emcdda.europa.eu/html.cfm/index5029EN.html).

Outside the medical context, drugs of abuse are separately regulated. In the UK, the Misuse of Drugs Act 1971 groups illegal drugs into three classes (A–C). Possession and supply of class A drugs carries the highest penalties and of class C drugs the lowest. Class A drugs include heroin, cocaine, ecstasy, methamphetamine and hallucinogens, class B most other stimulants, cannabis and codeine, and class C benzodiazepines, ketamine and anabolic steroids.

6.8   REPORTING ADVERSE EFFECTS

Both the UK's Medicines and Healthcare products Regulatory Agency and the licensing agency of the United States, the Food and Drugs Administration, maintain registers for adverse drug effects. These are important for patient safety and their analysis can result in added warnings, monitoring requirements (such as blood tests during clozapine treatment because of the agranulocytosis risk), or even withdrawal of a drug's licence. Such registers rely on the cooperation of clinicians who are encouraged to report any observations of important adverse events, especially those not or rarely documented before, to the relevant agencies and manufacturers. Patients can report adverse effects as well, but are normally encouraged to discuss this with their doctor or pharmacist beforehand. Special online forms are available. These can be accessed in the UK through http://www.mhra.gov.uk/Safetyinformation/Reportingsafetyproblems/Reportingsuspectedadversedrugreactions/index.htm and in the United States through http://www.fda.gov/Safety/MedWatch/default.htm.

Learning points

We have reviewed the principles of pharmacodynamics and pharmacokinetics. Pharmacodynamics describes the effect of a drug on the body. In the case of drugs acting on mental processes (termed psychoactive or psychotropic), these are mediated through the formation of complexes with receptors on or in neurons. The signal cascades triggered by these complexes will be explained in the Chapter 7. Neurotransmitters act as agonists at specific receptors, and their actions can be mimicked or antagonised by psychoactive drugs. Neurotransmitter action is also influenced by its removal from the synaptic cleft through transporter proteins and enzymatic degradation. Transporter proteins belong to several families of the solute carrier (SLC) superfamily and are important targets for antidepressant and stimulant drugs. Enzymes catalysing the breakdown of neurotransmitters are also therapeutic targets, for example in depression and dementia. Pharmacokinetics describes the effects of the body on the drug. These are important because drugs administered for therapeutic or recreational purposes will distribute in and be eliminated from the body according to certain kinetic processes. These are influenced by the function of the kidney and the liver, for example the CYP450 group of enzymes. Drug interactions and genetic variants can influence drug metabolism, resulting in plasma concentrations that are too low (thus not clinically effective) or too high (toxic). Prescribers, patients and carers need to be aware of the pharmacokinetics and toxicology of psychotropic drugs in order to prevent potentially severe side effects.

Appropriate medical monitoring, including the reporting of adverse effects, is therefore a prerequisite of a safe psychopharmacotherapy. Many psychotropic drugs also have a high potential of abuse and dependence and are therefore governed by specific guidelines and legal frameworks for the prescribing of controlled drugs.

Revision and discussion questions

- Explain the difference between a receptor antagonist and an inverse agonist.
- Describe the main mechanism for the removal of neurotransmitters from the synaptic cleft.
- Concentrations of homovanillic acid in the CSF of patients with Parkinson's disease can increase after oral levodopa administration – describe the intermediate steps.
- Discuss the challenges of psychopharmacological treatment in old age, in patients with physical illness, in patients with comorbid substance abuse and in suicidal patients.

FURTHER READING

The K$_i$ database of the Psychoactive Drug Screening Programme (PDSP) of the National Institute of Mental Health (NIMH) of the United States, which is hosted by the University of North Carolina (http://pdsp.med.unc.edu/pdsp.php)

Nestler, E. J., Hyman, S. E. and Malenka, R. C. (2009). *Molecular Neuropharmacology: A Foundation for Clinical Neuroscience* (New York and London: McGraw-Hill Medical).

NEUROTRANSMITTER RECEPTORS AND POSTSYNAPTIC SIGNALLING PATHWAYS

PREVIEW

Chapter 7 covers the postsynaptic actions of the major neurotransmitter (NT) groups, including receptor function and postsynaptic signalling pathways. We have encountered the main classes of NTs already in Chapter 2, and they are listed in Table 7.1 on p. 60, together with their main receptors in the CNS. The addition 'in the CNS' is important because many NTs also have effects in peripheral organs, for example the gut, kidneys or heart, which are not covered in this book, except where interaction with them leads to side effects of psychotropic drugs. In terms of their basic mechanism of action, two classes of receptors can be distinguished, the ionotropic (sometimes also 'ionotrophic') receptors, which are themselves ion channels, and the metabotropic receptors, which are coupled with G-proteins. The nicotinic acetylcholine receptor, the NMDA, AMPA and kainate glutamate receptors, the $GABA_A$, glycine and $5-HT_3$ receptors are the main ionotropic receptors of relevance to current psychopharmacological research. In addition, there are many ion channels that do not require activation by neurotransmitters (thus, are not 'ligand-gated') but will change their permeability for ions with changes in membrane polarisation ('voltage-gated' channels). In this chapter, we will first discuss the structure and function of the main ionotropic NT receptors and voltage-gated channels, followed by the metabotropic receptors and their second messenger cascades. We will finally learn about the neurotrophic signalling pathway, which converges at many levels with NT-mediated signal transduction.

7.1 IONOTROPIC NT RECEPTORS

We saw in Chapter 6 that membrane proteins with docking stations for ligands normally have a number of transmembrane (TM) domains with connecting intra- and extracellular loops (Figure 6.6 on p. 108). Whereas the loops provide the docking stations, conformation changes in the TM domains, which may lead to the opening of a central pore, are responsible for the changes in permeability that give the TM protein the function of a selective ion channel. The ionotropic NT receptors can be grouped into those with five subunits ('pentameric') ($GABA_A$, nicotinic, $5-HT_3$ and glycine) and those with four subunits ('tetrameric') (the ionotropic glutamate channels). The pentameric receptors have four TM domains in each subunit, the tetrameric receptors three.

7.1.1 Nicotinic acetylcholine receptor (nAChR)

The nicotinic receptor is assembled from alpha (α) (1–10), beta (β) (1–4), gamma (γ), delta (δ) and epsilon (ϵ) subunits, although not all of them may occur in humans. The alpha 1, beta 1, gamma, delta and epsilon subunits occur in the muscular nicotinic receptors at the neuromuscular junction, whereas the other subunits make up the neuronal receptors in various combinations. Receptors with only one type of subunit, e.g. $(\alpha7)_5$ (the subscript '5' denotes that five alpha 7 subunits are assembled) are called 'homomeric', receptors with mixed subunits, e.g. $(\alpha4)_2(\beta2)_3$ (Figure 7.1), are called 'heteromeric'. The nicotinic receptor is a non-selective cation channel. After agonist binding, a pore in the channel opens, through which potassium leaves and sodium enters the cell, with a net influx of cations and resulting depolarisation. This can lead to action potentials, either directly mediated by currents through nicotinic receptors or through activation of voltage sensitive ion channels. Some forms of the nicotinic receptor are also permeable for calcium in the activated state, especially $(\alpha7)_5$ and $(\alpha9)_5$, which can then exert second messenger functions (explained in Section 7.4.1) in the postsynaptic cell. Acetylcholine is the endogenous agonist for the nicotinic receptor. Nicotine binds with about equal affinity. The reason why the receptor is called 'nicotinic' is that nicotine, which has much lower affinity for the muscarinic receptor, is a more selective ligand. Keeping with the key-lock analogy introduced in Chapter 6, one could say that the NT (in this case acetylcholine) is the 'master key' that fits all its receptors, whereas the specific exogenous ligands (nicotine, muscarine) open the doors to individual rooms. Similar hierarchies apply to the ionotropic glutamate receptors (master key: glutamate; individual keys: NMDA, AMPA, kainate) and most other receptors, for which there are fewer (the respective natural NT) and more specific ligands. One major limitation of the 'key lock' model is that ligand–receptor kinetics are quantitative rather than qualitative. Thus, a high concentration of a ligand with lower affinity may open the lock in the same way as a low concentration of a ligand with higher affinity. Nicotine has highest affinity to the heteromeric $\alpha4\beta2$ subunits, which are ubiquitously expressed in the brain. Activation of nAChRs on dopaminergic neurons in the VTA stimulates dopamine release in the ventral striatum, which may be one of the mechanisms behind the rewarding and addictive properties of nicotine (Chapter 15). An interesting feature of ligand-gated ion channels, which is particularly relevant for the development of tolerance in substance misuse, is desensitisation. This term describes the progressive reduction or loss of biological responses to the binding of endogenous or exogenous agents after chronic exposure, as happens in long-term smoking. The exact mechanisms are not well understood, but some authors hypothesise a second 'desensitisation' gate in addition to the 'activation' gate (Karlin, 2002).

Figure 7.1

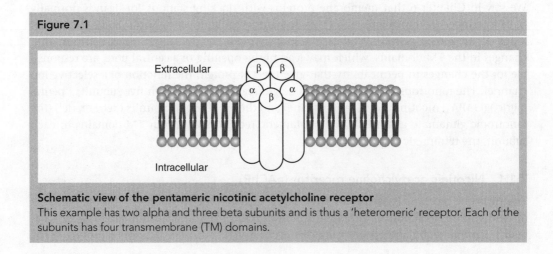

Schematic view of the pentameric nicotinic acetylcholine receptor
This example has two alpha and three beta subunits and is thus a 'heteromeric' receptor. Each of the subunits has four transmembrane (TM) domains.

7.1.2   GABA_A receptor

The GABA$_A$ receptor is also assembled from several subunits labelled with Greek letters and Arabic numerals. The most common type in the brain has two alpha, two beta and one gamma subunit. Activation by GABA leads to opening of a central pore, through which negatively charged chloride ions can leave the neuron, leading to hyperpolarisation and thus having an inhibitory effect. In addition to GABA, a number of direct agonists have been identified, which are mainly used in animal research. The agonist muscimol is found in hallucinogenic mushrooms and still sometimes used for recreational purposes, although this practice is associated with the added danger of ingestion of poisonous mushrooms. Positive allosteric modulators, each with their own binding site, include the benzodiazepines, barbiturates and z-hypnotics. Benzodiazepines and barbiturates have multiple pharmacological uses. Barbiturates have fallen out of favour as hypnotics but are still used as anticonvulsants in many parts of the world where the newer, more expensive drugs are not available. Benzodiazepines are used as hypnotics, anxiolytics, muscle relaxants, anticonvulsants and short-term sedatives and will be discussed in more detail in Part III (see Chapter 15 for a discussion of their abuse). Z-hypnotics (zolpidem, zaleplon, zopiclone) are used in the treatment of insomnia. Propofol is another positive allosteric modulator and has a medical use in short-term anaesthesia. Its abuse seems to have become more widespread amongst medical professionals, in particular. Several toxic substances have been identified as competitive (competing with GABA for its binding site) or non-competitive (blocking the ion channel at another site) GABA$_A$ receptor antagonists. The GABA system and especially the GABA$_A$ receptor have been implicated in the (reduced) formation of fear memories (Makkar et al., 2010), and alterations in the expression or sensitivity of GABA receptors feature prominently in biological models of anxiety disorders.

7.1.3   Glycine receptor

The glycine receptor is assembled from four isoforms of the alpha and a single beta subunit. Adult humans express heteromers of alpha 1 and beta units (Kuhse et al., 1995). In addition to glycine, several other amino acids also bind as agonists. The pesticide strychnine and caffeine are some of the competitive agonists. Like the GABA$_A$ receptor, the glycine receptor is a chloride channel and its activation leads to hyperpolarisation and thus inhibition of the postsynaptic neuron.

7.1.4   5-HT₃ receptor

Five different subunits (5-HT3A to 3E) have been identified for the only ionotropic serotonin receptor. The 5-HT3A subunit seems to be the only one that forms homomers, while all others form heteromers with this subunit. The 5-HT$_3$ receptor has structural and functional similarities with the nAChR, and it has been possible to design chimeric receptors from the extracellular domain of nAChR subunits and TM domains of the 5-HT$_3$ receptor that are activated by acetylcholine but then behave like 5-HT$_3$ receptors. Like the nAChR, the 5-HT3 is a cation channel and practically impermeable for anions. Whereas the A subunit has equal conductance for monovalent (sodium, potassium) and bivalent (calcium) cations, the B subunit is more selective for monovalent cations. The 5-HT$_3$ receptor is highly expressed in the dorsal vagal complex of the brainstem, which comprises the nucleus tractus solitarii, area postrema and dorsal motor nucleus of the vagus nerve (Barnes et al., 2009). These areas form a circuit for the control of the vomiting reflex, and 5-HT$_3$ antagonists like ondanset-ron are mainly used clinically for their anti-emetic (suppressing vomiting) properties, for example in cancer chemotherapy. 5-HT$_3$ receptors may be located both presynaptically (and thus enhance glutamate release through calcium influx) and postsynaptically (with direct depolarising effects).

7.1.5   Ionotropic glutamate receptors

The ionotropic glutamate receptors form another, tetrameric, superfamily of ligand-gated channels. They are all activated by glutamate, but each also selectively by their eponymous ligands (AMPA, kainate, NMDA). This is another example of the analogy between NT and master key explained above. The AMPA receptors are homo- or heteromers of the GluR1-GluR4 (new nomenclature: GluA1-4) subunits, and the kainate receptors are homo- or heteromers of the GluR5-GluR7 (GluK1-3) and KA1–KA2 (GluK4-5) subunits. Both classes are excitatory cation channels. Presynaptic kainate receptors also regulate glutamate release. The NMDA receptor family comprises heteromers of the NR1 (GluN1) and NR2 (subtypes NR2A-D/GluN2A-D) subunits, sometimes also the NR3 (subtypes NR3A-B/GluN3A-B) subu-nits. The main function of NMDA receptors does not seem to lie so much in fast excitatory signalling as in the integration of synaptic activity over space and time. In addition to gluta-mate binding to the NR2 subunit, the co-transmitters glycine or D-serine need to bind to the NR1 subunit for the cation channel to open. Through this need for coactivation, the NMDA receptor can integrate between different signalling pathways. In addition, depolarisation of the membrane, for example through activation of AMPA or kainate receptors, is required for activation of the NMDA receptor, which is blocked by a magnesium ion at resting membrane potentials. Because of these properties and increasing experimental evidence, the NMDA receptor has been assigned a key role in synaptic plasticity and cellular mechanisms of learn-ing, although AMPA seems to be important as well (Madden, 2002).

Several molecules act as antagonists at the AMPA and kainate receptors, but they are not in clinical use. Conversely, AMPA agonism (through positive allosteric modulation) is one of the mechanisms of so-called nootropic (enhancing mental power) drugs such as pira-cetam. Although still marketed for both clinical and preclinical stages of cognitive decline, these drugs generally have not shown clear benefits. More potent and selective AMPA ago-nists, 'ampakines', are currently in preclinical testing as cognitive enhancers. Several antago-nists of the NMDA receptor are of relevance because of their clinical use and illicit abuse. The anaesthetic drug ketamine is a non-competitive antagonist, which seems to have an activity-dependent effect (that is, it blocks the receptor only once glutamate has docked on). Ketamine can produce a psychosis that resembles that of schizophrenia more closely than those induced by amphetamines or hallucinogens because it also includes disorganisa-tion and first-rank symptoms. However, it is not clear whether the psychological effects of ketamine are in fact mediated by its anti-glutamatergic effect. For example, ketamine is also an agonist at the D2 receptor, which probably contributes to its psychotomimetic effects (Seeman et al., 2005). In addition, it was recently suggested that the hypnotic and some of the neurophysiological and behavioural effects of ketamine may occur through inhibition of the HCN1 (hyperpolarisation-activated cyclic nucleotide-modulated) channel (Chen et al., 2009). Ketamine, street name 'vitamin K' (not to be confused with the actual vitamin), is abused mainly for its hallucinogenic properties. The illegal drug PCP (phenylcyclohexyl-piperidine), street name 'angel dust', has a similar pharmacological profile to ketamine. The anti-dementia drug memantine binds non-competitively to the NMDA receptor and blocks the ion channel in its open state. It can thus inhibit the influx of calcium into the neuron, which can lead to over-activation and cell damage. This property may be the basis for its putative neuroprotective effects. Because memantine dissociates quickly from the receptor, physiological activation by glutamate is still possible, which may explain why memantine, unlike ketamine or PCP, is not normally psychotogenic.

7.2 VOLTAGE-GATED CHANNELS

Voltage-gated channels are ion channels whose opening depends on the membrane polarisation. The actual channel or pore is composed of four domains (D1-4) with six TM segments each (S1-6) (Figure 7.2). The channel (also called alpha subunit) is flanked by several auxiliary subunits (of which there are beta, gamma and delta types, dependent on channel type; see below). S4 is the voltage sensor. The extracellular loops between S5 and S6 form the pore and determine permeability for specific ions. The intracellular loop between D3 and D4 can

Figure 7.2

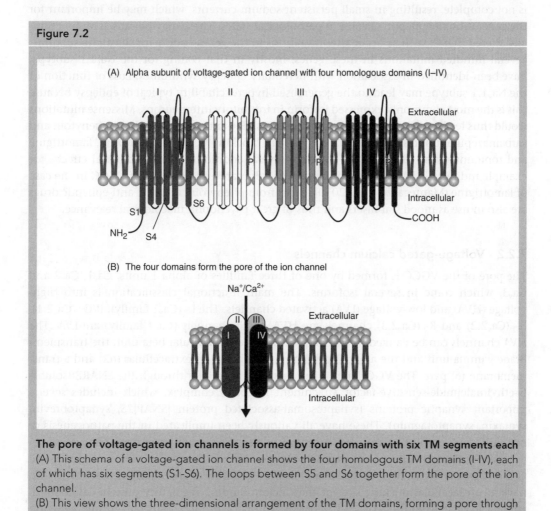

(A) Alpha subunit of voltage-gated ion channel with four homologous domains (I–IV)

(B) The four domains form the pore of the ion channel

The pore of voltage-gated ion channels is formed by four domains with six TM segments each
(A) This schema of a voltage-gated ion channel shows the four homologous TM domains (I-IV), each of which has six segments (S1-S6). The loops between S5 and S6 together form the pore of the ion channel.
(B) This view shows the three-dimensional arrangement of the TM domains, forming a pore through the membrane.

change its conformation to inactivate a voltage-gated sodium channel (VGSC). Voltage-gated calcium channels (VGCC) do not have such a pore inactivator. Instead, the intracellular loop between D2 and D3 forms a docking station for synaptic vesicles for the exocytosis of NT. The VGSC and VGCC are targets for many anticonvulsant and mood stabilising drugs and thus of particular interest for neuro- and psychopharmacology.

7.2.1   Voltage-gated sodium channels

Nine alpha unit isoforms have been identified for the VGSC ($Na_v1.1$–$Na_v1.9$). What type of VGSC is expressed by a cell depends on the stage of development (embryonic vs. adult), tissue (e.g. brain, peripheral nerve) and type of cell (neuron vs. glia). This alpha pore is flanked by two smaller beta subunits with a single TM segment (of the isoforms $\beta1$-4). VGSC are important for the propagation of action potentials. When the surrounding membrane is depolarised they open immediately (within a few hundred microseconds) to allow influx of Na^+ ions and are then inactivated within a few milliseconds. However, this inactivation is not complete, resulting in small persistent sodium currents, which may be important for the generation of epileptic seizures in pathological states. These may be caused by functionally altered VGSC, such as occur after mutations in the genes coding for the alpha subunits. Several hundred mutations in these genes, mostly in that coding for the $Na_v1.1$ subtype, have been identified in association with hereditary epilepsy syndromes. Loss of function of the $Na_v1.1$ subtype may lead to the generalised hyperexcitability typical of epilepsy because this is the most commonly expressed isoform in inhibitory interneurons. Missense mutations would thus lead to disinhibition of cortical circuits. The anticonvulsant drugs phenytoin and carbamazepine suppress seizures mainly through blocking VGSC. Valproic acid, lamotrigine and topiramate also block VGSC, but have several additional pharmacological effects, for example indirect GABA agonism in the case of valproate and blockade of VGCC in the case of lamotrigine (Mantegazza et al., 2010). Apart from phenytoin, all these anti-epileptic drugs are also in use as mood stabilisers and thus of great psychopharmacological relevance.

7.2.2   Voltage-gated calcium channels

The pore of the VGCC is formed by one of three families of alpha 1 units, Ca_v1, Ca_v2 and Ca_v3, which come in several isoforms. The main functional classification is into high-voltage (HVA) and low-voltage (LVA) activated channels. The L- (Ca_v1 family), P/Q- ($Ca_v2.1$), N- ($Ca_v2.2$) and R- ($Ca_v2.3$) channels are HVA, the T-channels (Ca_v3 family) are LVA. The HVA channels can be flanked by several proteins: the intracellular beta unit, the transmembrane gamma unit and the alpha-2/delta unit, which has an extracellular ($\alpha2$) and a transmembrane (δ) part. The VGCC are linked to synaptic vesicles through the SNARE (soluble N-ethylmaleimide-sensitive-factor attachment receptor) complex, which includes several important synaptic proteins (synaptosomal-associated protein [SNAP]25, synaptobrevin, syntaxin, synaptotagmin). These have all variously been implicated in the pathogenesis of mental disorders and certainly play a central role in the regulation of neural transmission. Specifically, the activation of exocytosis by N-type channels is important for the regulation of GABA release and that by P/Q-type channels for regulation of glutamate release. VGCC also have an intracellular docking site for the calcium-binding regulatory protein calmodulin, which can deactivate the VGCC after prolonged depolarisation, thus preventing depletion of NT stores. We have thus now assembled the molecular components to trace the whole process of neural signalling from NT release from a presynaptic neuron through the generation of EPSPs by ligand-gated channels, propagation of the AP through VGSC along the axon into the synaptic terminal and stimulation of NT release through VGCC.

The function of the LVA (T-type) channels is less well understood. As their name indicates, they need less depolarisation to open for calcium currents. This depolarisation can be produced by the hyperpolarisation-activated cation current (I_h), which is slower and weaker than the currents associated with APs. Once the I_h has reached the threshold for activation of T-type channels, the added depolarisation from the influx of Ca^{2+} is strong enough to trigger opening of VGSC and a burst of APs. However, it also triggers inward K^+ currents that restore hyperpolarisation. These regulatory cycles have a central function for thalamocortical circuits, for example for sleep/wake rhythms (Benarroch, 2010).

Mutations in genes for VGCC are responsible for epileptic syndromes and other neurological disorders, and several anticonvulsants target specific units. For example pregabalin and gabapentin bind to the alpha-2/delta unit of N and P/Q channels, which results in closing of the channel. The L-type channels are the targets for the antihypertensive 'calcium blocker' drugs like nimodipine, which is also being explored as treatment for bipolar disorder. The link between L-type VGCC function and bipolar disorder has been supported by a GWAS reporting association with a variant of the CACNA1C gene that codes for the α1 subunit of L-type channels (Ferreira et al., 2008).

7.3   METABOTROPIC RECEPTORS

The metabotropic or G-protein-coupled receptors (Figure 7.3) are not themselves ion channels, but effect conformation changes in ion channels through a cascade of chemical reactions on the intracellular side of the postsynaptic membrane (Figure 7.4). In addition their activation can lead to a variety of changes in the postsynaptic cell that will be described in Section 7.4. Because of these properties, metabotropic receptors are generally more suited

Figure 7.3

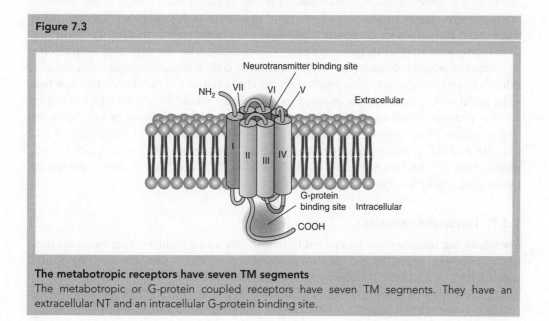

The metabotropic receptors have seven TM segments
The metabotropic or G-protein coupled receptors have seven TM segments. They have an extracellular NT and an intracellular G-protein binding site.

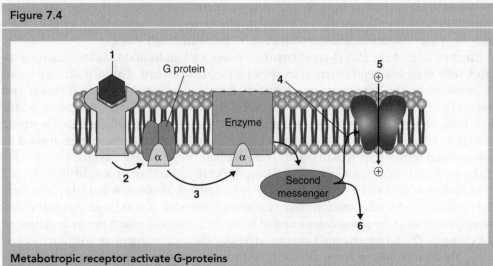

Metabotropic receptor activate G-proteins

After activation by a ligand (1), the metabotropic receptor activates a G-protein (2), which releases its alpha unit to activate a membrane-bound enzyme, for example adenyl cyclase (3) resulting in the up- or downregulation of second messengers, for example cAMP, conformation changes in ion channels (4, 5) and several postsynaptic chemical reactions (6). The further cascade is depicted in Figure 7.7.

for the modulation of neural activity and long-lasting plastic changes (involving changes in gene expression), for example during learning, whereas the ionotropic receptors (except the NMDA receptor) and voltage-gated channels can subserve fast neuronal signalling. The metabotropic receptors are all similar in their basic protein structure, with seven TM segments, an extracellular NT and an intracellular G-protein binding site (Figure 7.3).

The first step of the postsynaptic signalling cascade for all metabotropic receptors is activation of a G (guanine nucleotide-binding)-protein. G-proteins are a large family of membrane proteins, which are inactive when bound to guanosine diphosphate (GDP) and active when this is exchanged for guanosine triphosphate (GTP). Because the nucleotide–phosphate bonds are energy stores, this process is energy-demanding. The activated G-protein releases its α-subunit, which is coupled to GTP. This activated GTP- α-subunit complex stimulates or inhibits intracellular enzymes, depending on the characteristics of the G-protein. Most neuronal metabotropic receptors are coupled to G-proteins that either stimulate (G_s) or inhibit (G_i) the enzyme adenylate cyclase (AC) through conformation changes or to G_q-proteins that stimulate Phospholipase C-β (PLCβ) (Table 7.1). AC catalyses the conversion of ATP to cAMP and PLC converts phosphatidylinositol 4,5-biphosphate (PIP$_2$) into inositol (1,4,5) triphosphate (IP$_3$) and diacylglycerol (DAG). Cyclic AMP, IP$_3$ and DAG are important second messengers, whose functions will be described in Section 7.4.

7.3.1   Dopamine receptors

The dopamine receptors can be divided in to a D_1-like and a D_2-like family based on similarities of protein sequence and putative mode of action. The D_1-like receptors (D_1 and D_5) stimulate AC, whereas the D_2 receptor (and probably the other D_2-like receptors, D_3 and D_4) inhibits this enzyme, leading to increases or decreases in the intracellular levels of the second messenger cAMP (Figure 7.5). Although the D_1-like family is linked with a 'stimulating'

Table 7.1 Main classes of NTs and their neuronal receptors

Group	NT	Receptor	Type	Effect/2nd messenger
Amines (monoamines/catecholamines)	Dopamine	D_1 D_5	G_s-protein coupled	cAMP (upregulation)
		D_2 D_3 D_4	G_i-protein coupled	cAMP (downregulation)
	Norepinephrine/Epinephrine	α_1	G_q-protein coupled	IP_3 and DAG
		α_2	G_i-protein coupled	cAMP (downregulation)
		β_{1-3}	G_s-protein coupled ($\beta2$ also G_i)	cAMP (upregulation) ($\beta2$ also down)
Amines (monoamines/indoleamines)	Serotonin	5-HT$_1$ 5-HT$_5$	G_i-protein coupled	cAMP (downregulation)
		5-HT$_2$	G_q-protein coupled	IP_3 and DAG
		5-HT$_3$	Na^+ and K^+ channel	Depolarisation
		5-HT$_4$ 5-HT$_6$ 5-HT$_7$	G_s-protein coupled	cAMP (upregulation)
Amines	Acetylcholine	Nicotinic	Na^+ and K^+ channel	Depolarisation; Ca^{++}
		Muscarinic M_1 M_3 M_5	G_q-protein coupled	IP_3 and DAG
		Muscarinic M_2 M_4	G_i-protein coupled	cAMP (downregulation)
Amines	Histamine	H_1	G_q-protein coupled	IP_3 and DAG
		H_2	G_s-protein coupled	cAMP (upregulation)
		H_3	G_i-protein coupled	cAMP (downregulation)
Amino acids	Glutamate	NMDA (N-methyl-D-aspartic acid)	Na^+, K^+ and Ca^{++} channel	Depolarisation
		AMPA (α-amino-3-hydroxyl-5-methyl-4-isoxazole-propionate)	Na^+ and K^+ channel	Depolarisation
		Kainate	Na^+ and K^+ channel	Depolarisation
		mGluR$_1$ mGluR$_5$	G_q-protein coupled	IP_3 and DAG
		mGluR$_{2-4}$ mGluR$_{6-8}$	G_i-protein coupled	cAMP (downregulation)
Amino acids	GABA	GABA$_A$	Cl^- channel	Hyperpolarisation
		GABA$_B$	G_i-protein coupled; opens K^+ channel (hyperpolarisation)	cAMP (downregulation)
Amino acids	Glycine	GlyR	Cl^- channel	Hyperpolarisation

Continued

Table 7.1   Continued

Group	NT	Receptor	Type	Effect/2nd messenger
Peptides	β-endorphin (also enkephalins)	μ opioid receptor	G$_i$-protein coupled	cAMP (downregulation)
	enkephalins	δ receptor		
	dynorphin	κ receptor		
	Substance P	Neurokinin 1 receptor	G$_q$-protein coupled	IP3 and DAG

Abbreviations: cAMP = cyclic adenosine monophosphate; DAG = diacylglycerol; G$_{i,s}$ = inhibitory, stimulating G protein; G$_q$: 'q' is not an abbreviation but a label from the original ordering system of G proteins; IP3 = inositol triphosphate.

Figure 7.5

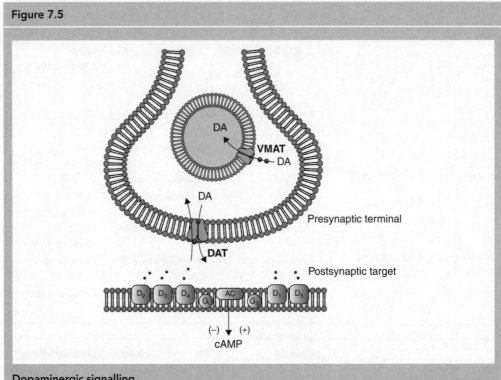

Dopaminergic signalling
The upper part shows the presynaptic dopaminergic terminal (see Figure 6.6). The lower part shows the postsynaptic membrane with dopamine receptors. Dopamine receptors can be coupled to inhibitory (D2–D4) or stimulating (D1, D5) G-proteins, resulting in decrease or increase of cAMP.

and the D$_2$-like family with an 'inhibitory' G-protein, this does not directly translate into excitation or inhibition of the postsynaptic neuron because second messenger cascades have complex effects. Activation of presynaptic dopamine autoreceptors inhibits the release of dopamine. Presynaptic blockade would therefore increase dopaminergic activity at the postsynaptic membrane, which explains why some dopamine receptor-blocking antipsychotics, given at low doses, can actually increase dopaminergic activity. *Autoreceptors* thus (down)regulate the release of their NT, whereas NT-binding to a *heteroreceptor* (for example a serotonin receptor on a dopaminergic cell or a dopamine receptor on a cholinergic cell) regulates the synaptic concentration of another NT. Presynaptic autoreceptors are located on the synaptic terminals and thus in the target area of a neuron's projection. Conversely, somatodendritic autoreceptors are located in the area of origin and regulate the firing of the neuron.

D_1 and D_2 receptors seem to be expressed ubiquitously in the brain. In the rat brain, the highest concentrations are found in the basal ganglia. There is some evidence for differential expression (more D_2 in substantia nigra and VTA, more D_1 in the amygdala), but the functional significance of this is not clear. The D_3, D_4 and D_5 receptors are less abundant and seem to be more selective for the limbic system. Autoreceptors are less frequently (if at all) expressed on VTA neurons that project to prefrontal areas (mesocortical pathway, see Chapter 1) than on those projecting to limbic areas (mesolimbic pathways) and other subcortical structures. This reduced potential for autoregulation may explain the higher firing rates of mesocortical neurons. Moreover, mesocortical neurons are less affected by antipsychotics. For example, chronic administration leads to a depolarisation block of the firing of other dopaminergic neurons, but has relatively little effect on the mesocortical system.

Dopamine is one of the main neuromodulators. Dopaminergic input from the substantia nigra to the striatum activates the direct basal ganglia pathway of extrapyramidal motor control, and dopaminergic deficits here lead to Parkinson's syndrome. Dopamine has also been implicated in reward learning, motivation and cognitive control. Whether the dopamine receptors contribute differentially to these functions is not well understood.

Many specific and less specific agonists and antagonists of dopamine receptors are in clinical use. Dopamine agonists such as bromocriptine or apomorphine are used for the treatment of Parkinson's disease (PD). They are ligands for all dopamine receptors, although some of them are more selective (e.g. bromocriptine for D_2 and D_3) than others. Dopamine antagonism is the main mechanism of action of antipsychotic drugs. Some of them are relatively selective for a specific receptor or family. For example, haloperidol and even more so sulpiride and amisulpride are selective for D_2 or D_2-like receptors. Another very specific D_2 and D_3 antagonist is raclopride, which is used for PET studies of dopamine receptor occupancy (see Box 7.1).

Box 7.1   Radioligand imaging

Most of the information about drug binding to receptors and transporters comes from in-vitro and animal studies. However, it is also important to test these models of drug action in the human brain directly. At present, the main techniques for such in-vivo neurochemistry are positron emission tomography (PET) and single-photon emission tomography (SPECT). Both are based on the detection of the products of radioactive decay from radioactively labelled tracers, so-called radioligand imaging. A radioactive isotope, for example ^{18}F (fluorine) for PET or ^{123}I (iodine) for SPECT, is added to a biologically active molecule in the radiochemistry lab. For example, ^{18}F can be added to deoxyglucose to yield Fluoro-deoxyglucose (FDG). FDG can be injected, crosses the blood–brain barrier and is taken up into cells through the same mechanism as glucose. However, unlike glucose, it is not metabolised further. FDG uptake thus provides a good measure of regional glucose utilisation in the brain (of course, it can be measured in other organs as well). ^{18}F is unstable, and one of its protons is converted into a neutron, yielding ^{18}O (oxygen, the element that precedes fluorine in the periodic table of elements). During this process, a neutrino and a positron are emitted. The positron will travel for a few millimetres and then react with an electron (annihilating each other) to yield two photons (gamma radiation), which move in opposite directions and can be detected by a special camera. The camera only counts photons that arrive at opposite ends at about the same time (coincidence detection). Because many such events will happen at about the same time and lead to random directions of gamma rays, the position of the emitter can be calculated as the crossing point of these lines (Figure 7.6) with a spatial resolution of a few millimetres.

Isotopes used for SPECT emit a single photon, which can be detected by a gamma camera. Here, the localisation of the emitter is determined through a device called a collimator, which is essentially an array of lead tubes interposed between the scanned object (e.g. the brain) and the crystal that detects the photons. The collimator blocks photons from reaching the detector crystal, unless they travel along certain directions. It thus allows for a linear reconstruction of the source of the emission. For three-dimensional images, the gamma camera has to be moved around the object, resulting in longer scan times than in PET. The spatial resolution is also lower, but SPECT is cheaper and more widely available. Its radionuclides have a longer half life than those commonly used in PET.

PET and SPECT enabled the first functional neuroimaging studies of changes in regional glucose uptake and blood flow during cognitive tasks and thus paved the way for cognitive neuroscience. This application has today been largely superseded by fMRI because of its higher spatial and temporal resolution and because it does not use ionising radiation. However, PET and SPECT are methods of choice for in-vivo neuropharmacology. The NT system that has been studied in most detail with radioligand imaging is the dopamine system, although there is also ample literature on the serotonin, acetylcholine, GABA, glutamate and opioid systems (Nikolaus et al., 2009a, 2009b). At the

Figure 7.6

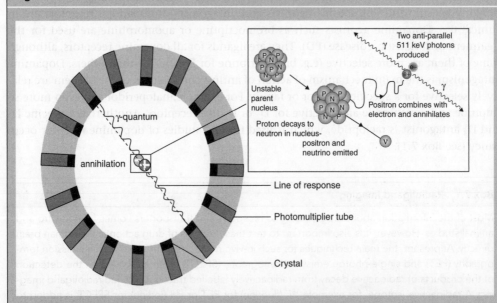

Principles of PET
The inset shows the radioactive decay of the unstable parent nucleus through conversion of a proton (P) to a neutron (N), emitting a neutrino (Greek letter nu, ν) and a positron. When the positron (e^+) encounters an electron (e^-), they annihilate, resulting in two photons (Greek letter gamma, γ), which can be picked up by the crystals in the detector ring (large picture).

Figure 7.7

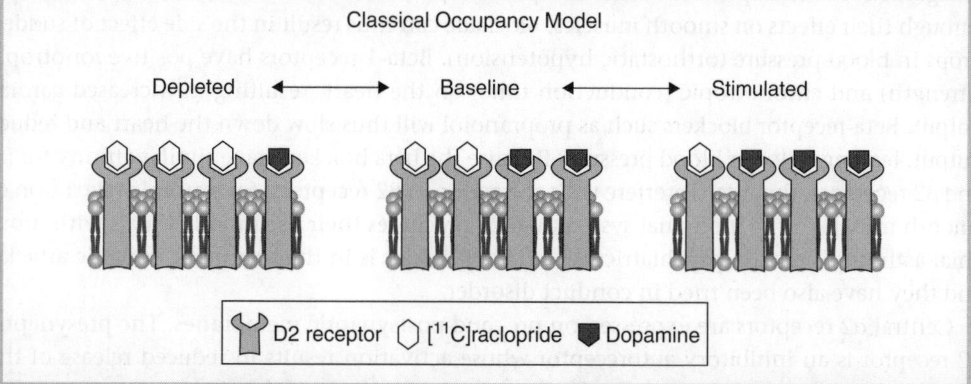

Classical Occupancy Model

Depleted ⟷ Baseline ⟷ Stimulated

D2 receptor [^{11}C]raclopride Dopamine

The classical occupancy model of PET radioligand studies

The occupancy model is the basis for the estimation of synaptic dopamine concentrations from the binding of radioligands to dopamine receptors. In the depleted state (lack of dopamine), more ligand (raclopride) can bind to D2 receptors, whereas less ligand will bind in the stimulated state, when more D2 receptors are occupied by dopamine. Emission of signal from the labelled raclopride thus allows inferences on local dopamine concentrations.

presynaptic level, dopamine synthesis can be assessed by measuring DOPA decarboxylase activity. Dopamine storage can be assessed through the uptake of ^{18}F-DOPA and through the binding of ^{18}F-dihydrotetrabenazine to VMAT-2, and reuptake through radioligands that bind to DAT. Synaptic levels of dopamine can be measured only indirectly through changes in receptor occupancy. Several D_2 receptor radioligands, including the antagonists[11] C-raclopride for PET and ^{123}I-IBZM (iodobenzamide) for SPECT are available. According to the occupancy model (Figure 7.7), higher ligand binding reflects lower synaptic dopamine levels and vice versa (Laruelle, 2000). However, baseline levels of ligand binding are difficult to interpret, particularly in clinical populations, because they depend on the density of postsynaptic receptors. Receptor density is a highly plastic process and can be modulated both in the short term by endocytosis and in the long term by gene expression regulation. Psychostimulant challenges may give a better picture of changes in dopamine levels. A single intravenous dose of amphetamine reliably decreases raclopride binding by 10–20%, probably through increasing synaptic dopamine levels. Similar effects were obtained after cocaine. Of particular interest, video game playing led to similar increases in synaptic dopamine, opening up interesting possibilities for measuring the reward system in humans. There is also some evidence that patients with schizophrenia have an exaggerated dopamine release in response to amphetamine.

7.3.2 Adrenergic receptors

The adrenergic receptors, which have norepinephrine (noradrenaline) and epinephrine (adrenaline) as endogenous ligands, are expressed in the central and autonomic nervous systems and peripheral organs such as heart and lungs. They are divided into an alpha and a beta family. The α1 receptor is coupled with a G_q protein and thus promotes IP_3 and DAG production. The α2 receptor is coupled with a G_i protein. Its activation thus leads to reductions in cAMP levels. The opposite effect is observed after activation of most beta receptors, which are coupled with G_s proteins. The multiple effects of activation or therapeutic blockade of adrenergic receptors in peripheral tissues go beyond the scope of this book, but a basic appreciation is important for an understanding of the side effects of psychotropic drugs that act on this system because many antipsychotics and antidepressants are alpha antagonists. For example, activation of alpha receptors leads to constriction of blood vessels through their effects on smooth muscles. Blockade can thus result in the side effect of sudden drops in blood pressure (orthostatic hypotension). Beta-1 receptors have positive ionotropic (strength) and chronotropic (conduction time) on the heart, resulting in increased cardiac output. Beta-receptor blockers such as propranolol will thus slow down the heart and reduce output, leading to lower blood pressure. Because the beta blockers have similar affinity for $\beta 1$ and $\beta 2$ receptors, they also interfere with the action of $\beta 2$ receptors, for example relaxation of smooth muscle in the bronchial system, which precludes their use in individuals with bronchial asthma. The main psychiatric use of beta blockers is in the treatment of panic attacks, and they have also been tried in conduct disorder.

Central $\alpha 2$ receptors are expressed on pre- and postsynaptic membranes. The presynaptic $\alpha 2$ receptor is an inhibitory autoreceptor whose activation results in reduced release of the NT into the synaptic cleft (negative feedback loop). Blockade of this mechanism, for example by the antidepressants mirtazapine or mianserin, thus results in more norepinephrine release. Conversely, agonism at the presynaptic $\alpha 2$ receptor, for example by clonidine or guanfacine, reduces central sympathetic tone. Clonidine and guanfacine are potential new treatments for ADHD and for Tourette's syndrome with ADHD symptoms.

7.3.3 Serotonin receptors

Of the six families of metabotropic serotonin receptors, two ($5\text{-}HT_1$ and $5\text{-}HT_5$) are coupled with G_i-proteins, one ($5\text{-}HT_2$) with G_q-proteins and three ($5\text{-}HT_4$, $5\text{-}HT_6$ and $5\text{-}HT_7$) with G_s-proteins. The $5\text{-}HT_1$ receptor has five subtypes in the brain (A, B, D, E and F). $5\text{-}HT_{1A}$ is the most widespread. It is expressed especially in the limbic system and raphe nuclei. Somatodendritic $5\text{-}HT_{1A}$ receptors, such as those expressed on raphe neurons, regulate a negative feedback loop. Thus, their activation, for example through the anxiolytic drug buspirone, leads to reduced firing of serotonergic neurons. Because $5\text{-}HT_{2A}$ heteroreceptors inhibit dopamine release by dopaminergic neurons, such activation of presynaptic $5\text{-}HT_{1A}$ receptors can result in disinhibition of dopamine release. Thus, $5\text{-}HT_{1A}$ agonists have positive and $5\text{-}HT_{2A}$ agonists have negative effects on synaptic dopamine levels. The $5\text{-}HT_{1B}$, $5\text{-}HT_{1D}$ and $5\text{-}HT_{1F}$ receptors are mainly known for their antagonism through sumatriptan, an anti-migraine drug. Very little is known about the function of the $5\text{-}HT_5$ receptor, which is chemically related to the $5\text{-}HT_{1D}$ receptor.

The $5\text{-}HT_2$ receptor is a key target for the new atypical antipsychotic drugs. For example, clozapine binds to the three $5\text{-}HT_2$ subtypes (A, B and C) with equal affinity. Its clinical effects on the serotonin system are supposed to be mediated through antagonism at the $5\text{-}HT_{2A}$ and possibly also the $5\text{-}HT_{2C}$ receptor. Although the atypical antipsychotics also block dopamine receptors, they are associated with lower occurrence of extrapyramidal side effects than typical neuroleptics such as haloperidol. One mechanism for this might be the disinhibition of dopamine release in the nigrostriatal pathway through $5\text{-}HT_{2A}$ receptor blockade (Stahl, 2008).

Ketanserin is a highly selective $5\text{-}HT_{2A}$ (and $5\text{-}HT_{2C}$) antagonist that is used in radioligand studies. The hallucinogenic psilocybin is a mixed $5\text{-}HT_{2A}/5\text{-}HT_{1A}$ agonist, and its psychotomimetic effect can be blocked by $5\text{-}HT_{2A}$ antagonists such as risperidone. Lysergic acid diethylamide (LSD) is a $5\text{-}HT_{2A}$ agonist as well, but also has high affinity for the other serotonin receptors except $5\text{-}HT_3$ and $5\text{-}HT_4$.

The GP$_s$-coupled serotonin receptors (types 4, 6 and 7) are targets for sumatriptan (ago-nist) and several antipsychotics (antagonists). A role in learning has been postulated, and both agonists (at the 5-HT$_4$ receptor) and antagonists (at the 5-HT$_6$ receptor) have been pro-posed as new agents for cognitive enhancement and dementia treatment, but hitherto this has not resulted in clinical use.

7.3.4   Muscarinic receptors

Muscarinic receptors (mAChR) are coupled to G$_q$- (M$_1$, M$_3$, M$_5$) or G$_i$-proteins (M$_2$, M$_4$). However, the postsynaptic effects can overlap because M$_2$ and M$_4$ receptors, in high concen-trations, can also stimulate protein kinase C (see Section 7.4.1). In addition, all mAChR can couple to G$_s$-proteins and thus stimulate cAMP production (Nathanson, 2008). Muscarinic receptors mediate parasympathetic effects in the postganglionic ANS (for example, M$_2$ recep-tors the slowing of the heart rate). They also regulate the activation of both sympathetic and parasympathetic neurons in the ganglia, jointly with the nAChR. These ANS effects are well-characterised and responsible for the anticholinergic side effects of many antipsychotics and antidepressants that are antagonists at the mAChR. Most anticholinergic drugs in clinical use, notably atropine, which is used in the emergency treatment of cardiac arrest, act indis-criminately on all mAChR subtypes.

The specific effects of mAChR subtypes in the brain are less well understood. Some hints may come from the distribution of mAChR expression in brain tissue. In the neocortex both M$_1$ and M$_2$ are expressed on postsynaptic membranes. However, in the hippocampus, the M$_1$ receptor is found mainly on the postsynaptic membrane, whereas the M$_2$ receptor is expressed on the presynaptic neurons of both cholinergic and non-cholinergic terminals. This suggests a dual role as autoreceptor that regulates the release of acetylcholine (ACh) and as heteroreceptor. For example, M$_2$ receptors can regulate the release of norepinephrine from noradrenergic neurons. Similarly, α2 adrenoreceptors on cholinergic neurons can regulate the release of ACh. M$_2$ is the main presynaptic autoreceptor in hippocampus and neocortex, and M$_4$ in the striatum (Nathanson, 2008). The M$_1$ receptor has been implicated in the cogni-tive functions that are impaired in Alzheimer's disease because of degeneration of cholinergic neurons in the basal forebrain.

7.3.5   Histamine receptors

The three types of histamine receptors that are expressed in the brain are coupled to G$_q$- (H$_1$), G$_s$ (H$_2$) and G$_i$ (H$_3$) proteins. The histamine system is unique in that histaminergic neu-rons are only found in a single nucleus in the brain, the tuberomammillary nucleus of the hypothalamus. However, histaminergic projections reach all parts of the brain. H$_1$ receptors are widely expressed in the human brain, with high concentrations in the arousal system, for example the thalamus, mesopontine tegmentum, the basal forebrain, locus coeruleus and raphe nuclei (Brown et al., 2001). In addition, H$_1$ receptors have been found ubiquitously in the limbic system and neocortex. Activation of H$_1$ receptors normally has excitatory effects on the postsynaptic neuron through modulation of voltage or ligand (NMDA)-gated chan-nels. H$_1$ activation can also lead to calcium influx and to the upregulation of the immediate early gene IEG c-fos (see Section 7.4). Antagonism at central H$_1$ receptors is the main mecha-nism for the drowsiness associated with the antihistamine drugs that are prescribed for their immunomodulatory role, for example to contain allergic reactions.

The H_2 receptor is co-localised with the H_1 receptor in some brain regions, for example the hippocampus. It is also expressed in high concentrations in the basal ganglia, locus coeruleus, raphe nuclei, VTA and substantia nigra. Thus, it is co-localised with the other amine NT receptors and may act synergistically with them (Brown et al., 2001). Activation of the H_2 receptor has an excitatory effect by blocking a calcium-dependent potassium channel that produces the slow after-hyperpolarisation responsible for the refractory periods after an AP. The H_3 receptor is ubiquitously expressed in neocortex, olfactory cortex, striatum and substantia nigra and mainly acts as a presynaptic auto- and heteroreceptor. Its activation reduces the release of histamine and several other NTs, probably through inhibition of VGCC.

Many antidepressants and antipsychotics exert sedative effects through histamine receptor antagonism. H_1 receptor blockade in the hypothalamus leads to increased feeding behaviour in experimental animals and may contribute to the weight gain observed after chronic administration of many of these drugs. Histaminergic activation of hypothalamic nuclei also leads to increased release of CRF, vasopressin and oxytocin and decreased release of GHRH and TRH. Although the complex interactions between antihistaminergic drugs and the endocrine system are not fully understood it is important to consider them as sources of potential clinical and side effects.

7.3.6   GABA_B receptor

The $GABA_B$ receptor is structurally similar to the mGluR group. It has two subtypes (B1 and B2) that can assemble to dimers in the membrane. The $GABA_B$ receptor is coupled to G_i-proteins and thus reduces cAMP levels. There are probably other postsynaptic effects as well, through which its activation stimulates the opening of potassium channels that bring the membrane potential closer to the equilibrium potential for potassium and thus to hyperpolarisation. Depending on the site on the cell, this can block VSSC and thus the propagation of APs or VSCC and NT release. Similar to the $GABA_A$ receptor, the net effect is one of neuronal inhibition.

The $GABA_B$ agonist baclofen is used as muscle relaxant to relieve spasticity (but can trigger epileptic seizures) and the agonist gamma-hydroxybutyric acid (GHB) is a general anaesthetic but also used as illegal drug. The $GABA_B$ receptor is currently also an interesting target for the development of new antipsychotic drugs.

7.3.7   mGluR

The metabotropic glutamate receptors can be divided into three groups based on sequence homologies and mode of action. Whereas the group I receptors ($mGlu_1$, $mGlu_5$) couple to G_q proteins, groups II ($mGlu_2$, $mGlu_3$) and III ($mGlu_4$, $mGlu_6$, $mGlu_7$ and $mGlu_8$) couple to G_i-proteins. Apart from $mGlu_6$, which is confined to the retina, all types are expressed ubiquitously on the brain's neurons, $mGlu_3$ and $mGlu_5$ also on glia. Group I receptors are generally postsynaptic and promote the activity of ionotropic glutamate receptors. Conversely, groups II and III are mainly found on the presynaptic membrane, where they act as autoreceptors and heteroreceptors (on GABAergic neurons) to regulate NT release. Although it has not been straightforward to develop specific agonists for mGluR subtypes because glutamate is a relatively simple molecule with limited degrees of freedom for variation and the NT binding site is relatively conserved across mGluR subtypes, several specific agonists and selective allosteric modulators are now available. Group II agonists in particular are being explored in preclinical studies for use in schizophrenia and anxiety disorders (Niswender et al., 2005).

7.3.8 Opioid receptors

Opioids and opiates bind to three classes of receptors, labelled with the Greek letters μ (mu), δ (delta) and κ (kappa). The corresponding genes are called OPRM1, OPRD1 and OPRK1. Each class has several subtypes that seem to result from post-translational modification because no gene variants have so far been detected. Opiates are alkaloids found in the opium plant, for example morphine, and opioids comprise a chemically heterogeneous group of endogenous (produced by the body) and exogenous substances with a similar pharmacological profile. The most important endogenous opioids are the beta-endorphins, met- and leu-enkephalin and dynorphin. Beta-endorphins have the highest affinity for the μ-, enkephalins for the δ- and dynorphins for the κ -receptor. However, the selectivity is not particularly high, and the opioids bind with affinities that are only one order of magnitude lower to their non-preferred receptors. Morphine binds to all opioid receptors, with the highest affinity for the μ-receptor. Morphine is the reference substance which serves as the yardstick to determine analgesic properties of opioids. For example the synthetic opioid fentanyl has about 100 times higher affinity for the μ-receptor than morphine and 100 times higher analgesic potency (meaning that a 100 times lower dose produces the same effect). In addition to the pharmacodynamic properties of the opioids (that is, affinity and selectivity for opioid receptors), their potency is also determined by pharmacokinetic effects (see Section 6.4).

The nociceptin receptor, encoded by the OPRL1 (opiate receptor-like 1) gene, is not an opioid receptor in the classical sense. Its endogenous ligand is the neuropeptide nociceptin, and several opioids are agonists. The nociceptin receptor is expressed ubiquitously in the brain and has been implicated in the regulation of pain and emotions, but a specific clinical use of its modulation has not yet been established. Another receptor that is sometimes grouped with the opioid receptors is the sigma receptor (types 1 and 2). This has historical reasons because before more detailed pharmacological characterisation and structural analysis, the sigma receptors were thought to be related to opioid receptors. The hallucinogenic dimethyltryptamine, which also activates monoamine receptors, is an endogenous ligand of the sigma-1 receptor. Various monoaminergic drugs, such as the SSRI fluvoxamine, also activate the sigma receptors, and both agonists and antagonists are being discussed as potential antipsychotics.

Opioid receptors are expressed in neocortex, limbic system, brain stem and spinal cord, with the following preferences: μ in the amygdala (except the central nucleus), thalamus and mesencephalon; δ in the olfactory tract and neocortex; κ in the basal forebrain, striatum and hypothalamus (Le Merrer et al., 2009). Based on the analgesic (pain-reducing) effects of opioids in humans and the reward properties tested in experimental animals, the opioid receptors have been implicated in the control of pain and reward learning. Opioids are clinically used for their analgesic properties, but intoxication can lead to life-threatening side effects such as respiratory depression. They are also important substances of abuse, and this aspect will be discussed further in Chapter 15.

7.3.9 Tachykinin and neurokinin receptors

Tachykinins are a large group of neuropeptides. Two preprotachykinin genes (A and B) encode longer peptide chains that are cleaved to yield the pharmacologically active forms. The A gene encodes the precursor of substance P and neurokinin A, and the B gene encodes the precursor of neurokinin B. These tachykinins preferentially activate the neurokinin (NK)

1 (substance P), 2 (neurokinin A) and 3 (neurokinin B) receptors. All NK receptors are coupled with a G_q-protein. Substance P has long been implicated in central pain processing. Because the NK_1 receptors are amply expressed in the extended amygdala, including the nucleus accumbens, and because NK_1 receptor knock-out mice are insensitive to the rewarding properties of opioids, it has been postulated that substance P is involved in the regulation of motivation and reward learning. The NK_1 receptor also appears to mediate stress responses (Commons, 2010). Because of these links with both the positive and the negative reinforcing pathways to addiction (see Chapter 15), NK_1 antagonists are being explored for a role in the treatment of various addictions (Heilig et al., 2010). NK_1 antagonists also have anxiolytic properties, and this is another clinical use that is currently explored, whereas NK_2 antagonists are under investigation as potential antidepressant agents.

7.4   SIGNALLING CASCADES IN THE POSTSYNAPTIC CELL

Compared to the electrical signalling through ion channels, which is fast (milliseconds to seconds) and binary (action potential 'on' or 'off'), the signalling through postsynaptic chemical modifications and modulation of gene expression is slow (minutes to days or even years) and continuous. It is crucial for plasticity and learning and plays a major role in the effects of psychotropic drugs and the development of mental disorders. For example, current neurobiological models of addiction explicitly include postsynaptic signalling cascades (Chapter 15).

7.4.1   Second and third messengers

The first step of signalling beyond that of the receptor is that of the second messenger (implying that the NT is the 'first messenger'). The main second messengers that are activated or inhibited by G-proteins are cAMP and IP_3. Ionotropic receptors can also act through second messengers, in addition to the direct alteration of membrane potentials. In this case, calcium is the second messenger. A key function of the second messengers is to activate enzymes that phosphorylate (kinases) or dephosphorylate (phosphatases) other proteins (Figure 7.8). Phosphorylation often activates a protein, which has given rise to the term 'kinase' (from Greek 'to move'), but can also deactivate it. These kinases and phosphatases are sometimes called 'third messengers'. Some kinases only phosphorylate specific amino acids in the peptide chains of proteins, for example the hydroxyl group of serine or threonine. Tyrosine-specific kinases are important parts of the signalling pathways of growth factors.

The central third messenger of the cAMP pathway and thus of metabotropic receptors coupled to G_s- or G_i-proteins is protein kinase A (PKA), a serine-threonine kinase. Its functions depend on the specialisation of the cell and the particular proteins that the kinase can activate. In muscle and liver cells, for example, modulation of enzymes regulating sugar metabolism leads to increased production of glucose. In the brain, its functions include spatial memory and fear conditioning. Both the direct modification of ionotropic glutamate receptors and the regulation of gene expression via cAMP response element-binding protein (CREB) have been implicated as underlying mechanisms (Abel and Nguyen, 2008). Kinases are themselves regulated in several ways, including phosphorylation by themselves (autophosphorylation) and other enzymes (which are then called 'kinase kinases'). PKA

Figure 7.8

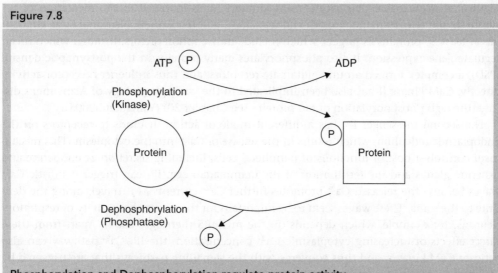

Phosphorylation and Dephosphorylation regulate protein activity
Many proteins are activated by phosphorylation by a kinase and deactivated by dephosphorylation by a phosphatase. The phosphorylation receives the required energy and the phosphate group from ATP, which is converted to ADP in the process.

also activates phosphodiesterase, the enzyme that hydrolyses cAMP and thus inhibits its own activation through a negative feedback loop.

One of the substrates that are activated by PKA is the dopamine- and cAMP-regulated phosphoprotein of 32 kDA (DARPP-32), which is highly concentrated in neurons that receive dopaminergic input. Activated DARPP-32 is a protein phosphatase inhibitor, but, depending on its phosphorylation site, can also block PKA in a negative feedback loop. The protein phosphatase 1, which is inhibited by DARPP-32, activates the Na/K-ATPase, the key enzyme for the restitution of the membrane potential after neuronal firing (see Chapter 2). The DARPP-32 pathway is thus considered one of the main mechanisms by which dopamine modulates the activity of its target neurons. DARPP-32 levels may be reduced in the frontal cortex of schizophrenia patients. Drugs that block D_2 or D_4 receptors, such as the antipsychotics haloperidol or clozapine, should lead to increased phosphorylation of DARPP-32 by disinhibition of cAMP production, and this is indeed what has been found in experimental animals. This pathway is thus of considerable interest for the development of new antipsychotic drugs (Molteni et al., 2009).

The protein kinases C (PKC) are a group of serine/threonine kinase isoforms or isozymes (structurally different forms of an enzyme that have the same catalytic function), most of which are activated by DAG alone or in conjunction with Ca^{2+}. It is the key third messenger for G_q-protein coupled receptors. Like PKA, the PKC pathway influences neural plasticity by changing gene expression. For example, the regulation of dendritic morphology, which is crucial for the formation of neural networks, is regulated by PKC.

Ca^{2+}/calmodulin-dependent (CaM) kinases are serine/threonine kinases that are activated by the presence of both Ca^{2+} and the calcium-binding protein calmodulin. They can thus be considered third messengers of the Ca^{2+} pathway. The CaM kinase most prominently implicated in neuronal plasticity is CaM kinase II. It is involved in the regulation of NT synthesis and release, neural growth and regulation of ion channels. Neuronal CaM kinase II has at least 50 proteins as targets, which include transcription factors, through which it can regulate gene expression. It also phosphorylates many proteins in the postsynaptic density (PSD), a complex formed around glutamate receptors, and thus influences receptor activity directly. CaM kinase II has also been implicated in the pathophysiology of Alzheimer's disease (through phosphorylation of tau protein, see Chapter 20) (Yamauchi, 2005).

The second messenger IP_3 has a different mode of action. It binds to receptors on the endoplasmic reticulum, which results in the release of Ca^{2+} into the cytoplasm. This mechanism controls a host of functions of peripheral cells, including secretion of endocrine and exocrine glands and the fertilisation of the mammalian egg. IP_3 can trigger dendritic Ca^{2+} waves because the released Ca^{2+} promotes further Ca^{2+} currents as it travels along the dendrite to the soma. These waves seem to be important for the pacemaker activity of respiratory neurons, for example, which depends on the mGluR5 (Berridge, 2009). Apart from these direct effects of increasing cytoplasmic Ca^{2+} concentration, the IP_3/Ca^{2+} pathway can also activate CaM kinases, and thus converge with the signalling pathways that are triggered by influx of Ca^{2+} from the extracellular milieu.

7.4.2 Modification of gene expression

We saw in Chapter 4 how genes (DNA) are transcribed into mRNA and then translated into proteins and how variants in coding parts of DNA can influence protein structure and function and thus lead to altered (for example clinical) phenotypes. This view suggests a strong genetic determinism, where the genetic code determines protein function, which in turn determines the phenotype. However, the genetic code can also be likened to an old book in a library. If its title is illegible or the book is not referenced in the library catalogue, readers may not find it and its beauty never appreciated. In order to be transcribed and translated, the DNA has binding sites for regulatory proteins. These binding sites are called 'response elements' or 'cis-regulatory elements' (from Latin cis = 'on the same side as') because they are located close to the gene whose transcription they regulate, normally within a few hundred base pairs. The regulatory proteins that bind to DNA and enhance or reduce the transcription of a particular sequence by activating or blocking RNA polymerase are called transcription factors. Many transcription factors need to be phosphorylated before they can bind to their response elements.

For example, the transcription factor CREB needs to be activated by PKA. It can thus be considered to be a fourth messenger of the signalling cascade that is initiated by G_i/G_s-protein-coupled receptors, for example the dopamine receptors. The DNA binding sites for CREB are called cAMP response elements (CRE) because they are a target for the cAMP pathway. Because CREs are found in many genes that are expressed in the nervous system, including those for neuropeptides and enzymes involved in the synthesis of NTs, CREB can have a multitude of effects on gene expression and neural plasticity. For example, it has been implicated in long-term potentiation (LTP), a process at the heart of cellular models of memory formation, and in the development of addiction. CREB also regulates the transcription of its own gene and those of other transcription factors. The phosphorylation of the amino acid serine at position 133 of CREB can also be effected by CaM kinase IV and a growth-factor dependent kinase. Thus, several signalling pathways can converge onto gene expression regulation by CREB.

7.4.3 Early and late genes

Several genes that are regulated by CREB belong to the family of 'immediate early genes' (IEGs). These genes were originally identified because their transcription could be induced in experimental settings where protein synthesis was inhibited (Miyashita et al., 2008). The conclusion was that the IEGs do not require previous activation of other genes and are thus in the first line of response of a cell to changes in the environment (e.g. those communicated by metabotropic receptors or calcium influx). In fact, IEG expression is normally low at baseline and very much depends on synaptic input. One of the IEGs activated by CREB codes for the protein c-fos. There is ample evidence that c-fos is a key mediator of the effects of CREB on neural plasticity (Loebrich and Nedivi, 2009). C-fos is a member of the activator protein-1 (AP-1) family of transcription factors. With c-jun, the product of another IEG, it forms a transcription factor that can then modulate the expression of other genes, called 'delayed effector genes', leading to more lasting changes in the shape and molecular mark-up of the postsynaptic neuron (Figure 7.9).

Not all products of IEGs are transcription factors. The gene products of the so-called effector IEGs can directly influence important cellular functions, such as growth (e.g. brain-derived neurotrophic factor, BDNF, see Section 7.4.4) and synaptic structure (Miyashita et al., 2008).

Figure 7.9

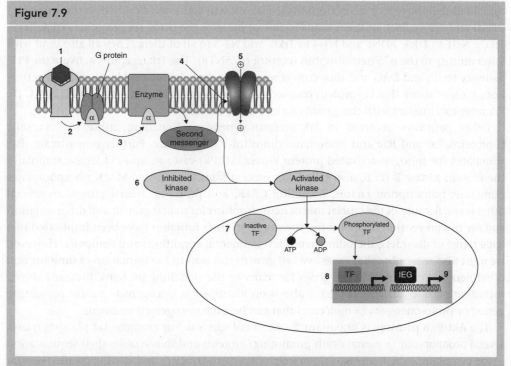

Second messenger cascades influence the expression of early and late genes
This figure follows on from Figure 7.4, no. 6. One of the triggered reactions in the postsynaptic cell is activation of a kinase. The kinase then activates a transcription factor, TF (7, see Figure 7.6). The activated (phosphorylated) TF, for example CREB, bind to appropriate stretches of DNA and promotes their transcription (8). Such binding sites for TFs are often coupled to immediate early genes (IEG), for example cFos. The protein product of the IEG can again act as TF to regulate the expression of other genes (9).

For example, the concentration of NT receptors in the neuronal membrane is not static, but activity-dependent, and its regulation is a key element of synaptic plasticity. Examples of IEG products that regulate receptor trafficking include the activity-regulated cytoskeleton-associated protein (Arc), which promotes the endocytosis (thus, removal from the membrane) of AMPA-type glutamate receptors and Homer-1a, which upregulates metabotropic glutamate receptors in the membrane (Loebrich and Nedivi, 2009). Because up- and downregulation of receptor expression in the membrane is a likely central mechanism for the long-term effects of psychotropic drugs, the IEGs and their encoded proteins are currently in the focus of research into drug development.

7.4.4   Neurotrophin signalling cascades

Neurotrophins are a group of structurally related growth factor proteins that stimulate growth, differentiation and/or survival of neurons. They are important in counteracting programmed cell death or apoptosis. They have a special class of membrane receptors, which are tyrosine kinases, meaning that they exert their further effects by phosphorylating the amino acid tyrosine in downstream proteins. There are many classes of tyrosine kinase growth factor receptors. Those for neurotrophins are called Trk (tropomyosin-related or -receptor kinase) receptors because they were initially identified with the help of the muscle protein tropomyosin. Mammals have four neurotrophins (Nerve growth factor [NGF], BDNF, Neurotrophin-3 [NT-3] and NT-4). Each of them binds to one or more of the three Trk receptors (TrkA, TrkB, TrkC): NGF to TrkA, BDNF and NT-4 to TrkB, and NT-3 to all of them. They all also bind with lower affinity to the p75 neurotrophin receptor (p75NTR). The Trk receptors activate the PLC pathway to IP_3 and DAG and thus converge with the cascade initiated by G_q-protein activation. We saw above that G_q-protein coupled receptors activate the beta form of PLC (PLC-β). Trk receptors interact with the gamma form (PLC-γ) instead.

Other pathways involved in Trk receptor-dependent signalling utilise the cytosolic G-proteins Ras and Rac and phosphatidylinositol-3 (PI3)-kinase. Further downstream, Ras stimulates the mitogen-activated protein kinase (MAPK) cascade, and PI3-kinase stimulates the Protein Kinase B (PKB, also called Akt protein family) pathway. MAPK phosphorylates numerous transcription factors, including CREB, and promotes neural growth in several other ways. Because of the crucial role of neurotrophins for neural growth and differentiation and for the prevention of apoptosis, alterations in their function have been implicated in a wide range of disorders, including neurodevelopmental conditions and dementia. However, we must also remember that excessive cell growth can lead to the formation of tumours and other neoplastic tissue, and the genes for many of the signalling proteins discussed above, including c-fos, c-Jun and Ras, have also been identified as oncogens (= cancer promoting genes) or proto-oncogens (= molecules that can become oncogens if mutated).

The Akt/PKB pathway is important for neuronal survival. For example Akt phosphorylates several proapoptotic (= neural death promoting) proteins and thus enables their sequestration in the cytoplasm, which prevents them from entering the nucleus and altering gene expression (Reichardt, 2006). The PI3-kinase pathway is also crucial for the ability of neurotrophins to determine the integration of signalling molecules into the cell membrane and thus help growing axons find their path to their target neuron. Akt/PKB is linked to the Glycogen synthase kinase (GSK)-3 pathway, which also regulates transcription, cell proliferation and death. Akt and GSK-3 have been implicated in the pathophysiology of schizophrenia because of reduced expression in post-mortem brains. Several antipsychotic drugs have activated the Akt pathway in experimental animals, but the mechanism behind this is unknown (Molteni et al., 2009).

Phosphorylation by GSK-3 inhibits glycogen synthase, and thus reduces storage of glucose into glycogen macromolecules. This process is disinhibited by insulin, which signals through another receptor tyrosine kinase that also uses Akt as intermediate messenger, inhibiting GSK-3. Insulin thus promotes glycogen synthesis from glucose. Lack of insulin sensitivity is at the heart of type II diabetes, which is associated with schizophrenia. It has therefore been proposed that alterations of the GSK-3 pathway are a common factor underlying diabetes and schizophrenia (Lovestone et al., 2007). This is one of many intriguing potential links between growth factor signalling cascades and neuropsychiatric diseases.

Learning points

We have learned how NTs and neurotrophins act on their target neurons. NTs act through ionotropic or metabotropic receptors. The nicotinic AchR, the 5-HT_3 and the glutamatergic NMDA, AMPA and kainate receptors are excitatory, whereas the $GABA_A$ and glycine receptors are inhibitory ionotropic receptors. All other identified NT receptors are metabotropic. Ionotropic receptors are ion channels and their opening or closing can directly influence membrane potentials and initiate action potentials. These are then propagated through the activity of VGSC. The conversion of this electrical signal into the chemical signal of NT release is triggered through Ca^{2+} influx through VGCC. The metabotropic NT receptors are coupled to G-proteins and activate or inhibit second messenger cascades. CAMP, IP3, DAG and Ca^{2+} are central second messengers. They activate protein kinases (third messengers), which can in turn activate or inhibit several proteins, including TFs (fourth messengers). TFs alter the expression of genes and thus crucially influence the protein composition of a cell. Some of the regulated genes are IEGs, which are particularly important for experience-dependent plasticity (e.g. learning). IEG can in turn encode TFs such as c-fos and c-Jun that activate delayed effector genes, leading to lasting cellular changes. Although these signalling cascades can regulate aspects of neuronal growth, the main group of molecules responsible for the regulation of neuronal growth, differentiation, migration and survival are the neurotrophins. These proteins act through receptor tyrosine kinases and stimulate several postsynaptic signalling cascades, some of which converge with those activated by metabotropic NT receptors. Because many of the therapeutic effects of psychoactive drugs take days or weeks to develop, changes in gene expression, rather than immediate effects on synaptic NT concentration, have been assumed to underlie their function.

Revision and discussion questions

- Describe the main second messenger systems.
- Explain the difference between metabotropic and ionotropic receptors.
- Discuss the relevance of gene expression regulation for psychiatric treatment.

FURTHER READING

Iversen, L. L. (2009). *Introduction to Neuropsychopharmacology* (New York: Oxford University Press).

Stahl, S. M. (2008). *Stahl's Essential Psychopharmacology: Neuroscientific Basis and Practical Applications* (Cambridge: Cambridge University Press).

Vyas, N. S., Patel, N. H., Nijran, K. S., Al-Nahhas, A. and Puri, B. K. (2011). The use of PET imaging in studying cognition, genetics and pharmacotherapeutic interventions in schizophrenia. *Expert Review of Neurotherapeutics*, 11, 37–51.

8 PHYSICAL THERAPIES

PREVIEW

The physical therapies described in this chapter comprise a varied group of non-pharmacological interventions that are nevertheless aimed at directly modulating the biological processes underlying a mental disorder. They range from the very 'low-tech' (sleep deprivation) to highly invasive procedures (deep brain stimulation). Their main use is in the treatment of depression, alone or in addition to pharmaco- and/or psychotherapy.

8.1 SLEEP DEPRIVATION AND LIGHT THERAPY AIM TO REBALANCE CIRCADIAN RHYTHMS IN DEPRESSION

Disturbance of circadian rhythm features prominently in pathophysiological models of depression. The severity of symptoms can fluctuate, normally decreasing over the day, and early morning awakening is common. One model that is supported by the earlier occurrence of REM sleep and reduction of slow wave sleep (these terms are explained in Chapter 19 on sleep and its disorders) in depression, posits a phase shift in the circadian oscillator that is out of phase with normal social rhythms. Light therapy, sleep deprivation and treatment with melatonergic agonists all aim to reset the circadian rhythm.

Light therapy uses a strong light source (up to 10,000 lx) with ultraviolet light filtered out for skin safety. The patient sits at a defined distance from 30 minutes to 4 hours per day, normally in the morning, and can read or engage in other activities, but has to look into the light briefly about once per minute because the effect is supposed to be mediated through retinal photoreceptor stimulation. Clinical benefits can already occur after the first few days of treatment and are particularly pronounced in Seasonal Affective Disorder (SAD) ('winter depression'). Light therapy can also alleviate symptoms of other forms of depression, normally in conjunction with other forms of treatment. Side effects can include eyestrain, headaches and agitation, and even induction (or unmasking) of hypomania has been reported. However, side effects are generally mild.

Sleep deprivation for the whole night or for the second half of the night over one or two consecutive nights has rapid antidepressant effects in about 60% of patients, and thus a response rate that is about twice as high (and much faster) than that achieved by antidepressant drugs. Unfortunately, the antidepressant effect normally does not last beyond the next full sleep. Sleep deprivation therapy is therefore generally combined with other treatments, for example an SSRI (Germain and Kupfer, 2008). It has been speculated that sleep deprivation activates the locus coeruleus at a time when it would normally be less active and can promote the expression of plasticity genes (Salvadore et al., 2010). There is also some indication that sleep deprivation may act through serotonergic and/or dopaminergic mechanisms and increase thyroid hormone release, in addition to its putative effects on the hypothalamic circadian pacemaker (Benedetti and Smeraldi, 2009).

8.2 ELECTROCONVULSIVE THERAPY INDUCES BRIEF GENERALISED SEIZURES

Electroconvulsive therapy (ECT) was originally developed for the treatment of schizophrenia based on the assumption that epilepsy was protective against schizophrenia (which, as we now know, is too simplistic: see Chapter 21). It is now still used in the treatment of a rare, severe form of schizophrenia (febrile catatonia), but mainly for treatment-refractory depression, that is, for patients who show no or only incomplete responses to several lines of pharmacological treatment. A brief current is induced in the brain that leads to a generalised seizure, lasting for up to one minute. Because of the unpleasantness and risk (e.g. of bone fractures) of the tonic-clonic movements caused by the seizure activity, modern ECT is conducted under muscle relaxation and ventilation. The current is normally confined to one hemisphere (commonly the non-language dominant) because bilateral stimulation confers little clinical advantage at the cost of increased risk of side effects. The main side effects are transient memory impairment and complications from the anaesthesia.

The acute course of ECT, normally approximately 12 sessions split over 4 weeks, has high clinical efficacy, with response rates of up to 70% (Merkl et al., 2009). However, relapse rates are considerable after abrupt discontinuation, and gradual tapering or maintenance treatment have therefore been suggested in order to increase the proportion of patients who stay in remission. One protocol for maintenance treatment consists in the administration of 10 more sessions over 5 months, tapering off the frequency from weekly to monthly. This regime yielded similar remission rates to a pharmacotherapy with nortriptyline and lithium (Kellner et al., 2006). Both compensatory increases in GABA and release of dopamine have been implicated as being responsible for the mood-enhancing effects of ECT, but there is no consistent evidence yet for neurochemical effects of ECT in humans. Animal models have demonstrated increases in mRNA for neuropeptides and even neuroplastic effects, for example hippocampal neurogenesis, of electrical stimulation protocols modelled on ECT.

TMS (see Chapter 2) is another less invasive, but also less effective, tool for electromagnetic stimulation of the brain. At high intensities it can also be used to induce seizures and would then have to be classed as equally invasive to ECT and need similar anaesthetic cover. This magnetic seizure therapy is still in the experimental stage. The aim is to obtain similar efficacy to ECT without the cognitive side effects.

8.3 VAGUS NERVE STIMULATION

Vagus nerve stimulation (VNS) is another, more invasive, approach to treatment refractory depression. VNS was introduced into the field of depression because mood improvements had been observed after its use in epileptic patients. The VNS device is inserted in a surgical procedure. The electrode is wrapped around the vagus nerve in the neck so as to send ascending impulses and is connected to a generator that is implanted in the chest wall, like a cardiac pacemaker. Typical stimulation parameters are trains of 20–30 Hz for 30 s, alternating with several minutes of pause. However, the patient can switch the device on or off through a magnet. The biological rationale and mechanisms of VNS are unclear. One possible mechanism is the stimulation of noradrenergic neurons in the locus coeruleus by the nucleus tractus solitarii, which is activated by vagus afferents (George and Aston-Jones, 2010). VNS has had therapeutic benefits in small uncontrolled studies, but not in the only double-blind trial (Daban et al., 2008). Side effects can arise from the surgical procedure and from the vagal stimulation. Effects on the laryngeal nerves are common (e.g. hoarseness) and respiratory problems have been reported as well, but cardiac or other autonomic side effects are relatively rare.

8.4   SURGERY AND DEEP BRAIN STIMULATION DIRECTLY INTERFERE WITH PUTATIVE PATHOPHYSIOLOGICAL NETWORKS

If a brain area or network is deemed to be hyper- or hypoactive in a mental disorder, the most direct remedy might be through surgery or direct electrical stimulation. The surgical approach may not cure the underlying problem but at least might contain the dysfunctional activation and thus reduce symptoms. Examples of this type of approach are the cases of callosotomy for severe intractable epilepsy, where the corpus callosum was cut to contain the spread of epileptic activity, which has given rise to the widely studied 'split-brain' phenomenon. However, in psychiatry the pathways by which dysfunctional activation spreads are rarely well established, and the success of surgical interventions has therefore been limited. Its main remaining use is for severe cases of obsessive compulsive disorder (OCD). Based on pathophysiological models of OCD (see Chapter 13), target tracts have been the anterior internal capsule, which connects the prefrontal cortex with the dorsomedial thalamus, the anterior cingulum and the substantia innominata, which contains fibres to the orbitofrontal cortex (OFC). A variety of surgical techniques have been used, including cuts, lesioning by thermal coagulation or local placement of radioactive probes. The approach is normally stereotactic, meaning that the instruments are brought to the target site under guidance by imaging, without direct inspection of the site by the surgeon, which makes the procedure less invasive. Recently, non-invasive radiosurgery with gamma rays ('gamma knife') has also been used for applications in OCD. All these approaches have been associated with good clinical improvement rates, with the largest evidence base for anterior cingulotomy. Although operative and postoperative complications can occur, the safety record of anterior cingulotomy has generally been good, apart from the occurrence of seizures in 1–9% of cases. It is still regularly used for treatment refractory OCD (Greenberg et al., 2010). However, remission may take 3–6 months and about 50% of patients will not respond.

Deep brain stimulation (DBS) follows a similar rationale: inhibitory protocols suppress hyperactive nodes, whereas stimulating protocols can activate underactive nodes. Current DBS protocols in psychiatry are modelled on the successful application of DBS in Parkinson's disease. Here, inhibitory high frequency (100 Hz) stimulation of the nucleus subthalamicus can have dramatic effects on motor symptoms. A main conceptual advantage over surgery is that the stimulation parameters can be adjusted to the clinical needs of the individual patient, and even dynamically adapted to clinical states. DBS of the ventral internal capsule/ventral striatum region has improved OCD symptoms in some patients, but this evidence has not yet been supported by a rigorous clinical trial (Greenberg et al., 2010). Based on functional imaging studies implicating dysregulation of the subgenual cingulate cortex in depression, DBS is also being piloted for use in depression. Case series of high frequency DBS of the subgenual cingulate showed symptom improvement in some patients (Mayberg et al., 2005), but this technique also awaits validation in larger controlled trials.

8.5 NEUROFEEDBACK IS A NON-INVASIVE WAY OF MODULATING BRAIN ACTIVITY

It has been known at least since Pavlov's famous classical conditioning experiments (Chapter 1) that physiological responses can be learnt. Operant conditioning even gives people (or animals) a way of regulating their own physiology. For example, biofeedback procedures, where participants receive feedback about physiological parameters such as heart rate or blood pressure, can be used to train people to attain some amount of control over these physiological responses. This may seem paradoxical at first after what we have learnt about the ANS, but perhaps less so when we consider the intimate links between the parts of the CNS involved in conscious, higher order cognitive operations, those involved in instrumental learning, and those providing central control to the ANS.

Biofeedback training need not be confined to peripheral physiological parameters. People can learn to regulate brain function directly as well. The most widespread tool for such training has been the EEG. It normally takes several – up to 30 – sessions of 30–60 minute EEG-neurofeedback until participants attain reliable control over a particular parameter of the EEG, for example the amplitude of the slow wave potentials, the sensorimotor rhythm or the ratio between alpha and theta activity, but they can then use this skill to control brain–computer interfaces (see Chapter 21). In psychiatric conditions where a particular EEG feature has been proposed as a potential biomarker, regulation of this feature may also confer clinical benefits. EEG-based neurofeedback has been used widely in treatment studies for ADHD, its main clinical application today, and substance abuse, and it has had some application in anxiety disorders and depression.

Another more recent neurofeedback approach is based on functional magnetic resonance imaging (fMRI, Chapter 2). This technique allows for a more detailed localisation of areas that are implicated in the generation of psychopathological symptoms. It has, for example, helped identify the auditory cortex activity accompanying auditory hallucinations in schizophrenia. It might also be used to identify areas that support coping, resilience and treatment effects (see Chapter 9). An fMRI-based intervention thus allows for direct targeting of specific brain areas that are supposed to be involved in the pathophysiology of the disease, compared to the more global measures that are the target of neurofeedback with EEG. For example, it can be used to train self-regulation of the brain's emotion networks (Johnston et al., 2011). This is particularly useful for diseases where components of the dysfunctional network have been well documented with functional imaging and other neurobiological techniques, such as the subgenual cingulate gyrus for depression. Furthermore, neurofeedback with fMRI might allow targeting patterns of interactions or functional connectivity between brain areas, which might be even more relevant in the pathophysiology of psychiatric disorders than the altered activity in individual brain regions. Finally, control of brain regions through fMRI feedback may be attained more quickly than the control of EEG features. Functional roles have been established for many brain regions, and patients may develop corresponding cognitive strategies to avoid the lengthy trial-and-error procedure of operant conditioning. First applications of fMRI-neurofeedback in the non-psychiatric clinical field (chronic pain) are encouraging (DeCharms, 2008), and clinical studies in depression and substance use disorders are currently underway (Figure 8.1). If successful, neurofeedback will be an attractive alternative to the more invasive brain stimulation techniques because of its expected lower risk, higher flexibility (the target area can be shifted more easily than an implanted electrode) and active engagement of patients. The latter provides a direct link with the neurobiological mechanism of psychotherapy, which will be the topic of the next chapter.

Figure 8.1

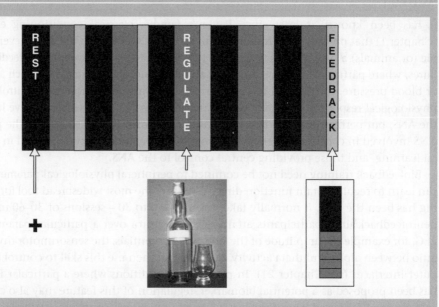

A potential clinical application of fMRI

Example of a protocol for a clinical application of fMRI-based neurofeedback for the control of alcohol craving. After the identification of a brain area or network that is active during craving with a symptom induction procedure, it would be the participants' task to downregulate activity in this area/network during the presentation of drug cues. They could gauge their success immediately from colour changes on a feedback display and thus learn self-control of the pathophysiological network. The hope is that this learnt control over brain activation aids motivated patients in the control of urges to consume the drug. Furthermore, the pairing of drug cues with downregulation of motivational brain networks should reverse some of the neurophysiological reinforcing processes implicated in the maintenance of addictive behaviour (Chapter 15).

Learning points

Physical therapies aim to normalise dysregulation of neural pathways and biological circuits in disorders such as depression or OCD. The 'low-tech' approaches of light therapy and sleep deprivation are effective, well-tolerated and easy to implement in clinical practice, but have only short-lived effects. ECT is very effective even in otherwise treatment refractory cases. It is mainly applied in short courses, and again clinical benefits have tended to taper off quickly, but new approaches with maintenance treatment seem promising. TMS, VNS, DBS and surgical lesions (in ascending order of invasiveness) all have documented clinical effects, although these have generally not been supported by randomised controlled studies (which are not really possible in the case of surgery). Treatment decisions will therefore always have to be based on a careful consideration of risks and potential benefits. New approaches that incorporate the active engagement of the patient into a neurophysiological or neuroimaging protocol with neurofeedback are conceptually appealing but still need to stand the test of time and clinical practice.

Revision and discussion questions

- Explain the rationale behind light therapy and sleep deprivation.
- What are the target areas for surgical intervention and deep brain stimulation in OCD and depression?
- What can neurofeedback add to psychotherapy?

FURTHER READING

George, M. and Aston-Jones, G. (2010). Noninvasive techniques for probing neurocircuitry and treating illness: Vagus nerve stimulation (VNS), transcranial magnetic stimulation (TMS) and transcranial direct current stimulation (tDCS). *Neuropsychopharmacology*, 35, 301–16.

Greenberg, B., Rauch, S. and Haber, S. (2010). Invasive circuitry-based neurotherapeutics: Stereotactic ablation and deep brain stimulation for OCD. *Neuropsychopharmacology*, 35, 317–36.

9 BIOLOGICAL EFFECTS OF PSYCHOTHERAPY

PREVIEW

This chapter describes the methods used to study the brain effects of psychological interventions. Most work in this area is currently conducted with functional neuroimaging techniques, but treatment-induced changes could be expected and potentially investigated at any level from epigenetics and cell biology to neural networks. Examples discussed include changes in brain activation after cognitive behavioural therapy for specific phobias and depression and comparisons between psycho- and pharmacotherapy. This chapter also briefly reviews the biology of the placebo effect and the rationale for augmenting psychotherapy with pharmacological agents.

9.1 PSYCHOTHERAPY CHANGES THE BRAIN

It may seem odd at first to have a section on psychotherapy in a book on the biological mechanisms of psychological disorders. However, the changes in affect, cognitive style, behaviour and generally in clinical state and everyday functioning brought about by psychological interventions need to be implemented through changes in the brain. Although it may be difficult to detect them with current scientific methods because of interindividual differences and the difficulty of controlling confounding variables, they should in principle be accessible to neuroscience. A deeper understanding of the way in which psychotherapies change the brain is of general importance for the scientific foundation of these techniques. There are practical implications as well. Although the best outcome measures of a psychiatric or psychological intervention will always be at the level of the clinical phenotype – for example, improvement of mood in a case of depression – these are sometimes difficult to define or obtain. This difficulty and the unreliability of self-report measures have triggered a quest for biological markers of treatment responses. Such markers could be obtained by psychophysiology, biochemistry, neurophysiology, radioligand receptor mapping or fMRI. Another clinical benefit of a deeper understanding of the brain mechanisms of psychotherapy might arise from the combination with drugs that target complimentary circuits. The comparison of the brain changes induced by successful psychological or pharmacological treatment in comparable patient groups is therefore of particular interest.

9.2 BEHAVIOURAL THERAPY AND MEDICATION FOR ANXIETY DISORDERS HAVE SIMILAR NEURAL EFFECTS

A classical example of behavioural therapy is the treatment of spider phobia. It is based on the assumption that the spider, which is not objectively dangerous for inhabitants of most industrialised countries, acts as a conditioned stimulus. Graded exposure, which is a key technique in the treatment of specific phobias, will then gradually desensitise the patient to the stimulus, and the unconditioned response will finally be extinguished. Animal learning studies allow researchers to make predictions about the brain circuits involved in this process. For example, if fear conditioning is mediated through the amygdala, extinction might result in decreased amygdala responses. Exaggerated limbic responses to spider images have indeed been found in fMRI studies of individuals with spider phobia, and preliminary results suggest that this response normalises after successful behavioural interventions. After a successful intervention, patients show no difference in their avoidance behaviour to control participants. We might thus have expected that the brain activity evoked by spiders changes with treatment. However, at least two different patterns of brain activity changes are conceivable: psychotherapy might lead to a normalisation of previously abnormal activation, or it may lead to the recruitment of additional areas. We would expect the latter to be the case particularly in psychological interventions with a strong component of cognitive restructuring.

The relationship between psycho- and pharmacotherapy can be studied best in disorders where both approaches are equally potent and commonly used. For example, in the study of social phobia a similar reduction in limbic activity during preparation of a public speech was observed in groups that were treated with antidepressants or a behavioural intervention. Converging effects of behavioural therapy and SSRIs on brain activation were also observed in OCD. Both treatments led to a reduction of previously increased resting blood flow in the basal ganglia. These results are conceptually very interesting because they suggest a specific chemical mechanism – serotonergic activation – for a behavioural intervention. However, this would need to be corroborated by evidence from direct molecular techniques, for example PET, because both treatments may also converge downstream from the serotonergic effects. A further clinical aim of such studies is to identify likely responders to different types of therapy by their baseline patterns of neural activation, allowing for an individualised therapy (Linden, 2006).

9.3   BRAIN EFFECTS OF COGNITIVE BEHAVIOURAL THERAPY FOR DEPRESSION AND ANTIDEPRESSANTS MAY DIFFER MORE

For patients with a simple phobia, symptom induction in the laboratory is relatively straightforward. Pictures or movies of the conditioned stimulus, for example spiders or needles, normally produce symptoms that mimic the clinical syndrome, as measured by self-report or psychophysiological parameters. Such symptom induction is also possible in social phobia (e.g. asking patients to prepare a public speech) or OCD (e.g. touching them with a supposedly contaminated object). Because these effects are transient, these procedures are commonly accepted as safe and ethically sound. The brain effects of such symptom induction are then studied in order to reveal hyper- or hypoactivated areas and assess treatment effects.

Depression is more difficult to model in the laboratory because of its multifaceted nature and lack of direct trigger. It is possible to induce specific affective states, for example sadness, through pictures, movie clips or stories. This mood induction seems to be particularly effective if autobiographically relevant material is used and when the participants are instructed to imagine themselves in emotionally charged situations (Martin, 1990). Functional imaging during sadness induction with these types of techniques has suggested a pattern of limbic over-activation and prefrontal under-activation. One of the over-activated areas was the subgenual cingulate, a main target area for DBS (see Chapter 8). However, mood induction models only a part of the depressive syndrome.

Most imaging studies of treatment effects in depression were conducted during the resting state rather than functional activation. This approach does not depend on symptom induction. Another advantage is that measures of blood flow or glucose metabolism with PET or SPECT yield quantitative parameters that can more easily be compared across time than the fMRI activations, which always have to be computed against some baseline. The main disadvantage of the resting state approach is that it is impossible to control the cognitive activity of patient during the 30 minutes or so of scanning, which will be reflected in the amplitude and distribution of brain metabolism.

Treatment effects in depression differed between pharmacological and psychological interventions. After Cognitive Behavioural Therapy (CBT), glucose metabolism was reduced in the prefrontal cortex and increased in the hippocampus. An inverted pattern was found after treatment with the SSRI paroxetine. The explanation may be that CBT decreases ruminations and other dysfunctional thought processes associated with prefrontal activity, whereas the SSRI would modulate emotional reactivity through suppression of limbic activity (Goldapple et al., 2004). However, these findings are not consistent across studies. For example Interpersonal Therapy (IPT), another psychotherapy frequently used for depression, led to similar reductions in prefrontal glucose metabolism as paroxetine treatment (Brody et al., 2001). One important methodological problem is posed by the absence of stable neuroimaging (or any other) biomarkers for most mental disorders, which makes it impossible to distinguish normal from pathological activation patterns. Another methodological problem is the comparability of psychological interventions across studies (or even across the patients of a single study) because of the importance of the relationship between the therapist and the patient. This may explain why to date the investigation of the neural correlates of psychodynamic therapies such as psychoanalysis is even less developed than that of its more formalized counterparts.

9.4   SPECIFIC PHARMACOTHERAPY CAN BE USED AS AN ADD-ON TO PSYCHOTHERAPY

Combinations of psycho- and pharmacotherapy are common in psychiatric practice. Although mild forms of depression and many anxiety disorders may respond to psychotherapy alone, many patients and clinicians prefer a dual approach. Because we are only beginning to understand the biological mechanisms behind effective psychotherapy, as discussed above, we know little about the way psychological and pharmacological treatment interact with each other. One particular approach is worth mentioning here, though, because it uses a drug that is not effective on its own, but only in conjunction with psychotherapy. D-cycloserine, a partial agonist at the NMDA receptor, has been used to enhance the effects of psychotherapy for acrophobia (fear of heights), social phobia and OCD. This is particularly interesting because the NMDA receptor is an ideal target for state dependent effects because of its complex activation requirements (see Chapter 7). It would thus make sense that 'pre-activation' by psychotherapy is required for D-cycloserine to have an effect, but this is still speculative at the moment. However, this example reveals some of the exciting potential of the further study of the brain effects of psychological interventions.

9.5   PLACEBOS CHANGE THE BRAIN

The placebo effect – improvement of clinical symptoms when patients think that they are treated with an active drug but in fact receive a substance without specific pharmacological properties (e.g. a glucose tablet) – is not confined to psychological disorders but has been observed across medical disciplines. Some of their effect may derive from the conviction of being treated with a potent medication, but it even appears when patients know that they have only a 50% chance of receiving the active drug, as in most double blind randomised controlled trials. In fact, informing the patient about the possibility of receiving a placebo is considered the only ethically acceptable form of placebo treatment. However, there is no evidence that placebos work when all patients receive them and are aware of this, but this may be because this design is not used in clinical trials. It is thus likely that several complex psychological and psychosocial processes play a role in the placebo response. The multitude of studies that showed effects not just on subjective measures of well-being but also on physiological parameters such as blood pressure or heart rate suggest that psychophysiological interactions mediate these effects. Neuroendocrine systems linking the stress response and the ANS control of the cardiovascular system are examples of potential mediators of such links between autosuggestion and physiology. Placebo responses can be particularly marked in the field of pain control. Intriguingly, similar effects to those of analgesic drugs on opioid receptors in the brain have been observed in PET studies of the placebo response (Benedetti et al., 2005).

Learning points

Psychotherapy is based on behavioural, cognitive or biographical rather than biological models of mental disorders. However, any psychotherapy exerts biological effects, and the challenge for current research is to elucidate them with non-invasive brain imaging, neurophysiology and neurochemistry. Some of the treatment effects predicted by pathophysiological models of anxiety disorders have indeed been observed in preliminary studies with fMRI, PET or SPECT. For example, limbic activation to symptom induction decreases after successful behavioural therapy of phobia, and blood flow in the caudate nucleus is reduced after treatment of OCD. The comparison of psychotherapy and medication effects is of particular interest and may lead to new ways of enhancing psychological interventions through specific neurochemical modulation.

Revision and discussion questions

- What learning models underlie behavioural therapy?
- Explain some of the techniques available for the investigation of biological correlates of psychotherapy effects.
- Will biological interventions ultimately replace psychotherapy?

FURTHER READING

Clark, D. and Beck, A. (2010). Cognitive theory and therapy of anxiety and depression: Convergence with neurobiological findings. *Trends in Cognitive Sciences*, 14, 418–24.

Derubeis, R., Siegle, G. and Hollon, S. (2008). Cognitive therapy versus medication for depression: Treatment outcomes and neural mechanisms. *Nature Reviews Neuroscience*, 9, 788–96.

Linden, D. E. (2006). How psychotherapy changes the brain: The contribution of functional neuroimaging. *Molecular Psychiatry*, 11, 528–38.

CLINICAL DISORDERS

10 SCHIZOPHRENIA AND RELATED DISORDERS

PREVIEW

The chapters of Part III deal with the mental disorders as defined by the current diagnostic classification systems, the ICD-10 and the DSM-IV. They all follow the same general structure, starting with a description of the clinical phenotype and natural history and some basic epidemiological facts (frequency of occurrence, age of onset, gender distribution). Many mental disorders have a high heritability, and each chapter provides an update on the current evidence for underlying genetic variants.

This is followed by sections on the available evidence for neural mechanisms of the various disorders or individual symptoms. The sections on brain structure and function review the evidence from neuroimaging, EEG and post-mortem studies, and the sections on neurochemistry integrate evidence from blood and CSF markers and inferences from mechanisms of drug action. For disorders with established or promising animal models, a separate section will be devoted to their discussion. Each chapter concludes with a detailed explanation of the mechanisms, clinical effects and side effects of the drugs used in the treatment of the disorder as well as an outlook on the development of new therapeutic agents.

This chapter on schizophrenia has an additional section on the history of the concept of this disorder or group of disorders, highlighting the contributions of the psychiatrists Emil Kraepelin, Eugen Bleuler and Kurt Schneider. It also devotes some space to the endophenotype concept because it has achieved its greatest prominence in schizophrenia research, although endophenotypes may be useful for any partly heritable disorder with a complex clinical phenotype. The effects of antipsychotics, which are all dopamine receptor antagonists, suggest a dopamine model of schizophrenia, and the evidence for such a model and its limitations are critically discussed. In addition to the mechanisms of treatment effects, the section on therapy describes the most important side effects of antipsychotic drugs and strategies for their management.

10.1 HISTORY OF THE CONCEPT

Schizophrenia is a fairly recent term for a very old phenomenon. Paranoia, bizarre behaviour, odd beliefs and strange perceptions and feelings have been documented in medical and literary writing since classical antiquity and were variously subsumed under the terms 'phrenesis', 'melancholia' or 'mania'. The German psychiatrist Emil Kraepelin (1856–1926) is credited with the first definition of what he called 'dementia praecox'. He thus described a disorder which presented with psychotic symptoms, such as auditory or tactile hallucinations or delusions of persecution, emotional blunting and stereotyped behaviour and had an unrelenting course towards deterioration, leading to early cognitive decline. In his system, the contrast was between dementia praecox and manic depressive illness, which he regarded as periodical and lacking the progressive deterioration found in his cases of 'dementia praecox'.

However, the syndrome described by Kraepelin did not always lead to rapid cognitive decline and was not confined to adolescence and early adulthood. The term 'dementia praecox' therefore did not seem ideal, and the Swiss psychiatrist Eugen Bleuler (1857–1939) suggested the name that is still in use today. The term 'schizophrenia' – Greek for 'split mind' – was used to denote the patients' failure to integrate their feelings, thoughts, memories and perceptions into a coherent whole. Bleuler believed that the more dramatic symptoms of schizophrenia that Kraepelin had described were accessory to its core features that included loosening of associations, ambivalence, inappropriate affect and autistic behaviour. Bleuler thus gave schizophrenia a much broader definition and also recognised subclinical forms of 'latent' schizophrenia. His ideas can be regarded as precursors of concepts of schizotypy and schizotaxia, which will be discussed in Chapter 14.

The first set of clinical symptoms that could be used by clinicians to support or reject a diagnosis of schizophrenia was provided by the German psychiatrist Kurt Schneider (1887–1967). Schneider classified highly specific symptoms that were of great utility for the differentiation of schizophrenia and other mental disorders as 'first-rank symptoms'. These included hearing one's own thoughts, hearing voices arguing or commenting on one's actions, or experiencing one's thoughts as being influenced or taken away by others ('Ichstoerungen', disturbances of the self or ego). Presence of any of these first-rank symptoms, in the absence of an obvious medical condition, made the diagnosis of schizophrenia very likely.

10.2   CLINICAL SYNDROME AND NATURAL HISTORY

All of these milestones in the development of the definition and understanding of schizophrenia influenced the systems of operationalised psychiatric diagnosis from the first version of the *Diagnostic and Statistical Manual of Mental Disorders* of the American Psychiatric Association in 1951 to the current DSM-IV (2000), and likewise the 10th edition of the WHO's international classification of diseases (1992). The basic idea of a separation of affective and schizophrenic psychoses goes back to Kraepelin, whereas the use of a set of clinical signs and symptoms to determine presence or absence of a specific disorder is based on the work of Bleuler and Schneider. The first-rank symptoms, in particular, play a prominent role in the catalogue of criteria for schizophrenia provided by both diagnostic systems. For example, both DSM-IV and ICD-10 regard hallucination of voices that give a running commentary on the patient's action or that engage in a dialogue as a sufficient criterion of schizophrenia. ICD-10 also puts special emphasis on Schneider's disturbances of the ego, such as thought insertion, broadcast or withdrawal (Table 10.1).

A commonly used distinction is that between acute psychotic or 'positive' and 'negative' symptoms. The DSM-IV explains the term 'positive' as 'excess or distortion of normal functions' and 'negative' as 'diminution or loss of normal function'. Hallucinations, for example, can be defined as perceptual experience in the absence of an adequate external stimulus, and thus represent an addition to normal perception. Conversely, the core negative symptoms of DSM-IV – affective flattening (loss of emotional reactivity), alogia (poverty of speech) and avolition (inability to initiate goal-directed actions) – all consist in a reduction of normal functioning. Because of their quantitative nature, they are difficult to separate from variants of normal behaviour, and they are less specific than the positive symptoms because they also occur in some types of mood disorders. However, the negative

Table 10.1   Criteria for schizophrenia in DSM-IV and ICD-10

	DSM-IV	ICD-10
Pathognomonic symptoms (1 sufficient)	Hallucinations in form of running commentary/ interlocuting voices	
	Bizarre delusions, for example loss of control over body	
		Though echo, thought insertion or withdrawal or thought broadcasting
		Delusional perception
Characteristic symptoms (2 required)	Delusions	
	Regular hallucinations in any sensory modality	
	Severely disorganised speech	
	Catatonic or disorganised[a] behaviour	
	Negative symptoms	
		Social withdrawal
Social/occupational dysfunction	Yes	Not specified
Duration	6 months, including 1 with characteristic symptoms	1 month

[a] In ICD-10 only in the additional criteria for hebephrenic schizophrenia (F20.1).

Source: The ICD-10 Classification of Mental and Behavioural Disorders : Clinical Descriptions and Diagnostic Guidelines, WHO (1992).
Diagnostic and Statistical Manual of Mental Disorders : DSM-IV-TR, American Psychiatric Association (2000).

symptoms have considerable impact on quality of life and the prospect of long-term social integration of the patient.

The positive symptoms can be further subdivided into the two categories paranoia and disorganisation. These categories are used to describe the most common subtypes of schizophrenia, the paranoid and the disorganised (in ICD: hebephrenia) types. Although this distinction is clinically meaningful and can help with prognosis (which may be better for paranoid schizophrenia than other types), it has not yet been supported by stable biological markers. Paranoia broadly describes the distortion of reality and includes hallucinations and delusions. Some delusions are internally consistent and could in principle be true, except that this is very unlikely in the specific case, such as the belief of a patient that he or she is under surveillance by international secret services. This type of delusion also occurs in other disorders, notably persistent delusional disorder. However, bizarre, clearly implausible delusions, such as the conviction that one is simultaneously living in two different ages, are highly typical of schizophrenia. Similarly, hallucinations can occur across a wide range of disorders, particularly neurodegenerative conditions and drug abuse, but certain types that reflect the feeling of being controlled by others are considered to be diagnostic of schizophrenia. Disorganisation can be inferred from patients' language or behaviour. Patients may talk incoherently, frequently change topic, give unrelated ('tangential') answers to questions and come up with new words or word combinations ('neologisms'). Disorganised behaviour is harder to define, and mere violation of social norms is not a sufficient criterion. However, behaviours that would be regarded as inappropriate in any culture or are clearly dysfunctional, such as the DSM-IV's example of wearing several overcoats on a hot day, can count as symptomatic. It has been proposed that a common factor of 'thought disorder' underlies disorganisation of speech and behaviour, and the two certainly correlate, but thought processes can only be inferred from the patient's speech and actions.

If symptoms of schizophrenia and of a mood disorder (see Chapters 11 and 12) occur during the same period of illness, a diagnosis of schizoaffective disorder should be considered. The DSM-IV defines schizoaffective disorder by a major depressive (depressive type) or mixed or manic (bipolar type) episode that occurs concurrently with symptoms of schizophrenia and for a substantial portion of the active and residual phases of the illness. In order to distinguish the depressed type of schizoaffective disorder from the negative symptoms of schizophrenia, pervasive depressed mood needs to be present. Because mood congruent psychotic symptoms can be part of major depressive (psychotic depression) or manic episodes, the diagnosis of schizoaffective disorder requires psychotic symptoms for at least two weeks without accompanying symptoms of mood disorder.

After a first episode of acute psychotic symptoms, the natural history of schizophrenia varies greatly. Although a small minority of patients are only affected by a single episode and recover fully, almost 90% of patients suffer from relapses, and most of them also from residual symptoms and psychosocial problems between episodes. Retrospective studies also revealed that most patients showed non-specific symptoms such as difficulties concentrating or social isolation several years before the first contact with the mental health services, and more specific symptoms such as magical ideation, odd beliefs and behaviour for 1–2 years before admission. This so-called prodromal phase is currently under intensive investigation with a view to determining the validity of psychometric (and biological) predictors of conversion to fully-fledged psychosis and identifying individuals that would benefit from early psychological or pharmacological intervention. Furthermore, retrospective studies found minor developmental abnormalities, affecting motor skills, social interaction and intelligence, ten years and more before onset of psychotic symptoms, that is, long before the putative prodromal period (Lewis and Levitt, 2002). These findings of early onset of presymptomatic precursors are of interest in the context of the neurodevelopmental hypothesis (Lewis and Lieberman, 2000), which assumes some neural changes associated with schizophrenia to be present from the perinatal period.

10.3   EPIDEMIOLOGY

The prevalence (cases per population) of schizophrenia seems to be fairly uniform across geographical regions and cultures at 0.5–1%, although social and cultural factors may influence the diagnosis. The annual rate of new cases (incidence) is estimated at between 15 and 50 per 100,000. Social class does not seem to influence the risk of getting affected, but proportions of patients are higher in lower classes due to downward social drift. Likewise, lower intelligence does not seem to be a risk factor, but the disease can have a negative effect on intellectual functioning and patients score on average ten points below their premorbid levels on standardised IQ tests. Age of onset is commonly between 16 and 35, with a median age of onset of 21 for men, and about five years later for women. The prevalence of schizoaffective disorder seems to be lower than that of schizophrenia. Its prognosis is generally better than that of schizophrenia, but social and occupational dysfunction is still common.

The causes of schizophrenia are unknown. Most models assume the joint operation of genetic, epigenetic and environmental factors, evidence for which will be discussed in detail in the relevant parts of this chapter. Research into the possible links between schizophrenia and specific infections has a long tradition. It has recently gained renewed interest because of the association of intrauterine and early childhood infections with schizophrenia (Lewis and Levitt, 2002). Specifically, exposure to influenza in the second trimester of pregnancy seems to constitute a risk factor. All other associations of schizophrenia with specific infectious agents, such as the link with maternal or the patient's own exposure to toxoplasma gondii, the infectious agent in toxoplasmosis, have remained controversial.

A possible role for infectious agents in the causal chain leading to schizophrenia would be compatible with the increasing evidence for abnormal inflammatory processes (Muller and Schwarz, 2006). How these might be linked to the neurochemical abnormalities implicated in schizophrenia (let alone its phenotype) is a matter of speculation. Animal models of the cellular and behavioural consequences of specific infections may provide further clues. For example, mice whose mothers were infected with the influenza virus showed behavioural abnormalities that may also be associated with schizophrenia.

10.4   GENETICS

It has long been noted that schizophrenia runs in families. Twin and adoption studies have determined that a considerable portion of this association is attributable to genetic factors. Furthermore, the risk for a monozygotic (identical) twin of a sibling with schizophrenia of developing schizophrenia themselves (the so-called concordance rate) is about 50%, whereas that for a dizygotic (non-identical) twin is about 17%, which is still higher than that for non-twin siblings (9%). Both shared environment and shared genes thus seem to contribute to the development of schizophrenia. Interestingly, risk of developing schizophrenia is also increased in relatives of patients with bipolar or schizoaffective disorder. These observations support a continuum model of schizophreniform and affective psychoses, which runs contrary to Kraepelin's original dichotomy of affective and non-affective psychoses, but might explain why the same antipsychotic drugs can be effective for schizophrenia and bipolar disorder.

The mode of inheritance is clearly different from the Mendelian patterns characteristic of monogenic disorders (e.g. Huntington's disease, see Chapter 4). Most psychiatric geneticists currently think that the genes associated with schizophrenia confer a predisposition to schizophrenia, perhaps even in a quantitative, cumulative manner. It would then be the combination of the genetic load with environmental (psychosocial, medical) risk factors that determines whether the disease will develop or not. The search for individual genes that contribute to the vulnerability for schizophrenia has utilised the two main techniques of molecular genetic analysis, linkage and association studies. Linkage studies revealed loci on chromosome 22q11–13 (which is also linked to bipolar disorder), 6p24–22 (the locus of the dysbindin gene, DTNBP1), 8p22–21 (locus of the neuregulin 1 gene, NRG1), 6q and 1q42 (locus of the Disrupted In Schizophrenia gene, DISC1). However, it is still an open issue which if any of these chromosomal regions (and others with preliminary evidence for a link with schizophrenia) will turn out to be true positives and yield disease genes.

10.4.1   Candidate gene studies

Until a few years ago, association studies used a candidate gene (rather than whole genome) approach. A large number of genes, which were selected for their relevance for the neurotransmitter systems implicated in schizophrenia, have been investigated for their association with schizophrenia, but few associations were confirmed in several independent studies. A polymorphism in the gene coding for the 5-HT_{2A} receptor (thymidine/cytosine exchange at nucleotide 102) is amongst those with the strongest evidence (Serretti et al., 2007), but only seems to confer a relatively small added risk (odds ratio of 1.2, that is the risk increases by approximately 20% compared to the overall population). Genes related to the dopamine system have also been implicated. Polymorphisms in both the dopamine receptor D2 and D3 genes (DRD2, DRD3) received support by various studies, but more recent evidence seems to suggest that the associations with dopamine receptor genes were false positives (Owen et al., 2004).

The ultimate aim of psychiatric genetics is to find associations of diseases, syndromes or symptoms with genetic alterations with known functional consequences. The valine-to-methionine (Val/Met) polymorphism at position 108/158 of the gene for catechol-O-methyltransferase (COMT) is an attractive target in this respect. The Met allele produces a lower activity form of the enzyme, which results in higher synaptic levels of dopamine. The prediction as to what allele would confer a risk for schizophrenia depends on what specific dopamine model of schizophrenia one adopts. If we assume a simple dose–response relationship between dopamine levels and schizophrenia risk (as might be suggested by the linear correlation between dopamine receptor affinity and antipsychotic effect of neuroleptic drugs), we would predict the risk of schizophrenia to increase with the load of the Met allele. However a more recent model suggests a U-shaped relationship between dopamine levels, at least in prefrontal cortex, and schizophrenia. In this scenario, the Met allele would be protective for those individuals who for other reasons have too little dopamine, and the Val allele would confer a risk in them. A series of studies in various populations have indeed suggested an association between the Val allele and schizophrenia, but these again seem to have been false positives (Williams et al., 2007). An even larger literature concerns the potential mediating effects of this polymorphism on cognitive function and treatment response. The current state of the evidence suggests that, if the COMT gene is involved in schizophrenia at all, it will be through a combination of polymorphisms at different sites, so called haplotypes.

The mechanisms through which the DTNBP1 and NRG1 genes confer a putative risk for schizophrenia are unknown because the specific mutations and their functional consequences are as yet unknown. Dysbindin binds to the proteins alpha- and beta-dystrobrevin, which are part of the postsynaptic dystrophin complex. However, dysbindin also seems to have presynaptic effects on glutamate metabolism. The NRG1 gene codes for several proteins, which are involved in axonal growth, synaptogenesis and glutamate metabolism. Its association with schizophrenia may thus be through its effect on neural development and glutamate function, which are both implicated in current pathophysiological models of schizophrenia.

10.4.2 Genome-wide studies

Results of major genome-wide association studies (GWAS) of schizophrenia were published from 2008 onwards. These have focused on common SNPs (with minor allele frequency >5%). Even larger numbers of participants than the several tens of thousands of the present studies will be needed to detect variants in rarer SNPs at genome-wide significance, and these studies will probably bring up further risk variants. Up to August 2010, at least four schizophrenia risk loci have been supported with genome-wide significance. These are in the genes for a zinc finger protein (ZNF804A), neurogranin (NRGN), transcription factor 4 (TCF4) and the major histocompatibility complex (MHC) gene family (Owen et al., 2010). Odds ratios generally range between 1.1 and 1.5. Assuming a population risk of 1% for schizophrenia, this would thus increase to between approximately 1.1 and 1.5% in carriers of a risk allele. This means that each individual locus only explains a small fraction of the heritability of schizophrenia, and that many risk variants of similar effect would have to be present to confer the genetic risk estimated from population and family studies.

The mechanisms through which these risk variants may contribute to the pathophysiology of schizophrenia are unknown. Although the ZNF804A protein is thought to be a transcription factor, little is known about its effect on brain function. Particularly high expression of ZNF804A was observed in the human amygdala and foetal brain suggesting a role in emotional regulation and neurodevelopment, respectively. Genetic imaging studies have suggested that healthy carriers of the risk allele may have lower functional connectivity between the hippocampus and prefrontal cortex and lower brain activation during theory of mind tasks, but the neurochemical mechanisms mediating this have not been elucidated. TCF4 is also a transcription factor, NRGN is a calmodulin-binding protein of the PKC pathway, and the MHC is involved in immune and autoimmune responses. Regulation of gene expression, second messenger pathways and inflammatory processes during neurodevelopment have all been implicated in pathophysiological models of schizophrenia, and thus a role for these genes and their products is conceivable.

The GWAS have also uncovered evidence for genetic loci that confer risk for both schizophrenia and bipolar disorder, for example the ZNF804A locus and a variant on the gene for alpha 1C subunit of the L-type voltage-dependent calcium channel (CACNA1C) (see Chapter 7). This genetic overlap is of particular interest because it calls the traditional 'Kraepelinian' dichotomy of affective and schizophrenic psychoses into question (Craddock and Owen, 2010). If disorders from both groups share genetic risk factors, it makes more sense to conceive of them as different expressions of a common genotype, where differences in the phenotype may be produced by additional genetic factors, environmental factors, or their interaction.

Another outcome of the genome-wide studies was considerable support for the association between schizophrenia and rare and large copy number variants (CNVs). CNVs are DNA loci between 1 kb (kilobase) and several Mb (megabase) in length (and thus affecting several genes) where individuals differ in the number of copies. For example deletion would result in only one copy (on the unaffected chromosome), duplication in three copies. The risk of schizophrenia is increased by about 20 times in carriers of a large (3 Mb) deletion on chromosome 22q11.2. This deletion also leads to velo cardio facial syndrome (VCFS), an autosomal dominant condition that is characterised by a cleft palate and cardiac, facial and endocrine abnormalities. VCFS is much rarer than schizophrenia (about 1/4000). Thus, although it increases schizophrenia risk much more than any of common variants, its contribution to the overall population risk of schizophrenia will be low (approx. 1/200 of all schizophrenia patients based on the above estimates). Other rare CNVs associated with schizophrenia with relatively large odds ratios (about 10) were found on chromosomes 1q21.1 and 15q13.3. The only schizophrenia-related CNV that affects only one gene is a rare deletion of the neurexin 1 (NRXN1) gene on chromosome 2p16.3 (Owen et al., 2010). This association is interesting because neurexins are cell adhesion molecules and instrumental in the development of the synaptic connections. A disruption of their function may thus constitute a model case for the neurodevelopmental and disconnection hypotheses of schizophrenia. However, as with all rare CNVs, we cannot necessarily assume that the same mechanisms are in play in the schizophrenia cases that derive their genetic liability from multiple common variants with small effects.

10.5 BRAIN STRUCTURE AND FUNCTION

The search for alterations in brain structure leading to psychotic illness is older than the concept of schizophrenia or dementia praecox itself. It was one of the main topics of the neuropathological research conducted by Kraepelin's contemporaries and the preceding generation, which was based on staining post-mortem brain tissue to make specific cells or structures visible and then examining it under the microscope. Kraepelin employed some of the greatest neuroanatomists of his time, including Franz Nissl, the inventor of the Nissl stain for cell bodies of neurons (Chapter 1), and Alois Alzheimer, the discoverer of the plaques and tangles that are now the hallmark of the eponymous dementia (Chapter 20). However, Kraepelin's own system was based on phenomenology and natural history rather than causes of psychotic illness, and he therefore showed comparatively little interest in its biological basis and virtually ended what Edward Shorter (Shorter, 1997) has called the 'First Biological Psychiatry'. This first wave of biological investigation of mental disorders had produced major breakthroughs in macroscopic and microscopic neuroanatomy, but had remained largely unsuccessful in describing brain correlates of specific mental disorders, excluding perhaps some of the clearly neurodegenerative disorders, such as Pick's disease, Alzheimer dementia or neurosyphilis (Chapters 20–21). The 'Second Biological Psychiatry' of the last five decades was initially driven by the success of pharmacological approaches, and the models built on them, but then seized on the opportunity to determine structural brain correlates of syndromes or symptoms when the techniques of non-invasive neuroimaging became available with the spread of computed tomography (CT) in the 1970s and magnetic resonance imaging (MRI) in the 1980s.

10.5.1 Neuroimaging findings

One of the first psychiatric discoveries that were made with the newly developed neuroimaging techniques was the enlargement of the lateral and third ventricles. This anatomical characteristic was specific to patients with schizophrenia compared with their siblings, occurred at the onset of the disease and was associated with poorer treatment response (Trimble, 1996). A recent study confirmed the specificity of ventricular enlargement compared to affective psychosis (McDonald et al., 2006). Importantly, the ventricle changes, and indeed all structural imaging findings, become statistically significant at group level, but cannot be used to diagnose schizophrenia on an individual basis. Changes in the ventricles cannot, of course, explain associations between brain structure and function in schizophrenia. However, they point to abnormalities in the migration of nerve cells that starts in the ventricular zone during brain development. Such a theory is at the heart of the current neurodevelopmental model of schizophrenia. The relative lack of family associations of the ventricle enlargement would support such a model. If only those members of families, who develop schizophrenia, show the phenomenon, ventricle enlargement would reflect the environmental stressors that trigger the disease, rather than the genetic predisposition. However, the recent study of ventricle enlargement in schizophrenia and bipolar patients and their relatives (McDonald et al., 2006) suggested that relatives of patients with familial schizophrenia (that is, with at least two known cases in the family) may also show this sign, and that it may therefore be a candidate endophenotype rather than a result of environmental influences.

Patients with schizophrenia as a group also show subtle loss of local brain volume in numerous areas, including the language and auditory areas of the temporal lobe, the attention and visuomotor integration areas of the parietal lobe, the memory and executive areas of the frontal lobe, and parts of the limbic system and the basal ganglia. Such volume loss has been reported for schizophrenia patients already during adolescence and was found to progress at a rate of up to 4% per year (Toga et al., 2006). Furthermore, even patients with prodromal schizophrenia show limbic alterations (Pantelis et al., 2003). However, at post-mortem examination there is often no difference in overall brain volume or that of structures implicated in the pathogenesis of schizophrenia, for example the frontal lobes (Highley et al., 2001), between patients and age- and intelligence-matched controls. Thus, brain degeneration does not progress at that pace across the lifetime in most schizophrenia patients.

10.5.2   Structure and function

Associations between structural changes and function have been most prominently established for the temporal lobes in association with auditory hallucinations. Patients with higher degrees of cortical atrophy also showed more severe and frequent hallucinations. Conversely, volume of temporal lobe white matter (WM) may be increased in patients with prominent auditory hallucinations (Shapleske et al., 2002). Such findings can be the starting point for an analysis of pathological networks, which can be aided by the use of diffusion tensor imaging (DTI), an MRI technique that utilises the restrictions on free movement of water molecules imposed by the myelin sheet of neurons in order to map the integrity of fibre tracts in white matter. The value most often used to characterise the integrity of fibres is fractional anisotropy (FA), which describes the degree to which displacement of water molecules varies in space. FA is decreased in schizophrenia in the frontal and occipital white matter, and in the fibre tracts of the uncinate fasciculus, cingulum and corpus callosum. These findings are commonly interpreted as evidence for anatomical dis- or hypoconnectivity. However, increased FA (and thus possibly increased connectivity) in the arcuate fasciculus (see Fig. 1.20, Plate IV), the fibre bundle linking Broca's and Wernicke's areas, was described for schizophrenia patients with chronic auditory hallucinations (Hubl et al., 2004). Hyperconnectivity between some areas is therefore a possibility in schizophrenia. Such hyperconnectivity may be the result of abnormal migration of nerve cells in the embryonic stage. Alternatively, pruning, the mechanism by which exuberant connections that form during postnatal brain development are cut back, may not work efficiently. In either case, findings of hyperconnectivity would support a neurodevelopmental model of schizophrenia. However, the DTI measures employed still await neuroanatomical validation, for example by post-mortem tracer studies.

Because the psychopathology of schizophrenia is intricately linked with language functions, perhaps more than that of any other mental disorder, changes in the dominant hemisphere have long been postulated. In most right-handers, the planum temporale, which comprises Wernicke's area in the dominant hemisphere, is larger and the Sylvian fissure longer on the left. This L > R asymmetry is also present in schizophrenia, but was found to be reduced in the majority of imaging and post-mortem studies (Crow, 1997). This reduction of planum temporale asymmetry may have its functional correlate in the multiple abnormalities of language, which are prominent in the characteristic symptoms of auditory verbal hallucinations (Oertel et al., 2010), odd speech, neologisms and pervasive in formal thought disorder. Deficits in comprehension have even been suggested to have high predictive value for the conversion to psychosis in the schizophrenia prodrome.

The non-invasive structural imaging techniques have produced detailed maps of grey and white matter and the changes that have been associated with schizophrenia. However, if we want to scrutinise the types of cells involved in more detail and find out about the molecular and developmental mechanisms of altered cortical structure and connectivity in schizophrenia, we will have to turn to the methods of post-mortem examination, histopathology and histochemistry.

10.5.3   Post-mortem studies

The most consistent feature of post-mortem studies of schizophrenia is that any changes are rather subtle. This is in striking contrast with the disabling nature of the disease, its pervasive psychopathology and often associated cognitive decline. There is normally no gross macroscopic abnormality, but even stereological measures of brain areas of interest such as the frontal or temporal lobes often do not reveal differences in regional brain volume. Several microscopic changes have been observed with some consistency. Gliosis, excessive growth of astrocytes after injury or inflammation of the brain, has been observed in the diencephalon and basal forebrain. Although this is not a primary change to neurons, it would be interesting in the context of inflammation and infection models of schizophrenia. However, it is probably unrelated to the pathology of schizophrenia as such, but produced by the other neuropathological abnormalities that are more frequent in the brains of schizophrenia patients than controls such as small strokes (Harrison, 1999).

White matter has also been investigated with histochemical methods. We need to keep in mind that subcortical white matter does not exclusively contain fibre bundles but also the interstitial neurons, which are remnants of the subplate of the foetal brain. There seem to be changes in the distribution of interstitial neurons – with relatively more in deeper areas of WM of dorsolateral prefrontal cortex (DLPFC) (Akbarian et al., 1996) and parahippocampal gyrus (Rioux et al., 2003) – in the patients' brains. These different patterns may reflect aberrant neural migration and thus support a neurodevelopmental model, but findings await replication in larger samples.

The investigation of cortical neurons has mainly targeted the frontal and the medial temporal lobes. There is insufficient evidence to support claims of overall changes in neuron content in the hippocampus. However, neurons seem to be smaller and more densely packed both in the hippocampus and in prefrontal cortex. The most likely reason for the higher neuron density in these areas is a reduction in neuropil, the axonal and dendritic processes of neurons in grey matter. These reductions in neuronal size and neuropil lead to a thinner cortical sheet in frontal cortex. Reduced neuron size, fewer spines and fewer inhibitory inputs were especially observed in layer III of prefrontal cortex, which is the main source of cortico-cortical projections (Harrison, 1999; Selemon, 2001).

Conversely, some subcortical areas (amygdala and striatum) showed reductions of neuron number but not density (Kreczmanski et al., 2007). These findings were not associated with illness duration and thus cannot be taken to indicate progressive neurodegeneration. Several studies reported fewer and smaller neurons in the dorsomedial thalamus, which is particularly interesting because of this region's projections to prefrontal cortex. However, these findings have more recently been called into question (Cullen et al., 2003).

The molecular analysis of post-mortem tissue has lent further support to models of altered connectivity in schizophrenia. Reductions of synaptic proteins have been observed in hippocampus, particularly for complexin II (which is found in excitatory neurons) and for neuronal growth associated protein 43 (GAP-43), a marker of synaptic plasticity (Harrison, 1999). Synaptophysin, which is ubiquitous across brain areas and neurotransmitter pathways and indicates the number of synapses, was found to be reduced in DLPFC, temporal lobes and thalamus in several studies, but findings were not always consistent. These synaptic changes and the reduction of dendritic markers would be compatible with findings of reduced neuropil and support the view that dysfunctional connections between and within cortical areas are a key component of the pathophysiology of schizophrenia. It would certainly be stretching the evidence to claim that schizophrenia is caused by permanent cortico-cortical or -subcortical disconnection – after all, many patients are symptom free for extended periods between acute episodes. However, the term 'dysconnection' (Stephan et al., 2006) may be appropriate to describe the molecular, microscopic and imaging findings of subtle alterations of the connectivity of grey and white matter in schizophrenia.

Both the early presence of structural changes identified by neuroimaging and the paucity of neurodegenerative findings at post-mortem have resulted in a paradigm shift, away from the Kraepelinian idea of dementia praecox as an early onset degenerative disorder to the view that schizophrenia is a developmental disorder with a genetic vulnerability and a set of environmental risk factors during pre- and postnatal development. Suggested risk factors include maternal viral infection, for example with influenza or rubella, season of birth (winter and spring), and complications during birth (Lewis and Levitt, 2002). According to the neurodevelopmental model, this interaction between genetic predisposition and early damage to neural circuitry results in a brain that is vulnerable to environmental stressors particularly during adolescence, when it undergoes its final maturation (completion of myelination, synaptic pruning) (Lewis and Lieberman, 2000).

10.5.4 Brain function: functional imaging and electrophysiology

The investigation of brain structure has yielded interesting insights in potential abnormalities of brain development in schizophrenia, but has failed to explain the specific symptoms of the disorder. There is possibly one exception, the grey and white matter changes in the temporal lobe and their association with hallucinations, but even here the anatomical data show considerable overlap between patients and controls, whereas symptomatically the two groups are clearly distinguishable. Thus, from the perspective of classical neuropsychology and the quest for structure–function relations, the contribution of structural brain research has been disappointing. With the development of cognitive neuroscience over the past 20 years, a new field of cognitive neuropsychiatry (Halligan and David, 2001) has emerged, which aims to operationalise psychiatric symptoms in experimental paradigms and investigate the underlying brain mechanisms with functional imaging and non-invasive neurophysiology (see Box 10.1).

Box 10.1 Social cognition in schizophrenia

General cognitive deficits are often disabling for the patients concerned and negatively affect their psychosocial rehabilitation. They have also been recognised as a poor prognostic factor and are therefore of importance for research and cognitive intervention in schizophrenia. However, the link with the initial clinical presentation and characteristic symptoms is not always straightforward to establish. Thus, the elucidation of their neural mechanisms may provide reliable diagnostic markers, but not necessarily insight into the mechanisms of the clinically most obvious features of the disorders. This link may be closer for cognitive deficits that are theoretically and/or empirically linked with specific clinical symptoms, such as deficits in social cognition and negative symptoms (Ochsner, 2008). The neural substrates of these deficits have recently attracted growing attention. Lee et al. (2006) scanned schizophrenia patients while they were reasoning about empathy and forgiving. Patients were scanned on two occasions, once during an acute episode, and once after recovery. The main change in brain activation was an increase in the left medial prefrontal cortex after recovery. This brain area has been implicated in self-referential and social judgements in a large number of studies. Altered neural mechanisms of social cognition have also been demonstrated for judgements about the social dispositions of others. When patients with paranoid schizophrenia had to rate the trustworthiness of faces, their activation in classical areas involved in emotional processing of faces, including the right amygdala and fusiform face area, was reduced compared to controls (Pinkham et al., 2008).

Decoding people's intentions through interpretation of their facial expression is a crucial component of social cognition. Less reliable decoding mechanisms may contribute to misinterpretations of the intentions of others, leading to suspiciousness or even delusions of reference and paranoia. There is some indication that patients with schizophrenia differ in their assessment of the emotionality of faces from the healthy population. Altered interpretation of facial expression may also contribute to the Capgras delusion, where people believe that a close relative has been replaced by an impostor. This phenomenon can occur in isolation, as part of schizophrenia or schizoaffective disorder, or in the course of neurological or neurodegenerative conditions (Josephs, 2007). Healthy people normally are aroused when they see the face of a familiar person, which is reflected in an increased skin conductance. Conversely, patients with Capgras syndrome do not differentiate between familiar and unfamiliar faces in this manner (Halligan and David, 2001). Of course, there are many cases where loss of emotional reactivity to familiar faces does not lead to the conviction that the familiar person has been replaced by an impostor. Perhaps patients who develop the Capgras delusion notice that somehow the familiar face does not 'feel' right but, rather than questioning their own lack of emotional response, seek the fault in the other person. Given the 'externalising' attributional style for negative events often observed in patients with psychosis, this would be a natural way of explaining the lack of emotional response to the familiar person.

It is important to learn more about the changes in emotional processes in patients with schizophrenia and other psychotic disorders, and to understand the resulting deficits in social cognition and interaction. This better understanding is needed for the development of psychological interventions that go beyond the focus on single symptoms and aim to help patient regain their ability to interpret actions and intentions of others and interact with them in a productive way.

Early functional imaging studies assessed resting blood flow and glucose metabolism with xenon-133 inhalation, SPECT and PET and found reductions in the frontal lobes, termed 'hypofrontality'. Such hypofrontality would be compatible with a model of dopamine deficiency in the mesofrontal system (in contrast with hyperactivity in the mesolimbic system), which could explain some of the cognitive and motivational deficits of schizophrenia. However, more recent studies with fMRI have demonstrated both hypo- and hyperactivity in the frontal lobes during cognitive tasks, for example of working memory. One interpretation of these findings is that the brains of schizophrenia patients compensate successfully for reduced capacity by over-activation or recruitment of additional areas during lower cognitive loads, but processing collapses when capacity limits are reached, which happens earlier than in healthy controls. An alternative approach measures brain activity with fMRI during the 'resting state', that is, without any specific task instructions. In this it is similar to the earlier metabolic imaging studies with SPECT or PET that assessed baseline glucose uptake or blood flow. The analysis of resting state fMRI data with data driven techniques such as independent components analysis can yield information about differences in the activity and connectivity of large-scale networks between schizophrenia patients and controls (Rotarska-Jagiela et al., 2010). It is attractive because it requires much less patient cooperation than functional imaging during task execution. It also lends itself to the comparison with measures of structural connectivity derived from DTI.

The non-invasive electrophysiological techniques (EEG, MEG) have the advantage compared to fMRI of real time resolution, but at the cost of much lower spatial resolution. Several potential biological markers of schizophrenia have been identified using the evoked (EP) and event-related potentials (ERP) of the EEG. The most widely investigated ERP in schizophrenia (and mental disorders generally) is the P300, The P300 or P3 is a classic 'event-related potential' (ERP). ERPs differ from EPs in that they are less dependent on stimulus properties than on the cognitive context or expectancy of the subject. For example, the P300 is recorded after rare 'oddball' events in repetitive stimulus trains and even when an expected stimulus does not occur, and thus in the absence of sensory stimulation. Another interesting feature of the P300 is that it can be evoked by visual, auditory, tactile and even olfactory or gustatory paradigms. Another cognitive potential that has shown abnormalities in schizophrenia and after the induction of model psychoses, for example with ketamine, is mismatch negativity, which is evoked by violations of regularity in auditory stimulus trains. However, it is not only the later components, those that occur 150 ms after a stimulus and later, that are disturbed in schizophrenia (Butler et al., 2005). A growing body of evidence from patients with schizophrenia indicates abnormalities of both early visual P1 (see Figure 2.9) and the early auditory P50 wave.

Another non-invasive electrophysiological approach to the study of brain function utilises time-frequency analysis of the EEG. In schizophrenia, deficits in oscillatory activity were identified particularly in higher frequency bands (the beta band, 15–30 Hz, and the gamma band, >30 Hz). These findings are of interest in the context of the putative role of synchronised gamma activity for cognitive and perceptual integration, and communication between neuronal assemblies in general (Uhlhaas et al., 2008). Synchronised high frequency activity crucially depends on intact inhibitory interneuron circuits. If these are dysfunctional in schizophrenia, as suggested by some of the post-mortem histochemical studies, a resulting failure to integrate neuronal activity temporally within and across areas may result in some of the cognitive deficit and even psychotic symptoms (Phillips and Silverstein, 2003).

The most direct evidence of the neural systems that contribute to the symptoms of schizophrenia has come from fMRI. Increased activity correlated with auditory verbal hallucinations (AVH) was observed in primary auditory cortex, corresponding to the subjective vividness of the experience (Dierks et al., 1999) (Figure 2.11, Plate V). The wider network of AVH comprised language areas in the frontal and temporal lobes and limbic areas, including amygdala and hippocampus. On this basis, we can tentatively build a neuropsychological model of AVH that suggests generation in speech production areas of the frontal lobe, with material retrieved from long-term memory through the hippocampus and receiving its affective connotation from the amygdala. These self-generated sentences, however, are not uttered but transmitted through the (possibly hyperconnected) arcuate fasciculus to temporal regions, including Heschl's gyrus, the site of primary auditory cortex. It is presumably at this point that the patient becomes aware of the AVH and attributes it to an external source.

Another important aspect of the physiological processes that lead to hallucinations is the relative timing of brain activation. The default mode of action (including speech) generation by the brain implements a forward model that anticipates which areas in the own brain would be affected by the action and suppresses them temporarily. This mechanism has been adduced as an explanation of why we cannot tickle ourselves. It may also explain why inner rehearsal of speech normally does not become audible. Such a suppression of auditory areas during inner speech may not occur in some patients with schizophrenia, leading to hallucinations. This could be reflected in instantaneous activation of prefrontal (supplementary motor area: SMA), language production (inferior frontal gyrus: IFG) and reception areas (superior temporal sulcus: STS, including the 'human voice area') during hallucinations, whereas this chain of activation proceeds over several seconds in the case of auditory imagery (Figure 10.1, Plate V). This information about timing differences was obtained through examining non-clinical voice hearers (individuals with pervasive auditory hallucinations but no other psychopathology and no functional deficits) and it is not clear how well it translates to the hallucinations experienced in schizophrenia (Linden et al., 2011).

This model is still very speculative and needs corroboration from larger patient samples. However, it has already led to partly successful attempts at attenuating hallucinations with transcranial magnetic stimulation over the temporal lobe. For further clinical applications of functional imaging in schizophrenia, one would probably need to identify specific neurotransmitter systems as being affected or incorporate molecular information from genetic imaging.

10.5.5 Endophenotypes and biological markers

The identification of the genes that confer a risk of a psychiatric disorder is often hampered by the heterogeneous clinical phenotypes. For example two individuals may both be diagnosed with schizophrenia, but not have a single symptom in common. One of the strategies to overcome this difficulty is based on the search for endophenotypes (Owen et al., 2004). These are physiological, anatomical or behavioural markers of a disorder that do not define the clinical phenotype and thus can also be measured in relatives of patients and in the general population (see Section 4.4.4). For a marker to be regarded as an endophenotype, certain criteria, such as heritability and co-segregation with the illness, have to be fulfilled (Gottesman and Gould, 2003). Behavioural endophenotypes are particularly attractive because they can be measured relatively easily in large samples. For schizophrenia, several behavioural endophenotypes have been proposed (Turetsky et al., 2007), including reduced Pre-Pulse Inhibition (PPI), errors on the antisaccade task and working memory (WM) deficits. However, these endophenotypes have so far not been associated with specific genes or, as in the case of the association of working memory deficit with a polymorphism in the COMT (catechol-O-methyltransferase) gene, have not been shown to reflect a straightforward association with schizophrenia (Williams et al., 2007). There is therefore a clear need for work towards further neurocognitive markers that may be more directly related to the clinical presentation of schizophrenia, and thus to its genotype.

Another non-invasive approach to identifying endophenotypes has used functional imaging and neurophysiology. Although schizophrenia patients are generally not impaired in the detection of targets in active oddball tasks, both the amplitude and latency of the P300 event-related potential can be reduced, particularly in the auditory domain. Weisbrod and colleagues (Weisbrod et al., 1999) found reduced amplitude of the auditory P300 both in patients with schizophrenia and their unaffected twins. The study of unaffected relatives (and/or unmedicated patients) is also important to rule out medication effects. Further support for P300 abnormalities across the schizophrenia spectrum came from studies of schizotypal personality disorder (Salisbury et al., 1996) and of healthy individuals with high scores on a schizotypy scale (Klein et al., 1999). The heritability of P300 amplitude has been estimated to be 60%. Although it is difficult to link a quantitative trait such as the amplitude of a component of the ERP with a categorical trait ('caseness' of schizophrenia), heritability is one of the prerequisites of an endophenotype, and the observation of these changes in relatives might suggest that P300 deficits are, indeed, a biological marker of schizophrenia. If this could be corroborated further, for example through the investigation of co-segregation in multiplexed pedigrees, the P300 might become an attractive trait to probe for association with specific genetic loci, which may then turn out to be relevant for schizophrenia as well. Because numbers of participants in ERP studies are normally too small to allow for genome-wide screens, this approach has so far only been taken with candidate genes. Associations with P300 alterations have been observed for several genes that are also implicated in the disease mechanism of schizophrenia or code for proteins that are targeted by treatment. These include the DRD2 and 3 and the DISC1 and 2 genes (Thaker, 2008). The next challenge will be to find associations with loci that have not yet been implicated in schizophrenia or other neuropsychiatric disorders, in order to fulfil the promise of the endophenotype concept that it will aid the discovery of new genes based on its more strictly defined and reliable phenotypes.

10.6 NEUROCHEMISTRY

10.6.1 Dopamine system

The success of modern biological psychiatry is mainly based on the effects of psychoactive drugs, and neurochemical models of mental disorders are largely derived from the pharmacological properties of these drugs. Specific pharmacotherapy of schizophrenia started at the beginning of the 1950s with trials of chlorpromazine, developed as an antihistaminergic drug, at the Val-de-Grace and Ste-Anne hospitals of Paris. It soon became clear that chlorpromazine had striking effects on psychotic symptoms, and several new substances that belonged to the same class of molecules, the phenothiazines, proved to have an antipsychotic effect as well. The same was true for another class of molecules, the butyrophenones, of which haloperidol is the most prominent example. It also emerged over the next two decades that the antipsychotic effect of these substances was not based on their antihistaminergic properties – antihistamines bring about sedation, but are not generally effective for psychotic symptoms – but on their effects on the dopamine system. Several lines of evidence pointed to dopamine. Patients developed side effects that resembled the clinical signs of Parkinson's syndrome, which research in the 1960s showed to be caused by a deficit of dopaminergic neurons in the substantia nigra. Moreover, Arvid Carlsson observed in 1963 that dopamine levels in the mouse brain changed after administration of antipsychotics. Finally, in the 1970s it was discovered that antipsychotics bind to dopamine receptors. In fact, the antipsychotic effect of phenothiazines and butyrophenones scales with their affinity to the dopamine D_2 receptor (DRD2). Other dopamine receptors also seemed to play a role; for example chlorpromazine binds to DRD1 in addition to DRD2, whereas clozapine, one of the more recent 'atypical' antipsychotic agents, binds to DRD4 rather than DRD2. The involvement of dopamine in schizophrenia is plausible because amphetamines, dopamine agonists, produce psychotic symptoms which bear some resemblance to the paranoid features of the disorder.

If antipsychotic effects are brought about by blocking dopamine receptors, a possible explanation would be that this blockade counteracts an excess of dopamine responsible for schizophrenia. Accordingly, researchers searched for evidence of increased pre-treatment dopamine levels in schizophrenia with a wide range of methods. As it is impossible to measure dopamine directly non-invasively in the intact human brain, several surrogate markers had to be employed. These included the levels of metabolic products of dopamine, such as homovanillic acid (HVA), in cerebrospinal fluid and blood and the numbers of postsynaptic dopamine receptors as measured with PET. Increased levels of the metabolites would indicate excess dopamine in the brain (although the alternative explanation that they indicate excess turnover of dopamine and thus levels would be lower in the brain cannot be ruled out). The PET measures of dopamine receptors, which are based on the binding of radioactively labelled ligands to the targeted receptor, are less clear in their interpretation. Although decreased binding may reflect decreased overall numbers of receptors, it may also indicate higher occupancy, preventing the tracer docking on to the receptor. Both scenarios would be compatible with increased overall dopamine levels, because downregulation of postsynaptic receptors is a frequent cellular response to increased neurotransmitter production by presynaptic cells. Increased levels of metabolites in CSF and blood and decreased tracer binding in PET would therefore be expected if excess dopamine was present in schizophrenia. However, results of these studies were rather disappointing. Levels of the dopamine metabolites HVA and DOPAC (dihydroxyphenylacetic acid) in blood and CSF were generally normal (Trimble, 1996), and D2 receptor PET studies comparing drug naïve first episode patients to controls did not reveal consistent changes.

The most consistent evidence for increased presynaptic dopamine comes from PET studies with [18F]fluorodopa, a radioactively labelled analogue of L-dopa. Like L-dopa, it is metabolised by DOPA decarboxylase. [18F]fluorodopa uptake thus provides a measure of dopamine synthesis and storage. It was increased by up to 20% in patients with schizophrenia and schizoaffective disorder, especially in the basal ganglia but also in prefrontal cortex and amygdala (Nikolaus et al., 2009b). It is important that some of these results were obtained from unmedicated patients because increased dopamine synthesis could otherwise be interpreted as a consequence of the dopamine receptor blockade.

Changes in presynaptic regulation of dopamine release have been assessed with SPECT studies of amphetamine challenge. Amphetamines are presynaptic activators of dopamine release but have stronger effects in schizophrenia patients than controls. Again, the increased dopamine release into the synaptic cleft after administration of amphetamines cannot be measured directly, but has to be inferred from the lower binding of radiotracers to postsynaptic dopamine receptors (Laruelle et al., 1996).

Treatment with DRD2 antagonists leads to reduced binding of the radiotracer, which allows for a quantitative estimate of the proportion of receptors occupied by the drug (see Chapter 7). DRD2 occupancy levels of up to 75% were observed already with low doses of haloperidol (2–4 mg). However, questions have to remain about the mechanism through which this receptor occupancy is converted into the clinical effects because the DRD2 occupancy is normally not related to treatment response and occurs already a few hours after the first dose of the drug, although the clinical effects often take weeks to develop.

Changes in dopaminergic activity may affect different pathways to varying degrees. An influential model postulates an association between the mesolimbic dopamine system and positive symptoms and between the mesocortical system, which includes projections to prefrontal areas related to executive cognitive functions, and the negative and cognitive symptoms of schizophrenia. Specifically, hyperactivity in the mesolimbic system would contribute to positive symptoms, whereas negative symptoms and cognitive decline would be caused by a hypoactive mesocortical system. Variations of this model postulate higher noise levels and thus less efficient signalling in dopaminergic projections to prefrontal cortex. Such a model might explain why antipsychotics with strong

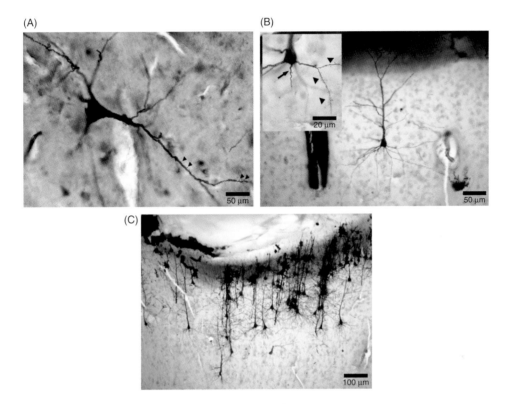

Figure 1.4, Plate I Golgi stains reveal the structure of neurons

(A) Golgi impregnation of an excitatory neuron in the basal nucleus of the amygdala. The arrows indicate the spines (sites of synapses from other neurons) on the apical dendrite.

(B) Golgi impregnation of a cortical pyramidal neuron (from layer II of area 22, a tertiary auditory field in the temporal lobe). The main image shows the selective staining of one whole neuron with all its projections against a background of many other faintly stained neurons. The Golgi method probably only stains one in a hundred or even fewer neurons. The inset shows the dendritic spines marked with triangles (as in preceding panel) and the axon marked with an arrow.

(C) View of the surrounding area of Figure 1.4(b), showing several Golgi stained pyramidal neurons in layers II and III of temporal cortex. The top of the image shows the pial surface and the bottom is at about the middle of the cortex (approx. Border between layers III and IV).

Source: Courtesy of Professor Ralf Galuske, Technische Universität Darmstadt and Max Planck Institute for Brain Research, Frankfurt, Germany.

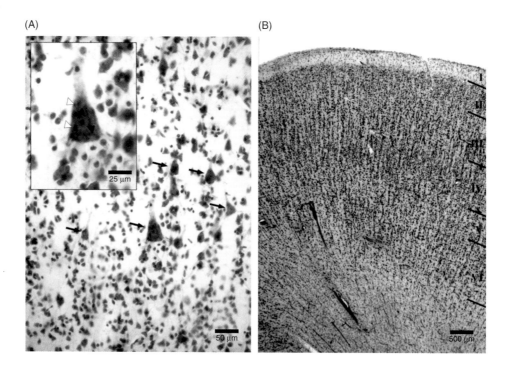

Figure 1.5, Plate II Nissl stains reveal cellular compartments

(A) Nissl stain in the cerebral cortex (area 22). The Nissl method is not selective for neurons but stains all cells. The dye, cresyl violet, binds to areas that are rich in nuclei acids (DNA and RNA). The thin arrow indicates pyramidal cells, against a background of much smaller (main circular) glia cells. The inset shows a magnification of a pyramidal cell. The filled triangle indicates the nucleus, with the nucleid acid-rich nucleolus, and the empty triangles indicate the rough endoplasmatic reticulum ('Nissl bodies'), which is covered with ribosomes, the site of protein biosynthesis.

(B) The Nissl stain reveals shape and density of neurons in cortex (area 22) and thus allows for the differentiation into layers. Note, for example, the pyramidal cells in layer III or the densely packed neurons in layer IV. A prominent layer IV is typical of sensory areas and receives afferents from the periphery or from earlier cortical areas.

Source: Courtesy of Professor Ralf Galuske, Technische Universität Darmstadt and Max Planck Institute for Brain Research, Frankfurt, Germany.

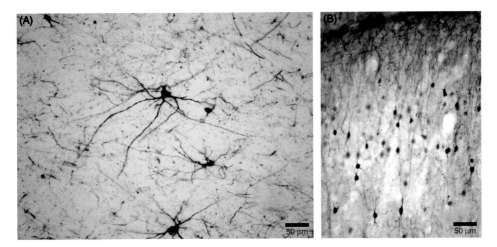

Figure 1.6, Plate II Immunohistochemical staining identifies specific types of neurons through molecular markers

(A) Inhibitory interneurons containing the calcium-binding protein parvalbumin in the basal nucleus of the amygdala.

(B) Inhibitory interneurons containing the calcium-binding protein calbindin in layers II/III of area 22. In both cases, the dye is coupled with antibodies to the protein of interest and thus selectively stains the neurons that contain this protein.

Source: Courtesy of Professor Ralf Galuske, Technische Universität Darmstadt and Max Planck Institute for Brain Research, Frankfurt, Germany.

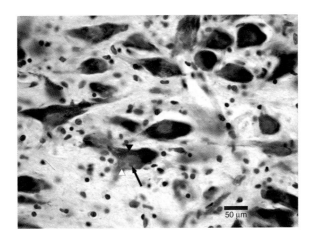

Figure 1.7, Plate III Nissl stain of the substantia nigra, pars compacta

Three types of cells can be distinguished: the small, circular glia cells, larger neurons with active protein synthesis in the soma and adjacent parts of dendrites, and neurons (white triangle, with black arrow pointing to its nucleus) that contain melanin (brown/black, black triangle), which indicates dopamine synthesis.

Source: Courtesy of Professor Ralf Galuske, Technische Universität Darmstadt and Max Planck Institute for Brain Research, Frankfurt, Germany.

(A)   (B)

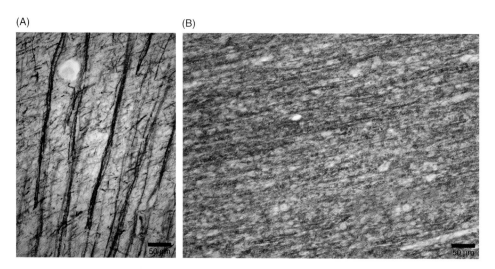

Figure 1.8, Plate III Silver impregnation of myelin sheaths
(A) Cortical axonal fibres (layer V of area 22).
(B) Subcortical fibre tracts. Note that axons and myelin sheaths are more densely packed in subcortical white matter. The preferred direction of fibres in a region of WM can be picked up non-invasively with Diffusion Tensor Imaging (DTI).

Source: Courtesy of Professor Ralf Galuske, Technische Universität Darmstadt and Max Planck Institute for Brain Research, Frankfurt, Germany.

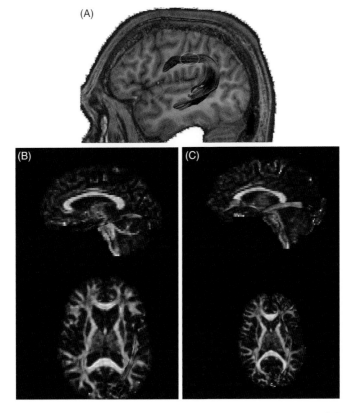

Figure 1.20, Plate IV Diffusion tensor imaging (DTI) reveals the fibre tracts of the brain
(A) The arcuate fascicle connects the frontal operculum with the planum temporale (PT) in the superior temporal gyrus and the area around the superior temporal sulcus (STS). In the dominant hemisphere it thus links the frontal with the temporal language areas. Reconstruction from Diffusion Tensor Imaging data against the background of a T1-weighted MRI (magnetic resonance imaging) scan of a brain.
(B) The inferior longitudinal fascicle connects the anterior temporal and the occipital lobes.
(C) The inferior fronto-occipital fascicle connects the frontal and occipital lobes. The front of the brain is left (on sagittal slices) or up (on axial slices).

Source: Courtesy of Dr Anna Rotarska-Jagiela, Frankfurt University (a) and Professor Derek Jones and Tim Vivian-Griffiths, Cardiff University (b, c).

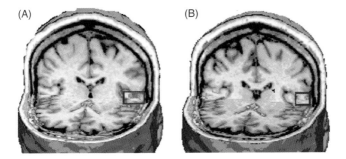

Figure 2.11, Plate V An example of fMRI mapping of brain correlates of psychopathology
In this experiment, patients with chronic schizophrenia were investigated with fMRI while they were experiencing auditory verbal hallucinations and reported their duration via button press. The brain maps show activity in auditory cortex during auditory hallucinations (A) and while listening to speech (B).

Source: Adapted from Dierks et al. (1999), with kind permission from Elsevier.

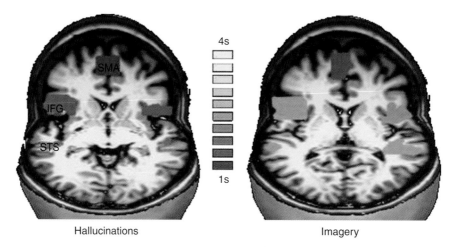

Hallucinations   Imagery

Figure 10.1, Plate V The brain networks of hallucinations and imagery investigated with fMRI
In this experiment, people with non-clinical hallucinations were investigated with fMRI while they were experiencing auditory verbal hallucinations (left). For comparison, control participants were scanned during active auditory imagery. The colour bar denotes the sequence of events (from 1 to 4 seconds) from a button press, by which the participant had indicated onset of hallucination. Activation of SMA (supplementary motor area), IFG (inferior frontal gyrus) and STS (superior temporal sulcus) was almost instantaneous, whereas there was a progression from frontal to temporal areas during auditory imagery, which was under participants' control (Linden et al., 2011).

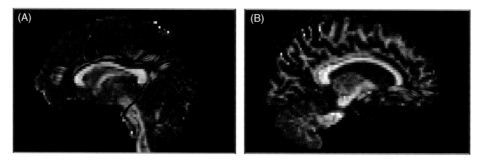

Figure 12.1, Plate VI Fibre tracts connecting important emotion centres
Diffusion Tensor Imaging (DTI) shows the cingulum (A) and the uncinate fasciculus (B), the main direct connections between the frontal lobe and the limbic system.

Source: Courtesy of Professor Derek Jones and Luke Dustan, Cardiff University, UK.

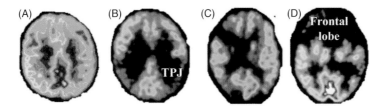

Figure 20.1, Plate VII PET distinguishes different types of dementia

Maps of glucose metabolism, measured with FDG-PET, in (A) a healthy control (aged 55), (B) a patient with Alzheimer's Disease (AD) (60), (C) a patient with vascular dementia (VD) (50) and (D) a patient with frontotemporal dementia (FTD) (69). Note that hypometabolism is most marked in the temporoparietal junction (TPJ) in AD and in the frontal lobe in FTD, but more diffuse in VD.

(A) Amyloid plaque   (B) Neurofibrillary tangle

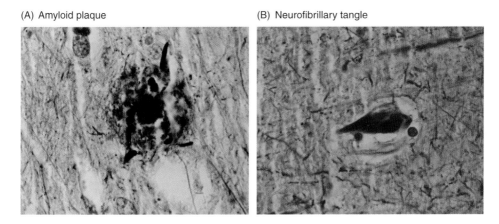

Figure 20.2, Plate VII Neuropathology of Alzheimer's Disease

(A) This silver stain after Bielschowsky shows intercellular amyloid accumulation ('senile plaque'). (B) The same staining technique shows a neurofibrillary tangle within a neuron.

Source: Courtesy of Professor C. Harker Rhodes, Dartmouth Medical School, USA.

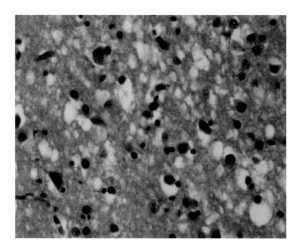

Figure 20.5, Plate VIII Neuropathology of CJD
Post-mortem brain slice from the cerebral cortex of a patient with CJD stained with haematoxylin-eosin. Haematoxylin (purple) stains DNA and RNA-rich tissue such as the nuclei, eosin stains protein-rich tissue such as cytoplasm and axons. Note the large vacuoles (literally empty spaces) within neurons that are characteristic of spongiform encephalopathy.
Source: Courtesy of Professor C. Harker Rhodes, Dartmouth Medical School, USA.

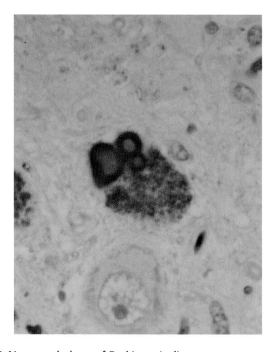

Figure 20.6, Plate VIII Neuropathology of Parkinson's disease
This post-mortem brain slice shows in the centre of the figure a Lewy body stained with histochemistry for its main molecular component, synuclein.
Source: Courtesy of Professor C. Harker Rhodes, Dartmouth Medical School, USA.

antidopaminergic effects can worsen negative and cognitive symptoms because they would further attenuate signalling in the mesocortical pathway. Although it may seem paradoxical that one dopamine pathway is over- and another under-activated, such differential effects are neuroanatomically plausible. Regulation by the glutamate system is one possible mechanism because glutamatergic cortico-tegmental input may regulate the VTA cells with limbic and neocortical projections differentially. However, little evidence has so far been obtained for such a differential dopamine model. Furthermore, the hope that partial dopamine agonists such as aripiprazole or 5-HT$_{2A}$ antagonists, which could theoretically have differential secondary effects on dopamine pathways (Chapter 7), would improve negative symptoms substantially has so far not materialised.

10.6.2   Serotonin system

The often severe and disabling motor side effects of the first generation of 'typical' antipsychotic drugs such as haloperidol led to the development of a new generation of 'atypical' antipsychotic agents, which have fewer extrapyramidal side effects, although clozapine is the only one where such motor side effects are negligible. This lower risk of motor side effects, which came at the cost of other side effects such as weight gain or rare cases of agranulocytosis, was related to lower specificity of the atypical antipsychotics for the D$_2$ receptor. These have a wider receptor binding profile than the typical antipsychotics, including in most cases antagonism at the 5-HT$_{2A}$ receptor. This serotonin antagonism has been implicated in the clinical efficacy of the atypical antipsychotics and led to pathophysiological models that allow for a contribution of multiple neurotransmitter systems to the neurochemical imbalance of schizophrenia. A potential role of serotonin hyperactivity would conform to the findings from experimentally induced psychoses, although the syndrome induced by the serotonin agonist LSD with prominent visual hallucinations and feelings of time dilation only remotely resembles schizophrenia. Post-mortem studies revealed lower expression of 5-HT$_{2A}$, but higher expression of 5-HT$_{1A}$ receptors in frontal cortex. Although such findings point to alterations in the serotonin system in schizophrenia, they have to be treated with caution because they are absent in young unmedicated patients and may only occur in the course of the illness (Harrison, 1999).

10.6.3   Glutamate system

Antagonists of the NMDA receptor such as phencyclidine (PCP) or ketamine produce the psychotic syndrome which perhaps most closely resembles schizophrenia, including its disorganised features. Reduced levels of glutamate or reduced or dysfunctional NMDA receptors have therefore been suggested as a pathophysiological feature of schizophrenia. Reduced glutamate levels have indeed been found in the CSF of patients with schizophrenia, and post-mortem studies showed that the main sites of glutamate reduction were in the hippocampus and the PFC. These findings were supported through in vivo studies of the glutamate metabolite N-acetyl-aspartate (NAA) with magnetic resonance spectroscopy (MRS) (Goff and Coyle, 2001). Glutamate receptors other than the NMDA receptor have also been studied in schizophrenia. Post-mortem studies showed reduced non-NMDA receptors in the medial temporal lobe (Harrison, 1999). Some evidence for lower expression of functionally relevant subunits of NMDA, AMPA and kainate receptors, mainly in hippocampus and thalamus, came from a study by Ibrahim and colleagues (Ibrahim et al., 2000). The reduced expression in the thalamus mainly concerned the dorsomedial nucleus, which is linked to PFC, and the centromedial nucleus, which connects to the limbic system. It thus affected those parts of the thalamus that are connected to brain systems that are implicated in the cognitive and emotional deficits of schizophrenia. There is also some intriguing evidence for a selectively reduced expression of the NR1 subunit of the NMDA receptor, which is crucial for its role in neural plasticity, in the hippocampus of schizophrenia patients.

The functional and behavioural consequences of under-expression of receptors or their subunits can be investigated with transgenic animals. Transgenic mice that produced only 5% of normal NR1 subunit levels were socially isolated, hyperactive and showed motor stereotypes. Although these behavioural abnormalities are not specific to schizophrenia and could equally occur in anxiety disorders, an intriguing link to schizophrenia is provided by the response to antipsychotic drugs in these animals (Goff and Coyle, 2001). This indicates that some of the clinical effects of antipsychotics are mediated by their interaction with the glutamate system. Although it is very difficult to provide direct evidence for this hypothesis, there is some indirect evidence from both human and animal experiments. Antipsychotic drugs, particularly atypicals, have been shown to reverse the behavioural (e.g. reduced prepulse inhibition) and neural (e.g. neurodegeneration) effects of NMDA antagonists. The molecular basis for such effects is still unknown, but both interactions between the dopamine and glutamate systems and direct agonism at the glycine binding site of the NMDA receptor have been proposed.

The growing evidence for glutamatergic deficits in schizophrenia motivated therapeutic trials with glutamate agonists. Agonists at the glycine binding site of the NMDA receptor (glycine, D-Serine, D-Cycloserine) and agonists at the AMPA receptor (ampakines) were added to neuroleptic treatment, with some encouraging effects on negative symptoms and cognitive performance. However, larger trials are needed to confirm their clinical effects. Direct agonists at the NMDA receptor are not suitable for clinical trials because of risk of excitotoxic neuronal damage and seizures. If the preliminary reports of reduction of negative symptoms and cognitive deficit under indirect NMDA enhancement with glycine analogues or ampakines are confirmed, these agents may ultimately come to have a place in pharmacotherapy as add-on to antipsychotics. Conversely, there is currently no prospect for their use as monotherapy because no effects on positive symptoms have hitherto been demonstrated.

10.6.4   GABA system

GABA is the main inhibitory neurotransmitter of the brain, and most inhibitory interneurons are GABAergic. Several studies have suggested alterations of the GABA system in the brains of patients with schizophrenia, providing evidence of a dysfunction of inhibitory interneurons. Post-mortem studies on brains of schizophrenia patients have shown reduced expression of the GAD67 gene, which codes for the 67-kD (kiloDalton) isoform of glutamic acid decarboxylase, which catalyses the synthesis of GABA (Chapter 2). Reduced concentrations of the GABA transporter 1 (GAT-1) were also observed. The reduced synthesis and reuptake of GABA mainly seems to affect the subset of interneurons (about 25%) in prefrontal cortex that contain parvalbumin, a calcium binding protein, which was also reduced in some layers of prefrontal cortex. These include the chandelier cells that form synapses onto axons of pyramidal neurons and modulate their spiking activity. Reductions in parvalbumin mRNA (but not in numbers of parvalbumin-expressing neurons) were also observed in specific layers of prefrontal cortex. This suggests that although numbers of interneurons may not be reduced in

Figure 10.2

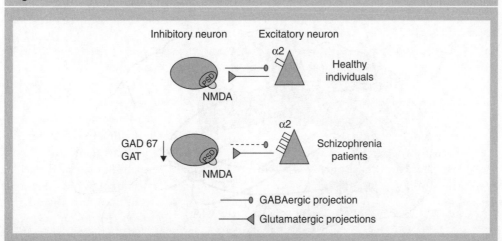

Inhibitory neuron   Excitatory neuron

Healthy individuals

NMDA

GAD 67 ↓
GAT

Schizophrenia patients

NMDA

──● GABAergic projection

──◁ Glutamatergic projections

Putative alterations of GABA signaling in PFC in schizophrenia

Top: Parvalbumin (PV)-containing interneurons (e.g. chandelier cells) inhibit excitatory pyramidal neurons through the release of GABA. The inhibitory interneurons are themselves regulated by gluatamatergic input, for example through NMDA receptors, from the excitatory neurons. In controls, the inhibitory neuron maintains sufficient GABA release and the excitatory neuron sufficient glutamate release to balance inhibition with excitation. Bottom: In individuals with schizophrenia, decreased NMDA receptor signalling alters the monitoring function of the inhibitory neuron, which downregulates its output, disinhibiting the excitatory neuron. This process is compounded by reductions in GABA-related proteins (PV, GAD 67, GAT1) and upregulation of GABA$_A$ receptor α2-subunits on the pyramidal neurons.

Source: Adapted from (Haenschel and Linden, 2011) with kind permission of Elsevier.

schizophrenia, they might be less effective. Such disturbed interneuron functioning may also contribute to the deficits in high frequency oscillatory activity discussed above.

Two main mechanisms have been proposed for the alterations in interneuron circuits in schizophrenia (Lewis et al., 2005). Reduced neurotrophin signalling through the TrkB receptor (see Chapter 7) may lead to reduced expression of GABA-related proteins. The TrkB receptor is expressed at particularly high levels on parvalbumin containing interneurons. Another mechanism may be through reduced glutamatergic signalling, particularly through the NMDA receptor. Administration of NMDA antagonists can lead to reduced levels of parvalbumin. This is an interesting example of potential links between the glutamate and GABA systems, which is important for pathophysiological models that are based on the interaction between these two NT systems (Figure 10.2).

10.6.5 Interactions between excitatory and inhibitory circuits

The dopaminergic neurons of the VTA that project to limbic areas (mesolimbic pathway) and the nucleus accumbens are under the control of glutamatergic inputs, GABAergic interneurons and several neuromodulators such as serotonin and CRF (Geisler and Wise, 2008). Assuming that the net effect of glutamatergic afferents to the VTA would be inhibitory (through interneuron activation), lower glutamatergic activity could lead to disinhibition of

Figure 10.3

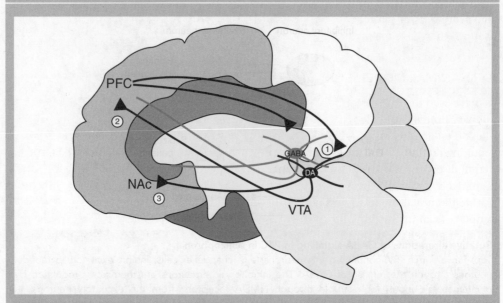

Interactions between glutamatergic, GABAergic and dopaminergic neurons in prefrontal cortex (PFC), ventral tegmental area (VTA) and nucleus accumbens (NAc)
Direct excitatory (glutamatergic) input from PFC onto DA neurons in the VTA that project back to PFC may constitute a positive feedback loop (1,2). Lack of glutamatergic activity in schizophrenia could then lead to hypoactivity in the mesocortical DA pathway (from VTA to PFC), which has been postulated as a mechanism of negative and cognitive symptoms. Activation of GABAergic projections to NAc (3) could have various effects, including the inhibition of cholinergic or dopaminergic cells in NAc, affecting motivational processes. Additional modulation (not shown) of mesocortical and striatal pathways may come from PFC indirectly through deeper brainstem structures, for example the pedunculopontine tegmentum.

the mesolimbic/mesostriatal pathway. At the same time, it might lead to attenuated activity of the mesocortical pathway because the VTA neurons that project to the cortex are under direct control of glutamatergic neurons and would thus receive less excitatory input. Dysfunction of the glutamate system could thus explain the putative imbalance between different dopamine pathways in schizophrenia. However, although the reciprocal projections between cortex and VTA seem to be relatively homogeneously glutamatergic (Carr and Sesack, 2000), the picture is far more complicated for the subcortico-mesolimbic-subcortico circuits. Furthermore, the roles of the inhibitory interneurons in the VTA and the GABAergic projections from VTA to the nucleus accumbens (NAc), which are both under the control of prefrontal glutamatergic input, are still unclear (Figure 10.3). Such a model of differential effects of glutamate on mesolimbic/mesostriatal vs. mesocortical dopaminergic pathways is thus still very speculative.

Glutamatergic projections from prefrontal cortex to the VTA and, directly or indirectly through the VTA, to limbic areas and the ventral striatum have also been implicated in the modulation of the dopaminergic stress response (Moghaddam, 2002). In this model, chronic stress leads to glutamatergic hypofunction in the PFC, which in turn has the net effect of reducing dopamine release in response to stress. This may explain some of the clinical features of relapse in addiction and of psychosis. Finally, lack of glutamatergic activation of inhibitory interneurons has been suggested to make the thalamus less effective as a sensory filter, thus facilitating flooding by sensory information that may be involved the perceptual and paranoid symptoms of schizophrenia. Direct GABAergic deficits are also a possible mechanism, although they have mainly been documented for the cortex rather than the thalamus.

10.7   ANIMAL MODELS

We have seen in Chapter 5 that it will never be straightforward to design animal models of complex human traits, let alone of mental disorders. After all, most psychiatric diagnosis relies on talking to patients about their thoughts and feelings, and this avenue is closed to us in our interaction with animals. Investigators therefore have to explore surrogate markers of mental disorders that tap into observable behaviour or biological measures and that can be exhibited by rodents. Schizophrenia is probably the mental disorder that is most difficult to capture in animal models. Most of its core symptoms are related to language, thought and complex social interaction and thus only accessible in humans. Efforts have therefore concentrated on behavioural features that are often associated with positive or negative symptoms. In the case of schizophrenia, candidate phenotypes include prepulse inhibition (PPI), electrophysiological markers of auditory gating and working memory deficits (Geyer, 2008). Healthy people normally show PPI of the auditory startle response, that is, they are less startled by novel sounds if they are closely preceded by a warning sound. In schizophrenia, this startle inhibition is often reduced. This effect may not be very closely related to the symptoms of schizophrenia or predict its course (Swerdlow et al., 2008), but it has the very attractive feature of being easily replicated in rodent models. Assuming that PPI is a trait of schizophrenia, these rodents would then show a behavioural feature of this mental disorder, whose biological correlates and response to treatment could then be further investigated.

Hyperlocomotion (moving about excessively and aimlessly under stress) can be regarded as a model of psychomotor agitation. Along similar lines, decreased interaction with conspecifics may be interpreted as analogue of social withdrawal, or decreased reinforcement by rewards as one of anhedonia. In the cognitive field, deficits of working memory or attention can be directly observed in animals, but these are much less specific for schizophrenia. One approach would then be to design animals with circumscribed behavioural or cognitive abnormalities that bear resemblance to features of schizophrenia and then assess them for possible biological differences.

Research so far has rather taken the converse approach, to design animal models based on putative pharmacological features of schizophrenia, such as dopamine receptor overexpression, psychostimulant supersensitivity or glutamate receptor deficits, or target genes implicated in the disorder. This work has provided partial support for both the dopamine and the glutamate model of schizophrenia. For example, transgenic mice with striatal DRD2 over-expression showed deficits in tasks associated with frontal lobe function (Kellendonk et al., 2006). But then, such an approach goes little further than studies of model psychoses in humans, where it is demonstrated that a particular neurochemical change can induce certain symptoms, which by no means proves that it has to be the mechanism that operates in schizophrenia. At least, if researchers induce symptoms resembling schizophrenia in animals by some pharmacological modification, they can use a much wider range of techniques to investigate the intermediate mechanisms than would be possible in humans.

The design of animal models by gene locus is potentially of higher aetiological relevance. If a gene that has been associated with schizophrenia is knocked out or otherwise manipulated and this leads to relevant symptoms, this can corroborate the association between the gene and the disorder. Moreover, such an approach allows researchers to investigate the mechanism of gene action by the analysis of downstream molecular and cellular effects. Even mouse models that do not affect risk alleles may help to identify new target alleles for research. The mouse model of Akt1-deficiency is a case in point (Akt1 is a protein involved in postsynaptic signalling cascades triggered by activation of DRD2 and neurotrophins, see Section 7.4.4). These mice showed increased psychostimulant sensitivity, as demonstrated by larger reductions of prepulse inhibition after administration of amphetamine. This association with a putative schizophrenia phenotype led to the search for genetic associations, which has produced preliminary evidence for association between schizophrenia and variants of the Akt1 gene (Arguello and Gogos, 2008).

The mouse models that were based on direct manipulation of risk alleles also produced chemical and behavioural features associated with schizophrenia. As mentioned above (Section 10.3), a region on the long arm of chromosome 22 has been identified as locus of risk alleles. Mouse models were constructed both for the deletion of part of chromosome 22 (22q11 microdeletion) and for some of the specific genes located there. Both the microdeletion of the entire locus and the knock-down (incomplete loss of function) of proline dehydrogenase resulted in memory impairment and abnormal PPI, as well as some of the neurochemical changes implicated in schizophrenia. Likewise, mice with NRG-1 knock-outs show both relevant neurochemical (reduced expression of NMDA receptors) and behavioural (reduced PPI) features. A mouse model of another currently favoured susceptibility locus, DISC (Disrupted in Schizophrenia)-1 on 1q42, yielded a working memory deficit but not the changes in neural migration expected on the basis of in vitro and developmental models (Arguello and Gogos, 2006).

Animal models can play an important role both in identifying the downstream functional effects of susceptibility genes and providing new candidate loci for association studies. However, they depend on the quality and specificity of the behavioural markers employed ('face validity'). If the behavioural markers of positive or negative symptoms reflect consequences rather than core components of the relevant symptom, their absence in a mouse model will not necessarily signify that the modelled gene does not contribute to schizophrenia. Conversely, if mutant mice show a particular behaviour, such as increased locomotion, this does not necessarily entail a functional relationship with the symptom of interest because the behavioural feature, although associated with the symptom, may constitute a non-specific reaction type. Consider the example of increased locomotion, which is a behavioural feature of a wide range of symptoms of disorders as diverse as schizophrenia, agitated depression, anxiety or ADHD. Furthermore, these behavioural reaction types may be results of convergent evolution rather than homology and thus reveal little about the underlying biology in humans.

10.8   TREATMENT

10.8.1   Antipsychotic drugs control psychotic symptoms by dopamine - receptor antagonism

Antipsychotics are drugs that reduce or control the symptoms of psychosis. Although the so-called positive (or classical psychotic) symptoms like hallucinations and paranoia often respond well to antipsychotic treatment, the effects are less clear on the negative and cognitive symptoms. This is one of the three main current challenges of antipsychotic drug therapy. The others are reduction of side effects/increase of compliance and differential therapy,

Figure 10.4

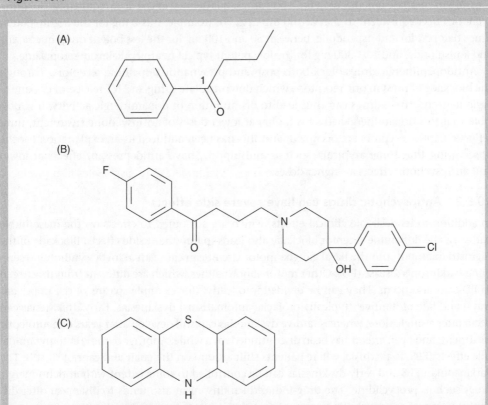

Examples of butyrophenone and tricyclic antipsychotics
(A) Basic structure of butyrophenone with a phenyl ring (left) and the 4-carbon butyryl chain with a ketone group at carbon 1. (B) Several substitutions of this basic structure lead to haloperidol. (C) Phenothiazines have a characteristic tricyclic structure, with two phenyl rings linked by a sulphur and a nitrogen bridge.

which presupposes rational tools for the decision about which drug will help which patient. Both these challenges address clinically significant issues because patients often just do not take the prescribed antipsychotic medication (non-compliance) because of side effects. Furthermore, many patients do not respond to the first drug they are prescribed and require treatment courses with several antipsychotics to get a clinical benefit.

Chemically, the first generation of antipsychotic drugs were butyrophenones, phenothiazines or thioxanthenes. The last two groups were collectively named 'tricyclic antipsychotics' because of their basic structure (Figure 10.4). The second and third generation atypical antipsychotics are chemically more heterogeneous, but many of them also have a tricyclic core.

All current antipsychotics are dopamine antagonists. They all bind to the D_2 receptor with varying affinity, and some have high affinity for other subtypes. For example, clozapine has higher affinity for the D_4 than D_2 receptor. The affinity of the 'typical' or first-generation antipsychotics or neuroleptics to the D_2 receptor is directly related to their potency. Drugs with higher affinity (lower K_i) have higher potency, meaning that a lower dose is required for the same antipsychotic effect. The 'chlorpromazine [CPZ] equivalent' has been established as a useful measure to compare potency of neuroleptic drugs. It is defined as the dose required for an antipsychotic effect equivalent to that of 100 mg CPZ. For example, it is 2 mg for the highly potent drugs haloperidol and risperidone, between 50 and 100 mg for the less potent drugs quetiapine and amisulpride, and 150–300 mg for the low potent typical neuroleptic levomepromazine.

Antidopaminergic drugs block both post- and presynaptic dopamine receptors. Through the blockade of presynaptic receptors, which downregulate firing and NT release of dopaminergic neurons, these drugs can thus lead to disinhibition of dopaminergic activity. It is possible that this dopaminergic effect is higher at lower doses of antipsychotic treatment, until all presynaptic receptors are occupied, and this has been adduced as an explanation for the observation that some atypicals, such as amisulpride, have antidepressant effects at lower and antipsychotic effects at higher doses.

10.8.2   Antipsychotic drugs can have severe side effects

In addition to its desirable clinical effects, which are attributed to effects on the mesolimbic pathway, the dopamine receptor blockade also leads to important side effects. Blockade of the nigrostriatal input into the basal ganglia motor circuit can cause an akinetic syndrome resembling Parkinson's disease (PD). Other motor abnormalities, which are different from those seen in PD, can also occur. They can be divided into 'early' (for example spasms of the upper airways) and late or 'tardive' (typically orofacial automatisms) dyskinesias. Early dyskinesias can occur after a single dose, whereas tardive dyskinesias can still develop after years of neuroleptic treatment, and even after it has been discontinued for a while. Another of these extrapyramidal side effects (EPS) is akathisia, where patients shift around on the chair and cannot sit still. The Parkinsonian EPS and early dyskinesias can be controlled to some extent with anticholinergic drugs such as procyclidine. The drug-induced Parkinsonism also tends to disappear after discontinuation of antipsychotic treatment, but this is often not a practical option. Conversely, akathisia and tardive dyskinesias tend to persist after discontinuation of treatment and do not respond well to pharmacological intervention, although beta-blockers can be tried for akathisia. Akathisia is not specific to neuroleptic treatment and can also be a side effect of antidepressant treatment and withdrawal, and the withdrawal from illicit drugs.

Neuroleptic malignant syndrome (NMS) is a life-threatening rare complication that can arise after treatment with all antipsychotic drugs. Its classic triad consists of rigidity, impaired consciousness and autonomic dysregulation (e.g. fever, tachycardia, sweating). It is also accompanied by characteristic laboratory parameters, such as increased creatine kinase levels in blood. Treatment in the intensive care unit is required and includes discontinuation of the antipsychotic, intravenous fluids and administration of the muscle relaxant dantrolene. Dantrolene blocks the ryanodine receptor on the sarcoplasmic reticulum. Activation of this receptor promotes the release of calcium into the cytosol of muscle cells through a mechanism paralleling that mediated by IP3 (see Chapter 7).

The mechanism behind NMS is unclear. Antipsychotics can affect cellular excitability in other ways as well. All antipsychotics can decrease the seizure threshold, which means that epileptic seizures can be triggered more easily, or even occur spontaneously. Fortunately, this is relatively rare compared to the high rate (up to a third for clozapine and olanzapine) of patients who show subclinical changes in their EEG. Changes in cardiac excitability have also been reported under all antipsychotics. Of most concern is the prolongation of the QT interval of the electrocardiogram (ECG), which can lead to life-threatening arrhythmias. This is the reason for the need to monitor the ECG in patients on antipsychotic treatment.

The blockade of dopamine receptors in the anterior pituitary leads to disinhibition of prolactin release, which stimulates milk production by the breasts. This can be experienced as a particularly unpleasant side effect by both female and male patients. Antipsychotics with antiserotonergic properties have this effect less because serotonin stimulates the lactotroph (see Chapter 3) and thus acts antagonistically to dopamine on prolactin release. There is also some evidence that antidopaminergic medication has a negative effect on cognition, although this is difficult to disentangle from the progressive effects of schizophrenia itself. This effect is thought to be mediated through dopamine receptor blockade on the meso-cortical pathway from the dopaminergic midbrain (VTA) to prefrontal cortex.

10.8.3   Atypical antipsychotic drugs have fewer motor side effects

The main reason for these side effects is that antidopaminergic agents that enter the brain from the blood circulation do not act in a spatially specific fashion and will thus disrupt dopamine effects both in the desired and undesired locations. One potential way around this problem is the use of partial agonists (see Chapter 6), which would have an antagonistic effect where dopamine concentrations are (too) high, and an agonistic effect where they may be (too) low. Because some models of schizophrenia posit an imbalance of dopamin-ergic activity between the mesolimbic (too high) and mesocortical system (too low) partial agonists, such as aripiprazole, may be effective antipsychotics with fewer side effects. They may also increase rather than decrease frontal dopaminergic activity and thus improve neg-ative and cognitive symptoms. However, the observed clinical effects of these drugs are less clear cut.

Another strategy is to influence dopamine release indirectly through the glutamate sys-tem. NMDA receptor activity suppresses dopamine release in the mesolimbic system but promotes it in prefrontal cortex, which may explain some of the similarities between model psychoses induced by the NMDA antagonists ketamine and PCP and schizophrenia.

The most important development so far in the quest to reduce the side effects of antipsy-chotic drugs has been the introduction of the so-called 'atypical antipsychotics'. These drugs are 'dirtier' than the typical neuroleptics in that they have effects on many NT systems in addition to dopamine. Most of the atypical antipsychotics are also antagonists at the 5-HT_{2A} receptor, and antagonism at 5-HT_{2C}, muscarinic, alpha-2-adrenergic and histaminergic receptors is also found frequently. Although this broader pharmacological profile brings scope for additional side effects, for example weight gain through histamine antagonism and several metabolic abnormalities through muscarinic antagonism, it may also explain why atypical antipsychotics at clinically effective doses carry a much lower risk of antidopaminergic side effects.

10.8.4   The dual mode of action of atypical antipsychotics: dopamine–serotonin interactions

The current model of atypical antipsychotic action posits that their ability to control psychotic symptoms with lower levels of EPS and their putative benefit for negative symptoms depend on the indirect dopamine agonism inherent in the blockade of 5-HT_{2A} receptors. Stimulation of 5-HT_{2A} heteroreceptors on dopaminergic neurons inhibits dopamine release. Thus, 5-HT_{2A} receptor blockade leads to higher dopamine levels. This dopamine-releasing effect can mod-ulate the general antidopaminergic effect of antipsychotics in two important ways. It would increase the relative activity of D_1-type receptors, which are blocked with less affinity by most

Figure 10.5

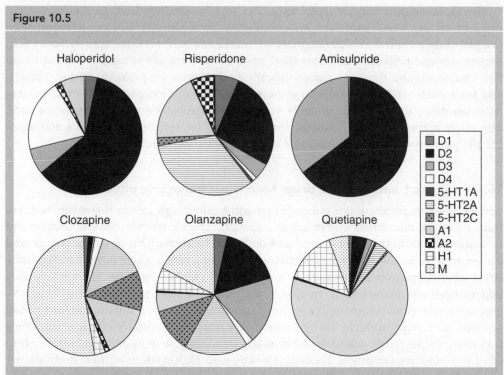

Receptor affinity profile of selected antipsychotic drugs
The pie charts show the relative affinity (1/K$_i$) of different antipsychotic drugs to neurotransmitter receptors. Note that haloperidol, a representative of the butyrophenone class, but also some of the 'atypical' antipsychotics (especially amisulpride) have very strong affinity for dopamine receptors, whereas others (risperidone, olanzapine and particularly clozapine) have relatively more affinity for serotonin receptors. The affinity profile also explains some of the side effects (e.g., note clozapine's high affinity for muscarinic receptors, which is matched by prominent anticholinergic side effects). It is worth remembering, however, that there are many different ways of measuring receptor affinities (e.g. in vivo vs. in vitro) and estimates can vary considerably across studies (for example for quetiapine and the alpha-1 adrenergic receptor, where lower affinities have also been reported).
Source: Data compiled from Arnt and Skarsfeldt(1998) and the PDSP K$_i$ database.

antipsychotics, over D$_2$-type receptors and it could lead to relatively higher dopaminergic tone in areas with higher serotonergic innervation. However, it is not yet known whether one or both of these mechanisms indeed contribute to the differences in clinical effects between typical and atypical antipsychotics. Indirect interactions between the serotonin and dopamine systems, for example through GABAergic interneurons, may also play a role (Di Giovanni et al., 2010).

10.8.5 Atypical antipsychotics have more anticholinergic side effects

Most atypical antipsychotics have higher relative affinity to muscarinic receptors than the typical neuroleptics (Figure 10.5) and thus cause more anticholinergic side effects at clinical doses. Blockade of muscarinic receptors disrupts signal transmission from parasympathetic neurons of the ANS to their effector organs, and thus any parasympathetic function can be affected. Muscarinic blockade has less effect on the sympathetic nervous system because the signal transmission in the autonomic ganglia uses mainly the nicotinic receptor, and sympathetic signalling to effector organs occurs through adrenergic receptors. Because the parasympathetic part of the ANS slows down the heart and promotes digestive processes, muscarinic blockade can result in tachycardia, reduced salivation, urinary retention and blockade of bowel movements. Anticholinergic drugs can also dilate the pupil (mydriasis) and lead to increased intraocular pressure (through blockade of the contraction of the ciliary muscle), which is dangerous in people with pre-existing narrow-angle glaucoma. Central anticholinergic effects can include disruption of cognitive functions, especially in the elderly, loss of balance, perceptual disturbance and even delirium. The central anti-cholinergic syndrome is a life-threatening complication of treatment with antimuscarinic substances. It can occur after intoxication but even after normal dosage, for example in slow metabolisers. It is characterised by any combination of vegetative parasympathetic symptoms and neuropsychiatric symptoms, which can include delirium and agitation but also impaired consciousness, even coma. Discontinuation of the anticholinergic drug and intensive care therapy are required. Anticholinergic side effects also occur after treatment with other muscarine receptor-blocking drugs, for example tricyclic antidepressants or the anticholinergic drugs used in the treatment of Parkinson's disease or drug-induced Parkinsonism.

10.8.6 Patients on antipsychotic treatment need to be monitored for metabolic syndrome

Weight gain of over 10% is a common side effect, particularly of atypical antipsychotic drugs. For example, it affects up to 40% of patients on clozapine or olanzapine and can severely compromise their willingness to take their prescription (compliance). The increase in weight does not seem to depend on the dose of the antipsychotic. Patients can also develop a fully-fledged metabolic syndrome, defined by the presence of three of the following criteria: obesity, increased fasting glucose, increased triglycerides (blood fatty acids), reduced HDL cholesterol (the form of cholesterol that reduces cardiovascular risk) and increased blood pressure. The metabolic syndrome is an important risk factor for the development of cardiovascular disease, for example heart attack, or diabetes mellitus. Patients with schizophrenia seem to have higher risk for metabolic syndrome anyway, compounded probably by their life-style (e.g. high rates of smoking), which is further increased by antipsychotic treatment, although it is presently not clear whether this is indeed higher after treatment with atypicals. Careful monitoring of metabolic and cardiovascular parameters is paramount during any antipsychotic treatment. The mechanism for these metabolic changes is unclear, but M_3 receptor antagonism has been implicated.

Diabetic ketoacidosis (DKA) and hyperglycaemic hyperosmolar syndrome (HHS) are rare medical emergencies that can be triggered by the use of atypical antipsychotics. DKA is a complication of diabetes, but can also be triggered in those with hitherto undetected diabetes or insulin resistance. Clinical symptoms are similar to those of other hyperglycaemic (with increased blood glucose levels) states and include nausea, vomiting, thirst, excessive passing of urine and abdominal pain. Ketones in blood and urine and blood acidosis are characteristic chemical features. HHS affects mainly older people suffering from type 2 diabetes mellitus and has a more insidious onset, which may include progressive deterioration of consciousness. Its characteristic laboratory findings include very high levels of blood glucose and high blood osmolarity. Both DKA and HHS can be fatal unless treated urgently with insulin and may require intensive care unit admission. Although they are rare complications of anti-psychotic treatment and occur far more often in other contexts, clinical psychiatrists have to be aware of them, and they exemplify the need to monitor metabolic states in patients on antipsychotics, particularly in those treated with atypical agents.

10.8.7   Different atypical antipsychotics have different side effect profiles

Amongst the commonly used atypicals, only clozapine has a negligible risk of EPS. Amisulpride and risperidone, in particular, can cause EPS in a dose-dependent manner. Ziprasidone and aripiprazole both have a relatively low risk of inducing metabolic syndrome and of anticholinergic side effects because of their low affinity to muscarinic receptors. Conversely, the incidence of weight gain and anticholinergic side effects is particularly high under clozapine and olanzapine. All antipsychotics can lower the seizure threshold, particularly the tricyclic antipsychotics and clozapine. Clozapine has the highest potential for seizure induction, and the cumulative risk after long-term treatment has been estimated to be up to 10%. This is an example of a dose-dependent side effect, where both the daily and the cumulative dose play a role in determining the risk. Other 'idiosyncratic' side effects are non-dose-dependent, and their occurrence seems to be determined by individual, unknown, mechanisms. A rare, life-threatening idiosyncratic side effect of clozapine is agranulocytosis (suppression of the production of white blood cells), which makes close monitoring of full blood counts necessary. Because of these side effects and monitoring requirements, clozapine, which is clinically rather effective, is normally considered only after one or two other antipsychotics have not produced a clinical effect. The choice of antipsychotic for a particular patient is normally made by weighing the particular clinical needs (e.g. severity of positive vs. negative symptoms, need for sedation) against the risk factors that may compound side effects (e.g. diabetes, obesity, pre-existing epilepsy) and will ideally be the outcome of a discussion with the patient and his/her carers.

10.8.8   Treatment in practice

Since the late 1950s (Healy, 2002), the basis of the treatment of schizophrenia has been the use of antipsychotic drugs. Antipsychotic treatment is normally initiated in the first phase of the illness, provided the patient comes to the attention of clinical services, and the first choice today in most cases would be an atypical agent. There may be some exceptions in patients who are acutely psychotic and need sedation in an inpatient setting, where initial treatment with a typical neuroleptic such as haloperidol combined with a benzodiazepine may still be required. The choice of the antipsychotic is driven by the aim to find the optimum fit with the patient's symptoms, although there is little systematic evidence for differential effects of different antipsychotics on positive or negative symptoms, and the need to consider the desired amount of sedation, side effects and pre-existing illnesses. It will normally be made jointly by the patient and his/her clinicians. Such a joint and informed decision- making process makes it more likely that the patient will be prepared to take the medication even in the face of unpleasant side effects (and thus increase compliance). Especially if symptom relief occurs, which can be expected after one to four weeks, patients can get the impression that they would now be able to manage without the medication and stop it, which can result in a relapse. If the first choice of antipsychotic has not produced a tangible benefit within 4–6 weeks at an adequate dose, another antipsychotic should be tried. Even an antipsychotic that is deemed not to have been clinically effective should not be stopped abruptly, though, in order to avoid rebound effects. It will normally be tapered over days or weeks while the new drug is introduced, a process called 'cross-titration'. After two unsuccessful treatment courses, clozapine may be the next option. Clozapine is often effective in such treatment refractory cases but is not recommended as first-line treatment because of its side effects and tight monitoring requirements of white blood cells. If no symptom relief is observed even after two months or more of clozapine treatment, augmentation with another antipsychotic, ideally with relatively specific DRD2 blockade, can be considered. Some patients are refractory even to such combinations, or become non-compliant or are lost to follow-up before the full treatment course can be evaluated. In patients with schizoaffective disorders, antipsychotics are often combined with mood stabilisers such as valproic acid. Combinations with antidepressants are also possible although their interactions with antipsychotics are poorly understood at the neurochemical level.

The pharmacological approaches need to be complemented with psychosocial interventions. Symptom-focused cognitive behavioural therapy may have some benefit, as do family interventions and psychoeducation. The aim of the treatment should ideally be the reintegration of the patients, who are often in the middle of job training or higher education when the disease breaks out, into society and to support them in their efforts to find stability in employment and relationships. Patients need to be educated about relapse risk and encouraged to keep engaging with mental health services through their remission in order to help them recognise early signs of a relapse. One to two years of ongoing antipsychotic treatment at therapeutic doses are normally recommended after a first episode, and patients who have experienced several episodes may need to take antipsychotics for their lifetime. The considerable side effects make the compliance with these suggestions relatively low. One way of improving treatment adherence is through the use of depot injections (e.g. on a fortnightly basis) of typical neuroleptics or risperidone.

EPS often need to be treated with anticholinergic drugs such as procyclidine. In addition, the potential for metabolic side effects makes it necessary to monitor cardiovascular risk factors such as weight, blood glucose, blood pressure and blood lipids. In sum, the treatment of schizophrenia is based on antipsychotic medication, which needs to be selected according to the patient's specific requirements and after a discussion of the possible side effects. If no response is achieved to the first antipsychotic, other antipsychotics and finally clozapine can be tried. If clozapine alone is not effective, it might be combine with another antipsychotic. Other augmentation options include anticonvulsant mood stabilisers and antidepressants, particularly for patients with schizoaffective disorder.

Learning points

Although the biological basis of schizophrenia has been a central topic of biological psychiatry for over 100 years, it is still essentially unknown. Many promising results have been obtained with structural imaging (e.g. ventricle enlargement, reduced temporal lobe asymmetry), radionuclide imaging (increased dopamine synthesis and response to amphetamines), genetics (several risk alleles with genome-wide significance) and neuroanatomical studies (abnormalities in neural development and several neurotransmitter systems). However, a unifying model has not been achieved, and none of the putative biological correlates is diagnostic in individual cases. The main biological models are derived from the antipsychotic effects of antidopaminergic agents and thus centre on the dopamine system and its modulation by other NT systems, for example serotonin, GABA and glutamate.

Antipsychotic drugs are dopamine receptor antagonists. They can be divided into the older 'typical' and the newer 'atypical' antipsychotics. The latter have a number of added pharmacological mechanisms, for example antiserotonergic, -cholinergic, -adrenergic and -histaminergic effects, which may explain why they are associated with lower levels of motor side effects. However, this comes at the expense of other side effects, for example weight gain. Finding ways of specifically modulating the parts of the dopamine system that may be altered in schizophrenia without affecting the others remains a challenge for future drug development.

The concept of schizophrenia has recently been criticised as being too broad or too narrow; too broad because it encompasses a range of clinically heterogeneous disorders, too narrow because it imposes an artificial subdivision onto a continuum of psychotic disorders ranging from the schizophrenia spectrum to the affective spectrum (e.g. bipolar disorder). From the clinical perspective, both the validity and the reliability of the diagnosis have been challenged. The usefulness of a diagnostic entity that encompasses disparate symptoms only loosely associated with each other is certainly questionable. Kraepelin's main justification for his concept of schizophrenia (dementia praecox), which he contrasted against manic-depressive illness, was based on the likely course of the disease and cognitive deterioration that was common to all patients. However, more recent studies of the natural history of psychotic disorders have shown that the course of schizophrenia is heterogeneous indeed and includes cases of complete recovery. Conversely, manic-depressive illness, or bipolar disorder, may lead to chronic deterioration and a residual state of cognitive and social impairment. Results from longitudinal studies of clinical outcome thus call the classical Kraepelinian dichotomy into question.

Might the clinical improvement under antipsychotic therapy then be a unifying feature for the diagnostic category? The reduction of symptoms achieved by antidopaminergic drugs is certainly the most impressive achievement of biological psychiatry as applied to psychotic disorders, and one on which most of the current pathophysiological models of schizophrenia are built. However, not all symptoms of schizophrenia respond equally well, for example negative symptoms less than paranoia or psychomotor agitation. Moreover, many patients do not respond to the first or even to several initially tested antipsychotic agents. These interindividual differences in treatment response have no obvious correlate in the symptom pattern of the patient, or receptor effects of the drug. Finally, acutely psychotic patients with bipolar disorder often also respond well to antipsychotic treatment. Antipsychotic drugs thus seem to do what their name says – they reduce psychotic symptoms irrespective of diagnostic category. If this is the case, their effects cannot be adduced in order to support the predictive validity of the concept of schizophrenia.

The strongest argument for schizophrenia as a diagnostic entity seems to come from its aetiological validity. It has been argued that the familial association concerns the syndrome rather than specific symptoms. If relatives of a patient with a particular set of symptoms, for example hallucinations and thought withdrawal, have a higher risk of developing schizophrenia symptoms in general rather than this specific set of symptoms, this would suggest the presence of a common underlying disorder. Similarly, if biological features of schizophrenia such as the increased ventricles are present regardless of subtype or symptom group, this would suggest common biological mechanisms upstream of the expression of specific symptoms. However, the concept of schizophrenia may still be too narrow. Relatives of patients with schizophrenia also have an increased risk of developing bipolar disorder, and some of the putative biological markers emphasise similarities, rather than differences, across the putative 'psychosis continuum'.

Any departure from the schizophrenia concept would have great impact on service provision, treatment and research of mental disorders. Up to now it has not been replaced by anything that clinical psychiatrists would find of equal value for their everyday practice, and most biological research still classifies patients according to DSM-IV or ICD-10 categories. The question of the validity of the schizophrenia concept in its present form will probably not be solved with purely clinical methodology. Firstly, none of the attempts at improving prediction of natural history and treatment response and aetiological classification by clinical subtyping has so far produced a consistent and replicated picture. Along similar lines, it has been proposed that more refined characterisation of patients for genetic studies will have to be based on neurocognitive endophenotypes (Jablensky, 2006). Secondly, the proposal of a psychosis continuum is largely based on genetic associations and biological similarities across the psychotic disorders. Any attempts at refining or redefining diagnostic categories will therefore likely combine clinical, psychometric and biological parameters.

If schizophrenia is indeed a disorder of neurodevelopment with biological and psychosocial consequences that can be detected before the onset of frank clinical symptoms, prophylactic treatment may be an option. Such an intervention, with psychological or even pharmacological means, requires markers with high predictive value in order to minimise the number of unnecessarily treated persons. Definitions of the schizophrenia prodrome and risk factors for transition to fully-fledged psychosis have so far been based on psychometric and cognitive tests alone (Klosterkötter et al., 2001). It will be an attractive new application for biological psychiatry to search for biological markers of the schizophrenia prodrome.

Of course, such diagnostic or classificatory contributions are only one aspect of the future of the biological psychiatry of schizophrenia. The other main task will be to move our understanding of the neurochemistry towards a multi-transmitter model that incorporates the abnormalities in the dopamine, serotonin, glutamate, GABA and possibly other systems and links them to neurodevelopmental processes. Human studies with neurochemical specificity (PET for in vivo and histochemistry and expression analysis for post-mortem studies) and aetiologically valid animal models will have to proceed concurrently for this endeavour.

Revision and discussion questions

- What is the evidence for the dopamine model of schizophrenia and what are its limitations?
- Is it possible to design useful animal models for complex mental disorders such as schizophrenia?
- Can model psychoses (drug-induced psychoses) help us understand schizophrenia?
- Should the diagnostic category of schizophrenia be abandoned? If so, what should replace it?

FURTHER READING

Sebat, J., Levy, D. L. and McCarthy, S. E. (2009). Rare structural variants in schizophrenia: One disorder, multiple mutations; one mutation, multiple disorders. *Trends in Genetics*, 25, 528–35.

11 DEPRESSION

PREVIEW

This chapter starts with a brief historical overview of the concept of mood disorder, which was separated from psychotic disorders in the late nineteenth century, and the beginnings of antidepressant treatment. It then describes the clinical syndrome of depression, which can occur in a single episode or become a relapsing remitting disorder. The review of the underlying biology focuses on three main areas: neuroimaging, neurochemistry and animal models. These various lines of evidence are integrated in the monoamine and neurogenic theories of depression. The monoamine theory is mainly derived from the effects of antidepressants, which all increase monoamine (mainly serotonin and/or noradrenaline) levels in the synaptic cleft. The effects of the various classes of antidepressants (reuptake inhibitors, monoamine oxidase inhibitors, presynaptic receptor blockers) and their side effects are discussed in detail.

11.1 HISTORY

Like schizophrenia, depression is a relatively recent term for states that have been described in ancient writings. Alterations of mood were traditionally subsumed under the concept of melancholy, which goes back to Hippocratic medicine with its doctrine of the body's fluids (blood, phlegm, yellow and black bile), which determine health and disease. Excess of black bile, 'melancholia', would lead to low mood, lack of motivation, enjoyment and interest and sometimes strange convictions, thus a picture very similar to the present definition of depression, except that some authors from antiquity through to the eighteenth century also associated it with particular intellectual or creative gifts (Linden, 1999).

Psychopathologists of the nineteenth and early twentieth century were mainly interested in the group of patients where depressive episodes alternate with those of elated mood, ideas of grandeur, excessive activity and hypersociability. This state, mania, appeared to be at the opposite end of the mood spectrum, and the alternation between depression and mania was termed 'manic-depressive disorder', and later 'bipolar' disorder (BD). In the classical Kraepelinian system, manic-depressive disorder was to be distinguished from dementia praecox, or later schizophrenia, not so much on the basis of presenting symptoms, which could overlap, but on the basis of the natural history. Kraepelin and his followers thought that patients with manic-depressive disorder recovered completely between phases, whereas those with dementia praecox showed chronic decline towards a residual state with emotional blunting and cognitive impairment. Newer longitudinal studies have shown that neither is exactly true, but the distinction between the schizophrenia spectrum and the mood disorders has persisted.

Patients with unipolar depression were underrepresented in the asylum of the nineteenth century, probably because families could cope with them more easily than with acutely psychotic patients. Affluent patients with depression would rally to the spa towns of central Europe, especially if somatic complaints were prominent, or, from the turn of the century, would seek the help of psychoanalysts. Biological treatment for depression therefore developed largely as a spin-off of the quest for a cure of psychosis. Electroconvulsive therapy (ECT), initially developed for schizophrenia, soon proved to have its main clinical use in the treatment of severe depression (Shorter and Healy, 2007). Similarly, the first antidepressants were developed when psychiatrists in the 1950s tried to improve the effectiveness of chlorpromazine and other antihistaminergic substances for psychosis. When the Swiss psychiatrist Roland Kuhn tried the chemically related substance that was later to become imipramine, the first antidepressant, in psychotic patients he did not get any antipsychotic effects, but instead some of the patients went into an elated mood. When tried with depressed patients, however, imipramine did lead to marked clinical improvements, and thus a new class of drugs, antidepressants, was serendipitously discovered (Healy, 1999). In another line of development, the American psychopharmacologist Nathan Kline pursued the clue from iproniazid, the anti-tuberculosis drug that blocks MAO and has antidepressant properties, that would lead to the development of MAOI antidepressants.

At about the same time as the pioneering work into antidepressants took place, major advances were made in the field of psychotherapy. Aaron Beck developed his cognitive behavioural therapy (CBT) as an extension of exposure-based behavioural therapy specifically for the treatment of depression. For many decades, psychological and biological approaches to depression seemed to be mutually exclusive and were rarely pursued by the same individuals in research and clinical practice. We have already discussed (Chapter 9) how recent changes in the thought patterns of both biological psychiatrists and clinical psychologists and the availability of new imaging methods have helped to bridge this artificial divide.

11.2   CLINICAL SYNDROME AND NATURAL HISTORY

The clinical syndrome of depression is characterised by low mood. Although mood can fluctuate during a depressive episode, the patient and others have very little control over it, and circadian rhythms seem to have a much larger impact than, for example, the patient's objective circumstances, or an offer to engage in activities the patient would normally enjoy. In addition to this lack of pleasure and even interest in normally enjoyable activities, patients often also show lack of motivation or drive and a variety of non-specific symptoms such as disturbed sleep, difficulty concentrating or loss of appetite. Patients are normally slow in all their activities, and can even be stuporous and almost not respond or act at all, but increased level of goalless activity, called agitation, is also possible. During severe episodes, patients may be vexed by thoughts of guilt and hopelessness, entertain thoughts of suicide and sometimes even act upon them. Depression is the single most common cause of suicide accounting for approximately 50% of cases in industrialised countries.

Depression is best described as a syndrome, which means that its diagnosis is not based on a single specific complaint, but on the presence of a sufficient number of symptoms that commonly co-occur in these patients. For an ICD-10 diagnosis of depression, a patient would be required to experience lowered mood, loss of interest and enjoyment and reduced energy, or at least two of these, over two weeks, and two other common symptoms for a mild, three to four for a moderate, and four or more for a severe episode (Table 11.1). A very severe form of depression is that where psychotic symptoms, such as the delusion of having sinned or hallucinations of voices accusing or slandering the patient, are also present.

Table 11.1   Criteria for depression in DSM-IV and ICD-10.

ICD-10	DSM-IV
Symptoms	*Depressed mood**
	Loss of interest and enjoyment
	Increased fatigue
	Reduced concentration and attention
	Ideas of guilt* and unworthiness
	Ideas or acts of self-harm or suicide, thoughts of death
	Sleep disturbance
	Disturbed appetite/weight change
	Pessimistic view of the future
	Reduced self-esteem and self-confidence
Features associated with somatic (ICD-10) or melancholic syndrome (DSM-IV)	Early morning awakening
	Mood worse in the morning
	Psychomotor retardation or agitation
	Weight loss
	Loss of libido

Notes: Five symptoms are required over a two-week period for an episode of Major Depression (DSM-IV). ICD-10 defines Depressive Episodes by a combination of the most typical (printed in bold face) and other symptoms. The number of symptoms determines the severity of the episode. Two typical and two other: mild; two typical and three or four other: moderate; three typical and four or more other: severe. If somatic features are present, a somatic syndrome can be diagnosed. These plus particularly severe forms of the symptoms marked by '*' are also criteria for the melancholic syndrome.

Source: American Psychiatric Association (2000)

As mentioned above, depression is a syndrome rather than a disorder, and a single brief depressive episode may not fulfil the criteria for a mental disorder. However, most depressive episodes are part of a more long-term pattern of affective changes, and up to 90% of patients with one depressive episode will experience another at some point, possibly years after recovery. Such a *recurrent depressive disorder*, where symptomatic episodes of normally several months alternate with symptom-free episodes that can last several years, would reflect the typical natural history of depression, but persistent or chronic forms without recovery periods are also possible, particularly in older age.

It is very rare for depression to persist throughout an individual's adult life without intervals of recovery. However, milder forms of low mood, often accompanied by feeling tired and exhausted, frequently develop into a chronic course, which is nowadays termed *dysthymia*, but was earlier known (and still is in the psychoanalytical literature) as neurotic depression.

11.3   EPIDEMIOLOGY AND GENETICS

The lifetime prevalence of depressive disorders is estimated at approximately 15%. Women are about twice as often affected as men, which means that at least one in five women suffer from depression at some point in their life. The first episode commonly occurs in the fourth or fifth decade, but there is a second peak of new onset of depression in the age group over 65. Prevalence was similar in studies in European countries and the USA, but some studies found lower levels in Asian countries, although this could be owed to methodological differences. In any event, depression is a major public health problem in the industrialised countries, and a growing problem in the developing world.

Most family studies of recurrent depressive or unipolar disorder (UD) found a relative risk for UD in first-degree relatives of 1.5–3. Thus, the genetic contribution to UD, although present, is much weaker that that to schizophrenia or bipolar disorder (BD). Furthermore, relatives of patients with UD do not seem to have a significantly increased risk of developing BD (Maier et al., 1993). Patients with an earlier age of onset (before 30) seem to have a higher likelihood of having a relative suffering from UD as well, suggesting that genetic liability leads to earlier onset. Patients with an early onset of depression also seem to have a higher rate of relatives with alcoholism, which may point to a weak genetic association between the two disorders. Twin studies suggest that shared environment played only a small role, but heritability was estimated at 37% (Sullivan et al., 2000) and higher. A considerable portion (about half) of the genetic liability of depression is shared with the personality trait of neuroticism, which has therefore been suggested as a useful quantitative trait or endophenotype for genetic studies of depression. Most researchers today are guided by the assumption that a genetic predisposition on the one hand and individual stressors and other aspects of the patient's unique environment on the other play equally important parts in the development of depressive disorder.

It will be important briefly to consider some possible meanings of 'genetic predisposition'. This may mean that alterations in one or several genes produce a liability to depression, to which the environmental stressors are then added, and if a sufficient number piles up, the individual develops depression. Such a model may not be far from the truth, at least if one considers the subjective accounts of many patients. However, it is also possible that genetic and environmental factors do not simply add up. For example, the genetic factors may sensitise patients to life events that otherwise do not contribute to depression, or may make them more likely to experience them, which would be examples of gene x–environment interaction (Kendler and Eaves, 1986).

Association studies with candidate genes have focused on polymorphisms in genes encoding receptors, transporters and enzymes involved in monoamine action and metabolism. The pharmacological effects of most antidepressant drugs, which indirectly activate one or more monoamine systems, suggest an important role for serotonin (5-HT) and norepinephrine in the pathophysiology of depression. A functional polymorphism in the gene for the 5-HT transporter has been associated with both BD and UD, as have other variations of this gene, but effects are small and some studies reported negative findings (Jones et al., 2004).

GWAS of UD with several thousand patients have so far produced only preliminary evidence of association, but GWAS with over ten thousand patients are underway. The best support has been achieved for SNPs in the ATP6V1B2 gene, which encodes an ATPase relevant for cell organelles and is adjacent to the VMAT gene on chromosome 8p21.3, the gene for mGlu$_7$, and the SP4 gene, which codes for a brain-specific transcription factor. The detailed functions of these SNPs are unknown, and the actual risk locus may be in an adjacent gene, for example the gene for the VMAT, which controls monoamine release from presynaptic stores. The group III mGluR, of which mGlu$_7$ is one, are presynaptic auto- and heteroreceptors (see Section 7.3.7) and thus can play a role in the regulation of monoamine release. Finally, knock-out studies in mice have suggested a role for SP4 in the integrity of hippocampal structures (Shyn and Hamilton, 2010). Thus, these loci from GWAS can be integrated in the main current biological models of depression, the monoamine model and the HPA-stress-hippocampal damage model. However, these links are still speculative and the risk loci, if supported in future sufficiently powered analyses, may very well provide insight into biological pathways that have not hitherto been considered.

11.4 BRAIN STRUCTURE

Affective disturbance is perhaps the most frequent and most often neglected psychiatric manifestation of neurological disease, and thus of great clinical relevance for neuropsychiatry (Chapter 21). It could also potentially provide cues as to the brain areas whose dysfunction leads to depression, even in those cases where no macroscopic brain abnormality is obvious, such as recurrent depressive disorder or BD. Depressive symptoms occur frequently (in up to a third of cases) in stroke, traumatic brain injury or brain tumour, particularly those affecting the frontal lobe and basal ganglia. Although such findings could potentially provide a lead to the role of these areas in maintaining emotional balance, caution is warranted for a number of reasons. The depressive syndrome is inherently heterogeneous, and focal lesions may predominantly produce symptoms that can be part of this syndrome, but also occur during a range of other mental disorders, for example psychomotor slowing and apathy after frontal lesions. Moreover, multiple sclerosis, a disorder with a diffuse lesion pattern and predominantly white matter pathology, can also present with depression early on. The same is true for physical illnesses affecting the brain such as acquired immunodeficiency syndrome (AIDS) or thyroid disease. Thus, a wide range of different lesion patterns affecting both grey and white matter can produce depressive symptoms, calling any straightforward structure–function relationship into question (Mayberg, 2004). Finally, the interpretation of affective changes in severely disabling neurological disorders is complicated by the occurrence of adjustment disorders with depressive symptoms, which are probably linked more directly with the dysfunctional coping mechanisms of the patient than with the function of the lesioned brain area.

There is thus relatively little basis to expect that evidence from neuropsychiatric cases of depression will highlight the brain areas that are involved in classical psychiatric depression as well. However, there are a number of structural imaging findings from patients with unipolar or bipolar depression, which are worth considering. Evidence for ventricular enlargement is weaker in affective disorders than in schizophrenia, and a considerable number of studies found no difference between patients and controls. Elderly patients with depression have so far been the only group where a sizeable majority of studies have reported enlarged lateral ventricles (Beyer and Krishnan, 2002).

Findings are also inconsistent across studies for most cortical areas. Yet, some confined areas have been suggested by several studies to be reduced. The subgenual area of the medial frontal lobe, the part of the anterior cingulate below the genu of the corpus callosum, was found to be reduced in both volume and metabolism in both BD and UD (Drevets et al., 1997). In fact, when metabolic activity is corrected for the effect of volume loss (the partial volume effect), it appears to be higher in depressed patients compared to controls and revert to normal after effective treatment (Drevets et al., 2004). The subgenual cingulate has recently received much attention because of attempts therapeutically to modulate its activity in treatment-refractory depression by deep brain stimulation (DBS) (Mayberg et al., 2005) (see Chapter 8). It may seem odd at first that a region with reduced volume should be hyperactive and produce clinical symptoms. However, if we consider that post-mortem studies have suggested that this volume reduction is owed to loss of neuropil (axons and dendrites) rather than a reduced number of neurons, we could explain such hyperactivity by disinhibition consequent upon loss of inhibitory afferents. The high-frequency DBS may then take over this lost inhibitory function and thus exert its therapeutic effect. Yet at the moment this account is entirely speculative, and the clinical effects of DBS on depression still await confirmation by a controlled trial.

Post-mortem studies have also assessed changes in the prefrontal cortex, both with histological and histochemical techniques. Several cell counting studies found reduced density of layer III neurons in the DLPFC. This layer receives input from other cortical areas and is thus important for maintaining circuits of information processing within the PFC. Histochemical studies provided evidence for a reduction of calbindin-positive GABAergic interneurons in layer I. These play mainly a role in the regulation of input into cortical areas (Hercher et al., 2009). Although reductions of markers of GABAergic activity have also been reported for schizophrenia (see Section 10.5.4), these concerned parvalbumin-positive neurons, which are more involved in the regulation of output. This intriguing dissociation of histochemical findings has so far not been integrated in models addressing the pathophysiological difference between mood disorders and schizophrenia.

The medial temporal lobe, particularly the hippocampus and the amygdala, has been specifically targeted by several volumetric studies because of the link between their presumed function in emotion regulation and associative memory formation and the clinical symptoms of depression. Furthermore, an attractive aetiological model, largely based on animal studies, has implicated hippocampal damage due to stress in the brain processes of depression. This may be linked to changes in neurotrophic signalling cascades, particularly through BDNF, which may be partly reversed by antidepressant treatment. Another neuroplastic system implicated by gene expression studies of depression is the fibroblast growth factor system, which is an important regulator of neurodevelopment (Mehta et al., 2010).

Post-mortem studies provide some evidence for general volume loss and reduction of neuropil (all tissue except the neuronal cell bodies, thus mainly axons, dendrites and glia) in the hippocampus. However, findings from structural imaging are inconsistent, with volume reductions, increases and no changes all being reported. A recent report also suggests that hippocampi are smaller already during adolescence in never medicated patients with early onset familial depression (MacMaster et al., 2008). Yet, small hippocampi have also been observed in traumatised individuals without depressive symptoms (Karl et al., 2006), and this finding may thus be a non-specific consequence of stress rather than a specific feature of the pathophysiology of depression. In the basal ganglia, several studies reported a reduction of the volume of the striatum (caudate nucleus and putamen) mainly in elderly depressed patients. A link between basal ganglia pathology and depression is also suggested by the high occurrence of depression in Parkinson's disease (up to 50%), but the apparent age effect would suggest that this may not be a primary pathology of psychiatric depression but an effect of the disease and/or medication, or a state marker of depression in the elderly.

Research in the 1980s suggested that a subgroup of patients with depression is suffering from increased secretion of cortisol and other signs of dysregulation of the hypothalamic-pituitary-adrenal (HPA) axis. This line of research has recently attracted renewed interested because of the HPA-stress model of depression, which will be discussed below. Structural imaging lent some support to changes in the HPA in depression. Both the adrenal gland and the pituitary were found to be enlarged in patients with depression, but it is as yet unknown whether this would normalise again after successful treatment or remission (Drevets et al., 2004). Gene expression studies have yielded an intriguing finding of increased CRF and CRF receptor gene expression in the paraventricular nucleus of hypothalamus, which would fit with the HPA model of depression (Mehta et al., 2010). Yet, as with most changes in the HPA axis, it will be difficult if not impossible to determine whether they are aetiological factors of depression or correlates of the stress resulting from depression, unless they are found in subjects with high genetic risk but no clinical symptoms.

11.5   STRUCTURE AND FUNCTION

Imaging of regional cerebral blood flow (rCBF) or glucose metabolism with positron emission tomography (PET) has indicated several functional abnormalities in the frontal lobes in addition to the changes in the subgenual ACC discussed above. In dorsomedial PFC, reduced flow and metabolism was observed in the dorsal ACC and the medial surface of the superior frontal gyrus. This area has been implicated in attenuation of emotional responses and defensive behaviour, but how its *hypo*activity would contribute to depressive symptoms is still an open question. The orbitofrontal (OFC) and ventrolateral prefrontal cortex (VLPFC) have been implicated in emotion regulation as well. These areas were hyperactive both in patients with depression during rest and in healthy individuals during induced sadness. Considering that orbitofrontal cells may be instrumental in modulating reward directed behaviour and extinguishing fear responses to aversive stimuli, their hyperactivation during phases of depression may reflect attempts to interrupt such aversive thoughts.

Depression may be associated with higher baseline activity in the amygdala. Several subgroups of patients with depression showed increased resting blood flow or glucose metabolism in this region and an attenuated response to emotional stimuli. Against the backdrop of higher baseline activity, lower responses in functional activation studies would be expected. One consequence of abnormally high amygdala activity may be that aversive memories are more deeply encoded in long-term memory, which would conform to the emotional biases on cognition that are often reported in depression (Gotlib and Joormann, 2010) where patients remember negative better than positive material. Such biases are important for cognitive models of depression that provide a foundation for cognitive behavioural interventions.

11.6   NEUROCHEMISTRY

11.6.1   Monoamine model

Like the dopamine model of schizophrenia, the monoamine model of depression receives its main support from the pharmacological effects of clinically effective drugs. All antidepressants increase the availability of the monoamines serotonin and/or norepinephrine, by blocking reuptake into the presynaptic cell, by disinhibiting the release of transmitter-filled vesicles into the synaptic cleft or by blocking enzymes that degrade monoamines. The monoamine deficit model of depression has been hugely influential. It is the standard model for the action of most antidepressants in clinical use and it has entered public awareness almost as a commonplace explanation of depression based on 'too little serotonin'. It is therefore worth examining more closely. The basic problem, as with all neurotransmitter models of mental disorders, is that we cannot measure neurotransmitter concentrations in the synaptic cleft directly, at least not in vivo. Such models will therefore be based on one or more of four main possible lines of evidence:

- changes in neurotransmitters or their metabolites that can be measured in more accessible tissues or fluids, for example blood serum, cerebrospinal fluid or platelets;
- induction of the disorder by inhibiting or stimulating the synthesis of the neurotransmitter in question;

- clinical effects of agonists or antagonists of the neurotransmitter;
- changes in receptor or transporter expression on the pre- or postsynaptic membrane as measured by PET or post-mortem histochemistry.

If patients with depression synthesise less serotonin or norepinephrine, as the standard version of the monoamine model would posit, they should also have lower levels of the metabolites of these neurotransmitters. 5-HT is metabolised through the monoamine oxidase pathway into 5-HIAA (see Chapter 2). The best evidence for reduced serotonergic activity comes from studies in people who committed or attempted suicide. For example, CSF levels of 5-HIAA were lower in those with a history of suicide attempts. Similarly, post-mortem studies indicate lower levels of serotonin and 5-HIAA in the brainstem of suicide victims (Mann, 2003). Histochemical studies reported an increase in the levels of tryptophan hydroxylase (TPH), the rate limiting enzyme for the synthesis of serotonin from tryptophan. Although this seems paradoxical, such an increase in TPH may be a compensatory response to the reduced serotonin levels (Hercher et al., 2009). Another way of probing serotonergic activity is through its effects on prolactin release. Serotonin stimulates prolactin release and increases of prolactin levels after administration of the serotonin reuptake inhibitor fenfluramine indicate serotonergic activity. This prolactin response is attenuated in people with a history of suicide attempt (Mann, 2003). Thus, various lines of evidence combine to suggest a serotonergic deficit in depressed patients who attempt or commit suicide, but many of these effects were also present in suicides with from other diagnostic groups, for example personality disorder. Based on this evidence it is therefore impossible to determine whether a serotonergic deficit would be a correlate of depression per se, or rather of suicidal behaviour.

Additional evidence for alterations in the serotonin system in major depression comes from PET studies with a specific 5-HT$_{1A}$ receptor ligand. These studies mainly revealed decreased receptor binding in cortical and limbic areas and the raphe nuclei. Because 5-HT$_{1A}$ autoreceptors regulate serotonin release (Feuerstein, 2008) their decreased expression could be a compensatory response to decreased serotonin levels in depression. However, PET does not differentiate between auto- and heteroreceptors, and other interpretations are thus possible. Radioligand studies of other 5-HT receptors or the 5-HT transporter in depression have not produced consistent results (Nikolaus et al., 2009b).

Finally, a direct link between the serotonin system and depression may be provided by tryptophan depletion studies. If this essential amino acid is missing from the diet, no new serotonin can be synthesised. Of course, this procedure is only temporary and normally consists in one night fasting followed by an amino acid drink that does not contain tryptophan, compared to the effects of one that does. Mild mood impairment has been observed after tryptophan depletion in healthy individuals, but worsening of depression in patients only in those who had previously responded to a serotonin reuptake inhibitor. This observation and the clinical experience that some patients respond better to catecholaminergic antidepressants suggest that different monoamine systems may be altered in different patients or different types of depression.

11.6.2 The neurogenic model of depression assumes damage to the hippocampus from chronic stress and hyperactivity of the HPA axis

There is increasing evidence from animal studies that chronic stress can lead to hippocampal damage, which has been correlated with cortisol levels and other markers of HPA activity. This hippocampal damage can be reversed by treatment with antidepressants or ECT. Both antidepressants and ECT have increased the number of dendritic spines and synapses, and even the proliferation of progenitor cells of hippocampal neurons in rodents and monkeys and may thus be able to stimulate neurogenesis, the creation of new neurons. The hippocampus is one of the few regions of the adult brain where such neurogenesis is thought to happen, and it is inhibited by stress. These new neurons take a few weeks to mature, which would correspond to the latency of the clinical effects of antidepressants. These pieces of evidence can be combined into an aetiological model of depression, where chronic stress, possibly going back to trauma in early childhood, mediated through hyper-activity of the HPA axis and insufficient negative feedback control (Figure 3.1), leads to hippocampal damage, which would then be the target for various antidepressant interventions (Figure 11.1). One problem with this model is that the symptoms of depression are not typical of hippocampal damage, which is classically associated with amnesia (Chapter 21), although it may explain some of the cognitive symptoms (Becker and Wojtowicz, 2007) and lead to affective symptoms through its involvement in Papez's circuit. Another problem is that the hippocampal effects have been consistently demonstrated only in animal models but not in patients with depression. Several modulators of the HPA axis have been explored for their potential therapeutic benefit, but have so far not resulted in clinical applications.

Figure 11.1

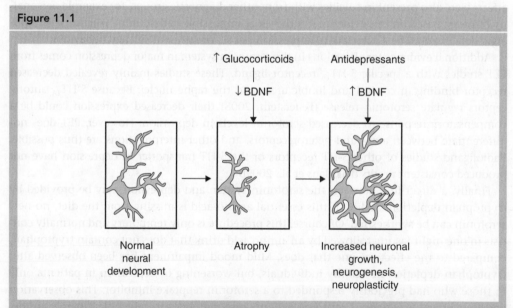

The hippocampus-stress model of depression
The schematic drawing shows the dendritic tree of a hippocampal neuron under normal development (left), atrophy (middle) and restitution of neuronal growth (right). Under chronic stress, alone or in combination with increased vulnerability from genetic and environmental factors and their interaction, increased glucocorticoid action and downregulation of growth factors may lead to hippocampal damage (middle). This process can be (partly) reversed by cessation of stress (e.g., through CBT, coping strategies, lifestyle adjustments), monoaminergic antidepressants or ECT. Note that most of the evidence for this model is still based on cellular and animal studies.

11.7 ANIMAL MODELS

Animal models of depression have served two main purposes: to elucidate disease mechanisms and to assess treatment responses. Most transgenic animal models of depression were designed to address aspects of the monoamine model. Serotonin transporter (SERT) knockout mice showed increased basal anxiety and stress responses. They have therefore face validity for some aspects of the depressive phenotype, but the construct validity of this model is unclear. After all, SSRIs and other serotonin reuptake inhibitors block SERT for an antidepressant effect. Thus, if SERT hypofunction was a causative mechanism in human depression, it would have to act through other downstream modifications of the serotonin system, for example receptor downregulation or densensitisation (where receptors are not activated regardless of ligand binding) because of constantly high synaptic serotonin levels. The SERT knock-out mouse can also be used to investigate the mechanisms of antidepressant drugs. These mice show no antidepressant effect to SSRIs, which confirms that SSRIs indeed have their effects through SERT blockade. Conversely, chronic administration of SSRIs leads to downregulation of SERT expression in rodents. Thus, the SERT knock-out mouse has reasonable face validity, unknown construct validity and negative predictive validity (therapeutic effects are inhibited). Like all mouse models based on a single gene, it is thus not likely to be a good mechanistic model for depression, but can be very useful for the study of treatment effects.

Knock-out mice have also been designed for serotonin receptors. 5-HT$_{1A}$ receptor knock-out mice should have increased levels of synaptic serotonin, but this has not yet been conclusively demonstrated. The phenotype of these mice shows some features of resilience against depression, for example shorter immobility times on the Porsolt Forced Swim Test and the Tail Suspension Test (see Chapter 5). However, it also shows anxiety-like behaviours (avoidance of novel and stressful situations) and memory deficits. The 5-HT$_{1A}$ knock-out mouse may be particularly useful as a model for antidepressant treatment effects, as well as resilience, because chronic SSRI treatment leads to desensitisation of 5-HT$_{1A}$ receptors, and blockade of these autoreceptors enhances antidepressant effects. SSRI administration initially reduces firing of serotonergic neurons because the serotonin that is kept in the synaptic cleft binds to autoreceptors. This effect is reversed after a few weeks when the autoreceptors are desensitised and finally a net effect of increased serotonergic activity ensues. This process is one of several explanations for the delayed clinical effects of antidepressants (Blier and de Montigny, 1994).

11.8 TREATMENT

11.8.1 Antidepressants are monoaminergic agonists

All antidepressants enhance monoaminergic activity in central synapses. They do so through three different modes of action: inhibition of reuptake, inhibition of enzymatic degradation and blockade of presynaptic autoreceptors. Antidepressants were originally classified by the chemical structure (tricyclic, tetracyclic, see Figure 11.2), but the more general classification today is by mode of action into selective or non-selective serotonin (SSRI/SRI) or noradrenaline (NRI) reuptake inhibitors, monoamine oxidase inhibitors (MAOI) or autoreceptor blockers.

Figure 11.2

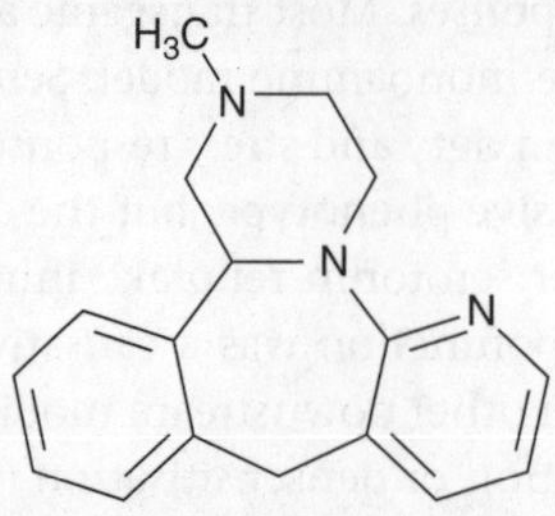

Mirtazapine is a tetracyclic antidepressant with a four-ring structure.

11.8.2 Most antidepressants are reuptake inhibitors

Most of the classical tri- and tetracyclic antidepressants are non-selective serotonin and/or noradrenaline reuptake inhibitors (and also weakly block dopamine reuptake) (see Figures 11.3 and 11.4). The 'selectivity' in the nomenclature refers to their action on other, non-monoamine receptors such as histamine or muscarine receptors, which are responsible for their side effect profile. Some TCA (e.g. desipramine and nortriptyline) have higher affinity for NET and others (particularly clomipramine) for SERT. Amongst the newer, more selective (meaning less anticholinergic or antihistaminergic effects) reuptake inhibitors, some are serotonin specific (the SSRI fluoxetine, citalopram and escitalopram, paroxetine, fluvoxamine and sertraline), whereas reboxetine is noradrenaline specific (NRI) and venlafaxine and duloxetine block SERT and NET almost evenly ('serotonin/norepinephrine reuptake inhibitor': SNRI). Bupropion is unique in being a combined noradrenaline and dopamine reuptake inhibitor (NDRI).

11.8.3 MAO inhibitors block the degradation of monoamines

Antidepressant MAOIs include the reversible MAO-A inhibitor moclobemide and the irreversible MAO-A and MAO-B inhibitor tranylcypromine. Selective MAO-B inhibitors are in use for the treatment of Parkinson's disease, because of their specific effects on synaptic dopamine levels, but they have no antidepressant effects. The idea behind the use of MAOIs for depression is that the blockade of monoamine degradation leads to longer dwell times for these NTs in the synaptic cleft, similar to the reuptake blockade discussed above. This higher availability of NTs in the synaptic cleft may either redress a pre-existing monoamine deficit or lead to compensatory postsynaptic adaptations that restitute the neuronal mechanisms that are dysfunctional in depression. For example, chronic inhibition of MAO leads to downregulation of both adrenergic (β_1) and serotonergic ($5HT_{2A}$) receptors. In addition to the inhibition of MAO-A and -B, tranylcypromine also directly promotes noradrenaline release through reverse transport at the NET. As with all other antidepressants, the discovery of the MAOI class has been serendipitous (through the early observation that the anti-tuberculosis drug iproniazid, which has MAOI properties, has antidepressant effects) and presently no direct evidence is available for an underlying monoaminergic deficit.

Figure 11.3

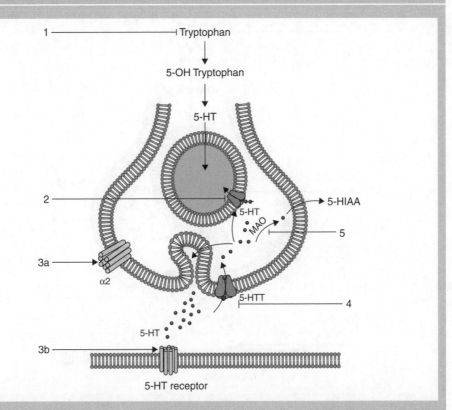

Effects of psychoactive drugs at a serotonergic synapse
The upper part shows a schematic drawing of a serotonergic terminal. Serotonin (5-HT) is released from the presynaptic cell and activates postsynaptic receptors (lower part). It is removed from the synaptic cleft by a transporter (5-HTT, also abbreviated SERT) and metabolised by MAO and other enzymes (see Figure 2.7). Various manipulations of this cascade for therapeutic and experimental purposes are possible. Restriction of tryptophan in the diet ('tryptophan depletion', 1) can model depression in vulnerable individuals. Inhibition of the VMAT and thus storage and release from presynaptic vesicles is the mechanism of action of reserpine, which is not in use any more as anti-hypertensive, but whose possible depressiogenic effects started the search for monoamine deficits in depression (2). Blockade of noradrenergic alpha-2 heteroreceptors by mirtazapine (3a) results in increased 5-HT release. Several psychedelic substances are 5-HT receptor agonists, whereas many of the atypical antipsychotics (Figure 10.5) are antagonists (3b). Blockade of the reuptake of serotonin (4) is the main mechanism of action for SSRI and many tricyclic antidepressants. MAO inhibitors (5) are other potent antidepressants.

MAOIs are very effective antidepressants, including in otherwise treatment-refractory cases. They have an activating effect and may be particularly suited for depressive syndromes with psychomotor poverty. Although they have few or no anticholinergic side effects, they are rarely used. The main reason seems to be that treatment with irreversible MAOIs requires a strict dietary schedule. MAO metabolises tyramine and other amines that are ingested with common foodstuffs, such as cheeses. Tyramine does not cross the blood–brain barrier but acts as a peripheral sympathomimetic agent by promoting catecholamine release. If tyramine levels

Figure 11.4

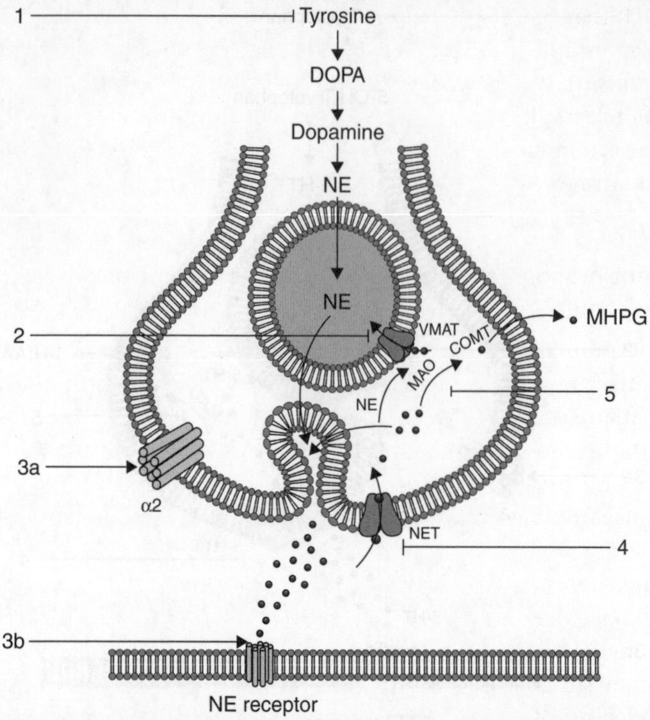

Effects of psychoactive drugs at a noradrenergic synapse
The upper part shows a schematic drawing of a noradrenergic terminal with the steps of biosynthesis from tyrosine (see Figure 2.6). Norepinephrine (NE) is released from the presynaptic cell and activates postsynaptic receptors (lower part). It is removed from the synaptic cleft by a transporter (NET) and metabolised by MAO, COMT and other enzymes. Restriction of tyrosine in the diet (1) is sometimes, but less commonly than tryptophan depletion, used as an experimental model of motivational states. For reserpine effects (2) see Figure 11.3. Blockade of alpha-2 receptors by mirtazapine (3a) results in increased NE release. Many psychiatric (e.g. Figure 10.5) and medical drugs bind to postsynaptic NE receptors (3b). Blockade of the reuptake of NE (4) is the main mechanism of action for SNRI and several tricyclic antidepressants. MAO inhibitors (5) block the metabolism of NE to MHPG. Further details of catecholamine metabolism are explained in Chapter 2.

increase because it cannot be metabolised by MAO, dangerous hypertonic crises can result. This is much less of a problem with reversible MAOI, which can be displaced from the enzyme by tyramine, and moclobemide treatment thus does not require dietary restrictions.

11.8.4   Mirtazapine is a noradrenergic and serotonergic agent with mainly presynaptic mode of action

Noradrenaline blocks the release of itself by activating presynaptic α_2 autoreceptors. It also inhibits the release of serotonin by blocking α_2 receptors on serotonergic neurons. These negative feedback loops are blocked by mirtazapine, which thus acts as an indirect noradrenergic and serotonergic agonist. Noradrenaline release in the raphe also activates serotonergic neurons via α_1 receptors. Mirtazapine blocks 5-HT_{2A}, 5-HT_{2C}, and 5-HT_3 serotonin receptors, which means that its net effect is mainly activation of 5-HT_{1A} receptors. Mirtazapine is a potent antidepressant, with relatively strong sedating effects from its antihistaminergic effects (H_1 antagonism). It can also be combined with an NRI because of the additive effects on noradrenaline release. Its main side effect, weight gain, is also related to the H_1 antagonism. Mirtazapine can induce agranulocytosis through an unknown idiosyncratic (non-dose-dependent) mechanism, requiring clinical and blood count monitoring.

11.8.5   Different monoaminergic profiles may be useful for different depressive syndromes

Depression is not a unitary disorder. Many symptoms from different categories – affective, cognitive, vegetative, motor – come together to yield a depressive syndrome. It has been proposed that patients can be divided into those where negative affective symptoms are prominent and those who suffer more from lack of positive emotions, also termed anhedonia, lack of drive and psychomotor poverty. Based on theoretical considerations, patients with prominent negative affect and anxiety might respond better to antidepressants with a predominantly serotonergic mode of action, whereas patients with anhedonia might need noradrenergic and those with psychomotor poverty dopaminergic agonists. However, clinical studies rarely make these subdivisions because of the considerable overlap between these syndromes in clinical practice, and thus empirical evidence for these predictions is difficult to obtain. They may still serve as guidance for the choice of first antidepressants in patients with a distinctive clinical syndrome.

11.8.6   Side effects can stem from monoaminergic actions or blockade of other NT receptors

The side effects of antidepressants can arise from the monoaminergic effects, in which case they can occur under both TCA and selective reuptake inhibitors. Another group of side effects stems from the blockade of muscarinic or histamine receptors and are thus associated with the TCA. Acute monoaminergic effects include agitation, headaches and a vegetative syndrome that can include nausea, sweating, diarrhoea, tachycardia and sexual dysfunction. Although sexual dysfunction can persist, most of these side effects are normally transient. It is important to remember that the initial activating effect, if not yet accompanied by mood improvement, can increase suicide risk. This has to be monitored carefully, and sedating medication, for example a benzodiazepine, may have to be added in the initial phase of antidepressant treatment. Whether antidepressants, particularly the SSRI, actually increase suicidal ideation and aggression (against self and others) is still a matter for debate. However, these concerns, particularly for children and adolescents, were serious enough for national regulators to demand that SSRIs carry a warning about potential increases in suicidal thinking and behaviour in this age group.

Activation of specific 5-HT receptors is associated with particular side effects: 5-HT_{2A} with anxiety, agitation and sexual dysfunction, 5-HT_{2C} with reduced appetite and sexual dysfunction, and 5-HT_3 with nausea, vomiting and headaches. This explains why these side effects are uncommon under mirtazapine, which blocks these receptors in addition to its enhancing effect on serotonin release.

A life-threatening central serotonin syndrome can arise after overdosing with serotonergic antidepressants, but also after normal dosage if several serotonergic drugs are combined (which is not recommended), or if metabolism is slowed down by other drugs that compete for the CYP system. The serotonin syndrome is characterised by rigor, neuromuscular hyperexcitation (rigidity, myoclonus, tremor, increased reflexes), and delirium. In addition, any of the vegetative symptoms of serotonergic activation can occur. Seizures and cardiac arrhythmia are particularly dangerous complications. In most cases, discontinuation of the serotonergic medication is sufficient. In severe cases, intensive care is needed to avoid progression to coma and organ failure. In these cases, the 5-HT_2 receptor blocker cyproheptadine can be used to antagonise the effects of serotonin.

The anticholinergic side effects of TCA are similar to those of the antipsychotics discussed above. Antihistaminergic effects include sedation and weight gain, and confusion in extreme cases. Alpha-1 adrenergic stimulation can lead to orthostatic hypotension (drop of blood pressure when getting up), which can result in a compensatory tachycardia. However, increases in blood pressure, potentially even hypertensive crises, can also occur under noradrenergic antidepressants, particularly the NRIs, SNRIs and bupropion. TCAs can have negative dromotropic effects on the heart, meaning that they slow down the signal conduction from the atrium to the ventricle. This can result in atrio-ventricular or bundle branch blocks in the ECG. After overdose, life-threatening tachyarrhythmias are possible, necessitating the need for 72-h cardiac monitoring. The cardiac risk associated with overdosing has been one of the main reasons for the declining popularity of TCA in the treatment of depression. However, some of the newer antidepressants (particularly venlafaxine at higher therapeutic doses) can also lead to cardiac arrhythmias.

A complete list of side effects and drug interactions of antidepressants would exceed the scope of this book. However, some side effects with poorly understood mechanism are worth mentioning here. Like all drugs, antidepressants can lead to allergic reactions, for example rashes, and will then have to be exchanged for a chemically different substance. TCA, the tetracyclic antidepressant mianserin and, as mentioned above, mirtazapine can induce agranulocytosis. All serotoninergic antidepressants can also impair platelet function, increasing the risk of bleeding, especially when they are combined with other drugs with anticoagulant properties such as acetyl salicylic acid (aspirin®). TCA and bupropion also reduce the seizure threshold, which limits their use in patients with pre-existing epilepsy. Patients treated with the SNRIs venlafaxine and duloxetine need to be monitored particularly carefully for potential hypertension. Finally, antidepressants can promote the production of AVP (vasopressin, see Chapter 3), also called antidiuretic hormone (ADH). This is called syndrome of inappropriate ADH hypersecretion (SIADH). ADH/AVP promotes renal fluid retention and thus lower serum osmolarity (concentration of electrolytes), particularly lower sodium levels. This can lead to dangerous complications, including cerebral oedema, seizures and coma. It is treated with discontinuation of the antidepressant, fluid restriction and, in severe cases, slow intravenous infusions of saline under intensive monitoring. In order to avoid SIADH or detect it early, regular electrolyte checks have to be part of a carefully monitored antidepressant regime.

Abrupt discontinuation of serotonergic antidepressants often results in a discontinuation syndrome with psychological (agitation, irritability, anxiety, depression), neurological (paraesthesias [odd sensations in the limbs], balance problems) and vegetative symptoms. Although these discontinuation symptoms are normally transient, they can be very unpleasant and make it difficult for patients to come off these antidepressants. Very slow tapering of the drug, often over months or years, will then be required.

11.8.7 Antidepressants can be combined or augmented with lithium or thyroid hormones

Only about a third of patients show a clinical response to the first antidepressant. If no clinical improvement has occurred after two months of treatment, it makes sense to change to another antidepressant from the same or from another group. If a response has occurred, but was incomplete, increasing the dose may also be an option, although this has been shown to be effective only for TCAs, MAOIs and SNRIs. If several attempts with a single antidepressant have been unsuccessful, a combination therapy may still be effective. In particular, pharmacodynamically complementary substances can be combined, for example mirtazapine with an SSRI or NRI for increased serotonergic or noradrenergic effects. Particular caution is needed because of the higher risk of central serotonin syndrome or hypertensive crises under such combinations. MAOI should not be combined with other antidepressants because of the danger of uncontrolled monoaminergic stimulation, for example serotonin syndrome.

Another way of increasing the clinical effect of antidepressant is through augmentation with lithium or thyroid hormones. The combination of an SSRI and lithium seems to be particularly effective. The thyroid hormone triiodothyronine can be added to SSRI or TCA with positive clinical effects. Although an underactive thyroid can independently lead to clinical depression (which is then easily remedied by substitution of thyroid hormones), the positive effects of augmentation occur even in patients with normal thyroid function. The exact mechanisms behind these augmentation regimes are unknown. Various other augmentation strategies, for example with the coenzyme 5,10-methylenetetrahydrofolate (MTHF) or with the anticonvulsant lamotrigine, are also being explored.

11.8.8 Use of antidepressants in other disorders

Serotonergic antidepressants are also used for the treatment of anxiety disorders. SSRI, SNRI and clomipramine seem to be equally effective. Treatment results are particularly good for panic disorder, but symptom improvement can also be expected in generalised anxiety disorder, obsessive compulsive disorder, social phobia and post-traumatic stress disorder (see Chapter 13). In milder cases, pharmacotherapy is normally the second choice after a course of psychotherapy, but in more severe cases medication is often used in addition to psychotherapy from the outset.

TCAs and SNRIs also have an established use in the treatment of various chronic pain syndromes, for example tension headache, neuropathic pain (e.g. in diabetes mellitus) or fibromyalgia. They can also be used for the treatment of somatisation disorders, where patients have various physical complaints, including pain, without a discernible cause. Their effectiveness may be explained by the high comorbidity of depression and somatisation. Sedating antidepressants (some of the TCA, for example amitriptyline and mirtazapine) can be used in the treatment of insomnia, especially when there are concerns about the use of benzodiazepines or z-hypnotics because of comorbid substance use disorders (Chapter 15).

11.8.9 Antidepressants in development target the monoamine system and several hormonal and neuropeptide systems

At least 30% of patients with MDD do not respond to standard pharmacological and/or psychological treatments, even after switching from several antidepressants (Rush et al., 2006), and a considerable number of those who do respond initially go on to develop a chronic relapsing-remitting disorder. These patients with no or only a partial response to standard treatments often enter a vicious circle of psychosocial decline with further deterioration of their mood and level of functioning. The search for new antidepressants, possibly using mechanisms of action not hitherto explored, is therefore of great clinical priority. Some of the substances under development still target the monoamine system, for example reuptake inhibitors of all three centrally acting monoamines (serotonin, noradrenaline, dopamine), although the fine-tuning of the balance between these different actions may be a challenge. The new antidepressant agomelatine (see also Chapter 19) combines 5-HT_{2C}-receptor antagonism, which leads to increased dopamine and noradrenaline release, with agonism at the melatonin receptor, which makes it particularly effective for sleep problems. Other experimental antidepressants are based on the models of HPA axis dysregulation and block the hypothalamic hormones (CRF or AVP antagonists) or the glucocorticoids directly. The neurokinin system is also a target for the development of antidepressants (see Chapter 7), although little direct evidence is available for its primary dysfunction in depression.

11.8.10   Treatment in practice

The treatment of depression combines psychosocial, pharmacological and physical interventions and needs to take account of the patient's individual, family, professional, social and financial circumstances. Comorbidities, most commonly with anxiety and substance use disorders, need to be considered as well. The first approach to mild to moderate depressive episodes can be based on low-intensity psychological interventions such as counselling or group physical activity programmes, although the latter are less widely available. If the patient does not experience tangible benefits, the options are a higher intensity psychological intervention (e.g. 20 sessions of CBT), medication or their combination. Patients with severe depression should be offered antidepressants from the outset. The first choice of antidepressant is commonly one of the SSRIs. If the patient does not experience some improvement after one month, or substantial improvement after two, another substance should be considered, for example another SSRI or NRI. There is some evidence that patients who do not respond well to one class of antidepressants respond better to a drug with a different pharmacological profile. Failing this, venlafaxine or another SNRI, mirtazapine, a reversible MAO inhibitor or a tricyclic antidepressant can be initiated. For patients who fail to respond to antidepressant monotherapy (treatment with a single substance) various augmentation regimes are available. The best evidence is available for augmentation with lithium, although thyroid hormone augmentation is also in clinical use and several folate preparations are available, although the jury is still out as to their efficacy.

Some combinations of two antidepressants are also possible, for example SSRI and mirtazapine, although increasing side effects need to be considered. For patients with psychotic features of depression, combination of an antidepressant with an atypical antipsychotic is an option. If psychotherapy or pharmacotherapy alone are not effective, their combination may still bring benefits. Finally, in treatment-refractory cases of severe depression, ECT can be an effective tool, at least for short-term symptom relief.

After remission of an episode, the antidepressant regime should be continued at the same dose, if tolerated well, for at least six months in order to reduce risk of relapse. For patients with high relapse risk (e.g. those with several previous episodes, residual symptoms or difficult psychosocial circumstances) continuation over at least two years is recommended. For patients who prefer not to take medication after remission or who do not tolerate the side effects, psychological interventions may also help reduce the risk of relapse.

Learning points

Depression is a common mental health problem, affecting up to 15% of the population of industrialised countries and leading to considerable personal suffering and socio-economic consequences. Its heritability, at about 37%, is lower than for most other major mental disorders, and environmental influences such as chronic stress and early trauma seem to play a major role in the development of depression. Although several neuropsychiatric syndromes can lead to depression, the localisation of affected brain areas is not consistent and most patients with major depressive disorder do not have any observable brain abnormalities. The strongest evidence for biological mechanisms of depression comes from the effects of antidepressant drugs, which are all monoaminergic agents. However, clear evidence for a primary monoaminergic deficit in depression is lacking. Furthermore, antidepressants take a few weeks to exert their clinical effects, when their effects on synaptic monoamine levels should be fairly immediate. This delay has been explained with differential regulation of inhibitory 5-HT_{1A} autoreceptors and 5-HT_2 receptors, as well as with postsynaptic effects on gene expression.

An alternative or additional way of explaining some of the findings from neurochemical and animal studies is through a dysregulation of the HPA/stress axis, whose overactivity might lead to hippocampal damage. Both pharmacological and non-pharmacological (ECT) treatments seem to have some neuroprotective effect on the hippocampus, but direct antagonists of the HPA axis have not been successful in clinical testing. At the moment, research is very active in linking the monoamine with the HPA model, and investigating how the environmental stress factors implicated in the genesis of depression might manifest in the developing brain.

Antidepressant drugs enhance monoaminergic (serotonergic, noradrenergic, and/or dopaminergic) neurotransmission. Most antidepressants inhibit the reuptake by blocking presynaptic transporters (TCA, SSRI, NRI, SNRI) or presynaptic receptors (mirtazapine). The other main mechanism of action is inhibition of the monoamine-degrading enzyme MAO (MAOI). Some antidepressants are selective for the serotonin or noradrenaline system, but it is still an open issue whether this translates into clinically distinguishable effects on depressive syndromes. The side effects of antidepressants stem from their monoaminergic effects (e.g. sympathomimetic and gastrointestinal effects) or from the blockade of other (mainly muscarinic and histamine) receptors. Antidepressants are used in a wide range of disorders in addition to depression, for example anxiety disorders and chronic pain. Treatment of depression is normally based on a combination of pharmacological and psychological approaches, and physical therapies, especially ECT, have a place as well, particularly for treatment-refractory patients and psychotic depression. New therapies based on brain physiology, including TMS, DBS and neurofeedback, still need to be fully tested for their clinical risks and benefits before their future role can be evaluated.

Revision and discussion questions

- What is the evidence for the monoamine model of depression and what are its limitations?
- What are the main mechanisms of action of currently used antidepressants?
- How might stressful life events affect the brain?

FURTHER READING

Ebmeier, K. P., Donaghey, C. and Steele, J. D. (2006). Recent developments and current controversies in depression. *Lancet*, 367, 153–67.

12 MANIA AND BIPOLAR DISORDER

PREVIEW

This chapter continues the review of the biology of mood disorders. It describes the syndrome of mania and its occurrence in bipolar disorder and reviews the results of recent genome-wide association studies. The section on brain structure and function discusses ways of assessing brain connectivity in relation to neuropsychological models of bipolar disorder. The section on neurochemistry centres on the cellular effects of lithium, the classical antimanic agent. Its clinical effect as well as those of the other antimanic and prophylactic drugs from the classes of anticonvulsants and antipsychotics are discussed in the treatment section.

12.1 CLINICAL FEATURES

The alternation of episodes of depression and mania, normally with intervals of recovery in between, constitutes Kraepelin's manic depressive disorder, today called bipolar affective disorder or *bipolar disorder* (BD). In ICD-10, a manic episode is defined by groundlessly and abnormally elevated mood. In addition, patients often display signs of increased energy, such as overactivity, fast talking, and decreased need for sleep. Loss of social inhibition and inflated self-esteem are also common (Table 12.1). Mania can occur with or without frank psychotic symptoms. If present, these often include grandiose, religious or persecutory delusions. Although many patients with BD do not experience psychotic symptoms during their manic or depressive episodes, BD is commonly classified as an 'affective psychosis'. How manic and depressive episodes, which in so many respects seem to constitute exact opposites, can be part of one and the same disorder and even coexist at the same time in 'mixed episodes' is a big conundrum of psychiatry and constitutes a challenge both for biological and psychological models. Some intriguing explanations have been attempted by theorists of evolutionary psychiatry (see Box 12.1). Some patients with BD only have recurrent manic episodes, without intervening depressed periods.

12.2 EPIDEMIOLOGY AND NATURAL HISTORY

BD is less common than unipolar depression and has a lifetime prevalence of approximately 1%. Age of onset is lower than that for recurrent depressive disorder, commonly between 15 and 30, and men are equally often affected as women. Bipolar II disorder, where episodes of depression alternate with hypomanic states (periods of elated mood that do not fulfil the criteria for mania), is more common (approx. 5% lifetime prevalence). Whether this is a milder form of BD, or a separate disease entity, is currently a moot case.

It is rare for manic episodes to be singular events, and 90% of them are followed by further manic episodes (thus constituting a diagnosis of BD), often alternating with depressive

Table 12.1 Criteria for mania in DSM-IV and ICD-10

ICD-10	DSM-IV
Core symptom	
Elevated mood (but may be irritable and suspicious instead)	Elevated mood (but may be irritable and suspicious instead)
Important symptoms for diagnosis	
Overactivity	Overactivity
Pressured speech	Pressured speech
Decreased need for sleep	Decreased need for sleep
Excessive optimism	
Inflated self-esteem	Inflated self-esteem
Flight of ideas	Flight of ideas
Distractability	Distractability
Perceptual disturbance	
Extravagant or inappropriate behaviour	
Reckless spending and other pleasurable activities with likely adverse consequences	Reckless spending and other pleasurable activities with likely adverse consequences

Note: A manic episode can be diagnosed when the core symptom and several (ICD-10) or at least three (DSM-IV) of the other symptoms are present for one week.

Source: World Health Organisation (1992)

episodes in a pattern that is relatively regular for the individual patient. Manic episodes are generally slightly shorter (median duration of four months) than depressive episodes (median duration of six months). The periods of recovery, which can be partial or complete, vary greatly in length from months to years. Contrary to Kraepelin's model, the progression of BD can lead to cognitive decline and residual states. The ca. 10% of BD patients who have four or more episodes of mania or depression in the course of one year fulfil the criteria for 'rapid cycling' and have a poorer prognosis than those with fewer episodes and longer periods of remission.

12.3   GENETICS

Family studies found a particularly strong genetic association for BD. First-degree relatives of patients with BD have a five to ten times increased risk of developing BD compared to the general population, resulting in an absolute risk of 5–10%. The concordance rate in monozygotic twins is even 60%, which means that if one twin suffers from BD, the other has a 60% chance of developing it as well. Advanced paternal age seems to be a risk factor. Structural mutations of DNA increase over the lifetime, and thus older parents have a higher probability of passing on de-novo mutations to their offspring. Thus, this would be a genetic risk factor that does not, however, increase heritability.

Relatives of patients with BD also have an increased risk of developing other affective disorders, notably bipolar II disorder and recurrent depressive disorder, and schizoaffective disorder. The question whether schizophrenia, too, is genetically associated with BD, is of great interest. Anecdotal reports of increased rates of schizophrenia in families with BD resulted in a conceptual challenge to the Kraepelinian dichotomy because such a genetic link would favour the hypothesis of a continuum between schizophrenic and affective psychoses. Studies of the frequency of schizophrenia in relatives of BD patients had conflicting results, and a considerable number did not find a relevant increase in the frequency of schizophrenia. Yet, it seems that schizophrenia is more frequent in relatives of patients with severe, psychotic forms of BD, which may explain the divergent findings of the previous literature (Vallès et al., 2000).

Like for most mental disorders with a substantial heritability, the mode of inheritance of affective disorders is complex and certainly not Mendelian. BD has been in the focus of genetic research over the past two decades, but no single risk gene has been identified. Several broad chromosomal regions have been linked with BD in family studies, including 4p16, 6q21–25, 12q23–24, 15q13–15, 18p11, 18q22–23, 21q22 and 22q11–13 (Berrettini, 2002; Jones et al., 2004; Craddock and Forty, 2006). Of these, 15q13–15 (Craddock and Lendon, 1999), 18p11 and 22q11–13 (the VCFS deletion, see Chapter 10) (Berrettini, 2002) are possible susceptibility loci for schizophrenia as well. Other rare variants implicated in both schizophrenia and BD include CNVs in the DISC1 (disrupted in schizophrenia 1) gene on chromosome 1q42.1. These findings seem to be at odds with the absence of common heritability for these two disorders. However, it must be remembered that most of these susceptibility loci are based on a very small number of studies, and often only one for each of the disorders. Furthermore, each of these regions is millions of base pairs long and thus contains multiple genes. Thus, even if linkage of both BD and schizophrenia to these loci was confirmed, they could still be associated with different genes. Finally, even if common susceptibility genes were identified for schizophrenia and BD, they might not directly code for the disorders, but for mediating factors or common phenotypic features. For example, schizophrenia and affective disorder share a higher likelihood of exposure to trauma, and may thus share variations in genes that control the exposure to such environmental factors.

GWAS have produced several new risk loci for BD. The strongest and best-replicated signals were obtained for loci in the CACNA1C gene on chromosome 12p13, which codes for the alpha 1C subunit of the L-type VGCC, and in the ANK3 gene on chromosome 10q21, which codes for the ankyrin-G protein. This regulatory protein is involved in the assembly of VGSC (Chapter 7). Voltage-dependent ion channels are targets of some of the drugs used in the treatment of BD, such as anticonvulsants and calcium channel blockers, and both genes are downregulated by lithium treatment in the mouse brain. Although the functional consequences of these new risk loci are only just beginning to be investigated (Erk et al., 2010), the genes and pathways implicated provide new interesting vistas on the pathophysiology of BD (Barnett and Smoller, 2009).

Box 12.1   Evolutionary psychiatry

Some disease genes are adaptive for certain types of environments and are thus positively selected in the populations exposed to these environments. The most famous example is the gene for sickle cell anaemia, an autosomal recessive blood disorder, which confers relative protection from malaria. Being heterozygous for this gene (and thus not affected by the disease) is therefore of adaptive advantage in areas with endemic malaria such as sub-Saharan Africa. It has been speculated whether similar mechanisms may apply to some features of mental disorders as well. Although mental disorders may be maladaptive in individuals displaying the full syndrome, individual features or attenuated symptoms may actually be adaptive in certain situations. Of course, there are important differences to the sickle cell anaemia scenario because most mental disorders seem to be equally frequent across the globe and thus geographical selection should not play a major role, and because mental disorders are only partly heritable and mostly not monogenetic. However, it is conceivable that individual genetic variants associated with mental disorders are adaptive and only become maladaptive and clinically relevant if too many of them occur in the same person.

Such adaptive analogues of psychiatric symptoms have been proposed for most mental disorders. For example, mania has been suggested to represent dominance and depression submission behaviours. A difference from the socially acceptable forms of such behaviours would be that they lack the foundations and perception by others, certainly in the case of mania. The stupor sometimes observed in severe depression or catatonic schizophrenia may be an extreme form of submissive behaviour, similar to the mammalian freeze response to threat. Dominance and submission are important stabilising factors for communities of social species such as humans because the hierarchies they create serve to minimise violent conflict resolution. Fear reactions also have both an adaptive function for the individual and a social function for the community, in signalling threat, and thus an altruistic element. Anxiety disorders may arise from exaggerated version of fear behaviour, and OCD, in particular, may still show remnants of such altruistic features.

Characteristic themes of delusions of patients with psychotic disorders have also been explained in an evolutionary context. Delusions of jealousy, which are more common in men than women, may reflect male preoccupation with fidelity of the mating partner in the face of uncertain paternity, whereas erotomania (delusion of being loved, often in relation to celebrities), more common in women, may reflect the search for a partner with high social standing.

The emerging field of evolutionary psychiatry, which has the aim of placing psychopathology in an evolutionary context, may fulfil many purposes. For example, understanding the biological basis of dominance behaviour in animals may provide insight into the biology of mania, assuming that these behaviours are homologous rather than merely analogous (Chapter 5). In addition to such direct parallels with animal research, evolutionary psychiatry might define behavioural endophenotypes as targets for genetic studies (Chapter 4). Finally, it may help patients understand the origins of their symptoms and evolutionary models could serve as a starting point for cognitive and behavioural interventions.

12.4   BRAIN STRUCTURE AND FUNCTION

The contribution of brain structural investigations to the understanding of the pathophysiology of mania and bipolar disorder is in many respects similar to the situation in depression (see Chapter 11). Mania can be produced by a multitude of brain lesions in neuropsychiatric conditions, for example the degeneration of the caudate nucleus in Huntington's disease or tumours in the frontal lobe, and these lesions may point to potential neuroanatomical pathways of the disease, for example fronto-striatal circuits. However, patients with BD rarely show abnormalities on gross anatomy, assessed with structural neuroimaging or postmortem techniques. The most widely reported structural imaging finding was enlargement of the third ventricle. Volume losses in medial thalamic or hypothalamic areas that form the walls of the third ventricle have been suggested to underlie this enlargement. A possible implication of the hypothalamus would be of particular interest because of the prominent somatic and autonomic symptoms, for example the disturbed circadian clock, present during both depressed and manic episodes. However, the study by McDonald (McDonald et al., 2006), which reported enlargement of lateral and third ventricles in schizophrenia, found no differences between psychotic BD patients and controls. The heterogeneity of the findings across studies and the effect of age suggest that ventricle size, if altered in affective disorders at all, would be a state rather than a trait marker. This view would be supported by the observation that relatives of patients with familial schizophrenia, but not those of patients with familial BD, also showed increased ventricles. However, we need to keep in mind that even these effects in schizophrenia are small and will never allow the identification of individual affected or at-risk cases, because of the huge overlap with the distribution in the healthy population. Another target of neuroimaging studies has been the amygdala, and although several studies have reported considerable volume reductions in BD patients, a recent meta-analysis has not confirmed this for adult patients (Usher et al., 2010).

Neuropsychological models of BD assume a deficient modulation of subcortical and limbic networks that mediate automatic responses to emotions by prefrontal regions involved in cognitive control and orbitofrontal regions involved in reward evaluation. Such models do not necessarily predict alterations in grey matter volume or microstructure, but would be equally (or even more) compatible with changes in the connectivity between areas. Connectivity is mediated through white matter tracts that can be investigated with structural MRI (e.g. diffusion tensor imaging, DTI) and post-mortem techniques. 'Functional' connectivity, the pattern of covariation of neural activity amongst brain areas, can be assessed with functional imaging or neurophysiological techniques. The 'connectivity' approach has been boosted by consistent observations of reduced volume of the corpus callosum in BD, although these are found to an even greater extent in studies of schizophrenia patients. Diffuse qualitative white matter changes, apparent as 'hyperintensities' on T2-weighted MR images, have also been observed. Such hyperintensities can result from a variety of pathological processes, including inflammation, demyelination and ischaemia. Although inflammatory processes have been implicated in pathophysiological models of BD, post-mortem studies have not produced consistent support for any particular type of pathology.

Amongst the connections between frontal and limbic areas, the uncinate fasciculus, which connects the OFC with the medial temporal lobe, has received particular attention. There is some evidence for diffusion abnormalities in this tract, which could result from aberrant fibres or a reduction of their overall number. Another fibre tract linking limbic areas is the cingulum, which surrounds the cingulate cortex (Figure 12.1, Plate VI). Changes in the anatomical

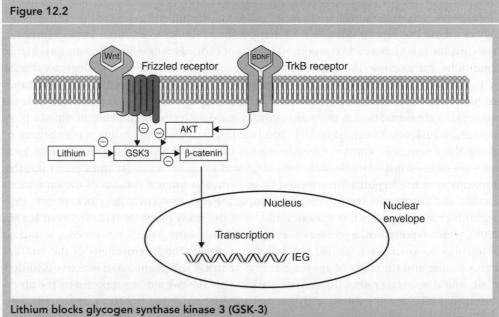

Figure 12.2

Lithium blocks glycogen synthase kinase 3 (GSK-3)
GSK-3 plays a central role in the Wnt and BDNF (brain-derived neurotrophic factor) signaling pathways. Lithium, activation of AKT by the TrkB receptor and activation of the Wnt pathway all inhibit GSK-3. This disinhibits beta-catenin, which can then activate the transcription of IEGs (see Figure 7.7).

connectivity that is mediated through these fibre tracts could also lead to altered properties of functional brain networks that are involved in emotion regulation (Mahon et al., 2010). However, they do not explain the time-varying nature of the symptoms of bipolar disorder.

12.5   NEUROCHEMISTRY AND MECHANISM OF DRUG ACTION

Like for the other classical mental disorders, there is as yet no biomarker for bipolar disorder, and studies of neurotransmitter metabolites or hormones have remained inconclusive. There is some evidence for reduced GABAergic activity from post-mortem studies. Both calbindin- (also implicated in depression) and parvalbumin- (also implicated in schizophrenia) containing interneurons were reduced in several limbic areas. One of the isoforms of GAD, the enzyme that catalyses the decarboxylation of glutamate to GABA in the mature brain (GAD67), was reduced in the hippocampus of BD patients. Reduced numbers of GABAergic interneurons and GABA synthesis would be compatible with reduced GABAergic activity (Martinowich et al., 2009). This reduced GABAergic activity may be one of the targets of valproic acid, a GABA agonist, and make it effective as a mood stabiliser.

Like in the cases of schizophrenia and depression, the main evidence for neurochemical models of BD is based on the biological effects of pharmacological treatment. Lithium inhibits several enzymes that are involved in the metabolism of inositol and might thus impact on the IP_3 signalling pathway (Chapter 3). Moreover, lithium and valproic acid reduce levels of PKC, a downstream target of the IP_3 pathway. Interestingly, one of the risk loci found in some (but not all) of the GWAS of BD was in the gene for diacylglycerol (DAG) kinase. This enzyme regulates levels of DAG, which is one of the second messengers of the IP_3/DAG pathway that leads to the modulation of PKC activity. Thus, there is both genetic and therapeutic evidence to implicate the IP_3/DAG pathway in BD, although the function of the risk variant is unknown and abnormalities in this pathway have not been demonstrated directly.

Lithium also affects the Wnt signalling pathway (Chapter 3) through inhibition of GSK-3. The Wnt pathway is important for neuronal and synaptic growth and plasticity. GSK-3 normally inhibits the downstream effects of this signalling cascade (Figure 12.2). Lithium thus has a disinhibitory effect, and there is indeed some evidence that it stimulates neuronal growth and hippocampal neurogenesis. Taken together with the evidence for reduced neural density and soma size in cortical areas from post-mortem studies (Schloesser et al., 2008), these treatment effects might suggest that BD is characterised by a loss and/or shrinkage of neurons that is reversed by lithium treatment. However, the post-mortem evidence is inconsistent and concerns only specific layers of cortex. The changes also do not seem to be progressive. Thus, models implicating neurodevelopmental abnormalities in BD are intriguing but need to be corroborated by further evidence.

Interestingly dopaminergic psychostimulants have opposite effects to lithium on these signalling pathways, in that they activate GSK-3 and PKC (Salvadore et al., 2010). These effects may explain some of the overlap of the behavioural and psychological features of stimulant abuse and mania. Although there is no direct evidence for hyperdopaminergic states in BD, the effects of antidopaminergic antipsychotics on manic symptoms (and even as phase prophylactic) and several animal models (see below) make such a link an intriguing possibility.

Patients with a history of BD are at increased risk of developing psychotic symptoms after glucocorticoid therapy (administered, e.g. for autoimmune disorders). This clinical observation has led to the assumption that the regulation of the HPA axis (e.g. through negative feedback mechanisms) is dysfunctional in BD. This assumption is supported by some animal models, which have shown mania-like behaviour in animals with increased expression of the glucocorticoid receptor, but not by consistent alterations of assays of HPA activity in humans, such as the dexamethasone suppression test.

12.6   ANIMAL MODELS

Behavioural features of mania in animal models have good face validity. Some of them, like hyperactivity and increased exploratory behaviour, directly oppose those of depression. Pharmacological and genetic manipulation of the dopamine system supports an involvement of this NT in both phases of BD. Depletion of the NT or its receptors leads to depression-like behaviours, whereas application of psychostimulants produces pictures that resemble mania, including hyperactivity and insomnia. In addition to various pharmacological manipulations, such symptoms can be induced by sleep deprivation. This model has good construct validity, at least as far as potential trigger processes are concerned, because sleep deprivation can lead to a switch from depressive to manic symptoms (Salvadore et al., 2010). The manic-like symptoms of sleep-deprived animals, including hypersexuality, irritability and aggression, could be reversed by lithium treatment, giving the model good predictive validity (Martinowich et al., 2009).

Two genetic animal models suggest links between BD and the glutamate and circadian regulation systems, respectively. Knock-out of the GLUR6 gene, which codes for the GLUK2 subunit of the kainate receptor (Chapter 7), led to aggressive and risk-taking behaviour and less anxiety in mice. Links between the glutamate system and BD are also suggested by the effects of lamotrigine and other anticonvulsants used in the treatment of BD, which lower glutamate release through inhibition of VGCC and VGSC. However, it is not clear what aspects of glutamate homoeostasis might be disturbed in BD.

Dysregulation of circadian timers in BD has long been suspected because of the rhythmicity of the disorder and the link with sleep deprivation and insomnia. A functional mutation of the CLOCK gene, which codes for a protein involved in the regulation of the circadian rhythms, indeed led to hyperactivity, insomnia and reward-seeking behaviour in mice, which are all features of mania, and reduced anxiety. Again these effects could be partly reversed by lithium (Martinowich et al., 2009). The regulation of circadian and other rhythms in BD is certainly one of the most promising target mechanisms for the further investigation of the elusive biology of this cyclic disorder.

12.7   TREATMENT WITH MOOD STABILISERS

12.7.1   Lithium modulates several postsynaptic signalling cascades

The effect of a mood stabiliser is supposed to depend on the mood state of the patient and the ideal mood stabiliser would normalise both depressive and manic states as well as preventing them from occurring in the first place. The combination of antidepressant and antimanic properties in the same drug seems paradoxical. However, it may be better to think of mood stabilisers not so much as antidepressants (which they are not, at least not as an effective monotherapy of unipolar depression) that can also lower mood in manic states, but as drugs that readjust the homoeostasis of the affective systems.

Lithium was the first mood stabiliser and fulfils all three of the above requirements. It alleviates depressive and manic episodes and is effective in reducing the number of episodes or phases of bipolar disorder. Lithium has an effect on several second messenger cascades. It blocks the enzyme inositol monophosphatase and thus reduces the availability of inositol for the synthesis of PIP_2, which has a negative effect on the DAG/IP_3 pathway. Lithium also seems to have complex effects on the cAMP pathway. It increases the activity of adenyl cyclase at baseline, but reduces its additional stimulation through G_s-protein activation. Such state-dependent effects are very attractive potential mechanisms for a drug that can have apparently opposite effects in different clinical states, but there is not yet any direct evidence linking depressive states with under- and manic states with over-activation of G_s-protein coupled receptors. Lithium also inhibits GSK-3 and thus disinhibits CREB and several other transcription factors (see Chapter 7). Animal studies suggest a direct link between GSK-3 inhibition and the behavioural effects of lithium. GSK-3 inhibition (as well as activation of neurotrophin signalling cascades) may also underlie the positive effect of lithium on the production of BDNF (Quiroz et al., 2010).

12.7.2 Lithium has a narrow therapeutic range

Lithium is generally tolerated well. However, some patients experience side effects, particularly initially. These can arise from lithium effects on the brain (e.g. tremor, cognitive impairment), kidneys (polyuria – passing great volumes of urine with low electrolyte concentration, polydipsia – increased thirst), bowels (diarrhoea) and hormonal systems. Cardiac arrhythmias can occur in rare cases, mainly with pre-existing heart conditions. Like the SSRIs (and carbamazepine), lithium can also induce SIADH in some cases. If side effects persist, another mood stabiliser may have to be chosen, although some of them can be controlled with additional medication (e.g. beta-blocker for tremor) or dose reduction. Renal, cardiac and thyroid dysfunctions have to be excluded before lithium treatment is initiated, and plasma levels (0.6–0.8 mmol/l for prophylactic effect, up to 1.1 mmol/l for antimanic effect) have to be monitored. Lithium has a particularly narrow therapeutic range (see Chapter 6). Signs of intoxication can occur from plasma levels of 1.5 mmol/l, and even at therapeutic concentrations, for example when other electrolytes are in imbalance. Lithium intoxication manifests itself with neurological symptoms such as tremor, psychomotor retardation and balance problems, and with nausea, vomiting and diarrhoea. Severe cases proceed to seizures and coma, in which case removal of the lithium from the circulation by haemodialysis may be required.

12.7.3 Several anticonvulsants are effective mood stabilisers

Several anticonvulsants (drugs used in the treatment of epileptic seizures), for example valproic acid, carbamazepine and lamotrigine, are also effective mood stabilisers. They can be used as the sole treatment of bipolar disorder, although there is better evidence for their antimanic and prophylactic properties than for their ability to curb depressive episodes. However, carbamazepine and lamotrigine, the atypical antipsychotics quetiapine and olanzapine and (with some limitations in the available evidence) lithium have all been shown to be superior to placebo in the treatment of bipolar depression, with similar effect sizes to antidepressants and without incurring the risk of affective switches (into hypomanic episodes) associated with antidepressants. These mood stabilisers or antipsychotics therefore seem to be safer options for the first-line treatment of bipolar depression than antidepressants (Van Lieshout and MacQueen, 2010).

The prophylactic properties are particularly well established for valproic acid. Most anticonvulsants modulate the opening of VGSC (see Chapter 7). They appear to block VGSC mainly after prolonged depolarisation or repetitive activation, such as occurs during a seizure, but not at normal resting potential. This may explain why they can prevent the spread of epileptic discharges without interfering with normal signal transmission. Some of the anticonvulsants also seem to act on VGCC. Their negative effect on cytosolic calcium and net inhibitory effect on action potential firing would affect glutamate release more than GABA. Valproate also seems to have a direct GABAergic effect by increasing GABA turnover (Rogawski and Löscher, 2004). GABA agonism (e.g. by benzodiazepines) is another well-known mechanism for the control of seizures, which is mainly used for acute treatment of a manic episode.

12.7.4 Anticonvulsants have important side effects and drug interactions

The activity-dependent, dynamic effects of anticonvulsants on neuronal excitability are an attractive property for a drug that is supposed to have state-dependent effects in the control of disordered mood. However, the pathophysiology of bipolar disorder is poorly understood but likely to be very different from that of epilepsy. For example, the characteristic EEG features of epilepsy do not accompany bipolar disorder, and the EEG does not change in any notable way between manic, depressive or euthymic episodes. It is thus an open question whether the cellular mechanism implicated in the antiepileptic effect also support the mood stabilising effect of anticonvulsant drugs.

Neurological side effects, for example sedation, are common in the initial phase of treatment with anticonvulsants but normally transient. Carbamazepine is prone to induce allergic skin reactions. These are normally benign, but carbamazepine (the same applies to lamotrigine and valproic acid) very rarely leads to Stevens-Johnson syndrome, a life-threatening skin condition, in which case it needs to be discontinued immediately. Carbamazepine can also lead to cardiac arrhythmia and should therefore not be used in patients with pre-existing cardiac blocks. Finally, like clozapine and some antidepressants, carbamazepine can suppress the production of blood cells in bone marrow and should therefore not be combined with other such substances. Carbamazepine induces CYP3A4 (Chapter 6) and can thus lower plasma levels of drugs metabolised through this pathway. Valproic acid can interfere with liver and, less commonly, pancreas function, necessitating regular control of the relevant enzyme levels. It inhibits CYP2C9 and glucuronyltransferases and thus interferes with both phases (oxidation and conjugation) of drug metabolism in the liver. It can thus increase the plasma levels of other drugs. One example is its blockade of the metabolism of anticoagulant drugs, which necessitates regular controls of coagulation parameters under such drug combinations.

12.7.5 Atypical antipsychotics have an increasing role in the treatment of mania and bipolar disorder

Atypical antipsychotics, for example olanzapine, aripiprazole, risperidone and quetiapine, are now in use for all phases of bipolar disorder. They have a unique role in the treatment of severe manic episodes, especially those with agitation and psychotic symptoms, where lithium or anticonvulsants alone are ineffective. They can be given on their own or in combination with lithium or an anticonvulsant. Some of the atypical antipsychotics are also effective in the prophylaxis of manic episodes (especially in patients who responded well during an acute manic phase) and in the treatment of depressive episodes. The mechanism behind the mood stabilising effects of some antipsychotics is not clear. However, it is of note that recent genetic and biological marker studies suggest a closer overlap between schizophrenia and bipolar disorder than previously thought (see Chapter 10), which may make it less surprising that the same drugs help in both disorders. The regulatory approval for antipsychotics for the indications treatment of manic and depressive episodes and prophylaxis varies between drugs and countries, and 'off label' use (use of a drug for an indication other than that for which is has regulatory approval) is relatively common. Because regulatory approaches vary between countries, and indications are constantly updated, we generally have not included lists of approved indications, and clinicians will have to consult the current national formularies and information issued by their relevant regulatory bodies.

12.7.6   Treatment in practice

The ideal medication for BD is one that controls both manic and depressive symptoms and prevents acute phases from occurring (phase prophylactic). The three drugs that are currently recommended in the UK (in the 2006 guidelines of the National Institute of Health and Clinical Excellence, NICE: http://guidance.nice.org.uk/CG38) as first-line monotherapy of BD, lithium, valproate and olanzapine, all fulfil this criterion, although they vary in their effectiveness for manic and depressive episodes. On the one hand, if new treatment is initiated during an acute manic episode, valproate or olanzapine may be favoured over lithium because clinical effects can be obtained faster. On the other hand, lithium may be more effective for depressive episodes and reduces the risk of suicide. If depressive episodes cannot be managed with a mood stabiliser or antipsychotic alone, an antidepressant can be added. Particular caution needs to be applied because of the risk of antidepressant-induced mood switches, which can drive a patient from a depressive directly into a manic episode. Antidepressant medication should therefore not be continued beyond the duration of depressive symptoms, and might even be stopped after only partial remission has been achieved. SSRIs seem to have a lower risk of inducing mood switches than TCAs (Salvadore et al., 2010). Patients with rapid cycling should not be prescribed antidepressants at all.

If one of the first-line drugs is not effective as a phase prophylactic or antimanic agent, combination of two first-line drugs is the next option. If even this is ineffective, a combination of lithium or olanzapine with carbamazepine or lamotrigine can be tried. For manic episodes with psychotic symptoms or severe agitation, antipsychotics may be superior to the other options. Risperidone and quetiapine are alternatives to olanzapine for this indication.

Psychosocial interventions also have an established place in the management of BD. Patients can be educated about the course of the illness and general measures aimed at reducing the number of episodes and their consequences, for example sleep hygiene and avoiding financial decisions, although this may be of limited use during acute manic episodes. Education of relatives and carers about the disorder may be equally important. Psychoeducative approaches or a formal course of CBT are important options for the management of depressive episodes and might be considered even at levels at severity that in unipolar depression would call for pharmacotherapy.

The prophylactic maintenance treatment with one of the first-line drugs should continue for at least two years after a diagnosis of BD has been established (that is, after the second episode) or even after a single manic episode if it has been severe. Longer maintenance treatment is recommended for patients with high risk of recurrence, for example those with a history of frequent clinical episodes.

Learning points

Bipolar disorder is a cyclic mood disorder with recurrent episodes of mania or alternations between mania and depression, interspersed with symptom-free intervals. The symptomatic episodes last several months and can be interrupted by intervals of months or years. A particularly fast alternation (at least four cycles per year) of symptomatic and symptom-free episodes defines 'rapid cycling'. Bipolar disorder affects about 1% of the population and is equally common in men and women. Its heritability is about 60%, and several loci of small effect have been identified in GWAS. Structural imaging and post-mortem investigation of grey matter has so far remained largely inconclusive, but there are interesting findings in white matter, for example in the fibre tracts linking prefrontal cortex with the limbic system.

As with most other mental disorders neurochemical models are based upon the pharmacological properties of clinically effective drugs. Lithium blocks GSK-3, and the resulting activation of transcription factors has been implicated in its therapeutic effect. The anticonvulsant mood stabilisers interact with VGCC and VGSC, but primary changes in these, if present, are probably subtle. Alterations of GABAergic interneuron firing have also been discussed. Another approach has been to design animal models based on behavioural features of BD, for example using sleep deprivation or selecting for hyperactivity and hypersexuality, and investigate their biological correlates. Dysregulation of internal timers, possibly caused by changes in the CLOCK gene, has also been discussed. However, no integrated model of neurochemical deficits in BD has been produced so far.

Lithium and anticonvulsants are the main mood stabilisers. They generally have better antimanic and prophylactic than antidepressant properties. Atypical antipsychotics are also increasingly being explored for a role in bipolar disorder, particularly in the control of manic episodes with psychotic features. Lithium, the anticonvulsants valproate, lamotrigine and carbamazepine and atypical antipsychotics are all recommended in use as mono- or combined therapies for BD, and the selection of the type of treatment will depend on the individual clinical profile.

Revision and discussion questions

- Describe the symptoms and course of a manic episode.
- What main treatments are available for bipolar disorder.
- Can mania be regarded as a particular type of creativity?

FURTHER READING

Brüne, M. (2008). *Textbook of Evolutionary Psychiatry: The Origins of Psychopathology* (Oxford: Oxford University Press).

13 ANXIETY DISORDERS

PREVIEW

Anxiety disorders include specific phobias, social phobia, separation anxiety disorder of childhood, generalised anxiety disorder, panic disorder, obsessive compulsive disorder and post-traumatic stress disorder. Although these disorders differ considerably in their clinical features, there is considerable comorbidity between them, and they seem to share some biological features. Their treatment (both psychological and pharmacological) also follows common principles, and the two main classes of drugs with anxiolytic properties, benzodiazepines and SSRIs, are used in many of these disorders. After a description of the clinical phenotypes, this chapter will therefore present the genetic, neuroimaging and neurochemical evidence in a comparative fashion and discuss the treatment options divided by drug classes rather than disorders. A specific interest of this chapter is the discussion of the brain's fear circuits and their significance for anxiety disorders. Many behavioural features of anxiety disorders can be modelled in animals with good face validity.

13.1 HISTORY

The group of anxiety disorders is probably the most common diagnostic category in psychiatry. Up to 30% of the population suffer from an anxiety disorder at some point in their lives. This category comprises specific and social phobias, generalised anxiety disorder (GAD), panic attacks, obsessive compulsive disorder (OCD) and post-traumatic stress disorder (PTSD). Some of these concepts have a long tradition, going back to Freud's theory of neuroses, whereas others have been recognised (or even appeared) only in the last decades, for example PTSD (widely recognised in the aftermath of the Korean and Vietnam wars but probably present already in veterans of World War II) and social phobia. All these disorders are linked by excessive fear in the absence of true danger that can be triggered by specific objects or situations and often leads to avoidance.

The first descriptions of anxiety disorders, agoraphobia and OCD were made by the German neurologist Carl Friedrich Otto Westphal (1833–90) in the 1870s. Sigmund Freud (1856–1939), the founder of psychoanalysis, singled anxiety out as a core neurosis and gave it a distinctly sexual interpretation. Distinct reactions to traumatic events such as railway accidents or combat experience were recognised since the middle of the nineteenth century and developed into famous concepts like 'hysteric paralysis' and 'shell shock'. But it was not until 1980 that PTSD was introduced as a diagnostic category into the DSM. It was and still is unique amongst the psychiatric diagnoses in that it could be completely determined by a single environmental event (Healy, 1993). Social phobia first appeared in the same third edition of the DSM. These new disease entities have triggered questions about the distinction between pathology and normality like perhaps no other psychiatric diagnoses. About a third of male Vietnam veterans with direct combat experience later suffered from PTSD. PTSD may thus be a common reaction to uncommon stressors. The criterion for classifying it as 'pathological' would then be its maladaptive nature rather than its frequency of occurrence in response to relevant triggers. PTSD is set apart from other anxiety disorders by the relative rarity of the triggering events, but social phobia may be less easily distinguished from normality. Where does 'normal' (socially acceptable and adaptive) shyness end and where does social phobia/social anxiety disorder begin? Here, the criteria will very much depend on subjective distress, which in turn will be influenced by the expectations of work and society. Although all diagnostic concepts in psychiatry are to some extent subject to cultural change, this seems to apply particularly to anxiety disorders. An additional interesting aspect is whether diagnoses gain public recognition in parallel with the development or adaptation of drugs for their treatments, as has been argued for social phobia (Lane, 2007).

13.2   CLINICAL SYNDROMES

A common feature of anxiety disorders is the exaggerated anxiety reaction to objectively innocuous stimuli or situations (or in the absence of such triggers). Like all emotions, the anxiety reaction has psychological/experiential (feeling anxious), physiological (correlates of heightened arousal, such as increasing heart beat), cognitive (focus on potential triggers, lack of concentration) and behavioural (e.g. avoidance) components. One main classification of the anxiety disorders follows the triggering stimuli or situations. In the *simple* or *specific phobias* the anxiety reaction is triggered by a specific object (e.g. spider, blood) or situation (e.g. fear of heights). Two specific phobias have been singled out as separate syndromes, *agoraphobia* (fear of being in open or closed places or being part of a crowd) and *social phobia* (fear of contact with other people, or of public speaking). In PTSD the triggering situation is a traumatic experience in the past that is re-experienced in the imagination, whereas in OCD the anxiety reaction is triggered by the actual or imagined contact with contaminated objects or lack of control over potential danger. Panic attacks may not have any discernible trigger (although comorbidity with agoraphobia and social phobia is high), nor does the more pervasively anxious and worried state of GAD. *Separation anxiety disorder*, which can occur in both children and adults, shares features of the phobias and of GAD.

13.2.1   Specific phobias

In specific phobias, the presence, expectation or even thought of an object or situation that does not constitute real danger nevertheless triggers an anxiety reaction. Patients will feel uncomfortable in this situation or the presence of the object in question and try and escape from it and/or avoid it. If this is not possible, they may show sign of symptoms of a full-blown anxiety reaction, even amounting to a panic attack. Specific phobias can be subdivided into those related to animals, for example spiders or dogs, situations, for example being in open or confined spaces, or under public scrutiny, natural environment, for example fear of heights, and injury, for example fear of dental procedures or venepuncture. Although all these triggers are objectively innocuous they may be linked to situations that entailed danger during evolution and still do in a natural habitat (see Box 12.1 on Evolutionary Psychiatry). For example, certain types of spiders are poisonous to humans, or fear of heights may have been a useful safeguard against too adventurous exploration of the environment (these days it mainly restricts the recreational activities of those affected, at least in industrialised countries). Fear may be a natural antidote to exploratory behaviour, and every species probably needs a balance between conservative and novelty-seeking traits in order to survive in stable but also adapt to changing environments. Phobias may just be the extreme of the conservative and avoidant spectrum of behaviours, whereas mania, ADHD and addiction may be the extreme and pathological states of the novelty-seeking behaviour.

The technical term for a specific phobia is formed by adding -phobia to the Greek (sometimes Latin) name of the animal or situation. Thus, fear of spiders becomes arachnophobia, fear of heights acrophobia, fear of the night nyctophobia, fear of being naked gymnophobia, and fear of dental procedures odontophobia. There are many long lists of specific phobias, some of which sound outlandish and are probably quite rare, but in principle any object or situation could become phobogenic through fear conditioning. However, most phobias are probably not acquired through conditioning or some other experience of association of the trigger with actual danger, but arise from the interplay between innate fear programmes and environmental stress (it is noteworthy that most phobias are not manifest until adolescence or even adulthood, and thus do not constitute pure instinctive behaviour). The severity of specific phobias can be measured by questionnaires or by the delay until escape mechanisms come into force. For example, one test to assess treatment success in arachnophobia is based on the time that patients are prepared to keep a spider in their hand.

13.2.2 Social phobia

Social phobia is a situational specific phobia where fear is induced by real or anticipated contact with other people. This can apply to any type of social contact, but commonly large groups and performance under pressure make symptoms worse. For example, a patient may be perfectly capable of giving a presentation fluently and competently to a good friend. Yet when it comes to giving the same presentation to an audience of superiors or even colleagues, the patient becomes nervous and jittery and ultimately has to interrupt the talk in order to avoid a panic attack. Severe forms of social phobia are disabling and seriously impact on patients' socio-economic status because unlike spiders or heights, social interactions cannot easily be avoided and are an important requirement for positions in the services industry, which is by far the largest part of the Western economy. Certainly by the time a patient loses his or her job as a consequence of the inability to talk to colleagues, attend meetings or give presentations, it becomes clear that this syndrome goes far beyond the character trait of 'conventional' shyness.

13.2.3 Separation anxiety disorder

Here the trigger is separation from the home or the key attachment figures (e.g. parents, partner). The main preoccupation is then to stay in contact with the attachment figures, the desire to return home and related fantasies, and worry about losing them due to some kind of disaster. Separation can lead to physical symptoms such as aches and nausea, and patients may have nightmares about being separated from their loved ones or about catastrophes befalling the family. The problems experienced during actual separation may lead to a vicious circle, compounding the separation anxiety. Ultimately this may impact on the patient's academic development or professional life, for example refusal to go to school or undertake work-related travel. Although classically associated with onset in childhood, adult separation anxiety disorder is now increasingly being recognised and may actually be more common. Because in most cases of childhood-onset separation anxiety symptoms subside with time, adult separation disorder may be an independent entity.

13.2.4   Generalised anxiety disorder (GAD)

Patients with GAD may not exhibit the full anxiety syndrome all the time, but can be in a constant state of worry and heightened arousal. Although there are no specific triggers, their cognitive focus may be narrowed on specific areas of concern, such as money, health (their own or that of loved ones), death, job security or generally the future. Patients with GAD also frequently have physiological and somatic signs and symptoms, probably more so than in the specific phobias. One explanation may be that avoidance of the trigger is not a realistic option in GAD, and control of the thoughts and worries would have to be a result of a successful therapy.

13.2.5   Panic disorder

Panic disorder describes the frequent occurrence of panic attacks. These are relatively brief (seconds to hours) states of intense fear and physiological processes associated with the fight-or-flight response, such as increasing heart beat or hyperventilation, but also other somatic and neurological signs and symptoms such as nausea, chest pain, sweating, dizziness, and paraesthesias. It is an extremely worrying experience (often mistakenly interpreted as a heart attack by first-time sufferers) and may occur without an external trigger. However, serious medical, for example heart, conditions can trigger panic attacks, as can pharmacological agents (e.g. alcohol, caffeine, cocaine) and, of course, all the triggers of specific phobias.

13.2.6   Obsessive compulsive disorder (OCD)

OCD is a complex syndrome of behavioural, cognitive and affective symptoms. Patients often have a narrowed cognitive focus on particular objects or situations (obsessions). They may worry about contact with actual or supposed contaminated objects, especially objects that might entail danger under highly hypothetical circumstances (for example, an intravenous needle or a mercury-filled thermometer). Another common worry is that they may do harm to their own or others' life or possessions, for example by failing to switch off electrical appliances. Most patients are aware of the irrational nature of their fears but still are not able to control them. Even reassurances by others will rarely suffice to sway them, resulting in the subjective need to control the source of danger in an exaggerated manner, for example by washing their hands or checking the oven over and over again (compulsions). If control cannot be achieved, intense fear may be the consequence. Substantial psychosocial repercussions, such as inability to hold on to a job or relationship, may further impact on patients' well-being, leading to a vicious circle of social isolation and increasing time spent on routines that give only partial relief. Excessive hoarding is recognised as a special case of OCD, and there is substantial comorbidity with tic disorders, such as Gilles-de-la-Tourette disorder, where patients feel the compulsion to utter obscenities and suffer from involuntary movements. Obsessive symptoms also occur outside OCD and are part of many mental disorders, such as depression, personality disorders and the prodromal state of psychosis. However, the insight in the irrational nature of the obsessions, which is preserved in OCD, constitutes a marked difference to states of psychosis. In some patients, OCD may express itself mainly as a cognitive-affective disorder with prominent obsessions, in others as an executive-behavioural disorder with prominent compulsions, and in others as a combination of the two (Graybiel and Rauch, 2000). These different symptom spectra have led to the formulation of neuropsychological models, largely based on findings in patients with focal brain lesions presenting with OCD-like symptoms (see Box 13.1).

13.2.7   Post-traumatic stress disorder (PTSD)

The classic 'trauma' that triggers PTSD is an episode of danger to someone's life or physical health, such as coming under fire during combat, experience of a natural catastrophe or a severe traffic accident. Causing the death or mutilation of another person can also be such a trigger, which is a common problem in railway drivers because of the relatively high number of suicides committed on rail tracks. More recently, it has also been recognised that the mere presence at the site of an accident or the experience of comrades being hurt during combat can also be such a trauma. Actual bodily harm to the patient is therefore not a requirement for the diagnosis of PTSD to be made. According to the ICD-10, the triggering event is of a nature that would cause distress (though not necessarily PTSD symptoms) in almost everyone. Symptoms of PTSD can start from immediately normally up to six months after the event. They include cognitive (concentration), affective (irritability) and behavioural (inability to revisit the site of the accident or to face similar situations again) problems, and often the regular re-experience of the event (flashbacks and nightmares). If avoidance strategies cannot be implemented (e.g. in war zones) intense stress and anxiety reactions can result. The large variability in the propensity of people to develop PTSD after traumas of outwardly similar severity makes it likely that predisposing factors, such as personality factors and childhood experiences, play an important role.

13.3   EPIDEMIOLOGY

According to data from the United States, the lifetime prevalence for panic disorder is around 5% (1% with and 4% without accompanying agoraphobia) and for isolated panic attacks even over 20%. Most people with panic disorder and even over 60% of people with isolated panic attacks seek treatment at some point. Lifetime prevalence estimates for specific phobia and social phobia are around 12% each, 4% for childhood separation anxiety disorder, 7% for adult separation anxiety disorder, 6% for GAD, 7% for PTSD and 1–2% each for OCD and agoraphobia. Allowing for some double diagnoses, about 30% of the population thus experience symptoms of an anxiety disorder at least once in their life. Even the 12-month prevalence (occurrence of symptoms in any 12-month period) of anxiety disorders is high, at 18%, indicating that these disorders can affect patients' lives over long periods, although most of these cases are mild. Most anxiety disorders affect women more frequently than men. Women are 4 times more likely to suffer from agoraphobia and two to three times more likely to suffer from specific phobia, panic disorder, PTSD or GAD. The most reported triggers for PTSD are related to sexual abuse for women and to combat for men (although this may apply to only countries involved in military campaigns, and female/male ratios may be higher in other countries). Gender distributions are approximately equal only for OCD and social phobia. Specific phobias and separation anxiety disorder almost always start in childhood (mean age of onset: seven years), social phobia mainly in adolescence and other disorders in adulthood, mainly between 20 and 30. Interestingly, a history of anxiety disorder was reported considerably (about 50%) less in the over 60 age group (Kessler et al., 2005, 2006).

There are several possible explanations for this. Anxiety disorders may have become more common over the last decades (and thus, rates will be higher once the 30-year-olds of today have reached their 60s) or they may have been under-diagnosed in the past. For example, some of the diagnostic categories of today's DSM-IV appeared only 30 years ago (see above). Other explanations are that memory of symptoms experienced in the past fades away as people become older, especially when they never received a formal diagnosis, or that older people feel more embarrassed about reporting certain symptoms.

13.4   GENETICS

The evidence for a genetic contribution and for specific genetic loci seems to be strongest for PTSD amongst the anxiety disorders. Because the definition of a traumatic experience is fluid and depends on both subjective and cultural factors it is difficult to determine how many people experience a trauma in their lifetime and how many of them develop mental health problems as a consequence. It has been estimated that about 5–10% of those affected by a traumatic experience will develop PTSD. This relatively low (although it is higher for severe combat experience) number indicates that other factors, which may be psychosocial, genetic or otherwise biological, need to be present for a trauma to lead to PTSD.

Family or twin studies of PTSD are constrained by the difficulty of finding families or twin pairs where two members suffered trauma of similar severity but only one developed PTSD. The Vietnam Twin Registry afforded such an opportunity. Here, mono- and dizygotic twin pairs who experienced traumas during the Vietnam War could be examined for the occurrence of PTSD. Monozygotic twins were more likely both to suffer from the disorder than dizygotic pairs, with heritability estimated around 30%. However, some of this shared variance may have been explained by common personality factors such as irritability, which have a high heritability, rather than factors specifically related to PTSD (Norrholm and Ressler, 2009). In any event, the heritability estimates are relatively low compared to other mental disorders.

Candidate gene studies have focused on genes regulating neurotransmitter action and trafficking. The polymorphism in the promoter region of the serotonin transporter (SERT or 5-HTT) gene on the long arm of chromosome 17 with a long (L) and short (S) allele is the most studied genetic variant with respect to anxiety and anxiety disorders. S carriers have less expression of the SERT and consequently less 5-HT reuptake into the presynaptic terminal and higher 5-HT availability in the synaptic cleft. Several studies with PTSD patients found an association with the homozygous S genotype, but also indicated a gene × environment (G×E) interaction, where the S allele contributed to PTSD only when the trauma was severe and the available social support poor (Norrholm and Ressler, 2009).

Heritability estimates for GAD are similar to those for PTSD, at 30%, and indeed some of the inherited risk factors (both in terms of personality traits and in terms of the underlying genes) may be identical. For example GAD has also been associated with the low activity S allele. This may sound paradoxical in a disorder that is treated with drugs (the SSRI) that reduce reuptake. Because the main neurobiological change leading to clinical symptoms may not be the initial higher serotonin availability but the ensuing postsynaptic adaptations (e.g. receptor downregulation) the SSRI effects may not be so paradoxical, though.

The genetic contribution to the phobias is relatively small, with heritability estimates being highest for agoraphobia (36%) and as low as 10% for specific phobias. Panic disorder has higher heritability estimates of up to 60%, but candidate gene studies have not yielded any strong effects. Linkage studies, which pointed to a susceptibility locus on chromosome

15 near genes coding for GABA$_A$ receptor subunits, and genome-wide association studies may be more promising (Norrholm and Ressler, 2009). The situation is similar in OCD, where heritability may be moderate (in the range of 50%) but no risk genes are known. One reason may be that previous studies have mostly looked at genes associated with the disorder rather than genes that may be associated with symptom dimensions. Of the five proposed dimensions – symmetry/order, contamination/cleaning, checking, hoarding and somatic/sexual/religious obsessions – hoarding seems to be the most heritable. The situation in OCD is thus paradigmatic for many other mental disorders, including schizophrenia, where recent work has challenged the strict diagnostic categories on both clinical and biological grounds. If it can be shown that certain symptom dimensions are independent of others (for which there is good evidence), have different treatment response profiles (this is less clear) and different genetic/neurobiological correlates (almost nothing is known about this), a new – more dimensional or symptom-based – approach to diagnoses will be needed.

Another possible explanation for the general scarcity of specific genetic associations with anxiety disorders may be that gene effects and generally the underlying neurobiology constitute a risk to develop fear and distress in general, and that then the specific clinical phenotype is more related to the traumatic events or experiences and other environmental influences. It is therefore generally recognised in the field that future studies need to take G×E interactions and the genetic underpinnings of resilience ('immunity' against developing anxiety disorders after stress or trauma) more into account.

13.5   BRAIN STRUCTURE

Most information about altered brain anatomy and function in anxiety disorders comes from neuroimaging studies of patients with PTSD or OCD. The most consistent structural finding in PTSD has been reduced volume of the hippocampus, but not with a sensitivity and specificity that would allow for its use as a diagnostic marker. Reduced regional brain volume has also been reported for the ACC and insula. A major question in any mental disorder, but particularly in those directly resulting from a specific trauma, is whether such changes pre- or post-date the triggering event or onset of the disorder. In the latter case, numerous confounds may play a role, including psychotropic medication, hospitalisation and changing lifestyle and health behaviour. In the specific case of PTSD, are these brain changes a vulnerability marker or a consequence of the stress response? – which is a possibility because chronic stress has led to loss of hippocampal volume (mainly neuropil) in rodent models. The literature is inconclusive on this point. A study of Vietnam veterans with PTSD found smaller hippocampi also in their unaffected, non-combatant twins, pointing to the role as a risk factor. However, another study with Vietnam veterans and their twins found volume reductions in the hippocampus, ACC and insula only in the individuals affected with PTSD, suggesting that this volume loss may be a consequence of combat stress and PTSD. This twin study methodology is based on the generally high heritability of brain volume and structural features.

Brain imaging work in OCD has focused on the circuits between striatum, thalamus, ACC and OFC that have been implicated in neuropsychological models of the disorder (see Box 13.1). Some studies with children and adults affected with OCD indeed reported increased grey matter in these regions as well as increased fractional anisotropy in the white matter tracts connecting them, for example the cingulum bundle. These circuits are of particular interest for OCD because they are also the main targets for the surgical treatment of OCD.

Both severing the anterior cingulum (cingulotomy) and the anterior part of the capsule interna (capsulotomy), which carries fibres connecting PFC and the dorsomedial thalamus, have shown some promise in otherwise intractable cases of OCD (Greenberg et al., 2010).

Box 13.1   Neuropsychological models of OCD

Symptoms of OCD such as ritualistic and repetitive behaviours or intrusive thoughts also occur in a wide range of neurological disorders. They represent the full spectrum of brain pathologies, including (post)inflammatory (Sydenham's chorea, arising after streptococcal infections; multiple sclerosis), neurodegenerative (frontotemporal dementia, Huntington's disease, Parkinson's disease), toxic (manganese), traumatic, ischaemic and inherited metabolic disorders (Lesch-Nyhan syndrome, which leads to overproduction of uric acid). However, the mainly affected areas show a clear pattern: the frontal lobe, the basal ganglia and their connecting fibre tracts. Taken together with the structural and functional imaging findings from OCD patients, these focal lesion data point to alterations in fronto-basal ganglia circuits as neurobiological substrate for obsessive and compulsive symptoms.

Functional neuropsychological models of OCD have been predicated on these circuits. The OFC, ACC and caudate nucleus have been associated with the evaluation of the rewarding or punishing consequences of stimuli or actions, the selection of appropriate actions and the learning of habits and action sequences, respectively. The reward expectancies mediated by the OFC may be faulty in OCD, and patients may rely on the short-term relief from performing ritualistic actions for want

Figure 13.1

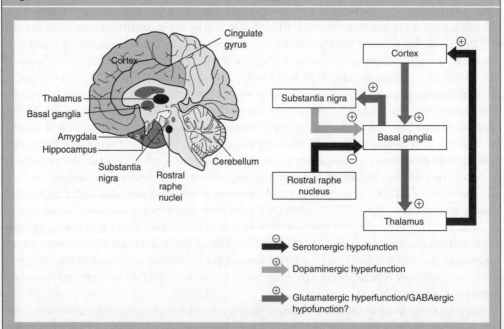

Putative circuits of Obsessive Compulsive Disorder (OCD)
Reduced serotonergic input from the raphe nuclei and increased glutamatergic and dopaminergic activity may result in positive feedback loops between basal ganglia, thalamus and (orbitofrontal) cortex that maintain compulsive behaviours.

of long-term goals of sufficient motivational strength. Disturbed action selection and lack of inhibition from the ACC may further promote compulsive behaviour. Reciprocal loops between frontal cortex and basal ganglia support the implicit learning of cognitive and motor patterns, which will often become automatic. Dysfunction of these circuits (see Figure 13.1) may result in intrusions of these normally automatic processes into the conscious thought patterns mediated by thalamocortical loops and contribute to obsessions (Graybiel and Rauch, 2000).

In addition to further non-invasive neurobiological work on the fronto-striatal-thalamic circuits in OCD with the aim of identifying biological markers, more detailed neuropsychological investigations, using paradigms that may constitute intermediate phenotypes such as sequence learning, motor inhibition, conflict resolution and executive control, will be needed to prove or disprove such a model.

The most prominent diagnostic category from the so-called 'OCD spectrum' is Tourette's syndrome (compulsive movements and utterances – motor and vocal tics), which is also supposed to be linked to basal ganglia dysfunction and treated with antidopaminergic antipsychotics. Other compulsive and obsessive disorders that have been subsumed into the OCD spectrum are trichotillomania (compulsive hair pulling) and body dysmorphic disorder (obsessions with one's appearance). This dimensional or spectrum approach is useful for a sub- or reclassification of disorders according to

leading symptoms, at least for research purposes, in order to improve the stratification of patients, and will hopefully help to uncover the neurobiological substrate if not of the OCD syndrome, then at least of obsessions and compulsions as separate symptom dimensions.

13.6   BRAIN FUNCTION

13.6.1   Fear circuits

The standard way of assessing changes in brain function associated with a disorder is through the comparison of brain activity or metabolism in a patient group with controls during some activation paradigm or the resting state. For anxiety disorders another approach is to study the brain mechanisms of fear responses in healthy individuals, for example after fear conditioning. The basic idea is that the short-term plasticity subserving fear conditioning can serve as a surrogate marker for the more long-term processes leading to the respective clinical disorders. Similar experimental approaches have been taken in addiction research, where changes in the brain's reward circuits may serve as surrogate markers, and in the study of mood disorder, although there is general agreement that (negative) mood induction will always mimic only a subset of the depressive syndrome.

We know from numerous functional imaging studies of the last 15 years (and even more abundant earlier and concurrent animal work) that the fear circuitry of the brain comprises the amygdala and hippocampus in the medial temporal lobe, areas in the frontal lobe, the nucleus accumbens in the ventral striatum, several thalamic nuclei, the ventromedial hypothalamus and brainstem areas such as the periaqueductal grey matter. The specific functions of the components of this network are still under investigation, but animal studies and functional imaging studies have suggested a role for the amygdala in fear conditioning and the execution of fear responses, whereas the OFC seems to be more involved in the overwriting of stimulus-fear response associations through extinction (Shin and Liberzon, 2010). Interaction between amygdala and hippocampus may underlie the heightened memory for contextual information acquired in fear-inducing or otherwise emotionally salient situations, for example where we were and what we did on 11 September 2001 ('9/11', the date of the terrorist attacks on the World Trade Center in New York).

Although the fear circuits of the human brain have been well explored, especially with paradigms of Pavlovian conditioning, these results have to be applied to human anxiety disorders with some amount of caution. With the possible exception of PTSD, we normally have no direct evidence of causation of cases of anxiety disorder by conditioning. For example, if a patient with agoraphobia develops a fear reaction to public transport, this is not normally the result of a series of actual threatening experiences (acting as hypothetical unconditioned stimulus) in this setting (thus making public transport the conditioned stimulus), but of a more subtle process that cannot be traced in all its details. Rather than being directly conditioned, public transport may here assume a symbolic role representing experiences of physical or mental confinement during childhood or other sensitive periods of developments. Even in PTSD, where the unconditioned stimulus (e.g. danger to one's life or physical integrity) can be identified, the conditioning process is different from those studied in most animal work because it can result just from a single exposure. Furthermore humans are likely to apply behavioural (avoidance) or cognitive (anticipatory anxiety vs. reappraisal) strategies to the fear-inducing situations, and thus disease models based on simple stimulus-reaction patterns are likely to fall short.

13.6.2 Patient studies

A common finding in patients with anxiety disorders and even people who may be at genetic risk (carriers of associated genetic variants, such as the 5-HTT promoter S allele) is higher activation of areas of the fear circuit, for example the amygdala, to emotional stimuli. At the same time extinction may be impaired, which has been reported for PTSD and other anxiety disorders. Exaggerated responses to emotional cues, impaired or delayed extinction learning, or impaired recall of extinction might then all be mechanisms that contribute to anxiety symptoms and their persistence.

The most interesting studies thus are those looking at the interplay between the different parts of the fear circuits. In PTSD there is some evidence for exaggerated responses in the amygdala and attenuated responses in the medial PFC and hippocampus. The dorsal ACC and insular cortex may also be hyperactive and thus support the learning of fear memories (Shin and Liberzon, 2010). In panic disorder and phobia hyperactivity in limbic and brain stem areas has also been observed. One intriguing question is now whether such hyperactivity will subside with successful treatment. Functional imaging studies both of resting metabolism and symptom induction have provided evidence for this type of plastic changes with successful psycho- or pharmacotherapy (Linden, 2006) (see also Chapter 9).

Functional imaging of patients with OCD has shown abnormalities in the same circuits implicated by structural imaging. Hyperactivity or -metabolism at rest was found in striato-thalamo-cortical circuits and could also be provoked with symptom induction (e.g. pretending to touch a patient with a contaminated object). Again, this hyperactivity is reduced with successful psychological, pharmacological or surgical therapy (Greenberg et al., 2010). Another potentially important clinical application of functional imaging would be to identify treatment responders (or even more relevant: distinguish between responders to different therapies) on the basis of their baseline metabolic activity. There is emerging evidence for associations between metabolic changes in the OFC and treatment success as well as correlations with pre-treatment metabolic activity. One study even found different patterns of correlation for treatment responses to CBT (higher OFC activity associated with better outcome) and drug treatment with the SSRI fluoxetine (lower OFC activity associated with better outcome) (Brody et al., 1998). However, it has so far been impossible reliably to distinguish responders and non-responders through their baseline levels of blood flow, glucose metabolism or functional activation. The non-invasive assessment of neurochemistry through magnetic resonance spectroscopy may provide an additional useful measure, and ultimately more than one neurobiological parameter may have to be adduced for sufficiently accurate predictions.

13.7   NEUROCHEMISTRY AND PHARMACOLOGICAL TREATMENT

13.7.1   Benzodiazepines have hypnotic, anxiolytic and muscle relaxant properties

The benzodiazepines are the largest class of anxiolytic drugs. They modulate the activity of GABA-$_A$ receptors. Whereas GABA binds to the receptor at the junction between alpha- and beta-subunits, benzodiazepines (and the 'z-hypnotics', Section 7.1.2) act on the benzodiazepine binding site at the junction between the alpha- and gamma-subunits. This explains why only receptors with a gamma subunit show effects of benzodiazepines. This positive allosteric modulation leads to higher sensitivity of the receptor to GABA and thus more inhibition of the postsynaptic neurons. Only receptors with alpha 1, 2, 3 or 5 (but not those with alpha 4 or 6) subunits are sensitive to benzodiazepines (Winsky-Sommerer, 2009). There is some evidence that, depending on the alpha subunit composition of the pentamer, activation of GABA$_A$ receptors will result in relatively stronger hypnotic (sleep inducing), anxiolytic or muscle relaxant effects. The different benzodiazepines vary greatly in their pharmacokinetics, with half lives ranging from 4–15 hours (oxazepam) to up to 30–40 hours (diazepam, chlordiazepoxide), with even longer half lives for the active metabolites. They all have a considerable potential for the development of dependency after chronic use. Side effects include excessive sedation and memory impairment. Overdosing can lead to coma and respiratory suppression and can be antagonised by flumazenil. Because of the muscle relaxation, benzodiazepines cannot be used in patients with myasthenia gravis, an autoimmune disorder where antibodies against the nAChR cause muscle weakness.

Benzodiazepines are effective in the treatment of many anxiety disorders, although antidepressants are the first choice for long-term treatment because of the lower addictive properties. However, benzodiazepines are often needed for the management of acute crises and a common adjunct to antidepressants (or to antipsychotics in the treatment of psychotic disorders where anxiety is a prominent problem). They are also used for severe cases of insomnia and other sleep disorders if sleep hygiene and psychological interventions have not produced the desired effect. Because of their hepatic elimination they have to be used with caution in patients with liver dysfunction, like all drugs that depend on hepatic enzyme systems for their elimination.

The acute symptoms of anxiety disorders generally respond to the GABAergic effect of benzodiazepines. Although this may point to a deficit of GABA availability or changes in GABA receptors, it could also simply reflect an inhibitory effect that is needed to counteract the overactivity of other systems. There is some evidence from PET and SPECT studies for reduced numbers of GABA$_A$ receptors in neocortical and limbic areas, but only half of the relevant studies reported this (Nikolaus et al., 2009b). The evidence was generally better for neocortical than limbic areas, and GABA$_A$ receptor downregulation was most consistent in PTSD.

It was accompanied by increased availability of dopamine in the striatum in OCD, which may suggest an imbalance between insufficient GABAergic inhibition and exaggerated mesolimbic dopaminergic activity in this disorder (Winsky-Sommerer, 2009). Antidopaminergic drugs, although not in the first line of treatment, are sometimes used in severe cases of OCD (alone or as add-on to serotonergic/noradrenergic drugs) and can also alleviate obsessive symptoms in psychosis.

13.7.2   The anxiolytic drug buspirone is a partial serotonergic agonist and indirect noradrenergic agonist

Buspirone is a partial agonist at $5-HT_{1A}$ receptors and inhibits presynaptic α_2 receptors, which results in increased noradrenaline release. Some, perhaps most, of its effects are mediated through its active metabolite. The net effects on the monoamine systems are thus similar to those of mirtazapine and it also has antidepressant (although not recommended as monotherapy) and anxiolytic properties. Its advantages over benzodiazepines are the absence of sedating or muscle relaxant effects, in cases where these are not desired, and the lower addictive potential. However, it is currently not clear whether buspirone is as effective for the long-term treatment of anxiety disorders as benzodiazepines or classical antidepressants. Although buspirone has not direct effects on muscarinic receptors, it is not recommended in patients with narrow-angle glaucoma. This exclusion also applies to benzodiazepines, although in both cases the pharmacological mechanisms for influences on intraocular pressure are unclear.

13.7.3   Pregabalin is a calcium channel modulator with anxiolytic properties

Pregabalin is an anticonvulsant that is also effective for generalised anxiety disorder and social phobia. It is also used for chronic pain syndromes, such as neuropathic pain and fibromyalgia. Pregabalin binds to the alpha2-delta subunit of VGCC (see Chapter 7) and can thus regulate neuronal excitation and NT release. Advantages over benzodiazepines for the treatment of anxiety disorders are the lack of addictive potential and the renal elimination (which makes it a safer option in patients with liver dysfunction). However, neuropsychiatric (e.g. irritability, memory problems), sexual and vegetative side effects are relatively common, especially during the early phase of treatment.

13.7.4   Adrenergic blockade alleviates some acute anxiety symptoms

The acute symptoms of anxiety disorders, particularly panic attacks, may also respond to drugs that block the beta adrenergic receptors ('beta-blockers'). These drugs were mainly developed to treat cardiac arrhythmias, high blood pressure and heart attack because of their antagonism of the beta-1 receptors of the heart. Stimulation of these receptors by adrenaline (epinephrine) leads to higher rate and volume of cardiac output, which fits with the general function of the sympathetic nervous system. However, it may also damage the heart, especially when it is already partly damaged by ischaemia, which is the rationale for the use of beta-blockers after heart attack. Beta-blockers that cross the blood–brain barrier, such as propranolol, can also antagonise noradrenergic transmission in the CNS, attenuating the flight/fight response that contributes to panic symptoms. Although beta-blockers have been used for panic disorder over several decades, it is still unclear whether their action is more due to their peripheral (and thus more related to its immediate effect on somatic symptoms such as palpitations or sweating) or central action. Acute symptom relief can come from relatively low doses (e.g. 40 mg of propranolol/day), although higher doses may be needed for more long-term effects. Propranolol is approved for the treatment of anxiety symptoms in the UK, but not in the United States. The symptomatic effects of beta adrenergic blockade may not inform us about any primary neurochemical abnormalities in anxiety disorders, because the heightened sympathetic tone for which they are effective may be a common pathway leading to pathological fear responses caused by a multitude of different environmental triggers and brain abnormalities. If a hyperresponsive noradrenergic system enhances fear memories and constitutes a risk factor for PTSD it may be possible to prevent the psychological consequences of trauma by emergency treatment with beta-blockers. However, no consistent clinical results for the prophylaxis of PTSD have so far been demonstrated. Furthermore, discussions have arisen as to whether such treatment – which essentially blocks the consolidation of memories – constitutes undue interference with people's personalities, especially if used in a preventive manner.

13.7.5 Treatment in practice

The mainstay of chronic pharmacological treatment of anxiety disorders is through antidepressants with serotonergic and/or noradrenergic activity. Social phobia, panic disorder, GAD and PTSD can all be treated with SSRIs, but often require higher doses for symptom improvement than depressive syndromes. For example, the maximum daily dose of citalopram in the treatment of depression is normally 40 mg/day and higher doses would be used only in particularly severe cases, whereas in anxiety disorders doses up to 60 mg are needed fairly regularly. Of the tricyclic antidepressants (TCA), clomipramine, which has the highest affinity of all TCAs for the serotonin transporter, has traditionally been used for OCD. At clinical doses, clomipramine also blocks the norepinephrine transporter and has antiserotonergic, antiadrenergic, anticholinergic, antihistaminergic and antidopaminergic effects. The resulting side effects have caused it to be less frequently used nowadays than the SSRIs. Buspirone is used as an add-on to other serotonergic drugs, or as monotherapy for GAD. Because of its partial agonist effects on somatodendritic autoreceptors it can inhibit firing of serotonergic neurons, and it is presently not entirely clear how these effects would be synergistic with the serotonergic effects of SSRIs.

13.7.6 Treatment and pharmacological models

There is no non-invasive method for the direct assessment of synaptic serotonin. Investigations with SPECT and PET (Chapter 7) have therefore used transporter and receptor binding to obtain estimates of relative serotonin levels. Both depletion and elevation of serotonin have resulted in reductions of presynaptic transporter binding in experimental studies, whereas postsynaptic 5-HT$_{2A}$ receptor binding seems to be inversely related to serotonin levels. Such changes in radioligand binding can be caused by downregulation of protein expression, particularly in response to chronically altered neurotransmitter levels, or competition between the radioligand and the neurotransmitter for binding sites (where the ligand shares the binding site on the receptor or transporter with the NT). The best documented change in anxiety disorders is probably the decreased serotonin transporter binding in the brainstem, found in 50% of studies (Nikolaus et al., 2009b). Because these findings were obtained in drug naïve patients, they are not an effect of treatment with sero-tonergic substances. However, based on the experimental findings from serotonin depletion and treatment studies, reduced serotonin transporter binding may reflect both increased or decreased NT levels and these nuclear imaging findings are thus unequivocal with regard to models of serotonin hypo- or hyperfunction leading to OCD. Cortical 5-HT2A binding was reduced in one study of drug naïve OCD patients, which could indicate lower receptor numbers or higher intrinsic serotonin concentrations. In the same study, striatal binding of a dopamine D2 receptor ligand was also reduced, which may point to dopaminergic hyper-activity in OCD.

At present, it is therefore an open question whether serotonergic drugs are effective for symptoms of anxiety disorders because patients have a deficit in serotonin production or availability. As in other cases where we mainly infer chemical mechanisms from treat-ment effects (such as the antidopaminergic effects on schizophrenia symptoms) there are at least three other possible explanations: serotonin levels may be normal, but seroton-ergic drugs generally make people less anxious; serotonergic drugs specifically counteract a dysregulation in another neurotransmitter system, which has not been identified yet; the brains of patients 'expect' higher serotonin levels, for example because of altered transporter activity, receptor numbers or postsynaptic modifications, which again are still unknown. Most likely several of these mechanisms are at play, which may explain why the direct demonstration of neurotransmitter abnormalities in mental disorders has been so difficult.

13.8   ANIMAL AND EXPERIMENTAL MODELS

Animal models can contribute to the neurobiology of mental disorders in two main ways. A model can be selected for its face validity, by selective breeding for behavioural traits related to the disorder, for example exaggerated fear conditioning or suppressed exploratory behav-iour in the case of anxiety disorders (see Chapter 5). Animals that display the desired traits can then be investigated for neurochemical or neuroanatomical abnormalities with invasive tools (including microdialysis, a technique to probe extracellular NT concentrations) that are not available for human studies. The model can also be tested for its predictive validity. In the case of anxiety disorders, models of high predictive validity would show increased symp-toms with anxiogenic and decreased symptoms with anxiolytic drugs (e.g. benzodiazepines, serotonergic antidepressants).

Several of the standard tests of anxiety-like behaviour have shown good predictive valid-ity. The Elevated-Plus Maze (EPM) test probes the balance between exploratory behaviour and the fear of open areas. After administration of anxiogenic drugs, animals will spend more time in closed arms and explore the maze less, whereas the opposite effects have been observed after anxiolytics. Similarly, on the Open Field test, less exploratory behaviour, less time spent in the open, illuminated centre of the arena and more freezing are considered signs of anxiety and normalise after anxiolytic drugs. The Defensive Burying test assesses the natural tendency of mice to bury noxious stimuli, which is suppressed by anxiolytics. Exploratory vs. safety behaviour is again assessed in the Dark-Light-Box test, where anxious mice tend to stay in the dark area, and anxiolytics can increase exploratory behaviour. These behavioural models can thus help in the preclinical testing of new anti-anxiety drugs. It would be attractive also to learn from them about the neurobiology of anxiety disorders but we must not forget that none of them is supposed to model a whole anxiety syndrome (or, indeed, anxiety disorders at all), but particular traits of exaggerated fear responses or memories, which may also occur in anxiety disorders.

The other approach, which may be closer to the underlying neurobiology, is based on the construct validity of the model, thus starting from a putative biological mechanism. The most widely used rodent anxiety model of this kind is the serotonin transporter knockout (SERT$^{-/-}$) mouse or rat (Kalueff et al., 2010). The preliminary evidence for association between low activity SERT genotypes (e.g. the S-allele of 5-HTTLPR discussed above) and anxiety traits and disorders motivates the construct validity of this model. Both the chemical and the behavioural consequences of the absence of the serotonin transporter have been extensively tested. These animals have increased extracellular levels of serotonin (although reuptake is not completely abolished), but decreased levels in some tissues (as a consequence of the decreased reuptake and/or downregulation of serotonin synthesis). They also show a downregulation of 5-HT$_{1A}$ but not 5-HT$_{2A}$ receptors. The increased serotonin levels can lead to spontaneous serotonin syndrome in SERT knockout mice. In humans, the serotonin syndrome, which comprises autonomic symptoms such as increased heart rate, flushes, fever, motor symptoms such as tremor, rigidity, exaggerated reflexes, anxiety and even seizures is observed after overdoses of serotonergic drugs, combinations of two serotonergic drugs (e.g. and SSRI and a MAO) or serotonergic drugs with substances that interfere with its metabolism. Behaviourally, the SERT knockout animals show decreased social and exploratory behaviour and increased acute and chronic stress responses such as aversive behaviour and recall of fear memories. This animal model may thus bridge the explanatory gap between genetic variants affecting serotonin trafficking and anxiety-like behaviours. However, the animals also display depression-like behaviour such as increased immobility on the forced swim or tail suspension test. These findings confirm the key role for serotonin in both anxiety and mood disorders, but also suggest that other genetic or environmental factors need to come in to shape the specific phenotypes observed in clinical practice.

Another biologically plausible approach to animal models may be through pharmacological induction of particular behaviours. For OCD, this has been attempted through administration of the dopamine D$_2$/D$_3$ agonist quinpirole in rats. This model mimics some aspects of stereotyped and ritualistic motor behaviour (Szechtman et al., 1998). Such models can then be tested for predictive validity by observing the effects of anti-anxiety drugs of the animals' behaviour, or to evaluate new experimental treatments such as DBS (Winter et al., 2008).

Analogous to the experimental induction of psychosis ('model psychoses', see Chapter 10), panic attacks can be induced in humans by administration of cholecystokinin (CCK) receptor agonists, such as the tetrapeptide fragment CCK-4. CCK is a gastrointestinal peptide hormone that is secreted by the intestinal mucosa and stimulates the secretion of digestive enzymes from the pancreas. CCK also has ubiquitous receptors in the CNS and can thus be regarded as one of the neuropeptides. As a neurotransmitter, CCK has mainly excitatory effects, but it also mediates the release of other NTs. Its central physiological functions mediate satiety (see Chapter 16). The experimental panic model of CCK agonism has sparked research into possible neuropeptide abnormalities in anxiety disorders and the development of CCK antagonists as novel anxiolytic drugs, but results so far have remained inconclusive.

Learning points

Anxiety disorders are amongst the most common mental disorders. About 30% of the population of industrialised countries experience symptoms of an anxiety disorder at least once during their lifetime. Although mild forms are compatible with relatively normal everyday functioning, severe forms can seriously disrupt the patient's ability to work, engage in social contacts or hold on to a relationship. The phobias and GAD are characterised by prominent psychological and physiological anxiety symptoms. In the phobias, these are triggered by specific (real or anticipated) stimuli, situations or events. PTSD is characterised by a combination of cognitive, perceptual and anxiety symptoms, avoidance behaviour and irritability that occurs after a catastrophic event and can become chronic. In OCD, patients suffer from a combination of obsessive thoughts and compulsive behaviour, which they engage in although they know that their fears and actions to control them are irrational (a feature that distinguishes them from OCD-like symptoms in psychotic disorders).

Compared to other mental disorders, anxiety disorders have a relatively low heritability (up to approx. 30%) and thus environmental and biographical factors play a major role. Aetiological models based on learning theory implicate faulty fear conditioning as a possible mechanism. Correspondingly, abnormalities in the brain's 'fear circuits' linking the amygdala, other limbic structures, the thalamus and PFC have been observed in functional imaging studies of anxiety disorders. In OCD, cortico-striato-thalamic loops have been implicated in particular. Some of these abnormalities in brain activation normalised after treatment with pharmaco- or psychotherapy. Animal models of exaggerated fear responses have implicated deficits in GABA and serotonin transmission. This matches the two most widely used treatment approaches, with GABAergic (benzodiazepines) and serotonergic (SSRI) drugs. Physiological anxiety responses, particularly in panic disorder, can also be controlled by adrenergic blockade (beta-blockers), and both central and peripheral effects may be responsible. Anxiety disorders often respond well to psychological interventions, particularly (cognitive) behavioural techniques, and these would normally be tried before initiating medication except in severe cases.

Revision and discussion questions

- How might anxiety traits have evolved?
- How can dysfunctional fear circuits contribute to anxiety symptoms?
- What do animal models and clinical effects of benzodiazepines tell us about the GABA system in anxiety disorders?
- Can biology contribute to the distinction between 'normal' shyness as a character trait and social phobia?

FURTHER READING

Shin, L. & Liberzon, I. (2010). The neurocircuitry of fear, stress, and anxiety disorders. *Neuropsychopharmacology*, 35, 169–91.

14 BIOLOGY OF PERSONALITY DISORDERS

PREVIEW

Like Chapter 13, this chapter reviews a group of disorders. Personality disorders are linked by some common clinical features such as the age of onset and presumed persistence throughout life. Their specific features are quite distinct, and they can present with (often attenuated) forms of symptoms of most of the classical mental disorders. This is matched by considerable heterogeneity in their biological models. These are largely derived from the well-developed psychological theories of personality, but very little direct evidence is available from patient studies to support them. This chapter therefore gives ample space to the discussion of categorical and dimensional models of personality and how they affect the concept of personality disorders. The chapter also introduces some of the recently developed animal models of personality disorder, many of which incorporate the effects of developmental stress.

14.1 DEFINITION, CLINICAL PRESENTATION AND EPIDEMIOLOGY

The current concept of personality disorders was introduced by the American Psychiatric Association through the DSM-III in 1980. It rests on the idea that personality traits, which are conceived of as enduring patterns of convictions, behaviours and interactions with the environment, can be maladaptive. If people's convictions about themselves or others or behaviour towards individuals or society consistently violate norms and societal expectations or otherwise prevent them from a successful interaction with their environment, they can suffer distress or functional impairment. The distress can result in self-harm (for example in borderline [BPD] or narcissistic personality disorder), and functional impairment can arise in areas of relationships (again for example in BPD, or paranoid personality disorder), work (e.g. avoidant personality disorder) or activities (e.g. obsessive–compulsive personality disorder). Harm to others is also frequent in some personality disorders, notably antisocial personality disorder (ASPD) and its rarer subform psychopathy (Box 14.1). The DSM-III introduced a second 'axis' of description for the personality disorders to distinguish them from the more 'classical' mental disorders coded on axis 1. The personality disorders were deemed to be qualitatively different from the more periodic or cyclic axis 1 disorders because of their pervasiveness and chronicity. They were also deemed to have an earlier age of onset (going back to adolescence in almost all cases) and be more resistant to treatment (Trull and Durrett, 2005). These qualitative differences between axes 1 and 2 have more recently been called into question (Beauchaine et al., 2009), and there is considerable comorbidity between diagnoses from the two axes.

As basis for the diagnosis of personality disorder, the DSM-IV stipulates 'an enduring pattern of inner experience and behaviour that deviates markedly from the expectations of the individual's culture', which:

- manifests itself in at least two of the areas cognition, affectivity, interpersonal functioning or impulse control;
- is 'inflexible and pervasive across a broad range of personal and social situations'
- leads to 'clinically significant distress or impairment in social, occupational, or other important areas of functioning';
- is longstanding; and
- can be traced back to adolescence or early adulthood.

The DSM-IV and ICD-10 take a categorical approach to personality disorders. They assume that groups of commonly coinciding symptoms yield qualitatively distinct syndromes. Based on the symptoms that are present in addition to the general criteria, the DSM-IV recognises 10 different personality disorders, which it groups into three clusters (prevalence estimates in the general population in parentheses):

1. Cluster A ('odd-eccentric')
   - Paranoid personality disorder (0.5–2.5%)
   - Schizoid personality disorder (less than 1%)
   - Schizotypal personality disorder (SPD) (3%)
2. Cluster B ('dramatic-emotional')
   - ASPD (3% in males, 1% in females)
   - BPD (3% in females, 1% in males)
   - Histrionic personality disorder (2–3%)
   - Narcissistic personality disorder (less than 1%)
3. Cluster C ('anxious-fearful')
   - Avoidant personality disorder (0.5–1%)
   - Dependent personality disorder (unknown)
   - Obsessive–compulsive personality disorder (1%)

A summary of the diagnostic criteria for individual personality disorders is provided in Table 14.1. The ICD-10 applies similar general criteria and recognises most of the individual personality disorder categories. The narcissistic type is listed but not defined, and obsessive–compulsive personality disorder is not listed at all, probably because it can be considered to be an attenuated form of OCD. Similarly, although schizotypal disorder is a category of the ICD-10, its use is not recommended because of its overlap with either paranoid/schizoid personality disorder or schizophrenia. Psychopathy is a personality disorder that is not listed in either DSM-IV or ICD-10. The concept was introduced by Hare based on his work with offenders in the prison system (Hare and Neumann, 2008). Its diagnostic criteria are more stringent than those of ASPD, and thus its prevalence lower at about 1% of the population and about 15–25% of prisoners, compared to 50–80% for ASPD.

If the prevalence estimates given above are combined (and allowing for some comorbidity between personality disorders), about 10% of the population suffer from a personality disorder. If the concept of personality disorder as a pervasive, longstanding functional disturbance is accepted, the point prevalence is almost as high as the lifetime prevalence because only the

Table 14.1 Symptoms and signs of specific personality disorders (DSM-IV)

Cluster	Type	Symptoms
A	Paranoid	Suspiciousness, lack of trust, reads hidden meanings, bears grudges, perceives attacks on character or reputation
	Schizoid	Little interest in relationships/sexual experience/activities, solitary activities, lack of friends, indifferent to views of others, flat affect
	Schizotypal	Ideas of reference, odd beliefs, unusual perceptual experience, odd speech or behaviour, suspiciousness, inappropriate affect, lack of friends, social anxiety
B	Antisocial	Unlawful behaviour, deceitfulness, impulsivity, aggressiveness, recklessness, lack of remorse
	Borderline	Efforts to avoid abandonment, unstable interpersonal relationships and self-image, impulsivitiy, suicidal or self-mutilating behaviour, affective instability, anger, feels empty, dissociative symptoms
	Histrionic	Wants to be centre of attention, uses physical appearance, inappropriate sexual behaviour, shifting and shallow emotions, dramatic speech and expression of emotions, suggestibility, romantic fantasies
	Narcissistic	Grandiosity in fantasy (e.g. of success) and behaviour (e.g. sense of entitlement), exploitation of others, lack of empathy, envy, arrogance
C	Avoidant	Avoids personal and work relationships unless certain of being liked, preoccupation with criticism, inhibition when making new contacts, inferior self-image, low risk taking
	Dependent	Does not take responsibility, needs reassurance, lack of confidence in own judgements, actions and opinions, needs company, submissive and clinging behaviour
	Obsessive–compulsive	Preoccupation with orderliness, perfectionism, devotion to work, conscientiousness, hoarding of money and objects, lack of flexibility and efficiency

Source: American Psychiatric Association (2000)

part of life before the onset of the disorder is truly symptom-free. Based on point prevalence thus estimated, personality disorders would constitute the commonest group of psychiatric problems. Several of the DSM-IV categories have been criticised because of cultural biases, where the concept of a 'dependent' personality disorder, for example, is considered to be an expression of the individualistic tenets of Western society. However, the DSM-IV does take account of cultural differences and stipulates that behavioural changes have to be outside what is expected by the individual's culture and cause significant distress. Like most psychiatric diagnoses, the personality disorders are matters of cultural and societal convention because a person's distress will often be influenced by their environment's attitude towards their beliefs and social expectations set a benchmark for functional impairment.

14.2 HERITABILITY

Although the diagnostic entities as such do not appear to be heritable (findings on this topic are controversial and marred by small sample sizes of most twin studies), the underlying personality traits such as aggressive behaviour are. BPD is an exception with 35–70% heritability

(Beauchaine et al., 2009), but this may reflect the heritability of impulsive behaviour, with may also explain the considerable comorbidity with ASPD, and of emotional lability. Patients with BPD also have increased genetic risk for substance use and mood disorders, and those with SPD for schizophrenia. Environmental risk factors and G×E interactions have also been investigated, mainly for BPD and ASPD. Some of the G×E interactions implicated in aggressive behaviour will be discussed in Chapter 17 in the context of childhood conduct disorder. Disturbed relationships with parents, upbringing in single-parent families and childhood sexual or physical abuse have all been implicated in risk to develop BPD. A common framework to explain the link between these environmental factors and the emotional lability, unstable relationships and fear of abandonment could be through the early disruption of attachment, which may be particularly damaging if linked with genetic vulnerability (Steele and Siever, 2010).

Although personality disorders have classically been considered to be both pervasive and persistent, their course may be more benign than previously assumed, although some of the maladaptive personality traits may be more deeply entrenched than the categorical syndromes. Estimates are difficult to obtain, because many patients do not come to the attention of health services, but perhaps about half of patients may recover with time. However, there is still significant morbidity and mortality associated with some of the personality disorders, for example BPD where approximately 10% of patients commit suicide. ASPD has both significant mortality (suicide risk of approx. 5%) and rates of delinquency associated with it.

The genetic associations and clinical similarities highlight the putative association between cluster A personality disorders with psychotic disorders. This has been cited as evidence for a 'schizophrenia spectrum', which posits that schizophrenia symptoms are one extreme on a continuous spectrum of schizotypal traits. The relatively high proportion of magical beliefs (of which delusions might be the extreme form) and voice hearing (about 4%, of which psychotic hallucinations might be the extreme form) in the healthy population support such a notion, but many practitioners would question the usefulness of watering down the boundaries between illness and normal functioning. Cluster B is particularly associated with axis 1 mood, substance and impulse control disorders and cluster C with anxiety disorders. It has been proposed that, similar to the schizophrenia spectrum incorporating cluster A, the symptoms of cluster B group together with those of substance and impulse control disorders on an 'externalizing' factor. The externalizing spectrum has been found to have good validity at longitudinal observation and is likely to feature in the new DSM-V. An 'internalizing' factor has also been proposed for the DSM-V as a counterpart that would incorporate dimensions of anxiety and misery and thus cover cluster C and some of cluster B, but its validity is less clear. It may be more valid to split the 'internalizing' spectrum into a 'fear' factor representing the phobias and an 'anxious-misery' factor representing mood and generalised anxiety disorder and the corresponding personality disorders (Beesdo-Baum et al., 2009). These factors may be significantly more heritable than individual personality disorder categories and even than individual personality traits. For example heritability estimates for the externalizing factor have reached 0.8 (Beauchaine et al., 2009).

14.3   MODELS OF PERSONALITY

The concept of personality disorder is derived from the theory of personality or trait theory, which posits that each individual has characteristic patterns of thought, beliefs, emotion and behaviour that are stable across time and thus traits (to be distinguished from time-varying states). Although some of these traits like impulsivity may result in directly observable behaviour, most of them are measured by questionnaires and their validity will partly depend on the quality of questionnaire design. Human attitudes and behaviours can in principle be explained by a multitude of traits, but the aim is to find those that are most stable over time and least correlated with each other. Factor analysis is the statistical technique most commonly used. This approach can be very useful for understanding the biological basis of human behaviour because it might yield factors that are more heritable and have more stable biological correlates than individual features of observed behaviour. For any detailed discussion of the theory, assessment and biological investigation of personality readers are referred to textbooks in this area. We will confine the discussion here to a selection of influential personality models that are relevant to the next section on dimensional approaches to personality disorders.

At the descriptive level, interindividual differences in personality traits have been classified by the influential five-factor model (FFM), which can be documented with the NEO (neuroticism-extraversion-openness) personality inventory. The FFM describes personality along the dimensions of neuroticism (sensitive/nervous to secure/confident), extraversion (outgoing/energetic to shy/withdrawn), openness (inventive/curious to cautious/conservative), conscientiousness (efficient/organised to easy going/careless) and agreeableness (friendly/compassionate to competitive/outspoken). Heritability estimates fort the five factors range between 0.4 and 0.6. As seems to be the case generally with personality traits, the environmental contribution to interindividual variability is mainly explained by non-shared rather than shared environment.

The American psychiatrist C. Robert Cloninger proposed a personality model with four temperaments and three character traits. The term temperament refers back to ancient physiological theories about the composition of the body and its influence on patterns of behaviour. It is essentially equivalent to personality traits in the sense defined above, but incorporates theoretical ideas about their biological and genetic underpinning. Cloninger's temperaments are formulated in terms of animal learning literature and reflect responsiveness to positive ('reward dependence') and negative ('harm avoidance') reinforcement, exploration ('novelty seeking') and maintenance of learned behaviours in the face of frustration and fatigue ('persistence'). Initial ideas that reward dependence would be associated with noradrenergic, harm avoidance with serotonergic and novelty seeking with dopaminergic mechanisms were almost certainly too simplistic, but such models of associated neural systems can stimulate research into the neuropsychology of personality traits and the influence of genetic variants and drugs. One of the purposes of Cloninger's model was to explain vulnerability to mental disorder, and excessive novelty seeking has been associated with substance abuse disorders, and harm avoidance with anxiety disorders and depression. Reward dependence describes a tendency to engage in socially desirable behaviour that is found in patients with anxiety and mood disorders and cluster C personality disorders, but also in some patients with psychotic disorders, and widely in the general population. The heritability of temperamental features has been estimated at between 0.2 and 0.6 (Saudino, 2005). Cloninger's character traits represent the more cognitive side of his model and describe a person's sense of autonomy, cooperative attitude and self-transcendence and thus the intentional attitude to oneself, society and the universe. An individual's temperament and character can be measured with the Temperament and Character Inventory (TCI). In application to personality disorders, one might say that abnormal character traits correspond to the general criteria of personality disorder (e.g. lack of sense of autonomy, or the weak ego of psychoanalysis, which has long been linked to the parts of the neuroses that were the diagnostic precursors of personality disorder such as narcissism), whereas the temperaments define the specific DSM-IV cluster or category, except that Cloninger's model lends itself better to a dimensional approach (see Section 14.4).

Another neurobiologically driven personality model was proposed by the German-British psychologist Hans Jürgen Eysenck (1916–97) and developed further by Jeffrey Gray (1934–2004). Eysenck associated one of his main personality dimensions, extraversion, with differences in sensitivity of the ARAS (see Section 2.1). Lower response thresholds of the ARAS would explain why introverts are more easily aroused by the same environmental stimuli and situations than extraverts. He regarded the other dimension of his model neuroticism as linked to the limbic system. Gray's Reinforcement Sensitivity Theory (RST) postulated three main systems for the regulation of emotion, motivation and associative learning that would also form the basis for personality: a fight-flight-freeze system (FFFS) closely modelled on the partly noradrenergic pathways for the acute stress response (see Chapter 3); a Behavioural Approach or Activation System (BAS) implemented through dopaminergic projections from the VTA to the NAc, and on to the basal ganglia and neocortex; and a Behavioural Inhibition System for conflict resolution and monitoring of internal and external states (BIS). This has recently been linked to the 'default mode system' of neural activation, a network of brain areas arund the midline that commonly shows a high activity during the resting state. In this model, learning through positive reinforcement is a domain of the BAS, and the FFFS processes both conditioned and unconditioned aversive stimuli. The best evidence for a neurobiological substrate of personality exists for impulsive approach behaviours/novelty seeking, which have been linked with underactive mesolimbic dopamine pathways (Beauchaine et al., 2009). Yet even here the evidence is indirect, coming from animal models of substance abuse and stimulant treatment of ADHD.

Cloninger's novelty seeking and the related NEO construct of extraversion (and exploratory behaviour in animals) may also be linked to the 7-repeat (long) allele of a 48bp VNTR (variable number tandem repeat, see Chapter 4) on exon III of the DRD4 gene, which produces a less responsive receptor. However, not all studies replicated this association. The long alleles have been found more frequently in populations that migrated in prehistoric times, an interesting example linking genetics and the development of human cultures. The other reasonably well-replicated association between a personality trait and a genetic variant is that between high scores on the NEO for neuroticism (but not on the related Cloninger construct of harm avoidance) and the short allele of the 5-HTT promoter gene.

Personality traits may also be linked to cognitive biases. Individuals who score highly on neuroticism had better memory for negative and poorer for positive experiences and were faster for negative compared to positive self-referential judgements (Canli, 2008). Of course, such links establish only association, at best, not causation. It is conceivable that the cognitive biases, which themselves may be rooted in shifts in the balance between neurotransmitter systems, lead to differences in self-judgement and corresponding scores on personality questionnaires. We have recently shown such a link between a cognitive bias and a neurotransmitter system by comparing patients with Parkinson's disease on and off dopaminergic medication on a working memory task for emotional faces. Dopaminergic medication improved memory for angry but suppressed it for sad faces (Subramanian et al., 2010), which may have to do with its role establishing salience for critical information.

Although the biologically motivated personality models have stimulated research into the neurochemical and genetic substrates of behaviour none of them has thus far received strong empirical support. They should therefore be regarded as heuristic systems (that generate hypotheses for further research) rather than fixed models for behavioural or clinical classification, which still need to be empirically derived (e.g. from factor analysis of behavioural observations and self-reports) while our knowledge of the underlying neurobiology develops (Paris, 2005).

14.4   CATEGORICAL VS. DIMENSIONAL MODELS OF PERSONALITY DISORDERS

The current diagnostic systems have adopted a categorical approach to personality disorders where seven to ten qualitatively different disorders exist in parallel. Other models use hierarchies of severity, which brings a dimensional aspect into the categorical classification. The American psychoanalyst Otto Kernberg proposed the severity of the reality testing deficit as hierarchical principle. In his psychodynamic model, disrupted reality testing was also associated with less stable identity and immature (splitting) defence mechanisms. Thus, the quasi-psychotic forms (broadly overlapping with cluster A), BPD and ASPD would be regarded as more severe than the 'neurotic' forms of cluster C. A similar hierarchy was proposed by the American psychiatrist John G. Gunderson based on the degree of functional impairment. He distinguished the less severe 'trait disorders' (cluster C and histrionic personality disorder) from the intermediately severe 'self disorders' (remaining cluster B and schizoid personality disorder) and the most severe group of 'spectrum disorders' (remaining cluster A personality disorders).

Although these models are more theory-driven than the purely observational classification of personality disorders, they are still exposed to the critique that has been levelled against the categorical approach. Its validity has been called into question based on the considerable degree of comorbidity between and within personality disorder clusters, a lack of stability over time and low agreement between diagnostic instruments. Furthermore the low heritability of most personality disorder categories, which contrasts with the moderate to high heritability of personality traits, makes dimensional approaches attractive (Trull and Durrett, 2005).

Personality disorders can be described by individuals' scores on the dimensions of the FFM. For example low scores on conscientiousness and agreeableness and high scores on extraversion may define what is currently classified as ASPD. The advantage of such an approach may be that it might be easier to identify biological correlates and genetic mechanisms of the underlying dimensions rather than the superordinate categories. A general disadvantage of theoretically driven dimensional models is that they may not fully capture the clinical reality of patients' presentations. For example, suicidal behaviour or quasi-psychotic experience would be hard to capture as extremes on non-clinical scales (Beauchaine et al., 2009). However, a dimensional approach that starts from the clinically relevant features and then traces their attenuated forms in the healthy population, for example the schizophrenia/schizotypy continuum, would solve this problem.

Cloninger's model also maps well on to the current definitions of personality disorders. Cluster A would be characterized by low reward dependence, Cluster B by high novelty seeking and Cluster C by high harm avoidance. As indicated above, the general criteria for personality disorders could be replaced by low scores on Cloninger's character traits, and then the specific type established by the temperament scores. However, this will constitute real progress for biological research into personality disorders only if the approach is not confined to giving a more systematic basis for current diagnostic categories, but establishes trait markers with high heritability and/or stable biological correlates.

Another purpose of dimensional approaches to personality disorder may be to establish continuity with axis 1 disorders. Siever and Davis' (1991) model uses the dimensions of cognitive/perceptual organisation, impulsivity, affective instability and anxiety to describe both axis 1 disorders and personality disorders, which are assumed to be chronic and less severe versions with an earlier onset of the corresponding axis 1 disorders. A strong point of this model is that it can make prediction of biological features of personality disorders based on the findings in axis 1 disorders, which should also be present, albeit possibly in attenuated form, in the corresponding personality disorder. Based on models of cognitive disorganisation in schizophrenia, one would predict a glutamatergic mechanism for this dimension and based on the effects of SSRIs for anxiety a serotonergic mechanism for that dimension. However, evidence for associations between specific neurochemical pathways and the dimensions of Siever and Davis' model is still preliminary.

14.5   BIOLOGY OF PERSONALITY DISORDERS

Some of the biological studies into personality disorders have confined themselves to the DSM-IV or ICD-10 categories, whereas others have looked at the extremes of the personality dimensions discussed above. Neuroimaging studies have mainly been conducted with categorically defined groups. Patients with SPD may have lower average volumes of the superior temporal gyrus, which is of interest because of similar findings in schizophrenia, but overlap with controls is still considerable (Goldstein et al., 2009). Several studies comparing BPD patients with controls reported volume reductions in hippocampus, amygdala, OFC or cingulate, but patient numbers were relatively low. Smaller amygdala volumes may be a surprising finding at first because BPD patients clinically appear to be emotionally hyperresponsive. However, against the expectations, psychophysiological responses to emotional material were not enhanced in BPD, and the skin conductance response (SCR) was even lower than that of controls, indicating hypoarousal (Herpertz et al., 1999). Such a finding would be compatible with amygdala dysfunction because amygdala damage leads to attenuated SCR (Gläscher and Adolphs, 2003). Perhaps the clinical picture of BPD is explained better by blunting of affective responses than by hyperarousal models because these patients may need higher levels of stimulation to maintain their hedonic homoeostasis. The opioid model discussed below is based on similar considerations.

All the major neuromodulatory NT systems and stress (HPA axis) and reward (opioid) systems have been implicated in the pathogenesis of abnormal behaviour. The presumed heightened need for rewarding and novel stimuli associated with extraversion, novelty seeking and addictive behaviours (and thus 'externalising' disorders in general) has been linked to reduced sensitivity of mesolimbic dopaminergic pathways. Aggressive and antisocial behaviours have been linked to markers of low serotonergic activity such as reduced levels of 5-HIAA in CSF or a blunted response on the fenfluramine test (see Section 3.3).

Life with a personality disorder entails chronic social stress because one cannot fulfil social obligations (mainly clusters A and C) or encounters resistance to what others perceive as inappropriate behaviour (cluster B). An upregulation of chronic stress responses, for example through the HPA axis, might therefore be expected as a consequence of personality disorder. It might also contribute to its causation, for example as a response to the early traumatic experiences often implicated in BPD and other personality disorders, where heightened HPA responses may constitute a biological trauma memory. HPA axis activity can be measured with the dexamethasone suppression test (DST), where reduced suppression of cortisol release indicates overactivity (see Section 3.4). However, BPD alone does not seem to be associated with attenuated responses on the DST, but only in cases with comorbid major depression, where HPA dysregulation has been implicated independently (see Chapter 11). The DST can be combined with a CRF challenge, where higher release of ACTH and cortisol indicate overactivity of the HPA axis. However, a study of the combined DST/CRF challenge in BPD found enhanced ACTH release only in patients with history of childhood abuse, supporting notions of a neurobiological trauma memory (Rinne et al., 2002). However, patients with comorbid PTSD showed the opposite effect, which calls such an interpretation into question. Thus, there is presently insufficient evidence to support associations between BPD with or without PTSD and HPA axis dysregulation, and even the literature on associations between childhood trauma and HPA overactivity is inconsistent. Although the association between childhood trauma and BPD is well established, this cannot be the sole cause because 20–45% of BPD patients do not report childhood trauma, and 80% of individuals who experienced childhood sexual abuse do not develop a personality disorder (Bandelow et al., 2010).

Dysregulation of the endogenous opioid system in BPD has been proposed on theoretical grounds and may be supported by the effects of naltrexone in symptom reduction. Underactivity of the endorphin (and possibly overactivity of the dynorphin) system may explain both the anhedonia often encountered in BPD and the attempts to self-stimulate through drug abuse or frequent change of sexual partners. The fear of abandonment may also be linked to this system because social bonds and attachment are linked with the endorphin system. Conversely, kappa receptor stimulation (e.g. through dynorphin) can lead to derealisation and depersonalisation, which are also frequently reported by patients with BPD. Although this model is intriguing, direct evidence for changes in opioid levels or receptors in BPD has thus far not been provided.

Treatment effects in personality disorders do not provide clear clues to the underlying neurobiology. Pharmacological treatment is largely symptomatic and often not very effective. Anticonvulsants and antipsychotics have been used for aggression and impulsivity, SSRIs and anticonvulsants for emotional instability, and SSRIs and other antidepressants as well as antipsychotics for compulsive behaviour. Psychological interventions are still at the core of personality disorder treatment, but they, too, face low compliance and poor success rates.

Box 14.1   The brain of criminal offenders

Whether neurobiological changes predispose individuals to criminal behaviour is a question that may have important implications for the theory and practice of law (Silva, 2009). It is also of great relevance to psychiatrists and psychologists who testify as expert witnesses in court cases, especially where criminal responsibility needs to be determined. A person who committed a violent offence might have the defence of insanity available to them, when at the time of the offence they were suffering from a mental illness that precluded them from understanding the nature or wrongfulness of their action of, if they had such understanding, from acting upon it. The first scenario, also called 'cognitive insanity' may occur for example in patients with dementia or delusions and is available in most jurisdictions; the latter, also called 'volitional insanity' and more controversial and less widely used, would apply in severe cases of impulse control disorders. In such cases the expert witness would have to establish a diagnosis of a recognised mental (e.g. schizophrenia) or neurological (e.g. brain tumour) disorder and then show that this disorder led to a functional impairment resulting in 'cognitive insanity'. The extent to which personality disorders can serve as a basis for such a defence, has been intensely debated. On the one hand it might be argued that a defendant diagnosed with ASPD or psychopathy can very well distinguish between right and wrong and would thus have at best the defence of 'volitional insanity' on the basis of reduced impulse control available to them. On the other hand one might argue that this person lacks the neurobiological substrate for moral judgements, which could constitute the basis for a defence of 'cognitive insanity'. This debate, which has been fuelled by observations of changes to morality and behaviour after brain injury since the nineteenth century and by recent advances in structural and functional neuroimaging, currently centres around the search for stable biological markers of delinquency and the question whether these may predispose to or follow from deviant social behaviour.

Most research into neurobiological aspects of delinquency has used the psychopathy construct. It can be measured with Hare's revised Psychopathy Checklist (PCL-R), which assesses interpersonal and affective attitudes, life-style and antisocial behaviour. The most widely used techniques were structural and functional neuroimaging and psychophysiology, and studies normally compare individuals with psychopathy against controls regardless of history of criminal conviction, or criminals with psychopathy against those without or against controls. Thus, most of the extant work on the neurobiology of delinquency is really on psychopathy, which is closely associated with delinquency and an important relapse factor, but does not capture the full spectrum of conditions under which people commit violent crimes.

Much of the neuroimaging work has focused on the OFC and ventromedial PFC because patients with lesions to this region can resemble psychopaths on several dimensions. The neurologist Antonio Damasio, who has studied many of these patients, has termed this syndrome, which includes lack of empathy, impulsivity, abnormal moral judgements and blunted emotions, 'acquired sociopathy' (Gao et al., 2009). However, individuals with psychopathy, unlike medial PFC patients, are supposed to have high levels of predatory aggression, the type of aggression that is planned and goal-directed and not accompanied by heightened emotional arousal, in contrast to the more affective 'reactive' aggression that can be regarded as a normal defence mechanism (Wahlund and Kristiansson, 2009). Further differences are that medial PFC patients rarely display the levels of ruthlessness or callousness found in many psychopaths and they are severely impaired in their planning abilities (Kiehl, 2006). Thus, although several studies found reduced grey matter volume and altered metabolism in PFC, isolated prefrontal dysfunction is unlikely to account for the whole range of behavioural and affective abnormalities in psychopathy. Abnormalities in wider areas of the paralimbic system, which comprises the temporal pole, cingulated cortex insula and parahippocampal gyrus in addition to the OFC and can be regarded as an interface between the limbic system proper and the neocortical systems, may contribute to the development of psychopathy.

Another line of investigation has used autonomic responses, such as electrodermal activity (or skin conductance response, SCR). SCR reflects sympathetic activity and can be used to measure arousal levels and reactivity to emotional stimuli. The presence or anticipation of aversive stimuli leads to less pronounced sympathetic responses in psychopathic offenders (Herpertz et al., 2001). Such findings would be compatible with theories that assume reduced fear and sensitivity to punishment in psychopaths, which may make them prone to risky behaviour and less likely to adjust their behaviour based on previous failures or social sanctions (Gao et al., 2009).

At present the associations between neuroimaging or psychophysiological markers and specific patterns of thought or behaviour are not yet stable enough for any prospect of replacing the classical clinical and personality assessments used in forensic psychology and psychiatry. Furthermore, inferences from patterns of brain activity on mental states are rarely straightforward (Poldrack, 2006) and thus it may never be possible to use a brain scan to tell whether a person was capable of moral judgements or not. However, if stable evidence of neural deficits in psychopathy were to be provided, it cannot be excluded that one day here, as for patients who violate norms as a result of overt brain injury, rehabilitation will be emphasised over punishment.

14.6   ANIMAL MODELS

Because of the association of BPD and other personality disorders with childhood sexual or physical abuse and early experience of abandonment, animals exposed to environmental stressors during early rearing may be considered causal models of personality disorders. In rats, two patterns of nursing can be distinguished, based on the frequency at which the dam licks and grooms the offspring and whether she arches her back over them. The high licking/ grooming and arched back nursing (high LG-ABN) leads to higher expression of the oxytocin receptor in the medial preoptic area of the hypothalamus through epigenetic modification of a series of genes (Kaffman and Meaney, 2007). High maternal care thus predisposes to high maternal care in the offspring, which is often missing in BPD. High LG-ABN was also associated with increased glucocorticoid receptor expression in the hippocampus, which in turn leads to inhibition of the paraventricular nucleus of the hypothalamus and thus lower activity of the HPA axis. Maternal separation has largely opposite effects on the neuroendocrine system of offspring (Francis and Meaney, 1999).

Other models were based on the putative neurotransmitters involved in abnormal behaviour. $5-HT_{1B}$ receptor knock-out mice, which have higher levels of synaptic 5-HT because the presynaptic $5-HT_{1B}$ receptor inhibits NT release, are more aggressive than the wild type (Lesch and Merschdorf, 2000). Monkeys with the S allele of the 5-HTTLPR short/long polymorphism, which produce less serotonin transporter and thus again have higher synaptic NT levels, show excessive anxiety and aggression when reared under suboptimal conditions, demonstrating a G×E interaction that might be relevant for the understanding of the development of aggressive behaviour.

The formation of maternal attachment social bonds has been the subject of a prominent series of investigations by the American psychologist Jaak Panksepp. He demonstrated the crucial role of endorphin, whose levels increase during attachment and decrease during separation. The distress caused by separation, which animals signal by vocalisations, can be reduced by administration of opioids. Recent work also demonstrated abnormal reduced separation distress and preference for interaction with the mother in mice with a knock-out for the mu-opioid receptor (Moles et al., 2004). These results are intriguing because they provide the first steps towards a neurobiological model of attachment formation (Parsons et al., 2010), which may be disrupted in patients with BPD and other personality disorders (Bandelow et al., 2010).

Learning points

Personality disorders were introduced into the DSM in 1980. They are coded on a separate 'axis' (axis 2) from the classical mental disorders (axis 1) because of fundamental differences in course (less cyclic/periodic) and onset (normally earlier). They are defined by an enduring, pervasive and inflexible pattern of dysfunctional experience and behaviour. Specific personality disorders are grouped into clusters A ('odd-eccentric'), B ('dramatic-emotional') and C ('anxious-fearful'), although this categorical classification has been challenged by several dimensional personality models. Some personality disorders may represent attenuated versions of axis 1 disorders (e.g. SPD of schizophrenia), and some researchers have proposed a continuum of pathological experience across the population. Little is known about the biology of personality disorders. Based on animal models and neurochemical findings, under-activity of the serotonin system has been implicated in aggressive and antisocial behaviour and under-activity of the endorphin system in the heightened reward-seeking behaviour of patients with borderline personality disorder, but these models are not based on stable biomarkers. One promising avenue of research is to try to find biological and genetic correlates of behavioural traits rather than diagnostic categories. Pharmacological treatment of personality disorders is largely symptomatic, and psychotherapy is a central element in the management, although full remission is difficult to achieve.

Revision and discussion questions:

- Describe dimensional approaches to the study of personality
- Are the personality disorders "milder" versions of axis 1 disorders?
- Are changes in the brain responsible for criminal offences?

FURTHER READING

Canli, T. (2008). Toward a neurogenetic theory of neuroticism. *Annals of the New York Academy of Sciences*, 1129, 153–74.

Paris, J. (2005). Neurobiological dimensional models of personality: a review of the models of Cloninger, Depue, and Siever. *Journal of Personality Disorders*, 19, 156–70.

15 BIOLOGY OF SUBSTANCE-RELATED DISORDERS

PREVIEW

This chapter introduces the basic principles of substance-related (substance-induced and substance-use) disorder and then reviews specific clinical features and drug effects separately for the 11 classes of substances of abuse that are recognised by the DSM-IV. The chapter has dedicated sections on alcohol, stimulant (covering amphetamines and cocaine) and opioid abuse, and a final section on the remaining main substance classes of clinical relevance (cannabinoids, nicotine, hallucinogens, inhalants, benzodiazepines and other psychiatric drugs). In each case, the chapter aims to describe the epidemiology and genetics and distinguish neural mechanisms that may predispose to substance abuse from those that contribute to its maintenance and the changes following from the toxic effects of the substance. Each section concludes with a review of pharmacological and psychosocial treatment options.

15.1 CLINICAL CLASSIFICATION

Thanks to advances in medicine and chemistry, almost every person is exposed to a specific chemically defined substance at some point in their lives, and the majority of people in industrialised countries are long-term users of prescription drugs. Although the widespread use of medication has led to much better ability to control diseases and enhance quality of life, it has also resulted in harmful consequences from medication side effects. Through the increased availability of legal (and also illegal) drugs, abuse, overdosing (both accidental and purposeful) and dependence have also increased. Because so many people take prescription drugs and because no drug is completely without adverse effects it is important to distinguish these side effects from *substance-induced disorders*. According to the DSM-IV, the latter include intoxication and withdrawal and a number of neuropsychiatric syndromes that can also have other causes (delirium, dementia, amnesia, psychosis, sleep disorder, amongst others). The other main group of substance-related disorders are the *substance-use disorders*, which comprise abuse and dependence.

The DSM-IV defines 11 main classes of substances of abuse (see Table 15.1) for a summary of clinical effects and pharmacological modes of action), although it recognises that other substances, including prescription drugs, can have a potential for abuse and addiction as well, and that many patients would abuse substances from more than one class. Substance-use and substance-induced disorders are often intimately linked. For example, harmful use of alcohol may lead to frequent intoxications and ultimately to dependence and withdrawal symptoms and even to personality changes and dementia. All substances of abuse can potentially be ingested in intoxicating quantities (although intoxication is not formally a category for nicotine) and lead to dependence (although caffeine dependence is not a DSM-IV diagnosis). Withdrawal syndromes constitute DSM-IV diagnoses only for

Table 15.1 Classification of substances of abuse according to the DSM-IV.

Class	Examples	Typical acute effects	Intoxication	Typical effects of chronic abuse	Main pharmacological effect
Alcohol	Ethanol, contained in alcoholic beverages from 3 volume % (light beer) to >60 volume % (strong spirits)	Sedation, but also disinhibition	Aggression, impaired judgement, neurological symptoms (slurred speech, ataxia, coma)	Personality changes, depression, hallucinations, Korsakoff's syndrome, brain atrophy, dementia	Allosteric agonist at the GABA$_A$ receptor; Glycine receptor agonist; NMDA receptor inhibitor; 5HT$_3$ and nicotinic ACh receptor agonist; Direct actions on ion channels
Sedatives, hypnotics, anxiolytics	Benzodiazepines, e.g. diazepam (valium); Barbiturates, e.g. Phenobarbital (luminal); gamma-hydroxybutyric acid (GBH)	Sedation, anxiolysis	Respiratory depression	Personality changes, sleep disturbance, loss of motivation	Most are GABA$_A$ agonists, barbiturates also antagonists at the AMPA (glutamate) receptor
Amphetamines or similarly acting sympathomimetics	Examples: Amphetamine, d-amphetamine, methamphetamine ('speed'), 4-methylpropiophenone (mephedrone), 3,4-Methylenedioxymethamphetamine (MDMA, 'ecstasy')[a]; Methylphenidate (Ritalin); Phentermine and amfepramone (diethylpropion) (clinical use as appetite suppressants); Naphthylpyrovalerone ('NRG-1', not to be confused with neuregulin 1)	Activation, euphoria	Aggression, cardiovascular and gastrointestinal symptoms, respiratory depression, seizures, coma	Blunted affect, fatigue	Inhibit catecholamine reuptake/promote catecholamine release; MDMA particularly 5-HT; substituted amphetamines also promote glutamate release; amfepramone is precursor of ethcathinone, a selective NRI
Cocaine	Component of crack, coca tea	As for amphetamines	As for amphetamines	As for amphetamines	Monoamine reuptake inhibitor. 5-HT receptor agonist

Caffeine	Contained in coffee and caffeinated soft/energy drinks	Activation	Restlessness, cardiovascular (tachycardia) and gastrointestinal symptoms	None recognised	(1) Adenosine receptor blocker (2) Phosphodiesterase inhibitor (leads to accumulation of cAMP and thus enhances postsynaptic effects of catecholaminergic drugs)
Cannabis	Various preparations and extracts, e.g. marijuana, hashish, with psychoactive ingredient: Δ^9-tetrahydrocannabinol (THC)	Relaxation	Anxiety, euphoria, time dilation, impaired judgement, tachycardia	Blunted affect, loss of motivation, personality changes; can trigger psychosis in vulnerable individuals; associated with poorer cognitive function if started in adolescence (?)	Partial agonists on cannabinoid receptors (type 1 in brain)
Hallucinogens	Lysergic acid diethylamide (LSD), psilocybin, mescaline	Perceptual changes, synaesthesia, hallucinations, flashbacks	Similar to acute effects (broad therapeutic range); delirium (rare)	May trigger chronic psychosis	5-HT2$_A$ receptor agonists
Inhalants	Aliphatic hydrocarbons (butane, propane), aromatic hydrocarbons (toluene, xylene), e.g. contained in organic solvents; anaesthetic gases (nitrous oxide, enflurane); nitrites	Very variable, e.g. euphoria, hallucinations	Hypoxia, tachycardia (nitrites), organ failure, sudden death	Brain damage (especially white matter), medical complications, psychosocial and cognitive decline	Anaesthetic gases: NMDA antagonists; solvents: GABA agonists?

Continued

Table 15.1 Continued

Class	Examples	Typical acute effects	Intoxication	Typical effects of chronic abuse	Main pharmacological effect
Nicotine	Contained in tobacco	Both stimulant and relaxing properties reported	Gastrointestinal and respiratory symptoms, sweating, palpitations, seizures	Chronic bronchitis, emphysema, lung cancer (from smoking), cardiovascular damage	Agonist of nicotinic acetylcholine receptor; leads to release of adrenaline and noradrenaline through effects in ganglionic sympathetic neurons
Opioids					
Phencyclidine (PCP) or similarly acting arylcyclohexylamines	PCP ('Angel dust'), ketamine ('Vitamin K' or 'special K', not to be confused with the real vitamin K)	Dissociation, hallucinations, analgesia		Brain damage; Paranoia, hallucinations, aggression	

[a] Mephedrone and MDMA (and other amphetamine-derivatives, as well as tryptamines) are sometimes classified separately as 'entactogens' because of the tendency to increase the feeling of intimacy with others. However, they otherwise share most of the amphetamine effects, and may also have some overlap with those of the hallucinogens.

Source: The ICD-10 Classification of Mental and Behavioural Disorders : Clinical Descriptions and Diagnostic Guidelines, WHO (1992).

alcohol, amphetamines, cocaine, nicotine, opioids and sedatives, although psychological (e.g. for cannabis) and physiological (e.g. for caffeine) symptoms can occur during withdrawal from other substances as well. Further potential for intoxication and infection comes from additives (e.g. solvents in preparations of cocaine), mode of administration (AIDS and Hepatitis C risk from intravenous drug use), unknown dosage of illegally bought preparations (incidental overdosing) and aberrations in the production process (e.g. methanol produced by illegal distillation).

Substance abuse is not defined by the amount consumed (this is often denoted by 'harmful' or 'hazardous' use, particularly of alcohol), but by the behavioural pattern and psychosocial consequences of the substance use. In order to fulfil the substance abuse criteria, the consumption has to be recurrent and conflict with work, school, family or other social duties or the law, or occur in situations where it is physically hazardous, for example drink-driving. Substance abuse can persist for a long time, but often also progresses to substance dependence. Tolerance (increasing doses are needed to achieve the same physiological and psychological effects) and the development of withdrawal symptoms when sufficient doses are not maintained are the key features of physiological dependence. The psychological side of substance dependence is characterised by compulsive consumption and almost exclusive cognitive focus on the substance of abuse. For example, a patient might spend virtually all his or her time procuring, consuming and recovering from the substance, at the expense of work, social activities or hobbies, and despite having insight in the harmful nature of the habit and wishing to terminate it. Alcohol, opioid, sedative and stimulant use can all lead to severe physiological dependence, whereas this is not associated with cannabis and hallucinogens. Withdrawal symptoms commonly occur after sudden reduction of a chronic pattern of substance consumption. The characteristic alcohol withdrawal syndrome includes autonomic dysregulation (sweating and tachycardia), tremor, visual hallucinations, gastrointestinal symptoms, agitation, anxiety and seizures. Amphetamine and cocaine withdrawal typically lead to dysphoric mood, sleep problems, increased appetite and psychomotor changes (retardation or agitation). Opioid withdrawal in many ways is characterised by a picture opposite to its acute effects, with dysphoric mood, anxiety, aches, dilated pupils, but also gastrointestinal symptoms and in severe cases fever. Withdrawal syndromes can develop immediately but also within days of cessation of use (depending on the half life of the abused substance) and last for many weeks (particularly long in the case of benzodiazepines). Individuals need medical and psychological treatment, and severe cases can constitute medical emergencies. In the cases of sedatives and opioids, pharmacological management of withdrawal normally consists in the slow reduction of the substance of abuse or administration of a similarly acting substance in decreasing doses. Conversely, for stimulant and alcohol withdrawal the focus is on the pharmacological control of symptoms using substances from other classes (e.g. benzodiazepines for alcohol or antidepressants for amphetamine withdrawal).

The success of treatment for abuse or dependence can be measured by the scale and length of remission. The DSM-IV defines 'full remission' by the absence of any of the criteria for abuse or dependence and classifies under 'partial remission' those individuals who still meet one or more of those criteria, but not the number required for a diagnosis. 'Early' remission occurs between the first symptom-free month and end of the first year, and 'sustained' remission after the first year, although relapse is still possible, especially under conditions of stress or changing life events.

15.2   ALCOHOL USE DISORDERS

15.2.1   Epidemiology

Alcohol has almost become part of the daily staple of adults in most industrialised countries, and consumption is on the rise in developing countries as well. It is estimated that over two billion people worldwide regularly consume alcohol. Although most of them drink responsibly, alcohol is also the most widely used addictive drug. Because of the high acceptance of social drinking and the stigma associated with dependence many problem drinkers will not come to the attention of the health service, or only subsequent to medical complications. Estimates of the prevalence of alcohol use disorders therefore vary widely but have been as high as 15% for lifetime prevalence and 5% for 12-month prevalence of alcohol dependence. Annual healthcare costs alone have been estimated at £3 billion for the UK, and overall socio-economic costs, including loss of working hours, are probably an order of magnitude higher.

Alcohol consumption is higher and all types of alcohol-related disorders are more frequent in men than women. Teenage binge drinking is an increasing public health problem and, according to most studies, constitutes a risk factor for later alcohol-related disorders. The peak time for the development of alcohol dependence is between age 20 and 40. In most cases, this remains a chronic problem, and even after treatment only 30% of patients achieve long-term remission.

15.2.2   Genetics

Although family and social environment and wider cultural factors as well as the availability of specific substances shape the development and course of any substance use disorder, heritability estimates are generally moderate to high, for example about 50% for alcohol dependence. The comorbidity between alcohol dependence and other substance use disorders as well as other mental disorders is high, and some of this seems to be explained by shared genetic mechanisms. For example, about half the genetic vulnerability to heavy smoking is shared with alcohol dependence. For the non-substance-related disorders, shared genetic risk has been established for so-called externalising disorders (ASPD, ADHD, conduct disorder) but is less certain for internalising disorders (depression and anxiety) (Ducci and Goldman, 2008).

The specific genetic variants contributing to alcohol (and indeed any substance) dependence are still largely unknown. Genome-wide association studies have so far lacked sufficient power and not produced replicated results. Genome-wide linkage studies highlighted a region on chromosome 4p containing genes for subunits of the $GABA_A$ receptor and region on chromosome 4q containing the genes of the seven alcohol dehydrogenase subtypes. However, the specific risk loci for alcohol dependence have not been identified. Because of this dearth of replicated findings and general difficulty studying such a heterogeneous phenotype that is also heavily affected by comorbidity, one approach focuses on genetic mechanisms underlying putative alcohol-related endophenotypes. Such endophenotypes might be found at the behavioural (attention dysfunction, deficient executive control, aberrant reward processing) and brain level, but would have to be demonstrated in unaffected relatives as well in order to establish their independence from environmental effects and consequences of the substance abuse. Another promising approach would be to study the G×E interactions contributing to substance abuse and dependence (Ducci and Goldman, 2008).

Molecular genetics has also been applied to study potential factors predicting treatment response. Treatment with the opioid antagonist naltrexone has shown some promise in sustaining abstinence from alcohol, and those with a particular variant in the gene for the mu opioid receptor (see Section 15.4.2) might show a better response. Such approaches have been confined to pharmacological treatment, though (pharmacogenetics), and not included prediction of the response to different psychological and psychosocial approaches, which would be of practical interest because of the generally low responder rates and considerable time and cost involved in rehabilitation programmes.

15.2.3   Biological changes as a consequence of alcohol abuse

The most direct marker of ethanol consumption is its blood level. Ethanol is absorbed from the stomach and small intestine and metabolised to acetaldehyde in the liver at a rate of about 15 mg/100 ml blood/hour. After oral ingestion, peak blood levels are reached within two hours. Most individuals will not show overt behavioural effects up to blood levels of 50 mg/100 ml, but ability to drive or operate machinery may be affected below this level. Higher levels of ethanol can lead to euphoria and arousal or numbness and drowsiness, and neurological symptoms such as fine motor coordination problems, ataxia and dysarthria. Behavioural disinhibition, anger and aggression typically start at levels about 100 mg/100 ml, and levels above 300 mg/100 ml can lead to respiratory depression, coma and ultimately death. The dose-dependent effects of alcohol vary between individuals as a function of metabolism and tolerance.

Because alcohol is evenly distributed in body water (including blood) a man of 100 kg weight and body water content of 60% could reach a blood level of 50 mg/100 ml after consumption of 15 g of ethanol, which is about equivalent to 150 ml of wine with an alcohol content of 12 vol%. Because women are normally lighter than men and have lower body water content due to higher proportion of fatty tissues, they will achieve the same ethanol levels after less consumption. However, individual differences play an important role in the metabolism of alcohol as well. For example, individuals without (or with a deficient version of) the enzyme aldehyde dehydrogenase 2 (ALDH2), which metabolises acetaldehyde, experience intense unpleasant effects such as flushes and palpitations after even small amounts of ethanol and will often refrain from alcoholic drinks altogether. Genetic ALDH2 deficiencies are common in East Asian countries.

The metabolic effects of chronic heavy alcohol use can be traced with a number of biochemical markers. Increased levels of gamma-glutamyltransferase (GGT), aspartate aminotransferase (AST), alanine aminotransferase (ALT) or alkaline phosphatise (AP) can denote the associated liver damage. Increased levels of carbohydrate deficient transferrin (CDT), a protein for iron transport, are also a sensitive marker, but the mechanism of its elevation by alcohol is not yet known. Toxic effects of ethanol on erythropoiesis, the development of new red blood cells, are reflected in their increased mean corpuscular volume (MCV). Elevated GGT, CDT and MCV all have a good specificity (avoid false positives) of 80–90%, but only CDT approaches a reasonable sensitivity (avoid false negatives) of 60–80%. Chronic alcohol use can cause or aggravate a large number of medical conditions, affecting all organ systems, for example fatty liver, liver cirrhosis, pancreatitis, cancers of the gastrointestinal tract, cardiomyopathy, polyneuropathy, epilepsy, Wernicke's encephalopathy, Korsakoff's syndrome (amnesic syndrome) and dementia. Alcohol use by pregnant women can lead to foetal alcohol syndrome with growth deficiencies, characteristic facial features and mental retardation.

Chronic alcohol use leads to irreversible loss of cortical neurons (dendritic shrinkage that may revert with abstinence) and subsequent white matter loss. Brain volume loss may be particularly pronounced in the frontal lobe and cerebellum. Partly reversible white matter changes have also been observed both post-mortem and with diffusion tensor imaging. These may consist in loss and alteration of myelin sheaths, which could lead to slower and disrupted signal transmission and explain some of the cognitive and electrophysiological changes observed in long-term heavy drinkers. Microscopic bleeds in the mammillary bodies and other diencephalic regions are associated with Wernicke's encephalopathy, which is a life-threatening condition characterised by ophthalmoplegia (paralysis of eye movements), ataxia and confusion. This pathology is not directly caused by alcohol, but by the thiamine (vitamin B1) deficiency often associated with its chronic use because of imbalanced diet or interference of alcohol with the resorption and/or storage of thiamine. Even heavy alcohol use over relatively short time periods (e.g. repeated binge drinking) can lead to marked cell loss in the CNS. Possible mechanisms include the release of glutamate, which can damage neurons through excitotoxicity (glutamate binding triggers metabolic intracellular processes that lead to unsustainable ATP demand) or oxidative toxicity (glutamate receptor-activation induced production of free radicals), and the activation of microglia, triggering autoimmune processes in the brain.

15.2.4   Mechanisms of tolerance and dependence

15.2.4.1   Tolerance may develop through changes in receptor sensitivity or concentration

Chronic abuse of alcohol leads to tolerance and may develop into the compulsive drinking patterns characteristic of dependence. Most knowledge about the putative biological mechanisms underlying these physiological and psychological changes comes from animal studies of chronic ethanol administration, but without more compelling direct evidence from patient studies, which is difficult to obtain, we cannot be sure that these mechanisms also take place in human alcohol dependence. Changes in receptor concentration and/or sensitivity are a mainstay of most models of substance tolerance. In the case of alcohol, downregulation of $GABA_A$ receptors and reduced sensitivity of the benzodiazepine binding site have been hypothesised, but PET studies in humans have so far failed to provide consistent support for such a model. Another hypothesis that has received some support from animal studies is that downregulation of the cannabinoid CB_1 receptor contributes to the development of tolerance to alcohol.

Tolerance to alcohol and other drugs of abuse has also been studied with classical behavioural techniques. The presence of conditioned stimuli (e.g. when the animal was kept in the environment that was associated with substance availability) increased consumption of the substance (the US) both after Pavlovian and operant conditioning. There have even been anecdotal reports where doses of a substance that were normally tolerated became toxic when consumed in a new environment, and thus this learned aspect of tolerance may be of clinical relevance.

15.2.4.2   Dependence may arise through interplay of positive and negative reinforcing mechanisms

The brain mechanisms of dependence may be closely linked to those of tolerance. Dependence is hypothesised to develop through the interplay of two effects of alcohol, the euphoria induced by its consumption, mediated through mesolimbic dopaminergic pathways, and the negative affective consequences of its abrupt cessation, mediated through the amygdala (Moonat et al., 2010). Local administration of ethanol in the VTA leads to increased firing of dopaminergic neurons, and the uptake of ethanol (and opiates, nicotine, amphetamine and cocaine) from the blood into the brain results in increased dopamine concentrations in the nucleus accumbens, and mesolimbic dopaminergic activity has been related to the rewarding properties of ethanol in animal self-administration studies (Weiss and Porrino, 2002) (see Box 15.1). Chronic administration of ethanol in rats has led to changes in the dopamine system, notably upregulation of DAT and downregulation of tyrosine hydroxylase, the rate limiting enzyme of dopamine synthesis. Both these adaptations would lead to decreased synaptic dopamine levels, and this might be one explanation why, after chronic exposure, positively experienced psychological states need the constant administration of ethanol (dependence), and in ever increasing doses (tolerance). However, human evidence for such adaptive changes is less clear cut. The downregulation of the dopamine system may persist over months after withdrawal and thus constitute a biological risk factor for relapse.

Box 15.1   Neurobehavioural pathways to addiction

We have already encountered behavioural and neurobiological models aiming to explain the different substance-related disorders in term of an interplay of mechanisms that attract people to substance use and those that make it difficult for them to abstain because of feared or real aversive consequence. In terms of learning theory, the former can be conceptualised as positive, the latter as negative reinforcement. The evidence for such interplay from both clinical observations and animal models has led to the formulation of the theory of opponent motivational processes in addiction (Koob and Le Moal, 2008). Addiction here is understood as a dysregulation of the interplay between mechanisms promoting and inhibiting rewards that, under normal circumstances (e.g. when only natural rewards are available) leads to a negative emotional state. Because of downregulation of the reward pathways or upregulation of the aversive pathways higher rewarding inputs are needed (described as shift of the 'hedonic set point'), which cannot be achieved with natural rewards (Martinez et al., 2007), but only with the substance of abuse (or other compulsive behaviour in the case of non-substance-related dependence, e.g. pathological gambling). The idea that the hedonic set point (Koob and Le Moal, 1997) moves upward during the development of addiction is supported by studies of substance self-administration (Ahmed and Koob, 1998) and intracranial electric self-stimulation (Epping-Jordan et al., 1998). Rewarding electrical stimuli to the basal forebrain need higher intensities in operant conditioning schedules when animals are withdrawn from a substance, and lower intensities when they are also allowed to consume it. The main aspect of this theory that has remained speculative is the need for an 'anti-reward' system, which has been explained in terms of homoeostasis, that is the reward system would have to be limited on energetic grounds. The adaptive processes that result in the imbalance between the reward and 'anti-reward' system can be implemented through downregulation of reward pathways (e.g. dopamine receptor downregulation shown in animal studies) or upregulation of stress systems, such as increased CRF levels in the central nucleus of the amygdala, increased dynorphin in the NAc or increased norepinephrine in the BNST. Once the hedonic set point has been shifted in this way, some cellular memory traces seem to persist even after periods of abstinence, triggering renewed rapid dose increases after relapse, which is also observed in clinical settings.

Craving has been defined by the WHO as 'the desire to experience the effect(s) of a previously experienced psychoactive substance'. Two types of craving have been distinguished based on the positive/negative reinforcement models: reward craving, which is supposed to be related to dopaminergic and opioidergic dysregulation, and relief craving, which has been linked with GABAergic and CRF pathways. Craving (and resulting relapse) can thus be induced by primary and secondary reinforcers (priming with the substance or exposure to conditioned stimuli, called 'cues') and by stress. Alcohol relapse can also be triggered by nicotine, probably through a common pathway involving nAChRs in the VTA that mediate the reinforcing properties of alcohol cues.

The mesolimbic dopamine system has emerged as key pathway towards addiction, although maintenance of the hedonic properties of a substance may be non-dopamine-dependent and rely more on the opioid system (Le Merrer et al., 2009). The initial positive reinforcement processes for all recognised drugs of abuse seem to go through dopaminergic projections from the VTA to the ventral striatum. Such a central role of the mesolimbic system is enabled by its numerous interactions with the other neurotransmitter systems. It is modulated by serotonergic projections from the dorsal raphe, cholinergic projections from the pedunculopontine nucleus, glutamatergic input from prefrontal cortex and enkephalinergic input from the ventral pallidum. The dopaminergic projections from the VTA are also under local regulation by GABAergic interneurons that express mu receptors. Based on the three main mechanisms by which the drugs of abuse promote dopamine release in the NAc, Lüscher and Ungless (2006) proposed a functional taxonomy: (i) opioids, cannabinoids and GHB inhibit interneurons by binding to metabotropic receptors; (ii) nicotine, ethanol and benzodiazepines bind to ionotropic receptors (nAChR and GABA$_A$ receptor); (iii) stimulants and related substances target monoamine transporters (Figure 15.1).

Figure 15.1

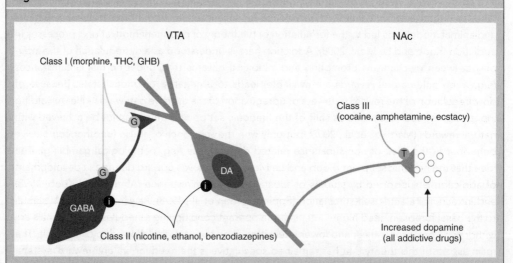

Addiction and dopamine

This schema summarises three ways in which drugs of abuse stimulate dopamine release in the Nucleus accumbens. Opiates like morphine, cannabinoids like tetrahydrocannabinol (THC), and gamma hydroxyl butyrate (GHB) inhibit GABAergic cells through G-protein coupled receptors (Class I). This leads to disinhibition of dopaminergic neurons. The second class of drugs binds to ionotropic receptors (nAchR in the case of nicotine, GABA receptors in the case of benzodiazepines, and a variety of receptors in the case of ethanol) and directly or indirectly activates dopaminergic neurons in the VTA. The third class has direct effects on dopamine reuptake and release.

Source: Adapted from (Lüscher and Ungless, 2006).

A synopsis of the animal studies of addiction thus yields at least three interacting systems that take the lead at various stages in the development of abuse, dependent behaviour and craving: a system for positive reinforcement learning based on the mesolimbic dopamine pathway; a system for negative reinforcement learning and stress avoidance based on limbic projections and central parts of the HPA axis; and the hedonic (mu and kappa) diencephalic opioid system. However, rodent models are prone to overlooking the influence of cognitive systems on human addictive behaviour. Thus, a fourth element may come into play – the (prefrontal) cortico-striatal system for executive control and behavioural inhibition – whose impairment may lead to the impulsivity that may be required for the initial stages of substance abuse to develop as well as for the later compulsive patterns. There are striking similarities between the behavioural syndrome observed after lesions to the orbitofrontal cortex and addictive behaviour, including shifts in value judgements, impulsivity and compulsive consummatory acts (Crews and Boettiger, 2009). Although there is little evidence for structural brain deficits (at the resolution detectable with current non-invasive neuroimaging techniques) preceding substance abuse the neuropsychological similarities are compelling and the neurocognitive disposition to addictive behaviour deserves more attention. Higher cognitive functions that may be unique to humans and other primates seem to be much more difficult to model in rodents than basic motivational processes, which is why self-administration, for example of cocaine, has also been studied in non-human primates (Beveridge et al., 2008).

The work on the interplay between neurotransmitter systems and common postsynaptic pathways (e.g. through the transcription factor CREB) has elucidated many commonalities between the mechanism of drugs of abuse and can explain some of the similarities in general behavioural patterns. It has also resulted in therapeutic approaches utilising these interactions, for example opioid receptor blockade to combat ethanol dependence. However, there are still important gaps in our knowledge, let alone in the availability of effective therapies. Regardless of the documented moderate to high heritability (and cross-heritability) of substance dependence, no reliable genetic markers have been identified. Furthermore, most neurobiological evidence concerns the consequences of drug use and comparatively little is known about possible neurobiological endophenotypes that may predispose to drug abuse. Finally, regardless of the convergent mechanisms at the level of the mesolimbic and other key motivational and emotional systems, all classes of drugs of abuse have their own physiological and psychological features, which are poorly explained by current biological models of addiction.

In addition to the positive reinforcing properties (desired states resulting from its administration) ethanol also seems to have negative reinforcing properties (undesired states such as anxiety and dysphoria resulting from its cessation), which are supposed to be mediated through the amygdala (particularly the central nucleus, CeA) and its extensions (e.g. the bed nucleus of the stria terminalis, BNST). A possible pharmacological mechanism for increased responsiveness of the extended amygdala after chronic ethanol use would be through corticotrophin releasing factor (CRF). CRF receptors may be upregulated after chronic alcohol use, and CRF antagonists have anti-anxiety effects during withdrawal in animals. A central role of CRF-releasing neurons of the amygdala would be supported by its projections to the basal forebrain and brainstem, allowing for interaction with other neuromodulator systems, and the well-established involvement of the HPA axis in the stress response, which has been implicated as a crucial factor in the development and maintenance of addictive drinking. CRF levels in parts of the extended amygdala are increased during ethanol withdrawal and normalised by renewed consumption (Weiss and Porrino, 2002). It has therefore been suggested that CRF antagonists might be developed for the treatment of alcohol addiction

(Moonat et al., 2010) and early phase clinical trials are underway (Jupp and Lawrence, 2010), but the problems are likely to be the same as facing the development of antidepressants targeting the HPA axis (see Chapters 3 and 11).

Endogenous opioids may play a role for both the positive and negative reinforcing functions of ethanol. Acute administration of ethanol increases the concentration of striatal endorphins, and naltrexone reverses the dopamine release induced by ethanol. The reduction of alcohol intake under treatment with opioid antagonists observed in both animals and humans may therefore result both from direct effects on the endogenous opioid system and indirect effects on dopamine concentrations. In contrast to the acute effects, chronic abuse of alcohol may lead to reduced endorphin levels, which may contribute to the aversive effects experienced after withdrawal.

15.2.4.3   Postsynaptic signalling cascades and regulation of gene expression have been implicated in substance dependence

Recent research has suggested that changes in a key intracellular pathway for the regulation of gene expression, through the transcription factor CREB, may be involved in both the positive and negative reinforcing mechanisms of alcohol dependence. Transcription factors bind to specific DNA sites (in the case of CREB: the cAMP-responsive element CRE) and promote their transcription, thus increasing the expression of the coded protein (Figure 7.7). They play a crucial role in the up- or downregulation of proteins such as receptors, transporters and growth factors, and thus in long-term synaptic plasticity. Several second messenger systems converge on CREB-mediated regulation of transcription, for example cAMP through protein kinase A (PKA) and calcium through calmodulin-dependent protein kinases (CAMK) II and IV. Other signalling cascades, for example that triggered by mitogen-activated protein kinas (MAPK), activate CREB (through phosphorylation to pCREB) as well. Chronic treatment with alcohol led to decreased levels of CAMK-IV and -CREB in rats (Kalsi et al., 2009), but acute administration may have the opposite effect (Figure 15.2). The gene for CRF is a target gene for CREB, as are those for neuropeptide Y (NPY) and brain-derived neurotrophic factor (BDNF), which are both reduced in chronically ethanol-treated animals (Moonat et al., 2010). Intracellular pCREB levels can be increased through PKA infusion, and this may reduce withdrawal symptoms in animals. However, it is currently not known whether pre-existing dysregulation of CREB may be a vulnerability factor for development of addiction after alcohol use. Other mechanisms for regulation of gene expression targeting DNA (histone acetylation, DNA methylation) or RNA (microRNAs) may also be altered after chronic alcohol exposure and are a topics of current research, matching the general interest in epigenetic mechanisms in biological psychiatry (Nestler, 2009).

15.2.5   Treatment

The traditional approach to the treatment of alcohol dependence is based on the maintenance of complete abstinence. Most people with a history of alcohol dependence need support with relapse prevention following withdrawal and throughout at least the early remission phase. Psychological interventions aim at reducing the focus on the positively reinforced properties of alcohol by concentrating on alternative goals (e.g. through motivational counselling (Cox and Klinger, 2004)) and at attenuating the negatively reinforced

Figure 15.2

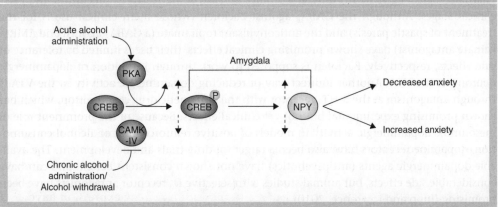

Putative effects on acute ethanol administration on CREB-mediated expression regulation
In this model (Wand, 2005), acute alcohol administration leads to activation of CREB through protein kinase A (PKA), whereas chronic alcohol intake or withdrawal have the opposite effect through blockade of calcium/calmodulin-dependent kinase IV (CAMK IV). CREB upregulates expression of neuropeptide Y in the amygdala, which is associated with decreased anxiety. Note that the chronic effects of ethanol seem to go in the opposite direction to the acute effects, resulting in higher ethanol intake needed to combat anxiety.

properties through alternative strategies for stress and anxiety management (e.g. relaxation techniques, CBT). Anti-anxiety medicines such as SSRIs can help with the latter approach. Disulfiram (Antabuse®) is a substance that specifically interferes with the rewarding effects of ethanol by blocking aldehyde dehydrogenase and leading to accumulation of acetaldehyde (although the exact mechanisms are not clear and it may also have effects on catecholamine metabolism). Disulfiram alone has no physiological effect, but intake of even small amounts of alcohol during disulfiram therapy can lead to a syndrome similar to that observed in people with genetic aldehyde dehydrogenase deficiency, including flushes, headache, nausea and drop in blood pressure. One approach is to administer very small doses of alcohol early in the treatment to evoke aversive effects and thus extinguish the reward memories associated with alcohol use. However, disulfiram has largely fallen out of favour because of mixed long-term effects in reduction of alcohol consumption, high rates of non-compliance and the potential for toxic effects, even death, from continued alcohol consumption during this therapy.

Other drugs can be used both in patients who still drink but want to reduce consumption or prevent return to heavy drinking and in those who are abstinent and need help with relapse prevention. The opioid antagonists naltrexone and nalmefene block the actions of the endogenous opioids released after ethanol intake (or in response to alcohol-related cues) and thus are intended to extinguish the conditioned drinking behaviour. This hypothetical model of its action is supported by a meta-analysis of treatment trials that revealed that, in addition to reduction of alcohol intake in those who still drink, naltrexone can also prevent relapse in abstinent drinkers. For the latter purpose, though, acamprosate seems to be the more effective medication. Although it is a GABA analogue, it exerts its main pharmacological effects through antagonism at the NMDA and mGlu$_5$ receptors and is hypothesised to counteract the sensitisation of glutamate receptors after long-term alcohol use as well as blocking the conditioned responses to alcohol-related cues during abstinence. Pharmacological agents with different profiles are also being tested in preclinical and early clinical stages. Although the GABA$_B$ agonist baclofen (whose main clinical use is for the treatment of spastic paresis) and the anticonvulsant topiramate (a GABA$_A$ agonist and AMPA/kainate antagonist) have shown promising clinical effects, their use is limited by tolerance or side effects, respectively. Baclofen is supposed to work through inhibition of dopaminergic neurons in the VTA. Another indirect way of reducing dopaminergic activity in the VTA is through antagonism at the 5-HT$_3$ receptor with the antiemetic drug ondansetron, which has shown promising experimental but not yet clinical effects. Because of the prominent role of mesolimbic dopaminergic activity in models of positive reinforcement of alcohol consumption, dopamine receptors have also been a target for drug trials and development. The available dopaminergic agents (antipsychotics) have not shown consistent benefit and can have considerable side effects, but animal studies with selective D$_3$ receptor antagonists have been promising (Jupp and Lawrence, 2010).

The clinical effect of even the established antidipsotropic (reducing the urge to drink) substances (acamprosate, naltrexone, disulfiram) is relatively low though, with a maximal risk reduction of 20% (Rösner et al., 2008). Combination with more effective psychological interventions or neurofeedback, combinations of substances with different pharmacological profiles (e.g. naltrexone plus acamprosate) and better selection of likely responders based on drinking patterns, personality profiles and genotype are promising avenues for future translational research.

15.3 STIMULANT ABUSE AND DEPENDENCE

15.3.1 Epidemiology

Rates of stimulant use and abuse have varied strongly between countries and over time, with particular subcultures promoting their use, although non-medical use of stimulants is illegal in most jurisdictions. The wider availability of amphetamines, for example as treatment for ADHD, and use of amphetamines and their derivatives as 'party drugs' (e.g. ecstasy) or performance enhancers has contributed to an increasing drug problem. Many established stimulants keep their main pharmacological properties after chemical modification. This has led to the practice of synthesising new substances derived from illegal drugs that enter the market for 'legal highs' until the authorities catch up with the new development and ban the new drug as well. The recent wave of use of naphthylpyrovalerone (marketed under the name 'NRG-1' or 'Energy 1'), which became popular in 2010 after the ban of mephedrone but was subsequently banned as 'class B' drug in the UK as well, is an example of this practice.

Lifetime prevalence of a single episode of amphetamine use in the USA was reported at 5%, and at 10% for cocaine, in the mid-1990s. Peak prevalence of stimulant use seems to be at secondary school and college age. Lifetime prevalence of amphetamine dependence was estimated at 1.5%, with 12-month prevalence being about 1/10 of that. This ratio is compatible with the observation that amphetamine dependence, unlike alcohol or opioid dependence, rarely lasts a lifetime. Lifetime prevalence of cocaine dependence was around 2% and 12-month prevalence about 0.6%. Both amphetamine and cocaine dependence are commonly associated with tolerance and increasingly unpleasant effects, as well as compromises on physical and mental health. Chronic amphetamine use may also lead to sensitisation, with smaller rather than larger doses required for the same physiological effects. Amphetamines and cocaine can be administered through a variety of routes. Most amphetamines are ingested orally or injected intravenously, but methamphetamine can also be taken nasally. Coca leaves are chewed in coca growing countries of South America, but cocaine preparations in use in industrialised countries are commonly snorted, inhaled or injected. Compulsive use in dependent individuals can follow different patterns, for example regular, daily or almost daily use, or episodic use, for example with binges during weekends.

15.3.2   Genetics

First-degree relatives of patients with amphetamine dependence have a five-fold increased risk of developing amphetamine dependence and also increased risk of developing alcohol, sedative, cannabis or cocaine dependence. Cross-risk between substances of abuse extends probably further, but data are not available for all combinations. Heritability estimates range from 0.4 for amphetamine to 0.7 for cocaine dependence. Although candidate genes might be reasonably sought amongst those coding for proteins involved in catecholamine synthesis, trafficking and signalling, no locus has been replicated so far. Preliminary evidence suggests association between a haplotype in the prodynorphin gene with reduced expression and cocaine dependence (Kreek et al., 2009). This is interesting because prodynorphin is the precursor of the endogenous opioid dynorphin, and blocks some of the rewarding properties of stimulants (Figure 15.3).

15.3.3   Neurobiological consequences of stimulant use

Amphetamines can be detected directly in urine for 1–3 days after a single use. For cocaine, the metabolite benzoylecgonine can be detected in urine for 1–3 days after a single dose and up to 12 days after chronic use. Chronic use of amphetamines (in animal studies also administration of a single high dose) leads to changes in dopaminergic and serotonergic neurons and synapses, including reductions in synaptic transmitter levels and receptor, transporter (DAT and VMAT) and synthesising enzyme (tyrosine hydroxylase and L-aromatic amino acid decarboxylase) concentrations (Yamamoto et al., 2010). Yet how the pharmacological effects of amphetamines as alternative substrates for catecholamine transporters (see Figures 6.6, 15.2) bring about these changes is still unclear. The observation that some of the neurotoxic effects are confined to amphetamines and not observed with methylphenidate may suggest that higher intracellular dopamine concentrations, resulting from disruption of storage in presynaptic vesicles (VMAT is blocked by amphetamines but not by methylphenidate), may play a role. Oxidative stress, excitotoxicity produced by glutamate release, activation of microglia and damage to the blood–brain barrier have been implicated as well (Berman et al., 2008; Yamamoto et al., 2010). Some of these mechanisms may also contribute to the hyperthermia classically observed after acute administration in animal models. Studies in non-human primates suggested that some of the neurotoxic changes to the dopamine system may be reversible through abstinence.

At the tissue level, changes associated with amphetamine use have included brain haemorrhages (after experimental doses in animals), gliosis (astrocyte hypertrophy and proliferation) and loss of cortical grey matter volume. Brain volume loss was even observed after exposure *in utero*. Some studies also found enlarged striatal volumes. The human findings were largely obtained in cross-sectional studies and may thus include changes predisposing

Figure 15.3

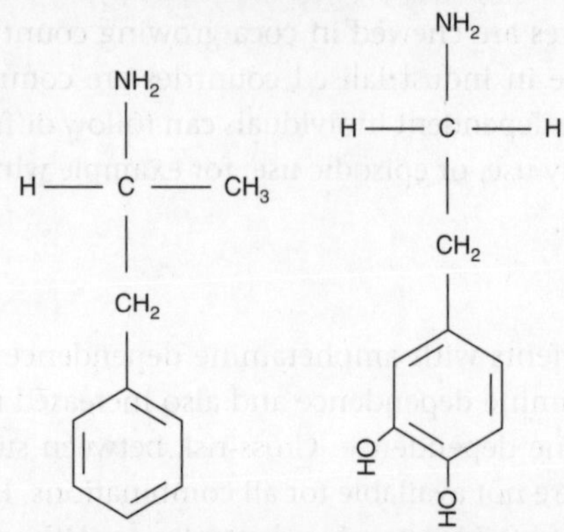

Amphethamine and dopamine share elements of their chemical structure
Structure of amphetamine (1-methyl-2-phenethylamine). Compare structure of dopamine on the right.

to (rather than following from) drug use, and longitudinal studies comparing brain volumes before and after onset of consumption would be needed to resolve this issue. These data are available only for ADHD patients treated with stimulants, where no longitudinal effect of treatment was observed (Castellanos et al., 2002). However, it is conceivable that the primary effects of the disease (the potential right-shift of the brain growth curve, see Chapter 17) and of the drugs cancel each other in ADHD patients. Furthermore, amphetamine concentrations similar to those obtained in ADHD treatment did have neurotoxic effects in baboons and squirrel monkeys (Berman et al., 2008). Thus, although no clinically relevant adverse effects on brain structure have been documented with medical use of stimulants, the scenario may be very different for unregulated illicit use and the vulnerability of the brain to stimulant effects may increase with age and other factors (e.g. concurrent HIV infection).

There is even less evidence base from studies in abusers of cocaine to assess possible long-term neurotoxic effects, but cross-sectional studies have also suggested widespread cortical (including cerebellar) volume loss. Rodent studies have suggested shrinking (pyknosis) and death (necrosis) of neurons as underlying processes. However, the brain atrophy induced by stimulant abuse may be less marked than that observed in chronic alcohol abusers, which can be almost pathognomic on clinical scans. Specific structural and functional deficits may underlie some of the neuropsychological changes following (but possibly already preceding) stimulant abuse. Impairments in executive functions, which include the ability to update task-relevant information, shift between operations and inhibit automatic responses, have been reported and may be associated with 'hypofrontality' observed in functional imaging studies. Both PET studies of blood flow during rest and fMRI studies of functional activation during inhibition paradigms (such as the 'Go/No Go test') found reduced prefrontal activation, which maps onto the course of metabolic deficits in cocaine self-administering monkeys, which starts in ventromedial prefrontal cortex and then proceeds to include dorsal prefrontal regions as well (Beveridge et al., 2008). Incidentally hypoactivation of mainly medial prefrontal regions, such as the anterior cingulate cortex, during inhibition tasks has also been observed in imaging and electrophysiological studies with ADHD patients (Linden and Fallgatter, 2009).

15.3.4   Mechanisms of sensitisation, tolerance and dependence

The molecular mechanisms of stimulant sensitisation, tolerance and dependence have been almost exclusively studied in animal models (rodents and monkeys). As expected, changes in the dopamine system played an important role. Behavioural sensitisation was associated with D_1 receptor activity. Plastic changes in postsynaptic neurons may be mediated through the cAMP/PKA signalling cascade, converging on DARPP-32 (dopamine- and cAMP-regulated phosphoprotein of 32 kDa), which inhibits protein phosphorylation and can thus regulate a wide variety of cellular processes (see Section 7.4.1). Activation of D_1 receptors enhances and that of D_2 and NMDA glutamate receptors reduces DARPP-32 activity and this pathway is thus considered to be a key link between the dopamine and glutamate pathways. Mice with a dysfunctional DARPP-32 pathway did not show sensitisation to the behavioural effects of cocaine. The long-term activation of DARPP-32 may be produced by the transcription factor delta-fosB through its target Cdk5 (cyclin-dependent kinase-5), which phosphorylates DARPP-32. Delta-fosB has been implicated as a key molecular 'switch' for drug sensitisation (Nestler et al., 2001) (Figure 15.4). It inhibits the synthesis of the endogenous opioid dynorphin, which inhibits reward mechanisms through binding to kappa-receptors. Delta-fosB thus disrupts a negative feedback mechanism in the mesolimbic dopamine system, which may explain its association with sensitisation and compulsive drug-seeking behaviour. The crucial role of the VTA-striatal projections is highlighted by experiments with repeated administration of amphetamine in the VTA of rats, which potentiated their locomotor responses to subsequent doses (Chen et al., 2009a).

Figure 15.4

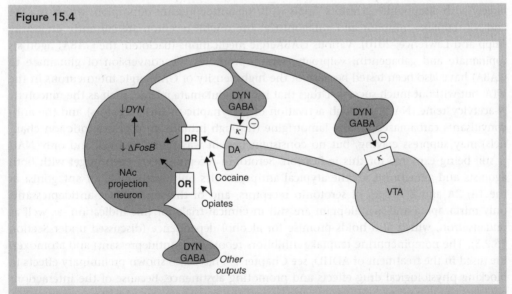

Postsynaptic changes mediating sensitisation

Indirect dopaminergic stimulation (dopamine receptors: DR) through cocaine and other stimulants or activation of opioid receptors (OR) leads to activation of the IEG Delta-fosB. This in turn down-regulates the expression of dynorphin (DYN), which normally inhibits dopaminergic neurons through postsynaptic kappa receptors. The overstimulation of reward related circuits thus essentially shuts down its own negative feedback control mechanism.

Source: Adapted from(Nestler et al., 2001) with kind permission. Copyright: National Academy of Sciences, USA.

Human radiotracer studies found decreased DAT binding after long-term methampheta-mine use and decreased SERT binding after MDMA use. Thus, the need for increasing doses during the development of tolerance might be explained by decreased concentrations of presynaptic monoamine transporters. However, the upregulation of mu opioid-receptors after cocaine abuse, which correlated with craving and risk of relapse (Martinez et al., 2007), is less easily squared with such a model. At the intracellular level, CREB has been proposed as a key transcription factor mediating tolerance and dependence. CREB activation in the nucleus accumbens has led to decreased interest in natural rewards (such as eating and drink-ing) in rodents, which mimics some aspects of the human addictive phenotype. The cellular functions of CREB are in many respects opposite to those of delta-fosB, which would fit with antagonistic processes underlying sensitisation and tolerance, but such transcription factor-based models appear almost too global to derive specific predictions regarding par-ticular types of drug addictions. Ultimately, neurobiological models of addiction will have to explain not only the heightened need for reward-inducing drugs, but also why these substances – alcohol, stimulants, cannabis, opioids, nicotine and so on – are normally not interchangeable for individual addicts.

15.3.5   Treatment

There is currently no established pharmacological treatment for stimulant dependence. Dopamine agonists of all classes (e.g. reuptaker inhibitors like methylphenidate, the MAO inhibitor selegiline, disulfiram in its capacity as dopamine beta-hydroxylase inhibitor, selec-tive DRD2 and DRD3 agonists, the partial DRD2 agonist aripiprazole) have been tried, but largely with disappointing results. Trials with the antidepressant bupropion, which is a DA and NE reuptake inhibitor and antagonist at the nAchR receptor, are currently underway (Jupp and Lawrence, 2010). Various GABAergic medications (baclofen; the $GABA_A$ agonists topiramate and gabapentin; valproate, which promotes the conversion of glutamate to GABA) have also been tested because of the high density of GABAergic interneurons in the VTA, but without much success. Drugs that inhibit glutamate release, such as the mucolytic N-acetylcysteine (NAC) (through activation of presynaptic mGlu1 receptors) and the anti-convulsants carbamazepine and lamotrigine (through inhibition of presynaptic ion chan-nels) may suppress craving, but no consistent benefit was found in trials and only NAC is still being explored for this indication. Serotonin receptors have been target with both agonists and antagonists Of the atypical antipsychotics only quetiapine, an antagonist at the 1A, 2A and 2C types of serotonin receptors, and of the serotonergic antidepressants only mirtazapine and escitalopram are still in clinical trials for this indication, as well as ondansetron, which also holds promise for alcohol dependence (discussed under Section 15.2.5). The norepinephrine reuptake inhibitors reboxetine (antidepressant) and atomoxet-ine (used in the treatment of ADHD, see Chapter 17) have also shown preliminary effects in blocking physiological drug effects and promoting abstinence. Because of the interactions between the dopamine and opioid systems and the partial success of naltrexone in reduc-ing alcohol consumption, this substance has also been tried for amphetamine dependence, with some preliminary success. A completely different approach to the treatment of cocaine dependence was based on a vaccine that stimulates the production of antibodies that bind to cocaine in the peripheral circulation and prevent its passage through the blood–brain barrier. This vaccination has been promising in reducing cocaine use but its effects can be neutralised by unmotivated patients through simply increasing the dose (Jupp and Lawrence, 2010).

This consideration highlights the general importance of combining any pharmacological approach to drug dependence with the appropriate psychological intervention and social support.

15.4   OPIOID-RELATED DISORDERS

15.4.1   Epidemiology

Because of the high rates of drug-related criminality and severe psychosocial problems associated with the abuse of opioids, which may eclipse those seen with other substances, estimates of the prevalence and course of opioid abuse and dependence are notoriously difficult to obtain. About 5% of the population of industrialised countries report at least a single episode of opioid use other than for prescription purposes. This use seems to peak in the third decade of life and affect men slightly more than women. Rates for abuse or dependence are estimated at 0.6–0.7% for industrialised countries and worldwide 0.4%. Terminologically we distinguish between opiates, which are chemically alkaloids found in opium or their synthetic derivatives, and opioids, which are molecules from different chemical classes that have similar pharmacological effects to opiates, that is they bind to one or more of the opioid receptors mu, delta and kappa. 'Endogenous' opioids are those (peptide-)opioids that are synthesised in the human body. Intravenous use of the opiate heroin and oral use of the opiate codeine or the opioid methadone are common forms of administration. There is also a longstanding and growing problem of dependence on opioids that are prescribed for chronic pain. This dependence persists beyond the point where the substance exerts its intended analgesic effect (and indeed, often in cases where its chronic use contributes to compounding the pain), and dose reduction is very difficult. A common substance used for the treatment of chronic pain and associated with these problems is tramadol, and its dependency problem may be increased by its SSRI- and SNRI-like properties.

Opioid dependence often has a chronic course with frequent relapses, and less than a third of patients achieve long-term abstinence. Medical complications are often severe, with annual mortality in long-term users as high as 2%. Some of the medical complications (e.g. hepatitis and HIV infection, tuberculosis and endocarditis) are associated with intravenous drug use, but the psychiatric and psychosocial consequences can occur with any substance and any type of administration. Although most cases of overdosing are observed with intravenous use, it can also happen through other routes of administration. Opioid dependence has considerable psychiatric comorbidities, particularly with other substance-use disorders and ASPD.

15.4.2   Genetics

The heritability of opioid dependence is moderately high at about 0.5. Although the genes for opioid receptors and endogenous opioids are obvious candidates, no conclusive association has been established. The A118G SNP in the OPRM1 gene, which results in a change from asparagine to aspartate at position 40 of the mu receptor (Asn40Asp), is considered to be a promising variant. However, findings on the association of the G-allele, the variant implicated in the treatment response to naltrexone in alcohol dependence, with opioid dependence have been mixed. Preliminary reports also exist for variants in the genes for the delta and kappa receptor, the 5-HT$_3$ receptor, galanin (a food intake regulator) and the metabotropic glutamate receptor mGluR$_8$ (Kreek et al., 2009). However, replication of these findings and results from GWAS are still lacking. There is also an increasing interest in epigenetic modifications, but so far tentative results are available only for treatment responses, where higher methylation of the OPRM1 gene may be associated with a better adherence to methadone treatment in former heroin addicts.

15.4.3   Neurobiological consequences of opioid abuse

Heroin, morphine and methadone can be detected for 1–3 days after use in urine, for up to 4 days in blood (and like most drugs – with LSD a notable exception – up to 3 months in hair). Heroin (diacetyl-morphine) is deacetylated into the active metabolites 6-monoacetyl morphine (6-MAM) and morphine. Most evidence on the consequences of long-term opiate/opioid use on the human brain is available for heroin. Cerebrovascular changes, including ischaemic strokes, and cortical atrophy have been described. As with the other drugs of abuse discussed above oxidative and excitotoxic damage from overstimulation of the dopaminergic and glutamatergic systems are possible mechanisms. Opiates bind to opioid receptors on GABAergic cells in the VTA and thus prevent release of GABA and inhibition of VTA dopaminergic cells, resulting in increased mesolimbic dopamine tone. Chronic opioid treatment also leads to CREB upregulation, which can trigger numerous further cellular processes. Apoptosis and suppression of hippocampal neurogenesis have also been observed in chronically opioid treated animals, but it is unclear how relevant the latter is in adult humans. The leukoencephalopathy associated with heroin inhalation is poorly understood in its mechanisms. In addition, brain damage may result from the administration route (e.g. infections resulting in brain abscesses) and associated medical conditions (e.g. HIV encephalopathy).

15.4.4   Biological mechanisms of opioid tolerance and dependence

The first studies of electrical self-stimulation in rats in the 1950s triggered research into the neurophysiological and neurochemical mechanisms of reinforcement. It was found that many of the reinforcement effects of electrical stimulation, for example in the septal region of the diencephalon, could be mimicked by self-administration of opioids. Research on specific opioid receptor agonists and antagonists has helped unravel their differential contribution, and it is now thought that activation of mu (and to a lesser extent delta) receptors leads to positive reinforcement, whereas activation of kappa-receptors has aversive consequences and promotes stress-induced drug intake (Le Merrer et al., 2009). Kappa-receptors would thus subserve the negative reinforcement component of maintenance of dependent behaviour.

Box 15.2   Animal models of addiction

Behavioural and neurobiological mechanisms of reinforcement can be studied with three classes of animal models. In self-administration schedules animals learn to obtain the desired substance through moving the manipulandum in a modified Skinner box (Chapter 5) where the food reinforcer is replaced with the drug (as pellets or with a device for local application in the brain). These schedules often also include the choice between different reinforcers and can thus probe discrimination learning and critical doses. Because drug intake is voluntary and often increases with time of exposure this model has good face validity for human drug abuse.

Place conditioning (Figure 15.5) is a Pavlovian paradigm that assesses approach (CPP) or avoidance (CPA) through pairing the drug (US) with environmental cues (CS). Animals will prefer the parts of the chamber that were paired with the rewarding properties of the drug (e.g. dopaminergic stimulation) and avoid those that were paired with aversive properties (e.g. kappa receptor stimulation by dynorphin). Because of its passive nature this paradigm has poor face validity, but the predictive validity is reasonable. For example, the CPP paradigm has shown that it is harder to condition with nicotine than with stimulants, which matches observations in humans (O'Dell and Khroyan, 2009). CPA can also be used to study the aversive effects of withdrawal.

Intracranial self stimulation (ICSS) is normally applied to the medial forebrain bundle, which connects the septal region with the midbrain. Animals can use the manipulandum to apply currents through the implanted electrode. A lower threshold for a reliable behavioural effect is determined first, and then how it changes under drug administration or withdrawal. Acute administration decreases the amount of current needed to motivate animals to engage in the conditioned behaviour (e.g. the lever press), indicating that the reward system has been pre-activated by the drug. In other words, the hedonic set point moves down. The opposite effects are observed during withdrawal, which has been described as increase of the hedonic set point.

Figure 15.5

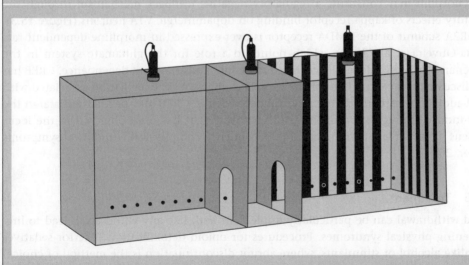

A three shuttle chamber
Sketch of a three shuttle chamber, which can be used for Conditioned Place Preference (CPP) tests in animal experiments. This setup can be used to investigate the rewarding and aversive properties of drugs because the experimental animals will learn to avoid the parts of the chamber paired with the aversive stimulus and prefer those paired with the rewarding stimulus.

Experiments with the conditioned place preference (CPP) paradigm, where specific stimuli, for example local drug administration, are associated with particular compartments of the cage (see Box 15.2), and with drug self-administration have demonstrated a crucial role for mu receptor activation in the VTA in positive reinforcement of opioid use. This does not apply to the delta receptor because mu but not delta knock-out mice cease to self-administer morphine into the VTA. The role of mu receptors in the Nucleus accumbens is less straightforward, and may be more important in the maintenance than in the development of dependent behaviour. Mu receptor activation in other parts of the ascending brainstem-basal ganglia-cortex pathways, including the ventral pallidum, periaqueductal grey matter (PAG, an important node in the pain pathways) and the pedunculopontine tegmental nucleus (a main component of the reticular activating system) is also involved at various stages of the development of opioid dependence, but the contribution of the amygdalar and thalamic opioid systems is unclear. The PAG may be more important for the development of physical dependence, whereas the VTA and NAc contribute more to the learned drug-related behaviours. Interestingly, morphine self-administration into the septal area is blocked by systemic pre-treatment with D_1 or D_2 antagonists, pointing to the close interaction between the dopamine and opioid systems.

The expression of the mu receptor does not change with long-term opioid treatment, but the precursor peptides for the endogenous opioids (proenkephalin and proopiomelanocortin, the precursor for endorphin, and prodynorphin) are downregulated in key areas involved in motivation and homeostasis such as the hypothalamus and striatum. This downregulation may contribute to the development of tolerance. Interestingly, endogenous opioids are upregulated by stimulant use, which may contribute to sensitisation to stimulants (see Section 15.3.4). Alternatively, upregulation of prodynorphin and dynorphin may constitute a regulatory negative feedback mechanism through the inhibitory effects of kappa receptor binding on dopaminergic VTA neurons (Figure 15.3). The NR2A subunit of the NMDA receptor is over-expressed in morphine-dependent rats (Cunha-Oliveira et al., 2008), which points to a role for the glutamate system in the maintenance of opioid dependence. Like for alcohol and stimulant dependence, CREB has been discussed as a central hub for the various changes in gene regulation associated with opioid addiction, particularly the physical dependence. CREB may be instrumental in the opiate-induced upregulation of the cAMP pathway that has been observed in the locus coeruleus in particular and implicated in dependence and physical withdrawal symptoms (Nestler, 2004).

15.4.5   Treatment

Opioid withdrawal can be particularly unpleasant and, like any withdrawal, lead to life-threatening physical syndromes. Procedures for opioid detoxification (like for sedatives but unlike alcohol or stimulants, where abrupt discontinuation is the method of choice) normally involve long-term dose reduction in small steps. Substitution therapy with other opioids, for example replacing heroin with methadone, is also common. However, if withdrawal symptoms do arise, they can sometimes be controlled with alpha$_2$ adrenergic drugs like clonidine, lofexidine and guanfacine or with GABAergic substances like baclofen or GHB (which, however, has its own abuse potential). Memantine has been tried for craving reduction based on the observation of NMDA receptor upregulation during dependence and withdrawal, but without clear benefit. Naltrexone has some effect in promoting abstinence but compliance in generally low. If complete abstinence is not expected, maintenance treatment with controlled administration of opiates or synthetic opioids is possible, but the debate on the best medical and legal approach to such substitution therapies continues, and legal regulation differs greatly across the world. Where approved, heroin can be administered under controlled conditions, reducing the risk of medical complications and overdosing and of drug-associated crimes. The standard substance for substitution therapy is the synthetic opioid methadone, which acts as mu receptor agonist and NMDA-receptor antagonist. Levo-α-acetylmethadol (LAAM), which has a similar mode of action but longer half life, was also in use but has been withdrawn from European and American markets because of rare cardiac side effects. It is still being used in clinical trials. The opiate derivative buprenorphine is a partial agonist at the mu receptor and a partial antagonist at the kappa receptor. Because of its partial agonistic it may have a better profile comparing analgesic and rewarding effects to sedation and respiratory suppression and accidental overdosing may be less likely than with methadone, let alone heroin. However, overdosing would be particularly difficult to antagonise because of its high affinity to the opioid receptors. Partial agonists also lead to less receptor adaptation than full agonists, but this has not been documented as a main mechanism of opioid addiction. This may explain why buprenorphine is no more effective than methadone or LAAM as a substitution treatment for opioid dependence (Jupp and Lawrence, 2010).

15.5   ABUSE OF OTHER SUBSTANCES

15.5.1   Cannabinoids

Cannabinoids extracted from the cannabis plant or their synthetic analogues are the illicit substances with the most widespread use in industrialised countries, and their use is tolerated in some legislations. Cannabinoids are smoked or ingested in various preparations, but the active compound in all of them is delta-9-THC, which activates the CB_1 and CB_2 receptors. The physiological agonists for these receptors are the endocannabinoids, for example anandamide and 2-arachidonoylglycerol. Cannabis is mainly consumed for its relaxing and mildly euphoric properties, and both effects can occur in more extreme forms during intoxication, in addition to perceptual disturbance and somatic symptoms. Reports of lifetime use range from 30–50%, with peak use in early adulthood. Lifetime prevalence of dependence is about 5%, and 12-month prevalence about 1%, which would indicate that the course is self-limiting in a considerable portion of abusers. Dependence is mainly psychological, although tolerance develops frequently leading to increasing dosage, and physical withdrawal symptoms have been reported. Comorbidity with other substance use disorders as well as with conduct and personality disorders and psychoses is common. Although many users go on to use other substances such as stimulants or opioids it is uncertain whether this is triggered by the previous cannabinoid use, as implied by the 'gateway drug' concept. The heritability of cannabinoid dependence is estimated at 50%. No results from GWAS are available, and the preliminary positive association results from candidate genes for the CB_1 receptor and a $GABA_A$ receptor subunit point to common risk shared with other types of substance dependence rather than specific risk for cannabis abuse (Agrawal and Lynskey, 2009).

The presynaptic CB_1 receptor is expressed particularly in basal ganglia, cerebellum and hippocampus. It is activated upon activation of the postsynaptic cell and thus retrogradely modulates neural transmission from both inhibitory and excitatory neurons through negative feedback loops. The net effect of acute cannabinoid administration seems to be excitatory, as evidenced by increased blood flow to cortical regions. Studies of the long-term effects of cannabinoids on brain structure and function have not produced consistent results. There is some indication that several cannabinoids can be neuroprotective, e.g. against oxidative damage, and preclinical (for AD) and clinical (for schizophrenia) evaluations are underway. Cannabinoids are also being explored as a treatment for chronic pain. Neuropsychological studies, which were mostly conducted in a cross-sectional design, suggest subtle deficits across a range of cognitive domains, but some of these, for example in executive functions and decision-making, may be part of the cognitive phenotype of vulnerability to substance abuse (Gonzalez, 2007).

Activation of the CB_1 receptor can lead to long-term depression (LTD) of mesolimbic dopaminergic neurons, which may contribute to the amotivational syndrome often observed with chronic use. It also facilitates LTD of inhibitory input and LTP of excitatory input into the hippocampus, which may form the basis for neuroplastic mechanisms of dependent behaviour. Knock-out and antagonist studies have shown that, like the mu receptor, the CB_1 receptor is involved in the reinforcement of dependent use of several classes of drugs. These include nicotine, ethanol and opioids in addition to the cannabinoids themselves. The endocannabinoid system may also be involved in the hedonic processes associated with stimulant and opioid use, and in the consolidation of drug-related behaviour and thus in relapse (Maldonado et al., 2006).

Several drugs that have shown promise for other addictions are currently being tried to support abstinence from cannabinoids, for example the GABAergic drugs baclofen and gabapentin. Dopaminergic (citicoline, which increases dopamine and muscarinic receptor numbers, and selegiline, a MAO-B inhibitor) and glutamatergic (NAC) drugs are also being investigated to correct putative hypofunction in these systems arising with chronic cannabinoid use, but trials are either ongoing or results were not available at the time of writing (Jupp and Lawrence, 2010). Current information about these and other trials is available on the website www.clinicaltrials.gov, a service of the National Institutes of Health of the United States.

15.5.2   Inhalants

Volatile compounds from very different chemical classes (for examples see Table 15.1) are inhaled for their psychological effects. They can lead to rapid intoxication both because of the direct effects of the substance and because of complications brought about by the mode of ingestion (e.g. asphyxia). The organic solvents that make up most classes of inhalants are lipophilic and thus enter neurons rapidly. Initial psychological and behavioural effects may include excitation, euphoria and disinhibition and with continued use hallucinations and symptoms of central depression such as slurred speech and dizziness, and ultimately coma and respiratory arrest. Because of the large number of different substances the acute effects vary widely, but medical complications are common and dangerous. Tolerance or withdrawal after long-term use is not frequently reported, but psychological dependence may occur. Inhalants are probably the drugs with the earliest age peak. Up to a quarter of young adolescents (up to age 12) in industrialised countries may have experimented with them, and rates are even higher in deprived and isolated communities. Chronic use is less frequent, but at 4% still makes them one of the major drugs of abuse in adolescents (Lubman et al., 2008), possibly because of their wide availability in legal products and low cost. Comorbidity with other substance use disorders and other mental disorders, particularly conduct disorder and ASPD, is common.

Chronic use may lead to cerebral and cerebellar atrophy and white matter changes, and to generalised cognitive impairment and neurological signs, which are partly reversible after abstinence. Many users are in their early teens and thus particularly vulnerable to the neurotoxic effects of inhalants, which may be responsible for the often dramatic changes on neuroimaging. Cell culture studies indicate that most inhalants antagonise NMDA receptors, particularly the NR1-NR2B subunit combination and nACh receptors and activate $GABA_A$, glycine and $5\text{-}HT_3$ receptors. Animal studies have demonstrated changes in gene expression, for example upregulation of NMDA and mu receptors, but whether these contribute to excitotoxic damage is not known. The reinforcing properties of inhalants are probably mediated through activation of dopaminergic VTA neurons and the resulting dopamine release in the NAc. Rodents can be conditioned to toluene and other inhalants. Animal models also produced evidence for cross-sensitisation with other drugs of abuse including ethanol, sedatives, PCP, cocaine and amphetamines (Lubman et al., 2008), which may partly explain the high rate of comorbid abuse of other substances. There is no specific pharmacotherapy to aid abstinence. In addition to standard behavioural addiction therapies, psychosocial help and treatment of any accompanying or underlying conduct or personality disorder will be important to attain long-term abstinence.

15.5.3   Hallucinogens

The group of hallucinogens comprises chemically heterogeneous substances, including lysergic acid diethylamine (LSD), the phenethylamines mescaline (3,4,5-trimethoxyphenethylamine) and 2,5-dimethoxy-4-methylamphetamine and the indole alkaloids psilocybin (O-phosphoryl-4-hydroxy-N,N-dimethyltryptamine) and dimethyltryptamine (DMT). LSD and the indole alkaloids are chemically related to serotonin (5-hydroxytryptamine), an indoleamine (Figure 15.6), and all hallucinogens act on serotonin receptors.

The hallucinogens, sometimes termed 'psychedelics', also converge in their psychological effects, producing altered states of consciousness and perceptual changes such as hallucinations, synaesthesia, altered body image, and euphoria. Heightened memories, regression into an earlier period of life and mystical experiences have also been reported.

Figure 15.6

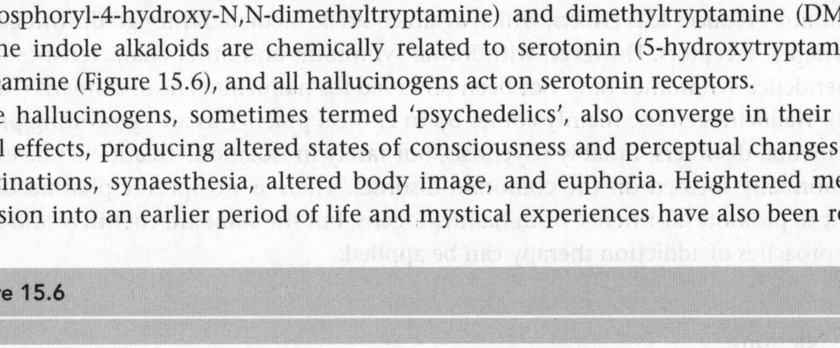

Serotonin and serotonergic hallucinogens a structurally similar
(A) Structure of lysergic acid diethylamide (LSD), (B) serotonin and (C) psilocybin.

After the initial euphoria, mood swings are common and can lead to intense dysphoria and anxiety ('horror trip') and psychotic experience. Uncontrolled behaviour is a potential source of accidents. Autonomic symptoms can result from sympathetic (tachycardia, hypertension, pupillary dilation, increases of blood sugar and body temperature) and parasympathetic (salivation, sweating, flushes) stimulation. Acute cognitive impairment has been reported, but is difficult to assess during the mental alteration. There is no evidence for long-term cognitive or neurological impairment from use of medium doses of LSD. Experience with the use of LSD is relatively common. In the mid-1990s 10% of US adults and adolescents reported having used a hallucinogen, with a peak at high school/college age. Hallucinogen use seems to be self-limiting in most cases, but can be comorbid with psychotic or personality disorders. Heritability is high at 0.6–0.8 but no genetic loci have been identified.

Orally administered LSD passes the blood–brain barrier, and animal studies suggest that it accumulates particularly in limbic and diencephalic structures and the pituitary. In cortex relatively high concentrations were measured in auditory and visual areas, which may explain the prominence of perceptual symptoms. LSD acts as a partial agonist on 5-HT_{1A} autoreceptors but also has high affinity for the other 5-HT_1 receptors and the 5-HT_{2A} receptor. Through its effect on presynaptic 5-HT autoreceptors it inhibits serotonin release and through its effect on 5-HT_{2A} coupled G-proteins it can regulate gene expression. The hallucinogens also increase dopamine release. Tolerance is a prominent feature of LSD and can develop after only 2–3 doses. Cross-tolerance between LSD, psilocybin and mescaline has been observed. Downregulation of 5-HT_{2A} receptor density has been suggested as a key mechanism. Such a mechanism is supported by the finding that the pre-treatment with SSRI or MAO inhibitors reduces LSD effects, which again could be mediated through downregulation of postsynaptic receptors. However, withdrawal symptoms and other characteristics of classical dependence syndromes have not been observed for hallucinogens in humans (Passie et al., 2008). Hallucinogen use mainly comes up in clinical practice as an aggravating problem of other mental disorders, notably psychosis, but rarely in isolation. Treatment correspondingly is normally focused on the comorbid disorder. There is no specific pharmacological treatment to promote abstinence from hallucinogens, but the standard cognitive and behavioural approaches of addiction therapy can be applied.

15.5.4 Nicotine

Amongst the substances of abuse, nicotine is responsible for the largest number of deaths (major cause of approx. 10% of deaths worldwide, compared to approx. 2.5% for alcohol). Over two-thirds of the population of industrialised countries report having used cigarettes and exposure to nicotine also occurs through other routes of administration (chewing tobacco, snuff). Although many chronic users start in their teens, lifetime prevalence increases further over life, driven by people who take up smoking later. The majority of regular smokers are dependent, and estimates of the point prevalence of nicotine dependence in the USA population are as high as 25% of adults. Dependency rates are higher in females than males (although consumption may be lower in females). Although regular nicotine consumption by adults has declined recently in the West because of public health campaigns and bans on smoking in public places, it seems to be on the increase in adolescents and in the developing world. Although most regular nicotine users report a desire to quit, and many try this regularly, less than a half attain long-term abstinence.

Heavy smoking leads to many and characteristic medical complications, including chronic bronchitis, emphysema, lung cancer, cardio- and cerebrovascular disease. It also has significant psychiatric comorbidities, notably with schizophrenia (80% of schizophrenia patients are also heavy or dependent smokers, and it has been proposed that this may be partly derived from attempts at self-medication). However, trials with nicotine receptor agonists to alleviate symptoms or cognitive problems of schizophrenia have so far been unsuccessful.

Nicotine dependence has a moderately high heritability (0.5–0.7). Although no associated genetic variants have been obtained from GWAS, higher activity variants of genes for nicotine metabolizing enzymes such as cytochrome P450 CYP2A6 are associated with higher nicotine intake and lower success in quitting. Genes coding for subunits of the nAChR and interactions between their variants have also been investigated for associations with nicotine dependence (Ray et al., 2009).

Tobacco smoke contains over 4000 different substances, many of which are toxic, for example chlorides, aromatic carbohydrates and heavy metals. The same toxic compounds are found in sidestream smoke (inhaled by others during 'passive smoking'). Because the majority of nicotine consumption occurs through smoking, the relative toxicity of nicotine and the other tobacco components cannot be determined from human studies. Although nicotine may enhance certain cognitive functions such as processing speed and memory after acute administration in both regular and non-users, the long-term effects on cognition are negative. Because nicotine passes through the blood–placenta barrier, smoking during pregnancy can affect the foetus. Intrauterine exposure to nicotine leads to reduced birth weight (on average by 200 g), increased infant morbidity and mortality, and deficits on cognitive testing.

Nicotine is a risk factor for the development of stroke. It also seems to contribute to clinically silent ischaemic lesions and white matter atrophy, which can lead to deficits in executive and other cognitive functions. Through its cerebrovascular effect nicotine is also a risk factor for the development of vascular and Alzheimer dementia. Smoking can also lead to direct neuronal damage through oxidative stress and apoptosis or inflammation. Animal studies have shown that cigarette smoke leads to an increase of reactive oxygen species (ROS) and nitric oxide (NO), which can damage lipids, proteins and DNA through oxidation and ultimately lead to cell death (apoptosis). Some of the cerebrovascular damage may also be mediated through NO, which can promote the formation of thrombi from leukocytes and platelets, which damage vessel walls (atherosclerosis).

Regardless of its amply documented long-term toxicity, nicotine has also been studied as a potential neuroprotective agent. Nicotine treatment of mice indeed reduced amyloid beta plaques, one of the neuropathological hallmarks of AD, but also promoted the phosphorylation of tau protein, another pathological feature of neurodegeneration associated with AD (Swan and Lessov-Schlaggar, 2007). It is therefore unlikely that nicotine will have a clinical role as an anti-dementia drug.

Like most if not all substances of abuse, nicotine acts through increased dopamine concentrations in the mesolimbic pathways. Nicotine has highest affinity to the α4β2 type of the nAChR. This stimulation switches VTA dopaminergic neurons from tonic to phasic firing mode, leading to higher dopamine release in NAc synapses. Nicotine also stimulates cortico-basal ganglia-thalamic circuits directly through cholinergic pathways, which may explain the positive short-term effects on attention. Nicotine also enhances activity of dopaminergic VTA neurons by stimulating the release of beta-endorphin and enkephalin, which bind to mu receptors on GABAergic interneurons in the VTA and thus reduce GABA release and disinhibit the dopaminergic neurons. We have already encountered this mechanism as one of the putative reinforcing pathways of opioid use (Section 15.4.4).

The chronic use of nicotine leads to increased mesolimbic dopamine levels (through greater release and/or reduced MAO levels) and upregulation of $\alpha4\beta2$ nAChRs and glutamate receptors in VTA and NAc. How this upregulation leads to tolerance and dependence is currently not clear.

Treatment to promote smoking cessation and abstinence is based on education and behavioural approaches. However, quit rates may be doubled through the additional use of pharmacotherapy. Nicotine replacement therapy through oral (chewing gum) or transdermal (patches) administration uses decreasing doses of nicotine to control withdrawal symptoms. Bupropion, an antidepressant that increases catecholamine release and blocks nAChRs, is also effective, but the behavioural mechanisms are unknown. The $\alpha4\beta2$ nAChR partial agonist and $\alpha7$ nAChR full agonist varenicline is intended to reduce craving and reward values associated with cigarette smoking. It is the most recent pharmacological aid to smoking cessation and has both FDA (Foods and Drugs Administration of the United States) approval and endorsement from the National Institute of Clinical Excellence (NICE) of the UK. Generally the advice is to combine pharmacological with behavioural approaches to maximise the chance of long-term abstinence. Like for cocaine, vaccines against nicotine are also in the trial phase. This approach seems to be safe because the antigen–antibody complexes do not pass the blood–brain barrier, and nicotine has no physiological function in the human body (the natural agonist at the nicotinic receptor is acetylcholine, with which this approach does not interfere). However, there is a theoretical possibility that vaccination will increase rather than decrease use (analogous to classical tolerance), and results from phase III clinical trials are still outstanding.

15.5.5   Addiction to sedatives and other psychiatric drugs

Prescription drugs are the second most common substances of abuse after the cannabinoids. Although classically abuse of prescription drugs has been more associated with later adulthood because of the generally higher prescription rates during that period, it is sharply increasing in younger age groups as well. Lifetime prevalence amongst US college students is now at 21%, and 12-month prevalence at 14%. Opiates and opioids prescribed for their analgesic properties or as cough medicine and benzodiazepines and other sedatives are probably the most widely abused prescription drugs, but abuse of prescribed stimulants, steroids and anticholinergics also poses important problems (Caplan et al., 2007). In addition, a wide variety of prescribed substances can lead to dependence after long-term or even short-term treatment in the absence of abuse (where the patient remains within the prescribed dosage and has no intention of using the substance for other than the prescribed purposes). In clinical psychiatry, this problem seems particularly challenging in the context of antidepressant drugs, where weaning off can be a very long process, requiring gradual dose reduction over months or years.

Although sedatives are also procured on the illegal market, abuse of prescription sedatives is common. Benzodiazepines are the most commonly prescribed sedatives in the West because of their favourable efficacy/safety profile over barbiturates. The more recently developed non-benzodiazepine 'z-hypnotics' were initially hailed as having a lower abuse potential but clinical, animal and molecular research has since challenged this view (Tan et al., 2010). Benzodiazepines activate $GABA_A$ receptors by allosteric modulation at the benzodiazepine binding site, whereas barbiturates at low doses have similar GABA-dependent effects through the barbiturate binding site, but at higher doses also directly activate $GABA_A$ receptors in the absence of GABA, which may explain their higher abuse potential. The z-hypnotics activate $GABA_A$ receptors through yet another mechanism in a subunit-specific fashion (see Chapter 7).

Benzodiazepines have desired properties as anxiolytics, hypnotics and muscle relaxants, and various drugs of this class differ in the relative strength of these effects. Intoxication can lead to coma and respiratory depression. In the elderly, medical complications resulting, for example, from falls under benzodiazepine treatment are not uncommon, and this age group can also react paradoxically (with agitation) even to low doses. Benzodiazepine effects add to and can be potentiated by those of other CNS depressants such as ethanol, antipsychotics, opioids and antidepressants with antihistaminergic properties. After long-term use cognitive deficits, for example in memory, have been reported, which were only partly reversible with abstinence.

Positive reinforcement of benzodiazepine use seems to occur through the common mesolimbic pathway of drugs of abuse. Benzodiazepines increase VTA dopaminergic activity and NAc dopamine release through disinhibition, specifically through the inhibitory effect of their binding to the alpha-1 subunit of $GABA_A$ receptors on VTA interneurons (Tan et al., 2010). The anxiolytic and stress-reducing properties of GABAergic activity in the limbic system seems to be another key factor in the development of sedative dependence, underlying the negative reinforcement mechanisms.

Treatment with antidepressants does not lead to a classical dependence syndrome because patients rarely develop tolerance or compulsive use, but withdrawal-type symptoms are common. Abrupt cessation of use leads to a discontinuation syndrome in up to 50% of patients, which comprises psychological (sleep disturbance, anxiety), neurological (sensory disturbance and imbalance), vegetative (nausea) and flu-like symptoms. Although, if recognised, this is easily treated with reinstatement of the antidepressant, it can make it very difficult for patients who wish to do so to come off the medication. The downregulation of 5-HT receptors brought about by chronic antidepressant use, which will result in low serotonergic tone when the enhancing effect of the antidepressant on synaptic serotonin levels is suddenly withdrawn, has been suggested as a possible mechanism. Plasticity of the cholinergic system may play an additional role in discontinuation of tricyclic antidepressants, which can result in Parkinsonism. Agitation and psychosis has been reported after discontinuation of dopaminergic and noradrenergic antidepressants, particularly MAO inhibitors, but the mechanisms of such paradoxical effects are not clear (Warner et al., 2006).

Learning points

Alcohol, sedatives, amphetamines and related stimulants, cocaine, caffeine, cannabis, hallucinogens, inhalants, nicotine, opioids and PCP are the main classes of drugs of abuse. Substance-induced disorders describe the direct psychological and physical damage caused by the drug, which can be acute, for example intoxication and withdrawal symptoms, or chronic, for example alcohol-induced dementia or amnesic (Korsakoff's) syndrome. Substance use disorders include substance abuse, characterised by recurrent consumption that conflicts with everyday functioning, and dependence, characterised by tolerance and withdrawal. Although most types of substance dependence have moderate heritability, reliable predisposing biological factors or gene loci have not yet been identified. This is in contrast to the clear biological evidence of the consequences of drug abuse, which vary by drug type, but can affect any organ in addition to the nervous system and have serious implications both for mental and physical health. The mechanisms leading to sensitisation, tolerance and dependence have been investigated in animal models. Changes in postsynaptic signalling cascades initiated by dopamine receptors have been implicated in the development of sensitisation, the exaggerated responses after repeated stimulus administration, which occurs particularly with amphetamines and related stimulants. The development of tolerance and dependence may be mediated by a shift in the 'hedonic set point' through an imbalance between (dopaminergic) positive and (serotonergic) negative reinforcement systems, although specific correlates of these changes have not been documented in humans. Treatment of addiction is based on combined psychosocial, behavioural and pharmacological interventions. The pharmacological component, which varies according to drug type, can consist in tapering of the drug of abuse or related substances (e.g. in benzodiazepine and opioid dependence), treatment of withdrawal symptoms with other drug classes (e.g. antidepressant treatment of stimulant withdrawal or benzodiazepine treatment of alcohol withdrawal), substitution treatment in cases where withdrawal is not possible or desired (e.g. methadone for opioid dependence) or anti-craving substances. Although the biological pathways of dependence show considerable convergence, particularly through the mesostriatal dopamine system, and some of the motivational treatment strategies can apply throughout, the specific consequences, monitoring requirements and drug treatment approaches vary across drug classes and require detailed knowledge of their pharmacological properties.

Revision and discussion questions

- Describe the concepts of tolerance, sensitisation, dependence and withdrawal.
- What are the common biological pathways of action of drugs of abuse?
- How well can animal models account for human drug addiction?

FURTHER READING

Jupp, B. and Lawrence, A. (2010). New horizons for therapeutics in drug and alcohol abuse. *Pharmacology & Therapeutics*, 125, 138–68.

Koob, G. and Le Moal, M. (2008). Review. Neurobiological mechanisms for opponent motivational processes in addiction. *Philosophical Transactions of the Royal Society B: Biological Sciences*, 363, 3113–23.

Le Merrer, J., Becker, J., Befort, K. and Kieffer, B. (2009). Reward processing by the opioid system in the brain. *Physiological Review*, 89, 1379–412.

Moonat, S., Starkman, B., Sakharkar, A. and Pandey, S. (2010). Neuroscience of alcoholism: molecular and cellular mechanisms. *Cellular and Molecular Life Sciences*, 67, 73–88.

Nestler, E. (2009). Epigenetic mechanisms in psychiatry. *Biological Psychiatry*, 65, 189–90.

PREVIEW

Although eating disorders and disorders of impulse control differ in many phenomenological features they are linked by a pattern of abnormal behaviour that is confined to specific stimuli (e.g. food in the case of eating disorders), situations (e.g. being in a shop in the case of kleptomania) or actions (e.g. hair pulling in the case of trichotillomania). This stimulus- or situation-specificity is shared by addictions or phobias. Impulse control disorders (ICD) also share behavioural characteristics with addictions (most obviously perhaps in the case of pathological gambling) and some proposals for the DSM-V have grouped them with other dependent syndromes as 'behavioural addictions'. For the eating disorders such a new classification would make less sense because the compulsive behaviours encountered here, for example the physical exercise of anorexia nervosa (AN) patients, do not result in a fully-fledged dependent syndrome as defined in the substance use disorders. Eating and impulse control disorders also share features with OCD. AN, for example, has a predominantly obsessive subtype, called the restricted type, and one with prominent compulsive features that manifest in binge eating. However, there are important differences in the associated personality types, with OCD patients normally scoring high on measures of harm avoidance and ICD (and substance use disorder) patients on measures of sensation seeking (Brewer and Potenza, 2008).

This chapter has one section on the eating disorders (anorexia nervosa, bulimia, binge-eating) and one on the behavioural disorders that are lumped together as ICD (kleptomania, pyromania, intermittent explosive disorder, pathological gambling and trichotillomania). Each section reviews the epidemiology, genetics and neurobiology of these disorders and discusses biologically motivated treatment strategies. Box 16.1 provides useful background to hypothesised altered molecular mechanisms in the eating disorders.

16.1 EATING DISORDERS

16.1.1 Clinical presentation and epidemiology

Low body weight is the hallmark of AN. It can be defined as a weight below 85% of the standard weight for age and height or, somewhat more strictly, as a body mass index (BMI: weight in kilograms/height in metres squared) below 17.5. Patients also are very preoccupied about their weight and consider themselves to be overweight against all objective evidence. They will try to reduce weight through dieting and excessive exercise. Amenorrhoea is also common, but this is true for other types of anorexia as well and may be a result of the weight loss. Classically anorexia (loss of appetite and consequently of weight) had been described in patients with severe and chronic physical illness such as cancer, and the term anorexia nervosa was introduced in Victorian times to indicate the non-physical or 'nervous' origin of the disorder. However, lack of appetite is not the reason for the refusal to eat, and is in fact rarely encountered in AN.

Based on the presence or absence of binge eating, AN can be further classified into a 'restricting' and a 'binge-eating/purging type'. 'Binge-eating' describes periodic intake of excessive amounts of food, often high calorie food. AN patients with this subtype will try and maintain their low body weight by avoiding the resorption of the ingested food through self-induced vomiting or other purging behaviour. The two subtypes are clinically different and pose different management challenges. They also seem to differ neuropsychologically because compulsive behaviour characterises only the binge-eating type. Finally, the underlying neural circuits may also differ because binge-eating AN (and the other disorders characterised by periodic overeating, bulimia and binge-eating disorder) share features with substance use disorders.

AN is ten times more common in females than males, with a lifetime prevalence in females of 0.5%. Comorbidity with depression and anxiety disorders is common. The onset is normally between age 14 and 18 and the course can be relapsing and remitting or chronically progressive, although single episodes have also been described. Progression from the restricting to the binge-eating subtype is not uncommon. If the weight loss is extreme, hospital admission and compulsory feeding may be required, and mortality is considerable in these cases. However, even with less severe cases, physical changes associated with malnutrition and low body weight such as bradycardia, hypotension and hypothermia, electrolyte imbalances, leucopoenia (reduced white blood cell count) or anaemia, ECG changes (most dangerously prolonged QT interval, which can lead to life-threatening arrhythmias), hormonal changes and osteoporosis may require medical attention. 50–70% of patients make at least a partial recovery (as indicated by normal weight and regular menstruation), but psychological features such as preoccupation with diet often persist. The heritability is high (0.5–0.8), but no associated genetic variants are available from GWAS. The personality characteristics associated with AN have been well studied and often observed to predate the onset of the disorder. They include perfectionism, harm avoidance, dysthymia, heightened interoception and obsessive compulsive traits (Kaye et al., 2009). Several of these personality traits have considerable heritability in their own right; they may hold some promise as endophenotypes for genetic studies of eating disorders at a dimensional level.

Bulimia (Greek for 'hunger of an ox') nervosa (BN), the other classical eating disorder, is characterised by binge-eating, but patients maintain normal body weight by measures to avoid food resorption ('purging type'), most commonly vomiting, or other compensatory behaviours such as exercise ('non-purging type'). Similar to AN patients, they are often obsessed with their weight and body image. The mean age of onset is slightly later than for AN, and lifetime prevalence is estimated at 1–3% for females and a tenth of this in men. Comorbidity with mood disorders has been documented, but the familiarity of BN is unknown, and reliable genetic associations have not been established.

Repeated or periodic binge-eating also occurs without compensatory behaviour and is then termed 'binge-eating disorder' (BED). Patients suffering from BED, which may be even more prevalent than BN, are commonly overweight (BMI between 25 and 30) or obese (BMI > 30).

16.1.2 Biology of eating disorders

Patients with AN often show marked alterations in major endocrine systems. These changes can be summarised as upregulation of the hypothalamus-pituitary-adrenal (HPA) axis and downregulation of the hypothalamus-pituitary-gonadal (HPG) and -thyroid (HPT) axes. However, they are associated with weight loss, revert when normal weight is regained, and are also present in patients who are underweight for reasons other than AN. Thus, the endocrine changes may be general features of anorexia or low calorie nutrition rather than specific markers of AN (Rask-Andersen et al., 2010). The same seems to be true for most of the documented macroscopic brain changes such as ventricular enlargement, which reverts with return to normal weight and may reflect reversible atrophy associated with reduced protein intake.

Several neurochemical pathways, both classical neurotransmitters and hypothalamic peptides involved in homoeostatic regulation, have been implicated in the dysregulation of feeding behaviour in eating disorders. Serotonergic activity can suppress appetite and produce sensation of satiety, and the anti-obesity drug sibutramine is a 5-HT reuptake inhibitor. There is some evidence that patients with AN have increased 5-HT_{1A} binding, for example in prefrontal and orbitofrontal cortex, on PET studies with receptor-specific ligands. Such increased binding potential may indicate increased receptor activity, supporting a role for 5-HT in the genesis of AN. Increased 5-HT_{1A} receptor binding is unlikely merely to be a result of low weight because it was also found *after recovery* from AN, but on that occasion only for the binge-eating type. Abnormalities of the dopamine system might also be expected because of the importance of this system for reward learning and because of the appetite-lowering effects of dopaminergic stimulants. There is little direct evidence for altered dopaminergic transmission in eating disorders, though. One PET study showed higher D_2 or D_3 (the ligand raclopride is selective for both these subtypes) receptor binding in remitted AN patients compared to controls, reflecting lower extracellular dopamine levels, higher receptor numbers, or both (Kaye et al., 2009). Such changes might lead to a hypersensitised dopamine system, which could correspond to a lowering of the hedonic set point, thus resulting in opposite effects to those implicated in addiction (see Chapter 15), which might explain some of the behaviours of the restricting type of AN. Some of the atypical antipsychotics have indeed shown some promise in alleviating obsessions and anxiety related to food intake. A presently still very speculative account might be that overstimulation of the dopamine system by natural rewards could trigger negative feedback loops (e.g. through the serotonin or dynorphin/kappa receptor pathways) with aversive affective consequences. Restrictive behaviours such as exercise and starvation could thus become negatively reinforced. An involvement of the opioid system was suggested by associations between AN and several SNPs in the delta receptor 1 gene, but initial hopes in naltrexone as an anti-anorexia drug were not fulfilled.

Such an account would be compatible with the biobehavioural model of AN proposed by Kaye et al. (2009), who use the 'prediction error' (see Chapter 2) rather than the 'hedonic set point' model but with similar consequences. They surmise that under normal homoeostatic conditions food cues generate a 'body prediction error' whereby the anticipated satiated body state is compared with the current body state, resulting in a signal to approach the food. Conversely, in AN patients these cues produce an avoidance signal because of the anticipated aversive consequences of food intake. Kay et al. (2009) propose the combined effect of enhanced serotonergic aversive signals and diminished dopaminergic appetitive signals as a mechanism.

Positive reinforcement mechanisms that lead people to assign value to food and feeding, mediated through the glutamatergic NMDA receptor, may also be disturbed in AN. In addition to such theoretical considerations, several findings from genetic association studies have implicated variation in the NMDA receptor subunits NR2B in AN. Potential risk variants have also been identified in the gene for SK3, a calcium-dependent potassium channel, which is responsible for the later component of the after-hyperpolarisation current and thus contributes to a neuron's refractory period. SK3 is upregulated by oestrogen, which may provide a link to neuroendocrine changes in AN. However, all these genetic associations have to be regarded as preliminary until confirmed by genome-wide studies.

Such tentative genetic associations have also implicated BDNF in AN. The restricting subtype was associated with the 66met (low secretion) allele of the BDNF gene, which is also associated with increased anxiety in an animal model, and BDNF serum levels were lower in AN patients and even in BN patients with normal body weight than controls, suggesting its independence from current nutritional state. However, recent results have called a simple association between eating disorder and BDNF into question. Reduced BNDF activity would only explain some of the behavioural traits of AN, but not the weight loss. Animal models with knock-out or reduced activity of BDNF or its tyrosine kinase B (trkB) receptor are hyperactive, anxious and hyperphagic and have increased rather than decreased body weight (Rask-Andersen et al., 2010). Although these various findings rule out a monocausal role for reduced BDNF levels in AN, its role as key regulator of brain homoeostasis and high expression levels in the hypothalamus make BDNF an attractive candidate for animal and genetic models of eating disorders.

The various hormones that mediate between gastrointestinal tract, fat tissue and the feeding centres of the brainstem and hypothalamus (Box 16.1) have been key targets for the biological investigation of AN, but little evidence for genetic associations or other primary abnormalities has been found. Levels of the anorexigenic hormone leptin are reduced in AN as a result of the reduced number of adipocytes and reverts (even overshoots, which can result in a rebound to starvation) with restoration of normal fat levels. One reason for the lack of biological trait markers of AN amongst the anorexigenic hormones may be that the primary deficit in AN does not consist in lack of appetite but in aversive responses to food intake.

The cannabinoid system has also been implicated in eating disorders. Activation of CB_1 receptors has orexigenic effects in animals, and produces craving for food in humans. Higher blood levels of the endocannabinoid anandamide have been found in AN patients (and BED) compared to controls, but not in BN. This could be an effect of the leptin reduction because leptin activates an anandamide-degrading enzyme, but the relationship between AN and endocannabinoids needs to be replicated in larger studies before further conclusions can be drawn.

A potential neuroimmunological link to eating disorders was suggested by the finding of heightened levels of the proinflammatory cytokine Tumour necrosis factor (TNF)-alpha in the blood of AN and BN patients. Unlike most hormonal markers, the altered TNF levels persisted beyond successful treatment and did not correlate with body fat (Nakai et al., 1999, 2000). However, this finding still awaits replication as well.

16.1.3   Animal models of eating disorders

In the absence of effective pharmacological treatments for eating disorders, animal models cannot be designed for predictive validity but have to be tested for their construct and face validity. A large number has been designed on the basis of supposed construct validity through modulation or knock-out of components of the appetite regulating and stress systems. Leptin or BDNF knock-out mice fall into this category, as does the administration of

CRH into the cerebral ventricles of experimental animals. The CRH model reproduces the hyperactivity and decreased feeding typical of AN, and also some of the associated physiological (downregulation of the HPG axis) changes (Kaye et al., 2009). However, there is presently no evidence that HPA dysregulation plays a causative role in human AN (rather than being a mere consequence). An example of an animal model selected for its face validity is hyperactivity with reduced feeding, which can be induced by food restriction in rats in a running wheel. At the behavioural level this suggests that hyperactivity may be an instinctive response to food restriction, for example for the purpose of foraging, which prevails over the homoeostatic need to reduce energy expenditure (Rask-Andersen et al., 2010). However, such animal models selected for their behavioural similarity with AN have not yet yielded tangible information about the potential biological mechanism.

16.1.4 Treatment of eating disorders

The main aim of AN treatment is the restoration of normal body weight. Behavioural interventions with structured refeeding programmes seem currently most promising, and medical supervision is important because of the rare but life-threatening refeeding syndrome (Attia, 2010). In adolescents, family intervention may bring additional benefit. Several antidepressants and antipsychotics have been tried both for acute treatment and relapse prevention, but only olanzapine has shown some promise for reducing feeding-related anxiety and restoring weight. The mechanism is unknown – its antiserotonergic, antidopaminergic and antihistaminergic effects have all been implicated – and it may be similar to that of the unwanted side effect of weight gain that is frequently observed when olanzapine is used for the treatment of psychotic disorders. Unlike for AN, where both antidepressant treatment and CBT have little proven benefit, these two approaches can be rather successful in BN. CBT delivered in specialist centres leads to a clinically significant reduction of binges in about one-third of patients. Fluoxetine in high doses (60 mg/day) is also effective, but less well tolerated. However, no added benefit has been gained from combining these two techniques. Future directions for translational research may target the different neurochemical pathways for motivation and behavioural control in order to develop new agents that will be more specific than the currently available neurotransmitters/hormones and precursor substances.

Box 16.1 Regulation of food intake and appetite

Food intake is essential to provide glucose and other sources of energy to the body, and insufficient motivation to seek for or ingest food would not be compatible with life. At the same time, overfeeding can have dangerous metabolic consequences, and the search for food needs to be balanced against other, for example reproductive, activities. It is therefore likely that mechanisms that regulating appetite according to the body's energy state would have evolved. These are implemented through signalling pathways from the gastrointestinal tract and adipose tissue to the brainstem and hypothalamus (Figure 16.1). One pathway is through the vagus nerve, which conveys satiety signals from gastrointestinal chemo- (e.g. CCK, released by the small intestine) and mechanoreceptors to the brainstem. Gastrointestinal peptide hormones also suppress feeding circuits in the hypothalamus directly, for example peptide YY, which is secreted by the intestinal mucosa and blocks the NPY receptor. Insulin also suppresses appetite through activation of hypothalamic insulin receptors, whereas the peptide amylin binds to the calcitonin receptor on cells in the area postrema of the brain

Figure 16.1

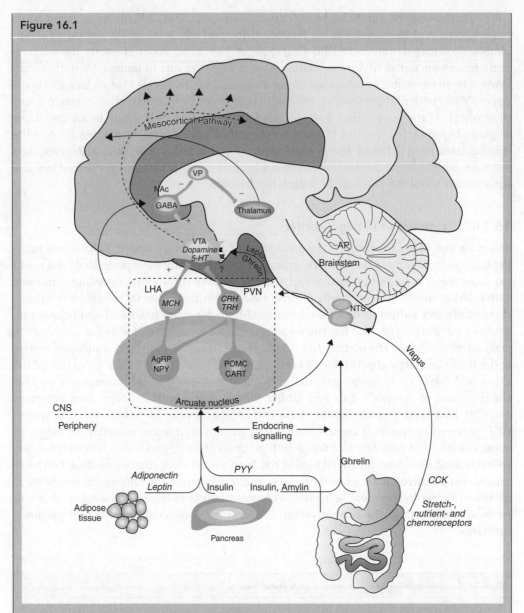

Regulatory pathways from the gastrointestinal tract and adipose tissue to the brain

This sketch summarises the signaling pathways from the gastrointestinal tract and adipose tissue to the brainstem and hypothalamus that regulate feeding behaviour. The vagus nerve (right part of figure) conveys satiety signals from gastrointestinal chemo- and mechanoreceptors to the brainstem (vagus nuclei and nucleus of the solitary tract, NTS). One chemical signaling substance is cholecystokinin (CCK). In addition to this vagal pathway, gastrointestinal peptide hormones, for example peptide YY (PTT), insulin and amylin suppress feeding behaviour directly by their actions on hypothalamic or brainstem cells. Another anorexigenic hormone is leptin, released by fat cells. Orexigenic (stimulate feeding) hormones include adiponectin, released by fat cells, and ghrelin, released by stomach and pancreas cells. Orexigenic neurons in the arcuate nucleus of the hypothalamus release growth-hormone-releasing-hormone (GHRH), Agouti-related protein (AGRP), NPY,

orexin 1 and 2 and Ghrelin, whereas anorexigenic neurons release CRH, proopiomelanocortin (POMC), leptin and the cocaine-and-amphetamine-regulated transcript (CART) group. Neurons of the arcuate nucleus project to the lateral hypothalamic area (LHA) and paraventricular nucleus (PVN). These in turn converge on the VTA, which sends dopaminergic projections to the NAc. The NAc sends inhibitory (GABAergic) signals to GABAergic neurons in the ventral pallidum (VP) that inhibit the mediodorsal thalamus, a main source of (excitatory) input to the OFC (Kringelbach & Rolls, 2004). Thus, activation of the NAc by mesocortical dopamine signals leads to disinhibition of the thalamus and net activation of the OFC. If homoestatic regulation is disrupted, overactivation of this circuit may result in compulsive feeding behaviour. Note the overlap of the final (basal ganglia – thalamus – OFC) pathways with those implicated in OCD (see Figure 13.1).
Source: Adapted from(Rask-Andersen et al., 2010) with kind permission of Elsevier.

stem. Fat cells release leptin, which is also anorexigenic, and adiponectin, which has the opposite effect through receptors in the hypothalamus and brainstem.

The decision whether to continue feeding or not depends on the interplay between orexigenic and anorexigenic neurons in the arcuate nucleus of the hypothalamus. Orexigenic neurons release GHRH, Agouti-related protein (AGRP), NPY, orexin 1 and 2 and Ghrelin, whereas anorexigenic neurons release CRF, proopiomelanocortin (POMC), leptin and the group of peptides described as cocaine-and-amphetamine-regulated transcript (CART). AGRP is of particular interest for the understanding of possible similarities between eating disorders and addiction because it also seems to be involved in the regulation of ethanol self-administration and binge drinking, which are reduced in AGRP knock-out mice (Navarro et al., 2009). Neurons of the arcuate nucleus project to the lateral hypothalamic area and paraventricular nucleus. These in turn converge on the VTA, which projects to the NAc. The NAc sends inhibitory (GABAergic) signals to GABAergic neurons in the ventral pallidum that inhibit the mediodorsal thalamus, a main source of (excitatory) input to the OFC (Kringelbach, 2004). Thus, activation of the NAc by mesocortical dopamine signals leads to disinhibition of the thalamus and net activation of the OFC.

Several drugs and neurotransmitters that are not part of the core feeding pathways can also regulate appetite and food intake. Amphetamines are anorexigenic, an effect that may be partly mediated through the downregulation of NPY, whereas cannabinoids are orexigenic. Opioids seem to be involved in both homoeostatic and non-homoeostatic (hedonic) feeding. For example, injections of mu and delta agonists into the VTA and NAc promote feeding. Stimulation of mu receptors in the shell of the NAc enhances both the 'liking' (as measured by positive affective movements) and the 'wanting' (measured by increased eating) of food. Such areas whose pharmacological or electrical stimulation induces liking for a stimulus or other pleasurable experience have been termed 'hedonic hotspots' (Peciña et al., 2006).

It thus appears that food intake is regulated by at least three partly independent systems. The first is the vagal/hormonal-hypothalamic signalling system that is largely driven by the body's energy balance. The second is the hedonic or 'liking' system, which seems to be mediated (but probably not exclusively) by the opioid system and depends on afferent pathways conveying taste and smell information. These indeed do interact with the opioid system at various levels. Already the first synapse of the gustatory pathway in the nucleus of the solitary tract is modulated by opioids, and the opioid-rich parabrachial nucleus of the pons may be the first level where it interacts with circuits for homoeostatic feeding (Le Merrer et al., 2009). Although the sensory processing of taste and smell is a prerequisite for hedonic signals, the pleasantness of food may only be decoded in higher multimodal areas such as the OFC (Kringelbach and Stein, 2010). The third system would be the motivational ('wanting') system that integrates between the body's current state (energy balance, opportunity to pursue other goals) and the hedonic properties of the available food and probably involves dopaminergic, mesolimbic and mesocortical projections. Depending on the complexity of the organism, we may also postulate further systems, for example a largely limbic system that encodes potential aversive consequences of particular foods, and a cognitive control system that guides socially appropriate feeding behaviour and long-term health goals, for example dieting.

16.2   DISORDERS OF IMPULSE CONTROL

16.2.1   Clinical presentation and epidemiology

Although deficits of impulse control are often encountered as part of larger and more pervasive syndromes such as those that lead to a diagnosis of ASPD or schizophrenia, a number of disorders are defined by the inability to resist relatively specific and isolated impulses. Those are intermittent explosive disorder (IED; aggressive impulses), kleptomania (impulse to steal), pyromania (impulse to set fire), pathological gambling (impulse to gamble) and trichotillomania (impulse to pull out one's hair). These disorders are further defined by their deleterious consequences, for example destruction of property in IED or serious debts in pathological gambling, and the gratification and relief of tension associated with the impulsive act. Furthermore, for a diagnosis from this group to be made it has to be ruled out that the actions were intended to obtain a primary gain, for example stealing coveted items from a shop or setting fire for an insurance claim.

The diagnostic criteria for ICD, particularly pathological gambling (PG), resemble some of the formal criteria for substance dependence, The criterion 'needs to gamble with increasing amounts of money in order to achieve the desired excitement' (DSM-IV) is analogous to the tolerance criterion for substance dependence and 'is restless or irritable when attempting to cut down or stop gambling' describes psychological withdrawal syndromes. Together with the cognitive (e.g. constant preoccupation with gambling) and motivational (craving) features, stress relief, compulsive nature of the pursuit regardless of adverse consequences, and psychosocial consequences (e.g. lying, stealing, fraud) shared with substance abuse, these characteristics have resulted in the proposals to group ICD with the substance-related disorders as 'behavioural addictions' in the forthcoming DSM-V (Potenza, 2008).

IED, kleptomania and pyromania are very rare, but trichotillomania is probably underdiagnosed and may have a lifetime prevalence of 0.5%. Pathological gambling has even been estimated to affect up to 3.5% of adults, and an even higher proportion of adolescents and college students. It is currently not clear what contribution the internet has made to these relatively high rates. New syndromes such as 'internet addiction' or compulsive buying are being discussed, but the usefulness of pathologising phenomena that are under a strong cultural influence has also been questioned (Frascella et al., 2010). Impulse control disorders have a family association amongst themselves and with other mental disorders, for example substance abuse (pathological gambling) or OCD (kleptomania), but reliable estimates of their heritability are available only for PG (approx. 0.5) (Brewer and Potenza, 2008). Non-pathological gambling (e.g. where gambling is one of several forms of occasional entertainment, with controlled bets that do not increase over time) is a very widespread practice in which about half of the population engage (estimates for the UK), and even more if those who play the state lottery are included (Chase and Clark, 2010).

16.2.2 Biology of impulse control disorders (ICDs)

The study of the mechanisms underlying ICDs is hindered by the dearth of direct evidence of biological abnormalities. Most of the available evidence comes from studies of PG, and analogies with substance abuse and animal models often have to be adduced. Nevertheless, the study of the neurology of impulse control and its deficits has recently made considerable progress thanks to the tools of non-invasive neuroimaging (Box 16.2).

Various NT systems have been implicated in PG. Amphetamine can prime gambling-related stimuli and enhance motivation to gamble. The observation that amphetamine can also prime cocaine use has been cited as evidence for commonalities between PG and substance dependence (Brewer and Potenza, 2008). Further support for dopaminergic models of PG comes from the clinical observation that levodopa or dopamine agonist treatment of Parkinson's disease (PD) can lead to compulsive gambling, as well as disinhibited eating and sexual behaviour.

A role of the glutamate system has been suggested by preliminary clinical effects of N-acetylcysteine, which increases glutamate turnover, for both PG and cocaine craving. Both serotonergic hyper- and hypofunction have been implicated in impulsivity based on the clinical effects of SSRIs. Experimental studies with tryptophan depletion in healthy individuals indeed found decreased inhibition of prepotent motor behaviour on the continuous performance task. Motor impulsivity is the main problem in trichotillomania, but it is too early to say whether experimental tasks of motor inhibition may constitute a potential endophenotype. Serotonergic deficit may be less relevant for PG because tryptophan depleted participants do not discount delays excessively, which would reflect impulsive choice behaviour that is closely related to PG. As with all pursuits with a strong hedonic component, opioids have been implicated in gambling, and associations with beta-endorphin activity have indeed been reported. Consequently, opioid antagonists have been tried with some success in PG, supporting a role for dysregulation of the hedonic part of this system.

In addition to dysfunctions of the dopaminergic/opioid regulated VTA/NAC system, cortico-striatal circuits have been implicated in PG. It has been proposed that the maintenance of dependant behaviour is based on transition from directly reward-related processing in the ventral striatum to habit formation, which relies on plasticity in the dorsal striatum. The behavioural disinhibition that is also characteristic of ICD might then be implemented in dysfunctional prefrontal activity and fronto-striatal circuits. For example, the steeper delay discounting found in PG has been associated with deficient function of the ventromedial PFC (VMPFC).

Although there may be considerable overlap in the neural circuits for impulsivity and compulsivity, Fineberg et al. (2010) have proposed two partly segregated pathways, one involving the caudate nucleus (dorsal striatum) and OFC for compulsive behaviour (which has also been implicated in OCD, see Chapter 13), and one involving the shell of the NAC (ventral striatum) and VMPFC/ACC driving/inhibiting impulsive behaviours. Although OCD is characterised by harm avoidance and ICD by reward seeking, which can be regarded as two opposite ends of a safety/risk spectrum, Fineberg et al. emphasise the shared feature of behavioural disinhibition, which might result from deficient frontal modulation of striatal circuits common to both groups of disorders. Links between the neurobiological mechanisms of impulsivity and compulsivity are also suggested by the genetic association between kleptomania and OCD and by the dynamically changing balance between impulsive and compulsive features and behaviours in the same individuals.

16.2.3 Treatment of ICDs

Many patients with ICD do not primarily go through classical mental health pathways but come to attention through the forensic system. Their rehabilitation is thus often marred by the associated delinquency. The prognosis is best if patients take up offers from the health service or self-help associations while they still have a reasonable level of psychosocial functioning. In analogy to Alcoholics Anonymous, Gamblers Anonymous have set up self-help groups, which have some effect. Psychological interventions for PG have generally been modelled on the substance dependence field and include brief psychoeducative interventions, CBT and motivational therapy. Antipsychotics and anti-depressants do not have consistent benefits, but the opioid antagonists naltrexone and nalmefene and the glutamate modulator N-acetylcysteine can reduce gambling urges (Frascella et al., 2010).

Box 16.2   Near misses and small gains – cognitive distortions and reward processing in PG

In classical addiction models (see Chapter 15), absence of the substance of abuse produces craving, to which the dependent person responds with consumption, which brings immediate reward and at least short-term relief, even if aversive consequences may dominate in the long run. Getting addicted to gambling – if PG is a behavioural addiction – must work through somewhat different processes. After all, reinforcement is seldom immediate (more often than not a gambler will carry home less than his/her bet), and may not materialise at all. It is therefore unlikely that the development of compulsive gambling is driven solely by classical mechanisms of operant conditioning/ reinforcement learning. Cognitive factors indeed seem to play a role as well. People generally tend to assume order even in random processes, as evidenced by the common assumption that after a series of heads the next toss of the coin is more likely to produce a tail. Gamblers overestimate their chances of winning because they believe that games of chance involve some skill ('illusion of control') or that they were very close to winning ('near misses') and will win, given another chance. These processes can fuel a habit of gambling even in the face of continued losing (Chase and Clark, 2010). Of course, a near miss is as much a loss as any other, but it is common knowledge amongst designers of fruit machines that building in a certain (higher than would randomly occur) proportion of near misses (e.g. two apples in a row and the third just coming in sight) increases gambling times. The neural correlates of the response to near misses have now been investigated with fMRI both in non-gamblers and in problem gamblers. Both groups showed increased activation for near compared to full misses in the ventral striatum, in the same region that was also activated by wins compared to losses. It can be speculated that dopaminergic reward signals underlie this activation, although fMRI is, of course, not specific for any neurotransmitter, and thus that the 'rewarding' properties of near misses fuel the cognitive distortions that give rise to habitual gambling.

Although the brain activation patterns during near misses are similar (although this was not formally compared in the studies) between non- and problem-gamblers, other circuits seem to work differently in those who have formed a habit of gambling. During a simulated gambling task in fMRI, patients with PG showed lower activity in VMPFC than controls (Reuter et al., 2005). Lack of controlling signals from this area could explain impulsive behaviour and would be compatible with findings in patients with medial prefrontal lesions who often have difficulties in financial decision-making. It was slightly more surprising that the gamblers also showed reduced ventral striatal activation. However, against the background of the above considerations we may assume that it is not the gambling itself but the (irrational) expectation of wins what produces the reward. The reduced striatal activation may reflect the fact that, with time, small gains become less rewarding, explaining the common observation that over time pathological gamblers place higher and higher bets.

Learning points

Anorexia nervosa (AN), bulimia nervosa (BN) and binge-eating disorder (BED) are the most important eating disorders. They are defined by dysfunctional eating behaviours in combination with body weight, which is lowered in AN, normal in BN and increased in BED. Females are more affected than men by an order of magnitude. Although heritability seems to be considerable (estimates go up to 0.8 in the case of AN), no stable genetic associations have been identified. Although several hormonal imbalances have been implicated particularly in AN, causative biological factors have not yet been demonstrated. Theoretical models have proposed a shift in the hedonic set point in the opposite direction to addiction for AN, particularly the restrictive type. This could be mediated through changes in the dopaminergic and opioid systems. The focus of treatment of AN, which can become a medical emergency because of weight loss, is on the restitution of normal body weight through behavioural interventions. Patients with BN may also benefit from antidepressants or CBT, but no specific drug treatment is available for any of the eating disorders.

Pathological gambling (PG) is the commonest ICD, affecting over 3% of adult males. It can also be caused by dopaminergic treatment of PD. Thus, the dopaminergic projections from the VTA may be involved, which is the basis for most current biological models. However, dopaminergic blockade with antipsychotic drugs does not reduce gambling urges effectively. PG continues to be a serious problem, and new approaches combining behavioural and pharmacological interventions will be required to contain it.

Revision and discussion questions

- Describe some of the signalling molecules involved in the regulation of homoeostatic feeding.
- What is the difference between AN and BD?
- Is pathological gambling an addiction?

FURTHER READING

Chase, H. and Clark, L. (2010). Gambling severity predicts midbrain response to near-miss outcomes. *Journal of Neuroscience*, 30, 6180–87.

Rask-Andersen, M., Olszewski, P., Levine, A. and Schiöth, H. (2010). Molecular mechanisms underlying anorexia nervosa: focus on human gene association studies and systems controlling food intake. *Brain Research Reviews*, 62, 147–64.

17 MENTAL DISORDERS OF CHILDHOOD AND ADOLESCENCE

PREVIEW

The mental disorders of childhood and adolescence are a clinically and biologically heterogeneous group that are mainly joined by an age of onset between infancy and early adolescence. The autism spectrum disorders almost invariably persist into adulthood, whereas ADHD and conduct disorder have a more varied natural history, where some patients develop adult forms (adult ADHD or antisocial personality disorder) while others show at least a partial remission by late adolescence. They all have a high heritability, which is why their genetics is covered in detail in this chapter. The chapter also reviews the extensive literature on animal models and endophenotypes of ADHD and autism. The section on conduct disorders has a particular focus on G×E interactions and their contributions to the biology of delinquency. The genetic syndromes associated with autism (Rett, Fragile-X, Angelman, Prader-Willi and Bourneville Pringle/tuberous sclerosis), which are clinically important and may provide leads to biological mechanisms that can explain autistic features) are described in a separate box.

17.1 ATTENTION DEFICIT/HYPERACTIVITY DISORDER

17.1.1 Clinical presentation and epidemiology

Attention-deficit/hyperactivity disorder (ADHD) has had a relatively short history as a diagnostic category and certainly caught the public eye only in recent decades, but descriptions of impulsive, inattentive and distractible children go a long way back, and treatment with amphetamines was pioneered as early as 1937. Although the phenomenon seems to be old, nomenclature has changed considerably. Initially the behavioural disturbances were subsumed under the group of learning disabilities. The second edition of the DSM introduced the 'Hyperkinetic Reaction of Childhood' in 1968. The term ADHD was introduced in the DSM-III-R in 1987.

As implied by the name, ADHD is characterised by two clusters of symptoms, related to inattention and hyperactivity-impulsivity. These symptoms have to exceed the behavioural problems normally observed at a comparable level of development, and some of them have to be present before age 7, although the diagnosis may be made several years later based on retrospective appreciation of the child's development. Behaviour is disturbed in more than one setting, normally at home and at school (or work, for adults) and interferes with family life, social contacts and school or work performance.

The inattention is often first picked up at school, where children will make careless mistakes because they do not sufficiently attend to detail. However, problems also arise during play when children fail to conduct one activity to the end and rather continuously switch from one task to another, or when they forget or do not stick to rules. Particular problems arise during homework and other tasks that require sustained attention. Individuals can also be distractible and forgetful. Hyperactivity can manifest in preschool (e.g. not listening to stories), school (e.g. not sitting still in the classroom) and play contexts (e.g. inability to play quietly). Excessive talking is also common. Frequent interruptions of conversations, premature responding during lessons and failure to wait for one's turn during games are all considered signs of impulsivity. Normal cognitive maturation includes the ability to learn reward associations over longer times and accept that a particular behaviour will not be rewarded immediately, and this development is delayed (and potentially never completed) in ADHD. Several cognitive paradigms address aspects of ADHD and may aid the development of endophenotypes, for example the Go/No-Go or continuous performance task for impulsivity and delay discounting tasks for altered reward responsiveness.

If one of the symptom clusters is prominent, subtypes of ADHD ('Predominantly Inattentive Type' or 'Predominantly Hyperactive-Impulsive Type') can be diagnosed. ADHD is estimated to affect 6% of children and is more frequent in males, with male to female ratios varying between 2:1 and 9:1. Thirty to fifty percent of patients are supposed to maintain symptoms into adulthood. In a small proportion of patients, symptoms may also start first during adulthood. In order to improve the distinction between ADHD and other problems of child behaviour and schooling, the DSM-IV has a list of nine symptoms, six of which have to be present. This results in considerable heterogeneity in clinical samples, which may make the investigation of the biological foundations difficult and has evoked criticism of the reliability and validity of the disease concept. However, the familial association and response to stimulant treatment suggest that at least some biological mechanisms are shared between ADHD patients.

17.1.2 Genetics

Twin studies have yielded high heritability estimates (around 0.8) for ADHD. It is likely that individual genes make only small contributions and that genetic association is higher for symptom dimensions than for the whole disorder. Although GWAS have not yielded any risk loci with whole-genome significance, several promising susceptibility loci were identified in candidate gene studies. These include the long allele of the 5-HTTLPR polymorphism of the serotonin transporter gene (see Chapter 13), VNTRs (variable number tandem repeats) in the 3′ UTR (10-repeat) and intron 8 (6-repeat) of the DAT1 gene, the 7-repeat allele of the VNTR in exon 3 of the DRD4 gene, the 148-bp allele of a dinucleotide repeat on the 5′ flank of the DRD5 gene and several loci in the gene for the Synaptosomal-associated protein 25 (SNAP25) (Gizer et al., 2009).

The DAT1 gene on chromosome 5p15 was an obvious target for candidate gene studies because the standard drug for ADHD, methylphenidate, blocks DAT and thereby increases synaptic dopamine levels. There is preliminary (but not consistent across studies) evidence that the 10-repeat 40-bp VNTR in the 3′ UTR and the 6-repeat 30-bp VNTR in intron 8 may be associated with higher protein levels, which would fit current pathophysiological models of reduced dopamine availability in ADHD. The 10-repeat allele may also be associated with a better response to methylphenidate in ADHD patients. A particular interest in variation in the DRD4 gene on chromosome 11p15.5 was motivated by its association with the personality traits of novelty seeking and impulsivity. There is also preliminary evidence for reduced cortical thickness in carriers of the 7-repeat allele. The other dopamine receptor most consistently implicated in genetic risk for ADHD is DRD5, but the main risk locus is outside the transcribed region and functional consequences thus unknown. Of the other NT systems, the most stable association has been found with variation in the serotonin transporter gene. Candidate gene studies are increasingly transcending the boundaries of proteins that are specific for a particular NT system (e.g. most receptors and transporters) and include genes coding for proteins regulating synaptic plasticity and neuronal growth. For example, SNAP25 is present on the cytosolic side of the presynaptic membrane and forms part of the complex facilitating exocytosis. An association between SNAP25 and ADHD symptoms is also supported by a mouse model that lacked one copy of the SNAP25 gene and displayed hyperactive behaviour. However, before confirmation of the candidate loci in GWAS any evidence for association between specific genes and syndromal ADHD remains preliminary.

17.1.3   Brain structure and function

The brains of children with ADHD are on average smaller (but with considerable overlap with controls such as to make this unsuitable as a diagnostic test). This reduction seems to persist into adolescence but not into adulthood. Regional volume reductions were found consistently in the cerebellar vermis, which is an interesting overlap with findings in autism, corpus callosum and the basal ganglia (caudate nucleus and globus pallidus). Radioligand studies also identified local decreases in blood flow and increases in dopamine transporter (DAT) in the striatum of ADHD patients. A unifying interpretation of these findings would be that reduction of dopaminergic neurons and/or increased concentration/activity of the DAT results in reduced dopaminergic firing, which is reflected in lower metabolic signals. There is some evidence that both blood flow and fMRI signals in the striatum are sensitive to dopamine availability, but direct demonstrations of such abnormalities in brains of ADHD patients through post-mortem examination are still missing.

17.1.4   Neurochemistry and drug treatment

Evidence for abnormalities in the dopamine system in ADHD comes from the clinical effects of methylphenidate, a blocker of the dopamine transporter, and from indirect measures of dopaminergic neurons and activity, such as the volume reductions in the striatum and globus pallidus and hypoactivation of reward circuits in functional imaging paradigms (discussed in Section 17.1.5). Furthermore, DAT knock-out mice show hyperkinetic behaviour resembling hyperactivity in ADHD. However, there is no direct evidence for dopamine depletion in ADHD, and a positive effect of dopaminergic drugs could also be explained by compensation for deficits elsewhere.

Currently three main classes of drugs are used in the standard treatment of ADHD: methylphenidate, amphetamines and NRIs. The first two are clinically grouped together as 'stimulants'. The psychostimulants are a chemically and neuropharmacologically heterogeneous group, which also comprises caffeine and nicotine, the illicit drugs methylenedioxymethamphetamine (MDMA) (street name 'ecstasy') and cocaine and modafinil. Modafinil is used in the treatment of narcolepsy (a type of excessive daytime sleepiness, see Chapter 19) and was in use as an alternative treatment for ADHD before it lost its approval in children and adolescents because of side effects.

Methylphenidate, which exists in a number of isomers, of which d-threo-methylphenidate is the pharmacologically active form, blocks the reuptake of DA and NE and thus increases catecholamine levels in the synaptic cleft. It is available in preparations with fast (e.g. Ritalin®) or slow (e.g. Concerta®) release. The slow-release preparations vary in the proportion of fast/slow release methylphenidate. Their aim is to reduce the number of administrations across the day and minimise the potential for abuse. Methylphenidate is a racemate (racemates are equal mixes of D- and L-enantiomers of a molecule, which are mirror symmetric, but can have different chemical effects). D- or dextromethylphenidate is not as widely available as the racemate, but may have fewer side effects and 'rebound' problems after discontinuation. Methylphenidate is the substance of first choice for the treatment of ADHD in cases where psychological and educational measures alone are insufficient. It should not be used in children under the age of 6. It is normally tolerated well, provided doses are increased slowly, but side effects such as headaches, sleep disturbance or irritability are common particularly during the early phase. Because of its sympathomimetic properties methylphenidate can increase blood pressure and heart rate and should not be used in patients with cardiovascular disorders. Methylphenidate also has anticholinergic side effects, and thus the same exclusion criteria need to be applied as with other anticholinergic drugs.

Amphetamine is another stimulant that blocks the DAT and promotes dopamine release from presynaptic vesicles (see Figure 6.6). It is available for the treatment of ADHD in different enantiomeric combinations (e.g. Adderall®). Similar cautions apply as for methylphenidate, and the addictive properties of stimulants have been discussed in Chapter 15. The NRI atomoxetine is an alternative option for the treatment of ADHD, particularly where emotional disturbance is prominent.

The α_2 adrenoceptor agonist guanfacine may become another non-stimulant treatment for ADHD. It is an unresolved conundrum why drugs that increase synaptic norepinephrine levels (atomoxetine, through reuptake inhibition) and those that decrease it (guanfacine, through activation of α_2 receptors that block NT release) should have similar clinical effects in ADHD, and this tells us that any models that implicate mere monoaminergic deficits are probably simplistic. The interest in non-stimulant drugs is driven by the potential for abuse and development of drug dependency associated with the stimulants, although the general view is that stimulants have the stronger clinical effects. The abuse potential seems to be lower with the new slow-release (once-daily) and precursor preparations.

Amphetamines increase synaptic catecholamine concentrations by at least three mechanisms. They are competitive substrates for the DAT and thus slow down reuptake. After their own uptake into the presynaptic neuron they replace catecholamines from vesicular stores, resulting in retrograde transport into the synaptic cleft. Finally, they act as MAO inhibitors (Heal et al., 2009). In prefrontal cortex (PFC), which lacks DAT, the increase of catecholamines in the synaptic cleft is produced by the affinity of amphetamines and methylphenidate to the NET, which is the main mediator of DA reuptake in PFC. Blockade of the NET is also the mechanism by which atomoxetine enhances dopaminergic activity, but this effect seems to be limited to PFC because in other brain regions, notably the basal ganglia, DA reuptake is governed by the DAT, to which atomoxetine has no significant affinity. This lack of subcortical dopaminergic effect may also explain the generally lower clinical efficacy of atomoxetine.

Long-term therapeutic stimulant use seems to be tolerated relatively well, with less than 2% of patients discontinuing treatment because of side effects. However, because of the short history of large-scale stimulant use in the treatment of ADHD longitudinal studies with a follow-up into adulthood are still lacking. Because of the documented effects of stimulant use on development (growth reduction after long-term therapeutic use, possibly as a consequence of appetite suppression) and the considerable toxicity in high doses further monitoring of possible behavioural and neurobiological consequences is needed (Berman et al., 2009).

17.1.5 Endophenotypes and animal models

Changes in the neural circuits for motivation that lead to altered reinforcement learning have been proposed as endophenotypes that might bridge the gap between putative dopaminergic deficits and the clinical phenotype and can also be studied in animal models. It has been noted for a while that patients with ADHD prefer smaller immediate rewards over larger delayed rewards. This is normal in preschool age, but during the early school years children commonly learn to balance the amount of a reward against the time to its achievement, a faculty called delay discounting by behavioural economists. The capacity to discount delays depends on intact short- and long-term memory systems and the correct interpretation of and reaction to reinforcement schedules. Although the cognitive component of this task is probably preserved in ADHD – there is no evidence for specific deficits on any standard neuropsychological tests, only higher variability across trials (Klein et al., 2006) – the motivation side may be impaired. Alternatively, children may learn the reinforcement schedules but be unable to follow them because of the tendency to impulsive behaviour and impaired self-control.

A failure to learn stimulus–reward associations might be caused by insufficient phasic dopamine responses to positive reinforcers, which during normal learning produce a 'cellular' reward where the 'real' reward is delayed and thus reinforce behaviour associated with delayed rewards (Chapter 1). Although it is impossible to measure such phasic firing of dopaminergic neurons directly in humans, fMRI studies have produced evidence for reduced anticipatory striatal signals in ADHD. Such a failure to anticipate rewards may lead to some of the symptoms of the inattention cluster such as failure to sustain mental effort (Tripp and Wickens, 2009). After all, the motivation to learn in school, unlike kindergarten play, is derived from the association with rewards that come at a much later stage and often are promised to occur only during adulthood (e.g. a place at university). It is presently unclear where impulsivity would fit into such models – whether it is a consequence or a cause of insufficient responses to delayed rewards.

The most common animal models of ADHD start from toxic effects or lesions that can result in ADHD-like behaviour and increased amphetamine sensitivity in rodents, such as perinatal heavy metal exposure or treatment with 6-hydroxy-dopamine (6-OHDA), which destroys most dopaminergic neurons in the substantia nigra. These models have good face and predictive validity (symptoms improve after amphetamine or atomoxetine administration) but limited construct validity because neither heavy metal exposure nor widespread loss of dopaminergic neurons has been associated with human ADHD. Nevertheless, the 6-OHDA model is still in widespread use to investigate the specific effects of dopaminergic denervation on monoamine transmitter systems (Kostrzewa et al., 2008). New promising modelling approaches include those based on ADHD risk genes (like the DAT knock-out mouse mentioned above) or based on putative behavioural endophenotypes such as the impaired reinforcement learning.

17.2   AUTISM (AUTISTIC DISORDER AND ASPERGER'S DISORDER)

17.2.1   Clinical presentation and epidemiology

Autistic Disorder and Asperger's Disorder belong to the group of pervasive developmental disorders in DSM-IV. These are deficits in the development of motor, cognitive and social skills that manifest in the first years of life, sometimes after a period of normal development (as in the case of Rett syndrome). Patients with these disorders often show some degree of learning disability (or mental retardation in American terminology), as measured by a subnormal (under 70) IQ. However, in autism the impairment of social and communication skills is relatively more prominent, and many patients with Asperger's Disorder can have IQs in the normal range. The pervasive developmental disorders (and learning disabilities/mental retardation) also have some overlap in the clinical presentation and intellectual development with a range of neurological and general medical conditions, such as perinatal hypoxic brain damage, congenital infections or chromosomal aberrations such as Down's syndrome, but in these cases the diagnosis is typically aided by a specific medical history and/or neurological and physical signs.

Autistic Disorder was first described by the Austrian-American psychiatrist Leo Kanner in 1943. It is the early infantile form of autism, often manifesting in the second year of life and by definition before the age of 3. It is characterised by severe and sustained impairment of communication, notably language development, and social interaction. The affected children may not speak at all, and those who do develop language skills may have a stereotyped speech pattern, monotonous prosody and idiosyncratic (private) vocabulary. They may not be interested at all in social interaction or friendship or, if they are, lack the skills to maintain them, for example in non-verbal communication. They may also have impaired ability to understand others' needs and reduced empathy. Experimentally, this is classically tested with 'theory of mind' (ToM) tasks (see Box 17.1). The behaviour of affected children is often repetitive and ritualistic, and minor changes to daily routines may trigger catastrophic reactions. They may be preoccupied with a narrow range of interests, and even develop some special skills or specialist knowledge.

Box 17.1   Theory of mind, joint attention and the brain

We have no direct observational access to other people's minds, and thus do not know whether people will experience the same as we do when they see something they describe as 'red' or when they watch a movie and later tell us that it was 'enjoyable'. This is a property of so-called 'first-person' experiences which are by definition private and can only be communicated in symbolic form, for example through language or bodily expression. Our ability to infer the mental states of others from their behaviour, communication, the situational context and our own previous experience develops gradually during childhood. Imitative behaviour and differentiation between intentional and unintentional acts are generally considered important milestones on this path. Complex social functions such as empathy and ability to experience others' emotions vicariously may be an outcome of this development that played an important role in shaping human society, but recent research has also shown a surprising level of theory of mind in great apes. Deficiencies in the understanding of the intentions of others may result in communicative and behavioural differences such as those observed in autism, and impaired performance on theory of mind (ToM)- and related tasks has indeed been observed consistently. Perspective taking can be assessed already in toddlers with picture sequences like the 'Sally and Ann comic strip' (Frith and Frith, 1999). This story introduces two characters, Sally and Ann. Sally puts her ball into a basket and then leaves the room. Ann then moves the ball into a box. The question is where Sally will look for the ball when she returns. Here, the observer has to predict a person's (in this case Sally's) action based on her presumed mental state. The observer has to abstract from her own knowledge (that the ball is in fact in the box) and take the perspective of Sally who cannot know this.

Another related aspect of cognitive development is that of reaction to others' gaze and the capacity to attend to the same object as another person. Infants start following their mother's gaze at three months of age but the capacity to shift the gaze and point to the same object the mother is looking at only emerges from nine months (joint attention). This capacity is crucial to the learning of phoneme–object associations and thus of language. Shared attention, which involves the mutual checking of gaze directions to ensure that both are looking at the same object, evolves later. This capacity is important for the acquisition of interactive communication skills. Finally, it is estimated that children become capable of ToM at about 4–5 years of age (Itier and Batty, 2009) (Figure 17.1).

The interpretation of gaze cues seems to depend on the co-activation of brain areas involved in face processing (fusiform face area, FFA, and superior temporal sulcus, STS) and those involved in the control of eye movements (frontal and parietal eye fields). This might indicate that mental

Figure 17.1

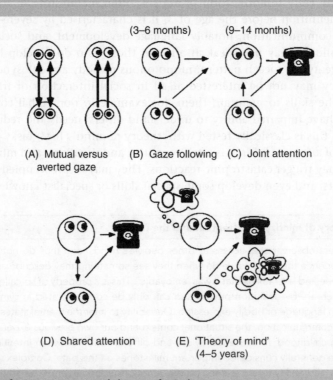

(3–6 months)   (9–14 months)

(A) Mutual versus averted gaze   (B) Gaze following   (C) Joint attention

(D) Shared attention   (E) 'Theory of mind' (4–5 years)

Development of joint attention and theory of mind

Infants prefer mutual over averted gaze (A) from birth. They can follow their mother's gaze from 3-6 months (B) and become capable of joint attention, that is, fixating the same object as someone else, between 9 and 14 months (C). Shared attention, that is interacting about an attended object, evolves later (D), and the basic set of social cognition skills is complete with the development of ToM between years 4 and 5 (E).

Source: From Itier and Batty (2009) with kind permission of Elsevier.

rehearsal of the other's gaze direction is needed in order to direct attention to the right object, along the lines of the mirror neuron hypothesis (see Box 1.4). ToM tasks have consistently activated areas in the medial prefrontal cortex that are also activated by other operations that involve reflection on the self and comparison with others. The amygdala may also play a role in both ToM and joint attention, but patients with amygdala lesions generally show more pervasive deficits of emotion processing and social communication as well.

This specialist knowledge can reach an impressive extent in patients with Asperger's disorder, which was first described in 1944 by the Austrian paediatrician Hans Asperger. It is distinguished from autistic disorder by the normal development of language and a normal cognitive and behavioural development up to the age of 3. Although Asperger's disorder is a chronic and disabling condition, particularly affecting the ability to form social and personal relationships, with a significant comorbidity with depression, the prognosis is much better than that of autistic disorder and many patients lead an independent life as adults.

Autistic disorder is much rarer than ADHD or conduct disorder with an estimated prevalence of 5–10 per 10,000, but is still one of the more common pervasive developmental disorders. The course is chronic, and two-thirds of patients will require full-time care as adults, and few will attain full independence and regular jobs. The prevalence of Asperger's Disorder is probably somewhat lower (estimates range around 2–5 per 10,000). Both have a higher (approx. 4:1 for autistic disorder, 8:1 for Asperger's disorder) proportion of males. Autistic disorder, Asperger's disorder and the DSM-IV category of 'Pervasive Developmental Disorders Not Otherwise Specified' (PDDNOS), which describes an atypical and commonly less severe course of autistic symptoms, are sometimes combined into a new class of 'Autism Spectrum Disorders' (ASD), based on the view that transitions between them may be fluid and that a dimensional conceptualisation may be more promising in the quest for biological markers than the traditional categorical approach.

17.2.2 Genetics

Autism has a high heritability, estimated at around 0.7. The high heritability of symptom domains (communication problems, social problems, repetitive behaviour) but low inter-domain correlation has suggested that these may be independent genetic risk factors. However, other studies yielded support for a single continuously distributed factor defining the autism spectrum. Autism has a special position in psychiatric genetics in that a number of known genetic variants can lead to autistic syndromes in the context of development syndromes. These include fragile-X syndrome, Rett syndrome, Angelman syndrome and tuberous sclerosis. These syndromes are defined by characteristic phenotypes and are caused by specific genetic variants. The proportion of affected individuals who also display a full autistic syndrome ranges from 20% (tuberous sclerosis) to 100% (Rett syndrome) (Box 17.2). However, they all overlap with autism in that they lead to developmental delay and can have other shared features, for example sleep disturbance. Thus, although the associated genetic variants have a complete penetrance for their respective syndromes (e.g. trinucleotide repeats in the FMR1 gene and fragile-X syndrome; mutations in the TSC1 or TSC2 genes and tuberous sclerosis), their penetrance for autism is incomplete. This opens up important avenues for neurobiological models of autism. It is important to identify common mechanisms through which the different syndrome-related genes operate, in particular with regard to the overlap between their phenotypes, which includes seizures and cardiac abnormalities in addition to the common risk for autism, pointing to common pathways in electrical conduction and neural transmission (Abrahams and Geschwind, 2008). Thus, even if the rare genetic variants of ASD-related syndromes may account for only 1–2% of autism cases, they can make a major contribution to the understanding of the underlying neurobiology and the development of animal models with high construct validity.

Box 17.2   Syndromes associated with autism

Fragile-X syndrome

Fragile-X syndrome (FXS) is caused by a trinucleotide (CGG) expansion in the gene for the FMR1 (FXS and Mental Retardation 1) protein on the X chromosome and affects between 1/3000 (male) and 1/6000 (female) births. This leads to methylation, resulting both in failure to express the protein and in a local constriction of the chromosome, which appears 'fragile' in light microscopy. FMR1 has been implicated at various levels in synaptic plasticity and neural development. Affected individuals have characteristic facial features and other physical anomalies as well as developmental delays and autistic symptoms such as social avoidance and perseveration. Males have large testicles (macro-orchidism).

Rett syndrome

Rett syndrome is rarer than FXS (<1/10000) but also more disabling. In most cases it is caused by de novo mutations in the gene for MECP2, a transcription factor, on the X chromosome. MECP2 is involved in the regulation of excitatory and inhibitory synapses, LTP and synaptic plasticity in cortex and hippocampus and hippocampal short-term synaptic depression. Most males affected by the mutation die in utero or in the first few years of life. In females, who probably partly compensate with their functioning copy on the X chromosome not affected by the mutation, development is normal in the first months of life, followed by stagnation or even regression of motor and language skills. Stereotypic hand movements and seizures are common, and both reduced limb (hand and feet) and brain growth (with characteristic microcephaly) can occur. The communication deficit and behavioural disturbance overlaps with the autistic syndrome.

Angelman syndrome

Both Angelman syndrome (AS) and Prader-Willi syndrome (PWS) are linked to an imprinted region on chromosome 15q11–13. Imprinted regions are expressed exclusively either from the maternal or the paternal chromosome. In AS the maternal copy is lacking, which affects paternally silenced genes, particularly the gene for UBE3A, which belongs to the ubiquitin complex and subserves protein degradation. The paternal copy of the UBE3A is not silenced in all tissue, but in some parts of the brain including the hippocampus. Reduced cerebral UBE3A expression may also be linked to non-syndromal cases of ASD. The incidence of AS has been estimated as between 1/10,000 and 1/20,000 births. The higher susceptibility to seizures, developmental delay and motor stereotypes overlap with autism, but the individual's demeanour is usually sociable.

Prader-Willi syndrome

PWS is caused by a lack of the paternal copy of the imprinted region, and thus maternally silenced genes will be affected, but it is not entirely clear which specific genes are relevant. The incidence is similar to that of AS. Hypotonia (lack of muscle tone) is noticed early, and facial features are characteristic. Hands and feet are small. Hypogonadism and hyperphagia, leading to early obesity, point to endocrine abnormalities. The overlap with the autistic/OCD phenotype can be seen in repetitive and ritualistic behaviour, and intellectual development is delayed and subnormal. Growth hormone treatment can relieve some of the physical signs.

Tuberous sclerosis complex (formerly Bourneville's disease)

Tuberous sclerosis complex (TSC) is inherited in an autosomal dominant fashion, although *de novo* mutations in one of the responsible genes, TSC1 on chromosome 9 and TSC2 on chromosome 16, are also common. Its incidence is around 1/10,000 births. TSC is characterised by benign tumours in the brain (Baskin, 2008) and other organs, for example skin or kidneys. The brain tumours lead to learning disabilities and seizures, and an autistic syndrome has been found in at least 20% of patients, but ADHD- and OCD-like syndromes can also occur.

Other rare genetic variants, mainly inherited or *de novo* (occurring in the affected individual for the first time in the family history) CNVs, may account for an additional 10–20% of ASD cases. Relatively common inherited CNVs are the duplication of chromosomal region 15q11-q13, which is also a locus for Angelman syndrome (Box 17.2), and the deletion of 22q13. Such cytogenic findings merely constrain the search space for specific genes that may be altered in the disorder, but further work has suggested the genes for ubiquitin protein ligase E3A (UBE3A), involved in protein digestion, and $GABA_A$ receptor beta 3 subunit (GABRB3) to be affected on chromosome 15, and the synaptic scaffolding protein SHANK3 on chromosome 22, which is also affected by *de novo* mutations associated with ASD. Another important *de novo* CNV is a 500 kb deletion on 16p11, present in ca. 1% of ASD cases.

The majority of cases of ASD are not associated with a single genetic variant but with small contributions from multiple common variants. These may lead to the disorder when a certain threshold is exceeded and additional environmental factors (there is speculation on a role of perinatal damage, for example from viral infections, similar to schizophrenia) are present. Because the rare variants and additive effect of the common variants lead to similar clinical phenotypes it is thought that they operate through common neurobiological pathways, for example abnormal synaptic function and brain connectivity (Abrahams and Geschwind, 2008).

Linkage studies have produced few loci with genome-wide significance and no identified specific genes. Because this might partly be due to the heterogeneity of clinical cases and the overlap with the healthy population on symptom dimensions of the autism spectrum, the focus has shifted to the definition of more homogeneous subgroups (e.g. by gender, leading symptom, physical features such as macrocephaly, neurological problems such as seizures) and the investigation of putative endophenotypes, such as language development, which may be delayed in unaffected relatives of ASD patients as well. The identification of genes associated with such endophenotypes, termed quantitative trait loci (QTL), may elucidate the contribution of common variants to ASDs. Future work is also likely to explore the genetic basis for the comorbidity between autism and ADHD.

17.2.3 Brain structure and function

In his original 1943 paper Kanner had noted the high proportion of large heads in his patients. Later quantitative comparisons between autistic and control children have consistently found increased head and whole-brain sizes. About 20% of individuals with ASD have macrocephaly (defined as head circumference above the 97th percentile). The volume increase seems to be particularly marked in early childhood (2–4 years) and differences were smaller or absent in older children and adults (Penn, 2006). One possible explanation is that genetic or developmental factors lead to exaggerated brain growth in the first years of life, which then leads to behavioural and cognitive abnormalities. The same or other factors may later lead to relatively slower growth, possibly adding further to delayed development. However, because the majority of ASD patients still have brains with sizes in the normal range and the majority of individuals with large brains do not develop autism the association between brain size and autistic symptoms has to be regarded as weak at best. It is also worth noting that children with Rett syndrome have abnormally small heads (microcephaly). The main importance of the investigation of global brain volume may be to motivate research into the neurodevelopmental processes underlying excessive brain growth, which may involve increased neurogenesis, decreased apoptosis, decreased pruning (reduction of initially formed synaptic connections) and increased production of glia (Verhoeven et al., 2010). One intriguing (but still largely speculative) possibility is that individuals who later develop autism have higher levels of peptides that stimulate neuronal growth. There is preliminary evidence for increased levels of vasoactive intestinal peptide (VIP), BDNF and neurotrophin 4/5 (NT4/5) at birth (Nelson et al., 2001). Another speculation is that the increased use of the neuropeptide oxytocin to induce labour has contributed to the rising numbers of ASD cases over the past decades.

Studies of regional cerebral volume differences have mainly described local reductions in ASD. The best replicated finding may be the reduction of parts of the cerebellar vermis, but its functional significance is unclear. Changes in other areas have been postulated based on the putative functional association with features of autism. The temporal lobe has been implicated in language and emotion disturbances and although evidence for changes in the temporal lobe in ASD patients is sparse, lesions in the temporal lobe in tuberous sclerosis or temporal lobe damage from viral encephalitis or tumours can contribute to autistic symptoms. Further support for an association between temporal lobe structures and autistic symptoms comes from studies of macaque monkeys with bilateral medial temporal lobe lesions, who display features of the autistic phenotype such as reduced eye contact and motor stereotypes. However, these features are not specific for autism (e.g., they could equally model aspects of OCD or schizophrenia), and the contribution of amygdala lesions may be more through impaired learning of fear responses than through a direct impact on social behaviour (Penn, 2006). Reduced responsiveness of the amygdala to emotional cues in ASD has also been suggested by several functional imaging studies. The frontal lobe has been implicated in ASD because of three of its supported functions, which are impaired in autism, theory of mind, joint attention and executive dysfunction (see Box 17.1). Although some functional imaging studies of tasks that require cognitive control, holistic or self-referential processing have found reduced prefrontal activation and post-mortem studies have reported subtle abnormalities in cortical volume and substructure, the link between frontal pathology and autism is presently still largely hypothetical. Finally, some studies have reported increased volumes of the caudate nucleus, which have also been implicated in OCD, which might account for the prominent obsessive (narrowed interest) and compulsive (repetitive motor behaviour) symptoms in ASD. It will be promising to link the presently still disparate findings through longitudinal studies that can unravel the stages of abnormal brain development and combinations of volumetric and connectivity (diffusion tensor) imaging. The most stable finding on brain connectivity so far is reduced volume and fractional anisotropy in the corpus callosum, the main commissure between the two hemispheres.

17.2.4 Neurochemistry and drug treatment

There is no unifying neurochemical theory of autism. Changes in peripheral serotonin levels or markers of serotonin synthesis were inconsistent, but SSRIs may improve some of the OCD-like symptoms. However, these also respond to atypical antipsychotic drugs like risperidone, which has an antiserotonergic effect (in addition to its antidopaminergic properties and effects on several other receptors). Dopaminergic drugs, such as amphetamines, may worsen the clinical picture. However, changes in dopamine metabolites and central dopaminergic activity between ASD patients and controls have also been inconsistent. The quest for neurochemical markers of autism may be more promising in the field of neuropeptides. Both increased opioid levels and decreased receptor sensitivity have been described. One might speculate about an association between altered pharmacological pathways mediating pleasure and changes in the reward value of behaviours. This may cause the patients to replace normal social interaction with repetitive, self-focused and possibly self-injurious behaviour. However, treatment with opioid blockers has not resulted in long-term relief from such symptoms.

Oxytocin levels have been reported as decreased in several studies. Patients also showed changes in the ratios of the different precursor peptides. Alterations of oxytocin metabolism and function are attractive for psychobiological models of autism because of its fairly well-established role as a 'prosocial' hormone that promotes communicative and affiliative behaviours and trust. Acute treatment with oxytocin has indeed shown some promising results for repetitive behaviours (Hollander et al., 2003) and social cognition(Andari et al., 2010) but studies of its long-term effects are still lacking.

Anticonvulsant drugs are mainly used to control seizures, whose frequency increases during the first decade of life. About 8% of ASD patients without and 27% of those with mental retardation have comorbid epilepsy (values are even much higher if cerebral palsy is present in addition to mental retardation) (Levisohn, 2007). However, anticonvulsants such as valproic acid may also have a positive effect on behavioural disturbances in ASD. Because of the frequent sleep disturbance, circadian rhythm (melatonin) and sedation (antihistaminergic drugs) are also components of pharmacological intervention.

17.2.5 Animal models

Animal models can help elucidate the mechanisms by which single rare genetic variants (and in more complex models, their interaction) contribute to the autistic phenotype. They can also investigate the effects of environmental factors implicated in the genesis of autism, such as maternal stress, foetal exposure to valproic acid or prenatal viral infections, on brain and behaviour. Moreover, they can help towards an understanding of the contribution of the various neurotransmitter systems, growth factors and postsynaptic signalling cascades to the changes in synaptic plasticity and neural development associated with autism (Moy and Nadler, 2008). Genetically designed mouse models of autism were based on mutations or knock-out of syndrome genes (Box 17.2) or autism susceptibility loci. The environmental approach exposes the animal to the relevant noxious substances or situations. If environmental effects are contingent upon specific genetic variants, G×E interactions can be confirmed. Finally, the classical approach through selective breeding for behavioural traits can help identify hitherto unknown genetic loci and neurochemical pathways. Standard behavioural tests assess social approach and avoidance, stereotypic motor behaviour and reversal learning. Because symptom onset in autism is much earlier than in most other mental disorders behavioural assays for social behaviour at very early stages of postnatal development are needed, for example ultrasonic vocalisations in pups separated from their mothers (Moy and Nadler, 2008).

Fragile-X syndrome has been modelled with a knock-out of the FMR1 gene, but this mouse has a milder phenotype without any significant learning impairment. Conversely, the MECP2 gene null mouse, a model for Rett syndrome, initially developed normally but then deteriorated neurologically and died early and thus showed an even more severe phenotype. Interesting observations from this model were increased anxiety behaviour and upregulation of the HPA axis, which may also play a role in autism. The mouse modelling Angelman syndrome with a maternal loss of the UBE3A gene has seizures, coordination deficits and deficits in fear conditioning and spatial learning and thus captures the clinical phenotype relatively well. Mice engineered to model its sister syndrome, Prader-Willi syndrome, had decreased numbers of oxytocin-producing hypothalamic neurons, which lends further support to the association between this neuropeptide and developmental disorders.

17.3   CONDUCT DISORDER

17.3.1   Clinical presentation and epidemiology

Conduct disorder (CD) consists in the persistent violation of social norms and basic rules of behaviour towards others, although the perpetrator is intellectually mature enough to understand these norms and rules. According to the DSM-IV, four main groups of behaviours can be observed: physically harmful actions or threats, damage to property, deceit and theft and other serious violations of rules, for example at school. The aggressive behaviour is often initiated by the patient and can range from intimidation to severe physical violence, such as rape or in rare cases even homicide. It is often characterised by particular physical or psychological cruelty. CD seems to be on the rise, and both changes in the social fabric of Western societies and increased awareness and provision of services have been implicated in this process. Prevalence estimates range from 1 to 10% with higher rates in males than females, making this one of the most diagnosed conditions in child and adolescent mental health settings. Subtypes are defined by onset of the first symptoms prior to (childhood-onset) or after age 10 (adolescent-onset). Further, more dimensional subtyping into a callous-unemotional and reactive/threat-based type has been suggested. The prognosis of the childhood-onset type is worse, with higher rates of persistence and development of adult antisocial personality disorder. Children with a combination of CD and ADHD-features pose the highest risk for later offending. CD is generally a risk factor for the later development of mood, anxiety, somatoform and substance-abuse disorders. It can be grouped with oppositional defiant disorder (ODD), which describes a less severe form of persistent antisocial behaviour, into the class of 'disruptive behaviour disorders' (DBD).

17.3.2   Genetics

The heritability of antisocial behaviour is generally estimated at about 50%, but may be considerably higher (in the range of 80%) for the group with callous-unemotional traits (Viding et al., 2008). Adult-onset antisocial behaviour (as in the context of antisocial personality disorder, ASPD) also has a particularly high heritability. There is also considerable G×E interaction, meaning that carriers of genetic risk factors are particularly vulnerable to environmental factors. For example maltreatment and negative early parenting in general have a greater chance of leading to antisocial behaviour in children at genetic risk (Thapar et al., 2007). A Swedish adoption study found that environmental risk was associated with a 6% incidence of criminality in adulthood, genetic predisposition with 12%, but the combination of the two factors with a staggering rate of 40% who later became recidivist criminals. One specific gene has been identified as possibly mediating this G×E interaction, the gene for the Monoamine oxidase A (MAO-A) (Caspi et al., 2002), which metabolises the catecholamine neurotransmitters. The X-chromosomal MAO-A gene has a 30-bp VNTR in its promoter region, and its effects have mainly be investigated in boys because of the difficulty of determining the functional genotype in girls, who have two X chromosomes. The most common variants result in lower (3-repeat) or higher (4-repeat) protein expression. Several studies have now found additive effects of exposure to maltreatment and the low activity genotype on the development of antisocial behaviour (with a diagnosis of CD) and other mental health problems, whereas the MAO-A genotype had no effect in unexposed children. The joint influence of maltreatment and MAO-A genotype on antisocial behaviour is to date the most prominent case of G×E interaction involving a specific genetic variant. Environmental risk factors, e.g. maternal smoking, pregnancy complications and malnutrition (Dutch children whose mothers were affected by malnutrition in the 'hunger winter' of 1944/45 during the first and second trimesters of pregnancy were more likely later to develop ASPD), have been implicated as well.

17.3.3   Brain structure and function

Biological correlates of DSM-IV conduct disorder have been investigated by relatively few studies, but if the domain of antisocial behaviour is defined more broadly to include any type of delinquent, violent or aggressive behaviour in children and adolescents, the evidence base becomes more solid (Van Goozen et al., 2007). However, compared to neurochemical and neuroendocrinological studies, there is a dearth of brain imaging investigations of antisocial behaviour, particularly in children. Studies with functional imaging and peripheral physiology mainly in adults with antisocial behaviour (ASPD or psychopathy) have suggested blunted limbic and arousal responses to threatening stimuli as well as reduced blood flow, glucose metabolism and cortical grey matter in PFC. There is also preliminary evidence for reduced PFC volume in children with CD, but global volume changes at a single point of development, even if replicated, do not distinguish between delayed or impaired brain maturation. As in autism and ADHD, longitudinal comparisons between patients (ideally with pure DBD, without comorbid ADHD) and controls are needed to determine the time course of brain volume changes.

The best evidence so far for a possible association between functions of the ventromedial PFC and OFC comes from patients with focal lesions to these areas. These patients can show marked personality changes and develop deficits in moral reasoning and generally antisocial behaviour and a psychopathic disposition. Combined with these clinical changes, they also show experimental effects similar to those observed in ASPD, such as reduced arousal to threatening and otherwise socially relevant situations. However, as with all lesion models (and similar to animal models with good face validity), this does not imply that the same structures and mechanisms are at work in antisocial behaviour that is not a result of focal lesions. Disturbances in different parts of the brain pathways for decision-making, impulse control and arousal could, in principle, converge to result in similar clinical pictures.

17.3.4   Neurochemistry and drug treatment

Aggressive behaviour can be driven by reactions to perceived threat (impulsive or reactive type). Alternatively, it can be proactive and controlled, often coupled with reduced emotional reactivity (callous type). The first type may be linked to hyperarousal, the latter to attenuation of normal physiological responses, for example to the suffering of others. Any neurochemical findings, particularly related to stress responses, will be difficult to interpret regarding their causal role. Individuals with antisocial behaviour are exposed and expose themselves to stress-inducing situations, and higher exposure to neglect and violence could be cause and consequence (or both) of disruptive behaviour. Thus, the role of psychological and physiological habituation of the stress response in the genesis of conduct disorders can be clarified only with longitudinal studies, testing neurochemical and physiological parameters before the onset of symptoms and ideally before the onset of any environmental adversity.

Much work on the neurochemistry of aggression has focused on the endocrine systems. The association between testosterone levels and aggressive behaviour is robust in many animals, but less clear in humans, especially prepubertal children. One reason may be that testosterone is more associated with social dominance and group leadership than aggression per se (Van Goozen et al., 2007). Another is that gonadal androgens, such as testosterone, play a prominent role only from puberty onwards. In prepubertal children after the beginning of the 'adrenarche' at about age 6, androgens secreted by the adrenal glands, such as dehydroepiandrosterone (DHEA), its sulphate (DHEA-S) and androstenedione, are more important. Increased DHEA-S in particular was associated with antisocial behaviour, which is interesting because of its GABA-antagonistic properties (Van Goozen et al., 2007).

17.3.4.1   Neuroendocrine models

Cortisol levels can be reduced in both adults and children with antisocial behaviour. Reduced cortisol has even predicted aggressive behaviour occurring five years later. Cortisol reactivity to stress has also been found in DBD, and may differentiate DBD from ADHD chemically. Such lower baseline and induced cortisol levels could be caused by insufficient or hypersensitive negative feedback loops at any level of the HPA axis. One interpretation is that antisocial individuals have attenuated stress responses and thus a higher tolerance to stress. This neurobiological model would thus fit the unemotional, under-aroused type, who may be particularly resistant to behavioural interventions. If low cortisol levels are aversive, patients may try and increase them by deliberately getting into stressful, arousing situations, as predicted by the 'simulation-seeking theory' of aggression. However, low cortisol levels are almost certainly not the sole cause of antisocial behaviour and aggression because they are not part of the phenotype of adrenal insufficiency (Addison's disease). Furthermore, there is no evidence that administration of glucocorticoids improves antisocial behaviour, and such treatment would have considerable side effects because of its varied metabolic effects.

17.3.4.2 Models involving the ANS

The hypoarousal model of controlled antisocial behaviour would predict attenuated sympathetic activity at baseline and in response to novel or threatening situations. This has mainly been tested with peripheral physiological markers, mainly skin conductance (SCR, reflecting sympathetic activity) and heart rate (HR, where the parasympathetic and sympathetic systems have opposite effects). The most stable biological marker of antisocial behaviour in adults has been a reduced HR (Raine, 2002), although findings were less consistent in children. Lower SCR has also been reported consistently, although these measures have so far failed to distinguish between the reactive (supposedly 'hyperaroused') and controlled (supposedly 'hypoaroused') types in the predicted way. Assuming that attenuated markers of sympathetic system activity represent a chronic hypoaroused state, one interpretation would be that antisocial individuals fear the potential negative consequences of aggressive actions less (Raine's fearlessness theory), and another that they seek the physiological stimulation of dangerous or antagonistic behaviour to raise their arousal levels (Zuckerman's stimulation-seeking theory). Both mechanisms may be at play to raise the incentive value of antisocial interactions and tear down barriers of normal cognitive-emotional control in these individuals.

17.3.4.3 Serotonin model

In addition to changes in the noradrenaline system, which is involved in ANS control, serotonin has also been implicated in aggressive behaviour. Low levels of central 5-HT, inferred from metabolite levels in CSF or urine, platelet 5-HT concentration or receptor/transporter occupancy in radioligand studies, have been associated with aggressive behaviour in numerous clinical and experimental studies. However, the effects of serotonergic medication on aggressive behaviour have been mixed. It does not seem to work in ASPD or DBD, and some observations have even implicated serotonergic drugs (particularly the SSRIs, perhaps because of the generally lower levels of sedation compared to the tricyclic antidepressants) in the promotion of auto-aggressive (suicide) and aggressive behaviour, leading to increased scrutiny of their use in adolescents in particular.

17.3.5 Endophenotypes and animal models

Both reactive and spontaneous aggression can be assessed in animals by observing threatening behaviour and attacks on intruders and on animals that do not themselves pose a threat. Rats will normally try and discourage (smaller) intruders with threat cues and, if they do attack them, direct this to less vulnerable parts of the body. However, rats with glucocorticoid deficiency caused by removal of the adrenal glands attacked after fewer threat cues and focused on parts of the body that are particularly vulnerable. This abnormal aggressive behaviour was prevented by injections of corticosterone (Van Goozen et al., 2007).

The link between 5-HT and aggression has also been tested in animal models. 5-HT_{1A}-receptor stimulation, for example with buspirone, reduces aggressive behaviour, and 5-HT_{1B} knock-out mice are more aggressive towards intruders. Conversely, activation of the 5-HT_2 receptor seems to promote aggressive behaviour, as suggested by the anti-aggressive properties of the newer antipsychotic agents, most of which are 5-HT_2-receptor blockers. Low serotonergic activity in the raphe nuclei was also associated with higher numbers of attacks, but only with the 'natural' type of attacks on non-vulnerable targets and not with the predatory type of attacks on vulnerable targets. This may indicate that serotonin inhibits hypoarousal-driven aggression less well and explain why serotonergic drugs have so little effect in ASPD. One possible explanation is that the effects of the 5-HT system cannot unfold because of insufficient synergy from the HPA axis, with which the 5-HT system interacts at various levels.

In sum, although antisocial and aggressive behaviour can be modelled well in animals and numerous physiological and neurochemical correlates have been identified in both children and adults, including evidence for reduced stress responses and arousal levels, this has not yet translated into specific pharmacological treatments. Promising avenues for further research include a more dimensional, endophenotype-based approach (differentiating different patterns of aggression), longitudinal studies of cause–effect relationships and the development of more specific agents, for example targeting subtypes of 5-HT receptors. It will also be interesting to probe the potential causal role of physiological changes by targeting them with biofeedback techniques.

Learning points

Childhood is associated with a specific set of developmental and psychological syndromes. The most prevalent of these are ADHD, pervasive developmental disorders (including autism) and conduct disorder (CD). Heritability of ADHD and autism is high, and G×E interactions have been strongly implicated in the development of CD. Although disordered brain development has been implicated in all of these groups (most strongly in ADHD and autism), stable biological markers have not yet been identified. Brains of ADHD patients seem to be on average smaller, and those of patients with autism larger, than age-matched controls, but theses differences are not diagnostic and often disappear by adolescence. Candidate studies of ADHD and GWAS of autism have produced several interesting risk loci, which all seem to confer small effects. However, rare variants with large penetrance lead to a number of related developmental syndromes with characteristic physical and/or behavioural features, including fragile-X, Rett, Angelman and Prader-Willi syndrome. Although animal models and neurochemical findings have implicated altered dopaminergic signalling in ADHD and neuropeptides related to brain development in autism, stable findings in patients are still lacking. The mainstay of pharmacological treatment of ADHD is based on the dopaminergic properties of stimulants.

Stimulants are dopaminergic drugs used in the treatment of ADHD. They increase synaptic dopamine levels through reuptake inhibition (methylphenidate, amphetamine) and increased release from presynaptic storage vesicles (amphetamine). Although good effects on behaviour and learning are often reported in children with ADHD who did not respond to psychological and educational interventions, side effects have to be considered and treatment is not recommended for children under 6. There is also a growing use of stimulants for adults with ADHD, either as continuation of treatment from childhood or by way of a newly initiated therapy. Treatment of ADHD with atomoxetine follows a partly different pharmacological pathway (blockade of the NET and thus increase of both dopamine and noradrenaline levels). There is also a growing illegal market for stimulants as cognitive enhancers, for example during exam phases.

No specific pharmacological therapy is available for autism, although there is some hope that social behavioural deficits may respond to oxytocin, and antipsychotic or sedative medication may be required in severe cases. Multiple biological models have been proposed for conduct disorder and its adult equivalent, ASPD, including dysregulation of the HPA and HPG axes, heightened sympathetic tone in the ANS, and serotonergic deficit. Again, these models are intriguing and can inform further drug development, but are not supported by stable biomarkers.

Revision and discussion questions

- Explain similarities and differences between ADHD and autism spectrum disorders.
- How might endophenotypes inform research into the biology of ADHD?
- What is the evolutionary basis for aggression, and how might it explain conduct disorder and antisocial personality disorder?

FURTHER READING

Abrahams, B. and Geschwind, D. (2008). Advances in autism genetics: on the threshold of a new neurobiology. *Nature Review Genetics*, 9, 341–55.

Tripp, G. and Wickens, J. (2009). Neurobiology of ADHD. *Neuropharmacology*, 57, 579–89.

Van Goozen, S., Fairchild, G., Snoek, H. and Harold, G. (2007). The evidence for a neurobiological model of childhood antisocial behavior. *Psychological Bulletin*, 133, 149–82.

18

BIOLOGY OF SEXUAL AND GENDER IDENTITY DISORDERS

PREVIEW

This chapter describes a large group of disorders, which have very different individual and societal implications. For example the primary sexual dysfunctions (sexual desire disorders, sexual arousal disorders, orgasmic disorders and sexual pain disorders) are mainly matters for the patient, his or her partner and the therapist. Conversely, the paraphilias, particularly exhibitionism and paedophilia, may bring the affected individual into conflict with laws governing public order and the protection of minors and thus involve the legal system and various government agencies. Finally, the gender identity disorders bring up issues of the indication and availability of gender-transforming hormonal and surgical interventions. There is little direct evidence about the biological changes underlying these disorders, and this chapter therefore relies strongly on neuropsychiatric cases (e.g. patients with specific brain lesions displaying altered sexual behaviour or preferences) and inference from the hormonal regulation of standard sexual behaviour. It also reviews hormonal and other biological treatment approaches as well as the evidence for brain differences between the genders (mainly in the sexually dimorphic hypothalamic nuclei) and possibly early determinants of sexual preferences.

18.1 DEFINITION, CLINICAL ASPECTS AND EPIDEMIOLOGY

Disturbed sexual desire (libido) or functions are common problems in mental disorders leading to considerable loss of quality of life. Loss of libido and (male) impotence are also common side effects of psychoactive drugs, for example antidepressants or antipsychotics, and amongst the most frequent reasons for patients' non-compliance or requests to discontinue the medication. Impotence and reduced libido can also result from other common prescription drugs, for example beta-blockers, and from legal (nicotine, alcohol) and illegal substances of abuse. They can also be caused by a wide range of medical conditions, for example endocrine, neurological or vascular disorders, which are outside the focus of this book.

In addition to these secondary sexual dysfunctions ('Due to a general medical condition' or 'Substance-Induced'), the DSM-IV recognises four main groups of primary sexual dysfunction: sexual desire disorders, sexual arousal disorders, orgasmic disorders and sexual pain disorders. A second class of sexual disorders comprises the paraphilias, which are characterised by 'recurrent, intense sexual urges, fantasies, or behaviours that involve unusual objects, activities, or situations' (APA, 2000: 535). Examples are exhibitionism, fetishism and paedophilia. Gender identity disorders describe conditions where individuals are unhappy with their biological gender and desire transformation into the opposite sex.

About 50% of the sexually active population suffers from sexual complaints that map on to the DSM-IV conditions, but it is not known how many of them would fulfil the full diagnostic criteria. Disturbances of sexual desire describe more the psychological (lack of sexual fantasies or desire or even aversion and avoidance) aspects of sexual dysfunction, whereas disturbed sexual arousal is identified by changes in the physiological aspects of sexual activity, for example male erectile dysfunction. If desire and arousal/excitement are preserved, the next phase of sexual activity that can be affected is the orgasm, which can be delayed or absent in men and women (male/female orgasmic disorder) or accelerated in men (premature ejaculation). The sexual pain disorders dyspareunia (genital pain during, before or after sexual intercourse) and vaginismus (involuntary spasm of the outer vaginal musculature) normally lead to much reduced sexual activity and are often chronic.

The paraphilias are defined by promotion of sexual excitement through specific fantasies, behaviours or objects that causes clinically significant distress or impairment. The paraphilic setting may be obligatory with patients unable to obtain sexual satisfaction outside, but a proportion of patients engage in their paraphilic activity only episodically. Fetishism describes the use of non-living objects, and voyeurism, exhibitionism and frotteurism describe specific behaviours towards non-consenting/unsuspecting individuals that do not, however, normally involve actual sexual intercourse. Sexual sadism and paedophilia (sexual fantasies about or acts with prepubescent children) always involve elements of bodily contact and often actual intercourse. Paedophilic behaviour (including indirect acts such as the consumption of pornographic material) is generally illegal. The legality of sadism depends on the consent of the victim and the severity of the acts, but there is a high degree of criminality (e.g. rape) and potential for serious physical harm involved. Similarly, certain practices of sexual masochism (sexual excitement derived from fantasies or behaviours where the individual is made to suffer) are highly dangerous, for example the oxygen deprivation required for 'hypoxyphilia'. Many of the paraphilic preferences can develop during adolescence (although a minimum age of 16 and 5 years older than the child involved is required for a formal diagnosis of paedophilia) and the course is often chronic. Mental health professionals will encounter individuals with paedophilia or rapists with suspected sexual sadism mainly in a forensic setting. The formal diagnosis of paraphilia is rare, but the legal and illegal markets for associated material and paraphernalia suggest that these phenomena are more widespread than the clinical data would suggest. The often persistent and monomaniac pursuit of the paraphilic preference puts this group close to the disorders of compulsive behaviour.

About 1/30,000 adult males and 1/100,000 females want to change their gender through surgery. Individuals with gender identity disorders (GID), not all of whom opt for surgery, commonly find their secondary sex characteristics disgusting, and want to fill the role of a member of the opposite sex. Problems with gender identity at pre-school age do not necessarily dispose to GID but to homo- and bisexuality in males.

It is in the nature of the definition of the primary sexual dysfunctions that little is known about their biological origins because those with an identifiable endocrine, pharmacological or other medical cause would be classified elsewhere. Knowledge about possible mechanisms of abnormal sexual behaviour is largely indirect and derived from the observation of the effects of pharmacological intervention and focal brain lesions in humans and animals. Finally, post-mortem histological analysis has allowed some insight into possible neurobiological determinants of sexual orientation and gender identity.

18.2   NEUROPSYCHIATRY OF ALTERED SEXUAL BEHAVIOUR

Although hyposexuality is more common after brain lesions from trauma, tumour, encephalitis or other causes, hypersexuality and abnormal sexual behaviour resembling some of the paraphilias have also been reported. Klüver-Bucy syndrome (see Chapter 21) arises after lesions affecting both temporal lobes, particularly the medial parts including the amygdalae. It classically includes disinhibitions of eating and sexuality and the tendency to put objects in the mouth. At the same time, affected patients tend to be placid and docile. It has to be noted that hypersexuality and indeed paraphilia do not automatically imply violent sexual behaviour, and some of the features discussed in the context of antisocial behaviour (see Chapter 14) may combine with those underlying sexual disinhibition to yield sexual aggression.

The basal frontal lobe and diencephalon are the other areas where lesions have consistently (but still only in a small minority of patients) produced sexual disinhibition and related behaviour, for example exhibitionism. It is important to recognise possible neurological causes in the assessment of paraphilic behaviour. For example, exhibitionism can occur in patients with epilepsy, multiple sclerosis, Tourette's syndrome and Huntington's disease. Paedophilia has been reported in cases with hypothalamic tumours, temporal lobe dysfunction, epilepsy and hypoxic brain damage. A study from the 1970s found organic causes in about 15% of child molesters and mental retardation in about the same number of cases (Miller et al., 1986). Hyposexuality and loss of libido have been specifically associated with lesions to the hypothalamus and pallidothalamic projections, but pallidotomy in Parkinson's disease has also resulted in hypersexuality.

Baird et al. (2007) proposed a modular model of brain regulation of sexual behaviour that incorporated the information from animal work and human lesion studies. According to this model, the amygdala and basal ganglia mainly control the sex drive, whereas the hypothalamus controls the homoeostatic, and the septal region the hedonic side of the event. The frontal lobe is involved because it controls or inhibits the motor areas involved, and the primary and secondary somatosensory centres in the parietal lobe process the tactile information.

In sum, the neurological study of changes in sexual behaviour has identified central roles for the basal frontal lobe, hypothalamus and limbic system in the control of sexual drive, but it is unknown whether these same areas are damaged in the paraphilias of the DSM-IV.

18.3   PHARMACOLOGY AND TREATMENT OF ABNORMAL SEXUAL BEHAVIOUR

The pharmacological study of sexual reinforcement provides further insight into the control of sexual drive and arousal, but not necessarily into the mechanism of abnormal sexual preferences. Some of the basic reinforcement mechanism may be shared between sexual and feeding-related behaviour, and both can be studied with place preference conditioning in rodents. Low doses of opioids in the ventral tegmental area (VTA) enhance sexual behaviour in male rats and activity of the opioid system in the medial preoptic area of the hypothalamus is required for sexual reinforcement. Similar mechanisms seem to apply in social behaviours, such as bonding between partners and mother and child (Le Merrer et al., 2009). However, opioids also have an inhibitory influence on sexual behaviour, as does neuropeptide Y (NPY), which shifts the attention of experimental animals away from sexual to feeding-related behaviour. After all, the right balance between feeding and sexual activity is crucial for the survival both of the animal and the species, and generally these activities are in competition.

Both neurotransmitters and hormones regulate sexual arousal. Serotonin and prolactin inhibit and enkephalins, dopaminergic and noradrenergic agents, acetylcholine and oxytocin increase the sexual drive. The hormonal system dedicated to the regulation of sexual behaviours and reproduction is the hypothalamic-pituitary-gonadal (HPG) axis (see Chapter 3). The gonadal hormones and their pituitary (LH, FSH) and hypothalamic (LHRH) activators also have arousing effects. However, for LHRH this changes with long-term use, which leads to 'chemical castration' because of downregulation of LH and FSH secretion and consequently reduced production of gonadal hormones. In therapeutic application LHRH agonists are commonly combined with an antiandrogen in the first 1–2 months to counter any initial hyperarousing effects. The main antiandrogens are the progesterones cyproterone acetate and medroxyprogesterone acetate. Other substances that are occasionally effective in controlling paraphilic urges and reduce reoffending include the SSRIs or tricyclic antidepressants. Although less severe cases might be treated with SSRIs alone, those with a history of sexual aggression may need combination therapy with an antiandrogen, or even triple therapy including a LHRH agonist (Guay, 2009). The hormonal treatments have their own important side-effect profile, which is beyond the scope of this book, but can be studied in textbooks of clinical endocrinology or pharmacology or in the relevant drug therapy manuals.

Psychotherapy is almost always indicated in paraphilia where the patient wishes it but more difficult to apply in settings of compulsory treatment, for example for paedophiles who are imprisoned for sexual offences. Surgical treatment through castration is largely a method of the past because of ethical concerns although it may be the most effective technique to prevent reoffending. However, not all orchiectomised males are impotent and they can stimulate themselves with exogenous testosterone and thus surgical castration does not completely rule out sexual aggression (Guay, 2009). In practice, a combined psychotherapeutic and pharmacological approach will normally be chosen depending on the setting and resources available, which may be limited in some prison systems.

18.4   GENDER PREFERENCE

The neurobiology of sexual orientation has attracted a great deal of interest and controversy. Like for gender identity, a strong influence may come from intrauterine hormone levels, as suggested by the association of congenital adrenal hyperplasia (CAH, a group of inherited enzyme deficiencies that lead to the accumulation of androgens) with bi- and homosexuality in girls. Some studies have also suggested an element of (maternal) heritability in (male) homosexuality. Regarding brain structure, the suprachiasmatic nucleus SCN (Chapter 2.1) was found to be larger in homosexual than heterosexual men. This was also the case for the anterior commissure, which is also larger in women than men (Swaab, 2007). Conversely, the third interstitial nucleus of the anterior hypothalamus (INAH3) was larger in heterosexual men compared to women or homosexual men in one post-mortem study (LeVay, 1991).

The fraternal birth order effect – the rate of homosexuality increases in boys born later among brothers – has led to an immunological explanation (Quinsey, 2003). Exposure to some product of the Y chromosome during a previous pregnancy would trigger an immune response in the mother, which could affect future male foetuses (Swaab, 2007). Although very interesting from the perspective of evolutionary and social biology, the mechanisms behind changes in sexual orientation are not in themselves topics for biological psychiatry because homo- and bisexuality are not disorders. They may become relevant in a psychiatric context when partnership problems lead to distress, although this does not necessarily occur more frequently than in heterosexual partnerships, or when individuals suffer from intolerant attitudes of family or society.

18.5   NEUROBIOLOGICAL DIFFERENCES BETWEEN GENDERS AND GENDER IDENTITY

The sexual organs develop in weeks 6–12 of gestation. The presence or absence of the sex determining region on the Y chromosome (SRY), which codes for the testis-determining factor (TDF), determines whether the individual will be phenotypically male or female. Male sexual characteristics develop under the influence of testosterone and dihydrotestosterone, and female characteristics through their absence, and it is generally assumed that sexual orientation and preferences are largely determined before birth (Swaab, 2007), which poses a challenge to psychoanalytic models of sexual development (Friedman and Downey, 2008). For the understanding of possible prenatal mechanisms contributing to altered gender identity it is important to note that gonadal sexual differentiation occurs much earlier than that of the brain, which starts in the second trimester and is complete only in adulthood. Transsexuality may arise when these two phases are differentially affected, leading to mismatch between the gender of the sexual organs and that of the preferred self. Although no genes underlying gender identity have been identified, those Y-chromosomal genes that are expressed during foetal and early postnatal development and those X-chromosomal genes that escape inactivation in females are attractive targets for research into this mismatch, and the development of gender differences in the brain generally. Many gender differences in gene expression and splicing of transcripts have been observed in studies on drosophila, nematodes and rodents, but how they might potentially influence brain structure and function is unknown (Jazin and Cahill, 2010).

Several differences in hippocampal structure and function (e.g. hippocampus dependent learning, LTP) between sexes have been observed in rodent studies. Stress-induced hippocampal damage is larger in male compared to female rodents and monkeys. Although this issue has not been studied in humans, it may be relevant for sex differences in stress responses and associated mental disorders. Sexual dimorphisms in neurotransmitter systems, which have been observed for monoamines, opioids, vasopressin and GABA, may play a role as well. There is also preliminary evidence from human neuroimaging studies that the hippocampus is larger in women, whereas the amygdala is larger in men (Cahill, 2006).

The most consistent structural brain differences in the human brain have been observed in the hypothalamus, specifically the preoptic area, the second and third interstitial nucleus of the anterior hypothalamus (INAH), the BNST and the SCN. Such areas are called 'sexually dimorphic' (Section 1.4.10) (Quinsey, 2003). The central nucleus of the BNST is larger and contains higher numbers of its main cell population, somatostatin-expressing neurons, in hetero- and homosexual men than women. A post-mortem study that included brains of male-to-female (MF) transsexuals found similar levels to females in this group, suggesting that the cell number in this area is a possible correlate of gender- but not sex preference (Zhou et al., 1995; Kruijver et al., 2000). Similar findings have recently been obtained for the third INAH (Garcia-Falgueras and Swaab, 2008). However, such changes could be a consequence of the treatment normally administered to MF transsexuals, which includes oestrogens and eventually orchiectomy, leading to lack of androgens. Although the authors tried to address this issue with control cases, the small numbers of brains of MF transsexuals and even smaller numbers of control cases make these findings preliminary.

Although there is thus no definitive answer yet on whether these hypothalamic changes in transsexuality are primary or secondary, several lines of evidence converge to suggest early hormonal changes. Polymorphisms in the oestrogen receptor A and B genes and in the gene for aromatase (which catalyses the conversion of testosterone into oestrogen) have been associated with transsexuality. The association of female-to-male transsexuality (FMT) with polycystic ovaries (a common syndrome of female infertility associated with elevated androgen levels), CAH and menstrual changes implicate androgen exposure in FMT (Swaab, 2007).

Learning points

Sexual dysfunction is a common feature of mental disorders and a common side effect of many psychotropic drugs, particularly antipsychotics and antidepressants. Their management requires a holistic approach that includes counselling and psychosocial support and possibly a change of medication. Little is known about the biology of the disorders with primary sexual dysfunction (reduced desire, arousal, ability to experience orgasms, or pain associated with the act), and their treatment is in the domain of specialised clinics. Similarly, there is little direct evidence for biological changes in patients with paraphilias, who prefer unusual sexual objects, activities or situations, but evidence from patients with brain lesions who develop related syndromes has pointed to a possible role for the basal forebrain, hypothalamus and amygdala. Patients with paraphilias come to the attention of mental health services only in rare circumstances, and then often in a forensic setting, for example because of paedophilic crimes. Treatment is difficult, and the pharmacological tools include antiandrogens, LHRH agonists (leading to downregulation of gonadal hormones in the long term) and antidepressants. The biology of gender identity has focused on sexually dimorphic nuclei in the diencephalons. Gender identity disorders are of relevance to mental health professionals particularly when they are members of a team advising on gender changes.

Revision and discussion questions

- How might the biology of sexual desire differ from that of other natural and learnt rewards?
- What can we learn from sexually dimorphic brain areas and early hormonal changes about the nature/nurture debate on the development of gender identity?

FURTHER READING

Swaab, D. (2007). Sexual differentiation of the brain and behavior. *Best Practice & Research Clinical Endocrinology*, 21, 431–44.

19

BIOLOGY OF SLEEP DISORDERS

PREVIEW

The primary sleep disorders can be classified into disorders with abnormal sleep (dyssomnias) and those with abnormal behaviour during sleep (parasomnias). The dyssomnias are relatively common, but not much is known about their heritability. Functional imaging and particularly EEG have a central place in the investigation of the biology of sleep disorders, and sleep phases are defined by their EEG correlate, as explained in Box 19.1. The other available evidence comes from animal models with disturbed sleep and neurochemical models of sleep regulation, although direct evidence for neurochemical dysfunction is scarce. A wide range of pharmacological approaches is available to treat sleep disorders, and their indications, mechanisms and caveats are discussed in the final section of the chapter.

Box 19.1 Sleep phases

Sleep is not homogeneous. Although it may seem to us – at least those of us enjoying sound sleep – that we go to bed at night and wake up in the morning without much happening in between, any recording of physiological activity during sleep will reveal a phasic pattern (Figure 19.1). Periods of deep or slow wave sleep (SWS) alternate with increasingly long periods of rapid eye movement (REM) sleep, which take up most of the second half of the night and during which dreams are supposed to occur. The method used to monitor the sleep stages in clinical and research settings is called polysomnography (PSG). It involves EEG recording with a reduced set of electrodes in order to pick up the characteristic delta waves of SWS (also called non-REM [NREM] sleep). Eye movement frequency is recorded with electrodes beside the eyes (electrooculography, EOG) and muscle tone with electrodes on facial muscles (electromyography, EMG). Breathing rate is also recorded in order to identify OSA and other breathing-related sleep disorders. The physiological assessment of sleep is a multidisciplinary exercise, involving clinical neurophysiologists and respiratory physicians. Recordings are performed by specially qualified technicians (clinical physiologists) in sleep laboratories.

Neuroimaging has yielded further information on the physiology of sleep stages, but is challenging to perform while participants are asleep. Compared to REM sleep or waking, blood flow was globally reduced during SWS. Reduced firing rates of brainstem neurons and hyperpolarisation of the thalamus have been observed in animals during SWS. Such hyperpolarisation of the thalamus results in reduced excitatory inputs to the cerebral cortex, which would be in keeping with these metabolic findings, assuming that the reduced blood flow is secondary to reduced neuronal activity. REM sleep is under the control of cholinergic projections from the pontine tegmentum (PPT and LDT), which explains the reduction of REM sleep with anticholinergic medication. Correspondingly, the pontine tegmentum, thalamus, limbic system and several cortical areas show increased metabolic activity during REM sleep. The pattern of cortical activation and deactivation during REM sleep has also been adduced to explain dreams. Dreams involve uncontrolled sensory activation, mainly in the visual and auditory domains. The activation of occipitotemporal (sensory) cortices and deactivation

Figure 19.1

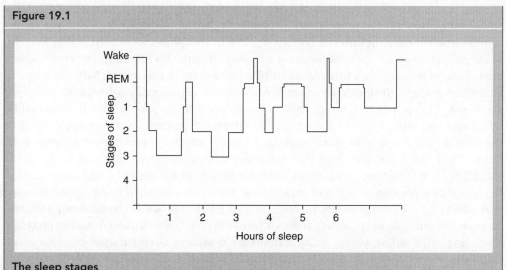

The sleep stages
This graph shows a standard nocturnal sleep recording, with several cycles of sleep of increasing (stages 1–3/4) and decreasing depth and increasing length of REM phases towards the morning.

of prefrontal cortex might explain such a phenomenology (Dang-Vu et al., 2007). A related area of research concerns the changes in dreams after focal lesions. Some reports suggest modality-specific decreases in phenomenal experience after lesions to sensory cortices. Because of the great importance of dreams in the theory and practice of psychoanalysis, this topic has attracted the interest of the emerging field of neuropsychoanalysis (Solms, 2011).

19.1 DEFINITION, CLINICAL ASPECTS AND EPIDEMIOLOGY

Patients with mental disorders often complain of disturbed sleep. The main reason that sleep disturbance does not feature more prominently in the diagnostic criteria is that it is not specific to any of the classical mental disorders, but it would be rare to find a patient with depression, for example, who is not intermittently or constantly suffering from sleep problems. The Hamilton Rating Scale for Depression, a common instrument for the assessment of severity of depression, for example, puts great weight on difficulty falling asleep, sleeping through, or early morning waking (early, middle and late insomnia). Many patients with mental and neurological disorders also suffer from sleep problems as a consequence of psychotropic medication. For example, many tricyclic antidepressants and antipsychotics have sedating effects, mainly through histamine antagonism, and can lead to excessive sleepiness. Sleep disruption is also a common side effect, for example, of antidepressants from all classes except mirtazapine and trazodone, antipsychotics, particularly aripiprazole, levodopa or beta-blockers. Disturbed sleep is also a common problem in substance abuse and can be the consequence of another medical condition.

The primary sleep disorders can be divided into dyssomnias (abnormal sleep) and parasomnias (abnormal behaviour associated with sleep). The dyssomnias include conditions with excessive (primary hypersomnia, Kleine-Levin syndrome, narcolepsy), diminished (primary insomnia) and disrupted (breathing-related and circadian rhythm sleep disorder) sleep. Reliable prevalence estimates are difficult to obtain. On the one hand many people complain of sleep problems without fulfilling the full diagnostic criteria of sleep disorder, which leads to overestimation; on the other, many people with clinical insomnia, hypersomnia or disturbed circadian sleep rhythm will take a long time to seek professional help, if they ever do. These problems explain the wide ranges of available estimates for lifetime prevalences, which are 1–10% for primary insomnia and up to 16% for primary hypersomnia. Both often have a chronic course, and the incidence of insomnia increases considerably with age. Kleine-Levin syndrome (KLS) is a rare recurrent hypersomnia, which is associated with hypersexuality, overeating and other forms of behavioural disinhibition. Its onset is in late adolescence or the third decade and it is often self-limiting. Males are affected three times more often than females, but KLS is not associated with increased testosterone levels (Schenck et al., 2007). Narcolepsy is a syndrome of excessive daytime sleepiness (particularly intrusions of REM sleep) and cataplexy (sudden loss of muscle tone, sometimes triggered by emotional arousal) that affects 0.5% of the population. Patients with narcolepsy show characteristic EEG features on the multiple sleep latency test. Nocturnal sleep is often disrupted, and hypnagogic (occurring while falling asleep) hallucinations are common. Sleep paralysis can also occur. Breathing-related sleep disorder (obstructive sleep apnoea, OAS) affects 1–10% of the adult population. Its incidence increases with age and body weight, and abnormal movements of the upper airways can often be documented. Circadian rhythm sleep disorder, inability to sleep during conventional times, affects up to 4% of the population with higher rates in adolescents and shift workers. The delayed sleep phase-type is most common and leads to daytime sleepiness unless the patients can adjust their life in a way that allows them to sleep from the early morning until noon (Panossian and Avidan, 2009).

The arousal type of parasomnias includes sleep terror disorder and sleepwalking disorder. Both are particularly common in children. Sleep terrors with autonomic arousal and panic occur always or often in 3% of children and sometimes in up to 15% (adults: less than 1%). Up to one-third of children have one episode of sleepwalking, and 1–3% sleepwalk regularly (adults: less than 0.5%). A common genetic factor for abnormal arousal during deep sleep has been suspected to underlie both disorders. Nightmare Disorder may be even more common than sleep terror disorder (especially in adults) and affects mainly REM sleep.

Enuresis (bed wetting) is another typical childhood parasomnia. It is not normally diagnosed before age 5, but then affects up to 8% of children regularly (adults: below 0.1%). It is strongly associated with ADHD. Conversely, REM sleep behaviour disorder (RBD) mainly affects men over 50 with a prevalence of 0.5%. Although normally REM sleep is associated with loss of skeletal muscle tone (see Box 19.1), this muscle atonia is lost and patients engage in complex motor activity, often apparently responding to the content of their dreams ('dream enactment'). Both REM sleep without atonia, which can be identified by the EMG trace on polysomnography, and dream enactment behaviour need to be present for a diagnosis to be made, but dream enactment is not specific for RBD and can also occur in other parasomnias, OSA, PTSD or substance abuse (Boeve et al., 2007). Nocturnal bruxism (teeth grinding or clenching) affects about 5% of children regularly. It is less common in adults, but can also be associated with a variety of brain lesions affecting cortex, basal ganglia and brainstem. Restless legs syndrome (RLS) is conventionally classified as a (neurological) movement disorder, but shares features with the parasomnias. The mainstay of RLS is an urge to move the legs, particularly during rest and at night, which can be triggered by unpleasant sensations and is relieved by movement.

The heritability estimates for the parasomnias range from 0.45 (nightmares) to 0.7 (enuresis). Enuresis has a positive family history in two-thirds of cases. Various modes of transmission have been discussed, but autosomal dominant transmission with high penetrance is the most likely (Hublin and Kaprio, 2003). However, sleepwalking (and the less severe form, sleep-talking) and enuresis are very common, affecting one-quarter or more of children, and can almost be considered normal features of development. Treatment would normally be sought only in severe or persistent cases. At the other extreme, sleepwalking or RBD may become forensically relevant where patients engage in sexually inappropriate or violent behaviour.

19.2   BIOLOGY OF SLEEP DISORDERS

19.2.1   Insomnia

Functional neuroimaging provides preliminary evidence for increased global glucose metabolism during non-REM sleep in primary insomnia, which would be compatible with theories linking insomnia to hyperarousal. In general, however, direct evidence for biological changes in patients with insomnia has been scarce and most biological theories are based on pharmacological effects on sleep (Table 19.1) and animal models. Because sleep is easily disrupted by pharmacological agents or environmental stimuli, a wide variety of animal models of sleep disruption is available. These can be used to test sleep-promoting effects of drugs (predictive validity), but not all have good face validity. Agonists of all of the arousing systems listed in Table 19.1 have been used in animal models of sleep disruption. Environmental stimuli commonly used to disrupt sleep include foot electroshocks, acoustic noise and changes of ambient temperature. Another common procedure for sleep deprivation used in rodents involves the use of a water tank where animals sleep on a platform or elevated grid and wake up during REM sleep because the atonia makes them touch the water. Such models can be used to assess physiological and behavioural consequences of sleep deprivation. For example, after such periods of disturbed sleep, rats will experience prolonged insomnia with stereotyped behaviour and aggressiveness. These models are mainly used for their predictive validity but have poor face validity for human primary insomnia because there the lack of sleep is not normally caused by the disrupting effects of external stimuli.

A particular problem in the design of animal models of sleep disorders is that general sleep patterns are very different across species. For example, the circadian sleeping pattern of humans is monophasic (that is, humans normally have one epoch of sleep per day) whereas it is polyphasic (multiple sleep/wave cycles per day) in rodents and cats. Furthermore many of the commonly used animals (e.g. rats and cats) are nocturnal and thus cannot model the arousing effect of daylight on humans. In addition to the methods for direct interference with sleep described above, insomnia can be induced in animals by stress (both conditioned and unconditioned stressors). Transferring rodents to a cage that still bears the vestiges of another conspecific ('cage exchange') appears to be a particularly strong unconditioned stressor, and rodents will initially not sleep in such an environment. This scenario may model the frequently observed problem humans have with sleeping in a new environment during the first few nights. Models that use pre- or postnatal (separation from the mother) stress may have even higher face and construct validity. These rats have disrupted sleep during their normal (daytime) rest period, which has been compared to the nocturnal hyperarousal of human insomnia. It has been proposed that the neonatal stress influences sleep patterns through the orexin system (Revel et al., 2009).

Because of the frequent co-occurrence of sleep problems and depression, animal models of depression that also show sleep disturbance (or animal models of sleep disorder displaying

Table 19.1 Pharmacology of sleep.

	Pharmacological mechanisms/pathways	Specific effects
(a) Substances with sedating effects		
GABA, galanin	Ventrolateral preoptic nucleus (VLPO) (see also Chapter 1)	
GHRH	Anterior hypothalamus/medial preoptic region	Promotes NREM sleep
Adenosine	Basal forebrain	
Melatonin	Pineal gland	
Prostaglandin D2		
(b) Substances with arousing effects		
Caffeine	Adenosine receptor antagonist	Increases latency to sleep onset and reduces sleep pressure
Acetylcholine	Basal forebrain; Pedunculopontine tegmentum/Laterodorsal Tegmentum	
Serotonin	Raphe nuclei	
Norepinephrine	Locus coeruleus	
Histamine	Tuberomammillary nucleus/Posterior hypothalamus	
Dopamine and psychostimulants	Ventral Periaqueductal Grey Matter (vPAG)	D_2-stimulation in basal ganglia may have opposite (sleep-promoting) effect (Vetrivelan et al., 2010)
Prostaglandin E2		
Orexins	Lateral hypothalamus, perifornical region	
Neuropeptide S	Cortex, hypothalamus, amygdala, thalamus	
Glutamate	Ascending Reticular Activating System (ARAS)	Promotes both wakefulness and REM sleep

behavioural features of depression) would be of particular interest. Chronic mild stress has been used to induce depression in rodent models, and these animals also have fragmented sleep and shifts from NREM to REM sleep, similar to patients with depression. More intense stress can induce full-blown insomnia. The link between stress and sleep disturbance seems to be mediated through the HPA axis; for example, CRF blocks the cytokine interleukin 1 (IL-1), which promotes NREM sleep.

19.2.2   Hypersomnia

Very little is known about the biological changes underlying primary hypersomnia. Dysregulation of the hypothalamus has been proposed on the basis of its central role for the sleep 'on/off' switch. However, structural brain scans of KLS patients (and patients with primary hypersomnia) are normal. There is some suggestion that the pathology underlying KLS is an autoimmune process (a disproportionately high number of patients have the human leukocyte antigen [HLA] subtype DQB1–201), but even if this is the case, it is unlikely to explain most cases of primary hypersomnia.

An autoimmune link has also been proposed for narcolepsy because of the high occurrence of HLA subtype DQ1B*0602. However, structural imaging and neuropathology have not yielded consistent findings of brain changes, although pathophysiological models have implicated the pontine tegmentum because of its role in the control of sleep states (Dang-Vu et al., 2007). The best replicated findings come from the histochemistry of the lateral hypothalamus, where loss of orexin-expressing neurons was reported both in human narcolepsy and in a dog model. Reduced CSF orexin-1 levels have also been reported, mainly in narcolepsy with cataplexy (Panossian and Avidan, 2009). Functional imaging has shown hypoperfusion in the bilateral anterior hypothalami, basal ganglia, limbic system and frontal regions, but it is not yet clear how these findings might be integrated into models of the disease. The most widely used animal models currently in use for narcolepsy are based on knock-outs of orexin or its receptors.

19.2.3   Changes in circadian sleep pattern

Circadian rhythm disorder (CRD) has a strong environmental component, with work patterns and psychosocial factors playing an important role. The biological mediators are poorly understood. Animals with lesions to the SCN may model some aspects of CRD because they have a disrupted circadian pattern of sleep but no change in overall sleeping time. The role of clock genes in disturbed circadian rhythm and other sleep disorders is currently actively researched, and G×E interactions may be of particular relevance here.

19.3   PARASOMNIAS

The biological investigation of the parasomnias is similar to that of the dyssomnias in that very little has been gleaned from the direct investigation of patients affected with the DSM-IV disorders. The parasomnias with dominant electrophysiological features, notably RBD, can be modelled well in animals. Other hints to potential neurobiological mechanisms may come from epilepsy. Many features of parasomnias also occur during epileptic seizures, including oral automatisms such as bruxism, uncontrolled motor activity such as wanderings and leg movements, fear and violent behaviour (Tassinari et al., 2009). However, like the brain lesions leading to parasomnia-like behaviour, the localisation of the epileptic foci has not permitted identification of anatomically constant generators.

Neuropsychiatry may provide interesting insights into the mechanisms of RBD, which is associated with Parkinson's disease. RBD may be associated with hypodopaminergic pathology even in non-PD cases because radionuclide imaging has shown signs of reduced dopaminergic neuron numbers (lower DAT and VMAT binding) in the striatum. RBD is associated with other neurodegenerative disorders as well, for example multi-system atrophy (MSA) or

Lewy Body disease (LBD), which all belong to the synucleinopathies (see Chapter 20). RBD mainly affects men over 50, who are vulnerable to cerebrovascular changes, which are thus frequently observed in this parasomnia. Here again, the pattern of localisation has not been consistent, but there is some evidence for an association with lesions to the pedunculopontine nucleus and laterodorsal tegmental nucleus, which contain key sleep-regulating circuits. Interestingly, RBD can co-occur with narcolepsy, which is characterised by increasing REM sleep intrusions in some inflammatory brain disorders (Boeve et al., 2007).

Animal models have contributed to our understanding of the interplay of brainstem circuits that can lead to REM sleep without atonia (RSWA). One of the functions of the magnocellular reticular formation (MCRF) is to send inhibitory pulses to spinal motor neurons. The MCRF is stimulated during normal REM sleep by 'REM-on' cells in the locus coeruleus complex (subcoeruleus in the cat or sublaterodorsal [SLD] nucleus in the rat). SLD nucleus lesions result in increased tonic EMG activity during REM sleep, either because of weaker MCRF activity or because of lack of direct inhibitory inputs from the SLD nucleus to spinal motor neurons (Boeve et al., 2007).

19.4   TREATMENT OF SLEEP DISORDERS

19.4.1   'Z-hypnotics' have a similar mechanism of action to benzodiazepines

Benzodiazepines such as diazepam (Valium®) and the non-benzodiazepine 'z'-hypnotics zolpidem, zopiclone and zaleplon are the main sleep-inducing drugs in psychiatric use. They are all agonists at the benzodiazepine binding site on the $GABA_A$ receptor, which is located between alpha and gamma subunits. The effect of the z-hypnotics may be more specific for $GABA_A$ receptors with an alpha-1 subunit, which may explain their selective hypnotic effects (they have little, if any, anxiolytic effect). However, unlike benzodiazepines, they do not seem to lead to altered sensitivity of the $GABA_A$ receptor after chronic treatment. This may explain a lower addictive potential, although there is as yet insufficient evidence from long-term use to be certain about this. The z-hypnotics have a low half life (under five hours) and no or only weakly active metabolites. They are therefore particularly suited for the treatment of early insomnia and carry less risk of hangover than benzodiazepines.

19.4.2   Melatonin regulates circadian rhythms

Melatonin (N-acetyl-5-methoxytryptamine) is produced from its precursor serotonin (5-hydroxytryptamine) in the pineal gland and released particularly during the night. It activates the metabotropic melatonin (MT) receptor. For sleep–wake regulation, the MT_1 receptor in the SCN is particularly relevant. Exogenous melatonin reduces sleep latencies and may be effective in disorders of sleep rhythm, for example jet lag. Melatonin is hepatically eliminated and should therefore not be used in patients with severe liver dysfunction. Caution needs to be taken in patients with intolerance to lactose because this is used as carrier substance. Otherwise side effects seem to be rare, but further clinical experience with long-term use is needed before its effectiveness can be evaluated fully.

Agomelatine is another agonist at the melatonin receptor. It is also a $5\text{-}HT_{2C}$-receptor antagonist. Because activation of this receptor on dopaminergic or noradrenergic neurons blocks catecholamine release, agomelatine is an indirect catecholaminergic agonist. Agomelatine is used as an antidepressant. It has no anticholinergic properties and therefore a better side-effect profile than the TCA. It also does not seem to lead to sexual dysfunction. While the antidepressant effects are probably mediated by the catecholamine release, the added melatonergic effect makes agomelatine effective for the treatment of sleep problems in depression without causing daytime sedation.

19.4.3 Treatment in practice

The treatment of primary insomnia is based on the three elements of sleep hygiene, CBT and pharmacological intervention. Pharmacotherapy should mainly be considered as short-term relief. The long-term use of hypnotics is indicated only in severe cases and where psychological interventions have failed. They are not considered to be a causal treatment of insomnia. The main yardstick for treatment success is the well-being of the patient, but several objective parameters can also be monitored, including the time it takes to fall asleep, number of awakenings during the night and the total sleep time (TST). For the pharmacological management of insomnia a detailed sleep history is important because drugs vary widely in their half life and therefore differ in their effects on sleep initiation and maintenance.

Next to the benzodiazepine and the newer Z-hypnotics, antidepressants are probably the most widely used group of prescription drugs. The tricyclic trazodone has been classically used for this indication, but very low doses of doxepine (6 mg or less per day compared to the 75–300 mg used for depression) may have an even better side effect/benefit ratio. At low doses, doxepine is a relatively selective histamine H_1 antagonist, which is the main mechanism presumed to underlie the sedating effect of antidepressants. Traditional antihistamine drugs like diphenhydramine may be less appropriate because of quickly developing tolerance and daytime drowsiness. Antipsychotics (e.g. quetiapine, olanzapine) and anticonvulsants (e.g. gabapentin) are also used for their sedating effects. A completely different mechanism would be addressed by orexin receptor antagonists, which are currently in clinical tests (Sullivan, 2010).

RLS responds well to dopamine agonists like pramipexole (an agonist at the DRD2,3,4 receptors). It is still unclear whether this addresses a primary dopamine deficit because molecular imaging studies have been inconsistent. Lack of iron, which is an important co-factor for tyrosine hydroxylase, has also been implicated in RLS.

Dopaminergic drugs such as the psychostimulants have also traditionally been used to treat the excessive daytime sleepiness of narcolepsy. The current treatment of choice, though, is modafinil. Although this substance is classified as a stimulant, its main effect may not be through the dopamine system. Modafinil also increases histamine levels and may increase orexin levels. However, its effect is partly orexin-independent, because it is also found in orexin knock-out mice. Cataplexy can be controlled to some degree through tricyclic or SSRI/SNRI antidepressants. The short-acting hypnotic GHB may be effective for both aspects of narcolepsy. All these options are symptomatic and probably not causal. However, a potentially causal therapy with orexin replacement would still need to be investigated.

Circadian rhythm disorders are difficult to treat. The main pharmacological agent is melatonin, which has some benefit for jet lag. Behavioural (chronotherapy – incremental delay of sleep onset) and physical (light therapy in the morning) therapies are also in use (Panossian and Avidan, 2009).

The standard treatment of RBD uses the benzodiazepine clonazepam. Dopaminergic drugs can also improve symptoms, but this effect is possibly due to suppression of REM sleep. Both activating (caffeine) and sedating (mirtazapine) substances can worsen symptoms of RBD, which underlines the complex interplay of sleep- and muscle tone-regulating circuits implicated in its pathophysiology.

Learning points

Disturbed sleep is a common complaint with many mental disorders, particularly depression. Secondary sleep disturbance and primary insomnia are treated with similar approaches, which include behavioural measures (e.g. sleep hygiene) and CBT in the first instance. These can be supplemented in severe cases by pharmacological approaches, including benzodiazepines, antidepressants and antihistamines. Although sleep can be modelled well in animal studies and comparisons with electrophysiological correlates of sleep phases are possible, the mechanisms of primary insomnia are still poorly understood. Amongst the hypersomnias, narcolepsy, which is treated with the stimulant modafinil, has been associated with deficits in the hypothalamic orexin/hypocretin system. Parasomnias share phenotypic features with epilepsy and are often characterised by disturbance of specific sleep phases, as in REM sleep behavioural disorder, which is treated with the benzodiazepine clonazepam. Both primary insomnias and sleep disturbance associated with mental disorders are major public health problems, and more research into the psychological, physiological and neurochemical mechanisms is needed with a view to designing more effective therapies.

Revision and discussion questions

- What are the characteristic features of dyssomnias and parasomnias?
- Discuss the clinical relevance of the different sleep phases.
- What can the sleep disturbances of neuropsychiatric disorders tell us about the biology of sleep?

FURTHER READING

Espie, C. A. (2002). Insomnia: Conceptual issues in the development, persistence, and treatment of sleep disorder in adults. *Annual Review of Psychology*, 53, 215–43.

Wilson, S. J., Nutt, D. J., Alford, C., Argyropoulos, S. V., Baldwin, D. S., Bateson, A. N. et al. (2010). British Association for Psychopharmacology consensus statement on evidence-based treatment of insomnia, parasomnias and circadian rhythm disorders. *Journal of Psychopharmacology*, 24, 1577–1601.

20 | AGEING AND DEMENTIA

PREVIEW

This chapter starts with a brief overview of psychological and neurobiological changes of normal ageing and then reviews the epidemiology, neuropsychology, biology and treatment of the different dementias, which are predominantly disorders of older age. The sections follow the standard subdivision into clinically, causally and/or neuropathologically defined syndromes (Alzheimer's disease, frontotemporal dementia, Parkinson plus syndromes, Creutzfeldt-Jakob disease, Lewy Body dementia, vascular dementia, normal pressure hydrocephalus and traumatic dementia). However, the chapter also touches on the recent molecular classification into amyloidopathies, tauopathies, synucleinopathies, prionopathies and ubiquinopathies, which runs partly orthogonal to the clinical syndromes.

20.1   SOME FACETS OF THE PSYCHOLOGY OF AGEING

Ageing is a lifelong process. Humans reach a state of physical, cognitive and neural maturation during their second decade (normally between 15 and 20 years of age), but physical fitness and some cognitive functions already start deteriorating in the fourth decade of life. Cognitive functions that decline naturally with age include psychomotor and cognitive speed, working memory, cognitive control (particularly inhibition) and flexibility, and the encoding of new material into long-term memory. Conversely, language functions and knowledge (retrieval of semantic information from long-term memory) are preserved and wisdom, a somewhat elusive function that combines knowledge and instinctive judgements based on lifetime experience, may even increase as people grow older. Considering the slower pace of most people's life after they retire from their job or other duties, these subtle cognitive impairments, which show up more on psychometric testing than in everyday tasks, may not be very functionally relevant. Personality and metacognitive changes have also been documented with ageing, especially a tendency to increased rigidity of thought and behavioural patterns. Emotional biases in perception and cognitive may also change, but evidence is inconsistent, and preferences for both positive and negative material have been reported. There is an increased tendency to dysthymia and reactive depression during older age as a consequence of the inevitable loss of partners or close friends, but generally no evidence for lower mood with advancing age.

20.2   NEUROBIOLOGY OF AGEING

Ageing, and ultimately death of cells and organisms, is a fundamental property of living beings, and the subject of intensive biological investigation at molecular, cellular and systems levels. The molecular mechanisms of ageing and cell death go beyond the scope of this book, but we will encounter some of them in the context of the processes leading to dementia. Whether dementia is a reflection of accelerated ageing of the brain, or a qualitatively separate process, is still a main conundrum of biological ageing research. Ageing can affect any part of the brain, although primary sensory and motor areas were relatively less affected in most studies. Volume loss in the basal ganglia, cerebellum, hippocampus and prefrontal cortex can start as early as the fourth or fifth decade, with some acceleration with advancing age. However, these changes correlate only modestly, if at all, with cognitive decline. White matter changes, which mainly consist in shrinkage and hyperintensities on MRI that likely reflect small ischaemic lesions, and particularly reduction of dopamine receptors may be more relevant to cognition (Park and Reuter-Lorenz, 2009). The quality and quantity of connections between cortical areas and input from subcortical systems may thus be more relevant than mere brain volume, at least up to a certain point.

20.3 DEFINITION AND SUBTYPES OF DEMENTIA

Dementia is a clinical syndrome leading to social or occupational dysfunction that is defined by the DSM-IV based on memory impairment and the presence of another neuropsychological deficit (aphasia, apraxia, agnosia or executive dysfunction). In contrast to developmental disorders the impairment constitutes a decline from a previously higher level of functioning. Importantly, the DSM-IV and the ICD-10, which has a very similar definition, do not make any assumptions about the underlying pathophysiology. Thus, dementia can be the result of a wide range of brain disorders. Reversible causes of dementia include normal pressure hydrocephalus, electrolyte imbalance, brain tumours, anaemia and metabolic encephalopathy. Of the irreversible or only partly reversible causes, some are degenerative. The main degenerative causes are (in decreasing order of prevalence) Alzheimer's disease (AD), Frontotemporal dementia (FTD) spectrum, Parkinson's disease, dementia with Lewy Bodies (DLB), Huntington's disease and Creutzfeldt-Jakob disease (CJD) and the other prionopathies. Non-degenerative causes include chronic intoxication with alcohol and other substances, chronic brain trauma (e.g. the dementia pugilistica of boxers), CNS infections (syphilis, AIDS encephalopathy), postencephalitic dementia (e.g. measles), chronic brain inflammation (e.g. multiple sclerosis) and vascular encephalopathy. This chapter includes the main (AD, FTD) and some of the rarer neurodegenerative conditions (DLB, CJD), vascular dementia (VD), normal pressure hydrocephalus (NPH) and dementia pugilistica. The other conditions, where dementia is normally preceded by other neurological or neuropsychiatric symptoms or syndromes, will be discussed in Chapter 21.

20.4 ALZHEIMER'S DISEASE

20.4.1 Epidemiology

AD is the most common form of dementia in the elderly. AD alone or combined with VD accounts for 75% of dementia cases. Its prevalence increases with increasing age, from 1% in the 60–65 age group to 40% in the over 85 age group. AD was first described by the German psychiatrist and neuropathologist Alois Alzheimer (1864–1915) in 1905. Alzheimer already noted the characteristic histopathological features, the extracellular plaques and intracellular neurofibrillary tangles. We now know that the plaques are accumulations of beta-amyloid protein, and the tangles of tau protein. Post-mortem studies sampling different stages of the disease have revealed a progressive loss of neurons in the basal nucleus of Meynert, entorhinal cortex and hippocampus, followed by association areas of the neocortex. Primary sensory and motor areas are affected last, except in the posterior cortical atrophy form, where occipital and posterior parietal areas degenerate early, leading to visual and visuo-spatial dysfunction.

20.4.2 Neuropsychology

Alzheimer's first patient, Auguste Deter (or Auguste D as she became known in the medical literature), already showed an advanced pattern of cognitive decline when he admitted her aged 51 to the Frankfurt asylum in 1901:

> She sits on the bed with a helpless expression. What is your name? *Auguste*. Last name? *Auguste*. What is your husband's name? *Auguste, I think*. Your husband? *Ah, my husband*. She looks as if she didn't understand the question (extract from the records with the patient's answers in italics, translated by Maurer et al. (1997))

The patient thus remembered only the most basic autobiographical fact, her given name, but not for example her married name. She had also lost orientation to time and had severe difficulty comprehending. She correctly named objects (and even recognised them with closed eyes) but then did not remember that she had just seen them. She had global aphasia, but partially preserved semantic knowledge (e.g. the colour of snow, the sky etc.). As part of his detailed assessment spanning several days, Alzheimer asked her to write her name and brief sentences, but she could do it only when she was reminded of every single word, which he classified as 'amnestic writing disorder'. He also noticed another striking feature about her writing; she used only the left half of the paper, as if she had 'a loss in the right visual field'. Auguste D also suffered from paranoia and auditory hallucinations and had behaved inappropriately and unpredictably, which had triggered her admission.

This first documented case of AD shows many of its characteristic neuropsychological features. Declarative memory is affected first, and semantic knowledge is often better preserved than autobiographical information. The latter tends to be lost with a temporal gradient, with information that was encoded earlier (e.g. during childhood) being preserved until later stages of the disease. There is often a profound short-term memory deficit at relatively early stages as well. Language problems arise at variable stages, but visuo-spatial problems, such as the hemineglect in the case of Auguste D, often arise early. These can be tested at the bedside with the 'clock test'. Once a patient has become unable to read the clock he/she has normally passed the watershed towards needing long-term care. This may be about the same time when patients start getting lost even in previously familiar surroundings. Difficulty copying figures and constructional apraxia (inability to handle and assemble objects) are further signs of visuo-spatial impairment. Conversely, visual and tactile recognition may be preserved until later stages, probably because sensory cortices are affected last. Psychotic symptoms and behavioural abnormalities normally start several years into the progression of cognitive decline, but a more dramatic course is possible as well.

20.4.3 Genetics

A small fraction of AD cases (less than 5%) are caused by mutations in the presenilin 1 (on chromosome 14) or 2 (chr. 1) or the amyloid precursor protein gene (chr. 21) and dominantly inherited. The remaining 'sporadic' cases have no clear mode of inheritance, but genetic factors seem to contribute to the risk. The best replicated genetic risk factor is the epsilon 4 allele of the apolipoprotein E (APOE) gene on chromosome 19. A variant in the apolipoprotein J (APOJ) gene on chromosome 14 (Harold et al., 2009) and other variants involved in cholesterol metabolism and immune responses (Jones et al., 2010) have also recently been implicated by GWAS. Having two epsilon 4 alleles increases the risk of developing AD by the factor 10 to 30. Apolipoproteins are crucial for the transport of lipids in the bloodstream, and less efficient isoforms (such as that coded by the epsilon 4 allele) may lead to less efficient transport and lipid accumulation in tissue. However, there is presently no strong evidence for changes in lipid metabolism associated with the epsilon 4 variant, and thus the mechanism by which this risk factor exerts its effect is still unknown. Furthermore, only 1–2% of the population are homozygous for the epsilon 4 allele, and over a third of AD patients carry no epsilon 4 allele. Thus, other risk factors need to be explored as well. Environmental risk factors seem to be same as for cerebrovascular disease (smoking, diabetes mellitus, high blood pressure, high cholesterol). Education might have a protective effect on disease onset and progression ('cognitive reserve hypothesis').

20.4.4 Neuroimaging

Once a clinical diagnosis of dementia has been established on the basis of history, examination and neuropsychological testing, the search for the cause is the next important step. Potentially reversible causes may be picked up by a full medical work-up including electrolyte, vitamin B12 and folate levels, a full blood count, and liver and kidney function tests. Neuroimaging is important to rule out space-occupying lesions, and where inflammatory processes are suspected, a CSF examination may be needed as well as blood tests for the relevant antigens or antibodies. EEGs may help identify some rare pathologies such as CJD. In most cases, however, no reversible cause will be found, and a neurodegenerative and/or cerebrovascular process will be most likely.

It is often not straightforward to establish the exact type of dementia based on diagnostic tests. Although hippocampal volume loss discriminates well between AD patients and age-matched healthy controls, the differences are less clear cut between AD and other types of dementia because these, too, can be associated with shrinkage of the medial temporal lobe. Functional imaging is more sensitive to the differences between the dementias because glucose metabolism, which can be measured with fluorodeoxyglucose PET, is affected in a regionally specific manner (Figure 20.1, Plate VII). Temporoparietal hypometabolism in AD can be contrasted with frontotemporal hypometabolism in FTD and a more diffuse pattern in VD. These metabolic changes match the progression of cortical volume loss and ensuing loss of neural activity.

PET can also be used to probe the pathophysiology of AD more specifically. For example, it can show the distribution of activated microglia, which is an indicator of local inflammatory processes involved in the neurodegeneration of AD. Although it is still unclear whether the activation of microglia, which essentially removes damaged neurons, is primary or merely a response to another process that leads to cell death, this PET technique is capable of identifying areas of progressive volume loss. Even more directly related to AD pathology, PET with a tracer called 'Pittsburgh compound B' (PIB) can detect accumulation of amyloid beta.

Changes in regional brain activity can also be probed by functional activation imaging, where patients perform a task while their blood flow (classically with PET using water with a radioactive oxygen atom as tracer) or oxygenation (with fMRI) is measured (Prvulovic et al., 2005). fMRI is more suited to longitudinal studies and studies of healthy ageing because it does not involve any radiotracers. These studies found that often patients at the early stages of AD have higher activation functionally relevant areas during task execution than controls. Similar observations were made comparing older and younger healthy individuals, and people with mild cognitive impairment (MCI) and controls. It can be interpreted as a mobilisation of cognitive resources in the face of increasing difficulty performing cognitive tasks. Once this reserve capacity is lost, patients may lose their ability sufficiently to recruit neural assemblies and consequently show a marked cognitive decline. These studies as well as purely clinical considerations reinforce the need to detect the precursors of dementia early with a view to potential early intervention and prevention.

20.4.5   Neurochemistry and neuropathology

The neuropathology of AD is characterised by the typical accumulation of beta-amyloid peptides in the intracellular space (plaques) and of tau protein inside neurons (neurofibrillary tangles, NFT) (Figure 20.2, Plate VII). Beta-amyloid or A-beta peptides are 40–42 amino acid long fragments of amyloid precursor protein (APP). The extracellular part of this transmembrane protein is cleaved by alpha- or beta-secretase, resulting in alpha- or beta-APP. The transmembrane residues can be cleaved further by gamma-secretase, and the longer residue that remains after beta-APP is split off then yields A-beta (Figure 20.3). This 'amyloidogenic'

Figure 20.3

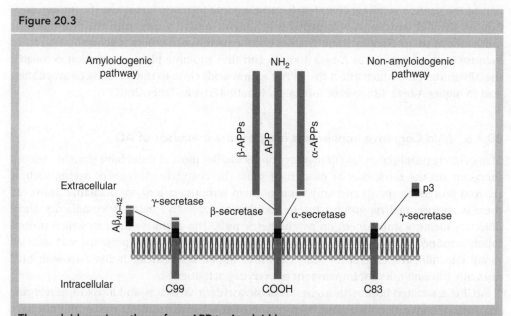

The amyloidogenic pathway from APP to Amyloid-beta

Amyloid precursor protein (APP) is cleaved by alpha- or beta-secretase, resulting in alpha- or beta-APP. The transmembrane residues can be cleaved further by gamma-secretase. In the non-amyloidogenic pathway, this results in protein p3, whereas in the amyloidogenic pathway, initiated by beta-secretase, this results in the 40–42 amino acid long A-beta fragments.

pathway is the target of multiple experimental therapeutic interventions (Masters et al., 2006), but exactly how accumulation of A-beta leads to cell death is still unknown. A-beta accumulation may not even be the primary pathogenetic mechanism, but rather a response to other mechanisms of neuronal damage, for example oxidative stress. Evidence for a primary amyloidosis that is at the heart of the pathophysiology of AD is best for the early onset familial cases (Swerdlow, 2007).

The intracellular tau protein is part of the cytoskeleton and in its phosphorylated form stabilises microtubules. The hyperphosphorylated form encountered in AD reacts with other tau protein rather than the microtubules and forms tangles, resulting in decay of the intracellular support structure. The crucial role of NFT in the pathology of AD is underlined by the correlation of cognitive decline with NFT load.

A-beta peptides and phospho-tau-protein can be measured in CSF. Decreased A-beta 42 levels, which may reflect the accumulation of this peptide in brain, and increased phospho-tau-protein have been found most reliably (Portelius et al., 2010). No single neurochemical test as yet has the quality of a biomarker, but combinations of neurochemical parameters hold some promise for an improved early diagnosis of AD (Hampel et al., 2009, 2010). The final validation of any putative biomarker of AD would still have to be against the detection of AD-typical histological changes on post-mortem brain examinations, but few research centres have the resources to conduct them routinely. Improved, and ideally non-invasive, biomarkers are also important for the early detection of MCI patients at high risk of conversion to AD, with a view to possible early treatment with anti-dementia agents.

The pathway from APP and A-beta can also explain the mechanisms by which the mutations in the APP and presenilin genes effect neuropathological changes. The presenilins form part of the gamma-secretase complex. Because gamma-secretase is not specific for any position on the APP residue, A-beta peptides at variable length result from the cleavage. The mutations in the presenilin 1 and 2 genes encode protein variants that generally lead to an increase in the A-beta 42 to A-beta 40 ratio and thus promote plaque formation. Similarly, the APP mutations, which affect the APP at amino acids close to the secretase cleavage sites, lead to higher A-beta 42 levels or A-beta 42/40 ratio (Ertekin-Taner, 2007).

20.4.6   Mild Cognitive Impairment is a possible precursor of AD

Many elderly people complain of memory problems, but most of them have normal memory functions (in the sense that at most they show the cognitive changes of ageing such as reduced processing speed) and only some of them fulfil the criteria for dementia. However, there is an intermediate group who, in addition to subjective memory complaints, show objective memory impairment on psychometric tests. The cognitive decline, which is commonly confined to the memory domain, is gradual and needs to be present for at least six months to fulfil the criteria for Mild Cognitive Impairment (MCI). Individuals with MCI normally have no relevant impairment of everyday activities.

MCI is associated both with higher rates of vascular risk factors and a risk of developing AD. Annual conversion rates have been estimated at 10–15%, but most studies did not have sufficiently long follow-up periods to determine whether all individuals with MCI will eventually develop AD. All the biomarkers discussed for AD are under investigation as potential biomarkers of MCI and/or conversion risk, including CSF A-beta and phospho-tau, ApoE genotype, homocysteine and lipid levels in blood, hippocampal volume on MRI and brain metabolism patterns measured with PET and SPECT. However, although several studies have shown differences in MCI compared to normal ageing on both structural and functional imaging, this research has not yet produced biomarkers that can predict conversion from MCI to AD with sufficient sensitivity and specificity.

20.4.7 Treatment

20.4.7.1 Acetylcholine-Esterase-Inhibitors (AChEI) combat the cholinergic deficit in Alzheimer's disease

Loss of cholinergic neurons in the basal forebrain is one of the pathological hallmarks of AD. Inhibition of the AChE, the main acetylcholine-degrading enzyme, increases synaptic acetylcholine levels and may partly remediate the loss of cholinergic innervation. The three AChEI in clinical use for AD and other dementias are donepezil, rivastigmine and galantamine. Donepezil and galantamine are reversible AChEI. Rivastigmine is a pseudo-irreversible inhibitor of AChEI (the chemical modification induced by rivastigmine is automatically reversed within a few hours) and its sister enzyme, butyrylcholine esterase (BChE). Galantamine is also a positive allosteric modulator of presynaptic nicotinic AChR, particularly those with α4 or α7 subunits.

Because α4 and α7 subunits are common in brain nAChR, galantamine has added central cholinergic effects through its effects on these receptors. BChE metabolises acetylcholine like AChE but is normally about ten times less abundant in the brain, and further away from the synapse. However, BChE is increased (and AChE decreased) in AD. The BChE inhibition by rivastigmine may thus have an added benefit, although clinically the effects of all three drugs on cognition tend to be similar (Wilkinson et al., 2004). The clinical effect is best documented in mild to moderate dementia, where the drugs may delay cognitive decline, or even produce temporary improvement of cognitive function. AChEI have been implicated in direct effects on the amyloidogenic pathway, tau phosphorylation and microglia activation, in addition to their cholinergic effects, but this is still speculative at present.

Side effects arise mainly from peripheral cholinergic effects and tend to be strongest for rivastigmine because BChE is abundant outside the brain and generally most severe during the initial phase of treatment. Gastrointestinal side effects, including nausea, vomiting and diarrhoea, are most common. The main cardiac side effect is bradycardia, which necessitates ECG monitoring, and sinoatrial or atrioventricular blocks are occasionally observed as well. Particular caution therefore needs to be applied in the treatment of patients with pre-existing heart conditions. Rarer central cholinergic side effects can include agitation, insomnia, seizures and hallucinations, and overdosing of cholinergic substances can even lead to cholinergic delirium. Generally, however, AChEI are well tolerated. Donepezil and galantamine are metabolised in the liver, and rivastigmine is eliminated through the kidneys.

20.4.7.2 Memantine is an NMDA antagonist with putative neuroprotective effects in AD

The damaged neurons in brains affected by AD are supposed to be particularly vulnerable to excitotoxicity, the apoptotic processes that can be induced by neuronal activation when energy stores do not suffice to maintain the electrolyte balance. Memantine is supposed to curb excitotoxicity by preventing calcium influx through non-competitive blockade of NMDA receptors. Normally, activation of the NMDA-receptor is regulated by the presence of magnesium, which blocks the channel unless the membrane is depolarised. This dual requirement for NMDA-receptor activation – membrane depolarisation in addition to the presence of an agonist such as glutamate – underlies its central role in neural plasticity and long-term poten-tiation (LTP), a major cellular mechanism for learning. However, if a neuron is chronically depolarised because of incipient metabolic damage, the regulatory role of magnesium will be lost and excitotoxicity can result. Because of its non-competitive binding, memantine will have most effects where intrinsic NMDA-receptor activation is highest, and its fast dissociation from the receptor seems to prevent the psychotic side effects seen with competitive NMDA antagonists such as ketamine or PCP (see Chapter 10). Moderate to severe AD can be treated with memantine, alone or in combination with an AChEI (Thomas and Grossberg, 2009), and its seems to have similar effects to AChEI in temporarily improving cognitive symptoms, and has also improved some of the behavioural symptoms associated with the later stages of AD. It has also shown promise in VD. Memantine has relatively few side effects, but should be avoided in patients with renal failure (it is eliminated through the kidneys) or epilepsy.

20.4.7.3   Development of new treatments

The AChEIs are aimed at restoring cholinergic function that is lost as a consequence of cell death, and memantine is supposed to prevent excitotoxicity in already damaged neurons. These pharmacological strategies are therefore symptomatic rather than causal. It would be attractive to tackle the pathophysiological cascade of AD at its root and prevent A-beta from accumulating in the first place. Various strategies, including inhibition of beta- and gamma-secretase and vaccination against A-beta, have been tried in preclinical and clinical studies (Lemere and Masliah, 2010), but because of lacking effect or unacceptable side effects none of these has yet reached the stage of therapeutic use. Reduction of pathological tau proteins is another target of current pharmacological research.

Although lifetime levels of cognitive activity may be protective against or delay the onset of dementia, a beneficial effect of cognitive training after the onset of clinical symptoms has not been shown. Cognitive rehabilitation, which differs from cognitive training in that it helps patients pursue individually selected cognitive or everyday goals rather than train-ing on standardised test batteries, may be more promising and has shown preliminary ben-efits on subjective ratings (Clare et al., 2010). With fMRI it is possible to evaluate the brain changes brought about by such interventions. For example, one can probe whether the train-ing of new cognitive strategies for a task involves the use of hitherto unused neural pathways (Van Paasschen et al., 2009).

There is no specific treatment for MCI. If it is associated with uncontrolled hyperten-sion, antihypertensive treatment may decrease the risk of developing dementia. There is no evidence that specific cognitive intervention or physical exercise programmes are ben-eficial, although general cognitive and physical activity may usefully be promoted as part of a healthy lifestyle. Most current evidence does not suggest a preventive effect of AChEIs (Chertkow et al., 2008), but the lack of biomarkers of conversion to AD has made it difficult to study this issue conclusively because of the low baseline conversion rate. This has trig-gered very active interest in biomarkers of MCI as outlined above (Section 20.4.5).

20.5   FRONTOTEMPORAL DEMENTIA

Frontotemporal dementia (FTD) accounts for approximately 10% of dementia cases. The typical age of onset is somewhat younger that that of AD (between 45 and 65) and degenera-tion affects the frontal and anterior temporal lobes at early stages. This pattern of neuronal loss is also responsible for the different neuropsychological profile, which is characterised by loss of executive functions and language problems early on. Complete frontal lobe syndrome with perseveration and disinhibition sometimes occurs. Memory deficit is present as well, but mainly affects retrieval processes. Conversely, visuo-spatial perception and construction, which are parietal lobe functions that are typically affected early in AD, are relatively preserved. FTD is also distinguished neuropathologically from AD by the much lower plaque load. FTD is part of the group of frontotemporal lobe degeneration (FTLD), which also includes the much rarer syndromes of primary progressive aphasia (PPA) and semantic dementia (SD). Primary progressive aphasia is caused by atrophy of speech production areas in the dominant hemisphere (Broca's area) and presents a non-fluent aphasia with word finding and pronunciation difficulties. SD is the sensory counterpart of PPA, with Wernicke's type of aphasia, where patients are impaired in the understanding of speech and retrieval of meaning of words, but can pronounce them fluently. It is commonly caused by atrophy of the planum temporale in the dominant or both hemispheres.

FTD proper can also have different clinical presentations depending on the site of atrophy. Orbitofrontal and temporal pole atrophy may lead to disinhibited behaviour, dorsomedial and -lateral atrophy to apathy and striatal lesions to stereotypies (Pickering-Brown, 2010). FTD has considerable heritability. About 40% of patients have another affected family member, which is more than in the other common dementias. Some families show an autosomal dominant mode of inheritance. Several FTD genes have been identified on chromosome 17, for example in the progranulin gene (Ahmed et al., 2007), but they explain under 20% of autosomally inherited cases. Patients with amyotrophic lateral sclerosis (ALS), a neurodegenerative disease with progressive loss of motor neurons that results in paralysis, have a higher rate of FTD. Some of the mutations on chromosome 17 that are associated with FTD also lead to Parkinsonism (FTDP-17).

FTD or FTLD is a clinical syndrome that can result from several neuropathological processes. Accumulations of proteins in the cytoplasm and axons of neurons had long been observed, and they were characterised by the presence of ubiquitin, a regulatory protein that binds to other proteins to mark them for degradation. This pathological subtype is therefore classically known as 'FTLD with ubiquitin-positive inclusions'. It has been recognised recently that the main protein contained in these inclusions is the 43kDa long TAR-DNA-binding protein TDP-43. TAR is a region of HIV RNA, to whose DNA equivalent TDP was first found to bind. TDP-43 thus seems to be a transcription factor, but its function in humans is not well understood. However, its accumulation in FTD seems to be an important stage on the path towards neuronal death. After this FTLD-TDP subtype, the next most common histopathology is aggregation of pathological hyperphosphorylated tau proteins in neurons and sometimes glia cells. This type is also called Pick's disease after the Prague psychiatrist Arnold Pick (1851–1924) who first described the ballooned neurons and intracellular protein aggregations (Pick bodies) characteristic of its histopathology. It is now known that these aggregations are composed of tau proteins. The consequences of this aggregation are probably similar to those of the tauopathy associated with AD.

The diagnosis of FTLD is based on clinical features, age of onset, exclusion of major cerebrovascular pathology and characteristic patterns of atrophy on cerebral imaging. However, the latter are not always present, and PET or SPECT imaging of local blood flow or glucose metabolism may be more sensitive (Figure 20.1), where it is available. Potential chemical biomarkers include reduced plasma or CSF progranulin levels or increased levels of TDP-43. However, these features are not universally present and there is little scope for them being developed into diagnostic markers because they depend on the specific neuropathological profile. For example, reduced progranulin is associated with the respective mutations in the gene on chromosome 17, and increased TDP-43 may only be found in the 50% of FTLD patients who have this neuropathological subtype. Thus its main function may be to differentiate FTLD-TDP from FTLD-tauopathy. Because there is presently no specific pharmacological treatment for any of the FTLD syndromes, the development of biomarkers may not have immediate clinical relevance. However, it is hoped that when specific interventions become available, which may very well be specific for neuropathological subtypes, such in-vivo markers will be useful (Pickering-Brown, 2010).

20.6 PARKINSON PLUS SYNDROMES

A group of neurodegenerative disorders combines Parkinsonian symptoms with cognitive decline and characteristic additional signs and symptoms. These are sometimes classified as 'Parkinson plus syndromes', although current aims are for a classification that is more based on the underlying pathology. In addition to dementia with Lewy Bodies DLB (see Section 20.8) and FTLD with comorbid PD, this group includes corticobasal degeneration (CBD), progressive supranuclear palsy (PSP) and multi-system atrophy (MSA).

CBD is clinically characterised by combination of Parkinsonian and other sensorimotor symptoms, for example ataxia and the sensation that one of the hands is 'foreign', termed 'alien hand syndrome', with specific neuropsychological deficits (aphasia, apraxia), progressive cognitive decline and behavioural and mood changes. The pathology, which is histologically defined as accumulation of tau protein, affects the basal ganglia, particularly the substantia nigra, and frontal and parietal cortex. It can be distinguished from DLB by the different neuropathology (tauopathy vs. Lewy Bodies in DLB) and different neuropsychological profile. Conversely it is harder to separate from PSP, which is also a tauopathy. Patients with PSP also show prominent Parkinsonian symptoms and ataxia as well as progressive cognitive decline, but the defining characteristics are the difficulty with coordinated eye movements (supranuclear ophthalmoplegia) and pseudobulbar palsy (difficulty swallowing [dysphagia] and articulating speech [dysarthria]). PSP also leads to prominent autonomic problems, such as urinary incontinence.

MSA is also characterised by combination of Parkinsonian, autonomic and cerebellar (ataxia) symptoms. It can be distinguished from CBD and PSP by the absence of their characteristic symptoms, and perhaps earlier and more dominant occurrence of autonomic symptoms such as genitourinary dysfunction in MSA. Cognitive decline and psychiatric symptoms can occur in the course of the disease. The pathology of MSA is characterised by alpha-synuclein aggregation.

The prognosis of all the 'Parkinson plus' syndromes is worse that that of PD, with a mean progression from symptom onset to death of 8–10 years. Only symptomatic treatment of the Parkinsonian symptoms (with dopaminergic drugs) is available, but they tend to respond less well than in classical PD. Because the Parkinson plus syndromes share pathological features with AD (tauopathy: CBD and PSP) and the group of synucleinopathies (MSA) it is hoped that patients will benefit from specific treatment for these two large classes of neurodegenerative pathology if and when they become available.

20.7 PRION DISEASE

Prion diseases or prionopathies are a group of rapidly progressive neurodegenerative disorders that are caused by misfolded proteins. A unique feature is that these pathologically altered proteins can be transmitted from one organism to another and induce similar molecular changes and thus cause the disease in the host. This transmission mode is similar to that of classical infections, which has led to the term prion, 'proteinaceous infectious agent'. Until the discovery of the prion mechanism by the American neuropathologist Stanley B. Prusiner in 1982 (Nobel Prize for Physiology or Medicine in 1997), it had been thought that infectious agents needed to contain DNA or RNA in order to replicate. Prion diseases can

Figure 20.4

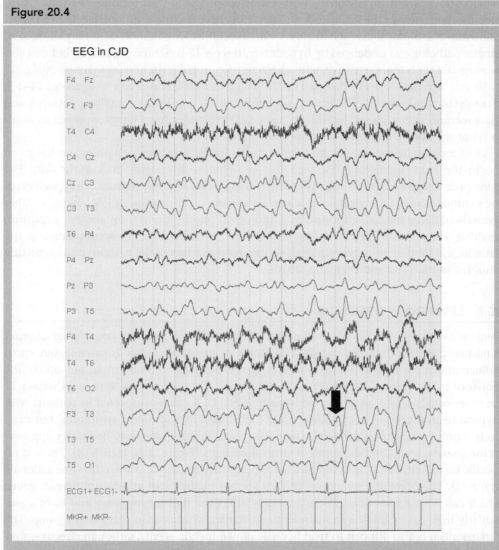

EEG in Creutzfeldt-Jakob Disease (CJD)

The EEG of this 55-year-old patient with rapidly progressive cognitive decline who was eventually diagnosed with CJD shows generalized slowing and left lateralized (odd numbers denote the left side of the head, even numbers the right) biphasic and triphasic (arrow) waves. Periodic bi- or triphasic waves are typical of CJD, although they are also often observed in other encephalopathies, most notably those of hepatic and other metabolic origin. Vertical dotted lines denote intervals of 200 ms and the bottom trace shows the amplitude calibration at 100 microvolts.

be transmitted from human to human through contaminated surgical instruments or tissue extracts. For example, right into the 1980s growth hormone (GH) for the treatment of growth deficiency was obtained from human pituitary glands (this has now been replaced by genetically engineered GH). Some prion diseases can also be transmitted from infected animals to humans through consumption of meat, for example scrapie in sheep or the bovine spongiform encephalopathy (BSE) in cattle known as 'mad cow disease', which gives rise to the 'new variant' of Creutzfeldt-Jakob disease (vCJD).

CJD is the most common prion disorder but still very rare in the general population. Whereas the – probably vanishing – vCJD can affect people in their twenties or thirties, most sporadic cases arise in the 7th decade or later. Cognitive decline is more rapid than in other dementias and motor signs such as ataxia and myoclonus are common. MRI may show basal ganglia pathology, as evidenced by hyperintensities on T2-weighted sequences, but can also be normal. EEG is more sensitive, with characteristic irregular sharp waves (Figure 20.4).

Several biomarkers can be detected in CSF. These include elevated levels of protein 14–3-3, a family of regulatory or 'chaperone' proteins that bind to other signalling proteins and share features with alpha-synuclein. Sporadic CJD progresses from symptom onset to death in about six months and there is no specific treatment.

The formation of vacuoles in the brain is the hallmark of the prionopathies and has given rise to the term 'spongiform' (sponge-like) encephalopathy (Figure 20.5, Plate VIII). The prion protein has a normal form, PrPc, which is expressed in many human cell types including neurons. The pathological process arises when the conformation of PrP_c changes, either spontaneously or through exposure to pathological prion protein from another organism, resulting in a pathological protein, for example PrP_{Sc} (scrapie protein). Accumulation of the pathological form of prion protein leads to structural changes of the neurons and eventually neuronal death (Frost and Diamond, 2010).

20.8   LEWY BODY DEMENTIA

Dementia with Lewy Bodies (DLB) accounts for about 10% of dementia cases. Its age of onset is normally in the 7th or 8th decade. The profile of cognitive decline is variable, but visual hallucinations are typical. Parkinsonian motor features are also common, but unlike the sequence in Parkinson's disease (PD), do not precede the cognitive decline (see Chapter 21 for more details on PD and Lewy Body pathology). DLB can be suspected in patients with atypical neuropsychological profiles, visual hallucinations and motor symptoms, but diagnosis is only possible post-mortem, where the typical intracellular Lewy Bodies are apparent in the somata, axons and dendrites of cortical neurons (Figure 20.6, Plate VIII). There is no specific treatment, but AChEIs can be tried for cognitive impairment with the same rationale as for AD. The psychotic symptoms of DLB are not treated with antidopaminergic agents, which can have paradoxical effects, adversely affect the motor symptoms and have a particularly high risk of leading to neuroleptic malignant syndrome in this patient group. The Parkinsonism is also difficult to treat because dopaminergic agents, although effective, may exacerbate psychosis.

20.9   VASCULAR DEMENTIA

Vascular dementia (VD) is the second most common form of dementia, and by far the most common non-degenerative form. It is caused by multiple (often small) strokes, often in white matter. This 'white matter disease' is also known as 'leukoaraiosis' (rarefication of white matter) or 'Binswanger's disease', after the Swiss psychiatrist Otto Binswanger (1852–1929) who first described the cerebrovascular pathology. Mixed pathology with AD is common (at least in 50% of VD patients), which has resulted in the proposal of a 'mixed dementia' category. Together AD and VD account for about 80% of dementia cases. AD and VD share many of the same environmental risk factors such as high blood pressure, high cholesterol, diabetes mellitus, smoking and high levels of homocysteine. Dementia is also a common consequence of major or 'strategic' stroke. Such strokes affect a functionally relevant of cortex or subcortical tissue in a way that disrupts its function sufficiently to cause symptoms that can be observed by clinicians and patients. An example is aphasia as a consequence of stroke of the anterior part of the middle cerebral artery territory in the dominant hemisphere, which includes the speech areas of the frontal operculum. Although dementias following from such clinically apparent strokes are also, by definition, of cerebrovascular origin, their neuropsychological profile is different (determined more by the location of the stroke) and they present a different type of challenge because of the disability often associated with major strokes. We will therefore discuss major stroke and its neuropsychiatric consequences in Chapter 21.

VD can affect the same cognitive domains as AD but its course is classically less insidious and more abrupt, fluctuating or stepwise, with each step of decline probably reflecting a subclinical stroke. Focal neurological symptoms, gait and incontinence problems are also typical. The diagnosis is made by a combination of clinical criteria and documentation of cerebrovascular pathology on cerebral imaging, ideally including T2-weighted MRI sequences. If strokes mainly affect the white matter underlying cortex – and thus the cortico-cortical fibre tracts – a 'cortical' type of VD may develop. The neuropsychological profile of cortical VD includes executive dysfunction (difficulties with the planning, initiation and organisation of activities), aphasia, apraxia and agnosia, and thus functions associated with the frontal, parietal and temporal neocortex. The 'subcortical' dementia caused by strokes in the white matter of the basal ganglia, which may also affect cortico-striatal and thalamo-cortical connections, also includes executive dysfunction, but also prominent mood and personality changes and difficulties with motor sequencing and learning. The prognosis of VD, as far as survival is concerned, is poorer than that of AD with median survival rates of four years from first onset of symptoms compared to seven years for AD (McVeigh and Passmore, 2006).

Although recurrence rates of major strokes can be reduced with anti-platelet agents like acetylsalicylic acid (Aspirin®) or clopidogrel (Plavix®), such secondary prevention is not available for the micro-strokes of Binswanger's disease. Primary prevention with reduction of vascular risk factors is therefore of the essence and a major public health challenge. Once clinical dementia has developed, similar treatment strategies as in AD can be tried because excitotoxicity would be expected also in VD, and reductions in cholinergic neurons have also been demonstrated, albeit not to the same extent as in AD. Consequently memantine and the three AChEIs have all shown some promise in preliminary clinical trials of VD and are currently under further investigation for this indication.

20.10   NORMAL PRESSURE HYDROCEPHALUS

Hydrocephalus (from Greek *hydro* = water and *kephale* = head) describes the widening of the inner CSF spaces (the cerebral ventricles). Congenital hydrocephalus can arise as a consequence of several developmental abnormalities. Acquired hydrocephalus can result from any condition that causes an imbalance between the production of CSF in the choroid plexus, its distribution in the ventricles, spinal canal, and cisterns and other subarachnoid spaces (outer CSF spaces), and its resorption into the venous blood stream. The most common causes of acquired hydrocephalus are meningitis, tumours and intracranial haemorrhages. Most of these conditions lead to raised intracranial pressure (ICP) because they obstruct the flow of CSF. ICP is normal or only temporally increased in NPH, which typically occurs without a preceding neurological condition (idiopathic) and accounts for approximately 1% of dementia cases. Its proportion increases with patients' age. The classical clinical triad of NPH consists of gait disturbance, urinary incontinence and dementia. The latter is of the 'subcortical' type with psychomotor slowing, inattention and executive dysfunction (Gallia et al., 2006). The syndrome has considerable overlap with VD, and vascular changes can be found on neuroimaging in the majority of NPH patients. Comorbidity with AD is also frequent. Both direct pressure on brainstem nuclei and ischaemic changes owed to impact on the cerebral circulation have been implicated in the pathophysiology of NPH dementia (Shprecher et al., 2008). Some patients with NPH will respond well to a permanent shunt that drains CSF from the cerebral ventricles into the peritoneum (ventriculo-peritoneal shunt) or right atrium of the heart (ventriculo-atrial shunt). The diagnosis of NPH and likely treatment response can be established by a lumbar puncture (spinal tap) with the removal of a large volume (30–50 ml) of CSF. Rapid symptom improvement after this procedure confirms the diagnosis of NPH and predicts good response to a permanent shunt. However, even patients who do not respond to such a therapeutic spinal tab may have NPH and respond to shunting. In the absence of randomised controlled trials, the individual benefits of shunting are difficult to assess and have to be weighted against the complications of surgery and the need for subsequent pressure adjustments. Generally, the gait problems seem to respond best and the cognitive decline worst to a shunting intervention. However, practitioners need to be aware of this diagnostic category because it is one of the potentially reversible dementia conditions in the elderly.

20.11   DEMENTIA PUGILISTICA ('BOXER'S DEMENTIA')

Dementia pugilistica or chronic traumatic encephalopathy (CTE) affects about 20% of professional boxers and also other regular participants in high-impact sports such as rugby or American football. It is supposed to arise from the multiple minor head traumas suffered in the course of a boxing career, and contusions, diffuse axonal injuries (Chapter 21), ischaemia and disruptions of the blood–brain barrier have all been suggested as mechanisms. Interestingly, the cognitive decline, which typically starts with memory impairment, may develop only after a latency phase of years to decades after the last trauma. This is very different from the effects of more severe traumatic brain injuries, where neuropsychological consequences are immediate and, if anything, improve over the first 1–2 years after the trauma. There is currently no good model for this latency between traumas and cognitive effects in dementia pugilistica. Psychotic symptoms, Parkinsonism and gait problems may also develop, suggesting global grey and/or white matter damage. Post-mortem studies indeed found global reduction in brain volume and size of the corpus callosum and enlarged lateral and third ventricles. Cortical atrophy affected the frontal, temporal and parietal but not the occipital lobes. Microscopically the tissue damage is characterised by neurofibrillary tangles with tau protein, similar to AD, and sometimes also beta-amyloid. These findings are interesting because they suggest that tauopathy may be a common final pathway for different causes of neurodegeneration. There is also some suggestion that CTE may increase the risk to develop AD or vice versa.

The microscopic changes affect Papez's circuit, leading to the emotional lability, and the hippocampal complex, leading to the memory problems. The substantia nigra, pars compacta, also degenerates, explaining the high proportion of cases with Parkinsonism. Because of the long latency period it is impossible to say when the traumatic changes become irreversible or what amount of exposure to head trauma may be safe. Calls for a ban on impact sports may not be realistic, but stricter guidelines on periods of rest after head trauma aiming to avoid a second trauma in quick succession, which is particularly deleterious, may go some way preventing CTE (McKee et al., 2009).

20.12   ALPHA SYNUCLEIN AS A COMMON FEATURE IN THE NEUROPATHOLOGY OF DEMENTIAS

The advances in molecular biology have called some of the traditional diagnostic boundaries of neurodegenerative disorders into question, even those that were primarily based on biological rather than clinical features. One example is the central role of alpha-synuclein (αSN). Fibrillar aggregates of this regulatory protein, which are found in neurons and glia, are a main component of Lewy Bodies. In addition to the Lewy Body pathologies (PD, DLB and the Lewy Body variant of AD, which may include up to 50% of AD cases), αSN pathology is also found in MSA. It is also associated with rare sporadic or autosomal recessive neurodegeneration with brain iron accumulation type-1 (NBIA-1), which affects children and leads to extrapyramidal motor signs, ataxia, dementia and premature death, and with Down's syndrome, the neurodevelopmental disorder caused by trisomy of chromosome 21. These disorders are classed as 'synucleinopathies' and distinguished from 'tauopathies' (AD and FTLD-tau), 'ubiquinopathies' (FTLD-TDP and ALS), 'amyloidopathies' (AD and amyloid angiopathy) and 'prionopathies' (see Table 20.1). However, even these molecular classifications are in flux. For example, ALS may be as much a 'synucleinopathy' as a 'ubiquinopathy' and AD falls into most of these categories. Furthermore, prion-type mechanisms of transmission of protein misfolding may extend beyond the classical 'prionopathies' (Frost and Diamond, 2010). More and more clues thus point to common basic molecular mechanisms of neuronal damage in the neurodegenerative disorders, but they also leave a major explanatory gap because, after all, some of the clinical syndromes and cascades of neural damage are very distinct. The neurodegenerative disorders with motor symptoms may indeed be a spectrum of disorders rather than pathologically distinct categories, with some commencing in the brainstem and leading to motor symptoms early on, and others commencing in the cerebral cortex and leading to early cognitive symptoms (Hindle, 2010).

Table 20.1   Molecular classification of neurodegenerative disorders that can lead to dementia.

- 'Synucleopathies': PD, DLB and the Lewy Body variant of AD
- 'Tauopathies': AD and FTLD-tau
- 'Ubiquinopathies' FTLD-TDP and ALS
- 'Amyloidopathies': AD and amyloid angiopathy
- 'Prionopathies': CJD and related disorders

Another possibility is that common pathological proteins such as αSN denote converging pathways of reaction to neuronal damage, as might be suggested by the αSN aggregations observed after acute traumatic brain injury. However, the association of mutations in the αSN gene with familial PD would suggest a more causal role for this protein (Lücking and Brice, 2000).

Cortical and subcortical (dopaminergic, noradrenergic) neurons express αSN, but its specific functions are still not very well known. It seems to be involved in the regulation of presynaptic vesicular dopamine storage, which is impaired in the mutant leading to familial PD (Dev et al., 2003), and of dopamine reuptake by the DAT. It also inhibits the phosphorylation (and thus activation) of tyrosine hydroxylase and thus reduces dopamine synthesis. This feature is shared by the 14-3-3 protein, which we encountered above as a biomarker of CJD, and which shares 40% of its amino acid sequence with αSN. 14-3-3 protein is a chaperone protein, meaning that it regulates the folding pattern of other proteins. Considering that misfolding is a key element in the presumed pathway from molecular changes to neuronal damage in most neurodegenerative disorders (Frost and Diamond, 2010), it would be attractive to propose that αSN, too, is a chaperone and that its pathological alteration would lead to misfolding of other proteins. There is, indeed, some evidence for a role of αSN as a chaperone protein (Bennett, 2005).

In sum, αSN seems to be involved in multiple pathophysiological pathways leading to neurodegeneration, and its pathological aggregates characterise a wide range of neurodegenerative disorders, particularly those with Parkinsonian features. However, whether these changes are secondary or causal for the neurodegenerative process still needs to be determined. A strict separation of 'synucleinopathies' and other types of pathology such as 'tauopathies' cannot be maintained because of the considerable clinical and neuropathological overlap between these groups.

20.13   ANIMAL MODELS

Most animal models of dementia start from a biological construct, for example amyloid pathology in AD. Because the biological cascades of AD-related pathology can to some extent be studied in isolation from the complex resulting behavioural changes, AD has not only been modelled in rodents but also in the fruit fly drosophila and the nematode worm *Caenorhabditis elegans* (Link, 2005). These animals do not naturally produce A-beta because their APP gene lacks the relevant sequence. Transgenic flies that produce A-beta 42 show behavioural deficits (olfactory learning and motor skills), progressive loss of neurons and a shortened life span. Neurodegeneration and vacuolisation, a typical feature of FTLD, was observed in flies with a FTDP-17-related mutation of tau protein. Conversely, complete knock-out of the tau protein gene had no effect, suggesting that its pathological effect in the 'tauopathies' is brought about by the toxicity of pathological forms of tau, not by lack of its physiological function. Thus, invertebrate models of neurodegeneration can give some hints as to the pathophysiological role of some of the molecules implicated in neurodegeneration. However, analogies to the functional role of these proteins in the more complex vertebrate brains have to be viewed with caution.

Mouse models of AD have started from the mutations associated with human familial AD in the APP and PSEN genes, allowing for a study of the cascade of pathological processes arising from the protein alterations. Over-expression of altered APP in the so-called Tg2576 mice, the most widely used mouse model of AD, results in increased A-beta 40 and 42, followed by plaque formation at about 1 year of age. Cognitive deterioration, measured with water maze learning, started at about the same time. Transgenic mice with mutations in the PSEN genes modelled the neuropathology of AD less well because, although A-beta 42 was elevated, plaques did not form. Neither APP nor PSEN mutant mice developed NFTs. Over-expression of mutant APP had to be combined with FTDP-17-associated tau protein gene mutation in order to achieve this. In these multiply transgenic mice, plaques developed at six months of age in neocortex and later in hippocampus and NFTs at one year in hippocampus and later in neocortex. These animals also showed cellular (altered long-term potential) and behavioural changes indicative of reduced neural plasticity. Although they thus model many of the cellular and behavioural changes of AD, the model may be artificial in that it combines mutations from two disease entities that are not required in conjunction for the human clinical phenotype. A model with good construct validity for the joint amyloid/NFT pathology in AD has thus not yet been found.

There are several other problems with inferences from rodent models to human AD. The processes of normal ageing seem to differ between humans and rodents. For example, no plaques and NFT are found in the normally ageing rodent brain, whereas they are part of normal ageing in humans. Furthermore, the time course of neuropathological and cognitive changes is different in the mouse models. Here behavioural deficits develop at the same time or before histological changes are detected, whereas in humans the first pathological changes can precede symptoms by years or decades. Finally, aetiologically valid models such as the Tg2576 mouse showed no loss of neurons. In order to model neuronal death in mouse models, multiple mutations are needed, which again differs from the human scenario where a single autosomal dominant mutation can lead to amyloidopathy and/or tauopathy with loss of neurons.

Although the animal models may have posed more questions than they have given answers to regarding the pathophysiology of neurodegenerative disorders, they are crucial for the evaluation of new treatment strategies. Animal experiments showed that the toxicity of A-beta was not confined to its role in plaques but that even soluble freely circulating A-beta 42 could be damaging. This has reinforced efforts to sequester A-beta by tagging it with antibodies, either through active (inoculation with parts of the peptide, followed by antibody production by the host) or passive immunisation (inoculation with the antibodies). These immunisation experiments led to reduction in plaque load and improvement of cognitive functions in several mouse models of AD. Although the first human phase 2 trials with active immunisation had to be discontinued because some patients developed autoimmune meningoencephalitis, trials with modified vaccination regimes, for example using passive immunisation that allows better control over antibody levels, are now underway (Elder et al., 2010).

Learning points

Dementia is a clinical syndrome of decline of memory and other cognitive functions that lead to functional impairment. It can be caused by a wide variety of primary brain and systemic pathologies, some of which are reversible. However, the majority of cases are caused by hitherto irreversible neurodegenerative processes. These are presently classified according to pathological features and/or specific neuropsychological and neurological profiles, resulting in the diagnostic categories of 'Alzheimer's disease', 'Vascular dementia', 'Fronto-temporal dementia', 'Dementia with Lewy

Bodies', 'Parkinson plus syndromes' and 'Prion disease'. Alzheimer's disease (AD) alone or in combination with vascular dementia is by far the commonest form. Its neuropathological hallmarks are intercellular plaques of A-beta protein and intracellular neurofibrillary tangles. Treatment with an AChEI or memantine can have a limited effect in slowing down the cognitive decline. Vascular dementia (VD) describes the cognitive decline brought about by progressive cerebrovascular white matter disease. Its progression is typically more gradual and symptoms more fluctuating than in AD. A 'cortical type' with prominent impairment of executive functions, language and praxis can be distinguished from a 'subcortical type' with personality and mood changes and learning problems. Diagnosis is based on documentation of cerebrovascular changes on imaging, and similar treatment strategies as in AD are being explored, although evidence for drug effects is still preliminary. Primary prevention of cerebrovascular risk factors is the main hope for reducing rates of VD, which is currently the second most common dementia. Frontotemporal dementia (FTD or FTLD) describes a group of clinical syndromes with neurodegeneration starting in the frontal and/or temporal lobes and a range of molecular pathologies. The most frequent pathological subtypes are FTLD-TDP and FTLD-tauopathy. The heritability is higher than in other common dementias, and there is currently no specific treatment.

Recent developments in molecular pathology have revealed considerable overlap between these categories. For example features of 'synucleinopathies' or 'tauopathies' are common to many of these disorders. Although only a small minority of the dementias are caused by autosomal dominant or recessive mutations, the resulting specific protein changes are informative as to the pathological processes involved and have been modelled extensively in transgenic animals. Current general treatment strategies are aimed at restoring depleted neurotransmitter pools (cholinergic for Alzheimer's disease and dopaminergic for Parkinson's disease and related syndromes) or at containing damage from excitotoxicity (memantine). More causal strategies, for example vaccinations against amyloid beta peptides involved in Alzheimer's pathology, are under development.

Revision and discussion questions

- What are major reversible and irreversible causes of dementia?
- How do the neuropsychological dementia syndromes relate to the underlying pathology?
- Are all irreversible dementias subtypes of the same neurodegenerative process?

FURTHER READING

Lemere, C. and Masliah, E. (2010). Can Alzheimer disease be prevented by amyloid-beta immuno-therapy? *Nature Reviews Neurology*, 6, 108–19.

Masters, C. L., Cappai, R., Barnham, K. J. and Villemagne, V. L. (2006). Molecular mechanisms for Alzheimer's disease: implications for neuroimaging and therapeutics. *Journal of Neurochemistry*, 97, 1700–25.

21 NEUROPSYCHIATRY

PREVIEW

As explained in this book's introduction, the decision whether to assign a brain disorder to neurology or psychiatry is a largely pragmatic one. We typically think that psychiatric disorders are under stronger environmental influences and linked to an individual's biography and psychosocial history, whereas neurological disorders have clear correlates in brain pathology. But then, all psychiatric disorders can be conceptualised as brain disorders as well, and many of them are highly heritable, more so than most neurological disorders. The border between the two fields is therefore fuzzy, and likely to change with more biological knowledge about mental disorders becoming available.

Clinicians who look after patients with stroke, epilepsy or traumatic brain lesions have long known that the psychiatric consequences of these disorders can be as severe and disabling as the physical and neurological impairments. These observations led to the development of a specialised field at the interface of neurology and psychiatry, called neuropsychiatry, which is concerned with the psychiatric consequences of neurological disorders. Up to 50% of patients will develop clinically relevant mental health problems after stroke or traumatic brain injury. Many of them will fulfil ICD-10 or DSM-IV criteria of mental disorders at least for a certain time. Adjustment disorder, organic personality disorder, depressive episodes and substance use disorders are the commonest diagnoses associated with brain lesions. Many of the signs and symptoms are non-specific and can occur after a wide range of pathologies and affected brain sites. There are, however, also several characteristic psychiatric syndromes associated with neurological disorders, for example the 'punding' behaviours in Parkinson's disease (PD) or Klüver-Bucy syndrome after Herpes-simplex-encephalitis.

Neuropsychiatry is of huge and increasing clinical relevance, because the prevalence of the underlying disorders will increase in an ageing population and the psychiatric consequences are difficult to treat. In the context of the present book, neuropsychiatry can also provide important insight into the brain pathologies that can underlie psychiatric signs and symptoms. Such knowledge is important for psychiatrists and clinical psychologists because alternative pathologies need to be ruled out before a diagnosis of the mental disorder is made. It can also inform the biological understanding of mental disorders, although the mechanisms underlying a classic mental disorder, such as depression, and affective disturbances after a brain injury, can, of course, be different.

The present chapter explains some classic syndromes that often occur after brain lesions from a variety of sources. It then describes some of the associated neurological pathologies and their management. Finally, the chapter addresses how they inform our pathophysiological models of psychiatric symptoms and syndromes. The aim will be to focus on neuropsychiatric syndromes that a trainee psychiatrist or clinical psychologist is likely to encounter rather than cover the whole field, which is vast because any neurological disorder can impact a person's mental health. The more specialist interests are covered in the comprehensive textbooks by Moore (2008) and Yudofsky and Hales (2008).

21.1 SYNDROMES

21.1.1 Delirium

Delirium is defined in the DSM-IV as a disturbance of consciousness and cognition. The disturbance of consciousness is typically a 'reduced clarity of awareness of the environment' with 'reduced ability to focus, sustain, or shift attention'. Typically, the cognitive disturbance would affect attention, memory, orientation, language and/or executive functions (planning abilities). Patients appear confused and in an intermediate state between wakefulness and coma. They often behave inappropriately. For example, a postoperative patient on a surgical ward may remove a feeding tube or intravenous lines and climb out of bed. Psychotic symptoms, predominantly delusions, thought disorder or visual hallucinations, often occur but are not obligatory for the diagnosis. Psychomotor changes are also common, and both hyper- and hypoactivity can occur, often in rapid alternation. Fluctuation is typical of the symptoms of delirium, and patients may have several lucid intervals in any 24-hour period. The sleep-wave cycle is disturbed, with fragmented sleep and sleeplessness (Yudofsky and Hales, 2008). Delirium shares features with dementia (particularly the cognitive disturbance) and psychotic disorders (particularly perceptual changes and persecutory delusions), but can be distinguished by its defining feature, the impaired level of consciousness. The onset of delirium is normally sudden and associated with an acute medical problem, but it can also develop insidiously as a consequence of a chronic condition such as dementia. Delirium is common in hospitalised patients, affecting about 10%, and older patients are at higher risk. It can be caused by a very wide variety of chemical disturbances and other medical conditions. Chemical disturbances include drug intoxication or withdrawal, changes in the electrolyte balance and over- or under-activity of endocrine systems. Prescription drugs, particularly those with anticholinergic effects, can be the culprit if taken in overdose. Neurological causes include TBI, epileptic seizures, brain tumours, stroke and infections affecting the brain (meningitis, encephalitis, brain abscess). Systemic infection can cause delirium as well, and in the elderly a common cause is insufficient fluid intake. A considerable portion of patients after surgery with general anaesthesia suffer from delirium, often after a 1–2 day interval.

The biological mechanisms of delirium are poorly understood. Because of the association of anticholinergic drugs with delirium, cholinergic hypofunction has been proposed as a mechanism. The overlap in cognitive symptoms between delirium and dementia, where the cholinergic acetylcholinesterase inhibitors have some effect would also support such a model. However, laboratory tests have not brought up any direct evidence of a cholinergic deficit, and cholinergic drugs are not an effective treatment for delirium (Hshieh et al., 2008). HPA axis over-activity and HPT axis under-activity have also been suggested because of the association of delirium with Cushing's syndrome (hypercortisolism) and hypothyroidism. However, there has been little empirical support for this, and the other functional extremes of these systems, Addison's disease (adrenal insufficiency leading to hypocortisolism) and hyperthyroidism can also lead to delirium. What seems to be clear is that the blood–brain barrier is affected and becomes more permeable, allowing toxic agents to enter the brain. This is probably an effect of the release of cytokines, which are mediators of inflammatory responses, which is a common global stress response and may explain why primary brain disorders such as local tumours and systemic infections can converge onto the same patho-physiological pathways and lead to very similar clinical phenotypes.

In addition to acetylcholine, imbalances in most other neurotransmitter systems have been implicated in delirium as well. Antidopaminergic antipsychotics such as haloperidol constitute the best medical treatment, and amphetamines can produce delirium. D_2-receptor stimulation inhibits acetylcholine synthesis. A hyperdopaminergic/hypocholinergic state is thus still the best neurochemical model of delirium although excess of norepinephrine or serotonin can also cause the condition. Studies of the localisation of strokes and other brain lesions associated with delirium have not produced a consistent pattern. Some evidence suggests a right hemispheric predilection. Because attention is partly lateralised to the right hemisphere, especially the parietal lobe, this may explain the severe attentional deficits of delirium. A central role for the thalamus, which receives cholinergic, noradrenergic and serotonergic projections from the brainstem and controls awareness, has also been supported by lesion studies. However, the majority of cases of delirium are not accompanied by a focal brain lesion, and the most characteristic neurophysiological feature is diffuse slowing of the EEG.

In sum, although the medical causes of delirium have been well studied and several neurotransmitter, neuroendocrine and neuroimmunological systems have been implicated, its exact pathophysiology is still poorly understood. Considering the generic treatment response to antidopaminergic agents, it seems likely that a common neurobiological pathway mediates the clinical manifestation of delirium caused by a multitude of brain and systemic pathologies.

21.1.2 Organic personality disorder

This profound change in personality is perhaps the most common and pervasive consequence of TBI and other brain lesions. The ICD-10 describes organic personality disorder (OPD) as a 'significant alteration of the habitual patterns of premorbid behaviour'. A DSM-IV equivalent is the 'personality change due to traumatic brain injury'. Characteristic features include emotional lability, irritability, apathy, disinhibition, suspiciousness and problems with concentration and goal pursuit. The DSM-IV accordingly further distinguishes a labile, disinhibited, aggressive, apathetic and paranoid type, although the combined type, where more than one of the features is prominent, is probably most common. Although patients often report low mood and sometimes express the wish to die (and occasionally even engage in self-harming behaviour), the clinical picture is different from that of depression. The periods of low mood normally last for hours or days rather than weeks or months and can be interrupted by periods of inappropriate cheerfulness. The cheerfulness, in turn, is different from mania in that flight of ideas and grandiose delusions are rarely present. Patients with organic personality disorder often show their emotions in a highly expressive fashion, which would be rare in depression. Although the emotional lability can respond to antidepressant drugs, treatment success is lower than in depression.

Organic personality disorder incorporates features of what is sometimes also described as 'frontal lobe syndrome', particularly the disinhibited and often socially inappropriate and hypersexual behaviour, executive dysfunction and apathy. Although a preponderance of these symptoms is often associated with lesions to the frontal lobes, they are not specific for this lesion site. The disinhibition overlaps with the loss of impulse control, which has been linked to orbitofrontal lesions. Apathy has been linked to anterior cingulate lesions, and loss of planning ability and other executive dysfunctions to the dorsolateral prefrontal cortex (Tekin and Cummings, 2002). Because all these prefrontal areas send self-regulatory projections to the thalamus via the striatum (caudate for DLPFC, ACC and lateral OFC; NAc for medial OFC) and the globus pallidus internus/substantia nigra, lesions at these sites can also produce 'frontal lobe syndromes'. This explains why they can develop in primary basal ganglia disorders such as Parkinson's and Huntington's disease. There is little evidence for the involvement of specific NT pathways in OPD, although the amotivational syndrome sometimes responds to dopaminergic medication.

21.1.3 Amnesic syndromes

Cognitive psychology teaches several basic differentiations of memory. Short-term or working memory, where information is stored and/or manipulated over seconds to guide a particular action, is distinguished from long-term memory, where information can be stored for life. The latter can be divided into declarative (semantic or episodic) and non-declarative memory. Semantic memory involves knowledge about the world, whereas episodic or autobiographical memory is concerned with personal experiences. For example, remembering that John F. Kennedy was the 35th president of the United States would be part of semantic memory. Remembering where one was when he was assassinated would be an episodic memory. Both are declarative because they involve conscious recollection and can be reported. Conversely, non-declarative memory can be probed only by implicit tests. For example, previous exposure to a stimulus may make us faster in reacting to a subsequent presentation (priming). Procedural learning and conditioning are also classified as non-declarative memory.

The neural substrates have been studied most extensively for declarative memory. One striking finding was that patients with bilateral hippocampal damage, such as the famous patient Henry Molaison, or 'H.M.', first reported by William Scoville and Brenda Milner in 1957, have severe difficulty encoding new material but can remember most events preceding the damage and anything learnt prior to it. Thus, hippocampal function is crucial for encoding new material into declarative memory, but not for the recall of the information, which may be stored in neocortical circuits, although the exact mechanisms are not clear. The neural substrates for non-declarative memory are probably less consistent and vary according to subtype. For example, fronto-striatal circuits have been implicated in procedural motor learning.

Loss of memory can affect the encoding of new ('anterograde amnesia'), the recall of old information ('retrograde amnesia') or both. The severity can be total ('dense amnesia') or partial. For the diagnosis of an amnesic disorder, it is required that memory function declines from a previous level, though not in the context of dementia or delirium, and affects social or occupational functioning. The main difference to dementia is that other cognitive functions remain largely intact.

Based on the main anatomical areas affected, three types of memory syndromes can be distinguished. H. M. showed the severe anterograde amnesia characteristic of hippocampal patients (and only some retrograde amnesia for events immediately preceding his operation). Lesions to diencephalic regions such as the mediodorsal thalamus or the mammillary bodies can give rise to Wernicke-Korsakoff syndrome, which consists in dense anterograde amnesia and retrograde amnesia. The retrograde amnesia has a temporal gradient, which means that events are remembered better the further they are in the past. Short-term memory loss, confabulations and a lost sense of temporal intervals are also common. A patient may place remembered events from the distant past into the current time to make up for the temporal gradient. Similarly, confabulations can be regarded as an attempt to fill gaps in memory. The exact functional contribution of diencephalic circuits to memory formation is still under investigation, but because of the important role of inputs from the basal forebrain it has been suggested that cholinergic mechanisms may play a role (Kopelman, 2002). The amnesias associated with frontal lobe lesions have a less characteristic presentation than those arising from medial temporal or diencephalic pathologies. However, a predominantly retrograde amnesia, based on failure to retrieve information, seems to be caused by damage to OFC, temporopolar cortex and its connection through the uncinate fascicle (Markowitsch, 1995). This dissociation between largely anterograde (hippocampal) and retrograde (fronto-temporopolar) amnesias supports the view that different brain structures support encoding into and retrieval from long-term memory.

21.1.4 Loss of impulse control and aggression

We have already discussed basic features of aggressive behaviour in Chapters 14 (ASPD), 17 (childhood conduct disorder) and 18 (sexual aggression). Aggressive behaviour can occur as a consequence of almost any mental disorder, particularly if auto-aggressive behaviours such as self-harming are included, and of substance abuse and intoxication. Aggression can be planned and premeditated, but in the context of brain lesions it is mostly a result of the lost ability to control impulses ('impulsive aggression'). Aggressive behaviour can be considered to be a particularly severe form of impulsivity. The main brain regions whose dysfunction has been implicated in the generation of aggressive behaviours are the PFC, hypothalamus and extended amygdala. We discussed the sexual disinhibition after bilateral medial temporal lobe (MTL) lesions, termed Klüver-Bucy syndrome, in Chapter 18. Generally, MTL lesions can lead to both increased and decreased aggressive tendencies. Temporal lobe epilepsy (TLE), which may be classified as hyperexcitability of the MTL, is a relatively frequent cause of aggression, and bilateral removal of the amygdalae for the treatment of TLE has reduced aggression in some cases. Aggression after prefrontal lesions normally constitutes an exaggerated response to environmental stressors, possibly because of disinhibition of limbic circuits. Similarly, the interictal (between epileptic seizures) aggression of TLE patients normally occurs in response to a trigger, whereas the ictal (during epileptic seizures) aggression or that associated with hypothalamic lesions is often spontaneous and undirected. Hypothalamic lesions of patients are normally not focused enough to disambiguate the role of individual nuclei, but animal studies have suggested that the ventromedial nucleus inhibits aggressive behaviour whereas the lateral hypothalamus promotes it.

The main neuroendocrine systems implicated in aggression are the HPA axis and the vasopressin system. In animal studies, levels of vasopressin outside the hypothalamus, for example the BNST, are associated with increased aggression, whereas levels in the hypothalamus are associated with higher anxiety and lower aggression towards conspecifics (Veenema, 2009). Administration of vasopressin in humans, which can be easily effected through a nasal spray, leads to a perceptual bias for threatening facial expression. This may, in turn, trigger aggressive expression or behaviour in the beholder. Depending on the executive control and quality of risk assessment, perceived threat can lead to low (if chances of winning are judged to be low) or high (if chances of winning are perceived to be high, rightly or wrongly) levels of aggression. This conforms to the clinical observation that the diencephalic and limbic regulators of the fight/flight response are under prefrontal control. Amongst the neurotransmitters, serotonin has been most extensively investigated in relation to aggression. Reduced markers of serotonin, such as lower levels of 5-HIAA in the CSF, platelet serotonin transporters, and serotonin in the brainstem on post-mortem examination have been found in individuals with a history of aggression, including those who committed or attempted suicide, which is a form of auto-aggressive behaviour. However, administration of the serotonin precursor tryptophan or of $5-HT_{1A}$ or $5-HT_{1B}$ agonists can reduce violent tendencies, which calls a simple association between low serotonergic activity and aggression into question. In order to reconcile these findings, it has been proposed that chronically reduced serotonergic activity leads to inappropriate aggression, whereas homoeostatic levels are required for adaptive dominance behaviour. The distinction between acute and chronic effects may also explain the disparate effects of SSRIs, which have been associated both with reduced and increased aggressive and auto-aggressive behaviour.

In sum, loss of impulse control and consequent hyperaggressive behaviour in response to minor stressors appears to be mainly associated with frontal lobe lesions and chronically low serotonin levels, whereas dysfunctions of the hypothalamus and amygdala, possibly mediated through altered vasopressin activity, can lead to spontaneous aggression.

21.1.5 Punding

'Punding', a term derived from the vernacular of Swedish drug addicts, describes a form of compulsive behaviour observed after the chronic dopaminergic stimulation of amphetamine abuse of PD treatment. It includes the fascination with and manipulation of particular familiar objects, for example repetitive assembling and disassembling or sorting or equipment, or repetitive vocalisations, such as humming, singing, doodling or even long soliloquies. These behaviours can occur at the expense of sleep and other physiological needs. Unlike the classical impulsive behaviours, punding behaviours are aimless and they are not associated with the same cycle of tension and relief. Punding shares features with OCD, and compulsive eating and spending are other related behaviours that can occur after dopaminergic treatment of PD (Ferrara and Stacy, 2008).

21.1.6 Klüver-Bucy syndrome

First observed in experimental monkeys after removal of both anterior temporal lobes, this syndrome is characterised by 'hyperorality' (tendency to put objects in the mouth), disinhibited and indiscriminate eating and sexual behaviour, placidity (or 'tameness' in animals) and profound visual agnosia ('psychic blindness'). The full picture rarely occurs in humans, and hypersexuality normally does not go beyond inappropriate sexual remarks (see also Chapter 18). Further work has shown that lesions to the amygdalae are most crucially involved in the development of Klüver-Bucy syndrome, which has been observed after a wide range of pathologies, including trauma, hypoxic brain damage, neurodegenerative, metabolic, inflammatory and neoplastic (mainly multicentric glioblastoma) disorders (Trimble et al., 1997). Limbic encephalitis (see Section 21.2.9) is another potential cause.

21.1.7 Gastaut-Geschwind syndrome

This syndrome is perhaps better described as a change in personality features or character than in terms of clinical symptoms. It is based on the observation that some patients with

TLE develop a particular interest in religious, moral and philosophical issues ('hyper-religiosity') and tend to write about these interests and their associated feelings extensively ('hypergraphia'). The thought and interpersonal behaviour of these patients has been described as 'sticky' because they adhere to particular topics and find it difficult to terminate conversations and encounters. These changes are accompanied by a loss of interest in sexual activities ('hyposexuality'). Although there is some indication that this personality type is weakly associated with the interictal (i.e. between seizures) phases of TLE (Trimble et al., 1997), no association with a particular anatomical structure has been established and the validity of this syndrome is still under debate.

21.2 PATHOLOGIES

This section briefly describes some of the key brain disorders that can give rise to neuropsychiatric symptoms and syndromes. This is neither a full list, nor intended to give justice to the complexity of the disorders. The main aim is to provide some background to the non-medical reader. Further information can be found in neurology textbooks such as *Adams and Victor's Principles of Neurology* (Ropper et al., 2009).

21.2.1 Traumatic brain injury

Traumatic brain injury (TBI) can be classified according to clinical severity or to the parts of the brain that are affected. The severity classification uses loss of consciousness (LOC) and post-traumatic amnesia (PTA, loss of memory for the events after the injury) as criteria. LOC of less than 20 minutes and post-traumatic amnesia of less than 24 hours define mild TBI, which is also called 'post-concussion syndrome' and is characterised by headaches, dizziness, sleep problems and fatigue, memory and concentration problems and emotional problems. Tinnitus or sensitivity to noise or light can also occur. Most patients recover after 3–6 months, but in some cases the symptoms can become chronic. The main treatment is through CBT.

LOC up to 1 day and PTA up to one week constitute moderate TBI, and beyond this the condition is classified as severe. After recovery of consciousness, all the symptoms listed for mild TBI can occur, but many patients who suffered moderate or severe TBI will go on to develop an organic personality disorder and/or show a deficit in impulse control. The specific neurological and neuropsychological deficits will depend on the type and location of the injury.

The classification according to type of injury distinguishes between bleeds, local tissue damage and diffuse axonal injury (DAI). Bleeds can occur at any tier below the skull – above the dura mater (epidural), between the dura mater and the arachnoid (subdural), between the arachnoid and the pia mater (subarachnoid), and intracerebral. Epidural and subdural bleeds are called haematoma because they result in a contained collection of blood, whereas subarachnoid and intracerebral bleeds are called haemorrhages. Subarachnoid and intracerebral haemorrhages can also occur without a traumatic lesion, as a consequence of aneurysms of large cerebral vessels or damage to small vessels, respectively. High blood pressure and other classical vascular risk factors increase the risk of spontaneous intracerebral haemorrhages, which are classified as strokes. Intracranial bleeds may not damage tissue directly, but through pressure and secondary vascular effects. For example, major complications of subarachnoid haemorrhage are the ensuing blood vessel contractions (vasospasms), which can result in ischaemic strokes.

Local tissue damage includes contusions (bruises) and lacerations (cuts), which are intermixed with small haemorrhages. These can occur below (coup) or opposite (contre-coup) the site of a blunt trauma. The OFC and temporal poles are most often affected, which explains the high rate of impulse-control deficits after TBI. DAI is caused by acceleration/deceleration trauma, for example during car accidents, where axons and small vessels are shorn and torn. DAI is not typically associated with specific focal symptoms but can lead to prolonged coma and persistent vegetative state (PVS) in severe cases (see Box 21.1). TBI is an acute medical and neurological emergency, and often needs immediate surgical intervention (e.g. for the evacuation of bleeds) and lengthy intensive care.

21.2.2   Hypoxic brain damage

The brain has very little tolerance to disruptions of oxygen supply, which happens when blood does not reach the brain (ischaemia) or does not carry enough oxygen (hypoxaemia). Global ischaemia can be caused by cardiac arrest, blood loss or strangulation, and hypoxaemia by respiratory failure, drowning or carbon monoxide poisoning. The reduction/lack of oxygen in tissue is called hypoxia/anoxia. Disruptions of oxygen supply of over five minutes result in permanent brain damage, and the hippocampi and basal ganglia are particularly vulnerable. Amnesic and motor syndromes are thus amongst the main consequences, but more severe cases can also result in PVS. The prognosis of coma due to TBI is generally better than that of coma due to hypoxic brain damage, possibly because the latter involves more intrinsic brain damage.

21.2.3   Stroke

Strokes are brain lesions caused by damage to the cerebral circulation. About 90% of strokes are ischaemic, meaning that they are caused by blocked blood supply to the brain, and the remainder are bleeds. Ischaemic strokes can result from cerebrovascular or cardiac disease. One common mechanism is through the gradual formation of a thrombus in the heart or one of the main arteries of the neck, which then gets dislocated downstream and clogs a vessel once the diameter becomes too small for it to travel through. Such thrombi can form wherever the normal flow of blood is disrupted, for example in the cardiac atria of patients with atrial fibrillation, or where the vessel wall is damaged, for example in atherosclerosis. High blood pressure, high cholesterol, diabetes, smoking and high levels of uric acid in gout are all common risk factors for atherosclerosis, which explains their association with stroke (as well as heart attack and other vascular problems). Atherosclerosis of small brain vessels can also lead to the small strokes of Binswanger's disease (see Chapter 20.9 on vascular dementia) and intracerebral haemorrhages.

Stroke is a medical emergency associated with high mortality and morbidity. The functional impairment and level of disability is determined by the size and location of the brain damage and associated brain oedema. Brainstem strokes affecting the respiratory centres in the medulla oblongata can lead to respiratory failure, and thalamic damage often leads to disturbed consciousness. Compression of the ventricles by large hemispheric strokes denotes poor prognosis, and if the oedema compresses the midbrain or cerebellar tonsils the outcome is almost invariably fatal. In ischaemic strokes, it may be possible to dissolve the thrombus early in order to open the blood vessel again and thus prevent most of the damage to the perfused tissue. Thrombolytic agents that reverse blood clotting can be injected into a vein and will then be transported to the desired site of action through the blood stream, or they can be injected locally by moving a catheter through the arterial system to the site of the thrombus. These procedures are still confined to specialised centres and have a high rate of side effects, mainly bleeding. Strokes from bleeds ('haemorrhagic strokes') can sometimes be treated by surgery in order to reduce compression and tissue damage.

The classic location for intracerebral haemorrhages associated with high blood pressure is the basal ganglia region. This often results in compression of the internal capsule and damage to the pyramidal tract, resulting in paralysis (total loss of motor function) or paresis (weakness) on the contralesional side. The middle cerebral artery (MCA) supplies the lateral frontal and parietal lobes, the anterior cerebral artery (ACA) the medial surface of the frontal lobe and the posterior cerebral artery (PCA) the visual cortex. MCA stroke can thus result in aphasia, if the dominant hemisphere is affected, contralesional motor deficits and neglect, ACA strokes to apathy and PCA strokes to contralateral hemianopia. Depending on the exact extent of the lesion, a wide variety of neuropsychological deficits and syndromes have been described, which are discussed in detail in textbooks of neuropsychology (e.g. Kolb and Wishaw, 1980). Post-stroke depression is common, affecting about one-third of patients. Although some reports have suggested that right frontal strokes are particularly often associated with subsequent affective disorder, any stroke can lead to mood problems, which suggests some global neurochemical dysregulation rather than local lesion effects as the cause. In addition, adjustment and difficulties coping with the disability may play a role.

21.2.4   Epilepsy

Epilepsy is a group of disorders characterised by periods of spontaneous excessive neuro-electric activity ('seizures') that lead to uncontrolled motor or sensory symptoms, loss of consciousness, altered behaviour or combinations of these. Seizures can be 'simple partial', 'complex partial' and 'generalised'. In partial seizures, the excessive neural activity remains confined to focal areas, whereas in generalised seizures it spreads, sometimes even to the other hemisphere. Simple partial seizures lead to relatively simple motor, sensory or visceral symptoms, such as involuntary movement of or sensation in an arm or nausea, and consciousness is unimpaired. Conversely, complex partial seizures, also called psychomotor or temporal lobe seizures, are characterised by loss of consciousness, either at onset or during the course of the seizure, and can lead to stereotyped motor behaviours such as nestling, but also complex activities such as walking about (Figure 21.1a). Ictal (i.e. during a seizure) aggression has also been reported and is particularly relevant for neuropsychiatrists and forensic experts. Generalised seizures include the type of seizures that most laypersons associate with epilepsy, tonic-clonic or 'grand mal' seizures. The typical grand mal seizure starts with a tensing of muscle groups, normally bilaterally (the tonic phase), following by rhythmic contractions. The upper or upper and lower limbs are most commonly involved. Seizures are accompanied by loss of consciousness and sometimes by tongue biting and loss or urine or faeces. Tonic-clonic seizures are normally self-limiting and last for seconds to minutes, but prolonged seizures or epileptic status (series of seizures where the patient does not regain consciousness during intervals) can lead to respiratory arrest. Shorter grand mal seizures can lead to medical complications as well and are a constant source of concern to the patients and their carers, for example because of the restrictions on professional and recreational activities. Generalised seizures that lead to isolated loss of consciousness, most commonly in children, are called absence seizures (Figure 21.1b). Generalised seizures with pure motor symptoms

Figure 21.1

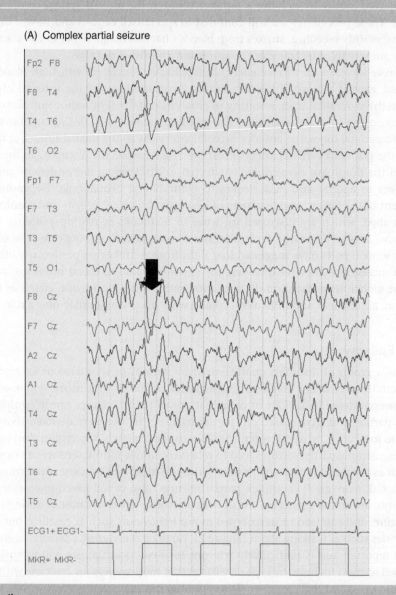

(A) Complex partial seizure

EEG in epilepsy

(A) EEG during a complex partial seizure – 29-year-old female patient with a history of Rasmussen encephalitis, a rare autoimmune brain inflammation. She developed complex partial seizures during which she is unresponsive and turns her head backwards. On this occasion the clinical event was preceded by right fronto-temporal sharp waves (even electrode numbers denote the right side of the head, odd numbers the left), indicated by the arrow.

(continued)

Figure 21.1

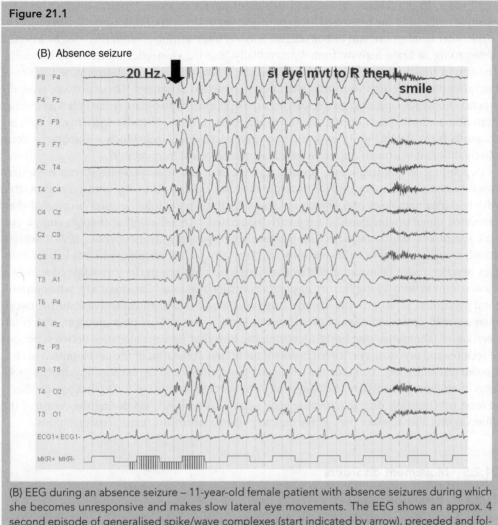

(B) EEG during an absence seizure – 11-year-old female patient with absence seizures during which she becomes unresponsive and makes slow lateral eye movements. The EEG shows an approx. 4 second episode of generalised spike/wave complexes (start indicated by arrow), preceded and followed by a normal trace. The bottom trace shows the calibration at 100 Microvolts.

include myoclonic seizures (very brief muscle jerks) and atonic seizures (loss of muscle tone that can lead to falls). Primary partial seizures can also become generalised (secondary generalised seizures). Epilepsy can occur as a consequence of any focal or diffuse brain pathology. Seizures are also common during intoxication with or withdrawal from substances of abuse. In most children or young adults who suffer from epilepsy the mechanism is unknown ('idiopathic' or 'cryptogenic'), and the classification of epileptic syndromes is largely based on their phenomenology and sometimes on the pattern of inheritance. Patients with learning disabilities also have a higher frequency of epileptic seizures.

Treatment is based on anticonvulsant drugs, which reduce neural excitability by increasing GABAergic and reducing glutamatergic activity, suppressing voltage-dependent calcium release and blocking sodium channels. However, complete freedom from seizures cannot be achieved in all cases. In particularly severe and treatment-refractory cases, surgical intervention, for example removal of the presumed focus or dissection of the corpus callosum to prevent spread to the other hemisphere, can be considered. Surgical intervention is often preceded by a period of recording of brain activity from intracranially inserted electrodes under video-telemetry. The aim of this procedure is to pick up clinically relevant seizures and determine the site of the excessive neural activation that will later be removed at surgery. These periods, typically around two weeks long, also give researchers the opportunity to obtain intracranial recordings from human participants during cognitive experiments. One particular challenge of epilepsy diagnosis is the distinction of epileptic from psychogenic seizures, which will require a completely different treatment approach based on psychological intervention.

Depending on the frequency, severity and focus of the seizures, epilepsy can have neuropsychological consequences, for example memory deficits. TLE, the syndrome associated with complex partial seizures, which are also called 'temporal lobe' seizures because of their presumed site of origin, are most frequently associated with behavioural changes and psychiatric symptoms, which can affect up to a quarter of patients (Trimble et al., 1997). Isolated visual, tactile or auditory hallucinations are classically part of seizures, whereas a more complex psychosis with delusions and affective symptoms develops in the interictal phases and is more common with a long history of poorly controlled seizures. Paradoxically, schizophreniform psychosis ('schizophrenia-like psychosis of epilepsy', SLPE) and affective disturbance can increase with optimised control of seizures in some patients. This phenomenon, which has been called 'alternative psychosis' (denoting the idea that patients alternate between periods of seizures and psychosis) or 'forced normalisation', was at the root of the development of electroconvulsive therapy (ECT) for the treatment of psychosis and depression. Psychiatric problems in epilepsy patients are therapeutically challenging because of the epileptogenic effects of most psychotropic drugs. Achieving good seizure control early on during the course of the illness is probably the best preventive measure against neuropsychiatric complications.

21.2.5 Movement disorders

21.2.5.1 Parkinson's disease

The movement disorders are a group of neurodegenerative or metabolic disorders that affect the extrapyramidal motor circuits of the basal ganglia and lead to exaggerated ('hyperkinetic') or diminished ('hypokinetic') motor activity. Parkinson's disease (PD), first described by the British apothecary James Parkinson (1755–1824) in 1817 as 'shaking palsy', is a neurodegenerative disease that affects primarily the dopaminergic neurons of the pars compacta of the substantia nigra. Clinical symptoms start when ca. 60% of these neurons are lost. With disease progression, serotonergic neurons in the raphe nuclei, noradrenergic nuclei in the locus coeruleus and cholinergic neurons in the basal nucleus of Meynert also degenerate. Most cases are sporadic, but about one-third of patients have other affected family members and about 1% are inherited in autosomal dominant or recessive fashion. Age of onset of symptoms is normally between 60 and 80 in sporadic cases, but can be much earlier, especially in inherited cases. The cellular pathology is characterised by abnormal accumulation of the protein alpha-synuclein, which forms the cytoplasmic inclusions first described by the German neurologist Friedrich Lewy (1885–1950) (Figure 20.6, Plate VIII). Alpha-synuclein seems to be a key component in the pathophysiology of a wide range of neurodegenerative disorders, which are sometimes termed collectively 'synucleopathies' (see Section 20.12). The lack of dopaminergic input to the striatum leads to changes in the balance between excitatory and inhibitory input into the direct and indirect basal ganglia pathways, which have increased inhibition of the thalamus by the internal globus pallidus as a net result. Because the thalamus is an important pacemaker for cortical motor regions, the symptoms of PD are largely hypokinetic, such as the characteristic shuffling gait or difficulty initiating movements. Tremor and rigidity are other characteristic signs. Neuropsychiatric consequences such as depression or dementia develop in up to 50% of patients after several years of disease progression. The dementia is characterised by psychomotor slowing, slow thinking, apathy and deficits in memory recall, which has been termed a 'subcortical pattern' because 'cortical' functions such as memory encoding and language are relatively preserved. Although PD dementia shares features with DLB (Chapter 20), the cognitive symptoms here follow the motor symptoms by several years, whereas the onset of cognitive and motor problems in DLB is synchronous. Behavioural abnormalities such as punding or pathological gambling and paranoid psychosis are a rare but important side effect of dopaminergic medication, which is the mainstay of treatment. In patients who do not respond well to treatment with dopamine agonists and/or levodopa (a dopamine precursor that passes through the blood–brain barrier), modulation of the basal ganglia pathways through deep brain stimulation may improve motor function but can also increase neuropsychiatric complications. Other major challenges to the neuropsychiatric management of PD are the excessive daytime sleepiness and narcolepsy-like features (see Chapter 19) that affect about a third of patients. These may also result from damage to the other neuromodulatory pathways and the orexin system (Arnulf and Leu-Semenescu, 2009).

21.2.5.2   Huntington's disease

Huntington's disease (HD) was first fully described by the American physician George Huntington (1850–1916) in 1872. It is an autosomally inherited (see Chapter 4), neurodegenerative disorder that starts in the caudate nucleus and results in chorea, irregular jerky movements that can lead to loss of balance and severely interfere with regular motor actions. At later stages visceral movements such as swallowing can also be impaired. Affective symptoms include both depression and mania, and obsessive-compulsive symptoms are also common. Because of the relentless course of the disorder, resulting in disability and dementia, and its impact on family planning, the associated psychosocial stress is considerable. HD affects between 1 and 5/100,000 in the general population. The responsible mutation affects a trinucleotide (cytosine-adenine-guanine (CAG), coding for the amino acid guanine) repeat region in the huntingtin gene on the short arm of chromosome 4. Healthy individuals have fewer than 35 repeats, over 40 lead to the development of HD, and intermediate numbers may or may not lead to symptomatic states. The function of huntingtin is unknown, but knock-out in mice is not compatible with life. There is no causal treatment for HD. Motor symptoms can sometimes be controlled with tetrabenazine, a VMAT antagonist that reduces dopamine release.

21.2.5.3   Wilson's disease

Wilson's disease was first described in 1912 as hepatolenticular degeneration (affecting the liver and the lentiform nucleus of the basal ganglia, which comprises the putamen and globus pallidus) by the British neurologist Samuel Wilson (1878–1937). It results from accumulation of copper in the affected tissues. In addition to liver and brain these can include the eyes, kidneys and the heart. The accumulation of copper is caused by mutations in the Wilson's gene on the long arm of chromosome 13. This gene codes for an ATPase that promotes the secretion of copper and its incorporation in the transport protein coeruloplasmin, which has characteristically low levels in Wilson's disease. Accumulation of copper in tissue can cause oxidative damage and eventually cell death. The neurological and psychiatric problems result from damage to the lenticular nucleus. Motor signs range from clumsiness to Parkinsonism and ataxia, and progressive cognitive deterioration, affective symptoms and psychosis can also occur if the disease is not adequately treated. The age of onset is commonly in childhood or adolescence, and 1–5/100,000 of the population are affected. Pharmacological treatment with chelators (copper-binding molecules) such as penicillamine is effective, but side effects, tolerance and paradoxical worsening of motor problems may pose problems. Treatment needs to be initiated as early as the disease is detected, even if patients are asymptomatic, because the liver and brain damage is not reversible.

21.2.5.4 Tourette's syndrome

Tourette's syndrome (TS) was first described by the French neurologist Georges Gilles de la Tourette (1857–1904) in 1885. This syndrome comprises chronic motor and vocal tics. Tics are involuntary movements, and only a limited number of them occur in any individual. Tics can be simple (e.g. blinking, barking) or complex (clapping, swearing), and may involve the repetition of the actions or verbalisations of others (echolalia, echopraxia). TS is highly comorbid with OCD and ADHD and can be severely disruptive to the patient's social activities, especially when others are not aware of the nature of the disorder. It affects about 0.05% of the population and commonly starts at primary school age. Although it is classified as a movement disorder and basal ganglia pathology has been implicated, its pathophysiological mechanisms are unknown. Pharmacological treatment is based on reduction of dopaminergic or noradrenergic activity, but there is no direct evidence for a primary hyperactivity of these systems. ADHD symptoms tend to respond better to pharmacological intervention than other symptoms of TS, and the available drugs are the same as those used for primary ADHD. The α_2 agonists guanfacine and clonidine, which reduce adrenergic tone, are in development for this indication as well.

21.2.6 Encephalitis

Infections of the brain (encephalitis) or brain and meninges (meningoencephalitis) can be acute and life-threatening or chronic and lead to progressive disability. Encephalitis caused by the Herpes simplex virus (HSV), for example, often presents initially with an acute psychosis, which can be accompanied by aphasia and seizures. The temporal lobes are normally affected uni- or bilaterally, and the focal damage is apparent on MRI (Figure 21.2a). HSV encephalitis also has characteristic EEG features (Figure 21.2b). The diagnosis is confirmed by detection of anti-HSV antibodies or virus DNA in CSF, but antiviral treatment needs to be initiated as soon as HSV encephalitis is suspected because any delay increases the risk of fatal outcome or irreversible hippocampal damage, which can lead to dense amnesia and the other syndromes associated with limbic pathology.

Acquired immune deficiency syndrome (AIDS), caused by infection with the human immunodeficiency virus (HIV), is an example of viral disease that can lead to chronic brain inflammation. AIDS encephalitis or encephalopathy leads to progressive dementia and can be associated with organic personality disorder, affective disorder and psychosis. Several mechanisms, including direct neurotoxic effects of viral proteins and release of proinflammatory cytokines by glia cells activated by the brain invasion of the virus, have been implicated in the pathophysiology of AIDS encephalopathy.

Up to the early twentieth century, syphilis (or lues) was one of the commonest causes of mental health problems, at least in the male population. Infection with the bacterium treponema pallidum affects the skin, internal organs and at later stages the spinal cord and brain. Chronic encephalitis, termed neurosyphilis or neurolues, is associated with characteristic eye movement signs, which allowed for a reliable diagnosis even before laboratory tests became available. It leads to progressive dementia, and psychiatric syndromes, particularly mania, are common. Although syphilis can now be treated effectively with antibiotics such as penicillin, there are still rare cases of neurosyphilis (sometimes in immuno-compromised patients, for example in conjunction with HIV infection), which are generally irreversible.

Another cause of chronic encephalitis which was close to eradication, at least in the industrialised world, but is now returning is infection with the measles virus. Encephalitis is a rare complication of measles, affecting about 1/1000 patients. Measles infection can also lead to the even rarer (1/100,000) sub-acute sclerosing panencephalitis (SSPE), which occurs with a

Figure 21.2

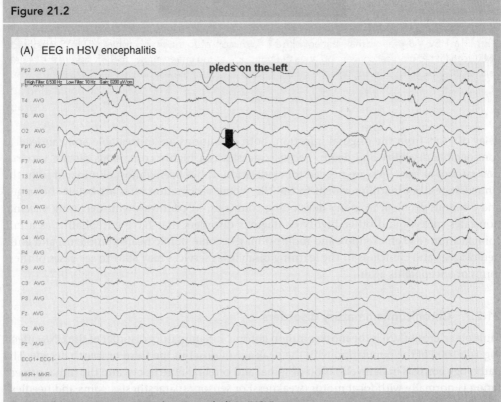

(A) EEG in HSV encephalitis

EEG and MRI in Herpes Simplex Encephalitis (HSV)

(A) EEG in HSV – 23-year-old female patient with a four week history of headache, altered behaviour and tonic-clonic seizures. The EEG shows left temporal periodic lateralised epileptiform discharges (PLED). The patient was diagnosed with Herpes Simplex Virus (HSV) encephalitis and treated with the antiviral agent acyclovir and the anticonvulsant carbamazepine. PLED are typical EEG features of encephalitis.

(continued)

Figure 21.2

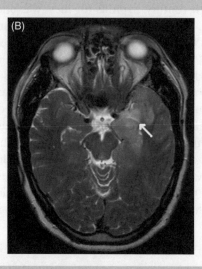

(B) MRI in HSV – 48-year-old male patient with a 4-day history of agitation and aphasia. This T2-weighted MRI scan (in radiological convention, thus the right side of the image shows the left side of the brain) shows the typical hyperintensity in the medial temporal lobe of the left hemisphere (arrow).

delay of years from the original infection. Both conditions are untreatable and can lead to considerable disability and death. Because measles is a highly contagious disease vaccination rates of at least 95% are needed for eradication. It has been almost eliminated from the United States, but is still prevalent in the UK, where vaccination rates are below the target, and a serious problem in many developing countries. In countries with declining vaccination rates measles and other highly contagious disorders that have encephalitis as a rare complication (e.g. chickenpox and mumps) may become public health problems, and child neurologists and clinicians in the learning disabilities services may start to see cases of these forms of encephalitis again.

21.2.7   Chronic inflammatory disorders

Multiple sclerosis (MS) is the most common chronic inflammatory disorder of the CNS, affecting 1–2/1000 of the population with the peak age of onset in the third or fourth decade. The pathology consists in demyelination of spinal and cerebral fibre tracts, and the initial presentation is normally with focal motor (weakness) or sensory (paraesthesias: 'pins and needles') symptoms. The course of neurological decline is highly variable. Many patients will initially experience isolated bouts of symptoms, which alternate with symptom-free periods ('relapsing–remitting course'). In other cases, the course may be progressive from the outset ('primary progressive') or after a relapsing–remitting phase ('secondary progressive'). Depression is common and may even precede neurological symptoms. Cognitive decline, fatigue and apathy are also important neuropsychiatric symptoms, whereas euphoria and psychosis are observed less frequently. Pseudobulbar affective disorder resembles the other organic mood disorders in that it is mainly characterised by emotional lability. It occurs after over ten years and is correlated with the amount of white matter lesions and cognitive decline.

The depression of MS patients is a major source of disability, and the associated motivational problems may compound motor disability and make rehabilitation more difficult. The severity of depression does not correlate with the degree of disability or duration of illness, but with the speed of progression. It may also be related to the amount of white matter damage in the frontal and temporal lobes. About 10% of MS patients make at least one suicide attempt. The pharmacological treatment strategies include the standard antidepressant drugs, but integration in a multi-professional service that incorporates physical and psychosocial rehabilitation needs and provides counselling on coping mechanisms is crucial, as with all organic mood disorders.

Systemic lupus erythematosus (SLE) is an autoimmune disorder that is in the remit of rheumatologists or nephrologists because it commonly first presents as arthritis or glomerulonephritis (a type of kidney inflammation). SLE affects about 75/100,000 with an age of onset normally above 50. SLE can affect the brain and then lead to cognitive decline, depression, hallucinations and organic personality disorder. These symptoms are associated with the activity of the disorder, that is, with the amount of autoantibodies produced, but not with the physical disability. Some psychotic symptoms can also arise as a consequence of the immunomodulatory therapy with glucocorticoids. In addition to the respective psychotropic drugs, control of the inflammatory process is crucial to the treatment of the psychiatric complications of SLE and other rarer systemic autoimmune disorders. Any first presentation of depression or psychosis in the elderly should trigger a somatic assessment, which needs to include the search for autoimmune disorders.

21.2.8   Brain tumours

Neoplastic tumours arise from the uncontrolled growth of a particular type of tissue. In tissues other than the CNS they are called 'malignant' if they spread through the blood or lymphatic systems and created metastases, and 'benign' if their growth is confined to the local area. In the brain this distinction is less clear. Although most brain tumours do not form metastases in other tissues, they may be highly destructive through diffuse infiltration of the brain, and surgical access may be risky if not impossible for many locations, particularly in the brainstem. Because of its high vascularisation the brain is also one of the main targets for metastatic tumours from other organs.

Tumours of neural tissue are rare (e.g. the medulloblastoma of childhood), and most primary brain tumours arise from the meninges (mengioma) or glia cells (glioma), for example astrocytes (astrocytoma) or oligodendrocytes (oligodendroglioma). Gliomas are staged into four degrees according to the level of destructive/infiltrating growth, and prognosis for grades 3 and 4 is generally poor. Grade 4 describes the highly infiltrative glioblastoma, which progresses rapidly and can lead to death within six months of the first presentation of symptoms. These initial symptoms are often psychiatric rather than neurological. In addition to the more generic syndromes of depression, apathy, personality change or psychosis, more focal neuropsychological deficits can occur, depending on the site of the lesion. The diagnosis is made through cerebral imaging (normally MRI), but other techniques may be needed to determine the exact type of the tumour, for example MR spectroscopy, angiography or even brain biopsy. Treatment varies according to the cell type of the tumour and may include surgery, chemotherapy and various types of radiation therapy.

21.2.9   Limbic encephalitis

Limbic encephalitis (LE) is one of the autoimmune encephalopathies, where the body produces autoantibodies against neural tissue. This group also includes the encephalopathy accompanying SLE discussed above (Section 21.2.7). Because it mainly affects the limbic system, behavioural and personality changes and psychotic symptoms are common. LE can be associated with tumours in other parts of the body, such as lung cancer, in which case it is called 'paraneoplastic' (occurring alongside a neoplasm or cancer). In most cases of LE, specific autoantibodies can be identified. These can target intracellular proteins, and some of them are closely associated with specific tumours, for example anti-Hu antibodies with small cell lung cancer. However, these antibodies can also be detected in patients with these tumours who do not develop LE or other paraneoplastic neurological syndromes, and probably make no direct contribution to the pathophysiological mechanisms underlying the neurological and psychiatric symptoms. Conversely, autoantibodies against cell surface proteins such as NT receptor or ion channel subunits likely play a central role in the development of neuropsychiatric symptoms. Antibodies against the voltage gated potassium channel (VGKC) (Figure 21.3), the AMPA receptor (GluR1 or GluR2 subunit, see 7.1.5) and against the B1 subunit of the $GABA_B$ receptor (see Section 7.3.6) have been identified in cases of LE, with or without an underlying tumour (Graus et al., 2010). A related neuropsychiatric syndrome, which is not classified as LE, has been observed in association with antibodies against the NR1 subunit of the NMDA receptor. Affected patients present with an acute psychotic episode, behavioural changes, potentially including aggression and violence, and progressive impairment of memory and consciousness. Disturbed movements,

---

Figure 21.3

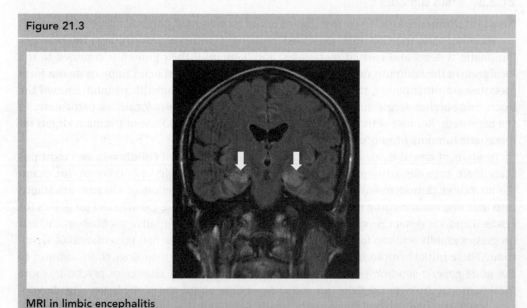

MRI in limbic encephalitis
The 63-year-old male patient presented with paranoia, impaired anterograde memory and fatigue. The FLAIR scan shows bilateral hyperintensities in the hippocampus (arrows), indicating an inflammatory process. Blood tests revealed anti-voltage gated potassium channel antibodies.

particularly catatonia, and autonomic failure can also occur. Females are predominantly affected and often also suffer from an ovarian teratoma, although non-paraneoplastic cases have also been observed (Nasky et al., 2008; Dalmau et al., 2011). The treatment of LE and other autoimmune encephalopathies often requires intensive care and involves several strategies of immune modulation (e.g. steroids, intravenous immunoglobulins) or removal of the autoantibodies (plasma exchange) as well as treatment of the underlying neoplastic disease, where present. For a general consideration of the treatment of the psychiatric syndromes of neurological disorders see Section 21.3.

21.2.10   Metabolic and toxic encephalopathies

A wide range of intoxications, for example with heavy metals or substances of abuse (see Chapter 15) and vitamin deficiencies can cause diffuse or focal brain damage. One example is Wernicke syndrome, which results from insufficient intake of vitamin B1 (thiamine) because of poor diet and is commonly associated with alcohol abuse. It involves relatively focal damage to diencephalic and brainstem structures such as the mammillary bodies, thalamus, and the nuclei of the oculomotor and abducens nerves. It presents with an insidious development of delirium, sometimes associated with nystagmus and/or ataxia. Untreated Wernicke syndrome is lethal in about 50% of cases. Treatment with high doses of intramuscular or intravenous vitamin B1 can have dramatic effects, and Moore (2008) poses the interesting public health question why vitamin B1 is not generally added to alcoholic beverages.

Metabolic encephalopathies are conditions where the intoxication is caused by accumulation of metabolites because of inability of internal organs to metabolise them further. The main reasons are renal (uraemic encephalopathy) or liver (hepatic encephalopathy) failure. Patients develop delirium and in some cases grand mal seizures. Asterixis (flapping tremor) and myoclonus (muscle twitching) are common signs. Whereas in hepatic encephalopathy ammonia seems to be most relevant, the toxin in uraemic encephalopathy has not yet been identified. The EEG shows generalised slowing and typical triphasic waves, but the pathophysiological mechanisms are unknown.

A group of metabolic disorders that often have an onset in early childhood and a poor prognosis results from abnormal storage of lipids in the brain and other organs. These lipid storage disorders can present with a wide range of neurological, physical and psychiatric symptoms (including learning disability or dementia) and are commonly discussed in textbooks of neurology, paediatrics or paediatric neurology. However, because in some cases they may have a primarily neuropsychiatric presentation and some forms do not start until adulthood, both child and adolescent and adult psychiatrists and psychologists need to be aware of them. Amongst this large group of liposomal storage disorders, metachromatic leukodystrophy, adrenoleukodystrophy and Niemann-Pick's disease type C occasionally have primarily psychiatric presentations, and changes in white matter and myelination and the resulting dysconnectivity of cortical region seem to be the underlying mechanisms (Sévin et al., 2007).

21.3   TREATMENT

Neuropsychiatric therapies often have to focus on syndromes because there is no pharmacological treatment for the underlying pathology (e.g. TBI, hypoxia, stroke), and thus many treatment principles apply across pathologies. Where it is possible, neuropsychiatric treatment will use the specific pharmacological agents that are indicated for the neurological disorder in question. For example, dopaminergic treatment of PD may, in addition to its effects on motor function, have desirable effects on mood states. Patients with brain injuries have a higher risk of developing side effects from psychotropic medication, especially cognitive impairment from anticholinergic effects. A high proportion of this patient group also suffers from symptomatic seizures, and seizure frequency can be increased or seizures induced by almost any psychotropic drug.

Emotional lability can be treated with SSRIs or anticonvulsant mood stabilisers, and mania with lithium. Deficits in motivation and arousal and sometimes cognition are improved with dopaminergic medication. Amantadine (which is also a weak NMDA antagonist), d-amphetamine, methylphenidate, modafinil and the D_2-agonist bromocriptine have all been used for this purpose. The injured brain is more vulnerable to side effects, though, which can include agitation, dysphoria and psychotic symptoms. However, the concern that these drugs lower the seizure threshold seems to apply only to amantadine (Yudofsky and Hales, 2008). Acetylcholinesterase inhibitors may also lead to small improvements of cognitive symptoms, similar to their effects in dementia.

In the pharmacological treatment of psychotic symptoms the higher vulnerability to develop Parkinsonian side effects needs to be considered. The antipsychotic agent risperidone has an acceptable balance between extrapyramidal and anticholinergic side effects. The psychotic symptoms associated with dopaminergic treatment of PD can often be controlled with the antipsychotic clozapine, which is not recommended in patients with focal brain lesions because of the relatively high risk of seizures. Antipsychotics work well for the symptoms of TS, but the α_2 adrenergic receptor agonists guanfacine and clonidine present an alternative, which may be preferable because of fewer side effects. Agonism at the presynaptic alpha$_2$ receptor of CNS neurons reduces the release of norepinephrine.

As for primary insomnia, benzodiazepines and z-hypnotics should be used only very restrictively for the sleep problems of brain injury patients. The sedating antidepressant trazodone, which has no anticholinergic effect (it is mainly a 5-HT$_{2A}$ receptor antagonist and 5-HT$_{1A}$ receptor partial agonist), is an alternative, but other important side effects such as the rare occurrence of ventricular arrhythmias or priapism (persistent painful erections) need to be taken into consideration.

Chronic aggression is perhaps the greatest challenge to the management of traumatic and other brain injuries. Atypical antipsychotics, anticonvulsants (carbamazepine, valproic acid), SSRIs and beta-blockers can all be effective, but in all cases will have to be evaluated against their side effects. High-dose treatment with a beta-blocker such as propranolol may be particularly effective, but patients with respiratory and several other medical disorders need to be excluded, and the cardiac effects of beta-receptor blockade monitored particularly carefully (Yudofsky and Hales, 2008).

Pharmacological treatment will never make more than a small contribution to the joint effort of the multidisciplinary team in the management and rehabilitation with brain injury patients. CBT and other psychological interventions are central in the management of emotional instability, anger and aggression. There is often a striking mismatch between (relatively little) physical impairment and major psychological effects. Frustration about the reduction in the level of functioning compared to the time before the injury and lack of activity and social stimulation play an important role in this and can be targeted with occupational therapy. Finally, social support and counselling for both patients and carers is particularly important in cases with brain injury or chronic neurological disorders.

Box 21.1   Persistent vegetative state, minimally conscious state, locked-in syndrome

Severe head trauma and other brain lesions, for example from anoxia, can initially lead to coma. This state resembles deep sleep, but even strong environmental stimuli cannot awaken patients who may at most show reflex movements to pain. Spontaneous breathing can be preserved, but other patients require continuous ventilation. The most severe form of coma has been termed 'brain death', which describes the irreversible loss of brain functions, where at most spinal reflexes are preserved. 'Brain death' is equivalent to the death of the person in most legal systems, even if it is possible to sustain cardiovascular and pulmonary functions mechanically for some time. If a patient survives but does not fully recover consciousness, two scenarios can emerge: persistent vegetative state (PVS) or minimally conscious state (MCS). Both are disorders of consciousness with partly preserved wakefulness but absent (PVS) or diminished (MCS) awareness (Bernat, 2009).

Patients in PVS breathe independently, can have their eyes open and move spontaneously, but not purposefully. However, they do not communicate and do not follow any commands. Thus, they do not seem to be aware of what is happening around them. Yet, they are not in coma because they act spontaneously and have an intact sleep–wake cycle. Patients with MCS respond variably and show some directed movements, but their communication is limited to simple gestures or verbal responses. Both PVS and MCS patients are bed-bound and totally dependent on 24-hour care. The dissociation of preserved wakefulness and impaired awareness is thought to be caused by the different neural representation of these functions. Wakefulness is supported by the ARAS, which is unaffected by patients with cortical or thalamic lesions, whereas awareness relies on cortico-thalamic systems. Wakefulness is a prerequisite for awareness but can be preserved without the latter.

Patients can stay in PVS or MCS for many years, and some can fully recover awareness even after years or decades. Determining prognosis is an important medical and ethical challenge. The ethical dimension derives from the question of whether essential life support, such as gastric tube feeding, may be withdrawn from patients who have practically no hope of regaining awareness. Some carers of patients in PVS have argued that maintaining physiological functions is compatible with the dignity of the person only if there is realistic hope that the patient will regain full consciousness, but others would argue that withdrawing support would be contrary to basic human rights. In addition to clinical features and the size and type of the original brain lesion, neurophysiological measures of brain responsiveness such as the P300 or mismatch negativity of the event-related potentials are being explored. Functional imaging can also be used to assess brain metabolism in PVS and MCS patients. Several case studies where PVS patients apparently followed commands to engage in specific mental activity during fMRI attracted widespread attention. In one such study, a patient was asked to imagine playing tennis, and higher motor areas duly showed activity during these instructions. Such findings suggest that purely clinical measures of responsiveness may underestimate the level of cortical activity. In this particular case, the diagnosis may have to be revised from PVS to MCS (Bernat, 2009). However, such reclassification will probably affect only a minority of patients. In a recent fMRI study only 10% of patients with disorders of consciousness showed signs of awareness (Monti et al., 2010). Because of the major impact of understanding the level of awareness of each individual patient on carers, family, and possibly for treatment and prognosis, these approaches are still very worthwhile.

Another disorder of communication but not of consciousness arises when the higher brain areas are separated from its output pathways by a stroke or other lesion of the upper brainstem. In this 'locked-in syndrome' patients are fully alert and aware, but may only be able to give 'yes' and 'no' signals through vertical eye or lid movements. In the very rare cases, where even these movements are no longer possible, for example as a consequence of late-stage ALS, communication can be attempted through Brain Computer Interfaces (BCIs) (Birbaumer and Cohen, 2007). BCIs use brain signals, picked up by EEG or fMRI, for the control of an output device, for example a computer mouse. If a patient is capable of controlling the relevant brain signal, he/she would also be able to give answers through the BIC. Patients can be trained to influence slow cortical potentials of the EEG or communicate through the P300. However, it is currently not clear whether it will be possible to train many of the total locked-in patients who would benefit most from these methods. An alternative might be the use of fMRI, where control of a spelling device may be possible without much training through the use of a set of mental imagery tasks (Sorger et al., 2009), but this has yet to be tested in clinical practice. Another interesting approach would be to try and extract information about mental activity directly from brain activity through a technique called multivariate pattern analysis (sometimes termed 'brain reading'). Yet this technique has so far been used only for relatively circumscribed sets of mental acts and not tested in real-life settings.

Learning points

This chapter reviewed some of the most common brain pathologies that can result in psychiatric symptoms. In some cases, there is a relationship between the affected areas and the type of symptoms, for example auditory hallucinations in temporal lobe epilepsy. However, more often the psychiatric problems resulting from neurological diseases will be non-specific and include mood- and substance-use disorders and impulsive/aggresive behaviours. In addition to the treatment of the underlying neurological disease, treatment of the psychiatric symptoms with psychotropic drugs and a general supportive rehabilitative and psychoeducative approach will be needed.

Revision and discussion questions

- Distinguish dementia from delirium and from amnesic syndrome.
- What do the neuropsychiatric symptoms of Parkinson's disease and side effects of dopaminergic treatment tell us about the functions of the dopamine system?
- How is the location of a stroke related to the neuropsychiatric consequences?
- Discuss new ways of communicating with patients who have minimal or no control of movements

FURTHER READING

Coetzer, R. (2010). *Anxiety and Mood Disorders Following Traumatic Brain Injury: Clinical Assessment and Psychotherapy* (London: Karnac Books).

Moore, D. P. (2008) *Textbook of Clinical Neuropsychiatry*, 2nd edition (London: Hodder Arnold).

Ropper, A. H. and Samuels, M. A. (2009). *Adams and Victor's Principles of Neurology*, 9th edition (New York: McGraw Hill).

Yudofsky, S. C. and Hales, R. E. (2002). *The American Psychiatric Publishing Textbook of Neuropsychiatry and Clinical Neurosciences*, 4th edition (Washington, DC: American Psychiatric Publishing.

Afterword: The Future of Biological Psychiatry

The development of chemically specific and reasonably well-tolerated drugs for mental disorders has been the big success story of biological psychiatry. Although many aspects of psychopharmacotherapy are unsatisfactory, for example the EPS of antipsychotics or the addictive potential of benzodiazepines, it has considerably improved the lives of the majority of patients, and modern concepts of psychiatry including community-based treatment would not exist without it. Where biological psychiatry has so far largely failed, however, is in providing diagnostically or prognostically useful biomarkers (except perhaps in the field of dementia) and clear evidence for the neural mechanisms of mental disorders. This is a puzzling outcome of over 150 years of research into the biology of psychological disorders, which has included ever more sophisticated post-mortem techniques, neurochemistry, electrophysiology, animal models and recently also the very powerful tools of non-invasive structural (MRI), chemical (SPECT/PET) and functional (fMRI, PET) neuroimaging. One reason might be that the tools that can be used in vivo in humans are still too crude, and that techniques with higher spatial and neurochemical resolution are required. Currently, the only way around this would be to combine and coregister PET and high resolution MRI in the same patients, and this (still very expensive) combination of methods is available in only a few research centres. Another reason might be that the phenotypes that are normally correlated with biological changes are too complex and heterogeneous. For example, the patient sample from any schizophrenia study will be composed of individuals with very different personal histories and indeed different, only partly overlapping symptoms. This could be addressed by careful subdivision of patients into clinical subtypes (e.g. paranoid vs. hebephrenic schizophrenia; melancholic vs. non-melancholic depression) or by the target search for neural correlates of specific symptoms. A third reason may be that investigators have not looked in the right places. The focus on specific neurotransmitters and their receptors, transporters and metabolising enzymes may have been a red herring suggested by the mechanisms of psychotropic drugs. This red herring may have led astray not only many years of candidate gene research, but also the search for neurochemical or histochemical (post-mortem) targets. Interestingly, the GWAS of most mental disorders do not prominently implicate any single NT system, but highlight potential risk loci on genes coding for proteins that regulate general synaptic and neural mechanisms. It would therefore be highly desirable to have non-invasive markers of synaptic function available in order to observe functional effects of these genetic variants. Recent genetic work also highlights the importance of rare variants (e.g. copy number variants) for disorders such as schizophrenia and ADHD, which means that the genes contributing larger effects to the genetic load differ greatly across patients. Again, this observation calls efforts to find a single (or small number of) gene for any mental disorder into question, and suggests that different protein abnormalities can result in a similar clinical phenotype.

The other major conundrum of biological research into mental disorders concerns the mechanisms leading to the occurrence and remission of symptoms. Such 'state markers' need to be separated conceptually from 'trait markers' that are present throughout a patient's life and possibly also in individuals at genetic risk. The search for valid and reliable state and trait markers of mental disorders is therefore a priority and should involve a joint effort of cognitive and basic neuroscience. Such markers can in principle be found at any level between the clinical phenotype and the genome, from behavioural tests down to epigenetic modifications. Much hope presently rests in the role of epigenetics as a mechanism linking early environmental influences with later neural and behavioural effects, but it remains to be seen just how powerful these explanatory tools will be. At present, though, we have almost no information about the psychological or biological mechanisms that trigger the onset of symptomatic episodes in the mental disorders with a relapsing and remitting course (schizophrenia, bipolar disorder, recurrent depressive episodes). The other main group of relapsing/remitting disorders in medicine are autoimmune disorders (e.g. multiple sclerosis, rheumatoid arthritis) and it remains to be explored whether some of the same biological principles apply in psychiatry.

Are there any new drugs or therapeutic strategies on the horizon? In the clinical chapters we learnt about several new pharmacological principles that are in preclinical and clinical testing, for example NMDA receptor agonists for schizophrenia, neuropeptides or HPA axis modulators for depression, oxytocin for autism or anti-amyloid vaccinations for Alzheimer's disease. All of these new drugs still need further evidence of efficacy and/or safety in order to be adopted by the licensing bodies. At present, therefore, the mainstay of the pharmacotherapy of mental disorders are agents that follow the traditional pharmacological principles of dopamine or dopamine/serotonin antagonism in schizophrenia, monoamine agonism in depression, and serotonin or GABA agonism for anxiety. The known targets of all these drugs are largely synaptic. The treatment of bipolar disorder is an exception because, in addition to presumed effects on the cell membrane, lithium has documented effects on postsynaptic signalling cascades, although it is not clear which mechanism underlies its therapeutic effect. Such an action at the level of postsynaptic signalling cascades is attractive because of the emerging evidence mentioned above that the classic mental disorders are probably not caused by changes in any single neurotransmitter system. It is hoped that further research into the cellular effects of currently used psychotropic drugs will reveal whether any of them have similar effects at the convergence points of second and further messenger cascades, or that substances with such effects will prove to be useful in other mental disorders as well. Another completely uncharted territory is the cellular mechanism behind psychotherapy. The last decade has seen a welcome increase in the interest in the neural changes produced by psychological interventions, and one practical outcome may be improved synergy between pharmacological and non-pharmacological treatments.

Pharmacotherapy (and this is largely true for other forms of therapy as well) is presently only available for the treatment and secondary prevention of mental disorders, but not for their primary prevention. Such a use would require substances that can prevent the outbreak of a disorder and predictive biomarkers to identify individuals at high risk. Trials are currently underway in patients at high clinical and genetic risk of schizophrenia to prevent the conversion from the prodromal syndrome to the full clinical phenotype through antipsychotic drug treatment or psychosocial interventions, and trying to prevent the conversion from MCI to dementia would be another such application. With conversion rates in the range of 20% or less per year, however, large numbers of patients and many years' duration are required in order for such trials to produce stable effects. Until such primary prevention of mental disorders becomes feasible, we have to acknowledge that current psychiatric and psychological treatment is symptomatic rather than causal.

At the beginning of this afterword I contrasted the comparative success of biological treatment with the hitherto disappointing results on biomarkers of mental disorders. These results are disappointing only from a purely clinical point of view because, in many other respects, the research into the biological underpinnings of mental disorders and its associated behaviours has been extremely fruitful. Many of the developments of cognitive, affective and social neuroscience, animal behaviour research, quantitative genetics and epigenetics were driven by research programmes in biological psychiatry, and they have contributed greatly to the understanding of the biology of human behaviour. We now have highly sophisticated methods available to test the fascinating new theories of the neural mechanisms of psychiatric syndromes and symptoms, many of which have been outlined in this book, which are likely to result in a very productive decade of scientific discovery and, hopefully, clinical advances in the biology of psychological disorders.

Glossary: Biological and Neuroanatomical Terms and Methods

Action potential (AP): Supra-threshold change of membrane potential, generated at the axon hillock, which is transmitted through the axon and leads to the release of neurotransmitters from synaptic terminals.

Adenosine triphosphate (ATP): A nucleotide composed of the organic base adenine, the sugar ribose (collectively termed 'adenosine') and three phosphate groups; the phosphate bond is a main source of energy for metabolic processes in the body.

Agonist: Molecule that promotes a chemical reaction or activates a receptor.

Allocortex: Cortex with less than six layers; classified as 'old' in evolutionary terms.

Alpha-amino-3-hydroxy-5-methyl-4-isoxazole propionic acid (AMPA): Specific ligand for one of the ionotropic glutamate receptors (the 'AMPA' receptor).

Amino acid: Class of molecules where a carbon atom is bound to an amino (NH2) and a carboxyl (COOH) group and a side chain of variable composition. Amino acids are the building blocks of proteins.

Amygdala: Almond-shaped nucleus at the anterior end of the medial temporal lobe, implicated in emotions and memory; part of the limbic system.

Antagonist: Molecule that inhibits a chemical reaction or the activation of a receptor.

Anterior cingulate cortex (ACC): Mesocortical structure of the medial surface of the frontal lobe; anterior part of the cingulate cortex, which forms a belt (Latin *cingulum* = belt) around the corpus callosum.

Ascending reticular arousal system (ARAS): A system of projections from the brainstem to cortex whose activation maintains wakefulness.

Autonomic nervous system (ANS): The part of the nervous system that regulates the functions of internal organs; collective term for the sympathetic and parasympathetic portions of nerves and their ganglia and nuclei. It thus comprises parts of the CNS and PNS.

Autoreceptor: Receptor for a specific ligand on the releasing cell; often subserves a negative feedback loop to control the release of that substance.

Axon: Part of a neuron, normally a single projection through which action potentials are transmitted to the neuron's target.

Baroreceptor: A type of mechanoreceptor inside vessels that is sensitive to changes in blood pressure.

Basal ganglia: Collective term for the grey matter nuclei that are embedded in the deep white matter of the telencephalon.

Basal nucleus (of Meynert): Area of grey matter in the basal forebrain, containing acetylcholine-producing cells.

Brainstem: Collective term for the evolutionarily older parts of the CNS along the axis of the body, the medulla oblongata, pons and midbrain; because all connections between the cerebral hemispheres and effector organs have to travel through the brainstem, its lesions often have severe neurological consequences.

Cell membrane: Structure of two layers of lipid molecules ('lipid bilayer') that surrounds cells and creates a barrier between the intra- and extracellular fluid; charged particles (ions) can pass the membrane through specific channel proteins, which are regulated chemically ('ligand-gated') or electrically ('voltage-gated').

Central nervous system (CNS): Collective term for the brain and spinal cord.

Cerebrospinal fluid (CSF): Fluid in the subarachnoid space surrounding the brain and spinal cord that provides mechanical protection to the CNS.

Chemoreceptor: Peripheral receptor (e.g. in some of the main vessels) that detects changes in the concentration of a range of chemicals.

Co-agonist: Ligand that is necessary but not sufficient for the activation of a receptor, for example D-serine in the case of NMDA receptors.

Conjugation: Part (Phase II) of drug metabolism in the liver; involves the addition of one of several residues (e.g. glucuronic acid, sulphates) to a polar group in the metabolite, rendering it inactive.

Copy number variant (CNV): Deletion or duplication of a stretch of DNA that may span several genes; can lead to quantitative and qualitative changes in gene expression.

Corpus callosum: Large fibre bundle (white matter) between the ACC and the lateral ventricles of the brain, containing most interhemispheric fibres.

Cranial nerves: Nerves arising directly from the brain and supplying mainly the head and neck.

Dalton: Unit of atomic mass (approximately the weight of one hydrogen atom); the unit kiloDalton (kDA) is often used in molecular biology.

Demyelination: Loss of the myelin protein forming the insulating sheath around axons; can result from inflammatory processes, for example in multiple sclerosis.

Dendrite: Part of a neuron, one of up to tens of thousands of projections that receive input from other neurons.

Deoxyribonucleic acid (DNA): Macromolecule that is main repository of genetic information in most living beings.

Depolarisation: Change of the membrane potential to a more positive value.

Diencephalon: Part of the brain situated between the telencephalon and the brainstem; comprises the thalamus and hypothalamus and thus contains crucial relay stations for sensory, cognitive and autonomic functions.

Diffusion tensor imaging (DTI): Method of MRI that provides information about the integrity of fibre tracts and allows for their reconstruction.

Dimer (Trimer ...): A molecule composed of two (three ...) subunits

Dorsolateral prefrontal cortex (DLPFC): Part of the lateral surface of prefrontal neocortex above the inferior frontal sulcus.

Electroencephalography (EEG): Recording of potential changes at electrodes on the scalp that reflect large-scale changes in synaptic potentials in the brain.

Elevated Plus Maze (EPM): A plus-shaped maze with two unprotected elevated arms and two enclosed arms; it allows the measurement of differences in time spent in the unprotected and protected arms, a surrogate marker of an animal's anxiety.

Endocytosis: Transport of molecules into the cell through the fusion of vesicles with the cell membrane.

Entorhinal cortex: Allocortical area in the medial temporal lobe with dense connections to the hippocampus, which it borders.

Epigenetics: The set of biochemical modulations of DNA that influence the activation or inactivation of genes; under discussion as a mechanism for heritability of acquired behaviours.

Eukaryotic cell: A cell with a nucleus (cells without a nucleus are 'prokaryotic')

Excitatory postsynaptic potential (EPSP): Depolarisation of the postsynaptic membrane; spreads electrotonically and can, through temporal and spatial summation, reach the threshold for triggering an action potential at the axon hillock.

Exocytosis: Removal of molecules from the cell through fusion of vesicles with the cell membrane.

Exon: Part of the gene that is transcribed into mRNA. Most genes have several exons, interleaved with 'intron' that are not transcribed and probably serve regulatory functions.

G-protein: Membrane-bound intracellular protein that is activated by Guanosine triphosphate (GTP).

Gene: Stretch of DNA that codes for one protein.

Genetic code: Triplets of bases of DNA or RNA are translated into specific amino acids.

Genome: The set of genes of an individual.

Glia cell: A non-neuronal cell of the brain, providing metabolic, structural or immunological functions

Glycolysis: Breakdown of glucose to pyruvate; under aerobic (= oxygen available) conditions this can be oxidised to acetyl-CoA (coenzyme A), which enters the Krebs cycle.

Golgi apparatus: Organelle that transports macromolecules such as proteins or lipids.

Haplotype (short for 'haploid genotype'): A set of closely linked allelic variants or genetic markers.

Heteromer/homomer: A molecule that is composed of several different/identical subunits.

Hippocampus: Sea-horse shaped part of allocortex in the medial temporal lobe, mainly implicated in the formation of memories; part of the limbic system.

Homoeostasis: The balance between metabolic processes required for survival of an organism.

Hydrophilic: 'Water loving', describes polar molecules that mix with water but are repelled by apolar parts of molecules, for example the long lipid chains of the cell membrane.

Hydrophobic: 'Water hating', the opposite of 'hydrophilic', describes apolar molecules that are repelled by water; also called 'lipophilic'.

Hyperpolarisation: Change of the membrane potential to more negative values.

Hypothalamus: Part of the diencephalon, containing central nuclei of the autonomic nervous system (ANS); also the origin of the hypothalamus-pituitary axis of hormone secretion.

Hypoxia: Lack of oxygen; can lead to irreversible damage to the brain and other organs.

Immediate early genes (IEG): Group of genes that have a low baseline expression rate; their expression is typically increased after activation of second messenger systems and is not under the control of other genes.

Inhibitory postsynaptic potential (IPSP): Hyperpolarisation of postsynaptic membrane; makes AP less likely.

Interneuron: Multipolar neuron with local projections, often inhibitory.

Ion channel: Protein that spans the cell membrane ('transmembrane') and can be permeable for ions (charged particles); their permeability may depend on the membrane potential ('voltage-gated ion channels') or activation by a ligand (ionotropic receptors).

Ionotropic (or ionotrophic): A receptor that is also an ion channel.

Ischaemia: Lack of blood supply; can lead to stroke.

Kinase: An enzyme that adds a phosphoryl group to a protein in order to activate or deactivate it.

Krebs cycle (or citric acid cycle): The sequence of chemical reactions that converts acetyl-CoA to carbon dioxide, yielding energy in the form of ATP; it is the last stage of the metabolism of glucose that starts with glycolysis.

Ligand-gated: An ion channel that is activated by binding of a ligand.

Limbic system: Group of allocortical and mesocortical areas and nuclei around the lateral ventricles (Latin *limbus* = border) that are involved in the formation of emotions and memories.

Lobe: One of four parts (frontal, parietal, occipital, temporal) of a hemisphere of the brain; the grey matter (cortex) of the lobes can be subdivided further into gyri.

Locus coeruleus: Nucleus in the pons, containing noradrenaline-producing cells.

Magnetic resonance imaging (MRI): Imaging technique that provides high-resolution information about anatomical structures, based on their water content and molecular composition. Functional MRI (fMRI) uses the same signal as MRI to trace local changes in blood oxygenation and is thus a marker of neural activity changes.

Mechanoreceptors: Receptors mainly located in the skin that register touch and pressure to the relevant organ.

Medial prefrontal cortex (MPFC): Medial surface of prefrontal cortex dorsal to the cingulate cortex; its posterior part, together with the medial surface of the premotor cortex, contains the supplementary motor area (SMA).

Membrane potential: The voltage difference between the intra- and extracellular milieu, produced by the distribution of charged particles on either side of the cell membrane; the reference is outside. The resting membrane potential is around -70 mV (millivolts).

Mesencephalon (midbrain): Structure between diencephalon and pons, containing descending and ascending fibres and nuclei (e.g. the nucleus ruber, part of the motor pathways, several cranial nerve nuclei, the superior and inferior colliculi).

Mesocortex: Subclassification of allocortex; five-layer cortex with considerable similarities to neocortex, for example found in cingulated and orbitofrontal cortex.

Messenger ribonucleic acid (mRNA): Product of transcription of DNA, serves as docking station for transfer RNA (tRNA); the right match between the base sequence of mRNA and tRNA, which carries amino acids, ensures that the genetic code is followed in the translation of mRNA into proteins.

Metabotropic: A receptor that is coupled to a G-protein.

Mitochondrium: Organelle that houses the central metabolic processes of the cell (conversion of glucose into the energy-storing molecule adenosine triphosphate, ATP).

Monoamine: A molecule with a single amine (-NH2) group; product of the decarboxylation (removal of carboxyl group -COOH) of an amino acid.

Morris Water Maze: A water-filled pool with a hidden escape platform; commonly used to test place memory in rats.

Myelination: Sheathing of axons by Schwann cells (PNS) or oligodendrocytes (CNS), which produces an insulating effect; this increases the speed at which an action potential travels.

N-methyl-D-aspartate (NMDA): Specific ligand for one of the ionotropic glutamate receptors (the "NMDA" receptor).

Neocortex (= isocortex): The six-layer cortex (sheet of grey matter) that covers most of the cerebral hemispheres; classified as 'new' in evolutionary terms.

Nervous system: The organ system mediating information transmission and coordinated activity between the sensory and motor systems and the control of the function of internal organs and bodily homoeostasis; the nervous system is divided into a peripheral, autonomic and central nervous system.

Neuron: Nerve cell, the main type of cell for signal conduction in the nervous system, which has projections for input (one or more dendrites) and output (normally only one axon).

Neurotransmitter: A molecule that is released from one neuron and induces chemical and electrical changes in another neuron or muscle cell; neurotransmitters come from different chemical classes, for example the monoamines dopamine, noradrenaline, adrenaline and serotonin.

Novelty-suppressed feeding test (NSFT): A test of feeding behaviour and novelty processing that measures the time until an animal (normally a rodent) starts eating familiar food in a novel environment.

Nucleic acids: Polymers (chains of identical subunits) of nucleotides. DNA and RNA are the most prominent examples; they are named for their abundance in the cell nucleus.

Nucleotide: Molecule composed of three subunits, an organic base, a 5-carbon sugar (pentose) and one to three phosphate groups.

Nucleus: 1. (Cell biology): Part of the cell, surrounded by its own membrane, which contains the chromosomes and is the site of DNA replication and transcription. 2. (Neuroanatomy): Subcortical area of grey matter, relay station for information transfer between cortex and periphery, for example the nuclei of the cranial nerves.

Open Field Test (OFT): A test of locomotor behaviour, where an animal (normally a rodent) has to explore a large new area.

Orbitofrontal cortex (OFC): Mesocortical structure in prefrontal cortex, above the orbits; implicated in reward processing and control of social behaviour.

Oxidation: Part (Phase I) of drug metabolism in the liver.

Penetrance: Frequency of the phenotype in carriers of a genetic variant.

Peripheral nervous system (PNS): The peripheral and cranial nerves and their ganglia outside the CNS.

Phenotype: Any set of features of an organism (e.g. colour of the eyes, height, intelligence) that is under the (partial – see 'penetrance') control of one or many genes (the 'genotype').

Phospholipid: Class of molecules whose defining elements are with one or more lipid tails and a phosphate head; to these additional central or peripheral component structures can be added; the phosphate head is hydrophilic, the lipid tails are hydrophobic, which aids their spontaneous assembly into bilayer structures such as the cell membrane.

Pituitary gland: Hormone-producing gland that receives releasing factors from the hypothalamus through dense vascular connection; its posterior part (neurohypophysis) secretes oxytocin and vasopressin and is part of the brain; its anterior part (adenohypophysis) produces and secretes several important hormones, summarised in Table 3.1.

Planum temporale: The upper side of the posterior part of the superior temporal gyrus, forming part of the lower bank of the Sylvian fissure; includes Wernicke's area in the dominant hemisphere.

Prefrontal cortex: Part of the frontal lobe, anterior to the premotor cortex; comprises the dorso- and ventrolateral and medial prefrontal cortex and the orbitofrontal cortex (further subdivisions such as dorso- and ventromedial and fronto-polar/rostral are sometimes used).

Premotor cortex: Part of the frontal lobe, anterior to the motor cortex.

Proteome: Term to denote the protein composition of a cell/organ/organism at a particular time, influenced by the part of the transcriptome that is actually translated.

Raphe nuclei: Nuclei in the pons and medulla oblongata, containing serotonin-producing cells.

Receptive field: The part of the environment covered by a neuron; for example, a neuron in visual cortex changes its firing in response to light emitted from its classical receptive field, but not to stimuli that are outside its receptive field (although this is a simplified model because of the presence of lateral connections).

Receptor: A molecule with a specific binding site for a ligand; binding of the ligand to the receptor according to the 'lock and key' principle normally changes the conformation of the receptor and triggers further electrophysiological and/or biochemical processes; receptors can be located on the cell membrane (pre- or postsynaptic, e.g. the neurotransmitter or growth factor receptors) or in the cell (e.g. many hormone receptors). Membrane receptors can be ionotropic, which means that they act themselves as ion channels, or metabotropic, which means that they modulate the activity of a G-protein and trigger second messenger cascades.

Reuptake: The active transport of a molecule, for example a neurotransmitter, from the synaptic cleft into the presynaptic cell; it is mediated by dedicated transporter molecules, for example the serotonin transporter, the dopamine transporter or the noradrenaline transporter (which also transports dopamine).

Ribonucleic acid (RNA): A nucleic acid whose nucleotides have ribose as their sugar; examples are messenger RNA (mRNA, the product of DNA transcription), transfer RNA (tRNA, which carries the amino acids for protein synthesis) and ribosomal RNA (rRNA, a main component of the ribosomes).

Rough endoplasmic reticulum: Membrane system ('reticulum' = net) covered with ribosomes, the sites of protein synthesis; also called 'Nissl substance'.

Second messenger: A substance that mediates the effects of a neurotransmitter or growth factor (the 'first messenger') on the postsynaptic cell; the enzymatic processes that lead to their production (adenylate cyclase for cyclic adenosine monophosphate or cAMP and phospholipase C for inositol triphosphate or IP3) depend on changes in G proteins that are controlled by metabotropic receptors; calcium, another important second messenger, can get into the cell through ion channels. The second messengers have further downstream effects (e.g. on kinases, transcription factors and immediate early genes).

Single nucleotide polymorphism (SNP): Genetic variant affecting a single base in the DNA; common SNPs are used to map the genome for genome-wide association studies.

Smooth endoplasmic reticulum: Membrane system that houses the synthesis of phospholipids, steroids and fatty acids (lipids).

Substantia nigra: Nucleus in the midbrain (mesencephalon), containing dopamine producing cells.

Synapse: Connection between two neurons that is commonly formed by the axon terminal of a 'presynaptic' and the dendritic membrane of a 'postsynaptic' neuron; these are separated by the synaptic cleft, which is around 20 nanometres (nm) wide.

Telencephalon: Largest part of the human brain comprising the cerebral hemispheres and basal ganglia; supposed to contain the most recent structures in evolutionary terms.

Thalamus: Large area of nuclei in the diencephalon; contains the key relay stations for sensory information from the periphery to the cortex, but is also part of important cognitive, motivational and motor networks.

Transcription factor: Proteins that bind to DNA and modify its transcription rate; a similar function for translation is fulfilled by microRNAs, which bind to specific stretches of mRNA and control its translation into proteins.

Transcriptome: The subset of genes that is transcribed in a particular cell/organ/organism at a particular time; measured through the mRNA content of a cell.

Transgenic: An organism whose genome has been manipulated.

Variable Number Tandem Repeat (VNTR): Area of the genome where individuals vary in the number of repetitions of a short (often only four base pairs) sequence.

Ventrolateral prefrontal cortex (VLPFC): The ventral part of the lateral surface of the prefrontal cortex, inferior to the inferior frontal gyrus.

Voltage-gated: An ion channel that changes its conformation in response to changes in the membrane potential (and thus does not need a ligand for its activation).

References

Abel, T. and Nguyen, P. V. (2008). Regulation of hippocampus-dependent memory by cyclic AMP-dependent protein kinase. *Progress in Brain Research*, 169, 97–115.

Abrahams, B. and Geschwind, D. (2008). Advances in autism genetics: On the threshold of a new neurobiology. *Nature Reviews Genetics*, 9, 341–55.

Ader, R. and Cohen, N. (1993). Psychoneuroimmunology: Conditioning and stress. *Annual Review of Psychology*, 44, 53–85.

Agrawal, A. and Lynskey, M. (2009). Candidate genes for cannabis use disorders: Findings, challenges and directions. *Addiction*, 104, 518–32.

Ahmed, S. H. and Koob, G. F. (1998). Transition from moderate to excessive drug intake: Change in hedonic set point. *Science*, 282, 298–300.

Ahmed, Z., Mackenzie, I., Hutton, M. and Dickson, D. (2007). Progranulin in frontotemporal lobar degeneration and neuroinflammation. *Journal of Neuroinflammation*, 4, 7.

Akbarian, S., Kim, J. J., Potkin, S. G., Hetrick, W. P., Bunney, W. E. and Jones, E. G. (1996). Maldistribution of interstitial neurons in prefrontal white matter of the brains of schizophrenic patients. *Archives of General Psychiatry*, 53, 425–36.

American Psychiatric Association (APA) (2000). *Diagnostic and Statistical Manual of Mental Disorders: DSM-IV-TR* (Washington, DC: APA).

Andari, E., Duhamel, J., Zalla, T., Herbrecht, E., Leboyer, M. and Sirigu, A. (2010). Promoting social behavior with oxytocin in high-functioning autism spectrum disorders. *Proceedings of the National Academy of Sciences USA*, 107, 4389–94.

Andreasen, N. and Pierson, R. (2008). The role of the cerebellum in schizophrenia. *Biological Psychiatry*, 64, 81–8.

Arguello, P. A. and Gogos, J. A. (2006). Modeling madness in mice: One piece at a time. *Neuron*, 52, 179–96.

Arguello, P. A. and Gogos, J. A. (2008). A signaling pathway AKTing up in schizophrenia. *Journal of Clinical Investigation*, 118, 2018–21.

Arnt, J. and Skarsfeldt, T. (1998). Do novel antipsychotics have similar pharmacological characteristics? A review of the evidence. *Neuropsychopharmacology*, 18, 63–101.

Arnulf, I. and Leu-Semenescu, S. (2009). Sleepiness in Parkinson's disease. *Parkinsonism and Related Disordors*, 15, Suppl. 3, S101–4.

Attia, E. (2010). Anorexia nervosa: Current status and future directions. *Annual Review of Medicine*, 61, 425–35.

Azevedo, F., Carvalho, L., Grinberg, L. et al. (2009). Equal numbers of neuronal and nonneuronal cells make the human brain an isometrically scaled-up primate brain. *Journal of Comparative Neurology*, 513, 532–41.

Baird, A., Wilson, S., Bladin, P., Saling, M. and Reutens, D. (2007). Neurological control of human sexual behaviour: Insights from lesion studies. *Journal of Neurology, Neurosurgery and Psychiatry*, 78, 1042–9.

Bandelow, B., Schmahl, C., Falkai, P. and Wedekind, D. (2010). Borderline personality disorder: A dysregulation of the endogenous opioid system? *Psychological Review*, 117, 623–36.

Barnes, N., Hales, T., Lummis, S. and Peters, J. (2009). The 5-HT3 receptor: The relationship between structure and function. *Neuropharmacology*, 56, 273–84.

Barnett, J. and Smoller, J. (2009). The genetics of bipolar disorder. *Neuroscience*, 164, 331–43.

Barros, L. F. and Deitmer, J. W. (2010). Glucose and lactate supply to the synapse. *Brain Research Reviews*, 63, 149–59.

Baskin, H. J. (2008). The pathogenesis and imaging of the tuberous sclerosis complex. *Pediatric Radiology*, 38, 936–52.

Bass, C. E., Grinevich, V. P., Vance, Z. B., Sullivan, R. P., Bonin, K. D. and Budygin, E. A. (2010). Optogenetic control of striatal dopamine release in rats. *Journal of Neurochemistry*, 114, 1344–52.

Beauchaine, T., Klein, D., Crowell, S., Derbidge, C. and Gatzke-Kopp, L. (2009). Multifinality in the development of personality disorders: A Biology x Sex x Environment interaction model of antisocial and borderline traits. *Development and Psychopathology*, 21, 735–70.

Becker, S. and Wojtowicz, J. (2007). A model of hippocampal neurogenesis in memory and mood disorders. *Trends in Cognitive Sciences*, 11, 70–6.

Beesdo-Baum, K., Höfler, M., Gloster, A. et al. (2009). The structure of common mental disorders: A replication study in a community sample of adolescents and young adults. *International Journal of Methods in Psychiatric Research*, 18, 204–20.

Benarroch, E. (2010). Neuronal voltage-gated calcium channels: Brief overview of their function and clinical implications in neurology. *Neurology*, 74, 1310–15.

Benedetti, F. and Smeraldi, E. (2009). Neuroimaging and genetics of antidepressant response to sleep deprivation: Implications for drug development. *Current Pharmaceutical Design*, 15, 2637–49.

Benedetti, F., Mayberg, H. S., Wager, T. D., Stohler, C. S. and Zubieta, J. K. (2005). Neurobiological mechanisms of the placebo effect. *Journal of Neuroscience*, 25, 10390–402.

Bennett, M. (2005). The role of alpha-synuclein in neurodegenerative diseases. *Pharmacology and Therapeutics*, 105, 311–31.

Berman, S., O'Neill, J., Fears, S., Bartzokis, G. and London, E. (2008). Abuse of amphetamines and structural abnormalities in the brain. *Annals of the New York Academy of Sciences*, 1141, 195–220.

Berman, S., Kuczenski, R., McCracken, J. and London, E. (2009). Potential adverse effects of amphetamine treatment on brain and behavior: A review. *Molecular Psychiatry*, 14, 123–42.

Bernat, J. (2009). Chronic consciousness disorders. *Annual Review of Medicine*, 60, 381–92.

Berrettini, W. (2002). Review of bipolar molecular linkage and association studies. *Current Psychiatry Reports*, 4, 124–9.

Berridge, M. (2009). Inositol trisphosphate and calcium signalling mechanisms. *Biochimica et Biophysica Acta*, 1793, 933–40.

Beveridge, T., Gill, K., Hanlon, C. and Porrino, L. (2008). Review: Parallel studies of cocaine-related neural and cognitive impairment in humans and monkeys. *Philosophical Transactions of the Royal Society of London. Series B, Biological Sciences*, 363, 3257–66.

Beyer, J. and Krishnan, K. (2002). Volumetric brain imaging findings in mood disorders. *Bipolar Disorders*, 4, 89–104.

Birbaumer, N. and Cohen, L. (2007). Brain–computer interfaces: Communication and restoration of movement in paralysis. *Journal of Physiology*, 579, 621–36.

Blier, P. and de Montigny, C. (1994). Current advances and trends in the treatment of depression. *Trends in Pharmacological Sciences*, 15, 220–6.

Boeve, B., Silber, M., Saper, C. et al. (2007). Pathophysiology of REM sleep behaviour disorder and relevance to neurodegenerative disease. *Brain*, 130, 2770–88.

Brewer, J. and Potenza, M. (2008). The neurobiology and genetics of impulse control disorders: Relationships to drug addictions. *Biochemical Pharmacology*, 75, 63–75.

Brody, A., Saxena, S., Schwartz, J. et al. (1998). FDG-PET predictors of response to behavioral therapy and pharmacotherapy in obsessive compulsive disorder. *Psychiatry Research*, 84, 1–6.

Brody, A. L., Saxena, S., Stoessel, P. et al. (2001). Regional brain metabolic changes in patients with major depression treated with either paroxetine or interpersonal therapy: Preliminary findings. *Archives of General Psychiatry*, 58, 631–40.

Brown, R., Stevens, D. and Haas, H. (2001). The physiology of brain histamine. *Progress in Neurobiology*, 63, 637–72.

Butler, P. D., Zemon, V., Schechter, I. et al. (2005). Early-stage visual processing and cortical amplification deficits in schizophrenia. *Archives of General Psychiatry*, 62, 495–504.

Cagnin, A., Brooks, D. J., Kennedy, A. M. et al. (2001). In-vivo measurement of activated microglia in dementia. *Lancet*, 358, 461–7.

Cahill, L. (2006). Why sex matters for neuroscience. *Nature Reviews Neuroscience*, 7, 477–84.

Canli, T. (2008). Toward a neurogenetic theory of neuroticism. *Annals of the New York Academy of Sciences*, 1129, 153–74.

Caplan, J., Epstein, L., Quinn, D., Stevens, J. and Stern, T. (2007). Neuropsychiatric effects of prescription drug abuse. *Neuropsychology Review*, 17, 363–80.

Cardno, A. and McGuffin, P. (2004). Quantitative genetics. In: McGuffin, P., Owen, M. J. and Gottesman, I. I. (eds), *Psychiatric Genetics and Genomics* (Oxford: Oxford University Press).

Carr, D. and Sesack, S. (2000). Projections from the rat prefrontal cortex to the ventral tegmental area: Target specificity in the synaptic associations with mesoaccumbens and mesocortical neurons. *Journal of Neuroscience*, 20, 3864–73.

Caspi, A., McClay, J., Moffitt, T. et al. (2002). Role of genotype in the cycle of violence in maltreated children. *Science*, 297, 851–4.

Castellanos, F., Lee, P., Sharp, W. et al. (2002). Developmental trajectories of brain volume abnormalities in children and adolescents with attention-deficit/hyperactivity disorder. *JAMA*, 288, 1740–8.

Chase, H. and Clark, L. (2010). Gambling severity predicts midbrain response to near-miss outcomes. *Journal of Neuroscience*, 30, 6180–7.

Chen, J., Chen, P. and Chiang, Y. (2009a). Molecular mechanisms of psychostimulant addiction. *Chang Gung Medical Journal*, 32, 148–54.

Chen, X., Shu, S. and Bayliss, D. (2009b). HCN1 channel subunits are a molecular substrate for hypnotic actions of ketamine. *Journal of Neuroscience*, 29, 600–9.

Chertkow, H., Massoud, F., Nasreddine, Z. et al. (2008). Diagnosis and treatment of dementia: 3. Mild cognitive impairment and cognitive impairment without dementia. *CMAJ*, 178, 1273–85.

Chrousos, G. (2009). Stress and disorders of the stress system. *Nature Reviews Endocrinology*, 5, 374–81.

Clare, L., Linden, D. E., Woods, R. T. et al. (2010). Goal-oriented cognitive rehabilitation for people with early-stage Alzheimer disease: A single-blind randomized controlled trial of clinical efficacy. *American Journal of Geriatric Psychiatry*, 18, 928–39.

Commons, K. (2010). Neuronal pathways linking substance P to drug addiction and stress. *Brain Research*, 1314, 175–82.

Cox, W. M. and Klinger, E. (2004). *Handbook of Motivational Counseling: Concepts, Approaches, and Assessment* (Chichester and Hoboken, NJ: John Wiley).

Craddock, N. and Forty, L. (2006). Genetics of affective (mood) disorders. *European Journal of Human Genetics*, 14, 660–8.

Craddock, N. and Lendon, C. (1999). Chromosome workshop: chromosomes 11, 14, and 15. *American Journal of Medical Genetics*, 88, 244–54.

Craddock, N. and Owen, M. J. (2010). The Kraepelinian dichotomy – going, going … but still not gone. *British Journal of Psychiatry*, 196, 92–5.

Crews, F. and Boettiger, C. (2009). Impulsivity, frontal lobes and risk for addiction. *Pharmacology, Biochemistry, and Behavior*, 93, 237–47.

Crow, T. J. (1997). Schizophrenia as failure of hemispheric dominance for language. *Trends in Neurosciences*, 20, 339–43.

Cullen, T. J., Walker, M. A., Parkinson, N. et al. (2003). A postmortem study of the mediodorsal nucleus of the thalamus in schizophrenia. *Schizophrenia Research*, 60, 157–66.

Cunha-Oliveira, T., Rego, A. and Oliveira, C. (2008). Cellular and molecular mechanisms involved in the neurotoxicity of opioid and psychostimulant drugs. *Brain Research Reviews*, 58, 192–208.

Cunningham, J., Yonkers, K., O'Brien, S. and Eriksson, E. (2009). Update on research and treatment of premenstrual dysphoric disorder. *Harvard Review of Psychiatry*, 17, 120–37.

Daban, C., Martinez-Aran, A., Cruz, N. and Vieta, E. (2008). Safety and efficacy of Vagus Nerve Stimulation in treatment-resistant depression: A systematic review. *Journal of Affective Disorders*, 110, 1–15.

Dalmau, J., Lancaster, E., Martinez-Hernandez, E., Rosenfeld, M. R. and Balice-Gordon, R. (2011). Clinical experience and laboratory investigations in patients with anti-NMDAR encephalitis. *Lancet Neurology*, 10, 63–74.

Dang-Vu, T., Desseilles, M., Petit, D., Mazza, S., Montplaisir, J. and Maquet, P. (2007). Neuroimaging in sleep medicine. *Sleep Medicine*, 8, 349–72.

De Leon, J. (2009). The future (or lack of future) of personalized prescription in psychiatry. *Pharmacological Research*, 59, 81–9.

DeCharms, R. (2008). Applications of real-time fMRI. *Nature Reviews Neuroscience*, 9, 720–9.

Deitmer, J. and Rose, C. (2010). Ion changes and signalling in perisynaptic glia. *Brain Research Reviews*, 63, 113–29.

Demarse, T., Cadotte, A., Douglas, P., He, P. and Trinh, V. (2004). Computation within cultured neural networks. *Conference Proceedings: Annual International Conference of the IEEE Engineering in Medicine and Biology Society*, 7, 5340–3.

Desbonnet, L., Waddington, J. and O'Tuathaigh, C. (2009a). Mutant models for genes associated with schizophrenia. *Biochemical Society Transactions*, 37, 308–12.

Desbonnet, L., Waddington, J. and O'Tuathaigh, C. (2009b). Mice mutant for genes associated with schizophrenia: Common phenotype or distinct endophenotypes? *Behavioural Brain Research*, 204, 258–73.

Dev, K., Hofele, K., Barbieri, S., Buchman, V. and Van Der Putten, H. (2003). Part II: Alpha-synuclein and its molecular pathophysiological role in neurodegenerative disease. *Neuropharmacology*, 45, 14–44.

Di Giovanni, G., Esposito, E. and Di Matteo, V. (2010). Role of serotonin in central dopamine dysfunction. *CNS Neuroscience and Therapeutics*, 16, 179–94.

Dierks, T., Linden, D. E., Jandl, M. et al. (1999). Activation of Heschl's gyrus during auditory hallucinations. *Neuron*, 22, 615–21.

Drevets, W., Price, J., Simpson, J. J. et al. (1997). Subgenual prefrontal cortex abnormalities in mood disorders. *Nature*, 386, 824–7.

Drevets, W. C., Gadde, K. M. and Krishnan, K. R. R. (2004). Neuroimaging studies of mood disorders. In: Charney, D. S. and Nestler, E. J. (eds), *Neurobiology of Mental Illness*, 2nd edn. (Oxford: Oxford University Press).

Ducci, F. and Goldman, D. (2008). Genetic approaches to addiction: Genes and alcohol. *Addiction*, 103, 1414–28.

Eiden, L., Schäfer, M., Weihe, E. and Schütz, B. (2004). The vesicular amine transporter family (SLC18): Amine/proton antiporters required for vesicular accumulation and regulated exocytotic secretion of monoamines and acetylcholine. *Pflügers Archiv European Journal of Physiology*, 447, 636–40.

Elder, G., Gama Sosa, M. and De Gasperi, R. (2010). Transgenic mouse models of Alzheimer's disease. *Mount Sinai Journal of Medicine*, 77, 69–81.

Epping-Jordan, M., Watkins, S., Koob, G. and Markou, A. (1998). Dramatic decreases in brain reward function during nicotine withdrawal. *Nature*, 393, 76–9.

Erk, S., Meyer-Lindenberg, A., Schnell, K. et al. (2010). Brain function in carriers of a genome-wide supported bipolar disorder variant. *Archives of General Psychiatry*, 67, 803–11.

Ertekin-Taner, N. (2007). Genetics of Alzheimer's disease: A centennial review. *Neurologic Clinics*, 25, 611–67, v.

Ferrara, J. and Stacy, M. (2008). Impulse-control disorders in Parkinson's disease. *CNS Spectrums*, 13, 690–8.

Ferreira, M. A., O'Donovan, M. C., Meng, Y. A. et al. (2008). Collaborative genome-wide association analysis supports a role for ANK3 and CACNA1C in bipolar disorder. *Nature Genetics*, 40, 1056–8.

Feuerstein, T. (2008). Presynaptic receptors for dopamine, histamine, and serotonin. *Handbook of Experimental Pharmacology*, 289–338.

Fineberg, N., Potenza, M., Chamberlain, S. et al. (2010). Probing compulsive and impulsive behaviors, from animal models to endophenotypes: A narrative review. *Neuropsychopharmacology*, 35, 591–604.

Fitzgerald, P. and Dinan, T. (2008). Prolactin and dopamine: What is the connection? A review article. *Journal of Psychopharmacology*, 22, 12–19.

Francis, D. and Meaney, M. (1999). Maternal care and the development of stress responses. *Current Opinion in Neurobiology*, 9, 128–34.

Frascella, J., Potenza, M., Brown, L. and Childress, A. (2010). Shared brain vulnerabilities open the way for nonsubstance addictions: Carving addiction at a new joint? *Annals of the New York Academy of Science*, 1187, 294–315.

Friedman, R. and Downey, J. (2008). Sexual differentiation of behavior: The foundation of a developmental model of psychosexuality. *Journal of the American Psychoanalytic Association*, 56, 147–75.

Frith, C. D. and Frith, U. (1999). Interacting minds: A biological basis. *Science*, 286, 1692–5.

Frost, B. and Diamond, M. (2010). Prion-like mechanisms in neurodegenerative diseases. *Nature Reviews Neuroscience*, 11, 155–9.

Fuxe, K., Dahlström, A., Jonsson, G. et al. (2010). The discovery of central monoamine neurons gave volume transmission to the wired brain. *Progress in Neurobiology*, 90, 82–100.

Gallia, G., Rigamonti, D. and Williams, M. (2006). The diagnosis and treatment of idiopathic normal pressure hydrocephalus. *Nature Clinical Practice. Neurology*, 2, 375–81.

Gao, Y., Glenn, A., Schug, R., Yang, Y. and Raine, A. (2009). The neurobiology of psychopathy: A neurodevelopmental perspective. *Canadian Journal of Psychiatry*, 54, 813–23.

Garcia-Falgueras, A. and Swaab, D. (2008). A sex difference in the hypothalamic uncinate nucleus: Relationship to gender identity. *Brain*, 131, 3132–46.

Geisler, S. and Wise, R. (2008). Functional implications of glutamatergic projections to the ventral tegmental area. *Reviews in the Neurosciences*, 19, 227–44.

Germain, A. and Kupfer, D. (2008). Circadian rhythm disturbances in depression. *Human Psychopharmacology*, 23, 571–85.

Gether, U., Andersen, P., Larsson, O. and Schousboe, A. (2006). Neurotransmitter transporters: Molecular function of important drug targets. *Trends in Pharmacological Sciences*, 27, 375–83.

Geyer, M. (2008). Developing translational animal models for symptoms of schizophrenia or bipolar mania. *Neurotoxicity Research*, 14, 71–8.

Gizer, I., Ficks, C. and Waldman, I. (2009). Candidate gene studies of ADHD: A meta-analytic review. *Human Genetics*, 126, 51–90.

Gläscher, J. and Adolphs, R. (2003). Processing of the arousal of subliminal and supraliminal emotional stimuli by the human amygdala. *Journal of Neuroscience*, 23, 10274–82.

Goff, D. C. and Coyle, J. T. (2001). The emerging role of glutamate in the pathophysiology and treatment of schizophrenia. *American Journal of Psychiatry*, 158, 1367–77.

Goldapple, K., Segal, Z., Garson, C. et al. (2004). Modulation of cortical-limbic pathways in major depression: Treatment-specific effects of cognitive behavior therapy. *Archives of General Psychiatry*, 61, 34–41.

Goldstein, K., Hazlett, E., New, A. et al. (2009). Smaller superior temporal gyrus volume specificity in schizotypal personality disorder. *Schizophrenia Research*, 112, 14–23.

Gonzalez, R. (2007). Acute and non-acute effects of cannabis on brain functioning and neuropsychological performance. *Neuropsychology Review*, 17, 347–61.

Gotlib, I. and Joormann, J. (2010). Cognition and depression: Current status and future directions. *Annual Review of Clinical Psychology*, 6, 285–312.

Gottesman, I. and Gould, T. (2003). The endophenotype concept in psychiatry: Etymology and strategic intentions. *American Journal of Psychiatry*, 160, 636–45.

Graus, F., Saiz, A. and Dalmau, J. (2010). Antibodies and neuronal autoimmune disorders of the CNS. *Journal of Neurology*, 257, 509–17.

Graybiel, A. and Rauch, S. (2000). Toward a neurobiology of obsessive-compulsive disorder. *Neuron*, 28, 343–7.

Greenberg, B., Rauch, S. and Haber, S. (2010). Invasive circuitry-based neurotherapeutics: Stereotactic ablation and deep brain stimulation for OCD. *Neuropsychopharmacology*, 35, 317–36.

Guay, D. (2009). Drug treatment of paraphilic and nonparaphilic sexual disorders. *Clinical Therapeutics*, 31, 1–31.

Guyenet, P. (2006). The sympathetic control of blood pressure. *Nature Reviews Neuroscience*, 7, 335–46.

Haenschel, C. and Linden, D. (2011). Exploring intermediate phenotypes with EEG: Working memory dysfunction in schizophrenia. *Behavioural Brain Research*, 216, 481–95.

Haenschel, C., Bittner, R. A., Haertling, F. et al. (2007). Contribution of impaired early-stage visual processing to working memory dysfunction in adolescents with schizophrenia: A study with event-related potentials and functional magnetic resonance imaging. *Archives of General Psychiatry*, 64, 1229–40.

Halligan, P. and David, A. (2001). Cognitive neuropsychiatry: Towards a scientific psychopathology. *Nature Reviews Neuroscience*, 2, 209–15.

Hampel, H., Broich, K., Hoessler, Y. and Pantel, J. (2009). Biological markers for early detection and pharmacological treatment of Alzheimer's disease. *Dialogues in Clinical Neuroscience*, 11, 141–57.

Hampel, H., Frank, R., Broich, K. et al. (2010). Biomarkers for Alzheimer's disease: Academic, industry and regulatory perspectives. *Nature Reviews Drug Discovery*, 9, 560–74.

Hare, R. and Neumann, C. (2008). Psychopathy as a clinical and empirical construct. *Annual Review of Clinical Psychology*, 4, 217–46.

Harold, D., Abraham, R., Hollingworth, P. et al. (2009). Genome-wide association study identifies variants at CLU and PICALM associated with Alzheimer's disease. *Nature Genetics*, 41, 1088–93.

Harrison, P. J. (1999). The neuropathology of schizophrenia: A critical review of the data and their interpretation. *Brain*, 122 (4), 593–624.

Harsh, V., Meltzer-Brody, S., Rubinow, D. and Schmidt, P. (2009). Reproductive aging, sex steroids, and mood disorders. *Harvard Review of Psychiatry*, 17, 87–102.

Heal, D., Cheetham, S. and Smith, S. (2009). The neuropharmacology of ADHD drugs in vivo: Insights on efficacy and safety. *Neuropharmacology*, 57, 608–18.

Healy, D. (1993). *Images of Trauma: From Hysteria to Post-traumatic Stress Disorder* (London: Faber and Faber).

Healy, D. (1999). *The Antidepressant Era* (Cambridge, MA: Harvard University Press).

Healy, D. M. R. C. P. (2002). *The Creation of Psychopharmacology* (Cambridge, MA and London, Harvard University Press).

Heilig, M., Thorsell, A., Sommer, W. H. et al. (2010). Translating the neuroscience of alcoholism into clinical treatments: From blocking the buzz to curing the blues. *Neuroscience and Biobehavioural Reviews*, 35, 334–44.

Hercher, C., Turecki, G. and Mechawar, N. (2009). Through the looking glass: Examining neuroanatomical evidence for cellular alterations in major depression. *Journal of Psychiatric Research*, 43, 947–61.

Herculano-Houzel, S. (2009). The human brain in numbers: A linearly scaled-up primate brain. *Frontiers in Human Neuroscience*, 3, 31.

Herpertz, S., Kunert, H., Schwenger, U. and Sass, H. (1999). Affective responsiveness in borderline personality disorder: A psychophysiological approach. *American Journal of Psychiatry*, 156, 1550–6.

Herpertz, S., Werth, U., Lukas, G. et al. (2001). Emotion in criminal offenders with psychopathy and borderline personality disorder. *Archives of General Psychiatry*, 58, 737–45.

Highley, J., Walker, M., Esiri, M., McDonald, B., Harrison, P. and Crow, T. (2001). Schizophrenia and the frontal lobes: Post-mortem stereological study of tissue volume. *British Journal of Psychiatry*, 178, 337–43.

Hindle, J. (2010). Ageing, neurodegeneration and Parkinson's disease. *Age and Ageing*, 39, 156–61.

Hollander, E., Novotny, S., Hanratty, M. et al. (2003). Oxytocin infusion reduces repetitive behaviors in adults with autistic and Asperger's disorders. *Neuropsychopharmacology*, 28, 193–8.

Hornby, P. (2001). Central neurocircuitry associated with emesis. *American Journal of Medicine*, 111 Suppl 8A, 106S–112S.

Hshieh, T., Fong, T., Marcantonio, E. and Inouye, S. (2008). Cholinergic deficiency hypothesis in delirium: A synthesis of current evidence. *Journals of Gerontology. Series A, Biological Sciences and Medical Sciences*, 63, 764–72.

Hubl, D., Koenig, T., Strik, W. et al. (2004). Pathways that make voices: White matter changes in auditory hallucinations. *Archives of General Psychiatry*, 61, 658–68.

Hublin, C. and Kaprio, J. (2003). Genetic aspects and genetic epidemiology of parasomnias. *Sleep Medicine Reviews*, 7, 413–21.

Ibrahim, H. M., Hogg, A. J., Healy, D. J. et al. (2000). Ionotropic glutamate receptor binding and sub-unit mRNA expression in thalamic nuclei in schizophrenia. *American Journal of Psychiatry*, 157, 1811–23.

Iscoe, S. (1998). Control of abdominal muscles. *Progress in Neurobiology*, 56, 433–506.

Itier, R. and Batty, M. (2009). Neural bases of eye and gaze processing: The core of social cognition. *Neuroscience and Biobehavioral Reviews*, 33, 843–63.

Jablensky, A. (2006). Subtyping schizophrenia: Implications for genetic research. *Molecular Psychiatry*, 11, 815–36.

Jansen, A., Nguyen, X., Karpitskiy, V., Mettenleiter, T. and Loewy, A. (1995). Central command neurons of the sympathetic nervous system: Basis of the fight-or-flight response. *Science*, 270, 644–6.

Jazin, E. and Cahill, L. (2010). Sex differences in molecular neuroscience: From fruit flies to humans. *Nature Reviews Neuroscience*, 11, 9–17.

Johnston, S., Linden, D. E., Healy, D., Goebel, R., Habes, I. and Boehm, S. G. (2011). Upregulation of emotion areas through neurofeedback with a focus on positive mood. *Cognitive, Affective and Behavioural Neuroscience*, 11, 44–51.

Jones, I., Kent, L. and Craddock, N. (2004). Genetics of affective disorders. In: McGuffin, P., Owen, M. J. and Gottesman, I. I. (eds), *Psychiatric Genetics and Genomics* (Oxford: Oxford University Press).

Jones, L., Holmans, P. A., Hamshere, M. L. et al. (2010). Genetic evidence implicates the immune system and cholesterol metabolism in the aetiology of Alzheimer's disease. *PLoS One*, 5, e13950.

Josephs, K. (2007). Capgras syndrome and its relationship to neurodegenerative disease. *Archives of Neurology*, 64, 1762–6.

Jupp, B. and Lawrence, A. (2010). New horizons for therapeutics in drug and alcohol abuse. *Pharmacology and Therapeutics*, 125, 138–68.

Kaffman, A. and Meaney, M. (2007). Neurodevelopmental sequelae of postnatal maternal care in rodents: Clinical and research implications of molecular insights. *Journal of Child Psychology and Psychiatry*, 48, 224–44.

Kalsi, G., Prescott, C., Kendler, K. and Riley, B. (2009). Unraveling the molecular mechanisms of alcohol dependence. *Trends in Genetics*, 25, 49–55.

Kalueff, A., Olivier, J., Nonkes, L. and Homberg, J. (2010). Conserved role for the serotonin transporter gene in rat and mouse neurobehavioral endophenotypes. *Neuroscience and Biobehavioral Reviews*, 34, 373–86.

Kammerer, M., Taylor, A. and Glover, V. (2006). The HPA axis and perinatal depression: A hypothesis. *Archives of Women's Mental Health*, 9, 187–96.

Karl, A., Schaefer, M., Malta, L., Dörfel, D., Rohleder, N. and Werner, A. (2006). A meta-analysis of structural brain abnormalities in PTSD. *Neuroscience and Biobehavioral Reviews*, 30, 1004–31.

Karlin, A. (2002). Emerging structure of the nicotinic acetylcholine receptors. *Nature Reviews Neuroscience*, 3, 102–14.

Kaye, W., Fudge, J. and Paulus, M. (2009). New insights into symptoms and neurocircuit function of anorexia nervosa. *Nature Reviews Neuroscience*, 10, 573–84.

Kellendonk, C., Simpson, E. H., Polan, H. J. et al. (2006). Transient and selective overexpression of dopamine D2 receptors in the striatum causes persistent abnormalities in prefrontal cortex functioning. *Neuron*, 49, 603–15.

Kellner, C., Knapp, R., Petrides, G. et al. (2006). Continuation electroconvulsive therapy vs. pharmacotherapy for relapse prevention in major depression: A multisite study from the Consortium for Research in Electroconvulsive Therapy (CORE). *Archives of General Psychiatry*, 63, 1337–44.

Kendler, K. and Eaves, L. (1986). Models for the joint effect of genotype and environment on liability to psychiatric illness. *American Journal of Psychiatry*, 143, 279–89.

Kessler, R., Berglund, P., Demler, O., Jin, R., Merikangas, K. and Walters, E. (2005). Lifetime prevalence and age-of-onset distributions of DSM-IV disorders in the National Comorbidity Survey Replication. *Archives of General Psychiatry*, 62, 593–602.

Kessler, R., Chiu, W., Jin, R., Ruscio, A., Shear, K. and Walters, E. (2006). The epidemiology of panic attacks, panic disorder, and agoraphobia in the National Comorbidity Survey Replication. *Archives of General Psychiatry*, 63, 415–24.

Kiehl, K. (2006). A cognitive neuroscience perspective on psychopathy: Evidence for paralimbic system dysfunction. *Psychiatry Research*, 142, 107–28.

Klein, C. and Ettinger, U. (2008). A hundred years of eye movement research in psychiatry. *Brain and Cognition*, 68, 215–18.

Klein, C., Berg, P., Rockstroh, B. and Andresen, B. (1999). Topography of the auditory P300 in schizotypal personality. *Biological Psychiatry*, 45, 1612–21.

Klein, C., Wendling, K., Huettner, P., Ruder, H. and Peper, M. (2006). Intra-subject variability in attention-deficit hyperactivity disorder. *Biological Psychiatry*, 60, 1088–97.

Klosterkötter, J., Hellmich, M., Steinmeyer, E. and Schultze-Lutter, F. (2001). Diagnosing schizophrenia in the initial prodromal phase. *Archives of General Psychiatry*, 58, 158–64.

Kolb, B. and Wishaw, I. Q. (1980). *Fundamentals of Human Neuropsychology* (San Francisco: Freeman).

Koob, G. and Le Moal, M. (1997). Drug abuse: Hedonic homeostatic dysregulation. *Science*, 278, 52–8.

Koob, G. and Le Moal, M. (2008). Review: Neurobiological mechanisms for opponent motivational processes in addiction. *Philosophical Transactions of the Royal Society of London. Series B, Biological Sciences*, 363, 3113–23.

Koolhaas, J. (2008). Coping style and immunity in animals: Making sense of individual variation. *Brain, Behavior, and Immunology*, 22, 662–7.

Kopelman, M. (2002). Disorders of memory. *Brain*, 125, 2152–90.

Kostrzewa, R., Kostrzewa, J., Kostrzewa, R., Nowak, P. and Brus, R. (2008). Pharmacological models of ADHD. *Journal of Neural Transmission*, 115, 287–98.

Kreczmanski, P., Heinsen, H., Mantua, V. et al. (2007). Volume, neuron density and total neuron number in five subcortical regions in schizophrenia. *Brain*, 130, 678–92.

Kreek, M., Zhou, Y., Butelman, E. and Levran, O. (2009). Opiate and cocaine addiction: From bench to clinic and back to the bench. *Current Opinion in Pharmacology*, 9, 74–80.

Kringelbach, M. (2004). Food for thought: Hedonic experience beyond homeostasis in the human brain. *Neuroscience*, 126, 807–19.

Kringelbach, M. and Stein, A. (2010). Cortical mechanisms of human eating. *Forum of Nutrition*, 63, 164–75.

Kruijver, F., Zhou, J., Pool, C., Hofman, M., Gooren, L. and Swaab, D. (2000). Male-to-female transsexuals have female neuron numbers in a limbic nucleus. *Journal of Clinical Endocrinology and Metabolism*, 85, 2034–41.

Kuhse, J., Betz, H. and Kirsch, J. (1995). The inhibitory glycine receptor: Architecture, synaptic localization and molecular pathology of a postsynaptic ion-channel complex. *Current Opinion in Neurobiology*, 5, 318–23.

Lane, C. (2007). *Shyness: How Normal Behavior Became a Sickness* (New Haven, CT: Yale University Press).

Laruelle, M. (2000). Imaging synaptic neurotransmission with in vivo binding competition techniques: A critical review. *Journal of Cerebral Blood Flow and Metabolism*, 20, 423–51.

Laruelle, M., Abi-Dargham, A., Van Dyck, C. H. et al. (1996). Single photon emission computerized tomography imaging of amphetamine-induced dopamine release in drug-free schizophrenic subjects. *Proceedings of the National Academy of Sciences USA*, 93, 9235–40.

Le Merrer, J., Becker, J., Befort, K. and Kieffer, B. (2009). Reward processing by the opioid system in the brain. *Physiological Reviews*, 89, 1379–1412.

Lee, K., Brown, W., Egleston, P. et al. (2006). A functional magnetic resonance imaging study of social cognition in schizophrenia during an acute episode and after recovery. *American Journal of Psychiatry*, 163, 1926–33.

Lemere, C. and Masliah, E. (2010). Can Alzheimer disease be prevented by amyloid-beta immunotherapy? *Nature Reviews Neurology*, 6, 108–19.

Lesch, K. and Merschdorf, U. (2000). Impulsivity, aggression, and serotonin: A molecular psychobiological perspective. *Behavioral Sciences and the Law*, 18, 581–604.

LeVay, S. (1991). A difference in hypothalamic structure between heterosexual and homosexual men. *Science*, 253, 1034–7.

Levisohn, P. (2007). The autism–epilepsy connection. *Epilepsia*, 48 Suppl. 9, 33–5.

Lewis, D. and Levitt, P. (2002). Schizophrenia as a disorder of neurodevelopment. *Annual Review of Neuroscience*, 25, 409–32.

Lewis, D. and Lieberman, J. (2000). Catching up on schizophrenia: Natural history and neurobiology. *Neuron*, 28, 325–34.

Lewis, D., Hashimoto, T. and Volk, D. (2005). Cortical inhibitory neurons and schizophrenia. *Nature Reviews Neuroscience*, 6, 312–24.

Linden, D. E. (1999). The natural and the supernatural in melancholic genius: A debate in sixteenth century Spanish medicine and its antecedents. *Medizinhistorisches Journal*, 34, 227–43.

Linden, D. E. (2006). How psychotherapy changes the brain: The contribution of functional neuroimaging. *Molecular Psychiatry*, 11, 528–38.

Linden, D. E. and Fallgatter, A. J. (2009). Neuroimaging in psychiatry: From bench to bedside. *Frontiers in Human Neuroscience*, 3, 49.

Linden, D. E., Thornton, K., Kuswanto, C. N., Johnston, S. J., Van De Ven, V. and Jackson, M. C. (2011). The brain's voices: Comparing nonclinical auditory hallucinations and imagery. *Cerebral Cortex*, 21, 330–7.

Link, C. (2005). Invertebrate models of Alzheimer's disease. *Genes, Brain, and Behavior*, 4, 147–56.

Loebrich, S. and Nedivi, E. (2009). The function of activity-regulated genes in the nervous system. *Physiological Reviews*, 89, 1079–1103.

Lovestone, S., Killick, R., Di Forti, M. and Murray, R. (2007). Schizophrenia as a GSK-3 dysregulation disorder. *Trends in Neurosciences*, 30, 142–9.

Lubman, D., Yücel, M. and Lawrence, A. (2008). Inhalant abuse among adolescents: Neurobiological considerations. British Journal of Pharmacology, 154, 316–26.

Lücking, C. and Brice, A. (2000). Alpha-synuclein and Parkinson's disease. *Cellular and Molecular Life Sciences*, 57, 1894–1908.

Lüscher, C. and Ungless, M. (2006). The mechanistic classification of addictive drugs. *PLoS Medicine*, 3, e437.

MacMaster, F., Mirza, Y., Szeszko, P. et al. (2008). Amygdala and hippocampal volumes in familial early onset major depressive disorder. *Biological Psychiatry*, 63, 385–90.

Madden, D. (2002). The structure and function of glutamate receptor ion channels. *Nature Reviews Neuroscience*, 3, 91–101.

Mahon, K., Burdick, K. and Szeszko, P. (2010). A role for white matter abnormalities in the pathophysiology of bipolar disorder. *Neuroscience and Biobehavioural Reviews*, 34, 533–54.

Maier, W., Lichtermann, D., Minges, J. et al. (1993). Continuity and discontinuity of affective disorders and schizophrenia: Results of a controlled family study. *Archives of General Psychiatry*, 50, 871–83.

Makkar, S., Zhang, S. and Cranney, J. (2010). Behavioral and neural analysis of GABA in the acquisition, consolidation, reconsolidation, and extinction of fear memory. *Neuropsychopharmacology*, 35, 1625–52.

Maldonado, R., Valverde, O. and Berrendero, F. (2006). Involvement of the endocannabinoid system in drug addiction. *Trends in Neuroscience*, 29, 225–32.

Mann, J. (2003). Neurobiology of suicidal behaviour. *Nature Reviews Neuroscience*, 4, 819–28.

Mantegazza, M., Curia, G., Biagini, G., Ragsdale, D. and Avoli, M. (2010). Voltage-gated sodium channels as therapeutic targets in epilepsy and other neurological disorders. *Lancet Neurology*, 9, 413–24.

Markowitsch, H. (1995). Which brain regions are critically involved in the retrieval of old episodic memory? *Brain Research. Brain Research Reviews*, 21, 117–27.

Martin, M. (1990). On the induction of mood. *Clinical Psychology Review*, 10, 669–97.

Martinez, D., Kim, J., Krystal, J. and Abi-Dargham, A. (2007). Imaging the neurochemistry of alcohol and substance abuse. *Neuroimaging Clinics of North America*, 17, 539–55, x.

Martinowich, K., Schloesser, R. and Manji, H. (2009). Bipolar disorder: From genes to behavior pathways. *Journal of Clinical Investigation*, 119, 726–36.

Masters, C. L., Cappai, R., Barnham, K. J. and Villemagne, V. L. (2006). Molecular mechanisms for Alzheimer's disease: Implications for neuroimaging and therapeutics. *Journal of Neurochemistry*, 97, 1700–25.

Maurer, K., Volk, S. and Gerbaldo, H. (1997). Auguste D and Alzheimer's disease. *Lancet*, 349, 1546–9.

Mayberg, H. S. (2004). Depression: A neuropsychiatric perspective. In: Panksepp, J. (ed.), *Biological Psychiatry* (Hoboken, NJ: Wiley-Liss).

Mayberg, H., Lozano, A., Voon, V. et al. (2005). Deep brain stimulation for treatment-resistant depression. *Neuron*, 45, 651–60.

McDonald, C., Marshall, N., Sham, P. et al. (2006). Regional brain morphometry in patients with schizophrenia or bipolar disorder and their unaffected relatives. *American Journal of Psychiatry*, 163, 478–87.

McKee, A., Cantu, R., Nowinski, C. et al. (2009). Chronic traumatic encephalopathy in athletes: Progressive tauopathy after repetitive head injury. *Journal of Neuropathology and Experimental Neurology*, 68, 709–35.

McVeigh, C. and Passmore, P. (2006). Vascular dementia: Prevention and treatment. *Clinical Interventions in Aging*, 1, 229–35.

Mehta, D., Menke, A. and Binder, E. (2010). Gene expression studies in major depression. *Current Psychiatry Reports*, 12, 135–44.

Merkl, A., Heuser, I. and Bajbouj, M. (2009). Antidepressant electroconvulsive therapy: Mechanism of action, recent advances and limitations. *Experimental Neurology*, 219, 20–6.

Meyer-Lindenberg, A. and Weinberger, D. (2006). Intermediate phenotypes and genetic mechanisms of psychiatric disorders. *Nature Reviews Neuroscience*, 7, 818–27.

Miller, B., Cummings, J., McIntyre, H., Ebers, G. and Grode, M. (1986). Hypersexuality or altered sexual preference following brain injury. *Journal of Neurology, Neurosurgery and Psychiatry*, 49, 867–73.

Miyashita, T., Kubik, S., Lewandowski, G. and Guzowski, J. (2008). Networks of neurons, networks of genes: An integrated view of memory consolidation. *Neurobiology of Learning and Memory*, 89, 269–84.

Moghaddam, B. (2002). Stress activation of glutamate neurotransmission in the prefrontal cortex: Implications for dopamine-associated psychiatric disorders. *Biological Psychiatry*, 51, 775–87.

Moles, A., Kieffer, B. and D'Amato, F. (2004). Deficit in attachment behavior in mice lacking the mu-opioid receptor gene. *Science*, 304, 1983–6.

Molteni, R., Calabrese, F., Racagni, G., Fumagalli, F. and Riva, M. (2009). Antipsychotic drug actions on gene modulation and signaling mechanisms. *Pharmacology and Therapeutics*, 124, 74–85.

Monti, M., Vanhaudenhuyse, A., Coleman, M. et al. (2010). Willful modulation of brain activity in disorders of consciousness. New England Journal of Medicine, 362, 579–89.

Moonat, S., Starkman, B., Sakharkar, A. and Pandey, S. (2010). Neuroscience of alcoholism: Molecular and cellular mechanisms. *Cellular and Molecular Life Sciences*, 67, 73–88.

Moy, S. and Nadler, J. (2008). Advances in behavioral genetics: Mouse models of autism. *Molecular Psychiatry*, 13, 4–26.

Muller, N. and Schwarz, M. (2006). Schizophrenia as an inflammation-mediated dysbalance of glutamatergic neurotransmission. *Neurotoxicity Research*, 10, 131–48.

Nakai, Y., Hamagaki, S., Takagi, R., Taniguchi, A. and Kurimoto, F. (1999). Plasma concentrations of tumor necrosis factor-alpha (TNF-alpha) and soluble TNF receptors in patients with anorexia nervosa. *Journal of Clinical Endocrinology and Metabolism*, 84, 1226–8.

Nakai, Y., Hamagaki, S., Takagi, R., Taniguchi, A. and Kurimoto, F. (2000). Plasma concentrations of tumor necrosis factor-alpha (TNF-alpha) and soluble TNF receptors in patients with bulimia nervosa. *Clinical Endocrinology (Oxford)*, 53, 383–8.

Nasky, K. M., Knittel, D. R. and Manos, G. H. (2008). Psychosis associated with anti-N-methyl-D-aspartate receptor antibodies. *CNS Spectrums*, 13, 699–703.

Nathanson, N. (2008). Synthesis, trafficking, and localization of muscarinic acetylcholine receptors. *Pharmacology and Therapeutics*, 119, 33–43.

Navarro, M., Cubero, I., Ko, L. and Thiele, T. E. (2009). Deletion of agouti-related protein blunts ethanol self-administration and binge-like drinking in mice. *Genes, Brain, and Behavior*, 8, 450–8.

Nelson, K., Grether, J., Croen, L. et al. (2001). Neuropeptides and neurotrophins in neonatal blood of children with autism or mental retardation. *Annals of Neurology*, 49, 597–606.

Nestler, E. (2004). Molecular mechanisms of drug addiction. *Neuropharmacology*, 47 Suppl. 1, 24–32.

Nestler, E. (2009). Epigenetic mechanisms in psychiatry. *Biological Psychiatry*, 65, 189–90.

Nestler, E., Barrot, M. and Self, D. (2001). DeltaFosB: A sustained molecular switch for addiction. *Proceedings of the National Academy of Sciences USA*, 98, 11042–6.

Nikolaus, S., Antke, C. and Müller, H. (2009a). In vivo imaging of synaptic function in the central nervous system: I. Movement disorders and dementia. *Behavioural Brain Research*, 204, 1–31.

Nikolaus, S., Antke, C. and Müller, H. (2009b). In vivo imaging of synaptic function in the central nervous system: II. Mental and affective disorders. *Behavioural Brain Research*, 204, 32–66.

Niswender, C., Jones, C. and Conn, P. (2005). New therapeutic frontiers for metabotropic glutamate receptors. *Current Topics in Medical Chemistry*, 5, 847–57.

Norrholm, S. and Ressler, K. (2009). Genetics of anxiety and trauma-related disorders. *Neuroscience*, 164, 272–87.

O'Dell, L. and Khroyan, T. (2009). Rodent models of nicotine reward: What do they tell us about tobacco abuse in humans? *Pharmacology, Biochemistry, and Behavior*, 91, 481–8.

Ochsner, K. (2008). The social-emotional processing stream: Five core constructs and their translational potential for schizophrenia and beyond. *Biological Psychiatry*, 64, 48–61.

Oertel, V., Knöchel, C., Rotarska-Jagiela, A. et al. (2010). Reduced laterality as a trait marker of schizophrenia: Evidence from structural and functional neuroimaging. *Journal of Neuroscience*, 30, 2289–99.

Owen, M., O'Donovan, M. and Gottesman, I. (2004). Schizophrenia. In: McGuffin, P., Owen, M. and Gottesman, I. (eds), *Psychiatric Genetics and Genomics* (Oxford: Oxford University Press).

Owen, M., Craddock, N. and O'Donovan, M. (2010). Suggestion of roles for both common and rare risk variants in genome-wide studies of schizophrenia. *Archives of General Psychiatry*, 67, 667–73.

Panossian, L. and Avidan, A. (2009). Review of sleep disorders. *Medical Clinics of North America*, 93, 407–25, ix.

Pantelis, C., Velakoulis, D., McGorry, P. et al. (2003). Neuroanatomical abnormalities before and after onset of psychosis: A cross-sectional and longitudinal MRI comparison. *Lancet*, 361, 281–8.

Paris, J. (2005). Neurobiological dimensional models of personality: A review of the models of Cloninger, Depue, and Siever. *Journal of Personality Disorders*, 19, 156–70.

Park, D. and Reuter-Lorenz, P. (2009). The adaptive brain: Aging and neurocognitive scaffolding. *Annual Review of Psychology*, 60, 173–96.

Parsons, C., Young, K., Murray, L., Stein, A. and Kringelbach, M. (2010). The functional neuroanatomy of the evolving parent–infant relationship. *Progress in Neurobiology*, 91, 220–41.

Partilla, J., Dempsey, A., Nagpal, A., Blough, B., Baumann, M. and Rothman, R. (2006). Interaction of amphetamines and related compounds at the vesicular monoamine transporter. *Journal of Pharmacology and Experimental Therapeutics*, 319, 237–46.

Passie, T., Halpern, J., Stichtenoth, D., Emrich, H. and Hintzen, A. (2008). The pharmacology of lysergic acid diethylamide: A review. *CNS Neuroscience and Therapeutics*, 14, 295–314.

Peciña, S., Smith, K. and Berridge, K. (2006). Hedonic hot spots in the brain. *Neuroscientist*, 12, 500–11.

Penn, H. (2006). Neurobiological correlates of autism: A review of recent research. *Child Neuropsychology*, 12, 57–79.

Phillips, W. A. and Silverstein, S. M. (2003). Convergence of biological and psychological perspectives on cognitive coordination in schizophrenia. *Behavioral Brain Sciences*, 26, 65–82; discussion 82–137.

Pickering-Brown, S. (2010). Review: Recent progress in frontotemporal lobar degeneration. *Neuropathology and Applied Neurobiology*, 36, 4–16.

Pinkham, A., Hopfinger, J., Pelphrey, K., Piven, J. and Penn, D. (2008). Neural bases for impaired social cognition in schizophrenia and autism spectrum disorders. *Schizophrenia Research*, 99, 164–75.

Poldrack, R. A. (2006). Can cognitive processes be inferred from neuroimaging data? *Trends in Cognitive Sciences*, 10, 59–63.

Portelius, E., Andreasson, U., Ringman, J. et al. (2010). Distinct cerebrospinal fluid amyloid beta peptide signatures in sporadic and PSEN1 A431E-associated familial Alzheimer's disease. *Molecular Neurodegeneration*, 5, 2.

Porter, R., Gallagher, P., Watson, S. and Young, A. (2004). Corticosteroid-serotonin interactions in depression: A review of the human evidence. *Psychopharmacology (Berlin)*, 173, 1–17.

Potenza, M. (2008). Review. The neurobiology of pathological gambling and drug addiction: An overview and new findings. *Philosophical Transactions of the Royal Society of London. Series B, Biological Sciences*, 363, 3181–9.

Prvulovic, D., Van De Ven, V., Sack, A. T., Maurer, K. and Linden, D. E. (2005). Functional activation imaging in aging and dementia. *Psychiatry Research*, 140, 97–113.

Quinsey, V. (2003). The etiology of anomalous sexual preferences in men. *Annals of the New York Academy of Sciences*, 989, 105–17; discussion 144–53.

Quiroz, J., Machado-Vieira, R., Zarate, C. J. and Manji, H. (2010). Novel insights into lithium's mechanism of action: Neurotrophic and neuroprotective effects. *Neuropsychobiology*, 62, 50–60.

Raine, A. (2002). Annotation: The role of prefrontal deficits, low autonomic arousal, and early health factors in the development of antisocial and aggressive behavior in children. *Journal of Child Psychology and Psychiatry*, 43, 417–34.

Rask-Andersen, M., Olszewski, P., Levine, A. and Schiöth, H. (2010). Molecular mechanisms underlying anorexia nervosa: Focus on human gene association studies and systems controlling food intake. *Brain Research Reviews*, 62, 147–64.

Ray, R., Schnoll, R. and Lerman, C. (2009). Nicotine dependence: Biology, behavior, and treatment. *Annual Review of Medicine*, 60, 247–60.

Reichardt, L. (2006). Neurotrophin-regulated signalling pathways. *Philosophical Transactions of the Royal Society, B Biological Sciences*, 361, 1545–64.

Reuter, J., Raedler, T., Rose, M., Hand, I., Gläscher, J. and Büchel, C. (2005). Pathological gambling is linked to reduced activation of the mesolimbic reward system. *Nature Neuroscience*, 8, 147–8.

Revel, F., Gottowik, J., Gatti, S., Wettstein, J. and Moreau, J. (2009). Rodent models of insomnia: A review of experimental procedures that induce sleep disturbances. *Neuroscience and Biobehavioral Reviews*, 33, 874–99.

Rinne, T., De Kloet, E., Wouters, L., Goekoop, J., Derijk, R. and Van Den Brink, W. (2002). Hyperresponsiveness of hypothalamic-pituitary-adrenal axis to combined dexamethasone/corticotropin-releasing hormone challenge in female borderline personality disorder subjects with a history of sustained childhood abuse. *Biological Psychiatry*, 52, 1102–12.

Rioux, L., Nissanov, J., Lauber, K., Bilker, W. B. and Arnold, S. E. (2003). Distribution of microtubule-associated protein MAP2-immunoreactive interstitial neurons in the parahippocampal white matter in subjects with schizophrenia. *American Journal of Psychiatry*, 160, 149–55.

Rogawski, M. A. and Löscher, W. (2004). The neurobiology of antiepileptic drugs. *Nature Reviews Neuroscience*, 5, 553–64.

Rösner, S., Leucht, S., Lehert, P. and Soyka, M. (2008). Acamprosate supports abstinence, naltrexone prevents excessive drinking: Evidence from a meta-analysis with unreported outcomes. *Journal of Psychopharmacology*, 22, 11–23.

Rotarska-Jagiela, A., Schönmeyer, R., Oertel, V., Haenschel, C., Vogeley, K. and Linden, D. E. (2008). The corpus callosum in schizophrenia-volume and connectivity changes affect specific regions. *Neuroimage*, 39, 1522–32.

Rotarska-Jagiela, A., Van De Ven, V., Oertel-Knöchel, V., Uhlhaas, P. J., Vogeley, K. and Linden, D. E. (2010). Resting-state functional network correlates of psychotic symptoms in schizophrenia. *Schizophrenia Research*, 117, 21–30.

Rush, A., Trivedi, M., Wisniewski, S. et al. (2006). Acute and longer-term outcomes in depressed outpatients requiring one or several treatment steps: A STAR*D report. *American Journal of Psychiatry*, 163, 1905–17.

Sack, A.T. and Linden, D. (2003). Combining transcranial magnetic stimulation and functional imaging in cognitive brain research: possibilities and limitations. *Brain Research Reviews*, 43, 41–56.

Salisbury, D., Voglmaier, M., Seidman, L. and McCarley, R. (1996). Topographic abnormalities of P3 in schizotypal personality disorder. *Biological Psychiatry*, 40, 165–72.

Salvadore, G., Quiroz, J., Machado-Vieira, R., Henter, I., Manji, H. and Zarate, C. J. (2010). The neurobiology of the switch process in bipolar disorder: A review. *Journal of Clinical Psychiatry*, 71, 1488–1501.

Saudino, K. (2005). Behavioral genetics and child temperament. *Journal of Developmental and Behavioral Pediatrics*, 26, 214–23.

Schenck, C., Arnulf, I. and Mahowald, M. (2007). Sleep and sex: What can go wrong? A review of the literature on sleep related disorders and abnormal sexual behaviors and experiences. *Sleep*, 30, 683–702.

Schloesser, R., Huang, J., Klein, P. and Manji, H. (2008). Cellular plasticity cascades in the pathophysiology and treatment of bipolar disorder. *Neuropsychopharmacology*, 33, 110–33.

Seeman, P., Ko, F. and Tallerico, T. (2005). Dopamine receptor contribution to the action of PCP, LSD and ketamine psychotomimetics. *Molecular Psychiatry*, 10, 877–83.

Selemon, L. D. (2001). Regionally diverse cortical pathology in schizophrenia: Clues to the etiology of the disease. *Schizophrenia Bulletin*, 27, 349–77.

Serretti, A., Drago, A. and De Ronchi, D. (2007). HTR2A gene variants and psychiatric disorders: A review of current literature and selection of SNPs for future studies. *Current Medicinal Chemistry*, 14, 2053–69.

Sévin, M., Lesca, G., Baumann, N., Millat, G., Lyon-Caen, O., Vanier, M. T. and Sedel, F. (2007). The adult form of Niemann-Pick disease type C. *Brain*, 130, 120–33.

Sham, P. and McGuffin, P. (2004). Linkage and association. In: McGuffin, P., Owen, M. J. and Gottesman, I. I. (eds), *Psychiatric Genetics and Genomics* (Oxford: Oxford University Press).

Shapleske, J., Rossell, S. L., Chitnis, X. A. et al. (2002). A computational morphometric MRI study of schizophrenia: Effects of hallucinations. *Cerebral Cortex*, 12, 1331–41.

Shin, L. and Liberzon, I. (2010). The neurocircuitry of fear, stress, and anxiety disorders. *Neuropsychopharmacology*, 35, 169–91.

Shorter, E. (1997). *A History of Psychiatry: From the Era of the Asylum to the Age of Prozac* (New York: John Wiley and Sons).

Shorter, E. and Healy, D. (2007). *Shock Therapy: The History of Electroconvulsive Treatment in Mental Illness* (New Brunswick, NJ: Rutgers University Press).

Shprecher, D., Schwalb, J. and Kurlan, R. (2008). Normal pressure hydrocephalus: Diagnosis and treatment. *Current Neurology and Neuroscience Reports*, 8, 371–6.

Shyn, S. and Hamilton, S. (2010). The genetics of major depression: Moving beyond the monoamine hypothesis. *Psychiatric Clinics of North America*, 33, 125–40.

Siever, L. J. and Davis, K. L. (1991). A psychobiological perspective on the personality disorders. *American Journal of Psychiatry*, 148, 1647–58.

Silva, J. A. (2009). Forensic psychiatry, neuroscience, and the law. *Journal of the American Academy of Psychiatry and the Law*, 37, 489–502.

Singer, P. (1989). All animals are equal. In: Regan, T. and Singer, P. (eds), *Animal Rights and Human Obligations* (Upper Saddle River, NJ: Prentice Hall).

Solms, M. (2011). Neurobiology and the neurological basis of dreaming. *Handbook of Clinical Neurology*, 98, 519–44.

Sorger, B., Dahmen, B., Reithler, J. et al. (2009). Another kind of 'BOLD Response': Answering multiple-choice questions via online decoded single-trial brain signals. *Progress in Brain Research*, 177, 275–92.

Steele, H. and Siever, L. (2010). An attachment perspective on borderline personality disorder: Advances in gene–environment considerations. *Current Psychiatry Reports*, 12, 61–7.

Stephan, K. E., Baldeweg, T. and Friston, K. J. (2006). Synaptic plasticity and dysconnection in schizophrenia. *Biological Psychiatry*, 59, 929–39.

Subramanian, L., Hindle, J. V., Jackson, M. C. and Linden, D. E. (2010). Dopamine boosts memory for angry faces in Parkinson's disease. *Movement Disorders*, 25, 2792–9.

Sullivan, P., Neale, M. and Kendler, K. (2000). Genetic epidemiology of major depression: review and meta-analysis. *American Journal of Psychiatry*, 157, 1552–62.

Sullivan, S. (2010). Insomnia pharmacology. *Medical Clinics of North America*, 94, 563–80.

Swaab, D. (2007). Sexual differentiation of the brain and behavior. *Best Practice and Research. Clinical Endocrinology and Metabolism*, 21, 431–44.

Swan, G. and Lessov-Schlaggar, C. (2007). The effects of tobacco smoke and nicotine on cognition and the brain. *Neuropsychology Review*, 17, 259–73.

Swerdlow, N., Weber, M., Qu, Y., Light, G. and Braff, D. (2008). Realistic expectations of prepulse inhibition in translational models for schizophrenia research. *Psychopharmacology (Berlin)*, 199, 331–88.

Swerdlow, R. H. (2007). Pathogenesis of Alzheimer's disease. *Clinical Interventions in Aging*, 2, 347–59.

Szechtman, H., Sulis, W. and Eilam, D. (1998). Quinpirole induces compulsive checking behavior in rats: A potential animal model of obsessive-compulsive disorder (OCD). *Behavioral Neuroscience*, 112, 1475–85.

Tan, K., Brown, M., Labouèbe, G. et al. (2010). Neural bases for addictive properties of benzodiazepines. *Nature*, 463, 769–74.

Tassinari, C., Cantalupo, G., Högl, B. et al. (2009). Neuroethological approach to frontolimbic epileptic seizures and parasomnias: The same central pattern generators for the same behaviours. *Revue Neurologique (Paris)*, 165, 762–8.

Tekin, S. and Cummings, J. (2002). Frontal-subcortical neuronal circuits and clinical neuropsychiatry: An update. *Journal of Psychosomatic Research*, 53, 647–54.

Thaker, G. (2008). Neurophysiological endophenotypes across bipolar and schizophrenia psychosis. *Schizophrenia Bulletin*, 34, 760–73.

Thapar, A., Harold, G., Rice, F., Langley, K. and O'Donovan, M. (2007). The contribution of gene–environment interaction to psychopathology. *Development and Psychopathology*, 19, 989–1004.

Thomas, S. and Grossberg, G. (2009). Memantine: A review of studies into its safety and efficacy in treating Alzheimer's disease and other dementias. *Clinical Interventions in Aging*, 4, 367–77.

Thomson, F. and Craighead, M. (2008). Innovative approaches for the treatment of depression: Targeting the HPA axis. *Neurochemical Research*, 33, 691–707.

Toga, A., Thompson, P. and Sowell, E. (2006). Mapping brain maturation. *Trends in Neurosciences*, 29, 148–59.

Torres, G., Gainetdinov, R. and Caron, M. (2003). Plasma membrane monoamine transporters: Structure, regulation and function. *Nature Reviews Neuroscience*, 4, 13–25.

Trimble, M. R. (1996). *Biological Psychiatry* (Chichester: Wiley).

Trimble, M., Mendez, M. and Cummings, J. (1997). Neuropsychiatric symptoms from the temporolimbic lobes. *Journal of Neuropsychiatry and Clinical Neuroscience*, 9, 429–38.

Tripp, G. and Wickens, J. (2009). Neurobiology of ADHD. *Neuropharmacology*, 57, 579–89.

Trull, T. and Durrett, C. (2005). Categorical and dimensional models of personality disorder. *Annual Review of Clinical Psychology*, 1, 355–80.

Tsankova, N., Renthal, W., Kumar, A. and Nestler, E. J. (2007). Epigenetic regulation in psychiatric disorders. *Nature Reviews Neuroscience*, 8, 355–67.

Turetsky, B. I., Calkins, M. E., Light, G. A., Olincy, A., Radant, A. D. and Swerdlow, N. R. (2007). Neurophysiological endophenotypes of schizophrenia: The viability of selected candidate measures. *Schizophrenia Bulletin*, 33, 69–94.

Uhlhaas, P., Haenschel, C., Nikolic, D. and Singer, W. (2008). The role of oscillations and synchrony in cortical networks and their putative relevance for the pathophysiology of schizophrenia. *Schizophrenia Bulletin*, 34, 927–43.

Usher, J., Leucht, S., Falkai, P. and Scherk, H. (2010). Correlation between amygdala volume and age in bipolar disorder: A systematic review and meta-analysis of structural MRI studies. *Psychiatry Research*, 182, 1–8.

Vallès, V., Van Os, J., Guillamat, R. et al. (2000). Increased morbid risk for schizophrenia in families of in-patients with bipolar illness. *Schizophrenia Research*, 42, 83–90.

Van Goozen, S., Fairchild, G., Snoek, H. and Harold, G. (2007). The evidence for a neurobiological model of childhood antisocial behavior. *Psychological Bulletin*, 133, 149–82.

Van Lieshout, R. J. and MacQueen, G. M. (2010). Efficacy and acceptability of mood stabilisers in the treatment of acute bipolar depression: systematic review. *British Journal of Psychiatry*, 196, 266–73.

Van Paasschen, J., Clare, L., Woods, R. T. and Linden, D. E. (2009). Can we change brain functioning with cognition-focused interventions in Alzheimer's disease? The role of functional neuroimaging. *Restorative Neurology and Neuroscience*, 27, 473–91.

Veenema, A. (2009). Early life stress, the development of aggression and neuroendocrine and neurobiological correlates: What can we learn from animal models? *Frontiers in Neuroendocrinology*, 30, 497–518.

Verhoeven, J., De Cock, P., Lagae, L. and Sunaert, S. (2010). Neuroimaging of autism. *Neuroradiology*, 52, 3–14.

Vetrivelan, R., Qiu, M. H., Chang, C. and Lu, J. (2010). Role of basal ganglia in sleep–wake regulation: Neural circuitry and clinical significance. *Frontiers in Neuroanatomy*, 4, 145.

Viding, E., Larsson, H. and Jones, A. (2008). Quantitative genetic studies of antisocial behaviour. *Philosophical Transactions of the Royal Society B: Biological Sciences*, 363, 2519–27.

Wahlund, K. and Kristiansson, M. (2009). Aggression, psychopathy and brain imaging: Review and future recommendations. *International Journal of Law and Psychiatry*, 32, 266–71.

Wand, G. (2005). The anxious amygdala: CREB signaling and predisposition to anxiety and alcoholism. *Journal of Clinical Investigation*, 115, 2697–9.

Warner, C., Bobo, W., Warner, C., Reid, S. and Rachal, J. (2006). Antidepressant discontinuation syndrome. *American Family Physician*, 74, 449–56.

Weisbrod, M., Hill, H., Niethammer, R. and Sauer, H. (1999). Genetic influence on auditory information processing in schizophrenia: P300 in monozygotic twins. *Biological Psychiatry*, 46, 721–5.

Weiss, F. and Porrino, L. (2002). Behavioral neurobiology of alcohol addiction: Recent advances and challenges. *Journal of Neuroscience*, 22, 3332–7.

Wilkinson, D., Francis, P., Schwam, E. and Payne-Parrish, J. (2004). Cholinesterase inhibitors used in the treatment of Alzheimer's disease: The relationship between pharmacological effects and clinical efficacy. *Drugs and Aging*, 21, 453–78.

Wilkinson, L. S., Davies, W. and Isles, A. R. (2007). Genomic imprinting effects on brain development and function. *Nature Reviews Neuroscience*, 8, 832–43.

Williams, H. J., Owen, M. J. and O'Donovan, M. C. (2007). Is COMT a susceptibility gene for schizophrenia? *Schizophrenia Bulletin*, 33, 635–41.

Winsky-Sommerer, R. (2009). Role of GABAA receptors in the physiology and pharmacology of sleep. *European Journal of Neuroscience*, 29, 1779–94.

Winter, C., Mundt, A., Jalali, R. et al. (2008). High frequency stimulation and temporary inactivation of the subthalamic nucleus reduce quinpirole-induced compulsive checking behavior in rats. *Experimental Neurology*, 210, 217–28.

World Health Organization (1992). *The ICD-10 Classification of Mental and Behavioural Disorders: Clinical Descriptions and Diagnostic Guidelines* (Geneva: WHO).

Yamamoto, B., Moszczynska, A. and Gudelsky, G. (2010). Amphetamine toxicities: Classical and emerging mechanisms. *Annals of the New York Academy of Science*, 1187, 101–21.

Yamauchi, T. (2005). Neuronal Ca2+/calmodulin-dependent protein kinase II: Discovery, progress in a quarter of a century, and perspective: Implication for learning and memory. *Biological and Pharmaceutical Bulletin*, 28, 1342–54.

Zachariae, R. (2009). Psychoneuroimmunology: A bio-psycho-social approach to health and disease. *Scandinavian Journal of Psychology*, 50, 645–51.

Zhou, J. N., Hofman, M. A., Gooren, L. J. and Swaab, D. F. (1995). A sex difference in the human brain and its relation to transsexuality. *Nature*, 378, 68–70.

Zubin, J. and Spring, B. (1977). Vulnerability: A new view of schizophrenia. *Journal of Abnormal Psychology*, 86, 103–26.

Index